ENVIRONMENTAL ECONOMICS

This intermediate-level undergraduate textbook in environmental economics builds on the microeconomics courses students take in their first year. It intentionally does not survey the whole field or present every possible topic. Instead, there is a clear focus on the theory of environmental policy and its practical applications. Most of the applied parts of the book deal with the economics of environmental policy in the European Union (EU) and in the United States. The book combines basic environmental economic analysis, such as the internalization of externalities, with recent developments in the field, including induced technical change and coalition theory. Moreover, topics from daily policy debates such as global warming are put into economic perspective. This is done in an intelligible form for advanced undergraduate students of economics, business administration, and related fields. Each part of the book contains a set of exercises and suggested solutions.

Alfred Endres is Full Professor of Economics at the University of Hagen, Germany, and Permanent Visiting Professor of Environmental Economics at the University of Witten/Herdecke, Germany. He has also taught at the Technical University of Berlin, Germany; Zhejiang University at Hangzhou, China; and the State University of New York at Buffalo. He held visiting appointments at the University of Florida and the University of California, San Diego. He is the author of 14 books on environmental economics, applied economics, and microeconomics, primarily in German. Professor Endres is a member of the Review Panel for the Swiss National Competence Center for Research on Climate Change and was a member of the Peer Review Committee for the Environmental Action Program of the EU. He is the author of numerous articles in journals such as the *Canadian Journal of Economics*, *Journal of Environmental Economics and Management*, *Journal of Industrial Economics*, *Public Choice*, and *Environmental and Resource Economics*.

Environmental Economics

Theory and Policy

Alfred Endres

University of Hagen, Germany

Translated by Iain L. Fraser

CAMBRIDGE UNIVERSITY PRESS
Cambridge, New York, Melbourne, Madrid, Cape Town, Singapore,
São Paulo, Delhi, Dubai, Tokyo, Mexico City

Cambridge University Press
32 Avenue of the Americas, New York, NY 10013-2473, USA

www.cambridge.org
Information on this title: www.cambridge.org/9780521173926

Originally published in German as Umweltökonomie by Wissenschaftliche Buchgesellschaft 1994
Second edition published in German as Umweltökonomie by Kohlhammer Verlag 2000
Third edition published in German as Umweltökonomie by Kohlhammer Verlag 2007
Revised and extended version published in English by Cambridge University Press 2011

Printed in the United States of America

A catalog record for this publication is available from the British Library.

Library of Congress Cataloging in Publication data

Endres, Alfred.
Environmental economics : theory and policy / Alfred Endres.
p.   cm.
Includes bibliographical references and index.
ISBN 978-1-107-00214-2 (hardback) – ISBN 978-0-521-17392-6 (pbk. : alk. paper)
1. Environmental economics.   I. Title.
HC79.E5E535   2010
333.7 – dc22   2010040743

ISBN 978-1-107-00214-2 Hardback
ISBN 978-0-521-17392-6 Paperback

Contents

v

Preface

Die Wissenschaft, sie ist und bleibt,
Was einer ab vom andern schreibt.
Doch trotzdem ist, ganz unbestritten,
Sie immer weiter fortgeschritten . . .

Our scholarship still is, and always will be,
rewriting what someone's already written;
yet all the same, it's progress that we do see,
whenever someone puts another bit in.

– Eugen Roth's Tierleben
[*Eugen Roths Animal Life*]
Munich, 1948–1949; tr. ILF, 2008

There is no doubt that environmental economics has greatly progressed since the appearance of the second edition of this book in 2000. In fact, it is these advances that persuaded me to thoroughly revise the text and extend it considerably. However, it is not necessary to establish whether environmental economics progressed in the manner cited previously or quite differently, nor do we need to go into the variances between the previous edition and this one in detail. For most readers of this book, the developments that led to the present state are not terribly important. (This is particularly so because the second edition is written in German.) Let us instead take this book as it is.

I investigate environmental pollution and environmental policy using the methods of microeconomics. The aim is to work out the economic structure that underlies the manifold practical problems and the attempts at solving them. Special attention goes to the incentive structure to which those making decisions of relevance to the environment are exposed because of market mechanisms, state regulation, and international institutions. A detailed discussion of the national or global environmental situation, individual environmental laws, or international environmental agreements is not the central concern of this book. So as not to let the fundamental discussion become detached from reality, however, connections with practical problems and approaches to solutions are continually made.

This book endeavors to go into the latest developments in the scientific and political debate. All the same, it is intended to be accessible to readers knowing "only" the very basics of economic theory – as conveyed in the first three semesters of a university economics program. I make no claim to have achieved this difficult combination of objectives, but keeping them in mind was always helpful while doing the work. Even "noneconomists" with the courage to skim confidently over the passages they cannot comprehend ought to, on the whole, be able to profit from the text. (I hope those passages are not too numerous or lengthy.) If so, the book may contribute to bridging the language barriers between "hard-core economists" and the "rest of the world." Particularly in the environmental sphere, where communication among different disciplines is indispensable, a "translation aid" would be extremely important.

Because environmental economics is firmly rooted in traditional microeconomics, the foundations of economic theory are dealt with in some detail in Part One. In my years of participation in the academic and political environmental debate, I have formed the impression that many communication difficulties are attributable to the failure to convey the basis of environmental economics in economic theory. The center of the first part is accordingly a presentation of the nature and optimality of market equilibria, fitted to the needs of the subsequent environmental economics analysis. The externalities that from the economic viewpoint are characteristic of environmental problems appear here as disruptions of the capacity of the market mechanism to bring about "socially optimal" results. The central environmental policy theme of "internalization of externalities" constitutes the attempt to restore the lost social optimality of the market system. In this presentation, particular weight is attached to developing the optimality concept as used in economics and, along with it, the value judgments underlying the concept of internalizing externalities. This part of the book is aimed particularly at the "noneconomists" among the readers. However, it may also be useful to "hard-core economists" because in their constant preoccupation with technical details of models, they may have lost sight of the fact that economics is not a natural or engineering science. In particular, it turns out that the optimality concept used in economics is not at all suited to formulating environmental policy objectives "objectively" over and above the jungle of divergent interests in a society. The locus of economically optimal environmental states instead depends *inter alia* on the preferences and incomes of those who are affected (in the broadest sense) by the state of the environment. It is also influenced by the state of technology. It, too, is shaped in a host of ways by social processes. Optimality is a social science concept.

Following clarification of the basic theoretical economic principles, Part Two presents and discusses the main strategies for internalizing externalities. It starts (in Chapter A) by discussing the model proposed by Ronald Coase (1960) of *negotiations* among the parties involved in an externality. Coase's ideas are fundamental to an understanding of the theory of externalities. They fit seamlessly into the economic theory of markets. Externalities appear as gaps in the market system, which can be closed by appropriately extending the scope of the market. In Coase's world, it is conceivable for someone causing an externality to compensate the damaged party and for the latter to allow the damaging activity. In contrast, though, an arrangement is also conceivable whereby the injured party pays the responsible party to reduce the externality. With this symmetrical treatment, Coase breaks the traditional role allocation in which the responsible party is *a priori* an offender and the injured party a victim. In that sense, this provocative approach by Coase has enlivened the welfare economics debate enormously. Related to Coase's thinking is the internalization of externalities through *liability law*, dealt with in Chapter B of Part Two. If the responsible party can be held liable for the damage caused to third parties, then it will take that into account correspondingly in decisions on the size and nature of its activities. The conditions on which the responsible party is liable to pay compensation for damages are laid down in detail in the "liability rule" in force. In this book, because of its high environmental policy relevance, the *strict liability rule* is covered in particular detail. For comparison, however, the *negligence rule* is occasionally brought in. As well as negotiations and liability rules, the Pigovian tax as an internalization strategy is also dealt with in Chapter C. According to this idea, the responsible party (polluter) must pay a levy per emission unit of the amount of the external marginal cost (estimated in the social optimum). To date, this "classical" strategy is influential in the "green tax" debate.

Internalization of externalities in a pure form is, for various reasons (set out in the text), very difficult in practice. The economics literature, accordingly, also deals exhaustively with the use of instruments serving less ambitious goals than the viewpoint of economic theory rather than internalization. The object in this connection is to see how far environmental policy instruments are suitable for attaining some set emission standard (not necessarily meeting the economic optimality criterion). The relevant instruments are accordingly termed "standard-oriented" instruments.[1]

The question addressed here is dealt with in Part Three. The extremely numerous "pragmatic" environment policy instruments discussed academically and politically are summarized in terms of three "prototypes," namely, *command and control* regulations, *emissions taxes*, and *transferable discharge permits*. They are considered in regard to their cost-effectiveness, their incentive effect in relation to the advancement of environmental technology, and their capacity for meeting the environmental policy objective precisely.

The presentations in the first three parts of this book explain the welfare economics foundation of environmental economics, its elementary building blocks, and the outlines of its architecture. This sets up the *basic model of environmental economics*.

---

1 Correspondingly, the internalization strategies might be termed "damage-oriented" instruments.

Of course, there are a large number of real problems with the environment and environmental policy that are not, or not adequately, depicted in this model. They are accounted for in the literature with corresponding extensions of the basic model (oriented to the explanatory objective of the given presentation). The question as to what representatives of the immense range of variants should be given consideration in an environmental economics textbook is, of course, difficult to answer. Ultimately, the selection will be determined by how the author rates their political relevance and scientific interest. Part Four of this book presents a motley group of enlargements to the basic environmental economics model. The pollutant interactions discussed in Chapter A give an example of how many ecological complications are ignored in the basic environmental economics model. We show by examples how ecological details can be "built in" to the economic model and how much this changes the results of the model. Another class of extensions consists of departures from the basic model, taking into account other reasons, apart from externalities, for "market failure" in one and the same model. This happens with environmental policy under conditions of imperfect competition and with the analysis of environmental policy with asymmetrical information, dealt with in Chapters B and C. A "broader broadening" lies in the way the social policy debate often looks at environmental policy, treated separately in the basic economic model, together with other policy areas. This interdependence is particularly telling in the debate on the interactions between environmental protection and employment. We take up this type of complication regarding the basic environmental economics model in Chapter D, with a discussion of a "double dividend" of green tax. Things are different again with the analysis in Chapter E of induced advances in environmental technology. In the basic economic model, this is rudimentarily dealt with under the concept of "dynamic incentive effect." However, the dynamic modeling of this in Part Four takes on so much of a life of its own as to break the bounds of the basic textbook model and may thus be termed an "extension." This estimation also applies to the analytical method used in Chapter E, which requires more technical knowledge on the part of the reader than the more illustrative presentations in the first three parts.

How far any particular area belongs to the basic model or to the extensions is ultimately a question of subjective assessment. Anyone may reasonably find some other assignment than the one chosen here more appropriate or more comfortable.

Much the same is true of the answer to the question of how the *economics of international environmental problems* is to be classified. Undoubtedly, they could also be seen as a broadening of the basic model and thus located in Part Four. However, we enter "another world" when the viewpoint shifts from the dichotomy between a (more or less well-informed) regulator and a host of the regulated to looking at the interaction among independent actors. This occurs systematically when analyzing international environmental policy. Here the construction of the nation-state, laying down and applying environmental law, is ultimately of no more use. Instead, account is taken of the fact that international environmental policy must be agreed to by (more or less free) sovereign states. The shift in the object of study corresponds with a change in analytical method. Traditional microeconomic regulatory theory is replaced by game theory. These considerations were decisive in not allocating international environmental problems to Part Four, as one of many extensions to the basic model but instead devoting Part Five exclusively to them. Other factors were the overwhelming importance of international environmental problems for current environmental and social policy debates, as well as the (correspondingly) large space allotted to the relevant discussions in this book. Because of the high topicality of the debate on global environmental problems, in this part we also pay special attention to not letting the theoretical economic considerations stand alone, instead adducing them for the assessment of practical international environmental policy. This is done specifically with the examples of an environmental economics analysis of the Kyoto agreement, the European Union's emissions trading scheme, and the vision of a U.S. greenhouse gas emissions trading system.

It was even easier than with international environmental problems to decide to deal separately in Part Six with *natural resources and sustainable development*, instead of putting them in Part Four as extensions of the basic model. Here the perspective clearly differs from the one taken previously in this book. Despite various departures and differentiations, the basic concept in the first five parts of the book is that alongside economic activity an undesired by-product (externality, emission) is produced, the amount of which is to be favorably influenced by regulatory or procedural policy action by the state (or a coalition of states). The *leitmotiv* of this influence is the internalization of externalities – whether in its pure form or in the "slimmed-down" version of standard-oriented environmental policy. Part Six of the book supplements this output-related viewpoint with an input-related one. The fact that every economic activity must take resources from nature becomes the focus of consideration. The problem lies in the exhaustion of resource stocks or in the damaging (if not indeed destruction) of the resource basis of human existence. The question that then arises is "What are the conditions for the durability of human existence?" The associated political *leitmotiv* is that of sustainable development.

So much for the overview of this book's program. Allow me, though, to present three more general considerations that are close to my heart:

- In educational and scientific policy debates, the "unity of research and teaching" is often dismissed as an outdated model that modern trendsetters leave to a few "dyed in the wool" old Humboldtians (likewise outdated models). Particularly in relation to Parts Four and Five (or to numerous other textbooks), it can be shown that this judgment is wrong. It is both possible and necessary to let the choice of themes dealt with in a basic book be determined by current research. The object and methods of this research can be conveyed within reasonable limits well this side of the cutting edge of active researchers, without expecting less specialized readers to put up with the indigestibilities of the research discourse.

- In the social policy debate, the place of ecological issues has in recent years been subject to rapid cyclical fluctuations. After a phase of *eco-hype*, such topics fell into an irresistible downswing, reaching a nadir toward the end of the twentieth century with the diagnosis of "environment is uncool."[2] More recently, the trend shifted again. We hear of the "return of ecology,"[3] and those who were too hasty in consigning environmental economics courses to the rubbish heap now look very passé. Given the present deep crisis in the world economy, and specifically in international financial markets, environmental issues are likely to slip further down the agenda of social policy debate. Of course, it would be desirable if the profession were not to respond quite so strongly to where the pendulum happens to be on its swing between ecoromanticism and ecoignorance. The efficient and responsible management of the scarce resource "environment" is an ongoing social task. Particularly in a sober view, it follows that environmental economics is due a prominent place on the priority list of economics teaching and research themes.[4]

- (Almost) in conclusion, we give one more word on the ways in which the environmental economics material is presented in various places in the book. Unquestionably, not everyone has to like my kind of humor. However, I do not share the oft-upheld (although mostly implicit) view that the personality of the author of an academic essay must completely disappear behind the subject matter. After all, in the course of cultural history, many have written on the function of irony in creating texts. To represent them all, here is Hanif Kureishi:

> We decided the film was to have gangster and thriller elements. . . . And the film was to be an amusement, despite its references to racism, unemployment and Thatcherism. Irony is the modern mode, a way of commenting on bleakness and cruelty without falling into dourness and didacticism. And ever since the first time I heard people in a theatre laugh during a play of mine, I've wanted it to happen again and again.   *– My Beautiful Laundrette*, London, 1986

---

2 Headline in *Die Zeit* No. 11, March 11, 1999, p. 1. (*Die Zeit* is a weekly highbrow newspaper published in Hamburg, Germany.)

3 Headline in *Die Zeit* No. 33, August 10, 2006, p. 1.

4 After all, 69.8% of economist respondents in a major survey by the *Verein für Socialpolitik* (German Economic Association) and *Financial Times Deutschland* (*FTD*) answered "yes" to the question "Should environment issues have a special place in economics, and should economic-policy measures always be tested for sustainability?" ("no": 21.3%, "don't know": 8.9%) (*FTD*, September 27, 2006, p. 2).

Let me add a final remark on style: In this text, not every actor has the same gender as the term by which the actor is referred. It should also be noted that entities such as "the polluter" and "the regulator" are thought of as companies, factories, political or administrative institutions, and so on. Referring to them as "he" is merely to avoid inelegant wording (e.g., "he or she," "his or her") and does not mean that the entity referred to is male.

Acknowledgments

This book is the product of a team effort. First, the text is the extended and updated version of the translation of my book entitled *Umweltökonomie* (Stuttgart: Kohlhammer Verlag, 3. Aufl., 2007). I am grateful that Kohlhammer Verlag unbureaucratically endorsed this translation. The book was translated by Iain L. Fraser, and I highly appreciate the splendid job he has done. The communication with Iain during the process of the translation improved my English a lot – and that was definitely necessary. I gratefully acknowledge the generous support of this translation by the Volkswagen Foundation, Germany.

Second, I am deeply indebted to Dr. Bianca Rundshagen, University of Hagen, for numerous helpful suggestions. Moreover, Dr. Rundshagen generously contributed exercises and solutions. This book would not be the same without Dr. Rundshagen's outstanding contributions. I also acknowledge the most helpful comments of four anonymous referees on an earlier draft of the manuscript. Naturally (and unfortunately), all remaining errors are mine.

My heartfelt thanks also go to Gabriele Debray and Daniel Limpinsel, University of Hagen, for providing excellent technical support throughout the multistage book preparation process. I am especially grateful to Professor Michael Faure, University of Maastricht, and to Dr. Uwe Fliegauf, Kohlhammer Verlag, Stuttgart, for their tireless support of this project.

Finally, I am happy to acknowledge the pleasant and fruitful cooperation of Scott Parris, Senior Editor at the New York Office of Cambridge University Press, and Ken Karpinski, Senior Project Manager at Aptara; I would also like to thank Kristin Lynch for her most competent copyediting.

Alfred Endres

Part One

The Internalization of Externalities as a Central Theme of Environmental Policy

A. Foundations

I. Object and Methods of Microeconomic Theory

Microeconomics is the science of *scarcity* and coping with the consequences of scarcity. Scarcity arises because the *resources* available to meet human *needs* are not enough to meet all existing desires. The concept of scarcity thus does not (only) refer here to the lack of essentials, but to any divergence between desire and reality. The central concepts of "needs" and "resources" are couched very broadly in modern economics.

The concept of need goes far beyond the area commonly termed "economic" in ordinary speech – namely, food, accommodation, clothing, and transport – to embrace needs often seen as "extraeconomic," such as those for a clean environment, internal and external security, and indeed even the longing for peace and harmony in a relationship.[1]

Similarly, the concept of resources is no longer confined in modern economics literature to the traditional factors of production – (paid) labor, capital, and land. Instead, natural (exhaustible or renewable) resources, as well as such elements as human knowledge and the work ethic in a society, are now taken into account.

A world of scarcity is necessarily one of conflicts over precious (because they are needed to reduce the scarcity) resources. No society is conceivable without mechanisms and institutions to settle these conflicts. The rules whereby scarce resources can be distributed among the all-too-numerous bearers of the all-too-numerous needs are varied. One might think of applying the law of the jungle, basic democratic deciding procedures, the market mechanism, or patriarchal (or matriarchal) allocations. Most societies practice a mixture of these allocation mechanisms, with

---

1 Cf. Becker (1993), as well as, e.g., Coyle (2007). Gary Becker won the Economics Nobel Prize in 1992 for his contributions to the further development of economics into a general theory of human behavior.

differing strengths of components. Modern economic theory has not only concerned itself overwhelmingly with the market as an allocation mechanism, but has also dealt with the other mechanisms mentioned previously (and still others).

For the (undoubtedly small) portion of the readership who doubt the relevance of the prior observations to environmental policy, let us clarify:

> Consider the airspace above a particular region as a scarce resource with various competing claims to it: firms would like to use the air as a medium to absorb their pollutants, whereas inhabitants would like to breathe it. The allocation mechanisms mentioned previously can also be used as institutions for settling this conflict.

Under the *law of the jungle* the emitters' "aggressive" mode of utilization would win out unrestrictedly against the "defensive" use intentions of the inhabitants.[2]

In the example case, the allocation mechanism of *authoritarian allocation* would mean that emission caps would be allotted to the firms. This would implicitly set a distribution of the scarce resource between firms and inhabitants.

Solutions oriented more or less to *market allocation mechanisms* would consist of such things as negotiations among potential polluters and potential pollutees[3] or the issuing of emission permits.[4]

A *basic democracy variant* might be a plebiscite on the emission level (or establishment or closure) of the relevant firms.

In connection with the analysis of mechanisms to decide the use of scarce resources and the benefits from their use, two questions are of particular interest for economic theory:

a) Which use of the scarce resources is arrived at in an economy as a whole as the outcome of the numerous decisions by individual decision makers?

    Here the point is to find out how the framework conditions under which the individuals take their decisions (e.g., technology or the legal system) affect the allocational outcomes. We call this part of microeconomics theory "positive analysis."

b) How is the allocational outcome established (or predicted) in the previous item assessed from the viewpoint of economic theory?

    This further-reaching program of microeconomics theory is termed "normative analysis."

---

2   The utilization of the air as a medium for absorbing pollutants limits the possibilities of using air at a quality favorable for breathing. In contrast, breathing does not limit emission possibilities. These statements must not, of course, be confused with the claim that a right conferred on inhabitants to breathe clean air does not limit emitters' possibilities of action. However, allowing such a right would go beyond the framework of the "law of the jungle" as an allocation mechanism. Where it is claimed in the text that under this law the utilization plans of the producers of the externalities would prevail, we are ignoring the possibility that those damaged prevent the emissions by force.

3   Cf. chapter A in part two.

4   Cf. section B.III in part three.

Many economists are particularly fascinated by comparing the actual result reached by a particular allocation mechanism with a "socially optimal" result. Of course, it is necessary for this undertaking to develop a criterion of social optimality. If an analysis of the market mechanism finds that the market outcome ("equilibrium") departs from the optimum, this gives the economist occasion to ponder possible correction mechanisms.[5]

We show in detail that the existence of environmental problems (in economic terminology, "externalities") establishes a divergence between market equilibrium and optimum. The "internalization of externalities" treated in part two of this book is nothing but an attempt to make economic policy corrections to the market mechanism with the aim of bringing equilibrium and optimum together.

Of course, the demand that politics should bring about an optimum position is – in the sphere of environmental policy as in any other sphere – for various reasons too ambitious. Nonetheless, it is worthwhile to operationalize the concept of optimality and discover structural causes of market mechanism failures by comparing the market equilibrium with the optimum. Even if, in reality, the optimum will perhaps never be reached, we might still provide guidance to environmental policy, which all too often has its view of what direction to take confused (comprehensible as this may be) by the undergrowth of everyday problems.

However, we are not going to recommend uncritically the optimality concept, or that of internalization of externalities used in economics, as an ideal instrument for creating the optimum situation. Instead, we also point out the catches with these concepts. To be sure, this critical presentation should not be misinterpreted as a negative attitude by the author toward internalization strategies. The suitability of the internalization of externalities as guidance for practical environmental policy has to be measured by comparing it with the alternatives actually available. As is established in more detail, the author takes the view that the internalization strategies (and other instruments developed on the basis of economic theory) are, for all their defects, to be placed fairly low on the inadequacy scale of rival environmental policy strategies.

Perhaps one *preliminary methodological observation* might be useful for representatives of other disciplines (than economics) among readers:

A typical feature of economists' approach to the questions discussed here (and others) is analysis by theoretical modeling. The point in economic theory is not to describe all individual cases of allocation problems occurring in the world in all their historically produced details. That would certainly be a tiresome and fruitless endeavor.[6] Instead, the point is to work out the common structure underlying various classes of individual cases (particularly regarding

---

5 The wording "occasion . . . mechanisms" has been deliberately couched cautiously: the fact that the market cannot bring about an optimum position does not at all mean that some other allocation mechanism would be capable of it.

6 Although, admittedly some people also find economic modeling theory tiresome and fruitless.

the incentive effects of framework conditions on decision makers). Here it is indispensable to abstract from many sorts of details of specific cases of application.[7] For example, the market for disposal work in the garbage sector certainly differs considerably from the market for bananas, and this, in turn, from the market for computer software. Nonetheless, all three areas come together under the category "market." Economic theory attempts to work out the common structure of the various markets (i.e., the "essence" of the market). For this, it develops such categories as specialization and exchange, supply and demand, efficiency and technical progress, and competition (or its absence). These play a role in all markets and can thus be used for a common understanding of the many and varied types of individual markets.

The outcome of the abstraction process discussed here is described in economic theory by "models." These are abstract cause-and-effect systems. They portray the interaction of the elements of reality considered important to the investigative object of the model in stylized form. Let us, for instance, consider as an example a model for explaining a firm's behavior. It consists of the following components:

a) Definitions (e.g., profit = revenue − costs)
b) Assumptions about the decision makers' objective (e.g., the firm aims at maximizing its profits)
c) Assumptions about the framework conditions under which the decision maker can come closer to its goal (e.g., the firm has a monopoly position)
d) Conclusions (e.g., the firm produces a quantity at which the marginal revenues are equal to the marginal costs)

The design of assumptions on which to base a model is a particularly important and difficult undertaking. On the one hand, the assumptions should be suitable for presenting the problem to be analyzed simply. After all, one of the most important tasks of the model is to reduce the high complexity of reality, which is often enough to drive the observer to despair. On the other hand, the assumptions must not be so simply conceived as to conceal "essential" aspects of the problem to be analyzed from the model's view. The construction of optimization models thus itself constitutes an optimization problem.

This optimization is not possible without a valuation by the analyst because he has to make a decision as to what aspects of the problem to be studied are in his view "essential" and what aspects can be ignored. The close connection arising here in relation to economic model building between optimization and valuation will come up again in discussing optimum emission or safety levels. Of course, the economist doing the analysis cannot in his valuation get by with "objective science" alone. Instead, he must also (regardless of his awareness of this) bring his own scientific and personal socialization into the process of model building.[8]

---

7   These are occasionally included in individual "case studies" applying the general theory.
8   These observations are also intended to counter the widespread view that economists are by nature heartless rationalists who (for that very reason!) should on no account be allowed any

Admittedly, the previous explanation of the "model" has come out rather abstractly – just like models themselves, by the way. This is not necessarily an advantage. We now try to make it more plain, availing ourselves of some support from the British novelist David Lodge. In his novel *Thinks* (London: Secker & Warburg, 2001), the protagonist explains what a novel is. Within the relevant passage, we replace the word "novel" with "economic model":[9] "In that sense economic models could be called thought experiments. You invent people, you put them in hypothetical situations, and decide how they will react. The 'proof' of the experiment is if their behaviour seems interesting, plausible, revealing about human nature" (Lodge, 2001, pp. 61–2).

II. The Equilibrium Concept in Microeconomic Theory

The concept of equilibrium is of considerable importance for environmental economics as applied microeconomic theory. However, its description can be kept brief because only the essentials are needed for a discussion of the topic at issue here. Further details can be followed up on in any microeconomics textbook.

Very hurried readers might be inclined to skip the discussion that appears after Figure 1. We take this inclination into account with our "lateral view." Perhaps

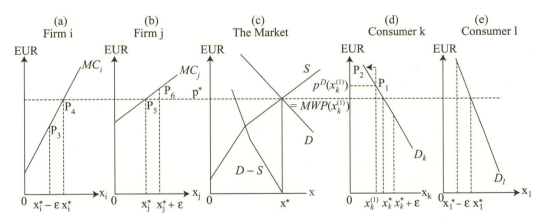

Figure 1

major influence in answering central questions on the life of human society. It is instead true that a good economist is marked by not only a sharp intellect, but also high sensitivity. Anyone regarding this as a contradiction should take heed from the fact that, in Japanese, the very same kanji sign is used for "feeling" and "intellect." (From Todd Shimoda, *The Fourth Treasure* (New York: Doubleday), 2002.)

9 The outcome of the terminological substitution process (economists love polysyllables!) can be seen: I've seen many a poorer definition of models. Here's a proposed topic for an evening fireside discussion: why do novels and economic models have common features? Where does the analogy end? The topic can then be taken up again a few weeks later for another fireside talk, when you have gotten further along in the book. Retrospective comparison of the records of the two discussions might be interesting.

the contemplation of this calligraphy will allow an intuitive (and thus extremely time-efficient) understanding of the equilibrium concept.

Lateral view 1: Well, everything in balance? *Source:* "Equilibrium," by L.J.C. Shimoda, taken from Todd Shimoda, *The Fourth Treasure* (New York: Doubleday), 2002. Reprinted with the artist's kind permission.

For a more detailed discussion of the equilibrium concept, we advise referring to Figure 1. It depicts in stylized fashion the market for any arbitrary product x of given quality.[10]

In this market, let there be perfect competition.[11] Let the supply side of the market be represented by two firms and the demand side by two households.[12] The supply and demand decisions of the actors in relation to the good x are coordinated as follows through the market.

For firms i and j, respectively, marginal costs of MC_i and MC_j, respectively, arise in producing product x.[13] It can be shown that the marginal cost curve of each firm

---

10   Of course, the quality is not really given, but to be determined endogenously. For reasons of simplicity, though, we do not bother setting out this aspect here. Cf., e.g., Hirshleifer/Glazer/Hirshleifer (2005).

11   The essential feature of the perfect competition market form is that no individual supplier or demander can influence the market price.

12   The restriction to two on each side is merely in order to keep the graphic portrayal as simple as possible. The generality of the statements remains unaffected thereby. Accordingly, the possible objection that the market form of perfect competition assumed here is incompatible with the assumption of such a small number of market participants is irrelevant in this context.

13   The marginal cost curves need not rise monotonically (still less linearly) with the quantity produced, as shown in Figure 1, but may take a different course (e.g., a U-shaped curve).

corresponds to that firm's individual supply curve.[14] The individual supply curves of the individual firms can be aggregated horizontally to give the supply curve, S, for product x on the market. For each of the two households, a monotonically falling individual demand curve D_k or D_l has been assumed. (To simplify the portrayal, linearity has also been assumed.) Horizontally aggregating *these* gives the demand curve, D, for this market.

The market equilibrium is, as we know, defined by the point of intersection of the supply and demand curves; that is, in Figure 1, an equilibrium situation arises at price p^* and quantity x^*. At the equilibrium price, firm i produces quantity x_i^* and firm j produces quantity x_j^*. For these quantities, the equilibrium condition for a firm aiming at profit maximization in the perfect competition market form, "price = marginal cost," is met.

At the equilibrium price p^*, household k demands quantity x_k^* and household l demands quantity x_l^*. The equilibrium position for a household at a given price for a product is defined by the point where the relevant household's marginal willingness to pay for the product equals the price of the product. This condition is rich in consequences for environmental economics based on microeconomics, and we accordingly explain it a little more.

The first thing important to an understanding of the household's equilibrium is that the level of the household's willingness to pay for a (marginal) additional unit of product can be read off for any original endowment of product x as an ordinate value on the corresponding demand curve.

We call the ordinate value on the demand curve the "demand price," p^D. Thus, for instance, the willingness of household k, if it already possesses quantity $x_k^{(1)}$, to pay for an additional (arbitrarily small) supply of good x can be read off as an ordinate value on the demand curve above $x_k^{(1)}$, namely, $p^D(x_k^{(1)})$.[15] We claim that the demand price is equal to the marginal willingness to pay (i.e., that $p^D(x_k^{(1)}) = MWP(x_k^{(1)})$ applies).

To understand this, imagine that things were otherwise, as follows.[16] Let us assume that the willingness to pay of household k for a marginal unit above its

---

Monotonically falling marginal cost curves are, of course, also conceivable, although they would go beyond the perfect competition model taken as the basis here. Cf. the passages on natural monopoly in many intermediate microeconomics textbooks, e.g., Landsburg (2002), Perloff (2007), Varian (2006), and the exhaustive presentations in Berg/Tschirhart (1988), a book still worth reading despite its relative age.

14 More exactly, the supply curve corresponds to the marginal cost curve in its rising part from the minimum of the average cost curve (not shown in Figure 1). This qualification is particularly important in the case of U-shaped marginal cost curves. For a more exact analysis in this context, the distinction between a long-term and a short-term cost curve would become important. For our discussion, however, we can ignore this distinction and content ourselves with referring to the relevant microeconomics textbooks.

15 The willingness addressed here to give money for a small additional amount of a given good is called "marginal willingness to pay."

16 The reader will already be suspecting that a "*reductio ad absurdum*" proof is coming up.

initial endowment $x_k^{(1)}$ is *below* the ordinate value on the demand curve at the abscissal value $x_k^{(1)}$ (i.e., is smaller than $p^D(x_k^{(1)})$). Then the household would not buy the last unit $x_k^{(1)}$ at a price of $p^D(x_k^{(1)})$. Otherwise, it would be paying more for the unit (namely, $p^D(x_k^{(1)})$) than it is willing to (namely, $MWP(x_k^{(1)})$). This result would contradict the assumption of a rational individual aiming at utility maximization – and it is only the behavior of such individuals that is explained by the model being presented here. The marginal willingness to pay can accordingly not be below the demand price.

Let us now assume that the household's marginal willingness to pay is *above* the demand price. If that were so, it would be inexplicable that for only a very slight rise in the price of x above the demand price $p^D(x_k^{(1)})$ associated with quantity $x_k^{(1)}$, the household responds by refraining from buying the last unit. But it *does* do so, as can be seen in Figure 1 from the movement from point P_1 to point P_2. Thus, the marginal willingness to pay cannot be *above* the demand price.

Because we have established that a household's marginal willingness to pay cannot be either below or above the demand price, we must conclude that marginal willingness to pay and demand price are one and the same thing. We can accordingly read off a household's marginal willingness to pay from the demand curve.

This discussion shows one important property of the competitive equilibrium illustrated in Figure 1: in a competitive equilibrium, the *conflict* between the two demanders k and l over good x is resolved by the institution of the market in such a way as to bring about a distribution of the total quantity x^* produced between those interested for which both individuals' marginal willingness to pay is equal to the market price. Because the market price is (in the perfect competition model assumed here) equal for all consumers, the marginal willingness to pay of both demanders is equal at equilibrium.

Much the same argument as we have given in detail for the demand side can be applied to the supply side. Here the two firms i and j are competing for factors of production needed to produce the good x.[17] Each firm has "allotted" to it through the market that quantity of inputs that enables it to produce a quantity of output for which the price is equal to their individual marginal costs. Because in the perfect competition model the price is identical for all suppliers, at equilibrium the suppliers' marginal costs are also equal to each other. At the competitive equilibrium, thus, the "equimarginal condition"[18] is met on both the demand side and the supply side.

---

17 For an exhaustive presentation of this conflict, an explicit inclusion of factor markets in the consideration would be needed. However, due to the analogy with what has just been said for the conflict between the households on the goods market, we leave out this discussion for space reasons.

18 Term coined by Hartwick and Olewiler (1998, p. 200).

III. The "Social Optimality" of Market Equilibrium in the Ideal-Type Economic Model

We indicated previously that microeconomics (and, thus, also its child environmental economics) is not only confined to describing, explaining, and forecasting human behavior ("positive analysis"), but also makes an attempt at evaluation ("normative analysis"). This is not, though, to be taken to mean that the economist doing the analysis is to make his own preferences as to the relative desirability of goods and social situations the criterion for his assessment. *In this sense*, the economic analysis has to be value free. The normative approach is instead concerned with taking ideas about the determinants of social welfare and the nature of linkages among them that play an important part in society itself and make them operational. A *conditio sine qua non* of this is that the social welfare criterion applied must be made explicit. Then the attempt can be made to measure allocations (and institutions) brought about by society against society's own value conceptions. It may be possible in this way to disclose discrepancies that point to policy errors or provide bases for believing that social actors are actually pursuing different objectives from the ones they claim they are.

Looked at all around, forming a normative component is essential if economics is also to be a tool for the critical analysis of social situations and political decisions. The normative approach is not some special feature of economics among the sciences. Instead, an idea of what constitutes social welfare is generally regarded as indispensable to social orientation. It is merely that public debate uses another term, namely, the "common good." There is probably no society that attempts to get by without this concept.

In contrast, anyone who has attempted to make the concept of social welfare (the common good) operational and, if possible, identify the conditions of a *social optimum* (maximum social welfare) has to admit that this project suffers from grave fundamental problems and innumerable difficulties of detail. Here we have to say, undoubtedly, that the way is the goal.[19]

We want to pursue the environmental economics concerns of this book efficiently and therefore avoid the mazes of welfare economic theory. In this pursuit, we may be helped by a simple (and perhaps for this reason very popular in the literature) convention – by social welfare, we understand the sum of the utilities of all members of society. These utilities may be positive or negative. For negative utilities, the term "cost" has become customary.

---

19   The problems in mind here are treated in welfare economics literature under *social welfare criteria* (Pareto criterion, Kaldor-Hicks criterion, Scitovsky criterion) and *social welfare function* (Arrow's theorem, Black's theorem). Cf. Sohmen (1976). Although this book is now as old as some of the finer malt whiskies, it nonetheless plumbs the depths of welfare economics so thoroughly that for our context it is still worth reading today. Unfortunately, only German-speaking readers will able to savor it. Newer, also fine, and even in English: Feldman/Serrano (2005).

A situation is socially optimal if it maximizes the difference between a (positive) utility and its cost aggregated over all members of society. What we mean may perhaps become (even!) clearer if we narrow the previous extremely general question about the definition of a socially optimum situation to the previous example of producing a good x: the socially optimum production quantity is defined by the fact that the difference between aggregate utility and aggregate production costs is a maximum.

This concept immediately raises the next (extremely uncomfortable) question: how then is utility to be measured? With the convention we are considering, as an approximation for the utility deriving for an individual from the good x, we take that individual's willingness to pay for a supply of the quantity of the goods considered. If we are considering the provision of an additional (marginal) unit, then correspondingly the marginal willingness to pay will serve as a proxy variable. Not all individuals will derive positive utility from the good concerned. Some are instead burdened with costs, especially (but in the environmental economics context we must add *not only*) the producers. The willingness to pay for bearing costs is negative. Negative willingness to pay corresponds to the demand to be compensated for the loss of utility incurred. If a (marginal) additional unit of the good is concerned, then we talk about the marginal compensation demand, or marginal cost.[20]

Using the conventions briefly explained here, then, the answer to the previous question is that the socially optimal production quantity of good x is reached when the difference between the aggregate willingness to pay for x and the aggregate cost of producing x is a maximum.

Let us now consider the market allocation with perfect competition. We first consider the consumer as "beneficiary" of the production. Because the individual demand curve of each consumer, as explained previously, reflects that consumer's marginal willingness to pay, the aggregate demand curve on the market is a graphic illustration of the "marginal utility" (in the sense of aggregate marginal willingness to pay) that the consumers derive from this product. The marginal utility expressed as the marginal willingness to pay is henceforth called "marginal benefit." The area under the demand curve thus represents the total benefit consumers derive from the good x.

Let us now look at the cost side of the market equilibrium and consider the producer as "upholder" of production. In the ideal model that we (initially) consider here, the producer's marginal costs reflect the properly evaluated resource consumption arising from production of an additional unit of good x. The supply

---

20 In applied welfare theory (particularly in the area of *cost–benefit analysis*), *willingness to pay* is set against *willingness to accept* (demand for compensation). The terms *compensating variation* and *equivalent variation* are also frequently used. For more details on the relation between these concepts, cf., e.g., Ebert (2008), Kolstad (2000).The distinction between willingness to accept and willingness to pay will play an important part when it comes to discussing negotiations as an internalization strategy (part two, chapter A, of this book).

curve on the market thus ultimately represents the economic marginal cost for producing good x. The area under the supply curve is accordingly (for the moment disregarding fixed costs) to be considered as a graphic illustration of the total costs associated with producing good x.

Clearly, the optimality criterion of maximizing the benefit–cost difference is met where the difference in the areas under the demand and supply curves is a maximum. Putting it differently, the optimum quantity is defined by the fact that "marginal benefit" and marginal cost of x are equal to each other (a further "equimarginal condition"). But this is the case precisely at the intersection of the supply and demand curves. There the relevant marginal quantities (marginal cost and marginal willingness to pay) are also equalized *between* the supply and demand sides. We can thus see that in the ideal basic model of "perfect competition," the market mechanism will, at equilibrium, make available the socially optimum quantity of the good considered.

Going beyond this, we can see that the market mechanism will distribute consumption of the total socially optimum quantity produced in socially optimum fashion over the various consumers and allocate production of the total quantity optimally to the individual producers.[21]

Let us start by considering the demand side. We have pointed out previously that the equilibrium on the demand side is defined by the fact that the marginal willingness to pay of consumers are made equal to the market price through the adjustment of the quantities individually demanded. Let us now look at the social optimality of this outcome.

For this, let us assume that the distribution has been done, instead of in market equilibrium fashion, in such a way that household k receives ε units more (i.e., $x_k^* + \varepsilon$) and household l receives ε units fewer (i.e., $x_l^* - \varepsilon$) (where $x^* = x_k^* + x_l^* = x_k^* + \varepsilon + x_l^* - \varepsilon$ holds). Then (because the demand curves are falling ones) the marginal willingness to pay for good x is lower for household k than for household l. It would now be conceivable for both households to alter the starting position to the benefit of both. They might, for instance, agree that k would transfer to l ε units of good x at price p^*. Household k would be better off from this exchange because its marginal willingness to pay for each unit between x_k^* and $x_k^* + \varepsilon$ would be below the return payment per unit, namely, p^*. Household l would also be better off from the exchange. For its assessment of the value of each unit between $x_l^* - \varepsilon$ and x_l^* would be above the price p^* to be paid to k for it. Because, then, the initially assumed starting position $(x_k^* + \varepsilon, x_l^* - \varepsilon)$ allows a change that improves the utility of both participants, the starting position cannot have been socially optimum. After all, the socially optimal distribution is defined by the fact that the sum of the

21 The identity of social optimum and market equilibrium allocation, and the simplicity of demonstrating it through the meeting of the "equimarginal conditions," feed on the fact that we have assumed monotonically falling marginal willingness to pay and (at least in the neighborhood of the solution) monotonically rising marginal costs. Both assumptions are part of the folklore of economic theory.

benefits of both parties is a maximum. The readers may convince themselves that no further increase of the aggregate benefit over both consumers is possible once the market equilibrium allocation x_k^*, x_l^* is arrived at. The market equilibrium is, then, optimum in the previously defined sense on the demand side.

Similar arguments can be made for the supply side: let us assume that in the initial position the total quantity x^* offered by both firms i and j is produced by having i produce a quantity $x_i^* - \varepsilon$ and j a quantity $x_j^* + \varepsilon$. Then j's marginal costs would be higher than i's. If, starting from this initial position, firm i increases its production quantity to x_i^* and firm j reduces its production quantity to x_j^*, then the total quantity produced would remain x^*, but the total costs expended on it would fall. The additional costs arising for firm i (in Figure 1, the area P_3, $x_i^* - \varepsilon$, x_i^*, P_4)[22] are smaller than the cost reduction effects arising for firm j (in Figure 1, area P_5, x_j^*, $x_j^* + \varepsilon$, P_6). The costs (resources) saved to the economy could, following this rise in efficiency, be used to produce something useful (i.e., associated with positive willingness to pay). Accordingly, the starting position $(x_i^* - \varepsilon, x_j^* + \varepsilon)$ was not socially optimal. However, readers may convince themselves that this condition is met by the market equilibrium position x_i^*, x_j^*.

The *social optimality* of the market equilibrium in the ideal economic model was presented previously with extreme simplification. We could do this with a (comparatively) good conscience: the explanation ought for pedagogical reasons to be confined to those elements of the problem indispensable to the specific context of discussion ("internalization of externalities") here. Nonetheless, it is probably appropriate to note that a more penetrating analysis would convey a considerably more differentiated picture than the preceding text. We have already referred briefly to the problems of the concept of social welfare. It must be further mentioned that the presentation was always, for reasons of simplification, confined to circumstances in a single market. For this, the instrument of *partial analysis* (more exactly, partial equilibrium theory) was employed. However, a more differentiated treatment would have to take into account the interplay of processes on various markets (*total analysis*, or more exactly, general equilibrium theory). The attempt to depict a complete market *system* with all its interdependencies and assess its allocation outcome is something to which economic theory attributes fundamental importance. These efforts are rooted in the works of the very founding father of economics in, for instance, *An Inquiry into the Nature and Causes of the Wealth of Nations* (1776) by Adam Smith. They were perfected by Kenneth Arrow and Gérard Debreu, who each took the Nobel Prize in Economics for their contributions, in 1972 and 1983, respectively.[23]

---

22   By the expression $(x_i^* - \varepsilon)$, the point entered on the graph $(x_i^* - \varepsilon, 0)$ is meant. This abbreviated writing convention is used similarly in discussing all graphs.

23   Because of its complexity, the area of general equilibrium theory is generally not covered in introductory microeconomics textbooks. Endres/Martiensen (2007) and Feess (2004) endeavor (following Einstein's well-known motto) to give presentations that re-create the theory as simply as possible – but no simpler! Too bad these text books are written in German. For research in

We previously discussed the social optimality of an ideal market model with plausibility considerations supported by the model. By social optimum, we understood the allocation that maximizes social welfare. Social welfare was defined as the amount by which aggregate willingness to pay exceeds the costs.

In the mainstream of the following discussion, we retain this concept of social optimality. Sometimes, however (particularly for pedagogical reasons, as well as to be able to link up better with the relevant literature), it is appropriate to use a slightly different concept of social optimality. It is also current in the theoretical economics literature and is known as the *Pareto optimum*. The relevant criterion for the social assessment of situations is a social situation A is to be preferred to another situation B if in A at least one member of the society is better off and no other worse off than in B. Here how well off the individual is always has to be assessed by the individual him- or herself. This concept for the operationalization of the social welfare concept goes back to the Italian sociologist and economist Vilfredo Pareto (1848–1923) and is known as the *Pareto criterion*. According to the Pareto criterion, a situation is socially optimal ("Pareto optimal") if, starting from it, no further change is possible that would leave even one member of the society better off without making another worse off.

The Pareto criterion has the great advantage over the concept of maximization of social welfare as a sum of the individual utilities explained previously that it gets by without a *cardinal utility concept*. To employ the Pareto criterion, we need neither assume that the utility of a single individual can be quantitatively determined nor that a utility comparison among various individuals is possible. That is a load off the chest of a welfare economist trained in ordinal utility theory![24] The advantage the Pareto criterion has in getting by with weaker assumptions has its price, however[25]: in contrast with the idea of maximizing society's aggregate net welfare, the Pareto criterion suffers from the fact that there are infinitely many situations for which the criterion is not at all able to rank them by social desirability. It is by definition not possible to say according to the Pareto criterion whether state C or state D is socially preferable if in C one member of society is better off than in D but another worse. Moreover, there are infinitely many Pareto optima. It is not even the case that an arbitrarily chosen Pareto optimum state is always, according to the Pareto criterion, socially superior to an arbitrarily chosen non–Pareto optimum state.

the area of applied environmental economics, *computable general equilibrium models* are gaining importance. Cf., e.g., Conrad (2002), Conrad/Löschel (2005), Conrad/Schröder (1993), Kemfert (2005), Steiniger/Friedl/Gebetsroither (2007).

24 In section 2 of chapter B, we again consider the tensions between cardinality and ordinality of the microeconomic utility concept.

25 Our worldly-wise readers will know that the globe in which humans live consists of two zones. In one of them (the small one), the motto "The best things in life are free" applies; in the other (the big one), it is instead "There ain't no such thing as a free lunch." Obviously, economic modeling belongs in the second zone. This need not surprise us all that much, for however beautiful it doubtless is, it undoubtedly is not among the best things in life.

In the light of the environmental economics concerns of this book, we cannot devote any more space here to these welfare economics positions. You can easily follow them up if you need to, though, by looking in a microeconomics textbook for the piece on the *Edgeworth box*. You can find Pareto optimum states in hoards and shoals on the "contract curve" illustrated in this box. Non–Pareto optimum states are to either side of the curve, and there are infinitely many of them.

IV. Divergences between Equilibrium and Social Optimum Due to Externalities: The Problem of "Market Failure"

Of course, the economic model sketched out previously is a radical simplification of how things are in reality. Considering its extreme simplicity, it is perhaps surprising that this model can nonetheless manage to go some way toward portraying the important driving forces of economic action and the nature of economic institutions (e.g., striving after profit or utility, competition, and purchasing power on the market). In contrast, there is no doubt that it is far too crudely structured for direct application to economic or environmental policy.

For instance, it is obvious that in reality even *individual* suppliers can sometimes have considerable influence on the price of the product they make. This has considerable consequences for the optimality of the market equilibrium. In the extreme case of monopoly, the supplier achieves an equilibrium at which the marginal costs lie below the market price. At equilibrium, accordingly, marginal willingness to pay and marginal cost do not equal each other, so that the socially optimal production quantity is not achieved. Similarly, the optimality of the market equilibrium is disrupted by government intervention such as customs duties or taxes on products, which drive a wedge between the prices paid by consumers and received by producers. Here, again, a balance of marginal willingness to pay and marginal cost is not reached. The result is a misallocation. A further aspect important in real life (and in rather more complex economic models) but ignored previously is that actors do not have sufficient information available to act in the way explained. In particular, information (e.g., on the quality of a product) may be *asymmetrically* distributed between supplier and demander. If the demander is not able to observe all relevant features of the product before purchase, misallocations may result.

The economic theory about this goes back to George Akerlof's (1970) paper "The Market for 'Lemons': Quality Uncertainty and the Market Mechanism."[26] The author was awarded the Nobel Prize in Economics in 2001 for his trailblazing work in information economics. In the context of our discussion, concerned with the theory of externalities, we refrain from an exhaustive presentation and content ourselves with the following summary.

---

26 "Lemons" is an Americanism for poor quality products (especially used cars). See Macho-Stadler/Pérez-Castrillo (2001) on the economics of asymmetric information.

Lateral view 2: Economic theory of asymmetrical information – executive summary. *Source:* Steinmann/Westfalenpost, Hagen, 2000. Reprinted with the author's kind permission.

Unquestionably, the list of differences between reality and the ideal model sketched previously is long. It is part of the folklore of microeconomics textbooks. However, not every item on the list is of interest for every discourse. It should be recalled in this connection that economic model building specifically does not pursue the objective of depicting reality like a photo. We accordingly concentrate on the divergences between reality and model of most relevance to the analysis of environmental problems[27]: the previous ideal presentation (implicitly) assumed that only the producers and demanders are affected by production of good x (plus, of course, the market suppliers of the production factors needed to produce it).

Every cost or benefit effect associated with good x is, in this model, transmitted through markets: the benefit from consuming good x goes exclusively to the consumers that pay to buy that good on the market for it. The costs for producing it are incurred exclusively by the firms producing it, which are compensated for their expenditure by the market proceeds. To produce it, they use only production factors bought on the factor markets. *In the model for good x just briefly sketched, there are no relationships other than market relations.* This fact has to be seen as a drastic simplification, given the actual circumstances of reality. In economics, we call interdependencies between individuals mediated through markets "internal effects."

An "externality" arises, in contrast, where the utility position (for firms, profit position) of an individual depends directly (i.e., without mediation through the market mechanism) on an activity controlled by another individual. Taking this definition as a basis, it will immediately be found that every individual's life world contains a thick jungle of externalities. Not all these effects are relevant in our

27   Of course, various divergences between a simple model and reality may interact. Taking account of this, although important to analysis, complicates it considerably. The consequences of simultaneous occurrence of externalities and market power are discussed in part four, chapter B. An example of the internalization of externalities with asymmetrical information is discussed in part two, section B.IV, in the context of environmental liability insurance. A similar interaction is covered in part four, chapter C, in connection with internalization negotiations with asymmetrical information.

context, and there is by no means consensus in society about which ones are at issue. One example of an externality on which consensus might be possible is dust emitted by a firm.[28]

A monetary evaluation of the externality shows the external costs.[29] The total costs caused by the production, the "social costs," result from the sum of the private and external costs.

To explain the effects of an externality on the social optimality of a competitive equilibrium, we return to our previous example of the production of good x. Let us assume for simplicity's sake that there is a third household,[30] m, that suffers damage from the soot emission (however defined). We assume it is possible to give the amount of the damage in money units as a function of the quantity emitted. The effect of this extension of the model on the optimality of the market equilibrium and thus on the need for economic policy action can be presented through a confrontation of the previously discussed interests of firms i and j and households k and l, on the one hand, and of household m, on the other hand. In order not to let the presentation get inordinately complicated, we combine the previously mentioned interests of i, j, k, and l by joining together the supply curve and demand curve for good x from Figure 1. The demand curve, as explained previously, gives the gross benefit of the production of good x. The supply curve, as also explained previously, gives the cost of this production to the extent that it arises from consumption of marketed production factors. Accordingly, the difference between the two curves represents the marginal net benefit of the production if only participants coordinated through the market (i, j, k, l) are considered. In Figure 1 the joined D–S curve falls to zero at the point of optimum production (x^*) at which the supply curve intersects the demand curve. Instead of reading this curve in conventional fashion from 0 in the direction of increasing production quantities, we can also look at it the other way around (i.e., from x^* in the direction of 0). Then the curve shows us how high the net benefit becomes that society loses, to the extent that is represented on the market for x, when the production of x is cut back. These losses of benefit are nothing, but the marginal opportunity costs of a reduction

---

28   Unless stated otherwise, we assume that the emission level is strictly proportional to the production level. Because we can set standards for the measuring unit for emissions in such a way as to make the proportionality factor take the value 1, we use one and the same symbol for output and emission, x. In part three and part four, chapter B, however, it will sometimes matter particularly that output and emission are not in a fixed coupled relationship with each other. This is obviously important when discussing incentives to polluters to employ abatement technologies or develop them further. In such contexts, the symbol "E" is used for emissions, retaining "x" for the output.

29   Whether externalities can be valued in money terms is an anything but trivial question. There is a rich literature on the conceptual, methodological, and empirical aspects of monetization. Cf., e.g., Mäler/Vincent (2005). For a *fairly* skeptical view, see Diamond/Hausman (1994), and for an *extremely* skeptical one, Ackerman/Heinzerling (2004).

30   The restriction to one household once again does not restrict the generality of the statement.

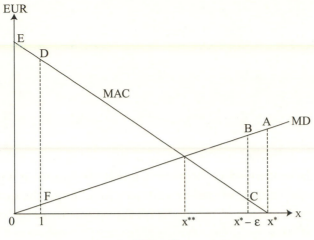

Figure 2

in the production level. As mentioned previously, we assume that the externality (here the producer's soot emissions) is strictly proportional to the quantity produced; the marginal abatement cost (MAC) curve is as shown in Figure 2.[31] Figure 2 also shows the marginal damage (MD) arising for household m, as a function of the level of production (emission).[32]

That clears the stage for us to put on the "internalizing externalities" show. By this, we mean charging the external costs to the polluter. If the internalization is successful, then the latter will take account in his allocation decisions of not only his private costs, but also the external ones (i.e., in total also the social costs). This brings private and social rationality into harmony. To further clarify these connections, we can determine the optimum level of emissions, in complete analogy with what we said previously about market equilibrium and the optimality criterion conventional in economics.[33]

The activity causing the externality must according to the logic presented previously be limited to the level at which the net benefit of the limitation is a maximum. This net benefit is the gross benefit less the costs of the reduction. Consider a reduction of the polluting activity x from the starting position x^* to a quantity slightly below that, $x^* - \varepsilon$. The gross benefit of reducing the activity by ε

31 If we imagine the curve being aggregated over a large number of firms, then it will have no kinks in it at all – well, hardly any.

32 The marginal damage curve has been shown rising monotonically. We cannot for space reasons go into the consequences arising from departing from this assumption. Cf., e.g., Burrows (2008); Perman et al. (2003), chs. 6 and 11; Xepapadeas (1997), pp. 44–51.

This figure appears – albeit with very different interpretations – *at least once* in *every* microeconomics textbook. As A. Leijonhufvud (1981) shows in his famous ethnological investigation of science, this is a kind of totem using by which the members of the *Tribe of the Econ* recognize each other and demarcate themselves from related (i.e., hostile!) tribes.

33 The externality caused by the emission is internalized precisely where the optimum emission level is reached (by charging for the external costs).

lies in the damage avoided thereby. Figure 2 symbolizes this effect by the integral (the area) below the marginal damage curve within the limits of integration $x^* - \varepsilon$ to x^* (viz. area $x^* - \varepsilon$, x^*, AB). The costs arising for society from this reduction are, in contrast, to be read off as the integral under the MAC curve within the same limits (viz. area $x^* - \varepsilon$, x^*, C). If the curves in Figure 2 correctly represent the circumstances of our example, then the gross benefit of a reduction in the externality (measured as damage avoided) by ε is clearly greater than the cost of reduction.

The socially optimum reduction level is attained if the quantity is cut back from x^* to x^{**}, where the difference between the benefit and cost of the reduction is a maximum. In other words, the marginal benefit corresponds to the marginal cost. The graph shows the optimum emission (production) quantity as the point of intersection of the MAC and MD curves. Here we see the analogy between the environmental economics concept of the optimum emission quantity and the traditional microeconomic concept of optimum production quantity. Both social optima are characterized by the equalization of marginal quantities that can be interpreted as respectively the marginal benefit and marginal cost of the quantity to be optimized.[34]

It is already becoming clear at this point that the environmental economics presented here constitutes a strict application of traditional microeconomics (with all its strengths and weaknesses). However, the *evaluation* of the market mechanism in accordance with this unitary optimality concept is diametrically opposite, where externalities are present, from that in the ideal model of perfect competition. Although in the latter the market mechanism is certified as having optimality, the market equilibrium (x^*) and social optimum (x^{**}) differ where externalities are present. When the allocation outcome of a mechanism departs from the social optimum, in economics we call this a "failure" of the mechanism. If the allocation mechanism concerned is, as here, the market system, we call that "market failure."[35]

This terminology brings a danger of misinterpretation if understood in terms of ordinary language. If a mechanism fails, one might think it should be replaced by another one as quickly as possible. However, one should let caution prevail here. It might after all prove (and it does) that no real allocation mechanism can meet the ambitious optimality criterion of maximizing social net benefit. If

34 The optimum emission quantity is defined here using marginal quantities (through the meeting of an "equimarginal condition"). A description in terms of total quantities would be of equal value: the optimum emission quantity is where the sum of total abatement cost and total damage is a minimum. The fact that with alternative shapes of the curves there are also optima that do not meet the marginal conditions explained in the text is mentioned here for the sake of completeness, but for space reasons we do not go further into it.

35 The theory of market failure takes up a lot of room in modern economics literature. As well as the externalities central to the discourse in this book, such issues as market power, asymmetrical information, network effects, and other reasons for market failure are exhaustively discussed. A broadly oriented critical discussion of the concept of market failure in its various modes is given in Cowen/Crampton (2002).

we reject all the concepts that do not meet the criterion, then nothing will be left. The literature accordingly tends to flank "market failure" by "governmental failure." Most recently, there has frequently been talk of "judicial failure" and even (horrors!) "science failure."

For practical economic or environmental policy, then, we have to live with the fact that we can choose only among imperfect allocation mechanisms, or perhaps combine these. The optimality concept serves us here only (but at least!) as a compass (occasionally flawed) to show us what direction the real allocation mechanisms and their combinations have to be changed in.

V. The Internalization of Externalities to "Restore" the "Lost" Optimality of Market Equilibrium

Defining equilibrium, on the one hand, and social optimum, on the other hand, and establishing that they diverge shows up a problem, but does not yet point any way toward solving it. Let us, once again, before we turn to paths to solution, summarize the insights we have gained into the social optimality of the competitive equilibrium in the ideal model and its suboptimality in the model with externalities:

a) The secret of the optimality of the competitive equilibrium in the ideal model is that every decision maker claiming a share of scarce resources must him- or herself bear the consequential scarcity he produces for others. Someone buying one unit of the scarce good x simultaneously causes two displacement effects by his purchasing decision. He prevents the production factors used to produce that unit from being employed in utility-creating fashion to some other end and prevents other consumers potentially interested in the unit of x from consuming it. These negative consequential effects of our consumer's decision are valued on the market through the marginal production costs for x and the marginal willingness to pay of the rival consumers. Now, it is central to our understanding of the optimality of the market equilibrium in the simple model that the market price for x at equilibrium simultaneously reflects both of these elements of renunciation.[36] We can see at this point in the discussion that the causation principle ("*polluter pays*" *principle*) inherent in environmental policy (at least in intention) is by no means to be regarded as an invention by ecologists critical of economics. The principle is, instead, a fundamental feature of the market mechanism itself. Where it functions optimally, its optimality is based precisely on the fact that our causer of scarcities is directly financially burdened with the scarcity consequences he causes for others. He is thus induced to bring these fully into his decisions.

b) Market failure in the presence of externalities is constituted by the breakdown of the polluter pays principle. By definition, a negative externality exists when a third party is adversely affected by a decision maker without the consequences

36   See Figure 1, where $p^* = MC(x^*) = MWP(x^*)$ holds.

of the decision rebounding on that decision maker. The internalization of externalities is meant to extend the causation principle as an essential feature of the market mechanism into this area. It is therefore important to understand that the internalization of externalities does not mean bringing some sort of ecological foreign body into the world of economics, but is instead a consistent application of economic principles to restoring the social optimality of the market mechanism.[37] It is in this (narrow) sense that the concept of internalization of externalities is to be understood here. The point is to burden the causer financially with the negative consequences of his action not initially covered by the market.[38]

The terms "social optimality" and "internalization" have often led to the misunderstanding in the literature that this amounts to portraying a "perfect world" pretending to a harmony that despises conflict-ridden reality.

However, the economic optimum is not some state of harmony in which all participants (or even only one of them) is unconditionally happy. It is much more the case that the economic optimality concept identifies the point at which the conflicts of interest among those involved become unbridgeable. If the optimum has not yet been reached, then (by definition) the existing competing claims for scarce resources can still be assuaged by reallocations that make at least one of them better off without detriment to the others, or even, with suitably clever redistributions, make all participants better off. If the optimum is then achieved, this does not mean that a state of universal happiness has been achieved, but only that any change making one individual better has to make another one worse off.

Thus, the optimum equilibrium in Figure 1 says nothing about whether consumer k is poor and would like to be rich, or whether both consumers are deeply unhappy at the fact that they can secure no more than x_k^* or x_l^*, respectively, of the desired good. Equally, the optimum position x^{**} in Figure 2 does not mark a position of harmony between the causer of the externality and the damaged party. Instead, the damaged party may complain bitterly at still having to endure x^{**} units of the externality, whereas the causer is still inconsolable at having had to reduce it from x^* to x^{**}.

The economically optimum state cannot remove the conflicts of interests among decision makers because it cannot remove the problem of scarcity. It can only (but this is already a great deal!) reduce the conflicts of interests to the lowest level

---

37   This statement is not to be confused with the expectation that the enthusiasm of "the economy" over the employment of instruments to internalize externalities will be great. Interest groups' attitudes to environmental policy in its various manifestations are studied by the *New Political Economy* ("Public Choice"). Cf., e.g., Halbheer/Niggli/Schmutzler (2006), Kirchgässner/Schneider (2003), Schneider/Weck-Hannemann (2005), Stavins/Pratt (2004).

38   There are a number of methods for inducing the causer of externalities to correct his behavior that are not "internalization measures" in the previously strict sense. These measures of "internalization in the broader sense" range from the pressure of public opinion to government commands and prohibitions. For an economic analysis of environmental policy instruments that are not in the narrow sense internalization strategies, see part three.

defined by the scarcity of the available resources. Suboptimal (inefficient) states produce more conflicts than necessary for any given resource endowment.

Various theoretical variants are available for the *internalization of externalities* (i.e., the charging of external marginal costs to the causer). The most important are as follows:

a) Negotiations on the level of externalities among those involved, in the sense of the paradigm developed by Ronald Coase (1960).

b) The creation of institutions regulating how far and on what conditions the causer of the externality has to pay the damaged party compensation for damages (liability law).

c) Charging the causer with the external marginal costs arising at the socially optimum position through a tax, on the paradigm of Arthur C. Pigou (1932).

We explained market failure as a consequence of externalities previously, and we go on in part two to deal with correcting it by employing internalization measures. It is assumed that the causer of the externality does not take it into account in deciding on the extent and quality of his activity as long as he is not having to face internalization strategies. In particular, he will make no contribution toward saving the environment out of mere respect for nature. Even knowing the fact that his consumption of the environment is encroaching on the welfare of other people will have no influence on his decisions. He can, therefore, be motivated to incorporate the externalities only *extrinsically*.[39]

The assumption that a decision maker is indifferent to the effects of his activities on others' welfare is *once again* just one of these unrealistic assumptions of neoclassical economic theory. In reality, after all, any child knows that people's utilities are interdependent. Thus, life is rich, and neoclassical economics is poor.[40]

Lateral view 3: Claudia and Gunhild Witzig's rich life takes them above neoclassical aridity. *Source:* Steinmann/Westfalenpost, Hagen, 2000. Reprinted with the author's kind permission.

---

39 On the economics of intrinsic motivation and the danger of suppressing it by extrinsic incentives, cf., e.g., Frey (2001), James (2005).

40 *Now let's be serious*: although interdependent utility functions are *side stream* in traditional economic theory, they cannot be overlooked. There is a wealth of approaches, ranging from Becker (1974) to (at the time of writing) Bergstrom (2006).

B. Implications of Making the Concept of Internalization Programmatic in Environmental Policy

Before we turn to analyzing individual internalization strategies in part two, we still have to work out what implications are associated with making the concept of internalizing externalities into an environmental policy program. The implications take it as a basis that making the concept of internalizing externalities (in the definition from economic theory used here) into an environmental policy program accepts the fundamentals of market logic and is to be employed in protecting the environment. Individually, the implications are as follows.

I. The Principle of Consumer Sovereignty

In the brief discussion of the economic optimality concept, the levels of various values (namely, production costs, environmental damage, and utility from the consumption of goods) played the fundamental part. A central notion in the concept of value that is the basis here is that the positive or negative value that a good or ill has for a decision maker can be assessed only by that decision maker him- or herself. The utility of a good to a consumer assessed in the economic model lies in that consumer's sense of utility. The utility concepts (preferences) of the decision maker are taken in economics (at any rate in the great bulk of the literature[41]) as given. The process of generating preferences, in particular, their determination by social interactions and learning processes, is not analyzed by mainstream economic literature, although undoubtedly of great importance for reality. Moreover, attention should be paid to the fact that the mainstream economics taken as a basis here assumes in order to simplify that individuals' preferences relate exclusively to the outcomes of the allocation process (and, thus, particularly to the provision of goods). As to the ways and means whereby the allocation outcome comes about, the individuals are, on the assumptions, indifferent.[42] These (and other) restrictions do not mean that traditional economic theory is worthless for explaining human behavior, but that it does not explain an important aspect of the dynamics of human societies and can therefore be only one voice (although in my view a very important one) in the polyphonic choir of explanatory approaches in the human sciences.[43]

---

41 However, economic theory is such a broad (and "biologically" so dynamic) field that it is always true that "there is nothing that there isn't." A subtle distinction is Cooter's (1991) between (endogenous) preferences and (exogenous) metapreferences, or see Ebert/v.d. Hagen (2002), with their distinction between (exogenous) preferences and (endogenous) taste.

42 That this can (must?!?) also be seen entirely differently is illuminated by the subtitle of Frey/Benz/Stutzer (2004): "Not Only What, But Also How Matters." Cf. also Frey/Stutzer (2005).

43 The separation made previously for the sake of clarity between "traditional economic theory" *here* and other "approaches in the human sciences" *there* (with nothing in between) yields a very fragmentary picture. In fact, what we see in the social and behavioral sciences is a fascinating process of mutual interpenetration in which (and how could it be otherwise?!) the parties involved

In a consumer's evaluation of the positive and negative utility of a good or ill, the decision maker's perceptions are essential. These are necessarily selective. However, we must warn against rejecting the principle of consumer sovereignty by referring to consumers' poor information about the properties of products and the negative effects of environmental impacts. Otherwise, there is a danger here of proposals for authoritarian solutions. In a democratic society, the valuations of single individuals should play a central part, even if they are not fully informed. Apart from the fact that the danger of abuse by an "expertocracy" would be considerable, the experts' level of information also has to be assessed skeptically. They can mostly see only one partial aspect of the complicated and interdependent problem of environmental or economic policy. Although they can accordingly make important contributions to the complex social communication process, they can in no way replace it. In relation to the role of economics in discussing problems of consumers' information level, it has to be stressed that considerable progress has been made here. Increasingly, "information economics," in which decision makers' degree of information is no longer treated as exogenously given, is being integrated into the "organism" of economic theory. Here the process of information production and processing is itself treated as an economic problem through which statements on the optimality of equilibriums are possible.[44]

II. Ordinality and Cardinality of the Concept of Utility: Willingness to Pay as an Approximation

If despite the reservations we accept (perhaps for lack of any better alternative) the concept of consumer sovereignty, then on the road to defining an optimum that is to be reached by internalization we are soon confronted with a new obstacle. Even if the utility estimates of those concerned are supposed to be decisive for the position of the optimum, that does not yet say how they are (conceptually and practically) to be measured. In modern microeconomics, utility is an *ordinal*, not a *cardinal*, concept.

In many areas of application (and research programs) of economic theory, it is also adequate to work with a utility concept according to which those concerned are in a position to order situations related to their degree of desirability without being able to evaluate the utility experienced thereby quantitatively or interpersonally comparably. But it is just this that is needed in order to define a social economic optimum, for instance, an optimum emission quantity. The statement that the optimum emission quantity is defined by the fact that marginal abatement costs and

can be changed radically. For instance (with particular reference to the links between economic theory and psychology), see the works of Frank (2004, 2008), Frey (2001), Frey/Osterloh (2002). The *Journal of Psychological Economics* continually prints articles that in the sense described are "(di)osmotic."

44 Cf., e.g., the introductory presentation in Varian (2006) or, more detailed, Macho-Stadler/Pérez-Castrillo (2001).

marginal damage are equal implies that both quantities can be indicated quantitatively in one and the same dimension. Apart from practical measuring difficulties, we have to first note the conceptual problem: both environmental damage and abatement costs involve losses of utility. The latter constitutes the losses of utility from refraining from using resources for alternative (e.g., consumption) purposes ("opportunity costs"). If the social optimum is defined as presented previously, then as an approximation to the utility, which strictly speaking cannot be measured as a cardinal, we take the *willingness to pay* (or demand for compensation, respectively) of the relevant decision maker. For the demand curve used previously, to evaluate consumer goods shows, as already explained, nothing else than the relevant consumer's marginal willingness to pay for the good. Analogously, the marginal damage curve in Figure 2 shows the concerned person's willingness to pay for a reduction in the damage. In another (related) interpretation, it shows the damaged party's demand for payment to tolerate the externality.

We have thus established that if the concept of internalizing externalities is used, then in environmental policy terms we are aiming at an optimum defined by economic criteria. The values used to constitute this optimum are *market values*. For marketable goods, the valuation made by an "ideal" market (i.e., in particular, one with perfect competition) is accepted. For goods not valued directly through markets, the valuation is made market analogously using the concept of willingness to pay.[45]

It is important to note that using market values, or substitutes for them derived by market analogous procedures, brings into the valuation, alongside the preferences of those concerned, also their *income* and *assets*. Obviously, a "rich" decision maker is in a position to manifest greater willingness to pay on the market than a "poor" one. We do not consider whether this is basically wrong; instead, each individual's valuation ought to go into the social evaluation with the same weighting. However, we would point out that the uncorrected use of willingness to pay as the value implicitly accepts the underlying income distribution.

III. From Individual Utility to Social Welfare: The Aggregation Problem

The explanation pursued so far of the implications of the optimality concept presented previously at the single individual's level has, of course, not yet dealt with all

---

45 The economic principles for valuing environmental goods using the concept of willingness to pay and the associated methods of empirical social research are, for space reasons, not discussed further in this book. A survey can be found in, for instance, the literature referred to in footnote 31. Carson et al. (2004) offer an interesting case study that makes the possibilities of employing monetary evaluation of environmental damage, and its problems, clear in exemplary fashion. The sources indicated previously take traditional welfare economics as the theoretical basis for valuing environmental damage. On the inclusion of unconventional economic theory approaches, cf. the articles in the special issue "Coping with Stated Preference Anomalies in Environmental Decision-Making" of *Environmental and Resource Economics*, Vol. 32, No. 1 (2005).

of them. The optimality of the supply of a particular good in an economy or of the emission level in a region has ultimately to do not with individual, but with social concepts. The step from the individual to the social evaluation is accomplished in economics by *aggregation*. The social value of an emission reduction is nothing but the sum of the valuations by all individuals benefiting from it. The social costs of this reduction are correspondingly the sum of the shortfalls from target suffered by the single individuals who have to bear the costs (opportunity costs) of this reduction. This concept has no room for an interest of "society as such" over and above the interests of its individual members. The underlying individualistic approach here may seem a matter of course to most members of today's Western societies. However, even those who accept it should be clear that it is not based on natural laws, but is an outcome of our cultural socialization. In other societies and/or other times, social welfare concepts may possibly determine people's lives.[46]

It must further be pointed out that with the aggregation method, the individuals' preferences are treated additively; this means that interdependencies that necessarily arise in the sociocultural communication process are left out of account.[47]

IV. Consequences

Let us consider the consequences of what we have said for internalization as our guiding principle of environmental policy. Internalization serves the objective of creating a socially optimum allocation of resources. In particular, the inability of the uncorrected market mechanism to produce optimum environmental quality levels is to be corrected. Contrary to widespread views in the literature, though, the optimum being aimed at is not some state to be defined by "natural laws" and with unchanging properties. Instead, it is rather a vague concept. Thus, the position of an optimum emission level depends on influences from various quantities.

From what was said previously, the following can be important determinants of the optimum:

a) Preferences of those affected by emissions
b) Consumer preferences for goods whose manufacture leads to emissions
c) Value that production factors used to reduce emissions have in other uses
d) Current state of the art in technology

---

46 In the literature, there has been much controversy over the underlying concepts of *utilitarianism* and *normative individualism*. In our context, there is unfortunately no room to go any further into these concepts; however, a critical discussion can be found in Binmore (2005).

47 On the economic role of communication, see, e.g., Frey (2001). In Reksulak et al. (2004), language itself becomes an object of study for economic analysis: the authors explain the development of the English language and its efficiency using the theory of network goods. On the importance of communication in interdependent decision situations (as analyzed by game theory), cf., Aumann/Hart (2003), Blume/Arnold (2004). For his contributions to game theory, Robert J. Aumann was awarded the Nobel Prize for Economics in 2005.

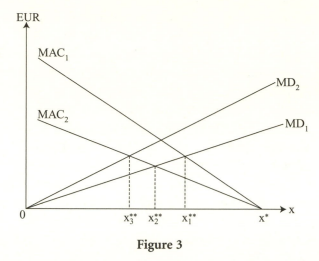

Figure 3

Correspondingly, the position of the optimum can shift with any change in the determinants.

Figure 3 shows how the optimum emission level defined by the intersection of curves MD_1 and MAC_1 falls from x_1^{**} to x_2^{**} if – say, because of technical progress – the MAC curve falls from MAC_1 to MAC_2.[48] If additionally the marginal damage curve rises from MD_1 to MD_2 – say, because the real income of the individuals concerned has risen (and the absence of the corresponding pollutant is a superior good) – then the optimum emission level falls further to x_3^{**}. Of course, movements in the opposite direction are also conceivable. Thus, a particularly upsetting report about the new "pollutant of the month," y, might push the pollutant shown in Figure 3, x, into the background in public awareness and lower the willingness to pay for its absence. Correspondingly, the marginal damage curve will fall. And this will raise the optimum emission value. An increase in optimum emission value might also come from a rise in the MAC curve. This might be due to, say, a rise in the cost of a production factor essential for x abatement technology. This cost increase may obviously be fully independent of environmental policy aimed at pollutant x. It might, for instance, be because demand for a product outside the environmental sector that needs the same production factor rises.

These few examples make it clear that the optimum emission level (optimum environmental policy) is not some exogenous quantity for the economy and society, but is itself defined endogenously through the interaction of innumerable quantities influencing it in a highly complex economic and social process. Internalizing externalities thus means aiming at a very highly mobile target.[49]

48 To understand the falling abatement costs with technical progress, it is advisable to depart from the simplifying assumption that the emissions are strictly proportional to output. We instead imagine that emissions might (in addition to means of output reduction) be cut by technical environmental protection measures. These may be oriented additively (e.g., installing a filter (but do not forget to switch it on!)) or integratively (e.g., raising the degree of combustion).

49 Let us take some drama out of this description by noting that even from the economic viewpoint, not *every* change in the optimum automatically necessitates an adjustment to the environmental

A further complication that comes along is that important influential factors among those mentioned not only change independently of environmental policy so that the latter has to respond to exogenous influences, but are also themselves influenced by environmental policy. Thus, environmental policy undoubtedly changes the income distribution, which is undoubtedly of interest for the location of the emission optimum.[50] Moreover, the choice of environmental policy strategies is decisive for the amount and direction of progress in environmental technology, which in turn, as explained previously, helps determine the location of the optimum.[51] Finally, the population's environmental awareness, which is important for the position of the *MD* curve (and thus of the emission optimum) not only affects the intensity and quality of the environmental policy, but is also in turn influenced by it.

Alongside these basic problems, we have to point out that optimality in the sense described can be reached only if *all* costs and benefits associated with the emission reduction observed are completely and correctly taken into account. This means, for instance, that all types of damage caused by the emission (e.g., damage to materials and buildings, aesthetic impairments, or health damage) have to be taken into account for all concerned, irrespective of how far away from the emission source they live. This requirement even extends to individuals that will be affected only in the future. Similarly, the costs of the emission reduction must also be taken fully into account. In particular, they must be set at the values that an ideal market mechanism would set them at. These "shadow prices" of the opportunity costs used in the emission reduction certainly differ from the market prices actually paid (distorted by, say, market power or government intervention).[52] Although there are a number of approaches to solving these problems, the difficulties are nonetheless considerable.

V. Nonetheless: Internalization of Externalities as an Indispensable Component of an Environmental Policy Vision

The severe conceptual and practical problems of internalizing externalities described previously ought not, in my view, lead to rejecting this approach as useless to environmental policy. It is often believed that instead of the "economic" internalization approach, environmental policy ought to be guided by extraeconomic criteria. This is, however, to overlook the point that the difficulties described

policy aiming at internalization. Here the utility of the policy change must be set against the policy cost (in the broadest sense). It would be interesting to investigate how far the costs of the policy change differ for various internalization strategies.

50 The connections between distribution and the position of the allocation optimum are explained in detail in part two, section A.II.1.

51 We go into this connection in section C.II. of part three in more detail (and in *yet* more detail in chapter D of part four).

52 For more on the concept of shadow prices and its importance to cost–benefit analysis in environmental protection, see, e.g., Young (2005).

previously that internalization has to deal with will undoubtedly turn up with other environmental policy concepts, too. Thus, any democratically legitimated environmental policy, whether it is called "economic" or not, has to live with the fact that people are imperfectly informed and their views about the values of scarce resources (environmental goods and marketable goods) are subject to constant change.

It is also wrong to counterpose the "economic approach" in environmental policy to "open social discourse" about environmental policy goals as alternatives, as occasionally happens in the academic debate. An open environmental policy discourse also improves the conditions for the success of the employment of economic environmental policy strategies. The better informed and more critical[53] the individual decision makers are, the better an economically oriented policy based on the autonomy of the individual will work.

Ultimately, the problems of the optimality concept in economics go back to the difficulty in a highly developed pluralist society of formulating objectives that are to apply to society as a whole. After all, such a society consists of many million people, each one of them already suffering from conflicting goals, and far more so having contrasting interests interacting along many dimensions while being linked with each other and dependent on each other in a world of interdependencies that is too complex to grasp properly. It is inevitable that an objective applying to a complex inhomogeneous society will in principle be problem ridden, hard to put into practice, and liable to change in course of time. This is something "economic" approaches suffer from no more and no less than "extraeconomic" ones. The objective of optimality of resource allocation developed in economics is, considering the Herculean nature of the task of formulating an objective for society, a thoroughly presentable one.

Moreover, it should not be forgotten that the policy alternatives are not either to pursue the goal of economic optimality, cost what it may, or else to ignore it. Instead, pragmatic (i.e., theoretically imperfect but practically applicable) formulations of the objective are possible. Examples can be found in the evaluation procedures of *cost–benefit analysis*.[54]

In addition, alongside the aspect of internalization as a *target* discussed so far, its nature as an *instrument* must also be included in the evaluation. The objective of optimizing resource allocation is aimed at, in internalization, by putting the costs of externalities onto whoever is causing them. Even if the amount of the

---

53 Being "critical" here (in contrast with what frequently happens in the environmental policy debate) does not mean just being able to criticize "industry." It instead refers to the ability to recognize to what extent arguments being presented in public are guided by special interests. Among these are the interests of the industry representative in downplaying the externalities arising from his production, but also the interest of the journalist (or academic!) in gripping reporting, or politicians' interest in boosting their own images.

54 Cf., e.g., Harris (2006), esp. ch. 6; Russell (2001), esp. chs. 5–8 and 15; or the presentations applied to the water sector in Young (2005). In the United States, cost–benefit analysis has taken on considerable importance in evaluating environmental policy measures; cf. Oates (2000).

costs of the externalities cannot be determined exactly, not all the causers can be determined, and it is only imperfectly possible to charge the costs of externalities found to the causers found, it may nonetheless be possible to put market-like forces at the service of environmental protection. Part three of this book shows where the use of environmental policy instruments that, strictly speaking, do not achieve an internalization of externalities but are nonetheless guided by that basic idea are better than other instruments in cost effectiveness and in their capacity to stimulate environmental innovation. Perhaps the environmental policy importance of internalization strategies should be measured not so much by whether they are in fact suitable for bringing about "optimality," but more by the practical contribution of the environmental policy instruments developed from them, which should be at the center of attention in the evaluation.

In part two, the most important internalization strategies are presented and evaluated. Here we always assume that the strategy, and the discussion in each case, is used *solely* for internalizing the externalities. The simultaneous employment of various strategies and/or the interactions between a strategy and other environmental policy regulations are not be an object of this discussion.

Exercises

Exercise 1.1
Explain the purpose of

 (i) a positive analysis
(ii) a normative analysis

Hint: Solve the problem by saying what the question is that positive and normative analysis, respectively, is supposed to answer.

Exercise 1.2
Discuss the following statement: "A theoretical model should approximate reality as close as possible."

Exercise 1.3
Which of the following assumptions has to be made in a model that formalizes the inefficiency of public good provision due to free rider incentives?

a) There are multiple players ($n \geq 2$).
b) The players are asymmetric (i.e., nonidentical).
c) The model has to be dynamic (i.e., a model with multiple decision stages).
d) The players have no possibility of contacting each other.

Exercise 1.4
Consider a perfectly competitive market of a good x with 100 firms on the supply side and 100 consumers on the demand side. There are 50 firms of type A with

marginal cost functions $MC_A = x + 10$ and 50 firms of type B with marginal cost functions $MC_B = 2x$.

Also, two groups of consumers can be distinguished. There are 50 consumers of type C with marginal willingness to pay given by $MWP_C = 20 - \frac{5}{3}x$ and 50 consumers of type D with marginal willingness to pay given by $MWP_D = 20 - \frac{5}{2}x$.

a) Determine the aggregate supply and demand functions (S and D).
b) Determine the market equilibrium (x^* and P^*).
c) Illustrate the market graphically.
d) Determine the level of social net welfare (defined as the amount by which aggregate willingness to pay exceeds the costs) in the market equilibrium.

Exercise 1.5

Consider an economy with a single firm. Let $x \in [0, 10]$ denote the emission level of the firm and $a = 10 - x$ the corresponding abatement level. Abatement costs are given by $AC(a) = 10a^2$. The expected value of external damages is given by $D(x) = 10x^2$.

a) Determine marginal abatement costs MAC and the marginal damage costs MD (as functions of x).
b) Determine the socially optimal emission level x^{**}.

Exercise 1.6

a) Define the terms "negative externality" and "positive externality."
b) Give some examples for positive and negative externalities.

Exercise 1.7

Consider the market described in exercise 1.4.

Now assume that the production of good x generates emissions that damage a third party. Total damage is given by $D(x) = 2x$.

a) Determine the socially optimal production level (x^{**}) analytically and graphically.
b) Determine the social welfare level in the market equilibrium and in the social optimum.

Exercise 1.8

Assume that the production of good x negatively affects the environment. The government analyzes the effects of a production tax t on the environmental quality using a partial analysis. Which (indirect) effects might be overlooked by the government?

Exercise 1.9

Discuss the following statement: "The social optimum (i.e., the allocation that maximizes social welfare) is a Pareto optimum."

Exercise 1.10
Discuss the following statement: "The income distribution within a country affects the individuals' willingness to pay for a certain level of environmental quality, but not the country's aggregate willingness to pay, because total income is the sum of the individual incomes and total willingness to pay is the sum of individuals' willingness to pay."

Part Two

Strategies for Internalizing Externalities

A. Negotiations

I. The Coase Theorem

As described in part one, where externalities are present, the uncorrected market mechanism leads to misallocations. The causer of the externality will, at an uncorrected equilibrium, produce an emission level x^* at which his profit (utility) is maximized, but the interests of those damaged are left entirely out of account. Perhaps the intuitively readiest response to this calamity is for the government to affect the polluter's emission level through direct controls.

In sharp contradistinction to this approach, Ronald Coase (1960) put the view in his famous essay that the misallocation could be rectified by direct interaction among those involved after the government has defined the rules of this interaction. This idea is often regarded as counterintuitive, but the basic notion can nonetheless be directly derived from the concept of the suboptimality of the uncorrected equilibrium. That is, if the uncorrected emission level x^* is not Pareto optimal, then this means by definition that changes in this starting position that leave at least one of those involved better off without any other being worse off are possible. There is thus potential here for welfare improvements, and a clever distribution arrangement can take advantage so as to make *all* participants better off. This potential runs out only at the optimum allocation. According to Coase, the prospect for achieving these potential improvements in condition, then, constitutes the motor for collaboration by the parties, with the object of bringing about optimality.

According to Coase's idea, collaboration between the parties takes the form of negotiations on the level of the externality (emission). It is central here to Coase's argument that the state should make a clear allocation of *ownership rights* (*property rights*) over the resource through which the externality is mediated (e.g., the air as an environmental medium). For this sets the framework for the ensuing negotiations:

a) If the polluter receives property rights to the environmental resource, then the situation reached at the uncorrected equilibrium, in which he produces the profit-maximizing level of the externality without negotiations, is clearly right and proper. Because the polluter has ownership rights in the resource, he can do with it what he likes – within the limits of the laws in force – without the consent of the damaged parties. It is central to Coase's argument, though, that the property right be *transferable*. If the damaged party wants to have the level of the externality reduced, he has to induce the polluter by making payments. Allocating ownership rights to the polluter brings him into legal possession of the scarce resource, and the damaged party has to buy some off him if he wants to possess some. The allocation of property rights in the environmental resource described here is termed the "laissez-faire rule."

b) Total allocation of the environmental resource to the polluter by an environmental policy decision of government is one extreme case of the construction of property rights. The opposite extreme is also discussed by Coase. Here ownership rights in the scarce environmental resource are assigned totally to the damaged parties. The damaged party can thus dispose of the utilization of the resource (i.e., possesses a right to be totally unharmed by the polluter). The "starting position" before negotiations among those involved is thus that the polluter may not cause any externality (i.e., must achieve a zero emission level). If he instead wants (at least partly) to control the environmental resource to use it as a medium for absorbing pollutants, he has to buy some from the owner, namely, the potentially damaged party. Borrowing from the associated term in the environmental policy debate, the "polluter pays" principle, we call this the "polluter rule."

Coase's suggestion is noteworthy in several respects. It should be noted that the strategy described here for internalizing externalities consists in making the environmental resource through which the externality is mediated into a marketable good by allocating property rights. The failure of the market mechanism is accordingly to be removed by extending the sphere of effectiveness of market allocation to the environment. Consistently, the government's role is limited to the task of defining the framework under which the individuals can decide and act. By allocating the property rights, the government only sets the initial endowment of those involved before the start of negotiations and lays down the ground rules for the latter. It is left to the participants to bring about the allocation outcome themselves.

However, it should not be overlooked that government, despite its rather modest role in comparison with interventionist approaches, nonetheless has considerable room for maneuver through the power to allocate property rights to the polluter or the damaged party. Certainly, government can and must implicitly make *value judgments* in allotting the property rights. Coase himself refrained from doing so. An important feature of his approach is the very fact that he does not treat a clear role assignment between a "polluter" and a "damaged party" as binding. The externality comes about through the interest conflict between the two parties, and in this sense, both are causers of the externality. Which side is right is ultimately a question of social values. Convinced advocates of the "polluter pays principle" in environmental policy who shrink in horror from the position described previously as the laissez-faire rule are recommended by the author to concentrate in endeavoring to understand Coase's property rights proposals on the other situation (the "polluter rule"). This might help avoid blocks to understanding. Sometimes it is also helpful for ecologically committed readers, when discussing the laissez-faire rule, to imagine a situation where an industrial country is harmed by emissions from a developing country.

Acceptance might also be promoted by the following presentation.

Lateral view 4: The practice of the Coase theorem. *Source:* Steinmann/Westfalenpost, 2000. Reprinted by kind permission of the author.

Before looking closer at the nature of the negotiating process and the outcome of negotiation, let us emphasize that Coase considered his model on the explicit assumption that there were no *transaction costs*. The (rather ambiguous) term transaction cost is, according to Coase, to be taken to be the cost of identifying those involved; the cost of the negotiations themselves; and the cost of establishing, executing, and monitoring the outcome of negotiations.[1] Let us point out that the clear definition of ownership rights itself helps reduce transaction costs.

Let us look at the interest positions of the two participants in negotiations under the polluter rule, using Figure 2 in part one, already employed in a different context previously. Here the causer cannot start emissions before concluding the negotiations. He thus has to bear the total costs of completely reducing the emission from x^* to zero. In Figure 2, these costs correspond to the area under the marginal abatement cost (*MAC*) curve between 0 and x^*. In the starting position, no costs for externalities arise for the damaged parties.

Now let us ask how a marginal increase in the externality (from 0 to 1 unit) would affect the welfare of both participants. If the polluter were allowed to emit one unit, he would be relieved of the corresponding abatement cost. These costs

---

1   We go further into the special importance of information costs as transaction costs in chapter C of part four.

can be read off in Figure 2 as the area under the marginal abatement cost curve. This is the area 01DE. The maximum payment the polluter could pay the damaged party for the right to emit one unit of pollutant would be precisely this amount of money. Then he would be giving up the entire advantage he derives from the corresponding permission to emit, in the form of compensation payments to the damaged party. He would refuse to pay a higher amount.[2] If the compensation payment actually made was smaller, then the potential polluter would be better off from the trading over the first unit of pollution.

Let us now look at the situation of the potential victim. If he puts up with emission of one unit of the relevant pollutant, he accepts damage. The size of this damage is shown in Figure 2 as the area under the marginal damage (*MD*) curve above the first unit emitted (i.e., as 01F). If the damaged party, as here for the moment assumed, has ownership rights over the environmental resource, then the minimum payment he will demand from the polluter for permission to emit one unit will correspond exactly to this amount of damage. He will not give the permission for any smaller compensation, and for any higher compensation he will derive a net increase in benefit from the negotiation.

Under the polluter rule discussed here, then, the allocation of ownership rights in the scarce environmental resource leads to a situation where the polluter's maximum willingness to pay for permission to emit (additional) units corresponds to the (marginal) costs for avoiding that emission. The limit to his willingness to pay can accordingly be read as the marginal abatement cost curve in Figure 2. In contrast, it is in the damaged party's interest to require in return for permission (for additional emission units) at least compensation for the damage suffered thereby. His limit in willingness to negotiate defined by this minimum compensation requirement can be read as the marginal damage curve in Figure 2. As long as the damaged party's minimum compensation demand under this rule lies below the polluter's maximum willingness to compensate, the parties can agree *in both of their interests* to an amount lying between these limits in order to increase the emission by one unit.

However, the fact is that increasing the emission level in the course of such negotiations leads to a lowering in marginal abatement costs and an increase in marginal damage.[3] As the negotiations go on, then, the room for negotiation will be increasingly narrowed by the fact that the damaged party's minimum compensation demand and the polluter's maximum willingness to compensate come closer together. No further reallocation by negotiations will be possible once a position is reached where the marginal damage equals the marginal abatement cost. This situation defines not only the outcome of negotiations, but simultaneously also

---

2   We assume that no one will voluntarily put up with a deterioration.
3   These curves are quite plausible, but not inevitable. For space reasons, we cannot go into the consequences of deviations for Coase's model. But cf. Burrows (2008) on the problem of nonconvexities in the theory of externalities.

the socially optimum emission quantity (as discussed in section A.IV of part 1). We can thus see that the outcome of negotiations is (under Coase's assumptions) optimal.

The brilliance of Coase's approach is that the very quantities that are decisive for an optimum situation and the equalization of which constitutes the optimum – namely, marginal damage and marginal abatement cost – become operative for allocations through the assignment of ownership rights via the medium of negotiation. We can see that there need not be any contradiction between brilliance and simplicity.

Very much as has just been argued about negotiations to allocate ownership rights to damaged parties, the negotiating process and outcome of negotiations can be explained for the laissez-faire rule. The actors on the internalization stage are the same; they have merely exchanged roles. If the polluter has the property rights in the environmental resource, then the damaged party has to compensate him for reductions in the externality starting from the uncorrected equilibrium x^*. The maximum compensation payment the damaged party is prepared to make for a marginal reduction in the externality corresponds to the marginal damage avoided through that reduction. For a higher compensation payment, the costs of negotiation would be greater than the benefit, a situation that the rationally acting decision maker of the theory avoids. If instead he succeeds in securing the reduction from the polluter for an amount of compensation below the marginal damage, then the net benefit of this reallocation is positive for him.

Correspondingly, the minimum payment that the polluter will demand under the laissez-faire rule for a marginal reduction in the externality will be the cost of the marginal abatement costs to be incurred for it. Following the tradition in the literature, the curves in Figure 2 show marginal abatement costs increasing and marginal damage decreasing with decreasing emission. If this correctly reflects circumstances in reality, then at starting position x^* the marginal damage will be higher than the marginal abatement cost. Those involved can then (assuming the absence of transaction costs) agree on a payment for reduction of emission by one unit that lies between the marginal damage avoided thereby and the marginal abatement cost incurred for it. If the emission is in fact reduced by the relevant unit to $x^* - 1$ and a corresponding compensation payment is transferred, then the utility position of both individuals has improved.

In connection with the emission reduction achieved (or proposed) in the course of these negotiations, the marginal damage falls and the marginal abatement cost rises. Once the emission quantity for which these two quantities are equal is reached, there is no compensation payment both can agree on with the aim of further reducing the emission. The outcome of negotiations under the laissez-faire rule will accordingly be x^{**}, the emission level at which marginal damage corresponds to the marginal abatement cost – the optimum allocation.

The consideration of Coase's ownership rights approach using economic theory thus leads to an initially surprising result. *Irrespective of which property law framework the government chooses, the negotiations lead to one and the same result for the emission level. This level is the socially optimum one.*

These statements are among the favorite (?!) theses of welfare economics of the past 50 years, and, in the literature, they are called the "Coase theorem."[4] This initially counterintuitive theorem can also be understood without the mathematical explanations commonly presented for it in the literature. The key to understanding it is that a polluter takes the amount of the damage he causes into account in his decision on the extent of emission in the same way, in principle following either of the property rights arrangements. On the polluter rule, the polluter takes it into account because he has to pay compensation for emitting.[5] On the laissez-faire rule, he takes it into account because he loses compensation payments from the damaged party when he emits. Although the polluter then incurs no monetary costs for emitting, as with the polluter rule, he does have opportunity costs. For the polluter's allocation decision, opportunity costs are just as relevant as monetary ones.[6]

For the following discussion, it is important to point out that the Coase theorem does not assert the total irrelevance of the ownership rights allocation by the state, but "merely" its *allocative* irrelevance. *Distributively*, in contrast, there is a fundamental distinction between the two opposite decisions by government on the ownership principle. The allocation of ownership of the scarce environmental resource is an important measure of distributive policy, which, in the case of the laissez-faire rule, is made in favor of the emitter and at the expense of the damaged party and, in the case of the polluter rule, in favor of the damaged party and against the polluter.[7]

Even if Coase's approach has fundamentally influenced the economic view of externalities, we must nonetheless warn against accepting the (implied) theorem he formulated unreservedly. Instead, there are a number of objections regarding its theoretical consistency and political applicability.

---

4   Cf. Coase (1960). In 1991, Professor Coase was awarded the Nobel Prize for Economics. Reference was made especially to this trailblazing work (and his equally important work titled "The Nature of the Firm" (1937)).

5   For the last unit, he can secure permission to emit in the course of negotiations; as compensation, he has to pay precisely the marginal damage.

6   For the last unit of emission covered by the outcome of the negotiations, he foregoes a compensation payment of just the amount of the marginal damage. The previous statements apply within the framework of the traditional microeconomic model. However, doubts as to the equivalence of costs and foregone benefit do come from psychoeconomics studies. Cf., e.g., Kahneman/Knetsch/Thaler (1990). Daniel Kahneman was awarded the Nobel Prize for Economics in 2002 for his pioneering work on integrating psychological and economic approaches.

7   The allocation of property rights determines *ceteris paribus*, the wealth distribution between the parties in the starting position. In the course of negotiation, the distribution is modified by reallocation and payment of the agreed compensation amounts. However, the following discussion on the connections between distribution and allocation remains, in principle, unaffected.

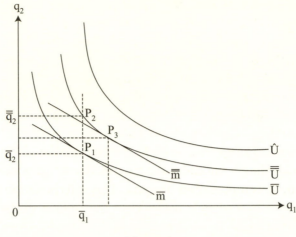

Figure 4

II. Critique and Extensions of the Coase Theorem

1. *Distribution and Allocation*

That the allocational outcome of negotiations on the level of an externality is independent of how the property rights are allocated, as asserted by Coase, presumes that allocation and distribution are independent. This is a very special assumption. We can make this clear by the example of the damaged party's position. The argument for the polluter would be similar. The marginal damage function expresses the (negative) marginal value of the emission to the damaged party. As explained previously, this value is not a utility in the sense of the ordinal microeconomics concept, but the monetary expression of this utility ("benefit"). Yet, the monetary articulation of preferences is indissolubly bound up with control of purchasing power. *Willingness to pay* depends not only on preferences, but also on *ability to pay*. Things are just the same with the demand for compensation. This connection, which already seems intuitively correct, can be clarified by a brief microtheoretical presentation. Figure 4 shows the classical indifference curve diagram for an arbitrary household.[8]

The indifference curves arrange all points (q_1, q_2) in the two-dimensional space of goods in accordance with the criterion of desirability for the household concerned.[9] Sets of goods (q_1, q_2) lying along an indifference curve provide the household with the same utility. The further away from the origin an indifference curve is, the higher the utility to the household of the set of goods represented on it. The underlying utility concept is ordinal.[10] The absolute value of the slope of an

---

8   Explanations can be found in any microeconomics textbook.

9   Of course, the presentation with only two goods does not affect the generality of statements made.

10 This means that the household can indicate which of two sets of goods it prefers to the other (or else whether it is indifferent between the two sets). It is, in contrast, not possible within

indifference curve at a point is called the "marginal rate of substitution" between the two goods q_2 and q_1. q_1 could stand for, say, a reduction in an externality (or for "the" quality of the environment), and q_2 might be a "common measure" (*numéraire*), a good made up of all other goods.

The marginal rate of substitution indicates the maximum amount of q_2 that the household is willing to give up in order to secure an (arbitrarily small) additional unit of q_1. Because consideration is referred to a single point, the marginal rate of substitution can also be interpreted as the minimum amount of q_2 the household will demand in order to give up an (arbitrarily small) unit of q_1. The marginal rate of substitution accordingly indicates, for a particular set of goods, the marginal willingness to pay or compensation demand. This interpretation of the slope of an indifference curve immediately makes clear the connection between this traditional microeconomics textbook argument and the problem considered here of internalizing externalities by allocating property rights.

The influence of distribution on allocation, central in the discussion of the Coase theorem, can be deduced by comparing the marginal substitution rates between the two goods q_1 and q_2 for two different sets of goods $(\overline{q}_1, \overline{q}_2)$, $(\overline{q}_1, \overline{\overline{q}}_2)$. Both sets of goods contain the same quantity of the first good, but the second set contains more of the second good. Referring to our example, the household enjoys the same environmental quality in both situations (represented by emission abatement level $\overline{q}_1$), but in the second state it has more wealth.

If the two goods q_1 and q_2 are normal (in the sense of "noninferior") goods, then with rising income the household will at equilibrium demand a larger quantity of both goods.[11] The income restriction on the household in its consumer decision is symbolized in the graph (for given prices of q_1 and q_2) by the negatively sloping straight line m. This "budget constraint" is shown as $\overline{m}$ for a higher income than for $\overline{m}$. As is not further explained here (because this is basic microeconomics), the household equilibrium can be shown graphically as the point where the relevant budget constraint is tangent to the highest attainable indifference curve. At the income implied in $\overline{m}$, the household equilibrium thus lies at point P_1. At the higher income implied by $\overline{\overline{m}}$, the household reaches point P_3. The graph illustrates the case of normal goods because at P_3 the equilibrium quantity of both goods is above the one at P_1. An increase in income will shift the budget lines in parallel. Because the equilibrium condition is that the relevant budget line in each case is tangent to the highest attainable indifference curve, it follows that the slope of the indifference curve at equilibrium at the lower income, P_1, is identical with the slope of the indifference curve at equilibrium with the higher income, P_3.

---

the framework of this utility concept to indicate the difference of the utilities to a consumer created by two sets of goods. With the cardinal utility concept, the definition of utility differences (and even their interpersonal comparison) is possible. Put more technically, the utility function for the ordinal (cardinal) utility concept is defined except for monotonically growing (linear) transformations.

11 For normal goods, the *Engel curves* have a positive slope.

Because the indifference curves are convex toward the origin ("law"[12] of falling marginal rate of substitution), it follows that the absolute value of the slope of the indifference curve at P_2 is greater than at P_1. We can thus see that on the standard assumptions of economic theory, the marginal substitution rate at P_2 is above the marginal substitution rate at P_1. The household's marginal willingness to pay for an additional supply of q_1, in units of the common measure q_2, will thus be higher the better endowed the household is with the common measure. In other words, for a marginal reduction of its q_1 consumption, the household will demand higher compensation in terms of q_2 the more endowed it is with q_2. These connections apply not only to the level $\overline{q}_1$ taken as an example in Figure 4, but also to any level of q_1.[13]

Applied to our example of the allocation of environmental resources, this means that the valuation in monetary units of the absence of an emission by a damaged party is higher at any set initial emission level the higher the damaged party's "wealth" is, as long as environmental quality is a "normal" good. Accordingly, the damaged party's marginal willingness to pay or marginal demand for compensation in negotiations will in general depend on his endowment of resources.

It is central to the criticism presented here that the government's decision about the allocation of property rights in environmental goods affects the resource endowment of the parties. On the polluter rule, the damaged party has a marketable asset assigned to it, and on the laissez-faire rule, he enters negotiations without this endowment. (It is only in the special case where environmental quality is a neutral good (i.e., one that is both inferior and superior) that it is admissible, then, to assume that the amount of marginal damage depends only on the initial emission level, but not on the distribution of property rights themselves.) If the connection addressed here is included in the considerations, then the equilibrium must be analyzed by employing marginal damage curves varying according to the ownership rights arrangements.

Figure 5 shows the consequences of the connection discussed here between distribution and allocation for the property rights solution to environmental problems. MD_I shows the marginal damage curve on the laissez-faire rule, and MD_{II} the corresponding curve for the polluter rule.

Because the damaged party's wealth is smaller on the first rule than on the second, MD_I lies below MD_{II}. If, then, the negotiating model explained previously

12 This is not really a law in the natural science sense, but more of an outcome of plausibility considerations. The consequences of concave indifference curves for the Coase theorem can be depicted by analogy with the previous presentation. For space reasons, however, we do not do that here.

13 The connections presented here for normal goods between distribution and allocation are reversed for inferior goods. For an inferior good, the *Engel curve* has a negative slope. If a good is neither inferior nor superior (or one might alternatively say both inferior and superior), then the *Engel curve* will instead be horizontal. It is only in this special case that the connections discussed in the text between distribution and allocation do not exist.

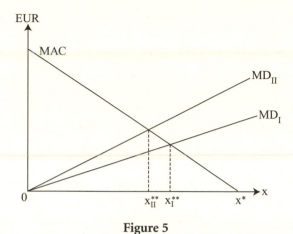

Figure 5

is applied to this situation, we have the result that the negotiation equilibrium will occur at a level x_I^{**} on the laissez-faire rule and at a level x_{II}^{**} on the polluter rule. It is plausible that x_{II}^{**} lies below x_I^{**} because the state's basic distributive policy decision makes the damaged party better off under the polluter rule than under the laissez-faire rule so that, on the first rule, he is a stronger partner in the negotiations. The damaged party will then be able to secure his interest in a clean environment better in the negotiations than with the smaller weight he can throw into the balance on the laissez-faire rule.

This criticism is not intended to claim that the optimality of Coase's negotiated equilibrium is not (in theory) independent of the property rights arrangement. By our argument, we are merely rejecting the part of the Coase theorem (or at any rate identifying it as a special case) that asserts the neutrality of the allocation outcome in relation to the basic property rights decisions. But just this partial rejection of the theorem is nonetheless significant because it illuminates, for the case of application to environmental economics, the general problem of the lack of uniqueness of the economic optimality concept as explained previously in part one. However, the finding of the optimality concept's lack of uniqueness ought not be confused with a claim that it is unusable in economic policy or environmental policy. What is instead being worked out here is that the government's decision of principle as to who is to get property rights in environmental resources is relevant not only to distributive policy, but also to allocation policy (and here also ecologically). One might in this connection speak of an upgrading of the state in modeling theory terms by comparison with Coase's approach. The state can (must!) not only distinguish between the various distributions, but also select an *optimum optimorum* out of the various socially optimum allocations, in accordance with its evaluation.

2. The Bilateral Monopoly between Negotiating Parties

Deciding on emission or its reduction by negotiation under various property law conditions displays – as explained previously – essential features of market alloca-tion. However, it should by no means be confused entirely with the functioning and outcomes of the competitive mechanism. One major distinction is that in the competitive market model, individual market participants cannot affect the market price, whereas in Coase's negotiation model, the price of emission or of reducing it is not laid down beforehand. Instead, the levels of (marginal) damage and (marginal) abatement costs merely determine the limits within which the price will lie. The agreements actually reached on compensation payment will depend on the parties' negotiating skills, and not least on their ability to tolerate the *status quo ante*. This status quo is, on the polluter rule, very unpleasant for the polluter and on the laissez-faire rule for the damaged party. The connection between the distribution of the gains of negotiation and "staying power" means that "combative" behavior may possibly be taken into account, whereby the opponent's position at the starting point is deliberately weakened. Thus, a polluter could, under the laissez-faire rule, run the damaging activity at too high a level, in comparison with his uncorrected profit maximum. It might even pay to take up new activities in order to "earn" compensation for stopping them again. Or a credible announcement might be useful to the polluter. Under the polluter rule, it might pay to engage in damaging activities (or announce one intends to) only to benefit from compensation payments by the polluter. The polluter is in a particularly poor position at the starting point under this rule, being subject to a total ban on emissions. Each individual damaged party has a strong power position because they have a "veto right" over emissions.[14] On either rule, it is thus conceivable that the party put in worse position by it at the starting point is under such duress as to joyfully accept an arrangement favorable to the stronger party.

We can thus see that both legal frameworks suggested by Coase contain the potential for a dangerous deployment of power alien to the world of perfect competition. The situation is more like a rather less congenial one such as bilateral monopoly – a game with an uncertain outcome.[15]

3. Polluters and Victims as Heterogeneous Groups: The Prisoner's Dilemma Problem

A further difficulty emerges when we consider that neither the polluters nor the victims constitute a homogeneous block with "collective interests." Both camps mostly consist of a multitude of individuals, among whom manifold conflicts of interests are conceivable.

For instance, for every member of the victim group, emission reduction under the laissez-faire rule is a *public good*. Each individual may say under these circumstances that while he benefits from the emission reduction, the extent of it does not

---

14   The allocational consequences of this sort of "holdup" position (also called "holdout") have been studied in the legal economics literature for a multiplicity of cases going beyond the Coase theorem. Cf. Schäfer/Ott (2004).

15   Although Coase – unlike many of his followers – did not fail to see the problems addressed here, he did rather trivialize it with his remark that they are merely "preliminaries to an agreement." Cf. Coase (1960, p. 7/8).

depend essentially on his contribution to the compensation amount. (The larger the damaged group is, the more justified this consideration.) It is accordingly attractive for the individual to downplay his own interest in emission abatement when the compensation amount is being "collected" and thus to benefit from enjoying it at lower cost (in comparison with his true willingness to pay). Each member of the damaged group is thus exposed to the fatal charms of the *prisoner's dilemma*.[16] If all members of the damaged group seek to adopt a free rider position, the actual compensation amount collected will not at all correspond to the valuation of an emission reduction by the damaged. The optimality of the negotiated solution assumed by Coase and others will thus be missed. *The problem of the market allocation of public goods apparently solved by the definition of property rights reappears as a conflict of interest within the victim group.* Coase (in contrast with most of his followers) avoids these problems by confining his argument to cases of *one* polluter and *one* damaged party. But the environmental problems of relevance in our context mostly affect a large number of individuals. The previous considerations show that a generalization of Coase's property rights approach to the typical case for environmental problems of many people involved is possible only to a very limited extent, so that the relevance of this approach to practical environmental policy is narrowly limited.[17] To solve these problems, the property rights approach to internalizing externalities would have to be supplemented by employing incentive-compatible "preference disclosure mechanisms." However, these display certain conceptual problems[18] and are likely to be costly in practical application.

4. Coase's Theorem and Environmental Policy: The Problem of Transaction Costs

As mentioned previously, Coase's analysis is done on the explicit assumption that no transaction costs are incurred. A critique of the Coase theorem within the model can thus not be based on the transaction cost argument. However, it must be pointed out that there is no consensus in the literature as to what costs that term is supposed to cover. This, of course, leads to a danger of "immunizing" the Coase theorem, as follows.

The reasons standing in the way of achieving the social optimum by negotiation can be annihilated using the transaction cost concept. This is true, for instance, of the problems listed previously of a bilateral monopoly between the parties or of the problems of overcoming the prisoner's dilemma within the groups involved. However, that would mean the concept of transaction cost would decay into a merely residual one and the Coase theorem would become a tautology: "an efficient allocation will be reached as long as the reasons that might block reaching it are not present." Whatever position we may take regarding these questions of economic

16 Part five of this book discusses the prisoner's dilemma in more detail.
17 It is interesting in this context that the number of those involved falls if the multiplicity of those affected is represented by two (or a few) states negotiating an international environmental agreement. On this, see part five of this book.
18 Cf., e.g., Laffont (2002), with many other references.

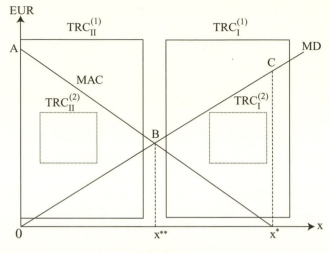

Figure 6

theory, for an assessment of the *practical* suitability of the property law approach going back to Coase for environmental policy, the existence of transaction costs cannot be ignored because in reality they are very significant.[19]

How high the transaction costs are in the property law treatment of environmental problems may differ from case to case. However, it is plausible for the reasons noted previously that they increase with the number of participants. Without being able to confirm this by empirical studies, I would venture the thesis that for many environmental problems the transaction costs exceed the possible "negotiating gain" (available for distribution among those involved).[20] That would make them prohibitive. On the polluter rule, the initial emission level of zero and, under the laissez-faire rule, the uncorrected equilibrium level x^* would continue to exist.

This situation is illustrated in Figure 6. To understand it, look at rectangle $TRC_I^{(1)}$ ($TRC_{II}^{(1)}$). It is intended to show the block of *fixed* transaction costs (by definition independent of the change in emission quantity agreed on in the negotiations) under the laissez-faire rule (or polluter rule, respectively). $TRC_I^{(1)}$ ($TRC_{II}^{(1)}$) is so arranged that the fixed costs arising under the laissez-faire rule (or polluter rule) exceed the maximum gains from trade to be achieved in the negotiations (i.e., when the equilibrium outcome of negotiations is reached), so that $TRC_{II}^{(1)} > 0AB$ and $TRC_I^{(1)} > BCx^*$ hold. The incentive to embark on negotiations is accordingly nipped in the bud by the threatened transaction costs (i.e., the parties remain stuck in the starting position of whichever rule applies).

It is quite different, in contrast, if while the transaction costs are fixed they are lower than the gains from negotiation. To illustrate this circumstance, consider the

---

19   The concept of transaction costs plays a key role in *institutional economics.* Institutional economics viewpoints on environmental policy are offered by Vatn (2005).

20   As a true Coasean, one ought to add: if it were otherwise, the negotiations would already have happened.

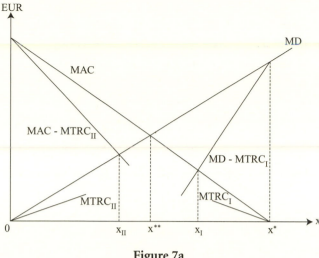

Figure 7a

fixed-cost blocks $TRC_I^{(2)}$ and $TRC_{II}^{(2)}$ shown in Figure 6 *as alternatives*. The existence of transaction costs at this level, although reducing the maximum net gain to be derived by the parties from negotiation in comparison with Coase's world without transaction costs, nonetheless leaves the allocation at the negotiated equilibrium unaffected. Just because these transaction costs are assumed to be independent of the emission level, the emission equilibrium that maximizes the negotiating parties' aggregate net benefit (negotiating gain less transaction costs) is at x^{**} (i.e., at the same point as in the model without transaction costs). A move from Coase's world without transaction costs to a world (closer to reality) with transaction costs thus does not destroy the validity of the Coase theorem, as long as the transaction costs are fixed and smaller than the gains from trade.

Let us now move from considering fixed transaction costs in the two versions presented previously to analyzing the effects of variable transaction costs on the negotiated equilibrium. Besides pedagogical considerations, plausibility viewpoints may also favor this variant of the model. Thus, a model with variable transaction costs can in a particularly simple way grasp the phenomenon, important for reality, that the parties do not possess perfect information about the relevant marginal damage and marginal abatement costs.[21] If we want to look into the allocational effects of this information deficit in the framework of Coasean negotiations, then it seems plausible to assume that the uncertainty of the parties as to the course of the curves rises with increasing distance between the emission level contemplated in the negotiations and the initial level. The associated increasing risks can be depicted pragmatically as transaction costs rising with the level of the change in emissions to be agreed. This is done in Figure 7a. Here not only the total, but also the marginal transaction costs are assumed to be increasing. $MTRC_I$ represents the marginal

---

21 A more exact (here, information economics) model is presented in chapter C of part four.

transaction costs under the laissez-faire rule, and $MTRC_{II}$ the marginal transaction costs under the polluter rule. The negotiated equilibrium under the laissez-faire rule lies where the marginal damage reduced by the marginal transaction costs corresponds to the marginal abatement cost (i.e., at x_I). For there, the expenditure associated with avoiding the last unit is precisely covered by the net benefit of this last unit (avoided marginal damage less marginal expenditure on negotiation).[22]

Analogously, with the polluter rule, the equilibrium when transaction costs are considered results from the equality of marginal damage and difference between marginal abatement cost and the marginal transaction costs arising under this rule (x_{II}). The existence of transaction costs thus has far-reaching allocational importance.

To defend the property law approach in environmental policy, we might now adduce the point that inclusion of positive transaction costs in the consideration changes not only the negotiated equilibrium, as explained on the basis of Figure 7a, but also the optimum. Because transaction costs mean just as much consumption of real resources as production costs or environmental damage do, they have to be included in defining the social optimum. If this is done, then on the laissez-faire rule allocation x_I emerges as both an equilibrium and an optimum. On the polluter rule, allocation x_{II} is both equilibrium and optimum.

This argument, however, overlooks the point that in defining an optimum, costs can be set only at their minimum value.[23] To include transaction costs in defining the optimum in connection with the property law approach in the same way as marginal production costs in testing the optimality of a market equilibrium output level, a property law arrangement would have to include an inherent incentive to minimize transaction costs, corresponding to the incentive a profit-maximizing firm has to minimize costs. But we cannot simply assume this without further ado.

Even within the property law approach, it is entirely possible for the transaction costs on the laissez-faire rule to differ from those under the polluter rule. Let us now show the consequences of such "rule-specific" transaction costs for the Coase theorem. We do so for a special case where the two property law arrangements differ *exclusively* in transaction costs. The costs that are not transaction costs (i.e., the sum of damage (D) and abatement costs (AC)) are assumed to be independent of the property law arrangement. This special case is shown in Figure 7b. The marginal transaction costs rise under both rules (starting from a value of zero)

22 The description leads to the same outcome if the transaction costs are added to the marginal abatement costs instead of deducting them from the marginal damage.

23 One of the many attractive properties of the market equilibrium is precisely the fact that producers' interest in profit guarantees that the minimum cost combination is secured. (Cf. also the account of the efficient allocation of a given production quantity over various producers in part one, section A.III. On the minimum cost combination for the production decision of a single firm, cf., e.g., the corresponding accounts in the microeconomic textbooks mentioned in footnote 13 in part one.)

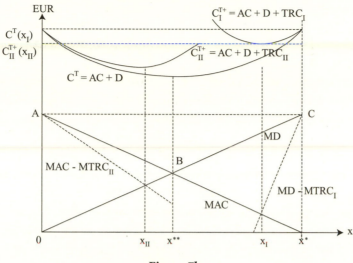

Figure 7b

monotonically with the distance of the emission quantity actually realized from the emission quantity at the starting position specific to the rule.[24] As explained previously, the starting position under the laissez-faire rule is x^*, and under the polluter rule, $x = 0$. Accordingly, $\partial MTRC_I/\partial\,(x^* - x) > 0$ and $\partial MTRC_{II}/\,\partial x > 0$ should hold, where $MTRC_I(x^* - x) = 0$ for $x = x^*$ and $MTRC_{II}(x) = 0$ for $x = 0$.

In addition, the marginal transaction costs for every level of transaction are assumed to be higher on the laissez-faire rule than for the polluter rule in this example. Accordingly, $MTRC_I(x^* - x) > MTRC_{II}(x)$ will hold for all values of x with $x^* > x > 0$. And $C_I^T(x^* - x) = C_{II}^T(x)$ should hold, where $C^T = AC + D$ for all values of x, where $x > 0$.[25]

This implies that without taking account of transaction costs, for any given level of change in emissions x, the negotiation gains on the laissez-faire rule are identical with those on the polluter rule. It also follows from the previous condition that $x^{**} = x^*/2$.

In Figure 7b, then, the triangle $0AB$ that illustrates the (maximum) negotiation gain on the polluter rule exactly corresponds with triangle BCx^* (mirrored in the vertical through x^{**}) that shows the (maximum) negotiation gain on the laissez-faire rule. In this specific situation, allocational preference should go to whichever property law arrangement shows the smaller transaction costs. In the situation depicted in Figure 7b, then, the polluter rule is socially optimal, but the laissez-faire rule is not. In Figure 7b, the equilibrium on the polluter rule attained in the model with transactions costs, x_{II}, is closer to the social optimum without transaction

---

24 No fixed transaction costs arise.

25 This is the formal expression of the assumption used previously that the total costs consisting of abatement cost plus damage are independent of the property rights arrangement.

costs, x^{**}, than the equilibrium attained with transaction costs under the laissez-faire rule, x_I. The total aggregate cost consisting of abatement cost, damage, and transaction cost, $C^{T+} = AC + D + TRC$, at equilibrium x_{II} is below the aggregate cost at equilibrium x_I. Accordingly, $C_{II}^{T+}(x_{II}) < C_I^{T+}(x_I)$ holds.

Although it is in contradiction with the Coase theorem, this connection can still be used constructively toward using a property law approach for environmental policy. It could be argued that this explanation furnishes the state with an additional criterion for deciding between the laissez-faire rule and the polluter rule. The government decision on the allocation of property rights should take into account not only an assessment of who the environmental resources "ought" to belong to on grounds of "justice," but also the differences in the level of transaction costs.

Thinking through the line of argument pursued here further, it nonetheless emerges that not only have differences in the level of transaction costs to be compared for the various property rights arrangements within Coase's approach. Instead, a transaction cost comparison also has to be drawn between the property rights approach (in its version including transaction costs) and other internalization approaches. This, of course, involves an empirical question that cannot be answered within the context of this book. However, it seems plausible that transaction costs for carrying out Coasean negotiations on environmental problems would as a rule be higher than for rival internalization strategies. This is true particularly where the number of participants is high. In my estimation, lower costs ought to be involved in estimating the damage caused by a power station using the ordinary economic evaluation procedures[26] and then charging them to the polluter in the form, say, of a tax, than in letting the polluter engage in negotiations with the many thousands of individuals affected.[27] Similarly, I believe that the costs of charging external damage from vehicle traffic to the state ought to be smaller than the expenditure on negotiations by drivers with street residents, pedestrians, other drivers, and others affected.

The number of polluters and victims involved is particularly high with global (and often also with other international) environmental problems. This makes transaction costs look particularly high and conditions for employing the negotiation approach particularly poor. However, it should be borne in mind that those involved in the conflict over the scarce resource of the environment – polluters and victims – do not mostly carry on in negotiations themselves in an international context. Instead, the (few) states act as representatives of their (many) citizens. The individual state can here be understood as an association (even if not an entirely voluntary one) for the lowering of transaction costs.[28] The "attorney" role that states play (willy nilly) for their citizens thus means that the transaction cost aspects of negotiations in the international context are particularly favorable, at least as far as the number of participants is concerned. However, the "price" of this lowering

26   Cf., e.g., Smith (2004), Turner et al. (2003).
27   It is possible that the numerous individuals affected may set up institutions to lower transaction costs.
28   This possible interpretation goes far beyond the discourse we are engaged in here.

of transaction costs might be that states are less able (and willing[29]) to formulate their citizens' preferences than are citizens themselves. If this criticism is important, then we have to ask whether the losses of welfare associated with it outweigh the transaction cost advantages secured via representation through the state.

It is to be further pointed out that compliance with an agreement by those signing an international treaty is considerably harder to ensure than within a country.[30] If treaty breaches can here be penalized only to a very limited extent, this will undoubtedly raise transaction costs in comparison with the national sphere.

So far, we have talked about the *existence* of transaction costs (in contradiction with the assumptions of the Coase model). We have not yet dealt with their *distribution* over those involved. But one specific transaction cost problem of the property rights approach might be precisely the fact that the transaction costs of various groups that should be involved in the negotiations are at very different levels. An asymmetrical distribution of transaction costs can lead to a misallocation. It is conceivable that groups with low transaction costs may agree to an arrangement that conflicts with the interests of a group that does not, because of the prohibitive level of transaction costs for it, take part in the negotiations. For instance, under a polluter rule, a polluter might reach an agreement with the immediate neighbors on the expansion of the damage-causing activity and the making of compensation payments. Individuals affected by the carrying of the pollutants to a distance, who are harder to identify and organize, might possibly have no influence on this decision. That would mean that part of society would have reached an agreement at the expense of another part of society (and thus also at the expense of the optimality of the negotiated outcome).

Previously, we looked at the effects of rule-specific transaction costs on the Coase theorem *ceteris paribus*. The polluter rule and the laissez-faire rule differed previously in transaction costs and only in transaction costs. We go beyond this simplifying assumption. Figure 7c illustrates a case where the total costs $C^T = AC + D$ at the starting position on the laissez-faire rule, x^*, are lower than the total costs at the starting position on the polluter rule ($x = 0$). It is certainly plausible that it is possible on this condition that the laissez-faire rule will be allocationally superior to the polluter rule, even if the transaction costs on the first rule are higher than on the second. Figure 7c shows such a case on the extreme assumption that the transaction costs on the laissez-faire rule are prohibitive. Here, then, on the laissez-faire rule, no change in the initial emission position will be achieved through negotiation (i.e., $x^* = x_\mathrm{I}$ holds). On the polluter rule, in contrast, in the same way as we discussed in Figure 7a and 7b, in the course of negotiations emissions can be raised from $x = 0$ to the equilibrium level x_II. In x_II, total costs including transaction costs ($C_\mathrm{II}^{T+} = AC + D + TRC_\mathrm{II}$) are at their minimum. The total costs arising at the negotiated equilibrium on the polluter rule (including transaction costs) are higher in the circumstances illustrated in Figure 7c than the

29   There are said to be some states that are not perfect democracies.
30   For more, see part five of this book.

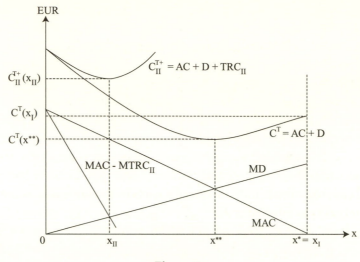

Figure 7c

total costs in the "immobile" starting position on the laissez-faire rule. Accordingly, $C_{II}^{T+}(x_{II}) > C_I^{T+}(x_I)$ holds.[31]

It can thus be seen that the (all too) simple rule of thumb for selecting property rights arrangements, namely, "choose the institution with the smallest transaction costs," may very well lead to error. A welfare comparison of various arrangements also depends on the transaction costs, but not only on these. Another important element in a welfare comparison is the situation from which negotiations start on the two alternative rules. Figure 7c illustrates the case where the starting position on the laissez-faire rule is already very close to the social optimum, whereas the starting position on the polluter rule is far from it. In the circumstances illustrated in Figure 7c, the laissez-faire rule is accordingly allocationally superior to the polluter rule because the advantage for the former rule in the starting position overcompensates for its drawbacks in transaction costs (as far as the welfare effects are concerned).

B. Environmental Liability Law

I. Introduction

Questions of liability law have for some time been analyzed from an economic viewpoint within the framework of the "law and economics" specialization.[32] There are numerous studies here with applications to the law of wrongful acts (tort law)

---

31 Because of the transaction costs, assumed to be prohibitive, the initial position on the laissez-faire rule will continue to exist ($x^* = x_I$). Without a change in the emission position, no variable costs will arise (i.e., $C_I^{T+}(x_I) = C_I^T(x^*)$ will hold). For the purposes of this discussion, we ignore the existence of fixed transaction costs.

32 The "classics" in this field are Landes and Posner (1987).

or product liability law.[33] The approaches presented are applied to the problem of environmental liability law.

Environmental liability law is to be taken to mean an institution (a set of regulations) establishing under what conditions and to what extent the causer of a negative externality has to pay compensation for damages to the damaged party. After what we said previously, it will immediately be clear that from an economic viewpoint, liability law constitutes an internalization strategy. If the polluter has to compensate the damaged party for damages, then he will take the external costs into account in his decision on the level and quality of production, just like the costs of production factors to be purchased on the market. Liability law causes him in this ideal case to evaluate initially external costs in the same way as internal ones (i.e., the externality is internalized).

Section II explains more precisely how liability law achieves a complete internalization effect, although (unfortunately) only under extremely restrictive conditions. It is argued that in this simple basic model, the optimality properties of the emission equilibria reached under liability law are even independent of the specific form of that liability law. As examples of such forms ("liability rules"), we present *strict liability* (*hazard (fault) liability*) and *negligence*. By "negligence," we mean a liability rule whereby the polluter has to compensate the damaged party for damage where the damage has been caused because the polluter has in his activities neglected "due care." However, where the damaging party has not acted negligently, he is exempt from liability. "Strict liability" (hazard liability), in contrast, means a liability rule whereby the polluter is responsible for any damage he has caused, irrespective of fault.

Section III shows how the suitability of liability law as a tool for internalizing externalities becomes less when it has to be employed under less ideal (i.e., more realistic) conditions. In distinction from the voluminous legal science discussion of liability law questions, we should make it clear that the interpretation of liability law in economic analysis as an internalization strategy focuses on the *preventive effects* of liability law, whereas in the legal analysis it is more the *distributive effects* that are to the fore.

For space reasons, we can deal with only one of these liability rules at any length. Because of the dominant role of strict liability in the environmental sphere in recent times, we confine the analysis, after presentation of the basic model (section B.II), of the *problems* of liability law as an internalization strategy (section B.III) largely to this liability rule. This is not to imply that strict liability is superior to fault liability in every respect. Although an exhaustive analysis shows many advantages of strict liability, a differentiated profile of the advantages and drawbacks of the two liability rules nonetheless emerges.[34]

33　"A tort is a wrongful act, other than a breach of contract, for which a civil law suit may be brought by a private person" (Landes/Posner, 1987, p. 1).

34　A more exhaustive comparative analysis of fault liability and strict liability can be found in Schäfer/Ott (2004) and in many other law and economics textbooks.

For an economic presentation, analysis, and evaluation of equilibria arising in framework conditions of liability law, it is of considerable importance whether the environmental problem at issue is a "unilateral externality" or a "bilateral externality."[35] A unilateral externality is defined by the fact that only the polluter (in legal terms, the "injuring party") is in a position to take economically meaningful measures to limit the damage. By definition, in unilateral externalities, the injured party has no influence over the amount of damage. Correspondingly, bilateral externalities are defined by the fact that both the injuring and the injured parties can take economically meaningful steps to lower the damage.[36] In the literature, environmental problems are typically treated as unilateral externalities, and traffic accidents, in contrast, as bilateral externalities. Of course, the classification of environmental problems as unilateral externalities is a gross simplification. For instance, a firm endangered by emissions can sometimes affect the level of damage through its location decision. Consumers can (presumably) affect the extent of health damage by air pollution through their smoking behavior. Despite these counterexamples, it may probably be said that in analyzing environmental problems, the attention is directed *mainly* at the polluter's activities and less at those of the injured party. Because analyzing allocation effects of the environmental liability rule is considerably simpler for unilateral externalities than for bilateral ones, we treat the environmental problem exclusively as a unilateral externality.[37] The usefulness of this simplification for our context is simply rated higher than the cost arising from the fact that this model construction systematically ignores possibilities for the injured party that may in a few practical cases be quite important.[38]

Before looking at the various liability rules as strategies for internalizing externalities, let us briefly demarcate this approach from the solution through negotiation (the property rights approach) discussed in chapter A. The literature sometimes treats property law and liability law approaches as synonyms. However, it is important to point out the following differences:

a) The property law approach has an arrangement, the laissez-faire rule, whereby the externality can be internalized by payments by the injured party to the polluter. There is no analogy to this rule in liability law.

b) If the polluter causes damage without having acted negligently, then under fault liability (the negligence rule) there is no compensation payment to the injured

---

35 These terms have been chosen by analogy with the terminology of "unilateral or bilateral accidents" customary in the law and economics literature in the economic analysis of accidents.

36 According to an alternative "technical" definition, unilateral damage is where the socially optimal level of every measure of adjustment to the external effect to reduce the damage by the injured party is zero.

37 An exhaustive discussion of the economic aspects of liability law for the case of bilateral accidents can be found in Endres/Lüdeke (1998) and Shavell (1987).

38 As we mention in part one, building economic models is an issue of assessing pros and cons, as well as one of optimization.

party (nor any other transfer between the two parties involved). There is no analog to this position in the property law approach.

c) The property law approach involves a voluntary solution. Property rights are transferable, but no one can compel the polluter under the laissez-faire rule, or the injured party under the polluter pays rule, to transfer the rights allotted to him in the initial position. It is different with liability law: the injured party (in contrast with the polluter pays rule in property law) cannot prevent the polluter from carrying on the activity associated with the externality. If the polluter nonetheless decides to exercise the activity concerned, the injured party has a legal entitlement to compensation. The difference in question has a number of interesting implications:

- In the property law approach, the limits of the negotiating parties' willingness to compromise (assuming rational behavior) are determined by the course of the marginal damage cost curves and marginal abatement cost curves, respectively. However, how the increased benefit from the move from the suboptimal initial position to the social optimum is, within these limits, to be divided between the parties is not determined *a priori*. In liability law, it is pre-decided that in the event of liability, the injured party should have the damage precisely compensated. The increased benefit of the move from the suboptimal initial position to the (in the ideal case, optimum) adaptive equilibrium under liability law thus accrues exclusively to the polluter. Let us assume, say, that the institution of strict liability leads allocationally to the same optimum outcome as the polluter pays rule in the context of property law. Then it follows that distributively the injured party will under liability law at best be so placed[39] as in the worst conceivable case under property law.[40] However, the injured party is always better off under strict liability than under the laissez-faire rule of property law.

- The fact that property law as a voluntary solution leaves the parties more freedom to maneuver than liability law may at first sight seem to the liberal observer to be an advantage. However, it should not be overlooked here that the greater freedoms of the party favored by the particular property law arrangement (the polluter under the laissez-faire rule, the injured party under the polluter pays rule) can be used in the way described previously

---

39 In the unilateral case, the injured party receives under the polluter pays rule at least a compensation payment of the amount of the damage. Under strict liability, the injured party receives (assuming full compensation) precisely this amount. In the bilateral case, not further discussed here, the injured party receives instead, under the polluter pays rule, at least compensation for his avoidance costs and the residual damage. Under strict liability, in contrast, the injured party's expenditure on avoidance remains uncompensated.

40 Interestingly, liability law arrangements nonetheless generally tend to be felt by a public sympathizing with the injured party as more acceptable ("fairer") than payments by the polluter to the injured party in negotiations on the Coase approach.

for "blackmail strategies." These possibilities of abuse exist to a much lesser extent under liability law.[41]

- In the property law approach, the parties face each other directly in the negotiations. The parties' subjective assessments of the amount of marginal damage or marginal abatement cost are accordingly solely decisive for the weight with which these enter the market-like coordination process. With liability law, in contrast, the level of payment that seems suitable for compensating a particular damage is ultimately determined by a third party, the court. Here there will generally be departures from the parties' assessments. In this case, the principle of consumer sovereignty basic to setting up the optimum resource allocation is infringed. Simple economic modeling treatments (section II) leave this problem out of account. For a more policy-relevant analysis, however, it cannot be ignored (section III).

- A further implication of the differing degrees of freedom allowed the parties under property law or liability law emerges in the case of bilateral externalities. Because the following discussion is confined to unilateral externalities, this point is only briefly mentioned here and ignored in the sequel. If the injured party also has ways of keeping the damage within limits, then on the property law conditions of the polluter pays rule he will use these only if the polluter's payment covers at least, besides the (in this case, correspondingly reduced) cost of the damage, also that of the action to limit the damage. Under strict liability, the injured party is, in contrast, compensated only for the cost of the damage. To induce him to make efficient use of the means of limiting the damage available to him, strict liability would have to be supplemented by a (carefully balanced) contributory negligence clause.

II. The Basic Economic Model of Environmental Liability Law

1. Emission Equilibria under the Negligence Rule

As mentioned previously, the negligence rule provides that the polluter is obliged to pay compensation for damages if and only if the damage is caused by his neglecting due care in his activity. The question arises (from both an economic and a legal viewpoint) of how the initially indefinite concept of "due care" can be made operational. Because we are analyzing liability law here as an instrument for internalizing externalities and considering the emission of a particular pollutant as an example of an externality, the due care must in our context be specified by setting a particular emission level. We accordingly imagine a particular threshold value being set for the polluter, keeping to which will protect him against damage claims from those affected. If the polluter exceeds this value, however, he is liable. In the economic basic model, which is the only one dealt with in this book for the case of the

---

41 The injured party may, however, enrich himself under strict liability if he can manage in the courts to win an amount of compensation exceeding the actual damage.

negligence rule, we take it that the polluter's conduct is regarded as not negligent as long as he does not exceed the socially optimum emission level. In other words, under the negligence rule, liability arises once the injuring party's emission level lies above the socially optimum level.

This construction is, of course, extremely restrictive. It presumes that the standard-setter knows the socially optimum emission level and has taken on board the underlying optimality concept enough to be willing to use it to operationalize the negligence concept. Because these assumptions are obviously problematic, a more exhaustive analysis of the negligence rule will also have to look at the allocational consequences of divergences between the rule defining due care and the socially optimum emission level. However, such an exhaustive discussion would go beyond the limits of this book.[42] We accept the heroic assumption that the standard of care is optimal so as to be able to present the essential features of the incentive effect of the negligence rule in small compass, at least "to a first approximation." We do so with some plausibility considerations, and then more precisely using a graphic presentation.

Let us put ourselves in the position of a polluter considering, under the liability law framework just described, the level of his emission. He will divide conceivable emission levels into three areas:

Area 1: emission levels below the emission standard set by government
Area 2: emission levels higher than the government-set standard
Area 3: the emission level corresponding exactly with the standard[43]

The decision maker now imagines scenarios describing his situation according to which of these three areas he moves his actual emission level to. He will here judge his situation more favorably the lower the costs to be borne by him in each case.

Let us compare areas 1 and 3. The liability rule in force provides that a polluter need pay no compensation as long as his emissions are confined to a level not exceeding the government-set standard. This criterion is met both by the whole of area 1 and by area 3 (precise compliance with the standard). The polluter has accordingly to bear only abatement costs (no damage costs) in area 1 or area 3. But any position in area 1 differs from the (unambiguous) position in area 3 by having higher abatement costs because the emissions are lower. A polluter aiming at cost minimization will accordingly rate every conceivable position in area 1 less favorably than the position of precise compliance with the standard (area 3). We may accordingly exclude area 1 as irrelevant to the decision.

Let us now compare areas 2 and 3. Area 2, in contrast with area 3, has both advantages and drawbacks for the injuring party. The advantages are that the

---

42 On this, cf. Endres (1989).

43 We call this an "area" in the interest of "lean terminology," although it is actually only the single point that separates the first two areas.

emission level in area 2 is higher than in area 3, so that the abatement costs for the polluter are lower. However, and this is the drawback of area 2 in comparison with area 3, in area 2, over and above abatement costs, compensation costs also have to be paid due to the liability.

If the decision maker entertains the idea of infringing the governmental standard (i.e., going for an emission level in area 2), he has to ask himself which of the infinitely many emission levels in this area is the most favorable for him. The answer is, of course, that the most favorable emission level in area 2 is the one where the sum of abatement and compensation costs is a minimum. The polluter's decision between areas 2 and 3 thus comes down to whether he sees it as more favorable in cost terms to comply precisely with the standard or to produce that emission level at which the sum of the care and compensation costs for infringing the standard is a minimum.

Because we assume that the regulatory standard has been set as a social optimum (i.e., is at the emission level at which the sum of abatement and damage costs is a minimum),[44] the most favorable infringement of the government standard for the polluter is a *minimum* one. The most favorable emission level for the polluter in area 2 is thus marginally above the government standard itself (area 3). If the polluter, then, does decide to infringe the standard, he can at best reach a position where his abatement costs are a slight amount lower than those to be borne when complying with the standard (because the emissions he produces are only minimally above those compatible with the standard). This minor saving on the abatement cost side arising from the (best possible for him) infringement of the standard is dearly bought, though, because the minor breach of standard means that he has to compensate the injured party for the whole of the damage arising at this emission level. It is, then, plausible that a decision maker aiming at cost minimization will in the liability law framework assumed here decide to comply precisely with the regulatory standard. Because the regulatory standard is, by definition, set at the socially optimum level, the polluter's emission equilibrium reached here is a social optimum.

This argument can be clarified using Figure 8.[45] In the area between the uncorrected equilibrium emission level x^* and down to just before the socially optimum emission level x^{**}, the polluter has to expect to pay the abatement cost *plus* damages. The decisive thing for his considerations on the level of care to choose will, then, in this area be the total of abatement cost (AC) plus damage (D) compensation. These costs are shown in Figure 8 as curve $C^T = AC + D$. For emission reductions down to x^{**} or further, there is no liability. In the region between 0 and x^{**}, accordingly, the abatement cost curve AC alone represents the costs of relevance to the polluter.

It is central to the model of the negligence rule presented here that the cost curve relevant to the polluter's decision shows a discontinuity at the (optimally set)

44   Cf. footnote 34 in part one.
45   Figure 8 is an amplification of Figure 2.

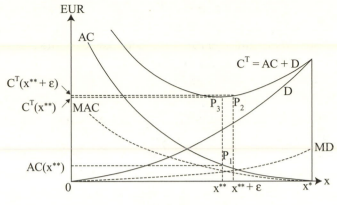

Figure 8

emission standard x^{**}. A marginal lowering of the emission level from $x^{**} + \varepsilon$ to x^{**} will spare the potential injuring party from taking account of the entire damage arising (from emission at level x^{**}) in his calculation.

The most favorable position for the polluter is, then, if he precisely complies with emission standard x^{**}. Then he will "be at" point P_1 in Figure 8. In this situation, the costs to be calculated will amount to $AC(x^{**})$. Were he to breach the emission standard, he could in the most favorable case reach point P_2 in Figure 8. He would then have to bear considerably higher costs, $C^T (x^{**} + \varepsilon)$.

If we assume that the polluter is aiming at minimizing costs, it follows that the pollutant level he will emit at equilibrium under the negligence rule will correspond to the economically optimum level x^{**}. At equilibrium, no compensation payment will be made to the injured party.

Strictly speaking, thus, the negligence rule is not an internalization strategy in the sense of the definition given in part one. For there, the internalization of externalities was defined as a policy in which the social optimality of the market equilibrium is achieved by charging the producers of the externality for the external costs. In somewhat looser language, the negligence rule is nonetheless called an internalization strategy because its use will (at any rate under the extremely simplified conditions of the basic economic model) produce the same emission level as internalization.[46] However, this statement should also be used with caution where it is not an individual polluter, but a polluting industry that is involved.[47]

2. Emission Equilibria under Strict Liability

In complete analogy with the previous discussion for the negligence rule, we can now depict the polluter's decision on emission level under strict liability, starting by using plausibility considerations and then giving a graphic presentation.

---

46   The negligence rule could, however, also be called "a system of regulations sanctioned by the liability threat."

47   Cf. the considerations in the next but one section (3).

Under strict liability, the polluter is liable irrespective of negligence. In relation to the situation contemplated here, this means that the polluter must always calculate the sum of abatement and damage costs, irrespective of the emission level. He will accordingly opt for the emission level at which the sum of these two costs takes on the smallest possible value. But the socially optimum emission level is defined by this very property. It follows, then, that the polluter will at equilibrium under strict liability produce the economically optimum emission level.[48] In Figure 8, the "ground rules" of strict liability have the effect that the total cost curve ($C^T = AC + D$) shows the costs relevant to the polluter's decision over the whole range of emission levels under consideration (from 0 to x^*). The minimum of this cost curve lies just above the socially optimum emission level x^{**}. The costs arising for the polluter in this situation amount to $C^T(x^{**})$; he "is at" point P_3 in Figure 8.

3. The Negligence Rule and Strict Liability Compared

In the simple economic model presented here, the negligence rule and strict liability lead allocationally to one and the same socially optimum outcome.[49] Distributively, however, the two liability rules differ fundamentally. At equilibrium under the negligence rule, the polluter is not obliged to pay damages because, by definition, he is not acting negligently in this situation. Those affected by the emissions must accordingly bear the damage themselves. With strict liability, in contrast, the polluter has to compensate the injured party in full for the damage. The latter is thus distributively better off here than under the negligence rule.

Accordingly, the allocational irrelevance of the liability rule in the simple basic economic model could be doubted by analogy with the argument presented previously in connection with the *Coase theorem*. Referring to the connection discussed exhaustively between distribution and allocation, the argument would be that the monetary equivalent of the environmental damage would have to be set higher under strict liability than under the negligence rule because the relevant party's capacity to pay under the first liability rule is above that capacity under the latter liability rule. The curve of expected damages in Figure 8 would thus depend on the liability rule. Because of the analogy with our previous argument in a property law context, we need not illustrate this point any further here.

We do, however, want to point out a related circumstance. This arises when we move from the picture of an individual polluter to one of a polluting industry. Under strict liability, the members of that industry would at equilibrium have to pay damages for the externality. The long-run equilibrium price of the product produced by this industry would thus also contain the initially external costs. It will be correspondingly higher than this industry's long-run price on the negligence rule, under which environmental damage need not be covered by the price because

---

48   This statement applies only for the case of unilateral externalities, the only one considered here. On the efficiency problems with strict liability in the bilateral case, cf., e.g., Endres (1989), Shavell (1987).

49   The analogy between these statements and the "Coase theorem" discussed in chapter A is evident.

no compensation obligation arises at equilibrium. The higher price of industrial output under strict liability means (assuming a negative slope of the demand curve) that the industry's *output level* under this liability rule will be lower than under the negligence rule. *Ceteris paribus*, accordingly, the industry's *emission level* at equilibrium will also be lower under strict liability than under the negligence rule.

A further difference lies in the information conditions for the relevant equilibrium to be an optimum. In particular, the standard-setting institution must in the case of the negligence rule know the care and damage curves. This condition is, of course, unnecessary for strict liability. Strict liability is accordingly superior to the negligence rule on the criterion of *informational decentrality*.[50]

4. Model Prerequisites

The simple economic model of liability law briefly presented previously (the "basic model") reveals major features of the incentive structure parties are subject to under the institutions of liability law. It is, however, based on a number of extremely restrictive conditions. It is in particular assumed that

a) The parties (polluter, injured party) take their decisions on the basis of "good" information. They know the content of the liability rule in force, including (if appropriate) the emission standard (due care standard). The polluter knows his own emission level, as well as the connections between this level and the abatement and damage costs. The institution setting the emission standard (legislature, judiciary) knows the actual and the socially optimum emission levels.[51]

b) The standard-setting institution uses its knowledge of the optimum emission level, in the case of the negligence rule, to define through that level the concept of due care.

c) The firms involved operate in conditions of perfect competition.

d) Damage and damage compensation payment are identical. This assumption implies, in particular, that monetary equivalents exist for all damage that may arise. It is further assumed that the causer and victim of any damage can be identified unambiguously (and at no charge).

e) The parties are risk neutral.

It is clear that there are considerable divergences between these model assumptions and circumstances in reality. Although we do not want to dispute in any way the pedagogical value of the basic economic model, it is nonetheless necessary

50 Complete informational decentrality would be where all that is needed for the equilibrium allocation to be an optimum would be that each decision maker know the costs "arising in his own house." However, this condition is not met by strict liability either. The potentially injuring party has to know the expected damage for the injured party.

51 Ott/Schäfer (1997) show on what conditions and (if possible) how optimum standards can emerge in the long term in the dynamics of judicial case decisions.

for a more policy-relevant analysis of the allocational effects of the environmental liability law to look at departures from the basic model. We accordingly look at the effect of assumptions in the economic model of liability law that are closer to reality about the location and optimality of emission equilibria. The following discussion is for space reasons confined to the case of strict liability.[52] This option is against the background of the considerably greater importance of strict liability in German environmental policy from the Environmental Liability Act, which came into force in 1991.[53]

III. Problems with Internalizing Externalities through Liability Law

The previous presentation did not distinguish between the level of damage and the level of the damage compensation payment. It was instead assumed that, in the event of a case of damage and liability, the polluter always has to compensate the injured party precisely for the damage. In practice, however, a number of influencing factors that may establish a divergence between the expected damage and the expected amount of compensation may operate. If an expected damage compensation payment calculated by the polluter is below the expected damage, we call this "damage discounting."[54] If, in contrast, the expected damage compensation payment calculated is above the expected damage, this is termed "excess" damages.

There are a number of reasons for divergences between the damage and the compensation. We concentrate on the case of damage discounting:

- Among the causes of this divergence may be *information problems.* These can arise because plant operators' activities are not (or at least not fully) observable. It is entirely possible for an actor to cause damage without being discovered. The plant operator may anticipate this and, in choosing the equilibrium level of care, use not the damage actually expected, but a value corrected by a factor for the likelihood of discovery (less than 1). Here, then, uncertain causality leads to a divergence between damage and compensation.[55] Information problems may also arise because the amount of damage is disputed by the parties in the courts. The plant operator will, of course, bring to bear arguments that make the damage seem smaller, whereas the injured party will argue in the opposite direction. Nor, of course, is the possibility to be ruled out that the court may

---

52 A corresponding analysis for the negligence rule can be found in Endres (1989).

53 For more on the German Environmental Liability Act, see section V.

54 That is to say that a "discount" is made on the damage. The intertemporal association usual with the concept of discounting in economics is not meant here.

55 If the causality is not immediately clear, the question arises as to who bears the *burden of proof.* To improve the allocative effects of liability law given uncertain causality, the law and economics literature offers the instrument (extremely unpopular with lawyers, to be sure) of "probability liability. . . . " For the basics of the construction of causality in economic theory of liability law, see Young/Faure/Fenn (2004).

end up setting the compensation figure wrongly (cf. Hiriart/Martimort/Pouyet 2004; Singh 2003).

- As well as information problems, *motivation* problems may also be responsible for divergences between damages and compensation. These arise where the transaction costs arising for claimants asserting claims for damages are higher than the expected compensation payment. In this context, the literature talks of "rational disinterest" of such parties in enforcing their claims.[56] This is particularly likely in the case of environmental problems, where the damage is spread over many parties. Rational disinterest may provide an argument for *class actions.*

- A third cause of damage discounting is *imperfect property rights.* Liability is a private law instrument in which the polluter compensates the victim for the monetary value of the damage caused. A necessary condition for the identity of damage and the compensation payment under private law is that all damages arise for particular persons who are entitled as victims to claim compensation. But this condition is not always met in practice. For instance, damage may arise in areas of nature where no property rights are defined. In the environmental policy debate, people talk here of "ecodamage." More recently, legal policy approaches have been developed that might be suitable for closing the internalization lacuna at issue here (or at least for beginning to). Thus, the environmental liability directive adopted by the European Union in the year 2004 and amended in 2006 concentrates on this very area of ecodamage and thus goes beyond the private law context. Here the state emerges as trustee of nature.[57]

- A further departure from the principle of full compensation arises where the polluter's liability is limited (and this constraint is binding in the case under consideration). Such *limitations of liability* are often already present in the legal provisions that regulate the liability. This is true of, for instance, the German Environmental Liability Act or the German Genetic Engineering Act.

  An upper limit to liability always results, irrespective of the acts regulating liability, from the fact that the liable assets of the polluting firm are (in different ways according to its legal form) limited. Because the damage discounting associated with a limitation of liability brings firms advantages, it is likely that they will also themselves actively promote circumstances that enable discounting. An empirical analysis has shown that the foundation of small, independent firms (with low-liability capital) in sectors hazardous to third parties has sharply risen

---

56 In general, on this common notion in the economic analysis of law, cf. Schäfer/Ott (2004).

57 One might accordingly deny that the EU directive is a liability law construction in the economic sense. Such doubts are strengthened by the fact that the directive provides mainly for restitution in kind instead of monetary transfers. Initial approaches to an economic analysis of the EU directive are offered by Swanson/Kontoleon (2004). For an economic assessment of restitution in kind versus monetary transfers, cf. Zervogianni (2004).

with the tightening up of liability law provisions.[58] The law and economics literature devotes considerable attention to the *judgment-proof* problem associated
with this. The point is to see how far the internalization effect of liability law can
be obtained with critically limited levels of firms' assets. Among possibilities
are extending damage claims to firms in particular contractual relations with
the polluting firm (e.g., in the form of *lender liability*), or various insurance law
constructions (on this, cf., e.g., Feess 1999, Feess/Hege 2000, Hutchinson/van't
Veld 2005, van Egteren/Smith/McAfee 2004).

A gap between damage and compensation has immediate effects on parties'
decisions as to their emission equilibria and the optimality of these equilibria.
The nature and extent of these repercussions is discussed here for the case of
strict liability. In the analysis, it makes sense to distinguish cases where divergences
between damage and compensation exist irrespective of the emission level from
cases where the difference arises only in particular subsets of emission levels. The
first-named case ("complete divergence") is dealt with in the next section. The
allocative effects of the complication mentioned last ("partial divergence") are
discussed in the section after that.

1. Complete Divergence between Damage and Compensation Payment

If the compensation payment to be made is, for one or more of the reasons mentioned previously, below the level of actual damage, this has effects on the polluter's
calculation of the most favorable emission level for him. In estimating these effects
we, in line with the traditional approach in economics, assume that the decision
maker is concerned solely with minimizing his costs. We do not assume that it is of
vital concern for him that the compensation he pays should make recompense for
a wrong that he has done to third parties.

It follows from this image of the decision maker that in our model of his calculation of the emission level he should choose, we should always use the compensation
payment rather than the actual damage level, as long as – as assumed here – the
latter is below the former.

In deciding what emission level to choose, the polluter will accordingly orient
himself by how the level of compensation payment depends on the pollutant emission level. He will also take account in his calculations of the size of the abatement
costs associated with particular pollutant levels. Ultimately, he will opt for the emission level that gives a minimum for the sum of abatement costs and compensation
payment. It is likely that the emission level meeting this condition is above the
optimum one for the overall economy, at which it is the sum of abatement cost and
damage actually arising that is a minimum.[59]

We can, then, say that under strict liability too high pollutant emission (compared with the optimum for the overall economy) will come about as soon as the
polluter can "discount" the damage (i.e., the compensation payment is lower than

58   On this, cf. Segerson (2000) and the sources indicated there.
59   A formal proof can be found in Endres (1989).

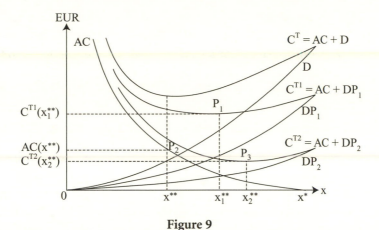

Figure 9

the damage). This partial charging for the damage through strict liability will lead to some reduction in emissions by comparison with the level without any environmental policy, but it must nonetheless be stressed that the object of internalizing externalities will be missed. The foregoing argument can be clarified still further on the basis of Figure 9.

C^T shows the total cost curve, as explained previously. It is made up of the abatement cost (AC) plus damage (D). For the damage compensation payment, lying below the damage, (DP), two examples are entered in the diagram.

"Weak" discounting leads to the curve lying "a little" under the D curve, DP_1. "Strong" discounting leads to the curve DP_2, lying "considerably" under the D curve. The relevant overall cost curve for the polluter with weak discounting under strict liability, C^{T1}, thus follows from the (vertical) aggregation of the abatement cost curve (AC) and the relevant damage compensation payment curve (DP_1). The equilibrium emission level x_1^{**} is defined by the minimum of curve C^{T1}. If the discounting is instead heavier, as with DP_2 in Figure 9, then $C^{T2} = AC + DP_2$ gives the relevant cost curve for the polluter under strict liability. In these circumstances, the polluter will decide for an emission level x_2^{**} that minimizes C^{T2}.

The further the compensation payment lies below the damage, the further above the optimum emission level the equilibrium emission level will be.

2. Partial Divergence: Partial Damage Discounting with Limitation of Liability

One important special case of a divergence between damage compensation payment and damage is set up by "limited liability." However, the allocational effects of limitation of liability cannot all be dealt with using the previous description of complete (i.e., done for every level of care) "discounting" of the damage by the polluter. In contrast with the previous presentation, here the expected damage compensation payment does not depart from the expected damage until the upper limit of liability is reached.[60] If, instead, the upper liability limit is exceeded

---

60   The previously mentioned special reasons for divergence (e.g., problems of the burden of proof) are ignored in the following analysis. It is typical for our presentation in this book that each

(i.e., the damage exceeds the maximum figure set for compensation), then the expected damage compensation payment is decoupled from the level of damage expected. The discounting thus applies only to part of the possible level of care. This point calls for separate presentation.

To understand the effects of a limitation of liability on a polluter's decision as to his emission level under strict liability, we must be clear that the limitation of liability has an important protective function for the decision maker. Particularly for high emission levels and associated high damage, it assures the polluter that nothing worse can happen to him than to have to pay the amount set as the upper liability limit. The possible emission level accordingly breaks down, for a polluter aiming at cost minimization, into two regions: the region where the damage D caused by his emission is greater than the maximum damage compensation payment DP^{max} defined by the liability limit, and the region where his emissions cause damage lying below the maximum compensation payment. The rationally acting decision maker will now seek to identify the most favorable cost position in each region and then select the *minimum minimorum* from those. In the region where the polluter cuts emissions so far that the damage caused lies below the maximum damage compensation payment, the analysis is similar to the previous. Here the optimum emission level for the polluter is where the sum of the damages and the abatement cost is a minimum.[61] Because in analyzing the upper liability limits we are disregarding all other departures from the basic economic model, this emission level corresponds to the optimum level for the overall economy. In the area where the emissions are so high that the damage is above the maximum damage compensation payment, the polluter has to calculate the sum of abatement costs and maximum compensation payment. It is central to an understanding of this calculation that the emission level affects the amount of only one of these parts of the sum. The abatement costs fall with increasing emissions, but the maximum compensation payment is independent of them. This means that the sum of abatement cost and maximum compensation payment is a minimum if the polluter avoids all emission abatement (i.e., produces his uncorrected equilibrium level x^*).

The polluter's decision thus reduces to a comparison of the cost burden arising for him at the socially optimum emission level with the cost burden for him when producing his uncorrected equilibrium emission level. How this comparison will turn out can, of course, not be said definitively at the level of abstraction chosen in this discussion. It depends on the course of the abatement and damage cost curves, to be determined empirically, and on the level of the upper liability limit applying in the given case.

---

of the departures from the basic economic model of liability law is considered separately. The simultaneous analysis of various divergences, with their effects on the internalization properties of liability law institutions, is definitely interesting, but would make the presentation far more complicated than an introductory text can afford.

61   We are here assuming that the liability limit is not binding for the relevant emission level (i.e., $D(x^{**}) < DP^{max}$).

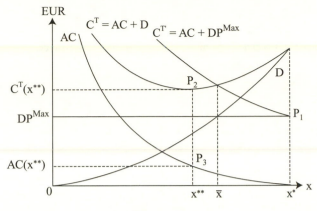

Figure 10

However, we can illustrate the connections graphically using Figure 10. The liability limit is entered as the horizontal straight line DP^{max}. If the polluter pays the total of abatement cost and maximum compensation payment, then he "moves" along the curve $AC + DP^{max}$ in Figure 10. In Figure 10, the sum of abatement cost and maximum compensation payment for emission levels between x^* and $\bar{x}$ lies below the sum of abatement cost and damage. In this area, then, the polluter will be oriented by the cost curve $C^{T'} = AC + DP^{max}$. If, instead, the emissions are below level $\bar{x}$, defined by the equality of damage and maximum compensation payment, then the damage will be below the maximum compensation payment. Between $\bar{x}$ and emission level 0, the polluter will accordingly orient him- or herself by the total cost curve $C^{T} = AC + D$.

We can see that the minimum for the total costs to be borne by the polluter in the region between x^* and $\bar{x}$ lies precisely at x^*. He then has no abatement cost (for x^* is his uncorrected equilibrium emission level), but must deduct the maximum damage compensation amount. In the illustration then, he "is at" point P_1 and bears costs at the level of DP^{max}.

In the area between $\bar{x}$ and 0, in contrast, the optimum position for the polluter lies at point P_2, at which the sum of abatement cost and damage is minimized (i.e., with emissions at the optimum level x^{**}).

If that is the way things are, as we assume in the curves shown in Figure 10, then it will be best for the polluter to use the protection of the liability limitation in order to do without any emission abatement. This outcome, of course, depends on the level of the liability limitation. The reader is asked to enter a liability limitation in Figure 10 that is high enough to induce the decision maker to move to the socially optimum emission level.[62]

---

62 The portrayal in Figure 10 has deliberately been kept simple. The result that for a sufficiently low liability limit the emissions are not reduced at all depends essentially on the point that a deterministic dependency between emission level and environmental damage is assumed. If the connection between emission level and damage is stochastic, the analysis becomes more

3. Other Problems

Previously, we dealt at length with the allocative problems of liability law brought by divergences between compensation and damage. The presentation concentrated on strict liability. We conclude by briefly mentioning a few other issues. Here the negligence rule is not left uncriticized either.

- The basic economic model assumes there is one plant operator whose activity is solely responsible for causing the damage ("monocausality"). In its application to environmental policy, however, we frequently have to do with multiple causation ("multicausality"). The joint polluters may be not only various plant operators, but also plant operators and injured parties. Taking multiple causality of damage into account considerably changes the outcomes regarding the internalization effect of liability law. In particular, it has to be stressed that strict liability loses the advantage of higher informational decentrality, in comparison with the negligence rule, in the case of multicausality. This is immediately obvious if we look at "bilateral damage" as a form of multicausality. If the damage is bilateral, then its expected value can be affected both by care activities by the potential polluter and care activities by the potential injured party. In general, for a socially optimum allocation, it is necessary that both parties make a contribution to preventing damage. Because with strict liability as introduced previously the plant operator is always liable, irrespective of the level of care he chooses, the injured party is in every case compensated for the damage arising. However, this eliminates any incentive for him to act with care himself. The equilibrium allocation under strict liability is socially suboptimal.[63] To heal this defect, strict liability must in the case of the bilateral damage here be considered as supplemented by a "contributory negligence clause" addressed to the injured party. This must, of course (by analogy with the care standard addressed to the plant operator in the basic economic model), be set at the socially optimum level. Similarly, strict liability must be supplemented by care standards where multicausality arises in the form of joint causation of damage by several plant operators.[64] Here, again, the advantage of the higher informational decentrality

complicated. Here it can be shown that liability limitation under strict liability need not lead to completely refraining from emission reduction, even if set very low. However, in this model at equilibrium a too high level compared with the social optimum will set in. The simplification in the previous presentation thus does not falsify the connection suggested here, but merely presents it in a particularly extreme case.

63   The existence of an equilibrium under liability law for bilateral damage is assumed without further ado in the literature. On these questions, see Endres/Lüdeke (1998), Endres/Querner (1995).

64   For more on this, see Feess/Hege (1998, 1999), Young et al. (2005). A solution efficient in the short term is also for each polluter to be responsible for the whole damage. This leads, however, to misallocation in the long-term equilibrium (cf. Feess/Hege (2002), Holmström (1982)). Moreover, such an arrangement would infringe the proportionality requirement and thus be difficult to enforce. The literature cited in this footnote and in footnote 63 has an

of strict liability in comparison with the negligence rule gets lost in the move from the monocausal to the multicausal problem.

- One restrictive assumption of the basic ideal model is that the competent bodies can manage to set standards of care at the socially optimum level. The information prerequisites for this are, of course, not generally met in the real world. It is accordingly needful to look at the allocational properties of legal provisions given suboptimal standards of care.[65] As was not to be expected otherwise, the analysis shows that considerable disruptions to the internalization effects of liability law can result from this. Let us for simplicity's sake assume a single case of monocausally caused damage. If the standard of care (compared with the social optimum) is set too low, the polluter will at equilibrium free himself of liability through precise compliance. The level of care reached is thus suboptimal. With a too high standard (in comparison with the social optimum), the polluter will "go along" as long as the costs of care arising thereby are below the sum of costs of care and expected damage arising at socially optimum safety. However, if the standard is so excessive that the costs of care arising from compliance exceed the sum of costs of care and expected damage at socially optimum care to be calculated by the polluter, then he will ignore the standard and let socially optimum care prevail. The excessive standard of care puts the polluter in the same position as strict liability. If against this background we compare strict liability and the negligence rule, then strict liability does of course have advantages. With monocausal damage, this liability rule obviates the need to define standards of care, so that the allocational problems arising with this definition also disappear. For multicausal damage, however, these problems catch up with strict liability. For the special case of multicausality cited previously, namely, bilateral damage, the problems arise with defining the injured parties' contributory negligence.

- Regarding the completeness of standards of care, things are similar as for their optimum level. The ideal internalization effects of the *negligence rule* suggested by the simple basic model can only arise if for every possible care activity a corresponding standard of care is also defined. This is, of course, extremely unrealistic. It is, for instance, very difficult to set standards for the level of the risk-loaded activity (e.g., production level). If the system of standards of care is imperfect in this sense, then it follows that the mix of care activities reached at equilibrium is suboptimal. Here, again, strict liability has advantages in the case of unilateral damage because in that system no standards of care need be defined. For bilateral damage, in contrast, with strict liability problems of imperfect *standards of contributory negligence* arise. The argument briefly presented here, for the case of given information on risk-lowering activities and given prevention technologies, also applies by analogy to the search

economic theory orientation. An economic analysis of liability in the case of multicausality with an orientation more toward legal practice can be found in Young et al. (2005).

65 An exhaustive model-based presentation can be found in Endres (1989).

for information and the further development of prevention technologies. For both important elements of risk management in a rapidly changing world, standard-oriented liability law gives no impulses of its own where it defines no standards.[66]

IV. Allocation Effects of Insuring Environmental Risk

1. *Preliminary Remarks*

If liability law establishes claims by those injured by externalities to compensation payments by the perpetrator, then an interest arises in insuring the corresponding risks.

Risk-averse potential polluters are prepared to transfer to an insurer, for a guaranteed payment (the premium), the risk of being called on to pay injured parties.[67] For injured parties, too, it is advantageous if the polluter is insured because this lowers the risk for them not to be compensated (or only partly) because of the polluter's inability to pay. In the interest of injured parties, accordingly, the state (in some cases) prescribes mandatory coverage for those engaging in activities hazardous to third parties. We have to ask, then, how the existence of insurance affects the internalization effect of liability law.[68]

For this discussion, the economic model of liability law used so far has to be slightly adjusted: the aspect of the uncertainty of the consequences of human decisions has not been taken explicit account of in the analysis. The model-based argumentation was done implicitly in conditions of a world of certainty. But the need for insurance is established only through the existence of uncertainty. We must accordingly bring the concept of risk into the model construction. This can most simply be done as follows:

a) As the activity, the equilibrium and economic optimum of which is considered here, we no longer take a firm's emission level, but the level of its "care activity" capable of reducing the likelihood of an accident and/or the extent of the damage caused by one. In practice, there is a multiplicity of technical and nontechnical safety measures that can be employed, alternately or combined with each other. To simplify, we assume the existence of one care activity, z.

b) To ease the transition from a model with certainty to one with risk, we assume that the decision maker is risk neutral, thus always guided in his considerations by the *expected value* of the risk-loaded quantities relevant to his decision. We go beyond this assumption in the next section.

---

66 See Endres/Bertram/Rundshagen (2007), Endres/Rundshagen/Bertram (2008) on the dynamic incentives of environmental liability law.

67 We do not distinguish between a party's risk and risk perception. It can be done: see the articles in the special issue "Risk Perception, Valuation and Policy" of the *Journal Environmental and Resource Economics*, Vol. 33, No. 3 (2006).

68 Cf. Faure/Hartlief (2003).

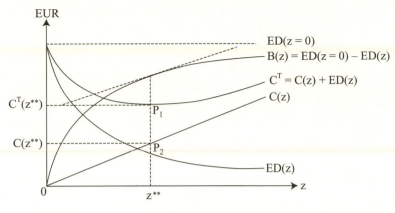

Figure 11

With these simplifying assumptions, it is easy to understand the internalization effects of liability law institutions in connection with risk-loaded activities in complete analogy with the basic economic model of liability law presented previously for the case of certainty. There are two effects associated with carrying out care activities in connection with risk-laden activity[69]: the higher the level of care activity reached, the higher the costs of care. In contrast, expected damage falls with increasing levels of care. The optimum care level is defined as having the sum of care cost and expected damage a minimum.

An equivalent description of the optimum care level can be arrived at as follows: carrying out the care activity brings costs and benefits. The costs are production costs, such as arise in carrying out any other activity. The benefits consist of the damage-lowering effect of the activity. The optimum care level is the one for which the difference between benefit and cost of this activity is a maximum. Figure 11 illustrates the concept of the optimum care level and the equivalence of the two formulations just presented.

For z^{**}, the sum of care cost and expected damage $(C(z) + ED(z))$ is a minimum. Similarly, at z^{**} the difference between the benefit curve $(B(z) = ED(z=0) - ED(z))$ and the care cost curve $C(z)$ is a maximum.[70]

Because of the far-reaching analogy with the model of emission abatement under certainty presented previously, the internalization effects of liability law in the basic economic model with risk is explained only briefly here. We confine ourselves to the case of strict liability. Here the potential polluter is oriented in the simple basic model to the cost curve $C + ED$. His cost minimum is at point

---

69   We consider only the care measures by the one engaging in the risk-laden activity, and thus, as in the model with certainty, consider only the case of unilateral externality.

70   Mathematically trained readers will see at a glance that the first-order condition for a maximum benefit–cost difference and a minimum of the sum of care cost and expected damage are identical. (The term $ED(z=0)$ is constant and therefore vanishes in the derivative, and the second-order conditions are met with the curve assumed here).

P_1, and this coincides with the overall economic cost minimum. At equilibrium, accordingly, he is at the economically optimum care level z^{**}.

2. Care Equilibria with Risk Aversion

To ease the move from the model with certainty to the model with risk, we have assumed in the above introduction that the decision-maker is risk-neutral. However, we cannot let an analysis of the internalization effects of insurance for environmental risks stop at this simplifying assumption because a risk-neutral decision maker has no interest in taking out insurance. An insurer can cover him for the risk of having to pay compensation to the victim only for a payment (premium) that *at least* covers the expected value of damage.[71] Because the risk-neutral polluter is by definition oriented to the expected value of damage, taking out insurance at a price at least as high as the expected value of damage is not attractive. The polluter will instead be prepared to take out insurance precisely if he rates the unfavorable possibility of actually having to make payments above the expected value after an accident higher than the favorable possibility of getting off with "below-average" payments. Such a polluter is "risk averse." He is willing to pay a "risk premium" for the insurance to take away the risk. Before we look at the internalization effect of concluding insurance for environmental risks, we must accordingly eliminate the assumption made previously that the polluter is risk neutral and replace it by the assumption of risk aversion.

For the risk-averse polluter, carrying out the risky activity is associated with both the expected damage and the risk burden. Thus, it follows that carrying out the care activity for him means the positive effect of lowering both of these elements. The benefit of the care activity is accordingly greater for the risk-averse polluter considered in this section than for the risk-neutral one considered in the previous one. Making the plausible assumption that the care costs are independent of the polluter's risk preference, it intuitively follows that the risk-averse polluter will carry out a higher level of the care activity at equilibrium than the risk-neutral one. Although this may please the environmentally concerned reader, it should nonetheless be pointed out that in the economic conception employed here, assessment of a decision maker's activity has to be done only through a comparison with the economically optimum decision. However, there are good reasons for society as a whole, the determinant of the economically optimum level of the care activity, to be less risk averse than the individual decision maker.[72] For simplicity's sake, we assume the extreme case where society as a whole is risk neutral, although each individual decision maker is risk averse. Then the level of the economically optimum care will not be affected by our change in assumptions about individual risk preferences. The previously defined care level z^{**} will accordingly continue to be economically optimum. However, at equilibrium, the risk-averse

---

71   Insurers have to live, too.
72   This may be because the risks of individual members of society balance out.

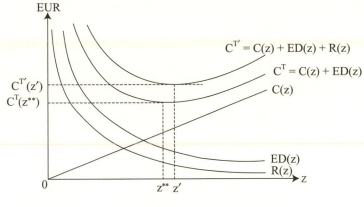

Figure 12

decision maker will be at a higher care level z', which minimizes the sum of care cost $(C(z))$, expected damage $(ED(z))$, and risk burden $(R(z))$. Regardless of how counterintuitive this may be for the environmentalist, even too high a care level constitutes a misallocation from the economic viewpoint.[73] Figure 12 illustrates the argument.

3. Care Equilibria with Insurance at a Fair Premium

We now bring the possibility of insurance into the model of the allocational effects of liability law. Here we assume in the first step that the premium to be paid by potential polluters is "fair" in the sense that it is equal to the expected damage. It is clear that the model of the allocational effects of liability law with risk-averse decision makers and the possibility of insurance at a fair premium is identical with the simple basic model in which the decision maker is risk neutral. Risk-averse potential polluters (on whom attention is concentrated in the case of the unilateral accidents assumed here) will under strict liability (all that is considered here) be willing to take out insurance at a fair premium $(p(z) = ED(z))$. For the polluter's overall costs fall by taking it out because the insurer takes away not only the expected damage, but also the risk burden, at a price that contains only the expected damage. The costs to be calculated by the polluter thus go down from $C(z) + ED(z) + R(z)$,

---

73 To reassure the agitated environmentalists among our readers, let us point out that the model discussed previously treats the polluter's risk aversion as the sole departure from the basic economic model. In reality, however, a number of departures operate together. As we have seen, these often mean that at equilibrium lower care (or analogously, higher emission) results than would be optimum. Analyzing the various divergences between reality and the basic model not successively as done here but simultaneously, the tendency to "overcare" arising from the polluter's risk aversion may prove a highly beneficial compensation for the many other incentives to "overnegligence." It should not be ignored here, however, that a simultaneous analysis of various divergences, however necessary it may be to arriving at economic policy decisions, would be complex and lengthy. Such an analysis cannot accordingly be presented within the limits of this book.

as explained in the previous section, to $C(z) + p(z)$, where $p(z) = ED(z)$ holds. Under these circumstances, the potential polluter will at equilibrium choose the level of care at which the sum of care cost and premium $(C(z) + p(z))$ is a minimum. Because of the identity of premium and expected damage, he will at equilibrium be at the economically optimum care level z^{**}.

4. Care Equilibria with Insurance with Moral Hazard

The model of insurance at a fair premium mentioned previously is based on (at least) three heroic assumptions: (1) that the institution of insurance incurs no (administrative) costs, (2) that the insurance company knows the connections between care level and expected damage, and (3) that the insurer can perfectly observe the nature and extent of the care efforts of each individual insured.[74]

Only then is it possible for the individual premium to be adapted to the damage expected by each potential polluter (dependent on his care efforts). We concentrate on the consequences of going beyond the previously mentioned assumption.

If the insurer cannot perfectly observe the care efforts of the insured potential polluter, then an information asymmetry arises between these two decision makers. As exhaustively shown in microeconomics textbooks, this information asymmetry produces a danger of *moral hazard*: the insurer's lack of knowledge of the care measures tempts the insured into dealing negligently with the risk.[75] The essence of the distortion of allocation brought into the model through insurance with information asymmetry and moral hazard can most simply be understood as follows: the less the insurer can observe the polluter's care behavior, the smaller the extent to which an (insured) polluter's care is reflected in premium reductions. Accordingly, the bigger the information asymmetry between polluter and insurer is the smaller is the reward firms receive for taking care measures. However, the insured always bears the *costs* of carrying out the care measures in full, irrespective of the insurer's degree of information. With increasing information asymmetry, then, the profitability of care measures for the causer of the risk falls.

Figure 13 singles out the *extreme case* in which the problem addressed here means that at equilibrium the polluter with insurance completely refrains from care measures. In interpreting Figure 13, we assume that the insurer cannot observe the potential polluter's level of care activity. In this situation, the premium cannot vary with the level of care. Instead, the insurer asks for a fixed premium at level $\overline{p}$.

Because on concluding the insurance the causer of the risk has to calculate only the care cost, but not the expected damage or risk burden, $C(z) + \overline{p}$ represents the cost curve of relevance to him in Figure 13. Because $\overline{p}$ is by the assumptions constant and $C(z)$ increases monotonically with z, it is minimum cost for the potential causer of the risk completely to refrain from care activities when taking out insurance $(z = 0)$. If in this situation no care costs arise $(C(z = 0) = 0)$, then the total cost

74   It is further assumed that the insurance firms behave in an economically competitive manner.
75   The extent of information asymmetries is, however, not given by nature, but can be controlled through the design of the liability law (cf. Feess/Hege, 2002).

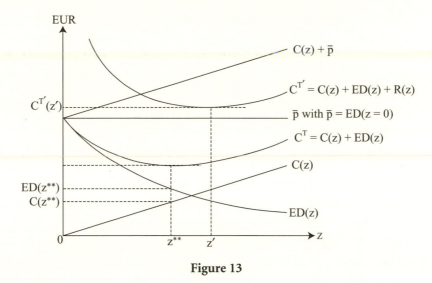

Figure 13

for the potential polluter in this situation amounts to $\bar{p}$. If the polluter did not take out the insurance, it would be most favorable for him to carry out the care activity at level z' for which the sum of the care cost, expected damage, and risk burden is a minimum. His cost burden would in this case be $C^{T'}(z')$. Because in Figure 13, $C^{T'}(z') > \bar{p}$, the causer of the risk will take out the insurance so that no care activity carried out is an equilibrium. Because in this equilibrium the insurer (working at zero administrative cost according to the assumption) makes no losses, the premium must cover the expected damage arising at equilibrium. Figure 13 shows $\bar{p} = ED\,(z = 0)$. The premium is accordingly, in the model discussed here with prohibitive information costs for the insurer (regarding the level of the care activity), still fair in the sense defined previously, but higher than the equilibrium premium $p = ED(z^{**})$ in the previous model with perfect information. This shows the misallocation brought about by the too low equilibrium level of care ($z = 0$ instead of z^{**}). The welfare losses from the divergence of the equilibrium from the social optimum are $ED(z = 0) - (ED(z^{**}) + C(z^{**}))$.

5. Care Equilibria with Insurance with "Own Risk" Excess and a Contractually Agreed Level of Care

The previous discussion shows that the problems of moral hazard associated with insurance can strongly affect the internalization effects of liability law. For the sake of completeness, however, we mention here that the equilibrium position in the case of insurance with moral hazard is not, even in the extreme case where the equilibrium care level is zero, to be assessed as unfavorably as the position arising with no employment of any internalization instrument. At the insurance equilibrium, at least those affected by the external damage are compensated. The distributive effects are – at any rate according to the value judgments dominant in our society – to be assessed more favorably than in the case of no internalization.

In addition, it should be pointed out that at the insurance equilibrium, the insurance premium is reflected in the price of the risk causer's products. In the long-term equilibrium, then, a risk-intensive industry will, as against the equilibrium with no employment of internalization policy, be pushed back, even in the case where the individual polluter's equilibrium care level is zero.

Despite these rather relativizing remarks, the problem of moral hazard still exists: the individual polluter's decision as to his care level has consequences for the expected damage. However, this effect is not charged to him in accordance with the polluter pays principle. The literature on insurance economics has developed a number of strategies for leveling out these shortcomings (at least in part). The most obvious method is to bring in an "own risk" element: if the insurance does not cover the whole damage but the polluter himself must pay part of it, then the profitability of carrying out care measures increases for the firm concerned. Even if we stay with the extreme case of a premium independent of the individual polluter's care level in the case of insurance with an own risk excess, alongside the cost of care there are also benefits of the care activity to the polluter. Increasing care activities reduce the expected value of the "residual damage" to be borne by the polluter and the risk burden associated with this prospect.

If, then, bringing in an own risk excess improves the internalization effect of liability law, as shown previously, one might conclude that it would be best to insure an own risk of 100% (i.e., to forbid the insurance of environmental risks).

However, this argument would not do justice to the essence of insurance. For considering liability law and insurance together, alongside the internalization effects of the institution under consideration, its effect on risk distribution must also be taken into account. If decision makers are risk averse, then insurance performs an economically useful function by taking on the risks. It offers a product for which positive willingness to pay exists (among both polluters and the injured parties). Within the framework of the extent of coverage made available by it, it takes away from polluters the risk of having to make payments above the expected value. On the other side, the taking out of insurance by the polluter reduces the risk for the victim of having to bear the damage without compensation (e.g., because of the polluter's lack of liquidity). We can thus see that the activity of insurance under conditions of environmental liability law brings about two tendencies, to be evaluated oppositely. On the one hand, it reduces (with asymmetrical information) the internalization effect of liability law, and on the other hand, it improves the distribution of risk. Accordingly, even an own risk excess is an ambivalent thing: with increasing own risk, the internalization effect of liability law improves, but the risk distribution deteriorates. To establish an economically optimum own risk level, these divergent tendencies would have to be weighed against each other – a difficult and interesting job, which goes beyond the limits of this study.

Insurers have responded to the problem of model hazard by various measures. Alongside the own risk excess, briefly addressed previously, insurance companies have the possibility of further developing the machinery of *risk analysis* and *risk management* and making more use of it. Here from an individual analysis of the risk position of its contractual partner, the insurer gains a picture of the level and quality of efficient (and actual) care measures of the potential polluter in question and thus combats the problem of asymmetrical information identified previously as critical. Carrying out the efficient mix of care measures is required in the insurance policy. In the event of an accident, if it turns out that these conditions were not complied with by the insured, then the insurer is exempted from its duty to compensate.

Of course, this sort of agreement is a potential source of inefficiency. The insurer's picture of efficient care measures need not coincide with the actual facts. Moreover, in specifying care measurers in the insurance policy, the insurer will concentrate on ones for which it is easier to check compliance with by the insured in the event of a claim.

Despite these shortcomings, it is obvious that the risk management described here will lead to considerable improvements over the position that emerged previously as the equilibrium when considering the basic model of insurance with model hazard. Through risk analysis, the insurance company breaks the assumption (catastrophic for the allocational outcome) that it cannot observe (affect) the insured's level of care. One interesting aspect that can only be alluded to here is that for insurance with a contractually agreed level of care the boundaries between strict liability and the negligence rule become fluid. If the legal provisions are for strict liability, then the polluter is (by definition) liable irrespective of the extent of his care. But whether the due compensation payment is made by himself or by the insurer is, in the case of insurance with a contractually agreed level of care considered here, very much dependent on his care behavior. The nature of this dependency will play an important part for a rationally acting polluter in deciding his level of care. Just as under the negligence rule with no insurance, complying with a particular level of care exempts him from payment. This is a strong incentive to comply with that level. We can thus see that the incentive effects of an insurance policy that contains agreements between insurer and polluter on care activities to be carried out are similar to those of the negligence rule without insurance. For the polluter's allocational decision, the package of care measures agreed with the insurer plays the same part as the standard of "due care" laid down by government or the courts in the case of the negligence rule. In a slightly exaggerated formulation, one might say that in the arrangement looked at here the polluter pays the insurance premium in order to move from the statutory strict liability to a privately agreed negligence rule that is more favorable to him in cost terms.

V. The German Environmental Liability Act

Since 1991, the German Environmental Liability Act (GELA) has been in force in the Federal Republic of Germany.[76] Previously, the relevant provisions were widely

---

76 On the importance of liability law for environmental policy in the European states and the United States, see Swanson/Kontoleon (2004).

scattered over the legal landscape. This led to a "mixed situation" of liability rules very opaque at least to nonlawyers (e.g., §823 of the Civil Code (BGB)), establishing the negligence rule, or §22 of the WHG (Water Resources Act), which (like §§25ff of the AtG (Atomic Energy Act)) establishes strict liability. Even though the GELA took a major step toward unifying the law, it must nonetheless be said that it by no means regulates the whole of environmental liability. Instead, the act applies exclusively to installations in its Annex 1 (which are mostly installations requiring permits under the Federal Pollution Control Act (BImmSchG)). In this introductory exposition, only two aspects of the GELA of economic importance can be singled out:

- The GELA enacts the strict liability rule.[77]
- The GELA has made it possible under certain circumstances to employ provisions of environmental law in cases of uncertainty as to the causation of damage.

Although the first point has already had light thrown on it by the previous statements on the allocational effect of strict liability (and its differences from the negligence rule), the second point calls for more exhaustive explanation. If an unambiguous demonstration of the causality of a particular activity in the occurrence of damage is a condition for liability and the burden of proof is on the injured party, then the internalization effect of liability law is severely limited. Because of the high barriers to be passed here by the victim, a polluter has to reckon with only a probability (lying more or less far below certainty) of having to pay compensation. The welfare-reducing effect of the resulting pattern of "damage discounting" was discussed in section B.III.1. Putting it rather strongly, one might say that the effectiveness of environmental liability law, in practice, stands or falls with its capacity to find a solution to the problem of attributing damage with uncertain causality. We briefly present the relevant provisions of the GELA and go on to outline an economic examination of the associated incentive effects. According to the GELA, the operator of an installation covered by the act is liable for damages where one of the following conditions is met:

1. The damage has undoubtedly been caused by the operation of his plant (certain causality).
2. His plant is, according to the facts of the individual case, capable of causing the damage produced. It is then assumed that the damage has actually been caused by the relevant plant (general presumption of causality pursuant to §6(1) of the GELA).

---

77 At least, §1 of GELA says so. We see that this statement is to be handled with some caution regarding the economic incentive effects of the statutory environmental liability provisions. It should be further noted that the liability is (by §16 of the GELA) limited to a maximum amount.

However, the operator can refute the presumption of causality under point 2 and thus free himself of liability if he can manage to bring one of the following proofs:

- The plant was operated *in accordance with regulations*, and operation took place normally (i.e., without any breakdowns; §6(2) of the GELA). Operation in accordance with regulations is to be understood in particular as compliance with environmental requirements. Because even with compliant operation as thus defined, accidents are not entirely excluded; therefore, it is best to interpret operation according to regulations and normal operation as two separate requirements.[78]
- There was another circumstance likely according to the facts of the individual case to cause the damage (§7 of the GELA). In interpreting this passage, however, it should be noted that other "GELA installations" (i.e., installations listed in Annex 1, as noted previously) than the plant used by the operator under consideration cannot be cited as other causal circumstances pursuant to §7 of the GELA. A plant operator in difficulties because of the GELA has to adduce natural phenomena or economic activities not covered by the GELA (and without being too farfetched) that might have caused the damage. He must further show that these other factors could have caused the damage alone (i.e., not merely in association with his plant). The legal literature calls this set of possibilities "alternative causality."

Let us now look briefly at the incentives these GELA provisions provide for damage prevention. We confine ourselves to the case of certain causality and the case of possible refutation of the presumption of causality by proving operation in compliance with regulations and freedom from breakdowns.

As stated previously, for damage with indubitable causality, strict liability applies. According to the account in section B.II, under this liability rule, the polluter will orient himself to the total expected damage. If strict liability under the GELA in a case of certain causality is applied to damage to that, without the GELA, §22 of the WHG (using strict liability, as mentioned previously) would have applied, then, at least in this stylized presentation, no additional preventive effect is to be expected from the GELA. The strict liability to which the polluter is subject is merely regulated at a different (additional) place. In contrast, when the GELA is applied in an area where the negligence rule previously applied, the picture is different. The allocational neutrality of the negligence rule and strict liability as presented in section B.II applies only to the special case (already explained there) where the negligence standard is set at the socially optimum level.

If, in contrast, the negligence standard is set too low (z_1^n in Figure 14a), then the introduction of the GELA increases the incentive to prevention. With a standard

---

78 We use this idea in the graphic presentations that follow. However, in the event of a breakdown, requirements will no doubt as a rule be infringed (especially regarding upper limits to pollutant emissions).

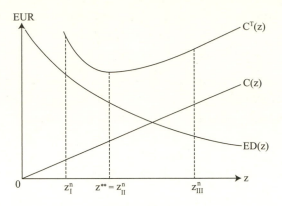

Figure 14a

previously set too high (z_{III}^n in Figure 14a),[79] introduction of the GELA gives no additional incentive to prevention.

We can also use the diagram for an economic interpretation of the refutation of the presumption of causality by proving operation in compliance with regulations.[80] For this, we assume that z_I^n, z_{II}^n, and z_{III}^n constitute three alternative possible minimum levels of care activity z embodied in environmental legal provisions (apart from the Environmental Liability Act). If the operator carries out the activity at the prescribed level in each case (and can also prove this), then his operation is by definition "in compliance with regulations." The causality presumption is then refuted and the operator exempted from liability. If the environmental law provision located outside the GELA prescribes minimum care level z_I^n,[81] then the operator must, for levels of care he employs between 0 and $z_I^n - \varepsilon$, calculate care costs and expected damage because he cannot show operation in compliance with the regulations and is thus liable. As from z_I^n, he need, in contrast, according to what has been said, pay only the care cost. In Figure 14a, accordingly, the cost curve of relevance to the plant operator jumps at z_I^n from C^T to $C(z)$. The operator reaches his cost minimum by exactly complying with regulations and correspondingly bearing costs at a level of $C(z_I^n)$.

We can thus see that the economic incentive effect of strict liability with a presumption of causality refutable by showing compliant operation is identical with the incentive effect of the negligence rule described in section B.II. Just as the negligence rule incentives' compliance with the standard of care concretized as

---

79 We assume here that the negligence standard applying before the GELA came into force was not defined so "excessively" high as to be ignored by a rational polluter.

80 To refute the causality presumption, normal operation *and* operation in compliance with regulations must be shown. Later in this chapter, these two elements are analyzed separately. In the previous passage (discussing operation in compliance with regulations), we therefore assume that no breakdown arises.

81 For levels z_{II}^n and z_{III}^n, the following argument applies by analogy.

"due care," the causality provision discussed here induces the polluter to comply with environmental standards that constitute operation in compliance with regulations. This makes it clear why we accompany the previous statement that the GELA brought in strict liability with some reservations. Although strict liability is codified in §1 of the GELA, its economic incentive effects correspond in several areas (here, uncertain causation and refutation of the general causality presumption by proving compliant operation) with those of the negligence rule. The allocational effects described here are certainly to be assessed positively where with unclear causality liability could not apply at all before the GELA came in. The expectation of social optimality of prevention (complete internalization of externalities) through strict liability (possibly) aroused by the reading of textbooks will however not be met.

After undoubted causality and uncertain causality with refutation of the general presumption of causality by proving compliant operation, let us now go on to look at the case of refutation of the presumption by proving normal operation (in the sense of no breakdowns). The two types of refutation are at first sight very similar, but their fine differences nonetheless lead to considerable consequences regarding incentive effects: with proof of compliant operation, compliance with the relevant provisions suffices to throw out the presumption of causality and thus avoid liability in the first place. Let us now assume that there were rules on avoidance of breakdowns analogous to those on compliant operation. If the operator complies with these requirements, then this is by no means sufficient to refute the presumption of causality. Instead, what is necessary is for no breakdown to actually occur. The incentive effects associated with this, and a comparison with those of proving compliant operation, are clarified in the next illustration.

Let us assume that a directive on avoidance of breakdowns prescribes safety measures z_s at level z_s^I. Let us further assume that the directive is accompanied by penalties adequate to induce the operator to comply.[82] The producer compliant with the directive now has to calculate the sum of the care cost and expected damage once the Environmental Liability Act is brought in. After all, in the event of a breakdown, compliance with the standard does not free him of liability to pay compensation. In contrast with proving compliant operation, compliance with the standard thus does not bring him the gratification of a sudden downward correction to his cost curve.

It follows that he will increase his efforts to curb breakdowns on introduction of the Environmental Liability Act from z_s^I to z_s^{**} if the standard (as was assumed

---

82 It would certainly be possible to incorporate these penalties in the previous description (cf., e.g., Endres (1991)). To keep things short, however, we do without this and assume *ad hoc* the existence of an effective penalty. Moreover, the penalty should be due as a fixed amount so as not to disrupt the polluter's marginal calculations depicted in Figure 14b. An allocationally equivalent assumption would be the one (remote from the model) that the plant operator would comply with the standard for ethical reasons (e.g., out of obedience to the law).

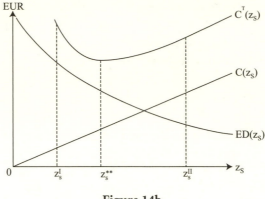

Figure 14b

for z_s^I) was set at too low a level by comparison with the social optimum (z_s^{**}). This intensification of the polluter's efforts at preventing breakdowns is by definition associated with an allocational improvement. If, in contrast, the standard regulating the breakdown prevention measures is more ambitious than the socially optimum safety level (as assumed in z_s^{II} in Figure 14b) and the firm complies with this standard (because of the threatened penalties) even before the GELA comes in, then the liability provision will not produce (positive or negative) an incentive to prevention. Things will stay with the traditional suboptimal (from the welfare economics viewpoint) allocation.

Our brief economic analysis of the regulations on the burden of proof in the GELA thus shows that the codification of liability rules chosen in it can under certain circumstances produce an effect that supports the enforcement of provisions on compliant operation. In the area of breakdown prevention, in certain circumstances, a prevention effect of the Environmental Liability Act itself going beyond the specific regulations might even arise. However, an empirical study by Schwarze (2005) was unable to show such an effect. Friends of the GELA hope that this is because of the "weak data position" (Schwarze, 2005, p. 258). The author himself presumes that, instead, regulatory overlap has meant that the Environmental Liability Act has not led to any measurable improvement in risk precautions. The specific safety provisions (in force irrespective of the liability law) have brought such a high level of safety that liability law was unable to develop any autonomous guidance effect.[83] In the literature, there has been considerable progress in designing a risk policy portfolio in which liability rules and safety requirements are optimally harmonized with each other.[84]

---

83 To better understand this explanation, one might look at Figure 14a. Here one would have to imagine that independently of the liability law, a safety standard prescribed a care level $\bar{z}$ for the firm that was above z^{**}.

84 Cf., e.g., Calcott/Hutton (2006), with many further references.

Well I'm standing by the river
But the water doesn't flow
It boils with every poison
You can think of.

–Chris Rea, "The Road to Hell: Part 2," 1989

VI. U.S. "Superfund" Liability

1. The Comprehensive Environmental Response, Compensation, and Liability Act (CERCLA)

The establishment of the Environmental Protection Agency (EPA) in 1970 was a milestone in U.S. national environmental policy. At that time, federal environmental legislation was focused on air and water pollution, with the Clean Air Act passed in 1970 and the Federal Water Pollution Control Amendments in 1972.

The problems of solid and hazardous wastes were tackled in a less comprehensive manner.[85] There were several laws that aimed to regulate the disposal of waste, but they contained many loopholes. For instance, the 1972 Amendments to the Federal Insecticide, Fungicide, and Rodenticide Act primarily addressed the production and use of pesticides, neglecting the disposal of unused pesticides. The Resource Recovery Act of 1970, in contrast, did not focus on the regulation of waste generation and management, but rather on helping state and local authorities establish waste disposal programs.

However, there was growing awareness in U.S. society that industrial processes were using increasingly more chemicals. Their (separate and combined) toxicity generated public fear. People were afraid of possible health effects and raised concerns about whether dangerous substances were properly handled and disposed of. During this time, many dump sites were discovered, and these discoveries received high publicity and much public attention. These sites often contained a precarious mixture of hazardous and solid wastes, contaminating soil, water, and air. Due to these problems and their public perception "(a) picture had emerged of a sector ripe for regulation" (Jenkins/Kopits/Simpson, 2009, p. 106).

The "final blow" for the established legislation on waste generation, transportation, and disposal came with the dramatic case of Love Canal, a site near Niagara Falls, New York. At this site, 2,500 people had to be evacuated in 1978 because of severe health problems and cancer risks attributed to the contamination of the site from past disposal practices.[86]

Policy makers reacted quickly to the catastrophe and to the societal alarm it triggered. In 1980, the Comprehensive Environmental Response, Compensation,

---

85 The following sketch of the evolution of U.S. solid and hazardous waste legislation is based on Jenkins/Kopits/Simpson (2009).

86 There is a fictional treatment of the Love Canal disaster in the novel *The Falls* by Joyce Carol Oates (2004).

and Liability Act (CERCLA), often called the "Superfund," was passed. The main features of this law are as follows.[87]

To induce proper management of risk at contaminated sites, CERCLA authorizes the EPA to take action against the damage and risk caused by hazardous substances (except nuclear material and petroleum). Particularly, the EPA may locate, investigate, and respond to land-based spills and other potential or actual uncontrolled releases of these substances. CERCLA enables the EPA to take two kinds of action: removals and remedials. The first category relates to quick "emergency cleanups," and the latter relates to cleaning up sites that generate problems that are, although grave, less pressing. The EPA is entitled to assess the risks posed by remedial sites and put them on the National Priority List (NPL). It can have a site cleaned, paying the bills using funds from the "Superfund." For the first 5 years of its operation, $1.6 billion was raised via special taxes. In 1986, the Superfund Amendments and Reauthorization Act (SARA) introduced new taxes in order to raise another $1.7 billion per year for an additional 5 years. In addition, costs for cleanup can be covered by contributions from potentially responsible parties (PRPs). (We return to this point.) Payments of PRPs often result from lengthy litigation processes or from (out of court) settlements. The latter are, in general, less time consuming.

By the end of 2007, the NPL contained 1,569 sites. Sixty-six percent of the sites were listed as "construction complete," meaning that all remedies at a site have been fully implemented.

This chapter is concerned with the economics of environmental liability law. Accordingly, the special structure of environmental liability chosen within CERCLA is of particular interest in this context. There are two main features distinguishing liability as used in CERCLA:

- *Joint and Several Liability*. The doctrine of joint and several liability applies to the case where two or more tortfeasors are responsible for an "indivisible harm."[88] In particular, this legal principle allows a plaintiff to sue the tortfeasors to fully recover the damages. Under CERCLA, any PRP may be held liable for the *entire* cost of cleaning up the respective sites and the damage caused by the contamination. Notably, the definition of PRP is quite comprehensive, including waste generators, transporters (or arrangers of transport), managers of waste landfills, and (past and present) property owners.[89]

   There are two obvious points that render joint and several liability particularly attractive to policy makers and the EPA. First, procedural costs are reduced if it is possible to collect the funds necessary for cleanup and compensation from

---

87 Again, we follow Jenkins/Kopits/Simpson (2009).

88 This is a particularly popular subject of research in *law and economics*. It is analyzed under the headings of "multiple injurers," "multiple torts," or "multiple causation." See the "classic" discussions in Landes/Posner (1987, ch. 7), and Shavell (1987, ch. 7), as well as the presentation in Kornhauser/Revesz (2009).

89 Lenders (not managing the site), innocent purchasers of the property, and (nonnegligent) consultants assisting in the cleanup are not PRPs.

just one of the parties that contributed to the damage. In contrast, legislation that would make each contributing party liable for an appropriate part of the damage would raise complicated questions with regard to attributing adequate shares. The EPA would have to go to court with a multitude of contributors instead of just one or those with "deepest pockets." Second, as a result of this, the risk of leaving damaged parties uncompensated and/or placing the burden on the taxpayer is reduced. However, the rule has often been criticized on the basis of justice. Many commentators consider it extremely unfair to make a single contributor pay for the total damage caused by this party, together with many others, who are then let off the hook scot free.

These problems of inequity are somewhat softened by the fact that the unlucky injurer who is made to pay as a result of a court's ruling under CERCLA (or agrees to do so in a settlement with the EPA) is entitled to sue other involved parties for *contribution*. If successful, he obtains partial recoupment from other PRPs. However, full recoupment, "indemnity," is ruled out.

- *Strict Liability*. Joint and several liability may be combined with both strict liability and negligence. Under CERCLA, defenses to liability are limited to cases in which the release of hazardous substances (or the possibility thereof) was caused by an act of God, acts of war, or acts/omissions of a third party with whom a PRP has no contractual relationship. It is worth noting that a party proving that it has not acted negligently does not constitute a defense to liability under CERCLA. So, demonstrating that it exercised reasonable care and conformed to the prevailing regulations does not help a PRP in its attempts to escape liability under CERCLA. Superfund liability is, therefore, a case of *strict liability*.

2. On the Economics of Joint and Several Strict Liability

a) Incentives to take care. In CERCLA, a particular mix of liability rules is applied: strict liability is combined with joint and several liability. What are the incentives to take care generated by this legal construction? We find out using a very simple economic model.[90] First, we consider what characterizes the socially optimal level of care for the case of multiple causation. Second, we analyze equilibrium care under strict liability in the case of multiple causation. Here strict liability stands alone, not combined with joint and several liability. We term this case "pure strict liability." Third, we compare the two aforementioned results with equilibrium care as achieved under joint and several liability combined with strict liability. This latter liability rule is analyzed in two alternative versions, one without and one with contribution.

We now turn to the first step. The socially optimal level of care has already been characterized previously in this chapter. Consider, for example, care level z^{**} in the analysis of Figure 14a. This level is socially optimal in that it minimizes the sum of the costs, $C^T(z)$, consisting of the cost of taking care, $C(z)$, and expected

---

90 The seminal contributions to the literature are Landes/Posner (1980) and Tietenberg (1989).

damages, $ED(z)$. The reason we have to take up this subject again is that the prior analysis dealt with the case of a single polluter, while in this context two or more polluters are at issue. The analysis must therefore be adjusted accordingly. To make things as simple as possible (applying the cost-effectiveness criterion to the design of economic modeling!), we confine the analysis to the case of two polluters. Of course, there are many possibilities with respect to how environmental damage may be caused by two polluters. We take the simplest case of multiple causation as given: it is assumed that expected damage depends on the aggregate care taken by the two polluters. Aggregate care, z, is the sum of the individual care levels of the two polluters, z_1 and z_2.[91] The condition that characterizes the socially optimal level of *aggregate* care in the case of multiple causation is simply the same as the condition for the optimal level of care taken by a single polluter, which we already know from the analysis in prior sections: aggregate cost associated with the environmental problem under consideration (i.e., the costs of taking care plus expected damages) must be minimal. An equivalent formulation is that for the optimal level of aggregate care, marginal expected damage equals marginal cost of care.[92] For the case of a single polluter, the socially optimal allocation is fully characterized by this statement. However, in the case of multiple causation, this statement is not sufficient to fully define the socially optimal allocation. The open question remaining in this latter case is how the optimal level of aggregate care is to be distributed between the two polluters in a socially optimal manner. The answer can be given intuitively using conventional economic wisdom: the total burden of taking care is distributed optimally between the two polluters when the individual contributions to taking care reach the very levels for which the respective marginal cost of taking care for each polluter equals that for the other polluter. This can be understood most easily by, for the time being, interpreting taking care to be simply the production of any commodity, such as apples or tons of steel. The economics of the socially optimal distribution of any given level of aggregate production among two firms that supply the good under consideration have been explained in part one, section A.II, of this book. The answer given there to the question of optimal production division is that the marginal production costs of individual firms have to be equal to each other. You may want to re-read this section, focusing in particular on the discussion of the supply side of the economy stylized in Figure 1.

We can summarize, then, that the socially optimal allocation is characterized by a level of aggregate care for which the aggregate marginal costs of care are equal to marginal expected damage and the individual marginal costs of care are equal to each other. This situation is illustrated in Figure 15a, where z^{**} is the socially optimal level of aggregate care and z_1^{**} and z_2^{**} are the socially optimal levels of individual care for the two polluters under consideration. It is worth noting that in the socially optimal situation, polluter 1 contributes more to aggregate care taking

---

91   More complicated forms of multiple causation are analyzed by Tietenberg (1989), and in part four, chapter A, of this book.

92   Again, we assume that the underlying functions are well behaved.

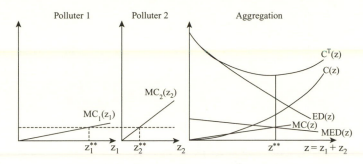

Figure 15a

than polluter 2, $z_1^{**} > z_2^{**}$. This is so because it is easier for the first polluter to take care than it is for the second one; MC_1 is flatter than MC_2.

Having established the socially optimal levels of aggregate and individual care as a point of reference, let us now turn to investigating equilibrium care under strict liability, the second step of this exposition.

We have analyzed the allocative implications of strict liability in the previous sections. However, to extend this analysis to an economic interpretation of CERCLA, the definition of strict liability first has to be adjusted to the context of multiple causation. The *law and economics* literature takes "the natural interpretation of strict liability"[93] in the case of multiple causation to be that each injurer is liable for a fraction of the damage jointly generated and that this fraction does not depend on the level of care taken by the polluter under consideration. To make things simple (again!), we assume that the two polluters must take equal shares (i.e., each has to calculate half of the total damage under strict liability). Accordingly, in striving to minimize costs, each polluter will choose a level of care for which the marginal costs of his individual care taking are equal to half of the marginal damage. Obviously, the equilibrium situation resulting from this kind of cost minimization will be different from socially optimal care, defined by each polluter equating individual cost of care to the full amount of marginal expected damage. Turn to Figure 15b for a somewhat more differentiated analysis.

Figure 15b is a reduced version of Figure 15a, showing only the marginal curves without the total ones. As a point of reference, you find the socially optimal level of aggregate care z^{**} at the intersection of the aggregate marginal cost of care and marginal damage functions, as in the third quadrant of Figure 15a. In addition, the individual marginal cost of care functions, $MC_1(z_1)$ and $MC_2(z_2)$, familiar from the first two quadrants of Figure 15a, are shown again in Figure 15b. The socially optimal care levels of the two polluters are defined by the individual marginal abatement costs being equal to marginal expected damage in the socially optimal situation, $MED(z^{**})$. These levels are again denoted by z_1^{**} and z_2^{**}, respectively. A new element in Figure 15b compared with Figure 15a is the curve denoting half of the marginal expected damage, $\frac{1}{2} MED(z)$. This is the marginal compensation payment each individual polluter has to calculate under strict liability, according to

93   See, e.g., Shavell (1987, pp. 164, 177).

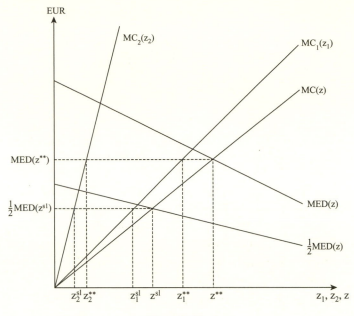

Figure 15b

the assumptions of this simple model. In equilibrium, each of the involved parties will increase care taking to a level for which his own marginal abatement costs are equal to half of the expected damage. The sum of this care taking will be defined by the point for which aggregate marginal cost is equal to half of the expected damage, $MC(z) = \frac{1}{2} MED(z)$. These individual care equilibria are denoted by z_1^{sl} and z_2^{sl} for the two polluters, respectively. And $z^{sl} = z_1^{sl} + z_2^{sl}$ denotes the aggregate equilibrium care level. It is plausible (and can be confirmed by exact modeling) that aggregate and individual equilibrium care levels are too low in comparison to socially optimal care levels (i.e., $z_1^{sl} < z_1^{**}$, $z_2^{sl} < z_2^{**}$, $z^{sl} < z^{**}$).[94] It is worth noting, however, that the aggregate equilibrium level of care under this liability rule, z^{sl}, is distributed cost effectively between the two polluters in the given framework. After all, the marginal costs of care of the two individual polluters are equal to each other (and to the level of half of the marginal expected damage, measured in the equilibrium situation, $\frac{1}{2} MED(z^{sl})$). This is a special result due to our assumption that the two parties share expected damage evenly.[95]

94 The equilibrium underprovision of care under strict liability in the case of multiple tortfeasors is quite evident in our example. Nevertheless, the example illustrates a case of "mild underprovision" due to the assumption that only two polluters are involved. Underprovision is grave in cases of many polluters being involved.

95 The implications of an uneven distribution between the two polluters can be easily assessed using the example of one polluter having to bear three fourths and the other only one fourth of the expected damages. In such a case, the distribution of care taking activities between the two parties will be distorted: the polluter carrying three fourths of the burden takes too much care compared to the cost-effective situation, and the polluter privileged by having to bear only one fourth of the expected damage takes too little care compared to the cost-effective situation. (Remark for the advanced reader: the equilibrium aggregate care level, given that the two tortfeasors share

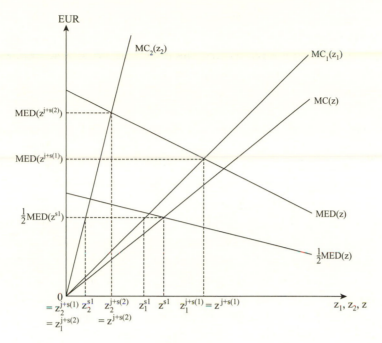

Figure 15c

We now turn to the third step of our investigation, the analysis of the incentives to take care under joint and several liability combined with strict liability. In a first substep, we analyze joint and several liability without contribution. The case of joint and several liability including contribution is analyzed in a (second) substep.

Consider joint and several liability *without contribution*: this means that one of the two parties under consideration is held liable for total damage. The other party gets away with paying nothing, and there is no chance for the first party to recover any part of the liability payment from the second party. For simplicity, we assume that the parties know in advance which of them will be sued for damages. Imagine that one of the parties has "deep pockets" and the other "no pockets at all." In this polar case, the wealthy party – in our example, let this be polluter 2 – will certainly be chosen to be sued for the damage. It is worth noting that in this example, it is the polluter with the higher marginal cost of care who is targeted to be liable for the entire damage. If this is known ex ante, polluter 2 will increase care taking to the level where his marginal cost of taking care equals marginal expected damage. The other party, aware ex ante that there will be no liability at all, decides not to take any care.

In Figure 15c, the second party's equilibrium care level, under joint and several liability without contribution combined with strict liability, is denoted by $z_2^{j+s(2)}$, and the equilibrium care level of the "judgment-proof" polluter 1, $z_1^{j+s(2)}$, is set

the damage evenly, will generally not be identical to the equilibrium care level in the case of a damage distribution of three fourths versus one fourth.)

to zero.[96] Because in this equilibrium polluter 2 is the only one to take care, the equilibrium care level of this polluter is identical to the aggregate equilibrium care level, $z_2^{j+s(2)} = z^{j+s(2)}$. It is obvious (and can be confirmed by exact modeling) that the aggregate equilibrium care level under joint and several liability combined with strict liability is smaller than the equilibrium aggregate care level under strict liability only, $z^{j+s(2)} < z^{sl}$. If we compare the equilibrium care level of polluter 2 across the two legal frameworks, then it is plausible that this polluter expands care if joint and several liability is added to a system of pure strict liability, $z_2^{j+s(2)} > z_2^{sl}$. After all, this institutional change means that the second polluter must balance the marginal cost of care against 100% of the marginal reduction of expected damages under the "new framework" compared to balancing marginal cost of care against 50% of the reduction in marginal expected damage under the "old framework." This should increase this polluter's enthusiasm to take care. However, the additional care taken by the second polluter, as a reaction to the envisioned change in the legal framework, does not completely make up for the fact that the incentive for the second polluter outright vanishes if the legal framework is changed from pure strict liability to strict liability combined with joint and several liability.

In addition to this "quantity effect" that distinguishes the equilibria attained under pure strict liability from those attained under strict liability combined with joint and several liability, there is a "cost-effectiveness effect."[97] Under joint and several liability, the aggregate cost of taking care is inflated compared to the situation under pure strict liability, for any level of care. This is so because any potential cost savings that may result from a division of labor between the two polluters in taking care are forsaken given that the liability rule is confined to targeting one polluter exclusively. A more formal way of expressing this is that in the equilibrium under joint and several liability combined with strict liability, the marginal costs incurred by the two polluters are not equal to each other in equilibrium. In contrast, under pure strict liability, an equilibrium is attained where the marginal costs of care for the two polluters are equal to each other, as we have shown previously.

The analysis of joint and several strict liability has been presented under the assumption that it is the "high-cost polluter," 2, that is held liable for the entire damage. For this case, it is straight forward to assess the consequences of a change from pure strict liability to joint and several strict liability *in terms of welfare*. We have seen that the equilibrium level of aggregate care under pure strict liability is too low compared to socially optimal care. However, the equilibrium care under joint and several strict liability is even lower. Therefore, considering this "quantity effect," it would seem that welfare decreases in moving from pure strict liability to joint and several strict liability. With respect to the "cost-effectiveness effect," joint and several strict liability is also definitely inferior to pure strict liability in terms of welfare (based on the assumption that the two responsible parties share

---

96   In this notation, the subscript number refers to the party taking care, whereas the superscript number refers to the party being held liable in this context.

97   The two effects interact but are dealt with separately for didactic reasons.

liability equally under the latter rule). So, each of the two effects that distinguish the two liability rules from each other suggests that joint and several liability is welfare inferior to pure strict liability.

So far, the analysis has been carried out based on the assumption that high-cost polluter 2 is the one with the "deep pockets." Now consider the alternative case of the low-cost polluter, 1, being liable for the entire damage under joint and several strict liability. In doing so, we can apply reasoning analogous to what has been said previously for the case of the high-cost polluter, 2, being liable. It follows that the equilibrium care level of the first polluter, $z_1^{j+s(1)}$, is defined by $MC_1 = MED$. The other polluter does not take any care at all, $z_2^{j+s(1)} = 0$. Obviously, we have a different "quantity effect" comparing the two liability rules than we have in the case of the high-cost polluter being liable: the aggregate equilibrium care level under joint and strict liability is higher than the aggregate care level under pure strict liability (but still lower than the socially optimal care level) (i.e., $z^{sl} < z^{j+s(1)} = z_1^{j+s(1)} < z^{**}$ holds).

With respect to the "cost-effectiveness effect," however, changing from the assumption of the high-cost polluter being held liable to that of the low-cost polluter being liable does not affect what we said previously: aggregate equilibrium care is split up cost ineffectively between the two involved parties under joint and several strict liability. Taking the two effects together, the welfare implications of going from pure strict liability to joint and several strict liability turn out to be ambiguous in the case of the low-cost polluter being held liable under the latter rule. The "quantity effect" works in the direction of a welfare improvement; the "cost-effectiveness effect" works in the opposite direction. Which of the two countervailing effects prevails depends on the specific forms of the cost of care and damage functions involved.[98]

Now, to wind up, we turn to the second substep of our analysis of joint and several strict liability. We assess how it will affect the results if joint and strict liability are designed *with contribution*. Here the party that has been held liable in the first place may recover part of the liability payment from the other party. The results in terms of equilibrium care depend on what magnitude the involved parties can expect contribution to take. The two polar cases are, on the one hand, that contribution will be zero and, on the other hand, that contribution will constitute

---

98 The case of joint and several strict liability being superior to pure strict liability in terms of social welfare may be counterintuitive to some readers. The possibility of this result is driven by the assumption that the care activities of the two involved firms contribute to the reduction of damage in an additive manner. Opposed to that, there are cases in which it is not effective in terms of damage reduction if just one of the involved parties increases care, *ceteris paribus*. Here only simultaneous upscaling of everyone's care is effective. The more the involved parties' care activities are interactive in this manner, the less likely is it that joint and several strict liability is superior to pure strict liability in welfare terms. See van Velthoven/van Wijck (2009) for different forms of care interaction in cases of multiple causation.

half of the damage.[99] In the former extreme case, the analysis will be exactly the same as that of joint and several liability with no contribution. In the latter extreme case, the analysis will be exactly the same as in the case of pure strict liability. These are the two cases that we have already analyzed. Let us assume, then, that contribution is between these two extremes in our example case. To be more concrete, we assume that the polluter being held liable in the first place is able to recover one fourth of the total damage from his "fellow" polluter. (To do so, we must slightly modify our initial assumption saying that the other polluter has "no pockets at all"(i.e., is completely judgment proof).)

A change in the legal framework from joint and several liability without contribution to joint and several liability with contribution will change the incentives of the involved parties to take care as follows. Due to his ability to recover, as has been assumed, one fourth of the damage from his fellow polluter, the polluter initially held liable for the total damage now balances the marginal cost of care with three fourths of the total damage under the new legislation. Consequently, his incentive to take care is somewhat reduced in comparison to the case of no contribution, where the entire damage had to be accounted for. On the other hand, the polluter who was not liable at all under the first legal framework balances the marginal abatement cost against one fourth of the aggregate marginal damage under the new legislation. As a result, this polluter's equilibrium care increases moving from pure joint and several liability to joint and several liability with contribution. In addition, because both marginal cost of care curves are assumed to be increasing in care, the cost ineffectiveness of the distribution of the aggregate care level between the individual polluters is somewhat reduced if we add contribution to joint and several liability. This is so because the decrease in the equilibrium care level of the polluter receiving compensation and the increase in the equilibrium care level of the polluter paying compensation, as induced by the envisioned change in the legislation, reduces the equilibrium difference in the individual marginal cost of care.

All in all, introducing contribution to a system of joint and several strict liability moves the equilibrium allocation of care somewhat in the direction of the equilibrium allocation of care under pure strict liability. The extent of this move depends on the share that the polluter being held completely liable under pure joint and several liability is able to recover from the second polluter when contribution is introduced. The higher this share, the more the equilibrium attained under joint and several liability with contribution resembles the equilibrium under pure strict liability.

b) Other incentives. In the previous analysis, we focus on the incentives to take care generated by alternative forms of liability law, particularly joint and several strict liability. This focus is warranted because in this context, the potential of liability law to serve as a means to internalize externalities is at issue. Moreover,

99   It is commonly presumed in the *law and economics* literature that the share of damage that a party that lost a contribution suit is required to pay would be equal to or less than the part it would be required to pay under pure strict liability.

joint and several strict liability is the specific form of liability chosen in the U.S. "Superfund" legislation. However, there are other incentives generated by liability law. These have been discussed in the literature in the context of joint and several strict liability with particular reference to the "Superfund" legislation. Although a detailed discussion is beyond the scope of this book, these issues should not be completely ignored.

- *Transaction Costs.* It has been argued in the literature that the possibility of a single polluter being held liable for the entire damage jointly caused by several polluters induces the polluter chosen for liability by the EPA to do almost anything to contest the EPA's claim. In addition to fighting the claim of the EPA, there is a considerable incentive to sue other companies for contribution. Of course, companies fighting the EPA and each other "tooth and nail" in court generate considerable transaction costs. Critics have claimed that the "Superfund" legislation with its arrangement of joint and several strict liability has contributed more to making lawyers happy than it has to cleaning up the environment. It has been reported that "Superfund" money having been used to finance expenses for legal fees and other transaction costs adds up to an amount that equals between 7% and 41% of expenses for cleanups.[100] An oft-cited example is that Detroit automakers sued more than 200 other companies and institutions, including the Girls Scouts, for contribution to a single clean-up (Goodstein, 1995, p. 226). However, how far joint and several liability (compared to other forms of liability) is responsible for the high litigation cost has been disputed. A particular point of dispute in this context is the question of whether joint and several liability discourages settlements. This would be an important issue because settlements save legal costs compared to taking the cases to court.[101]

- *The Brownfield Problem.* Imagine you are a real estate developer who is considering the acquisition of a certain piece of land. You are informed that the land may be contaminated and that, once you become the owner, you might be held liable for clean-up according to CERCLA rules. What would you do? An intuitively plausible reaction would be to not buy the land.

  In practice, many potential redevelopers have felt exactly that way. The consequence has been that these sites stay what they are – precarious "brownfields." This is a burden to communities in which these sites are located because they are sources of urban blight. Moreover, not using the sites causes high opportunity costs because precious rural locations are sacrificed as new industrial sites that would have been spared if the industry had been allocated to the brownfields.

  Responding to these problems, the EPA and local communities have taken steps to lift the *Sword of Damocles* of being held liable from prospective developers of brownfields. For instance, under certain circumstances, the EPA is

---

100 See Rhoads/Shogren (1998) for a theoretical discussion of this issue and for the empirical evidence mentioned previously.

101 In an empirical study, Chang/Sigman (2000) find no evidence for this common assumption.

willing to enter into a contract with prospective developers of brownfields that contains a "covenant not to sue" the prospective purchaser under CERCLA. Moreover, the Small Business Liability Relief and Brownfields Revitalization Act of 2002, which amended the "Superfund" legislation, provides an "innocent purchaser" exemption from owner liability under CERCLA to take the brake off brownfields redevelopment.

There is an intriguing economic puzzle among these issues. Using *introductory economics*, one might wonder why fallow brownfields cause a problem for market allocation in the first place. Is not contamination a dimension of product quality that should be reflected in the market price of a piece of land, like any other dimension of quality? More specifically, why do low land prices not sufficiently compensate potential buyers for the liabilities associated with the property? However, using more *advanced economics* reveals that efficient transactions of land are discouraged due to market imperfections and distortions generated by joint and several strict liability. This case is argued by Chang/Sigman (2007) and Sigman (2010) using theoretical analysis and empirical evidence.

- *The Decision for Judgment Proofness.* If the value of the assets of a firm is lower than the environmental damage generated by the firm, then it will be impossible to get full compensation. The firm is *judgment proof* to a certain extent. In the preceding discussion, we found two effects of judgment proofness for the equilibrium care level of the firm under consideration: in section III.2, we found that a limitation of liability (due to judgment proofness or other causes) may attenuate the incentives to take care, even in the case of a single polluter. In the case of multiple polluters, as analyzed in this section, another distortion of judgment proofness has been revealed. A judgment-proof firm is less likely to be targeted by the EPA to be exclusively liable under joint and several strict liability than a solvent firm. In the extreme case of a judgment-proof firm that is certain that it will not be targeted for liability, equilibrium care drops to zero. In the analysis given previously for a single polluter in section III.2, as well as for multiple causation in this section, it has been assumed that it is exogenously determined whether (and to what extent) a firm is judgment proof. In reality (as well as in more sophisticated economic models), it has to be acknowledged that judgment proofness is not a fact of nature to be humbly accepted but, in part, the consequence of economic decision making. In particular, it is attractive for firms to spin off the very parts of their economic activities that generate environmental risk into smaller firms that can drastically reduce liability through bankruptcy. There is empirical evidence suggesting that this is not just a theoretical possibility. On the contrary, it has been shown that more hazardous industries have more small firms with little assets, and more firms that are rather short lived.[102]

---

102 See Segerson (2000, p. 436) and the literature referred to therein.

C. Pigovian Tax

The idea of removing misallocations arising from a divergence between private and social costs by state intervention in economic activity goes back to the work of Arthur Cecil Pigou[103]:

"In general industrialists are interested, not in the social but only in the private, net product of their operations... self interest will bring about equality in the values of the marginal private net product of resources invested in different ways. But it will not tend to bring about equality in the values of the marginal social net products except when marginal private net products and marginal social net products are identical. When there is a divergence between these two sorts of marginal net products, self interest will not, therefore, tend to make the national dividend a maximum; and consequently certain specific acts of interference with normal economic processes may be expected, not to diminish, but to increase the dividend."[104]

Pigou suggested that the state should influence the behavior of those causing negative externalities through taxes and those causing positive externalities through subsidies (negative taxes). Taxes and subsidies should be rated just so that the polluter will in his own interest exercise his activity at a socially optimum level:

"It follows that, under conditions of simple competition, for every industry in which the value of marginal social net product is greater than that of the marginal private net product, there will be certain rates of bounty, the granting of which by the State would modify output in such a way as to make the value of the marginal social net product there more nearly equal to the value of the marginal social net product of resources in general, thus – provided that the funds for the bounty can be raised by a mere transfer that does not inflict any indirect injury on production – increasing the size of the national dividend and the sum of economic welfare; and there will be one rate of bounty, the granting of which would have the optimum effect in this respect. In like manner, for every industry in which the value of the marginal social net product is less than that of the marginal private product there will be certain rates of tax, the imposition of which by the State would increase the size of the national dividend and increase economic welfare; and one rate of tax, which would have the optimum effect in this respect."[105]

Taxes levied in line with Pigou's idea for internalizing externalities are called "Pigovian taxes." A.C. Pigou's proposal has been clarified and extended in the literature on externalities in a number of contributions. The following presentation of the Pigou approach has been kept brief because of its relatedness with the

---

103 Pigou, *The Economics of Welfare* (1920). Later, the 3rd edition (1932) is cited.
104 Pigou (1932, p. 172).
105 Pigou (1932, p. 224).

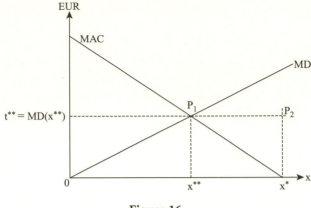

Figure 16

internalization strategies discussed exhaustively in chapters A and B and the emission tax covered in part three.

The core of Pigou's idea is to charge the producer of a negative externality a tax such that the tax rate corresponds to the external marginal cost arising at the socially optimum position. The incentive effects for the causer of the externality arising from the tax can more simply be explained on the basis of Figure 16. As already presented for other internalization strategies, the uncorrected equilibrium emission of the polluter firm is x^*. The economically optimum emission level is, in contrast, x^{**}. If for every pollutant unit emitted the polluter is now charged a tax at the level of $t^{**}(= MD(x^{**}))$, then additional costs for him at a level of $x^* \cdot t^{**}$ arise if he does not adjust his emission level. But this is not an optimum reaction for a decision maker aiming at profit maximization (and thus cost minimization). He can instead cut costs by reducing emissions. The most favorable amount of emission reduction for the polluter follows from a comparison of the marginal abatement cost with the Pigovian tax rate. For every additional emission unit avoided, he will, on the one hand, have expenditure of the amount of the marginal abatement cost but, on the other hand, save taxes at the level of the tax rate. It follows that he will, starting at x^*, abate emission as long as his marginal abatement cost (MAC) lies below the Pigovian tax rate (t^{**}). All in all, by optimal adjustment to the Pigovian tax, the polluter will cut costs by an amount corresponding in Figure 16 to the area $x^* \, P_2 \, P_1 \, x^{**} - x^* \, P_1 \, x^{**} = x^* \, P_2 \, P_1$.

He will, then, at his new emission equilibrium cut emission by precisely the amount for which the marginal abatement cost has risen to the level of the tax rate. In Figure 16, this condition is met at point P_1. Because the tax rate is precisely equal to the marginal damage at the social optimum, it is also true in the new equilibrium situation that the marginal abatement cost corresponds to the marginal damage. Thus, the equilibrium condition for the firm after introduction of the Pigovian tax is identical with the condition for the optimum emission level. The external effect has accordingly been internalized.[106]

---

106 In the literature, various disruptions to the internalization effect of a Pigovian tax have been disputed in modeling theory. From an economic theory viewpoint, particular interest attaches

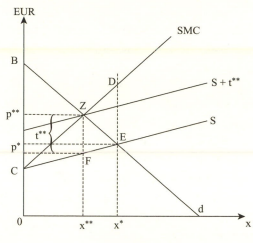

Figure 17

Further illumination on the mode of operation of the Pigovian tax comes from considering not a single polluter firm but the firms in a particular polluting industry as a whole. This makes clear the effects of Pigovian taxes on the market price of the commodity the production of which causes the emission.[107] For this, we consider the simple supply and demand diagram of Figure 17 for a commodity x, and to do so briefly take up the theoretical economic bases of environmental economics exhaustively presented in part one: the supply curve (S) shows the private marginal costs of producing x. SMC shows the social marginal cost of production. The integral under SMC gives the overall social costs (i.e., the evaluated consumption of resources caused by the production).

Disregarding income effects, we can use the integral under the demand curve (d) as a measure of consumers' willingness to pay for x. Let us accept willingness to pay as a monetary approximation for the benefit brought by x; then the contribution the production makes to social welfare can be shown in Figure 17 as the area between the demand curve and the social marginal cost curve.

As long as the demand curve lies above SMC, an additional unit of x brings a positive contribution to welfare. However, as soon as the SMC is higher than consumers' willingness to pay for an additional unit, the welfare contribution of the additional unit becomes negative. In Figure 17, the contribution of producing x to social welfare is a maximum for an output level of x^{**}. At x^{**}, the social marginal costs are equal to the marginal willingness to pay. The quantity x^* supplied at the competitive equilibrium is too high from welfare viewpoints. For x^*, it is only the

---

to the difficulties arising if a monopolistic (or oligopolistic) causer of an externality is regulated through a Pigovian tax. (On this, cf., chapter B, part four.) The allocational effects of negotiations between polluters and injured parties (in Coase's sense) have also been discussed in the condition where the polluter has a Pigovian tax imposed on him.

107 In this description, we assume that the relevant firms produce only one good and that the emission level is proportional to the production level.

difference between willingness to pay and private cost that is a maximum. The equilibrium social welfare (at x^*) in Figure 17 is smaller than the maximum social welfare (ZBC) by ZDE.

Let us now consider the effects of the Pigovian tax. The optimum tax rate corresponds to the difference between the supply curve and the social marginal cost curve above output level x^{**} (i.e., the distance ZF in Figure 17). If polluters have to face t^{**}, then the supply curve on the market will shift from S to $S + t^{**}$. The new market equilibrium x^{**} defined by the intersection of the new supply curve with the demand curve is identical with the optimum welfare position. The price of the relevant good rises, because of the tax charged, from p^* to p^{**}. The price increase brought by the Pigovian tax thus has the effect of shifting a part of demand away from the pollution-producing commodity x and – after the price increase – toward relatively less expensive substitutes.[108]

To be able to set a Pigovian tax at the optimum level and levy it, "government" has to know the marginal damage and marginal abatement cost functions used in the previous discussion. These high requirements on the degree of information of the tax-setting office are a major hindrance to the practical realization of the concept of a Pigovian tax: many kinds of damage are hard to measure and evaluate, for instance, because they concern psychological, health, or aesthetic areas. Moreover, the number of polluters and injured parties is often so high that covering all of them and exactly allocating damage to causes is extremely difficult. These difficulties are increased by the fact that for the Pigovian tax rate, it is not the marginal actual damage but the marginal damage at the social optimum that counts. Although it is possible that a tax rate oriented toward actual damage will after several iterations converge on the optimum tax rate,[109] this sort of process is time consuming and associated with misallocations. Moreover, because of the heavy uncertainty and discontinuity for firms that it brings, it is likely to be politically difficult to implement.

But even if immediate realization of a Pigovian tax (like other internalization strategies) thus faces considerable obstacles, it should by no means be dismissed as irrelevant to environmental policy. The practical importance of the Pigovian tax is that it is godfather to a number of more policy-relevant variants of the taxation of externalities. In particular, emissions tax on the price standard approach was born from the Pigovian tax.[110] On this concept, the high objective of internalizing externalities is dropped from the outset. The intention of this tax variant, modest from a theoretical economics viewpoint, is to lower the externalities (specifically,

---

108 That the substitute products are not only cheaper, but also more environmentally friendly than commodity x at issue is ensured only if environmental policy embraces *all* goods produced in the economy in its internalization efforts.

109 Especially where there are nonconvexities, this is, however, not certain. On this, see Burrows (2008).

110 Cf. Baumol/Oates (1971, 1988).

the emissions) to a politically set level. This approach is dealt with in part three, along with other methods aimed at the same objective.

One subproblem given much attention in discussing the Pigovian tax is the question of the symmetry or asymmetry of taxes and subsidies for internalizing negative externalities. Here the consequences are investigated that arise when government, rather than taxing the causing of negative externalities, subsidizes their prevention. It is frequently argued in the literature that subsidies bring the same effect as taxation.[111] An understanding of the thesis that taxes and subsidies are allocationally equivalent comes from Figure 16: let us suppose that in Figure 16, a subsidy rate s^{**} has been entered at the same level as the Pigovian tax rate t^{**} discussed previously. Starting from the initial emission level x^*, the polluter receives a subsidy of s^{**} for every marginally reduced unit of emission. As for the previous Pigovian tax, it is easy to see that on this condition it will be profitable for the polluter to cut emissions as long as the subsidy rate lies above the marginal abatement cost. The subsidy equilibrium will accordingly be reached at emission level x^{**}, the same as the tax equilibrium and the social optimum. The equivalence suggested here can also be appreciated by considering that, with both tax and subsidy, costs of the same amount arise for the individual polluter: with the tax he must pay directly an amount of t^{**} for a marginal increase in emission. With the subsidy policy, this happens indirectly because the marginal increase in emission causes opportunity costs at the level of the lower subsidy payment s^{**}. If $t^{**} = s^{**}$, then within the limits of the previous argument the allocational equivalence of tax and subsidy follows. However, the argument presented here falls short. It considers only the position of an individual polluter firm on a short-term analysis. On a long-term analysis, on top of the *marginal* conditions for equilibrium (here, t (or s) = MAC), there is a further central *total* condition: at the long-term competitive equilibrium, the gain is equal to zero for all firms in an industry.[112] If the firms in a competitive industry make profits in an (assumed) starting condition, this will attract new firms.[113] The access of new firms raises the supply quantity on the market. The equilibrium price thus falls (given a demand curve with a negative slope). The downward course continues until the price has fallen to the average cost of production. Then the overall profit has been swallowed up by the enlargement of the industry, and the incentive to entry by outside firms evaporates. The system comes to a point of rest, and the long-term equilibrium for the industry has been reached. These circumstances have considerable consequences for the comparison between the allocational effects of taxes and subsidies.

111 The analogy to the *Coase theorem* arguing that it is allocatively irrelevant who compensates whom in the process of internalization negotiations is evident. See chapter A.

112 A positive reward to the entrepreneur firms is accounted for as a component of cost. Further explanations on long-term competitive equilibrium can be found in any microeconomics textbook.

113 Free market access being among the constitutive features of a competitive market.

To understand this, let us assume that a polluting industry subject to a Pigovian tax is at the long-term equilibrium. The product price will then precisely cover the average costs (which contain the Pigovian tax), and the profit of the industry (and of each individual firm) is equal to zero. Now let the Pigovian tax at rate t^{**} be replaced by a subsidy at the same level, s^{**}. Although this does not affect the marginal cost of production, the average costs nonetheless fall on the day of the policy change. With the Pigovian tax, the average costs of production that firms have to calculate are above the average production costs in a world without any environmental policy, whereas with the subsidy they are below that. If (in accordance with the assumptions) in the starting position the firms under the Pigovian tax were earning no profit ("long-term equilibrium"), then the policy change will mean that "overnight" the polluting industry will be flowing with milk and honey. This starts outside firms moving (i.e., we "observe" an influx of productive resources into the polluting industry). Through the adjustment process described previously, this leads to an expansion in supply that will continue until the profits that have fallen into the lap of the polluting industry due to the policy change are exhausted and a new long-term equilibrium reached. Because we have assumed that the emissions are proportional to output, it immediately follows that emission at the long-term subsidy equilibrium will be higher than at the long-term Pigovian tax equilibrium. The quantity supplied (emission caused) at a subsidy equilibrium is not socially optimal because the product price is not sufficient to cover the social marginal costs of production.

The explanation for the long-term asymmetry in the allocational effects of Pigovian tax and subsidies and the negative assessment of the subsidy in welfare theory presented here has been known in the environmental economics literature for a long time.[114] Nonetheless, it is continually overlooked in the economic policy debates where lobby groups shop for subsidies. In assessing the economic policy debate, we previously assumed a form of subsidy particularly favorable to allocational effects, namely, a subsidy for avoided emission units. In real politics, it is more often quite different forms of subsidy that occur (e.g., on particular abatement measures or production factors), forms that are still more unfavorable in allocational terms.[115]

114 Cf. the first edition, which appeared as long ago as 1975, of Baumol/Oates (1988), cited in this book from the second edition, as well as the still earlier works of Bramhall/Mills (1966), Calabresi (1965), and Schulze/d'Arge (1974). The validity of the asymmetry argument adduced previously does not depend on the simplifying assumption (customary in the literature) that emissions are proportional to output level. Instead, the argument also applies if emission reduction measures going beyond the output reduction are incorporated into the model.

115 For instance, if a particular abatement technique is subsidized, this provides no incentive for a polluter to look for the economically most efficient combination out of the wide range of possible abatement activities.

Exercises

Exercise 2.1
Mention two important assumptions of the Coase theorem.

Exercise 2.2
Compare the interactions of individuals in the Coasean bargaining model with the interactions between individuals in a competitive market. What is the main difference?

Exercise 2.3
Could a bargaining solution also be realized if the government does not assign the property rights over a resource that is used by at least two citizens? If your answer is "yes," what would the solution look like?

Exercise 2.4
Assume that a factory and a fisher are settled at a river. The factory is settled upstream and dumps its emission into the river. This influences the catch of a fisher who lives downstream. The profit function of the factory is given by $\Pi_U = b \left(a E - \frac{1}{2} E^2 \right)$. The profit function of the fisher is given by $\Pi_D = d - \frac{c}{2} E^2$, with $d = 200$, $a = 10$, and $b = c = 2$.

a) Determine the socially optimal emission level E^{**}.
b) Starting from the noncooperative emission level (which depends on the property rights with respect to the river water), the two parties negotiate the transition to the socially optimal emission level.
   i) Assume that the polluter holds the property rights. Derive the noncooperative emission level E^* of the factory, the maximum payment the fisher could pay for the transition to the socially optimal emission level, and the minimum payment the factory will demand.
   ii) Assume that the fisher holds the property rights. Derive the noncooperative emission level E^0 of the factory, the maximum payment the factory could pay for the transition to the socially optimal emission level, and the minimum payment the fisher will demand.
c) In the following, assume that the liability law is applied to internalize the external costs. Discuss the implications of (i) strict liability and (ii) the negligence rule with socially optimal emission standard on the decision making of the factory. Plot the objective functions of the factory under both liability rules in a diagram.

Exercise 2.5
Discuss differences between the internalization of external effects by liability law and by Coasean bargaining.

Exercise 2.6
Consider an economy with two firms ($i \in \{1, 2\}$). Let $x_i \in [0, 10]$ denote the emission level of firm i and $a_i = 10 - x_i$ the corresponding abatement level.

Abatement costs of firm 1 are given by $AC_1(a_1) = 50(a_1)^2$ and of firm 2 by $AC_2(a_2) = 100(a_2)^2$. The expected value of social damages is given by $D(x_1, x_2) = 50(x_1 + x_2)^2$.

a) Determine the socially optimal individual and aggregate emission levels (x_1^{**}, x_2^{**} and $x^{**} = x_1^{**} + x_2^{**}$).

b) To induce the socially optimal emission level x^{**}, the government considers the introduction of a variant of the strict liability rule, where both firms have to pay 50% of the total damage cost. Determine the equilibrium emission levels of the firms under the described liability rule.

c) Propose an alternative variant of the strict liability rule that would induce the socially optimal allocation in the described economy.

Exercise 2.7

Assume that a producer A reduces environmental damages stemming from his production by a care activity x. The costs for this care activity are given by $C(x)$, with $C(0) = 0$, $C'(x) > 0$, and $C''(x) \geq 0$. Environmental expected damages are given by $D(x)$, with $D(x) > 0$, $D'(x) < 0$, and $D''(x) \geq 0$.

a) The government aspires the internalization of external costs by the negligence rule. State possible reasons for the care standard deviating from the socially optimal level.

b) Which consequences for the negligence rule care equilibrium arise from a suboptimal standard?

c) State possible reasons for a damage discounting (i.e., a positive difference between expected damages and the expected compensation payment).

d) Which consequences for the negligence rule care equilibrium arise from a damage discounting?

e) Let the cost and damage functions be given by $C(x) = 2x$, $D(x) = 8/x$ and the care standard by $x^S = 7/2$. Show that the standard chosen by the government differs from the socially optimal care level. Determine the equilibrium care level of the firm under the negligence rule.

f) In addition, the firm acts on the assumption that if a damage occurs, it only has to pay $9/16$ of the total damage. Determine the equilibrium care level of the firm under these assumptions.

g) Compare social cost in items (e) and (f) and the social optimum.

Exercise 2.8

Explain how a Pigou taxation induces a polluter (i.e., the producer of a negative externality) to choose the socially optimal activity level.

Exercise 2.9

How would you judge the chances for the implementation of the Pigou tax in practice?

Exercise 2.10

Consider an economy with a single firm. Let $x \in [0, 6]$ denote the emission level of the firm and $a = 6 - x$ the corresponding abatement level. Abatement costs are given by $AC(a) = 50a^2$. The expected value of social damages is given by $D(x) = 25x^2$.

a) Determine marginal abatement costs MAC and marginal damage costs MD (as functions of x), and plot both curves in a diagram.

b) Determine the socially optimal emission level x^{**} and the corresponding value of expected damages.

c) To induce the socially optimal emission level x^{**}, the government considers the introduction of an emission tax. Determine the socially optimal (Pigou) tax t^{**} and the corresponding tax load of the firm.

d) As an alternative environmental policy instrument to induce x^{**}, the government considers strict liability and the negligence rule with the emission standard x^{**}. Show that under both liability rules, the firm, which is assumed to be risk neutral, chooses the emission level x^{**}.

e) Compare the three instruments – emission tax, strict liability, and negligence – with respect to (i) information requirements of the government, (ii) planning security of the firm, and (iii) distributional effects. (Who bears the damage costs?)

Part Three

Standard-Oriented Instruments
of Environmental Policy

A. Introduction

In this part, we present and assess the types of environmental policy instruments that play an important part in the academic and political debate.

For a "fair" comparison of the properties of various instruments, it is indispensable for them to be dealt with in the same analytical framework.[1] In particular, it must be assumed that the alternative instruments are being used to attain the same ecological objective. The hypothetical nature of the *ceteris paribus* construction considered here is consciously accepted for this. It distinguishes this book from one concerned mainly with analyzing practical environmental laws. The uniform objective the instruments are to serve is presumed to be keeping a preset absolute emission ceiling ("aggregate emission standard") for a particular pollutant i within a certain region (per unit of time).[2] The environmental policy instrument is supposed to make the sum of the absolute emission quantities of all producers of the relevant pollutant in the region concerned not exceed this maximum. To distinguish them from the "internalization strategies" concerned with charging for the (monetized) external damage, the instruments for reaching the objective described are called "standard oriented."

Let us briefly pause for a "terminological warning": there is a possible source of confusion in how the term "standard" has been used in the literature. On the one

1 Comparing a mosquito's calorie consumption with an elephant's does not tell us much if the little one's consumption is measured in all-out attack flight and the big one's when it is already stuffed for posterity. As clear as the example from nature we have given may be, the principle of the equality of "other" influencing factors (the *ceteris paribus* principle) is nonetheless often ignored in economic analysis of environmental policy instruments.

2 The demarcation of environmental regions is (quite apart from the nature of the environmental policy instrument deployed) problematic, yet it is feasible in practice. The distribution of emissions within such a region is left out of consideration in the objective as just described. On this cf., e.g., the brief description in Perman et al. (2003, ch. 7.5), or for more detail, Geoghegan/Gray (2005).

hand, "standard" means an aggregate level of emissions. The goal of environmental policy is to make sure that equilibrium aggregate emissions do not exceed this target. It is in this sense of the term that we use the expression "standard-oriented environmental policy" in this book. On the other hand, the term "standard" has been used in the literature to denote an *instrument* of environmental policy. Here the standard is an upper emission limit addressed to the individual polluter. The standard in this sense is one of many instruments with which the standard in the former sense (the policy *goal*) may be achieved. To avoid confusion, we use the term "command and control" when referring to the individual emission standard in the instrumental sense.

The restriction to a single pollutant considerably simplifies the presentation. Of course, in reality, many pollutants have to be regulated through environmental policy. The limitation adopted here for pedagogical reasons does no harm as long as the pollutants are independent of each other in both their environmental effects and their abatement costs. In that case, what is said here about a single pollutant is representative of all pollutants; however, the generalization of statements derived from analysis of only a single pollutant is no longer acceptable once pollutants interact. Pollutant interactions are complicated to deal with both scientifically and economically. We initially ignore their existence, turning separately to this point in chapter A of part four. The regional targets in practical environmental policy are, in contrast with this construction, frequently formulated as immission limits. The following discussion nonetheless relates to emission values, for two reasons:

a) The immissions into a region must ultimately be controlled through emissions (not necessarily from the same region). Lowering emissions thus means hitting "intermediate targets" on the road to lowering immissions. The "tall chimney policy" highlights the point that neglecting this connection might have fatal consequences.

b) An emission-oriented policy is analytically simpler to deal with than an immission-oriented policy. The findings arrived at remain unaffected in an immission-related analysis. The latter only calls for a few extensions to the emission-oriented analysis, which are addressed in section C.III.7.

In this book, the following types of standard-oriented environmental policy instruments are examined in detail:

a) Command and control
b) Emission taxes
c) Transferable discharge permits[3]

For pedagogical reasons, these instruments are treated as alternatives in the context of this introductory presentation. We accordingly do not address the complications of combining them. This is a modest approach that readers are already

---

3 Synonym: tradable emission certificates.

familiar with from our discussion of internalization strategies in part two.[4] We also largely confine ourselves to a general discussion of the range of environmental policy instruments. However, specific aspects of individual areas of application (e.g., the specifics of certain environmental media such as air, water, and soil) are considered marginally.

Command and control is taken to mean a policy that prescribes an absolute maximum for each producer of the relevant pollutant in the region concerned for the emissions to be produced (per unit of time). The sum of the individual emission ceilings results in the regional emission maximum laid down. Of course, such requirements do occur in practical environmental policy in many varieties, departing from this definition. Where statements made apply to variants differing from the "prototype" of command and control presented here, we mention that specifically in each case.

An *emission tax* (charge, duty, levy) will mean a policy where each producer of the relevant pollutant in the region has to make payments to the state for the quantity emitted. The charge rate (tax per unit of emission) is constant and is equal for all emitters. The rate is set so as to bring about an adaptation response by the individual polluters that will limit their combined pollutant emissions to the preset emission target. When a tax variant differing from this "prototype" is addressed, it is explicitly mentioned.

Transferable discharge permits mean a policy where polluters who want to emit a particular quantity of pollutant in the relevant region are required to possess the corresponding quantity of emission permits (certificates). A total quantity of permits with nominal values adding up to the regional emission ceiling is auctioned among the relevant polluters.[5] In each case, mention is made in the discussion where there are departures from this "prototype" of permits.

When we talk about environmental *policy* instruments, "policy" means *governmental* influencing of firms' emission behavior. The literature also discusses how far environmentally friendly behavior can be induced by consumers' "voting" on the markets for goods (or by workers or capital providers on the factor markets).

---

4   A glimpse at an analysis of the simultaneous operation of various instruments could however be gleaned from chapter B of part two. In dealing with the negligence rule and negligence rule aspects of insurance policies, it came out clearly that liability law standards of care and command and control provisions are closely related to each other in terms of the economic incentives they generate.

5   In the literature, transferable discharge permits are often deemed to be "the market solution" to environmental problems. However, it is clear from the mere definition of transferable environmental permits that this assessment has to be interpreted cautiously. The total quantity of emissions of the relevant type allowed in a permit policy is not determined on the market, but laid down by government. It is "only" the price of the permits and the equilibrium distribution of emission rights among emitters that is determined by the market mechanism. Despite this important restriction, we may retain the terms usual in the literature because, in comparison with the nonmarket instrument of source-specific requirements predominantly used in practical environmental policy, environmental permits are a "relatively market-oriented" instrument.

Environmentally aware consumers might value the "environmental performance" of goods through their purchasing behavior in a way perceptible to their suppliers. This point is undoubtedly interesting, but the properties (and problems) of the guidance mechanism just mentioned are so different from those of governmental action that there is little use discussing them jointly.[6] The author instead follows precepts of prudent self-restraint (please note!) and refrains from presenting them in this book. The differences in creative possibilities between governmental decision makers and consumers can be spotlighted as follows:

- *Aim and Means.* For the state as decision maker, it is realistic to set an environmental policy target in the sense described previously (i.e., aim at a definite aggregate emission level in a region). It has means (e.g., definition and enforcement of requirements, emission charges) that are in principle suited to attaining the objective. For the individual consumer as decision maker, in contrast, it makes no sense to aim at such a goal. His influence is too small. To the extent the emissions involved arise from the production of goods the consumer demands, although he may send a signal, the supplier cannot hear it because it is drowned out acoustically in the white noise of the market. If the goods involved are instead ones the consumer does not demand, then he has no influence anyway. This is true of many consumer goods and as a rule for all investment goods.
- *Incentive.* Because the environmental effect of demand behavior depends on the totality of all consumers' decisions, the individual consumer is open to the temptation to act as a free rider. Even if he values the environment, he is subject to an incentive to consume an (otherwise attractive to him) environmentally intensive good, for instance, to drive his private car to work. He or she then enjoys the individual advantages without perceptibly deteriorating environmental quality for himself. Government as the "agent" for society as a whole is not exposed to this tension between individual and collective rationality – at any rate, as long as national environmental problems are being addressed.[7]
- *Information.* If consumers want to control emissions through their demand for products, then they have to know what materials the relevant products (including precursors) are made of and how emission intensive their production is. However, government can in principle regulate emissions directly at the source (as long as production is domestic).

This is not intended to mean that the effects of consumer behavior on environmental quality are not worth talking about (or investigating). Instead, it is certainly

---

6 Contributions to the explanation of environmentally friendly behavior not induced by governmental regulation can be found in, e.g., Baumgärtner/Faber/Proops (2002), Baumgärtner/Faber/Schiller (2006), Menges/Schröder/Traub (2005), Schaltegger/Burritt (2005), Schaltegger/Wagner (2006), Ziegler/Schröder/Rennings (2007).
7 The incentive issues facing the individual state in the area of international environmental policy are dealt with in part five of this book.

interesting to ask on what conditions the free rider issues addressed previously may be obviated. It is, moreover, worthwhile indicating areas where the information problems just mentioned are not so burdensome. Again, the importance of government instruments for lowering the cost of information would have to be analyzed here.[8] The previous observations are meant merely to make it clear that consumer influence on environmental quality ("buying green") is very different as a subject of scientific investigation from governmental environmental policy. The reader can then, hopefully, understand that we content ourselves with referring to the relevant literature instead of going intensively into these problems.[9] Much the same – as already mentioned in connection with internalization strategies in part two – applies to the question of whether decision makers behave in an environmentally friendly way merely for the sake of doing good (*intrinsic motivation*). Even readers who may be disturbed by narrowing the presentation down to *extrinsic motivation* will undoubtedly admit after reading the following brief treatment that sometimes it is the only way.

Lateral view 5: Extrinsic motivation – an attempt at saving honor at least. *Source*: Steinmann/Westfalenpost, Hagen, 2000. Reprinted with the author's kind permission.

Following this digression, let us get back to command and control, emission taxes, and transferable discharge permits as manifestations of governmental environmental policy. All three types of instruments are variants of a "weak" form of the "polluter pays principle," according to which the producer of emissions should pay the cost of abating them. The prototypes of taxes and permits, moreover, belong to the "strong polluter pays principle" because the polluters have to pay costs for emissions not avoided ("residual"). The instruments presented previously

---

8 Among these are voluntary forms of ecological informational differentiation (seals of environmental approval and the like) and governmental requirements to disclose certain ecologically relevant information. Cf., e.g., Baksi/Bose (2007), Cohen/Santhakumar (2007), Engel (2004, 2006).

9 Cf., e.g., Brennan (2006), Dietz/Stern (2002), Eriksson (2004), Krarup/Russell (2005). One particularly interesting question is what effects the existence of "green consumers" may have on the optimum design of environment policy instruments. Going into it would, however, break the bounds of this basic environmental economics textbook. Cf. Bansal (2008), Nyborg/Howarth/Brekke (2006).

are considered as "prototypes" and examined in divergent versions,[10] according to the following main criteria:

a) Cost effectiveness
b) Dynamic incentive effect
c) Ecological precision

Of course, the list of criteria could be extended, for instance, to cover aspects of administrative flexibility or of regional and sectoral economic issues as well as competition policy.

Cost effectiveness means the capacity of an instrument to reach the set emission target at minimum cost.[11]

Dynamic incentive effect means an instrument's ability to induce environmentally advantageous technical progress.

Ecological precision means an instrument's capacity for reaching the set target level precisely. Testing instruments against this criterion brings out the specific requirements for that instrument that let perfect precision in hitting the target be achieved. Attention here must go particularly to requirements relating to the level of information and the flexibility of environmental policy decision makers. Of course, environmental policy decision makers will in practice not possess complete information (say, on the polluters' abatement costs). Analyzing ecological precision yields conclusions on divergences between the emission target and the actual values achieved by alternative environmental policy instruments that arise from imperfect information.

The discussion of environmental policy instruments is structured as follows. First, the basic ideas of the three central types of instrument are presented in several variants (chapter B). Second, the suitability of the main types of instruments on the basis of the criteria defined previously is discussed (chapter C). In analyzing all instruments, it is assumed that the corresponding governmental rules will be complied with by all polluters. This presumes that their conduct is monitored[12] and noncompliance punished. The range of sanctions runs from cease and desist orders to fines to plant closures. The former produce only a slight incentive to obey the law because they involve no penalty for past excesses. The latter often lack credibility

---

10 It is particularly interesting here how applications-related variants of the "prototypes" discussed here may be constructed to be optimally adapted to the specific requirements of various environmental problems. This aspect is made clear in chapter C of part five of this book, using the example of European CO_2 trading. However, a more exhaustive discussion of this question would go beyond the bounds of this book, aimed primarily at presenting the basic connections.

11 By "costs," it is emission abatement costs that are meant. On the transaction costs of environmental policy, cf., e.g., Challen (2000), Mäler/Vincent (2005, vol. 3, ch. 25), and various articles reprinted in Tietenberg (2001, vol. I, part 2).

12 Economic implications of imperfect monitoring possibilities are dealt with by, e.g., Arguedas (2008), Feess/Schumacher (2006), Goulder/Schmutzler (1997), Macho-Stadler/Pérez-Castrillo (2006), Russell (2001, ch. 11), Schmutzler (1996a, 1996b).

due to their severity. With fines, it is assumed that they are high enough to induce a rational polluter to compliant behavior.

B. Types of Environmental Policy Instruments

I. Command and Control

The most intuitively obvious type of instrument is *command and control.* If we know that unacceptably high emissions are caused by a particular production process, nothing is more obvious than to directly regulate the level of these emissions at the polluter. Faithful to the biblical saying "if thine eye (or somebody else's?) offend thee, pluck it out," command and control methods thus act on the individual emission source as the cause of the trouble.[13]

The prototype of the requirement is – as explained previously – taken to mean a policy of assigning absolute emission ceilings to individual firms. In practical environmental policy, requirements can take various forms. The biblical saying comes closest to factory closure (!). What is common, though, is setting emission and/or immission thresholds that appear feasible according to the given *level of technology* ("state of the art"). Compliance is to be guaranteed particularly through licensing procedures for new installations. However, subsequent orders for older plants are also common. The threshold values may be formulated in absolute terms or in relation to a basic unit (e.g., 1 m^3 of exhaust gas). In addition, state-of-the-art production and/or waste treatment technologies are often prescribed, standards for end products and/or inputs laid down, or location bans imposed. Command and control requirements dominate practical environmental policy everywhere in the world. One example is the Clean Air Policy in the Federal Republic of Germany, using the German Federal Pollution Control Act (BImSchG).[14] The BImSchG obliges those building or operating potentially environmentally hazardous installations so to design their activities such that

a) No harmful environmental effects, serious detriment, or annoyance can be caused.

b) Precautions, particularly through state-of-the-art emission abatement measures, are taken against harmful environmental effects.

c) Residues occurring are if possible not only eliminated, but also used.

13 The Swedish economist Karl Gustav Cassel noted as long ago as 1922: "(It) has always been the natural thing to try and prevent all troubles and nuisances in the life of the community by forbidding them to occur . . . " (Money and Foreign Exchange after 1914; we cite the English translation, published in 1923). This observation was made in relation to the political attractiveness of state price controls.

14 The U.S. "analog" to the German BImSchG is the Clean Air Act. We return to this in the next section in connection with controlled emissions trading (cf. section III.2.a).

The framework set by the BImSchG can be supplemented by the federal government via statutory order or general administrative provisions. For instance, this has been the case with the *Large Incinerators Order* (GFAVO) or the *Technical Instructions for Clean Air* (TA Luft).

The essential requirement in German clean air policy to use state-of-the-art technologies can also be found in many variants in the environmental policies of other countries. Among examples are the concepts of "best practical means" in Britain or "best available control technology" in the United States. A common feature of regulations referring to the state of the art is that they operate faster and more firmly with new installations than old ones.

II. Emissions Taxes

The direct approach of imposing a requirement is opposed to the indirect one of fiscal charges. Here the carrying out of activities that affect the environment is not directly limited, but rather made more expensive for the polluter. This is done by imposing a charge on the emitted quantity of a pollutant, the quantity of a production factor employed, the quantity of final product produced, or the like. In the following statements, we assume that emissions are the basis for assessing the charge.[15] As mentioned previously, with the emissions tax discussed here, the emission level aimed at is no longer the object of economic balancing between the benefits and costs of consuming the environment. Instead, the emission target is set "exogenously." In contrast with the Pigovian tax, the charges discussed here do not in the strict sense serve to internalize externalities. The approach is accordingly often called the "price standard approach" in the literature.[16] To reach the target, the emissions of the relevant pollutant are subjected to a constant charge at a rate identical for all polluters in the region. The policy presented in the introduction as the "prototype of emission charges" is thus identical with emissions tax in the sense of the price standard approach.

It is intuitively clear that the amount of emission reduction with which firms affected by the environmental charge will respond to its being levied will depend on the level of the "charging rate" (charge per emission unit). If the rate is ∞, then they will respond very strongly; if it is zero, then they will not respond. The proper charging rate for the price standard approach is defined precisely by its inducing the firms concerned as a whole to cut emission to the exogenously set emission

---

15 A precondition for taxing emissions is knowing how much pollutant is emitted. Giving emission declarations on the basis of the polluter's own measurements seems a generally practicable procedure. Of course, occasional checks by the environmental authorities by measurements or input analyses will be necessary. Advanced technology even makes continuous measurement of emissions possible. A policy of requirements or permits tied to emissions also needs the quantities emitted to be known.

16 This term goes back to Baumol/Oates (1971). Cf. also Baumol/Oates (1988). As in many environmental economics texts, the terms "emissions tax" and "emission charge" are used synonymously.

target. The difficulty of determining the correct "tariff" is discussed in detail later. Each firm will compare the charge it has to pay per unit of pollutant emitted with the cost of avoiding one unit of pollutant. This may be done by, say, redesigning the production process, possibly by using recycling or building in filters, or even by stopping production. The cheaper a firm can cut emissions, the likelier it will be to decide to avoid paying the charges by instead cutting emissions.

Practical examples of emission charges are harder to find in Germany or elsewhere than command and control requirements. Nonetheless, there are now regulations in many states that contain elements of the price standard approach.[17] This is, for instance, the case with the German Water Pollution Control Charges Act (*Abwasserabgabengesetz*). This act makes water polluters pay certain rates for each unit of damage they cause. The units of damage are calculated according to the amount of waste water and its quality. The attempt is made to take account of the differing properties of materials by raising the damage units associated with a unit of pollutant according to its hazardousness. However, it must be stressed that the Water Pollution Control Levy Act is for various reasons not a pure fiscal charge within the meaning of the "prototype" described previously. It is instead supplementary to the machinery of administrative penalties and must be considered in association with the Water Resources Act (*Wasserhaushaltsgesetz*). A combination of elements of tax policy and command and control is common in the practical environmental policy of many countries.

III. Transferable Discharge Permits

1. Conceptions

A further element in the range of environmental policy instruments is the defining of marketable rights to use the environment.[18] These may take the form of emission or immission rights. The simpler variant, emission rights, is discussed.

The basic idea is for a political decision maker to set an emission ceiling for a particular pollutant for a certain area and for distribution of the rights to use this "environmental capacity" among (chiefly industrial) users of the environment to be regulated through a market. This is done through a government body splitting up the right to emission within the set limit into many partial rights to emit a corresponding fraction of the total emission quantity, certifying them in the form of *tradable emission permits*. A polluter is entitled to emit a particular quantity of

---

17   Cf., e.g., Harrington et al. (2004), and the homepage of the Regional Environmental Center (www. rec.org/). However, the taxation variants used in practice often show no connection between the charging rate and an operationally definable environmental policy target. Moreover, they are often associated with command and control policies that disrupt the incentive effect of the charges. The closest to the pattern of an emissions tax presented in the theory are the SO_2 and CO_2 taxes in Sweden and Norway and the CO_2 taxes in Finland and the Netherlands.

18   This concept is rooted in the "classical" works of Dales (1968a, 1968b).

the relevant pollutant only if in possession of an appropriate quantity of permits. For the procedures whereby polluters can obtain permits, there are two proposals.

a) **Auction.** In the first variant, the governmental institution issuing the permits auctions them to the highest bidder among polluters. This results in a market price for the emission rights that produces similar incentive effects as an emissions tax. Emitting becomes more expensive, and firms are compelled to treat the environment as a production factor in economic terms. Each firm now has to compare the price for the permits required for particular activities with the cost of abating emissions. Firms easily able to abate emissions will be more likely to refrain from emitting because abatement is cheaper for them than buying a corresponding quantity of emission permits. Firms for which protecting the environment is costly will instead be more likely to have occasion to buy emission permits, even if they are dear. This ensures – as with an emissions tax – that the scarce resource of environmental capacity to absorb a particular pollutant is guided precisely into the use of it that is most urgently needed.[19] Apart from this relatedness, the most important difference between an emissions tax and emission permits is that with a certificate policy the direct setting and implementation of an aggregate emission ceiling is ensured.

In view of the urgency and long lastingness of the environmental problem, it is important in assessing the permit idea to know that the emission ceiling set at any given moment may very well in the course of time be lowered politically. If permits made out with *no time limit* are issued, then the overall level of emissions can be controlled by devaluing the amount of emissions certified by a permit from period to period. On expiry of a period, for instance, the owner will only have the right to emit, say, 90% of the annual quantity stated on the permit. In the interest of firms' planning security, however, the levels of devaluation must be announced in good time. Of course, expectation of a devaluation of the emission rights certified in the permits will affect the supply of them on the market. That is, firms will be more likely than in a system without devaluation to "hoard" for later use permits freed in consequence of action to protect the environment, instead of offering them on the market. As well as devaluing the permits, government may also tighten the emission standard by withdrawing permits from circulation through an "open market policy." This would, of course, bring an element of the common burden principle into the permit concept.[20] Lowering of the emission threshold could further be achieved by allowing permits to also be bought by individuals aiming at

19   The criterion for the extent of urgency being willingness to pay. Cf. the discussions in part one.
20   In contrast with traditional forms of the common burden principle, however, here the criterion of cost effectiveness would be met. If a firm sells emission rights at the market price to the government body operating the open market policy, then it is in its interest to effect the emission reduction this necessitates at minimum cost. If the state were to reimburse the costs of emission reduction or the costs of a particular procedure for reducing emissions, the incentive to cost minimization would instead be absent. Nor would emission reduction effected by the state itself offer any guarantee of cost effectiveness.

a lower emission threshold. In this context, there is a touching report in the *New York Times* for March 31, 1995: a group of law students (!) from various universities bought at auction 18 (out of 176,400) SO_2 permits offered under the U.S. Acid Rain Program (see section 2). Their declared objective was to leave these emission rights unused. Self-confidently (and/or ironically – who can tell?) their spokesman declared: "We're trying to force the price up by taking as many off the market as we can." Such "private actions" are likely to remain mostly at symbolic level[21] or not to occur at all. The campaigners are faced with free rider problems that do not arise for the polluters. If a polluter acquires an emission permit, then he has a right to emissions that he can use exclusively. The market in emission rights thus provides him with a private good for which incentives to disclose willingness to pay exist. If, in contrast, an individual citizen buys a permit to leave it unused, he thus improves the emission situation not only for himself, but also for all inhabitants of the relevant region. He would then be paying for the provision of a public good. Here problems of strategic behavior would arise.[22]

If *time-limited permits* are issued, the overall emission standard can be brought down by reissuing only a certain proportion of the expiring permits. In the case of a time limitation, however, attention must be paid to ensuring the principle of protection of vested rights by enabling firms to buy emission permits that allow them to operate their plant for its expected residual useful life. In the interest of intertemporally consistent design of a permit system with limited lifetimes, it would always have to be possible to buy emission rights for future periods. A comprehensive system of futures markets would accordingly have to be institutionalized.

Of course, the auction procedure sketched here may bring considerable financial burdens and uncertainties for the firms. Moreover, the problem of market power over such a market in permits is intensively discussed in the literature.[23] Finally, considerable legal problems might arise from a move from the traditional command and control policy to one of auctioned permits.

b) Free issue. For these reasons, the following alternative[24] to the permit auction procedure has been proposed. Instead of bringing in environmental permits at an "H hour," at which no decisions have yet been taken as to the emission needs of various polluters, they in fact affect a specific situation in which polluter firms operate licensed plants that are producing emissions. The basic idea of the second

---

21 "Symbolic" is not, of course, identical with "meaningless." Cf. the quantitative assessment on the example of the U.S. "Acid Rain Program" (see section 2.b) in Israel (2007)). A constructive analysis of the issuing of emission rights to citizens can be found in Ahlheim/Schneider (2002).

22 In critical cases, free rider problems may be obviated by mobilizing solidarity among those involved. Moreover, environmental associations with high purchasing power may play a part. Finally, an individual firm might take certificates that harm it off the market.

23 Cf., e.g., Sturm (2008).

24 The two procedures may also be combined. See the discussion of EU emissions trading in chapter C of part five.

allocation procedure is to give each polluter permits for the right to emit as much as they are allowed to under the existing command and control policy and make these transferable.[25] This procedure whereby rights conferred implicitly by a command and control policy are made explicit and fungible is called "grandfathering" in the literature.[26]

Of course, in contrast with auctions, this variant of permit policy no longer satisfies the previously mentioned "strong" form of the polluter pays principle: those firms that are allotted permits gratis pay the cost of emission abatement but not that of residual emissions. Obviously, issuing a permit for the actual current emission does not improve environmental quality but merely avoids an increased burden of the pollutant regulated. This is already noteworthy as long as the economy of the relevant region is growing. For instance, if an established firm wants to expand, it has to ask itself whether it will abate the necessary emissions by cost-effective measures or else appear as a purchaser on the permit market. The latter will be the case where other emitters of the same pollutant in the region concerned can abate emissions more cheaply than the expanding polluter. These will offer on the market the permits that the expanding firm is demanding. Although in this version of the permit idea polluters initially obtain their permits free of charge, the market in certificates here as with the first version exercises a compulsion to deal in economic terms with environmental resources. Potential demanders of certificates will seek efficient abatement techniques in order to avoid the costs of those permits. Potential suppliers of permits will try to find efficient abatement technologies in order to make profits from an offer on the permits market. Of course, the announcement of an allocation of emission rights covering the actual emissions of each firm creates an incentive at the time of introduction of the emission rights system to make these actual emissions be as high as possible. This move can be avoided or weakened if earlier periods are chosen as a standard, or if actual emissions must be kept within the framework of the command and control provisions in force. An improvement in the emissions position in relation to the pollutant concerned might, as with the auction version of the permit concept, be attained by, say, devaluing the emission rights over the course of time. If emissions are to be cut by a particular percentage not only in the course of time, but also from the time of introduction of the permit policy, this might be done from the outset by allotting the firm only a corresponding fraction of its actual emissions as a transferable emission right. This

25 This favors old polluters over new ones. This is often regarded in the literature as defensible on grounds of protection of vested interests. An advantage going beyond protection of vested interests will arise for old polluters if the rights have no time limit. The old emitter may then retain, without having paid for it, the right given him under the command and control policy only for the lifetime of the plant, but then sell it on.

26 Besides the "grandfathering" dealt with here, free allocation may also take the form of "benchmarking." Emission certificates for a given plant are allocated in a quantity that would be needed for a plant of this type meeting the "state of the art." We ignore "benchmarking" as a variant of free allocation and concentrate on the case of "grandfathering."

procedure would (especially in respect of reequipment costs) be more cost effective than the proposal made in the literature to cut the emissions down to the target level through traditional emission requirements on each individual emitter, and then issue transferable emission certificates on the basis of the reduced emission value.

The two versions of the permit concept differ, according to what we have just said, in the determination of the "initial endowment" of the polluter with permits. What is common to them is the institutionalization of markets in emission rights, the price of which will lead to economic utilization of environmental resources.

2. Practical Examples: Emissions Trading Systems in U.S. Environmental Policy

Examples of practical environmental policy that have taken on major elements of the permit idea are now fairly numerous.

Moreover, there is no other environmental policy instrument that has been so well documented and evaluated by every rule of art in the literature as environmental permits. This is probably because the tradable permit policy has always been a "favorite child" of many environmental economists. This preference was by no means shared by most other participants in the environment policy debate. Instead, representatives of politics, business, and administration have pooh-poohed the idea as a pipe dream, remote from reality. Accordingly, much political resistance had to be overcome before the first attempts at implementing it in practice were ventured on. In contrast with what the common (nasty) rumors maintain, most economists are not only interested solely in their pet ideas, but also in how these stand up when acted on in real life.[27] This interest acted as a strong stimulus to work on the evaluation of practical tradable permit schemes. *Honi soit qui mal y pense:* we assume that sympathy for a permit policy has not clouded the piercing scientific gaze of the evaluators.

An overall view of the tradable permit variants employed by various countries to solve environmental problems suggests a division into "cautious" and "bold" programs. In the former, the transfer of emission rights comes after verification of the individual case by the competent authority. The transaction comes about mostly bilaterally between one supplier and one demander. Frequently, there is even

---

27 Of course, economic theories are never converted into practice "1:1." (Much the same is true of the ideas of other sciences.) This is totally unavoidable because the one and only reality and an economic model are fundamentally different constructs. See also our methodological observations in part one of this book (and the Kafka quote in the epigraph to part one). A further reason for the divergence, however, is that a "faithful" application of economic theories would often be detrimental to the interests of influential social groups. These then endeavor (mostly with some success) to set up distinctions and "exceptional circumstances" that protect them from the consequences of economic rationality. Environmental policy as an outcome of the competition and collaboration of societal interests is studied in the *New Political Economics* (Public Choice). Cf., e.g., Halbheer/Niggli/Schmutzler (2006), Kirchgässner/Schneider (2003), Polk/Schmutzler (2005), Schneider/Weck-Hannemann (2005), Stavins/Pratt (2004).

a transfer of emission rights between emitting plants of one and the same firm. In the "bold" variant, in contrast, a market in emission rights running along stock market lines is set up. Here many suppliers and demanders are present.

Environmental policy with emission permits is a recent approach in comparison with command and control or emission taxes. It is often accordingly the case that – following precepts of prudence – a permit policy is first introduced in the cautious version. In the course of application, there are learning effects that may be used to optimize the framework conditions of the program and its ground rules. If things work out successfully, overall confidence in the system's functionality is built up. At a later stage, the cautious variant is then extended into a bold one (which does not then need all that much boldness). A pioneering role in practical application of permit programs has been played by the *U.S. Environmental Protection Agency* (EPA). In particular, it has given a market economy shape to clean air policy.[28] From the many emissions trading programs now implemented in various countries, we accordingly single out two U.S. ones. We select "controlled emissions trading" as an example of a "cautious" program in the previous sense, and the U.S. Acid Rain Program as an example of the bold variant. The U.S. "Acid Rain Program" covers markets in SO_2 and NO_x emission rights. Here we concentrate on SO_2.[29]

Our presentation of controlled emissions trading and the SO_2 component of the Acid Rain Program is kept brief. It serves merely to show by example what shape the idea of emission permits, which may initially appear abstract to many readers, can take on in reality. For an exhaustive environmental economics evaluation of the programs, we are not far enough along in this part. The requisite theoretical scaffolding is not offered until chapter C. For the application of the theoretical evaluation machinery, we choose a different practical variant of the permit model, European CO_2 emissions trading. Because the EU certificates market is a supra-national environmental policy instrument (even though obviously of enormous national importance), we discuss it in part five on international environmental issues. We decide on this particularly because of the close connection between the Kyoto Protocol and emissions trading, although the discussion might equally well have fit in at the end of part three of this book.

a) Controlled emissions trading in the United States. As was usual, U.S. clean air policy initially used command and control instruments exclusively. The U.S. Clean Air Act (1970; amended in 1977 and 1990) set air quality targets to be reached by particular dates, using command and control policy. Unsatisfactory experience

---

28   Most recently, there have also been a number of relevant programs and initiatives in water purity and biodiversity policies. Current information can be found on the EPA homepage.

29   A comprehensive assessment of both programs is offered by Burtraw et al. (2006), on which, in particular, the following description is based. This and a number of other programs are presented and evaluated in Harrington et al. (2004), Harrison (2002), OECD (2004), Schwarze/Zapfel (2000).

with this policy then induced the legislature and the EPA to develop, as from 1977, economic incentive instruments that borrowed from the idea of tradable emission permits. The basic idea of the controlled emissions trading policy is that firms whose emission abatement does better than the governmental requirements receive emission credits for this additional effort. On certain terms, these credits can be used to fall below the government requirements elsewhere. This transferability of emission rights between different installations constitutes the common feature between controlled emissions trading and tradable environmental certificates. Various different modes of controlled emissions trading policy can be distinguished[30] :

- *U.S. Bubble Policy.* Here the governmental environmental authority sets an emission standard for a local airspace (bubble), regarding a particular pollutant. If there is only one firm emitting in this bubble, then on certain conditions it will be left up to it to decide how to meet the governmentally set emission limit. It can thus decide, knowing its plant's processes, where it can most cheaply abate emissions. If several firms emit the relevant pollutant in the bubble, then they can come to an agreement among themselves as to which one will use which proportion of the set emission framework. The setting up of such a bubble must be authorized by the environmental agency. Applicants have to show credibly that the emission and immission position will not be worsened by the bubble.
- *U.S. Offset Policy.* This policy transfers the basic idea of tradable emission permits from already existing emission sources to new ones being set up. If, for instance, a new firm wants to settle in a polluting area, then it can look for a firm already established there that will sell it the right to emit the quantity of the relevant pollutant it would have to produce. The older established firm then has to demonstrate corresponding emission reductions. If a firm cannot immediately find a use for a credit created by an extraordinary emission reduction, it can, in many U.S. states, deposit it in a "bank." Only plants meeting particular requirements regarding the technological state of the art are allowed to take part in the policy outlined here. That means that elements of command and control policy – with all their problems – are combined with elements of permit policy. In the offset policy, the emission reduction must always exceed the emission increase calculated against it (by a factor of, say, 1.2). Thus, each balancing transaction improves the emission position.

With the development of controlled emissions trading, expectations came to be associated with the concept: its advocates expected a revolution in clean air policy, whereas critics doubted the concept's practical applicability. In practice, controlled emissions trading has proved to be implementable. It has not, however, brought about a basic renewal of clean air policy.

---

30   Cf. the summary presentation in Klaassen/Nentjes (1997), with further references.

b) The U.S. Acid Rain Program. An example of use of the permit model going beyond the controlled emissions trading described previously in both economic and ecological importance can be seen in the 1991 amendment to the U.S. Clean Air Act. Here, as part of the "Acid Rain Program," a far-reaching transfer of SO_2 (and NO_x) emission rights was enabled, especially among energy-producing firms.[31] We confine the following description to SO_2.

In total, the quantity of emission permits issued was calculated to reach an emission reduction of 10 million tons from 1980 levels by the year 2010. This corresponds to a reduction by more than 50%. The emission limit was negotiated in the extraparliamentary area in a harmonious arrangement among a trio of government bodies, industry associations, and environmentalist associations. Industry had offered a reduction of 8 million tons, and the environmentalists called for 12 million. The emission rights, allotted to firms on the grandfathering system, are made out for a particular calendar year, but unused rights can be carried on into the future. This *emission banking* has attained considerable importance in practice. The program reached its target in two phases. Phase 1 began in 1995, covering the 110 "dirtiest" coal power stations, with a total of 374 plants. With the beginning of phase II in the year 2000, all other coal power stations (with an output of 25 MW or over) were covered, as well as smaller power stations burning coal with particularly high sulphur content. Altogether, 1,420 plants are covered. At the start of the second phase, the endowments of the emitters already covered in the first program phase were drastically cut (by a good half). In 2005, the EPA continued the program for combating acid rain by issuing the U.S. Clean Air Interstate Rule (CAIR). This is a program (again in two phases) that further tightens the emission targets for SO_2 (and NO_x). Over and above that, the area of application of permits trading is further extended. Phase I of CAIR is to start in 2010, and phase II in 2015.

Firms found in the annual audit to have actual emission quantities above the levels certified in the permits pay fines of $2,000 per ton, and in the following year, lose emission rights in the amount of the excess. One particularly noteworthy feature of the program is that the EPA always retains a small portion (2.24%) of the emission rights allotted to each firm and offers them to the highest bidder in a national auction.[32] Here we can see a combination of the two procedures mentioned previously for initial allocation of tradable emission rights. Since the market opened, it has had a lively history. The number of transactions has steadily increased, according to EPA indications. Between 1994 and 2003, in 27,290 transactions, 166.9 million emission rights (for 1 ton each) were traded. When the program started, most transfers were between associated firms or within a single firm. With increasing market experience (and thus market acceptance), however, the proportion of trading between economically unassociated firms rose sharply, and in recent years, it has been stable at around 50% of the total value of transactions.

---

31   Cf. the exhaustive description and economic analysis in Burtraw et al. (2006).
32   Private bidders for emission rights are also admitted to the auction.

The price of emission rights initially fell steadily after the program opened. In this phase, it was far lower all around than had been forecast. The market opened at prices around $150 and, in 1996, reached its lowest level with figures of around $70.[33] Since then, the market has shown a rising price trend. In it, "quiet" market phases can be clearly distinguished from "turbulent" ones.

In the quiet phases, the price rise had a size that allowed "normal" interest on the capital tied up in the form of emission rights deposited in the bank. A price development that follows this pattern points to an intertemporal market equilibrium: if the value of emission rights kept in the bank were to grow faster than the value of a comparable financial investment, then it would be attractive to beef up the permit account at the expense of the financial account. For this, additional certificates would be demanded. This would force the prices for permits upward. If, instead, the value of the stock of permits held were to rise at a slower rate than that of the financial investment, then correspondingly a process of price reduction would get going.[34]

In the turbulent phases, exogenous "disruptions" lead to abrupt price increases. The most important exogenous disruptions can be divided into two groups: changes in environmental policy regulation and stormy events on the energy markets. One example of the former is the price hike between 1999 and 2000 related in the literature to the beginning of the second phase of the Acid Rain Program and further tightening of environmental standards by the Clinton administration. This category of determinants of price rises also includes the presumption that the CAIR program briefly referred to previously is responsible for the recently observable price rises. However, the price rise in 2004 is explained by determinants in the second category. In particular, it is attributed to the sharply rising natural gas prices in this phase and the associated sharp rise in demand for coal-generated power.

The central argument for employing market-oriented instruments in environmental protection (e.g., for tradable emission permits) is the expectation that these instruments can let environmental policy targets be met at considerably lower cost than by command and control requirements.[35] Correspondingly, considerable

---

33   Here and later in the part, all prices indicated are given in U.S. dollar values in the relevant year.

34   The equilibrium condition for the stock of permits kept in the bank implied here follows the same principle as the *Hotelling Rule* in the area of the economics of exhaustible resources (cf. part six of this book and, e.g., Perman et al., 2003, Tietenberg, 2008). According to the Hotelling Rule, an intertemporal market equilibrium for an exhaustible resource is defined by the fact that the resource price rises over time at a rate corresponding to the interest rate. If the actual price path is higher than the path meeting this condition, then the old saying "oil in the ground appreciates faster than money in the bank" will apply. This situation will be an incentive for a supplier of the resource to delay offloading the stock until the intertemporal equilibrium condition is met. The same is true, but with the opposite sign, if the starting position can be described as "oil in the ground appreciates slower than money in the bank."

35   There are more details on the theoretical economic background to this expectation in section C.I, "Assessment of Environmental Policy Instruments," under the heading "Cost Effectiveness."

space is allotted in the literature to the question of how high the cost savings for the certificate-based Acid Rain Program have been in comparison with an "ecologically equivalent" command and control arrangement. It is hardly surprising that there is no completely uniform picture here. After all, in answering the question, it is not possible to compare the costs actually incurred from two programs carried out in parallel: one through command and control and the other using permits. Instead, the point is how the costs actually incurred with the permit policy applied in the Acid Rain Program relate to the costs that *would* have arisen if the same SO_2 abatement target[36] had been reached through a command and control policy. The comparison calculation thus necessarily contains a hypothetical ("contrafactual") pillar. The question "what would have happened if...?" is certainly hard to answer not only in real life, but also in the world of science. Burtraw et al. (2006) give references to a whole gallery of relevant works. These tackle the issue addressed previously with the most varied methods of empirical economic and social research. All round, there is qualitative agreement among the various studies to the extent that the cost advantages of the permit policy are seen by all as "considerable." If we are to believe the thorough studies by Carlson et al. (2000) and Ellerman (2003), then the SO_2 part of the Acid Rain Program will have saved around 55% of the cost of an ecologically equivalent command and control policy.[37] This value is particularly noteworthy for its high level because the studies mentioned do not suffer from the following imperfection of prior simulation calculations in cost comparisons among environmental policy instruments. Previously, it was usual to empirically estimate the minimum costs at which the environmental policy target set could be reached. It was then simply and hastily assumed that a perfect market in permits would be capable of achieving this cost minimum at equilibrium. The costs of the command and control policy were then compared with that. Often, it was further assumed that the command and control policy took no account at all of cost concerns. Accordingly, those studies had in two ways been constructed in a biased way in favor of the market-oriented policy. Command and control policy was stylized as completely ignorant about costs, whereas permit policy was identified from the outset with the ideal state (defined according to cost-effectiveness criteria). In contrast, the studies mentioned here assume a command and control policy that is highly sophisticated as to the requirements of economic emission abatement ("enlightened command and control approach" (Burtraw et al., 2006,

---

36 By which we mean (in line with the bulk of the literature) the concept of ecological equivalence between permit and command and control, in the sense that both instruments are pursuing the same target for aggregate reduction in pollutant emission. One might, however, also include interregional (and intertemporal) pollution *distribution* in the equivalence criterion.

37 Of this total cost advantage, 80% is attributed to the more efficient use of given possibilities of emission abatement with permits. The remaining 20% is attributed to the technical progress induced through the market mechanism. (This latter connection is further discussed in section C.II under the heading, "Dynamic Incentive Effect," and is gone further into in chapter E of part four.)

p. 264)). On the one hand, account is taken of the fact that the permit model *de facto* introduced fails to hit the minimum cost combination. Of course, nobody need believe the outcome of such estimations down to the "last nickel and dime." On the other hand, the attempt to venture quantitative statements about the cost comparison is essential. In the studies mentioned, the authors have clearly derived their quantitative statements in accordance with the best of their knowledge and belief and by applying the newest available scientific methods.

From the environmental economics viewpoint, it is interesting to ask to what the departures of the actual permit program from the minimum cost abatement solution are to be attributed. The studies that have looked into this question without exception make individual state regulations on the energy business and other regulations responsible for the market actually established lagging behind the possibilities of an ideal permits market. These regulations establish high incentives for firms to comply with emission ceilings by input substitutions or by using exhaust gas desulphurization plants, even where these measures are more costly than buying permits.[38] One major reason for this is that the firms have to pass on gains (cost savings) made through permits trading to the consumer by cutting prices. The cost-based system of power price regulation is responsible for this. Moreover, expenditure on exhaust gas desulphurization and input substitution (especially the use of low-sulphur coal) can be claimed as capital costs. The authorizing authority responsible for energy prices allows a *fair rate of return* on this to be calculated into those energy prices. Expenditures on emission rights are instead classed as variable costs for which no return through the energy prices is allowed.

Despite the restriction indicated previously, though, the fact remains that the Acid Rain Program is much more in line with the principles of market environmental policy than controlled emissions trading. It is also noteworthy that the regulations that hinder market forces from developing fully are motivated in controlled emissions trading in environmental policy terms. In contrast, the (far more generously assessed) room for the development of market forces in the Acid Rain Program is restricted on energy policy grounds. The optimum harmonization of governmental regulations interacting with each other is both interesting in economic theory and necessary from an economic policy viewpoint.

In conclusion, we would recall that the programs singled out here are only examples of applications of the tradable permit idea to practical environmental policy. A wealth of information on the market organization and market development of all U.S. trading programs can be found on the homepage of the EPA (http://epa.gov/airmarkets/) (last accessed July 18, 2010). One permit policy that receives much attention in the literature alongside the two examples taken here is the Californian RECLAIM Program.[39]

---

38   Cf. also the studies cited in Burtraw et al. (2006, p. 265).
39   Cf., e.g., OECD (2004, ch. 2).

C. Assessment of Environmental Policy Instruments

After sketching the essential features, we now assess the individual instruments of environmental policy in accordance with the criteria set out initially.

I. Cost-Effectiveness

She works in the tax office, he says. And she dissects her fish a way he's never seen it done. With maximum efficiency. Four short elegant incisions, that's all. The cutlery is left almost clean. The fillets are left nicely arranged on her plate. You had to have seen it . . .

       – Gregor Hens, *Himmelssturz* [*A Fall from Heaven*], btb, München, 2002

The cost effectiveness of an environmental policy instrument is taken to mean its capacity to induce polluters to comply with any set emission target at the lowest possible abatement cost. The incentive to minimum cost emission abatement is a central criterion of assessment: if many resources are unnecessarily used up on environmental protection, then welfare losses will arise because the wasted proportion of the resources has to needlessly be taken away from other uses. A proper distribution of cost-effectiveness gains over the economic subjects affected by a regulation also means that cost-effective instruments improve the prospects of reaching ambitious ecological targets.[40]

We now discuss the cost-effectiveness properties of the three types of instrument presented previously. Let us consider the situation of a single polluting firm affected by an environmental policy instrument and then the totality of polluter firms regulated.[41]

1. The Individual Polluting Firm

If a *command and control policy* demands that the polluting firm cut its emissions by a particular amount or percentage, or to a particular ceiling, then there is every reason for the firm to seek the lowest-cost method for achieving the called-for emission reduction. This is at any rate true if the company's objective is profit maximization.[42] The addressee's position is different where the requirement does

---

40   See section III.3.

41   With all the instruments, the question arises of how far small emitters ought to be counted among the polluting firms regulated by the given instrument. For reasons of implementation costs, it sometimes seems to make sense to exclude small polluters from the regulation. Up to what emission level an emitter can be treated as negligible is, of course, controversial in the individual case. In particular, it must be recalled that the small emitters may together be responsible for a considerable emission level. Often, it may be advisable to regulate small emitters through instruments that, although weaker in terms of cost effectiveness, stand out for their lower costs of monitoring.

42   We always use this assumption for simplicity reasons. For the statement just made, the weaker assumption of cost minimization suffices.

not impose an emission target, but instead orders a particular procedure for production or for emission reduction. That narrows down the firm's room for maneuver in seeking the lowest-cost way of reducing the emissions. A cost-effective solution will accordingly not always be arrived at. It would be conceivable for a firm that knows cheaper ways of achieving the emission reduction measures for its sector than those prescribed by government to seek to convince the authorities of that and bring about a corresponding change in the regulations. But this sort of trek through official channels is cumbersome, and success is in the first place uncertain.[43] That reduces the incentive to seek information about possibly available economically more favorable processes.

A *tax* on emissions produces an incentive to individual economic cost effectiveness. The emissions producer will here weigh up whether he can manage to abate a unit of pollutant at a cost lower than the tax burden resulting from emitting that unit. He will accordingly abate emissions as long as the emission abatement cost for an additional unit abated lies below the tax rate.[44] The calculated gain from emission reduction resulting from the saved tax burden less the abatement cost is largest for the minimum abatement cost. This argument makes it clear that emissions as the basis for calculating the tax are superior to other bases for tax calculation in terms of the breadth of the incentive to cut emissions: with an emissions tax, the firm will save taxes if it cuts emissions. The means whereby it brings about reductions are irrelevant for the amount of tax saving. A whole range of reduction possibilities – ranging from input substitution through recycling processes – and the use of filters to output reduction or substitution will be considered by the firm. If, instead of the emissions, it is the product manufactured in an environmentally hazardous fashion that is taxed, then the only incentive to environmental protection lies in lowering the quantity of the taxed good produced. The incentive to cost minimization is accordingly restricted, to the detriment of the firm and of the environment.[45]

If, in order to be allowed to emit, the firm has to buy *tradable permits*, then the same incentive to individually economically cost-effective behavior arises as with an emissions tax. The role of the tax rate is then taken on by the permit price. It is obvious that this individual economic incentive to minimize costs will still remain if polluting firms do not need to bid for the permits at auction, but rather receive a certain amount of them allocated gratis and may then sell them on.

43 If the cheaper process is also applicable to other firms, problems of the individual supply of public goods are added. These may possibly be overcome by business associations.

44 In this book, we discuss polluters' adaptation to an environmental policy instrument on the assumption of certainty. On the economic theory of environmental policy, instruments under uncertainty, cf., e.g., Krysiak (2008), Perman et al. (2003, ch. 8), Pindyck (2007), Wesseler/Weikard/Weaver (2003).

45 In special cases, a departure from emissions as the basis for calculating tax may be necessary where measuring or estimating them is too expensive. This case will often arise in the case of pollutant emissions caused by private households. Also, the object of environmental policy may in the case of particular substances lie not, as assumed previously, in cutting the emission of them but in reducing any use of those substances. In such cases, input taxes may be appropriate.

2. The Totality of Polluting Firms

Going from consideration of an individual polluting firm to an analysis of the totality of emitters of a particular pollutant in a particular region, we are presented with the problem of the cost effectiveness of an environmental policy instrument in the following way: a set total emission level for the quantity produced by the emitters of a particular pollutant in a single region can be achieved in arbitrarily many ways. The total permissible emission level can be distributed in many different ways over emission levels of the individual polluters. In other words, the total reduction in emissions that has to be made in order to lower the actual emission level to the desired value can be achieved in various ways through individual firms' efforts at reduction.

The cost-effective distribution pattern will be precisely the one where the emission reduction quantities "allotted" to the individual polluters minimize the total cost of emission reduction calculated over all polluters. An essential fact for the nature of the minimum cost distribution of a given emission target over several polluters is that the emission abatement costs of the individual polluters will as a general rule have different levels.[46] This follows from the fact that emitters of the same pollutant may, for instance, be of various ages or sizes or operate various production processes, often producing different final products. The minimum cost distribution of a total emission reduction quantity aimed at among individual polluters is characterized by the fact that firms will take a larger proportion of the total quantity to be reduced the easier (i.e., at lower cost) they can abate emissions.

This feature of an efficient situation cannot be brought about by a "one-size-fits-all" *command and control policy*. For instance, if a requirement states that all firms have to cut their emissions by 50% in order to achieve a total emission reduction of 50% in the relevant region, achieving the goal will be paid for at too high a cost if the firms involved have different marginal abatement cost (MAC) functions.

Of course, command and control need not necessarily take quite such a crude form. Instead, attempts may be made to take account of the polluters' differing cost structures. If, for instance, it is presumed that firms have smaller abatement costs the bigger they are, then a graded form of the requirement will seem advisable. The total emission target will be achieved by, say, forming three size classes of firms and compelling "big" firms to make greater cleanup efforts (absolutely and relatively) than "midsize" ones, whereas "small" firms will be commanded to make the lowest efforts. This sort of grading can lead to a reduction in the total cost of reaching the target. It is, however, doubtful that a criterion like the size of a firm can always be a good indicator of the level of abatement costs. Particularly for firms of various ages

---

46 Numerous studies show a considerable range for many and various pollutants among abatement costs for different plants and processes. A recent example is a report released by McKinsey & Company, entitled "Reducing U.S. Greenhouse Gas Emissions: How Much at What Cost?" However, the report was received rather diffidently by American environmental economists. See http://gei.newscorp.com/resources/files/mckinsey–howmuchatwhatcost.pdf (last accessed July, 23, 2010).

and differing production, applying this rule of thumb may prove wrong. Even if these objections did not exist, there would be the problem with graded command and control that firms with differing abatement costs within the classes formed would be treated equally by the requirement because, with the aim of cost minimization, they would have to make differing cleanup efforts. A cost minimum can be reached through emission requirements only if an individual requirement is imposed on each firm and this is exactly adjusted to the firm's abatement costs. Of course, fine-tuning the command and control in this way would cause considerable costs. In particular, the authority imposing the requirements would have to know the abatement cost of each individual firm. This is an extremely restrictive condition.

Because the emission reduction a firm would be compelled to make under an individual "made-to-measure command and control policy" aiming at cost minimization would be the higher the lower is its abatement cost, the firm would be deprived of the impetus to seek efficient environmental protection. Indeed, it would have every occasion to exaggerate its abatement cost. We must then regard it as established that a command and control environmental policy for emissions will not be a minimum cost way of achieving the targeted goals.

In an *emission taxation policy*, the transition from considering an individual emitter of a particular pollutant to considering all regulated emitters of this pollutant in a region produces no difficulties regarding the criterion of efficiency. Since with a tax the individual polluter's emission quantity is left up to economic calculation, here firms' individual differences in reduction costs can result in differing emission reduction quantities by individual firms. The effect of an emission charge is, as explained previously, based on the fact that each polluter will in his own interest compare the cost of abating every unit of pollutant with the tax cost of emitting that unit. For firms with lower abatement costs, the comparison will be more likely to be in favor of abatement than for firms with high abatement costs. The emissions tax will accordingly, because of individual firms' profit-maximizing adjustments, lead to various abatement levels differentiated precisely according to the firms' individual abatement costs. This is the very essence of the cost minimum.

The same mechanism operates with the instrument of *tradable emission permits*: the higher a firm's emission abatement costs are, the higher permit prices it will be prepared to pay at auction. Thus, ultimately, the firms will buy more permits the higher their emission abatement costs are. The firms' abatement levels will be higher the lower their abatement costs are. The minimum cost distribution of emission abatement activities will also be arrived at where the permits are not auctioned but initially distributed gratis. As long as a firm's abatement costs (for one additional unit of emission) are below the price on the permit market, the firm will carry out abatement activities and sell the thus "liberated" permits profitably on the market. A firm with emission abatement costs (for one additional unit of emission) lying above the permit price will, in contrast, refrain from abatement activities and instead purchase the emission right on the permit market, again in the interest of profit maximization. In this way, the minimum cost distribution of

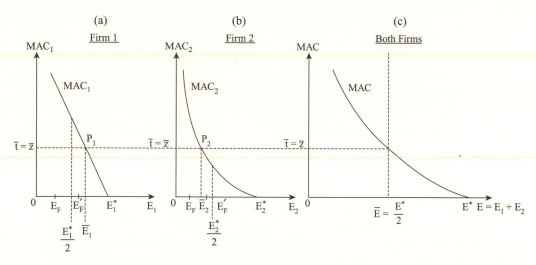

Figure 18

the set total emission quantity over the individual polluters will be arrived at, with the firms' abatement efforts graded according to the criterion of their abatement costs.[47] The cost-effectiveness advantages of the tradable permit policy (and of the price standard approach) in comparison with command and control have been explained here in purely theoretical terms. In chapter B, we refer to empirical estimates in connection with the presentation of practical variants of the permit idea. A third element in the efficiency comparison is simulation calculations. We cannot do more here than refer to the relevant literature.[48] The findings and their convincingness cannot be discussed here for space reasons.

3. Graphic Depiction

The connections explained previously can be shown more precisely in a diagram. Figure 18 is to be read as follows: in a region, pollutant E is emitted by a number of firms.[49] For simplicity reasons, Figure 18 shows only two of these firms. With no environmental policy interference, the quantity emitted by firm 1 will be E_1^*

---

47 The room for maneuver in cost saving created by the possibility of transferring emission rights is limited where the firms – as we mention, for instance, in describing the offset/bubble version of the permit concept – have to meet individual requirements related to the technological state of the art. The same effect arises where firms have particularly high emission reduction standards set for them. (In the extreme case where aggregate emissions have to be cut to zero, the emission rights solution merges into the emission requirements solution.)

48 Cf. the works reprinted in Tietenberg (2001, vol. I, part 1).

49 Previously, we emphasized the importance of possibilities of emission reduction over and above cutting production level (e.g., using filtering technologies). We are accordingly departing in the illustration from the practice predominantly employed in this book, and for simplicity reasons, using one and the same symbol (x) for output level and emission level. For the emission level, we use the symbol E in part three.

(cf. Fig. 18a), the quantity emitted by firm 2 E_2^* (cf. Fig. 18b), and thus the total quantity emitted, will be $E^* = E_1^* + E_2^*$ (cf. Fig. 18c).

The costs arising for firm 1 (firm 2), where emissions are reduced starting from $E_1^*(E_2^*)$, are shown in its marginal abatement cost curve MAC_1 (MAC_2). This shows the cost of each additional emission unit cut. Its shape, rising in the direction of zero, represents the assumption that abating additional emissions becomes more difficult with an increasing level of abatement already achieved. The (variable) total costs of firm 1 (2) are shown by the area under the MAC_1 (MAC_2) curve in Figure 18.

The marginal abatement cost curves assume that each individual firm employs the emission reduction methods in minimum cost fashion.[50] The marginal abatement cost curve MAC in Figure 18c shows the minimum marginal cost of abating emissions at the level of the totality of emitting firms. Here, then, for each level of the pollutant emitted in total over the region, the amount that a (marginal) emission reduction will cost in the most favorable case, whatever firm makes the reduction, is entered. The total marginal abatement cost curve MAC is defined as the horizontal aggregation of the individual firms' marginal abatement cost curves MAC_1 and MAC_2. Now let the aim of the regional environmental policy be to cut emissions by half.[51] The consequences arising for the emitting firms from reaching this target with alternative environmental policy instruments can now be determined from Figure 18.

One-size-fits-all command and control, treating all emitters equally, converts the overall target of halving emissions into standards that oblige each individual firm to halve its emissions. Firm 1 (2) thus cuts emissions from $E_1^*(E_2^*)$ to $E_1^*/2(E_2^*/2)$. The costs arising here for firm 1 (2) are represented in Figure 18 by the area below the MAC_1 (MAC_2) curve within the limits $E_1^*(E_2^*)$ and $E_1^*/2(E_2^*/2)$.

The two firms' differing marginal abatement costs in the situation forced by the command and control arrangement ($MAC_1(E_1^*/2) \neq MAC_2(E_2^*/2)$) reveal that here the halving of the regional emission level has been bought at an unnecessarily high cost (i.e., that cost-ineffective environmental policy is being pursued). It is easy to see from Figure 18 that the total costs incurred (i.e., by firm 1 and firm 2 together) for the same regional emission reduction are lower if firm 1 cuts one (marginal) unit less (i.e., is allowed to emit $E_1^*/2 + 1$), whereas firm 2 abates one unit more (i.e., now emits only $E_2^*/2 - 1$). For the cost-cutting effect of this "shuffling" of emissions between the firms, which is irrelevant to the total emission quantity, arising for firm 1 here is higher than the cost-raising effect for firm 2. Of course, the marginal abatement costs rise for firm 2 because of the emission abatement quantity, now one unit higher. The MAC of firm 1 (initially operating with higher

50 Against the background of what was said previously, this assumption means granting rather a lot to the capacities of command and control.

51 This sort of emission reduction target spread over all firms assumes that the firms' emissions can (e.g., because of the spatial closeness of the emission sources) be treated as interchangeable in their environmental effect.

costs), in contrast, falls because of its abatement quantity, which is one unit less. The shuffling of one emission unit to be cut thus leads to a reduction in the total costs of reaching the regional emission target, but it narrows the potential for savings to be achieved by further reshuffling. The shuffling process can continue to lower costs until the firms' MACs have become equal to each other. It is only if the starting position defined by the one-size-fits-all command and control policy ($E_1^*/2$, $E_2^*/2$) is modified enough for the firms to be operating with equal marginal cost ($\overline{E}_1$, $\overline{E}_2$) that the cost minimum will be achieved. Thus, the situation brought about by such an omnibus command and control policy will in general be inefficient.[52]

If the exogenously set target of halving regional emissions is to be reached through an *emissions tax*, then the right emissions tax rate, in Figure 18, will be $\overline{t}$.[53] Each firm will now consider how far it is better for it to abate emissions than pay taxes. Firm 1 (2) will cut its emissions to level $\overline{E}_1(\overline{E}_2)$, for which its marginal abatement cost is equal to the tax rate.[54] For up to this adjustment equilibrium, the marginal abatement costs are lower than the tax, whereas beyond that they are above it. The costs arising for firm 1 (2) from the environmental policy using emissions taxes are made up of two elements: the (variable) environmental protection costs are represented in Figure 18 by the area under their marginal abatement cost curves within the limits E_1^*, $\overline{E}_1(E_2^*, \overline{E}_2)$. On top of this is the tax burden to be borne by the firm, appearing in Figure 18 as the rectangle $0\overline{E}_1P_1\overline{t}(0\overline{E}_2P_2\overline{t})$. Because both firms are induced by the tax to bring about a situation where each of their marginal abatement costs is equal to the tax rate, their marginal abatement costs in this situation are also equal to each other. As explained previously, this equality is the characteristic feature of a minimum cost distribution of the total necessary emission reduction over both emitters. The emissions tax is accordingly cost effective.

Figure 18 can also clarify the question of tax-free amounts (as envisaged in many emissions tax proposals): if the tax-exempt emission amount is below the lowest equilibrium emission level of a firm ($\overline{E}_2$ in Figure 18), and is, say, E_F, then the tax-exempt amount will in the context under discussion here[55] be allocationally irrelevant. Tax rate $\overline{t}$ will bring the same equilibrium levels $\overline{E}_1$ and $\overline{E}_2$ as in the case without a tax-free amount. If the exempt level is instead higher than $\overline{E}_2$ (e.g., between $\overline{E}_2$ and $\overline{E}_1$ at E_F'), then the cost effectiveness of the emissions tax will be adversely affected. Firm 2 will cut its emissions not to $\overline{E}_2$, but only down to the exemption level E_F'. Further reductions would only bring it costs, but no tax savings. Despite this lower emission reduction by firm 2 to achieve the set regional

---

52   The one-size-fits-all command and control policy would bring about an efficient outcome only if for proportional emission reduction there were identical MACs. This would, in particular, be the case if all firms were to have identical marginal abatement cost functions.

53   The problems of finding this tax rate are dealt with in section C.III.

54   If the marginal abatement cost curve shows a jump in this area (in contrast with Fig. 18), the firm will attempt to come as close as possible to balancing the tax and the marginal abatement cost.

55   Dynamic aspects of tax-exempt amounts are discussed in section C.II.

emission target, the emissions tax would have to be set higher than $\bar{t}$ in order to induce firm 1 to make a corresponding reduction beyond $\overline{E}_1$.[56] Ultimately, firm 1 would show higher marginal abatement costs at equilibrium than firm 2. Here, then, an emissions tax with an exemption amount would bring about a cost-ineffective equilibrium position.

If the set target of halving regional emissions is to be attained using the instrument of *auctioned emission permits*, then the environmental authority will create emission rights to a volume of $E^*/2$ emission units (say, $E^*/2$ permits, each for one emission unit). In Figure 18c, then, the vertical line above $E^*/2$ will be the supply curve for emission permits. It takes a vertical course because the supply quantity is set exogenously (i.e., is, in particular, independent of the price of the permits). Demand for permits by each individual firm will be determined by the permit price and the marginal abatement cost: for any given permit price, it is best for a firm to avoid just enough emissions to make its marginal abatement cost equal to the permit price. For the remaining emission quantity, it will require permits. For every firm, thus, the marginal abatement cost curve is identical with the permit demand curve. The total demand by both firms is accordingly shown in Figure 18c by curve *MAC*. If conditions of perfect competition obtain on the market,[57] then an equilibrium price of $\overline{z}$ will be arrived at. At this price, firm 1 (2) will demand permit quantity $\overline{E}_1(\overline{E}_2)$, which will bring its marginal abatement cost into agreement with the equilibrium price of the permits. The remaining emissions will be abated. As with the emissions tax, the marginal abatement costs of both firms become identical at the permit equilibrium (i.e., the environmental policy target is achieved cost effectively). The financial burden on the firms will correspond with that for the emissions tax. If the permits were to be not auctioned but issued gratis, for instance, by endowing firm 1 (2) initially with $E_1^*/2$ ($E_2^*/2$) permits, then under competitive economic conditions firm 2 would at equilibrium sell $E_2^*/2 - \overline{E}_2$ ($= \overline{E}_1 - E_1^*/2$) emission rights to firm 1 at a price of $\overline{z}$. The financial burden on the firms would be lower than with an auction[58] : on top of the environmental protection costs (the level of which is independent of the permit allocation procedure), all that arises for firm 1 with gratis allocation is the expenditure for permits at a level of $\overline{z}(\overline{E}_1 - E_1^*/2)$, instead of the amount of $\overline{z}(\overline{E}_1)$ to be paid with the auction procedure. For firm 2, the total expenditure is indeed smaller than the environmental protection cost because it has $\overline{z}(E_2^*/2 - \overline{E}_2)$ proceeds from selling its permits. In contrast, with the auction procedure, it would have had to spend $\overline{z}\overline{E}_2$ on buying certificates on top of its abatement costs.

---

56   If the tax-exempt amount is close enough to $\overline{E}_1$, then it can even prevent the regional emission target being attainable through the emissions tax. The environmental policy will then fall into an "exemption trap." This is always the case where the exemption figure lies above $\overline{E}_1$ and $\overline{E}_2$.

57   It should be recalled that the limitation to two polluter firms is purely for the sake of graphic simplicity.

58   Corresponding to lower revenue for the state.

In the environmental policy debate, it is sometimes pointed out that the instrument of tradable emission permits can lead to a departure from the equality of marginal abatement cost and permit price that guarantees cost effectiveness. If over the course of time growth, inflation, and/or technological change occur in the region concerned, then in Figure 18 the *MAC* curve (and thus the equilibrium price) would have to be corrected correspondingly. For instance if, *ceteris paribus*, a third emitting firm comes in, then the *MAC* curve in Figure 18c will move rightward. The equilibrium price will rise although the environmental policy target is unchanged. If the two established firms have not foreseen this development, then they may have technologically fixed on a particular level of emission reduction on the basis of the expected price, which will later, in the light of the actual price, prove to be suboptimal. Correcting this will bring about frictional costs. However, one must add to this argument the point that the problem of a suboptimal pattern of industrial environmental protection installations can also arise with any other environmental policy instrument (e.g., command and control). A proper comparison between permits and command and control in relation to the argument of fixing technology at the wrong level would, for command and control, too, have to start from the point that the regional environmental target – as assumed in the argument relating to permits – is not changed when the third firm comes in. Then the requirements imposed on the two established firms would have to be tightened correspondingly.[59] The same suboptimality of fixed technology would then arise as with permits.

The same applies to the tax policy: the existence of a third firm is compatible with the set emission target only if the tax rate is raised. The problem addressed here is not, then, confined to the permit policy, nor is it specific to environmental protection. Rather, it arises with all technical fixes if the surrounding conditions change in course of time.

Previously, we sang the praises of cost effectiveness loud enough for everyone to hear. The readers of this book expect nothing else! To meet the obligation to truthfulness (which also means "completeness"), we must add the following qualification: sometimes *cost ineffectiveness* may also have its special charm. This has been established by the author in an experiment on himself (a method the potential of which *experimental economists* have not yet properly recognized!). As proof, we supply the following photo. It shows the author engaged in converting the second edition of the German version of *Environmental Economics* into the third one.

---

59 A command and control arrangement that did not do so (something ecologically questionable) cannot be compared with the permit arrangement described in the text, but with an arrangement where the permit supply would be correspondingly expanded when the third firm comes in. In this case, both instruments would buy avoidance of the inefficiency of fixing the technology at the cost of softening the emission target.

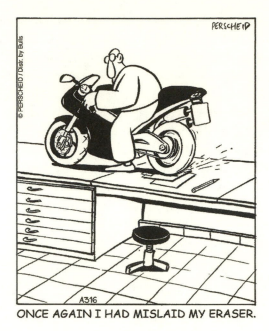

ONCE AGAIN I HAD MISLAID MY ERASER.

Lateral view 6: A.E. demonstrating the bottomless charm of cost ineffectiveness. *Source*: Perscheid "Abgründe" [Chasms]. Reprinted with the author's kind permission.

II. Dynamic Incentive Effect

The analysis of the cost effectiveness of environmental policy instruments previously assumed that processes for emission reduction and their costs are given and unchanging. The question was ultimately whether an environmental policy instrument was capable of inducing firms to employ given processes to the "proper" extent. Of course, the state of environmental technology and its implementation in industrial practice is by no means given, but depends on many factors. Among these factors is the pattern of environmental policy instruments. The question accordingly arises of their dynamic incentive effect: how far do the instruments differ in their capacity to induce the development and deployment of environmental technology progress? Progress in environmental technology occurs, according to a definition prevalent in the economic literature, when it is possible to achieve higher emission reductions at the same cost or the same emission reductions at lower cost.[60]

It must be explicitly pointed out that the object of the discussion is couched much more narrowly than would be the case with a general discussion of economic aspects of environmental technology progress. The point is whether environmental policy instruments are differently able to arouse the interest of emitters in discovering new possibilities for environmentally friendly production methods and developing them further until ready for practical application. Our analysis leaves

---

60 Doubts about this operationalization are indicated by Bauman/Lee/Seeley (2008). And in more differentiated fashion, Baker/Clarke/Shittu (2008).

the contributions of governmental research and development institutions out of consideration (as presumably tending to be independent of the instruments). The influence of the environmental protection industry is dealt with only marginally. A farther-reaching question than the one of the ranking of instruments in terms of the *strength* of their dynamic incentive effect would be the one of the ranking of instruments in terms of their ability to provide for the *optimum* dynamic incentive effect. Because answering it is quite complicated, the necessary discussion does not fit into part three of this book, which is confined to the fundamentals of environmental economics. We accordingly defer it to chapter E of part four. That discussion differentiates according to optimum technical progress within the framework of the internalization approaches as presented fundamentally in part two of this book and to optimum technical progress within the framework of the standard-oriented approaches basically dealt with in part three.

If firms face a *command and control policy* that prescribes emission ceilings for them, then it makes sense for them to look for new processes that allow the emission limits to be complied with at lower cost than traditional abatement techniques.[61] This need not necessarily be through additive (end-of-pipe) measures. Instead, in the course of technical change in a company, there may well be an integration between technical progress in environmental and production respects. However, with this kind of environmental policy, firms have no reason to develop and introduce techniques leading to a reduction of emissions below the governmentally set ceiling.[62] The expenditure that would involve would not produce any gain. Overfulfillment of the emission standard can at best happen as a by-product of an innovation in production technology.

The problem of the modest dynamic incentive effect of command and control policy is intensified if it is combined with the prescription of a "technological state of the art."[63] Here the attempt is made to adjust the environmental protection requirements for new plant to advances in technological development.

However, it must be noted that technical progress, like any other economic activity, can be promoted or slowed down by incentives. A policy that requires firms to comply with the technological state of the art operates against its objective of bringing a dynamic element into determination of the thresholds on one important

61　If the emission limit is not in absolute units but expressed as pollutant intensity, then a new technique might even achieve the emission limit, to the detriment of the environment, at higher absolute emission output.

62　Unless they anticipate an imminent tightening of the thresholds, independent of their own activities, or want to maintain a certain "safety distance" from the governmental standard.

63　According to § 3(6) of the German Air Pollution Control Act (BImSchG), the technological state of the art is "the state of development of advanced processes, installations or operational techniques that allows the practical suitability of a measure for limiting emissions to be seen as guaranteed. In determining the technological state of the art, comparable procedures, installations or operational techniques that have been successfully tested in operation are in particular to be taken into consideration." The U.S. Clean Air Act defines the state of the art as the "best available control technology."

point. Because the requirements on the emitters are more restrictive the more advanced the methods recognized as the technological state of the art are, they have strong motives for opposing technical progress rather than promoting it. Here, then, the forces of the market system are not only not used, but also even steered into counterproductive tracks. The incentive structure of this policy induces firms not to make use of possibilities of improvement clear to the insider (but hard for the outsider to perceive). Moreover, the technological state-of-the-art policy delays replacement of old, environmentally burdensome plant. An individual emitting firm will even hesitate to introduce an environment technology innovation that seems economically profitable in a particular production process if it has to reckon with the government treating that as proof that this process now represents the technological state of the art. It might then be made compulsory in other production processes of this firm where it is not profitable.[64] It sounds paradoxical in this context when the architects of the technology-related command and control policy who have dreamt up the counterproductive incentive structure complain that a "cartel of silence by senior engineers" among emitters is slowing down progress in environmental technology. The "technological state of the art" might encourage the development of technical progress by emitters at best in the special case where a company rates its own environmental technology ability as considerably higher than its competitors. It might then pursue a combative policy of innovation in environmental technology by employing technical innovations in the hope that this will lead to the imposition of requirements its competition cannot bear. The question is whether there may not be some safer and cheaper method of competitive squeeze-out. The role of driver of technological advance has with this arrangement presumably to be played by government bodies and the "environment protection industry." For members of this latter industry, there is an incentive to develop effective emission abatement installations and endeavor to have the corresponding processes or emission levels recognized as the technological state of the art. The regulations will then ensure the spread of these developments in new installations. If particular processes developed by the environmental protection industry are fixed on as the "technological state of the art," one might, however, expect this to result in a favoring of the development of end-of-pipe technologies, at the expense of integrated environmental protection.

Consideration of the economics of incentives thus argues against the idea that the concept of the "technological state of the art" is likely to promote the dynamism of a command and control policy. Expectations in this direction are probably based on confusing an "ordinary language" understanding of the concept of the "technological state of the art" with the "official" one. In ordinary language, the term suggests imposing the *best possible* abatement process in each case and thus achieving *maximum emission reduction*. The official "technological state of the art" – the

---

64   This incentive structure may have the consequence that even offering subsidies will not induce firms to make the innovations for which the government hopes.

one that can actually be converted into regulations – lags far behind the one in ordinary language, however. Apart from the considerations presented previously, the following reasons are decisive for a divergence between the "ordinary language" and "official" concepts of the technological state of the art:

a) Putting the official technological state of the art into regulations is a time-consuming matter. When those responsible hear about application of an advanced process, its transferability to other cases has to be discussed. Once a decision is taken, with the inclusion of expert advice, then it has to be converted into regulations. This may take the form of a direct obligation to apply the process or the enactment of corresponding emission thresholds. The regulations sometimes have to go through long official channels. Once the technological state of the art has been established, although it is possible for the authorities to set thresholds that go significantly beyond those laid down in the regulation, it is difficult in practice. Because much time passes before such regulations are revised (in the case of the German air quality regulations, for instance, more than 10 years), this means that a sizable bit of rigidity is built into the thresholds. Altogether, the many processes of information, decision, codification, and amendment lead to considerable delays.

b) Provisions on the technological state of the art can be imposed without major problems only in the case of new installations. Experience shows that for old plants, it is considerably harder. Even when the attempt is made – as was done with the German Clean Air Regulations – to require old plants to be brought up to the technological state of the art, once the updating time limits have expired, the new technology will once again be yesterday's state of the art. Expecting a "permanent revolution" of environmental technology in old plants from this would be totally unrealistic.

c) The definition of the concept of the "technological state of the art" is by no means independent of *economic considerations*. According to the predominant verdict of legal commentators, a technology that is not economically "defensible" cannot be the technological state of the art. The state of the art can accordingly be seen in this light not as a finding of engineering fact, but as the outcome of a weighing-up process. In defining it, the emitters are involved. They pay attention that (at least) the requirement of proportionality is kept to in burdening business with protecting the environment. If a policy of imposing the technological state of the art were to ignore economic concerns, then one ought not to be surprised at a growth of shortfalls in implementation beyond the current position and a flood of legal proceedings.

Considered all round, accordingly, the policy of prescribing the latest technological state of the art can in general be expected to produce slowdown effects. Here, then, a well-intentioned environmental policy instrument is working against the reaching of its own objective.

If *emissions taxes* are employed, then there is an incentive to introduce innovations that lower the cost of protecting the environment. This incentive is not, however, in contrast with a command and control requirement, confined to complying with a particular emission target. Instead, the tax institutionalizes steady pressure on emitters to keep lowering emissions. Every unit of emission that can be avoided using improved environmental technology will, after all, spare the firm that much tax. Firms will thus increase their profits if they can develop processes that bring the costs of emission reduction below the corresponding tax burden. This connection exists irrespective of the level of emission reduction that has currently been achieved. Every firm accordingly has an incentive to mobilize its intimate knowledge of its production process with an eye to making innovations that protect the environment and to deepen that knowledge. This incentive extends to both new and old plants. Of course, as well as in-house innovations, demand for innovations from the environmental protection industry will also be promoted. Over time, the emission level brought about at a constant tax rate will *ceteris paribus*[65] steadily improve because of innovation stimulated by the taxation policy. If the aim of the environmental policy is to maintain a constant emission level or achieve a slower decline in that level, the tax rate would have to be correspondingly lowered over time. That would then weaken the dynamic incentive effect of this instrument.

Where *tradable emission permits* are used as the instrument of environmental policy, there is at the outset the same financial incentive to innovation as with a tax: the more emissions are reduced by progress in environmental technology, the more firms will save on permit costs. They can sell their permits freed up by technical advances to other firms. However, an improvement in abatement technology will mean that *ceteris paribus*[66] the pressure on the permits market will slacken: if emitters manage by introducing advances in environmental technology to abate increasingly more emissions (and thus save spending on permits), then demand for the permits will fall. Their price will fall, thus also reducing the dynamic incentive effect of this instrument.[67] Here the rigid setting of an emission target as a structural feature of the permit solution shows its effects. If this effect is undesired, government will have to take emission rights off the market (by buying them, devaluing them, or cutting back the renewal of time-limited permits), thereby tightening up the emission standard.

This is also true of the U.S. *offset* and U.S. *bubble policies* as pragmatic variants of the permit idea: if the emission target is not tightened over time, then demand for emission rights will disappear in times of economic stagnation once

---

65   As is explained in more detail, economic growth and inflation act against this effect.

66   The effect described may be weakened or (over-) compensated for by growth of the emitters established in the relevant region or by an increase in the number of emitters.

67   This is often overlooked in the literature. With the market form of perfect competition assumed here, the permit price depends on the innovation behavior of the totality of emitters, but not on that of an individual emitter.

the regional target has been achieved. Additional emission abatement is uninteresting for firms because no takers are available for the emission credits it would give them. If instead demand is stabilized by tightening the emission standard and/or by economic growth, then the "production" of emission credits through environmental protection is a rewarding business for firms. This is what the concept of emission permits in all its variants lives on. For the tightening of emission thresholds mentioned here, however, in the pragmatic implementation of the permit idea in the form of controlled emissions trading (cap and trade) in the United States, the following problem arises: the reference level of emissions, starting from which the emission reduction aimed at by exchange transactions is calculated, is defined by a path over time of governmentally sought emission reductions in the direction of particular target figures. This time path cannot however be regarded as autonomous (i.e., independent of the nature and extent of the transfer transactions). The extent of the "reasonable further progress" that this time path complies with instead also depends on technological change induced by the transfer transactions. (To be precise, even the level of realistic targets itself or the date they can be achieved by depends on this change.) Here strategic problems now arise for each individual firm. If an environment-saving innovation that sets emission rights free is possible at some particular point in operations, this will initially look like an attractive thing to do because the firm might be able to sell the rights to an expanding or new company in the same region. However, the potentially innovative firm has to ask itself whether its own innovation may not change the regulatory authorities' view of "reasonable progress" in emission figures. That would then lead to a speeding of the pace at which all firms would have to cut their emissions. This feedback, unpleasant for the innovative firm, between its own emission-cutting activities and the emission reference level by which the authorities measure these activities, also might tempt the company into refraining from the innovation.[68] The dilemma, hardly completely soluble, with determining a time line for tightening up emission thresholds lies in the point that, on the one hand, it cannot take individual successes in innovation as a criterion (because that would discourage efforts at such successes), whereas, on the other hand, it cannot be independent of these successes (because otherwise either unmeetable reduction requirements would be imposed on firms or their capacity to cut emissions would be understimulated).

A few major aspects of the dynamic incentive effects of environmental policy instruments just explained verbally are depicted in Figure 19.[69] The point of Figure 19 is to compare the profit situation of an emitting firm (1) with two alternative

68 The incentive structure looks different in the (unlikely) case where the firm – a point addressed previously in connection with command and control – pursues a "combative" innovation policy. The importance of the strategy of "raising rivals' cost with environmental policy" (a variant of the popular game "Beggar my Neighbour") in the international context is discussed in Körber (2000).

69 We confine ourselves to a simple illustrative presentation. A more exact analysis comes in chapter E of part four of this book. See also Requate (2005a, b).

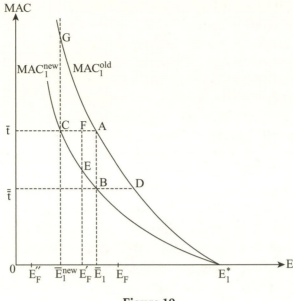

Figure 19

environmental technologies and their various environmental policy instruments.[70] $MAC_1{}^{old}$ ($MAC_1{}^{new}$) shows the firm's marginal abatement costs before (after) introducing the advance in environmental technology. The profit enhancement coming from introduction of the superior technology is taken as an indicator of the incentive for implementing the technology. We accordingly attribute the biggest innovatory impetus to the instrument that brings about the biggest difference in profit between the old and the new technology. Of course, in the firm's profitability calculation, its costs have to be deducted from the proceeds of the technical advance. Because these costs are equal for the instruments, they are irrelevant for distinguishing among the instruments and are ignored. Comparison between the dynamic incentive effects of instruments can be done effectively only if instruments for reaching the same goal are being analyzed.

In the static context, the requirement that the instruments should be aimed at the same objective needs no further elucidation. Things are different, however, in the context discussed here of variable abatement cost functions. We present three alternative concepts of target equivalence, discuss the implications of each for the dynamic incentive effect of alternative environmental policy instruments, and finally evaluate their environmental policy significance.

Target Equivalence Concept (a). It would seem obvious to treat the instruments as equivalent if, prior to the technical change, employing each of them would

---

70   Let emitter 1 again be one of many emitters (subject to competitive conditions). The situation of other emitters is not shown in Figure 19, for simplicity's sake. Figure 19 can also, by analogy with the previous statements, be interpreted as showing an emitting industry in a competitive economy.

reach the same emission target $\overline{E}_1$. In interpreting Figure 19, we accordingly assume that the firm considered must in the command and control case meet emission target $\overline{E}_1$ to comply with the governmental regulation. In the case of an emissions tax the firm is assumed to be subject to a tax rate $\overline{t}$. In the case of a permit policy the firm is assumed to participate in a market with a permit price of $\overline{z}\ (=\overline{t})$. If under *command and control*, the firm moves from the old technology to the new one, then it will save abatement costs represented in Figure 19 by the area E_1^*AB. With an *emissions tax*, the firm would save the same amount if it continued to emit $\overline{E}_1$. Under the new technological conditions, however, it is most favorable for it to cut its emission below $\overline{E}_1$ to $\overline{E}_1^{new}$ because the new marginal abatement cost in this area is below the tax rate. Accordingly, to this saving, we must further add the tax saving (less the costs of the additional emission abatement) represented in Figure 19 as the area ABC. Altogether, then, there is an "incentive area" E_1^*AC. The incentive to move from the old technology to the new one is thus greater with the emissions tax than with the corresponding imposed requirement.[71] However, the previous statements apply only if the emissions tax rate is not lowered following the improvement in environmental technology.[72]

Target Equivalence Concept (b). One might take the tax equivalent to an imposed requirement $\overline{E}_1$ to be, instead of the tax $\overline{t}$ looked at previously that leads to standard $\overline{E}_1$ *before* the technological adjustment, a tax rate $\overline{\overline{t}}$ that brings about $\overline{E}_1$ *after* the innovation. It is also important with this different definition that on the condition assumed here of many emitters of E, a single emitting firm cannot influence the tax rate by its innovation decision. If we regard the lower tax rate $\overline{\overline{t}}$ as equivalent to an imposed requirement of $\overline{E}_1$, then the situation of the representative firm (1) between the old and new technology has to be compared at the given tax rate $\overline{\overline{t}}$. This comparison shows, on the basis of Figure 19, that the incentive to innovation with the tax rate at rate $\overline{\overline{t}}$ is less than that with the imposed requirement for $\overline{E}_1$. For the innovation savings from the imposed requirement, amounting to E_1^*AB, correspond to savings of only E_1^*BD for $\overline{\overline{t}}$.[73]

Target Equivalence Concept (c). Previously, we measured the target equivalence of environmental policy instruments according to whether they reach the same emission level (a) before or (b) after introduction of the technological advance. The third way of regarding environmental policy instruments as

---

71 The dynamic incentive effect of *permits* can be described analogously to that for the emissions tax.

72 For the permit policy, it would have to be assumed correspondingly that the permit rate is kept constant (e.g., by open market operations). There, then, repeated government intervention is necessary, whereas with the tax an automatism has been set up.

73 For permits, we already pointed out previously that *ceteris paribus* progress in environmental technology automatically leads to price falls that weaken the dynamic incentive effects of the instruments.

equivalent in the context of their dynamic incentive effect is if they lead to the same innovation equilibrium before *and* after the innovation. Of course, there does not exist an emission level set by an imposed requirement that is in this sense equivalent to a single emissions tax rate because the same emissions tax rate will lead to different emission equilibriums if technology changes. In the sense of our equivalence definition (c), then, the consequence of imposed emission requirements (graded over time) is always equivalent to some emissions tax rate.[74] We can use Figure 19 to illustrate the simplest case of this sort of grading of emission requirements, namely, a two-stage requirement: with the old technology, emission requirement $\overline{E}_1$ applies, but when the new technological possibilities become known, requirement $\overline{E}_1^{new}$ does.[75] Thus, the emission quantities agree before and after introduction of the technical advance under both environmental policy instruments. As in concept (b), the dynamic incentive effect of the imposed requirement (here in the sense of a graded requirement) is higher than that of the tax. The tax-specific incentive area explained previously is E_1^*AC, in comparison with the incentive area E_1^*GC for the graded imposed requirement.

How are things, now, with the environmental policy relevance of our three concepts of target equivalence? In answering this question, we pay particular attention to the (rather unconventional) equivalence concept (c).

We must point out that the two-stage model in Figure 19 is favorably "tailored" for the dynamic incentive effect of command and control. After introduction of its second stage, the world in the model comes to an end, but the real one does not. The dynamic incentive of an emissions tax continues in reality, even after the new technology is introduced. To not break the bounds of a target-equivalent pattern of command and control and taxation within the meaning of concept (c), we should really have to imagine an unending sequence of imposed requirements. If, however, the sequence terminates, in the last period the incentive structure seamlessly turns into the position described under concept (a). This highlights the relevance of concept (a). In a context with an open time horizon, accordingly, equivalence interpretation (c) requires environmental policy to be impressively mobile. A further aspect of the environmental policy relevance of the alternative interpretations of the concept of target equivalence of environmental policy instruments can perhaps best be grasped if we stylize the process of progress in environmental technology into three stages:

1) Invention (birth of a new idea)
2) Innovation (incorporation of the new idea into a practical context)
3) Dissemination (spread of the innovation in procedural practice)

The construct of graded command and control employed in concept (c) seems to have its greatest environmental policy relevance in the area of dissemination. Here

---

74   Or, analogously, a consequence of quantities of emission rights issued as permits.
75   Analogously, in the two stages, differing quantities of permits would be issued.

a new process in environmental technology becomes known, and the point is now to promote its further dissemination in production. In this situation, it is conceivable for the authority putting forward the environmental policy to announce that on a particular date it wants to introduce more ambitious requirements that will take account of the better emission abatement possibilities of the new process.[76] For with dissemination problems, the environmental authority has a knowledge (or at least an idea) of the technical possibilities of the new process and the costs associated with applying it. It can accordingly formulate an adequate standard for the new process.

However, the conditions for the graded command and control arrangement pictured in concept (c) are as bad as possible in the area of invention. By definition, before its invention, the process is unknown in terms of its effectiveness and cost. Formulating a realistic standard (adequate to the technical and economic possibilities after invention and development as a practical application) is accordingly impossible. To stimulate inventions, in contrast, an emissions tax as in concept (a) is a realistic concept with comparatively favorable incentive properties. It follows that command and control has its forte in terms of dynamic incentive effect in the area of dissemination (and innovation, in a more limited way), whereas taxation has it in the area of invention (and innovation, in a more limited way). In other words, taxation seems (comparatively) more effective the stronger the element of the unknown in the problem to be solved is.

However, the importance of the criterion of the dynamic incentive effect is less the greater the certainty of knowledge of the technical and economic properties of new processes is (in particular, the governmental authority's knowledge). Once the new process is known, the authority can simply order its application or compliance with a threshold value oriented to this process.[77] If transgressions are appropriately punished, then considerations of the incentive effects for the firms to make technical changes are in any case irrelevant. The authority pursuing the environmental policy is dependent on mobilizing emitters' inventive spirit just where the superior processes are as yet unknown (or very far from practical application). This lessens the environmental policy interest of the criterion of dynamic incentive effect in this area. One might even assert the view that the possibility discussed previously of bringing about tighter threshold values through "dynamic command and control" has not been given the right heading under the criterion discussed here of dynamic incentive effect. The point with this criterion is to see how far environmental policy instruments are capable of putting firms' *own interest* at the service of environmental policy progress. This is just what does not happen with the previously discussed graded command and control policy arrangement (regarding

---

76 Let us note in passing that the reference to the known new process will facilitate the political (and perhaps also legal) implementability of the tighter regulations.

77 If environmental policy is ultimately concerned with achieving tighter environmental policy objectives, then in any case permits would be preferable to command and control from an economic viewpoint. They achieve the lower emission level equally reliably (cf. section C.III), but at lower cost (see section C.I).

the tightening of thresholds[78]). Here progress in environmental technology is not generated by an intrinsic dynamic but ordered by government (on the assumption that the new processes are known to the environmental authorities).

In conclusion, we may state the following: a generally valid ranking of environmental policy instruments by their dynamic incentive effects is not possible. However, taxation (and, with limitations, permits) is superior to command and control precisely in the areas where the greatest environmental policy importance attaches to dynamic incentive effect.

Figure 19, already heavily exploited, further enables us to clarify the dynamic incentive effect of tax-exempt levels. For this, let us again look at the case considered initially of a tax rate set at $\bar{t}$ irrespective of the state of environmental technology. Here three classes of tax-exempt amounts can be distinguished in Figure 19:

a) If the emission quantity exempt from tax is above the equilibrium level $\overline{E}_1$ that the firm would have reached with the old technology, say, at E_F, then the dynamic incentive effect of the tax is low. For all that the firm saves by moving to the new technology is the emission abatement cost difference for abating $E_1^* - E_F$ units of emission. Because of the exempt amount, the new technology will not lead to abatement activities, with corresponding tax savings, going further than E_F.

b) If the emission level exempt from tax is between $\overline{E}_1$ and the equilibrium level $\bar{E}_1{}^{new}$ that the firm would have achieved with the new technology without the exempt amount, say, at E'_F, then the dynamic incentive effect is stronger than in the first case but weaker than in the case without a tax-exempt amount. With E'_F, the firm will, using the old technology, reduce its emissions down to $\overline{E}_1$, but with the new technology down to E'_F. On top of the abatement cost saving from the new technology amounting to E_1^*AB, there will also be a tax saving (less the additional abatement expenditure) of *ABEF*.

c) If the tax-exempt emission quantity is below $\bar{E}_1{}^{new}$, say, at E''_F, then initially there will be the same dynamic incentive effect E_1^*AC as in the case without an exemption amount, made up of abatement cost saving plus tax saving. However, the two-stage construction of Figure 19 distorts the picture: technical progress does not consist in a single transition from an "old" to a "new" process but is a continuous process. Over time, this process can mean that the "new" marginal abatement cost curve in each case moves so much leftward that its equilibrium emission level $\overline{E}_1$ lies on the left of E''_F. The process of technological progress would then ultimately have made an "unobjectionable" tax-exempt amount of class (c) into an "objectionable" example of class (b). The wandering of the tax-exempt amount may in course of time even go as far as class (a).

---

78 A firm's own interest under command and control in new processes that reach a given threshold value cheaper has already been evaluated previously.

III. Ecological Precision

1. *Exogenous Emission Standards*

By the ecological precision of an environmental policy instrument, we mean its capacity to achieve a set emission standard for a region precisely.[79]

On this definition, a *command and control policy* should at first sight be rated favorably. Because the emission level is equally the objective and the point of impact of a governmental action, every emission standard aimed at ought to be achievable with high precision. Particular importance attaches to this feature in situations of environmental crisis and with highly hazardous pollutants. If in the case of the latter the point is not merely to cut emissions while having regard to economic aspects, but to prevent the occurrence of damage absolutely, then a ban on emission or production is the suitable instrument of environmental policy. Of course, there are problems here with measuring and monitoring emissions, which are indispensable for disclosing transgressions of the governmental requirements.[80] But these arise with the other instruments anyway.

However, the degree of ecological precision meant here can be reached only if the requirements are formulated as absolute emission ceilings for firms, as is assumed by the "archetypal" requirement discussed primarily. If we instead merely limit the "burden" (pollution intensity per basic unit; e.g., x mg SO_2 per m^3 of exhaust gas or x mg lead per liter of petrol), then the total emission level achieved will depend on the duration and intensity of operation of the licensed installations. With economic growth, moreover, the number of installations emitting the pollutant in question may increase. Because these determinants of emissions quantity are not checked by the concentration-oriented command and control policy, the emission standard ultimately achieved also lies out with full control by this policy. To achieve a constant emission level in the region in question, the limits formulated in terms of the burden must always be adjusted to fluctuations in the level of economic activity – a hardly feasible requirement.

The ecological precision of the *taxation solution* suffers from the fact that the emission levels aimed at are not the immediate object of the policy, but are to be reached indirectly through the polluters' adaptations to the prices of emissions set by the government. If the taxation solution aims at a particular emissions outcome in a region, then there must be some idea of the adjustment behavior of the firms affected by the levy. Because, as described previously, a profit-maximizing polluter will endeavor to adjust his marginal abatement cost to the tax rate, a knowledge of the polluter's abatement costs is necessary for the targeted setting of the emissions tax rate.

Strictly speaking, the marginal abatement cost curve, as shown in Figure 18c, would have to be known for the totality of all emitters of the relevant pollutant in the

79   The distribution of the emissions inside the region is not taken into account here.

80   Economic aspects of duties on firms to disclose information and monitor emissions have been paid much attention to in the literature. See the references in footnote 12.

region in question. The marginal abatement cost curve in Figure 18 comes from the horizontal aggregation of the individual marginal abatement cost curves. Of course, the information prerequisites for this kind of procedure are unrealistically high. Pragmatically, one might proceed by constructing an image of a few representative polluter firms on the basis of published information from them about production, size, age, etc., and, on that basis, make a simulated calculation for the totality of polluters. Here errors in estimation are inevitable. If the marginal abatement costs are lower than presumed, then the emission target will be overfulfilled. If they are higher, then it will not be reached. In both cases, the ecological precision is inadequate, although in the first case the ecological effectiveness is higher than planned. However much ecologists might welcome this, it will nonetheless annoy the firms concerned because reaching the exact target would have meant lower costs.

If government wants to correct the gap between the desired and the actual position, it will have to alter the tax rate accordingly. Of course, even the corrected assumptions about actual marginal abatement costs might be wrong, making a multiple trial-and-error process necessary. Into the bargain, the aggregated marginal abatement costs are affected by growth by the polluter firms, entry of new ones, and changes in manufacturing and environmental technologies. If, for instance, new emitters come into the region, the marginal abatement cost curve in Figure 18c will shift rightward. If the original tax rate $\bar{t}$ met the target and remains valid, the emission limit will now be exceeded. In addition, inflation in an economy changes the relative prices for emitting and eliminating emissions. If the prices for preventing emissions rise over time, the tax burden at a constant tax rate will become increasingly smaller in relation to the marginal abatement cost, so that the abatement incentive from the tax will steadily decline. To maintain a constant emission standard, the tax rate would have to be continually adjusted to the foregoing changes (or its net effect on total emissions would). Because setting tax rates is a difficult and time-consuming political process, the call for continual revision seems unrealistic.[81] The polluters would point out that continual adaptation to changing tax rates is costly. Adjusting to a particular tax rate has as a consequence technical decisions that cannot necessarily be changed readily.

A *tradable permit solution* avoids the ecological uncertainties just mentioned.[82] Because the number of permits issued is limited to the target emission value, this can

81   However, the problems of altering tax rates might be somewhat mitigated by skillful institutional arrangements. Thus, it has been suggested that environmental laws should merely lay down the environmental targets aimed at. The tax rates could be adjusted by subordinate authorities in accordance with a target performance comparison of environmental quality. This would also be a way to avoid time-consuming statutory amendments aimed at changing the tax rate. A still farther-reaching idea is to set up an institution in the environmental sphere that can change tax rates the way the Central Bank does with discount rates.

82   This advantage, in comparison with emission taxes in terms of certainty of ecological effect, is, however, bought at the cost of uncertainty in the cost effects. Although an upper limit to marginal abatement costs is known *a priori* with a tax (at which polluters will switch to paying the tax), the level of marginal abatement costs emerges only at equilibrium for emission permits.

never (legally) be exceeded.[83] This is an important fact for the environmental policy debate: in it, emission permits and the pragmatic forms of controlled environmental trading are often rejected because it is erroneously assumed that these market-oriented instruments will leave the level of permissible emissions up to "the laissez-faire of the market." This is often imagined as a sort of "trading in indulgences," in which well-off emitters buy from citizens their right to a clean environment. Properly understood, however, a permit system sets an emission ceiling just as much as the "prototype" of the command and control requirement allotted priority here does. It is only a market economy matter to the extent that the distribution of the available quota of emission permits is decided in decentralized fashion through the mediation of market prices.

In contrast with an emissions tax, the government here need not know the marginal abatement cost in order to exactly reach the target. The running of plants at different capacities, changes in regional economic structures, inflation, etc., do not in the permit solution have the consequence of adversely affecting ecological precision. The effects of these happenings are reflected in the permit price but not in the emission level: if, say, demand for the right to emit rises in the region because new pollution producers have come in, this development cannot lead to an increase in emissions because the number of emission permits is set exogenously. Instead, the additional demand for emissions will result in a rise in demand for the permits. The resulting increase in the price of emission rights will depress the emissions of established firms and thus create room for emissions by new ones within the emissions framework set by the environmental policy target. (Of course, the rising permit price will mean that the emission demand by the new firms will always end up smaller than it would have been at the lower price.)

One central distinction between an emissions tax policy and a tradable permit policy is, then, that the latter frees the environmental authority from the burden of having to repeatedly take the environmental policy initiative again following changes occurring in the economy.[84] The statement made previously that tradable permits will automatically guide the scarce resource of the environment toward its most urgent use (as evaluated by the market) thus remains true even if the relative urgencies change over time.

Even if, as explained previously, with a tradable permit arrangement emissions cannot rise above the government-set regional threshold, the introduction of permits may nonetheless lead to a rise in *actual* emissions: if the quantity of emission rights allotted to firms is measured not on the basis of the pollutant quantities they actually emit but of the emission quantities allowed them under the regulations in force, the transferability of emission rights may lead to the mobilization of emission

---

83 It could at most be undershot, if citizens buy permits and do not use them, so as to improve the emission position. Cf. what was said in section B.III.

84 The allocation of automaticity and intervention between permits and tax is thus a mirror image in terms of ecological precision of the one discussed previously for dynamic incentive effect. Cf. footnote 72.

reserves. If firms own emission rights that they are not actually using, then these dormant rights will be awakened to new life if they are sold to firms that will use them. Of course, it cannot be ruled out that the firms offering the rights might have used them themselves again at a later date, an option they lose by selling them. If the possibility of activating emissions is seen as ecologically dangerous, the set emission target could be lowered accordingly.

One particular problem with ecological precision arises for all instruments if the exogenously set emission target is to be adjusted to seasonal or even daily fluctuations in the environment's assimilative capacity. One interesting suggestion for how this could be accomplished with a permit policy links up with water rights arrangements already employed by the U.S. state of Colorado. The basic idea is not for all tradable emission permits to contain an absolute right to emit, but for there to be various permit classes allowing emissions at differing probabilities. The probabilities are associated with expectations as to the state of the relevant environmental medium (flow velocity, temperature, etc.). Firms absolutely dependent on emissions at a particular point in time will assemble a portfolio of permits with a higher proportion of guaranteed emission rights than will firms with more flexible emission needs. The latter might tend more to take up classes of (cheaper) emission rights with a lower probability of utilization. This system might also be transferred to the area of private car transport. Instead of regulating car volume on smog days according to arbitrary criteria (allowing driving only by vehicles with even or uneven numbers), permission to drive would be tied to the urgency of the driving need as evidenced by the permit market. The efficiency properties of the permit solution would be conserved in this system. Moreover, the flexibility of emission abatement technologies would be promoted by such a system.

2. Time Needed for Adjustment

It is important in assessing an environmental policy instrument to know not only whether a set emission target can be achieved by it, but also how quickly it will reach the goal. If adjustment time is incorporated into consideration of the ecological properties of instruments, then a problem arises for command and control. Out of concern for technical or business difficulties, the requirements as to the abatement technology state of the art are frequently couched less ambitiously (or less consistently applied) for old plants than for new ones. This produces an incentive for plant operators to increase the remaining useful lifetime or the intensity of utilization of old, emission-intensive plants. Command and control thus leads to delay in the environment-protecting effects it induces. The advantage of a command and control policy often claimed in the literature, that it works more quickly, thus seems doubtful in light of this argumentation.

Price incentives like those resulting from taxes and tradable permits in contrast lower the attractiveness of operating old emission-intensive plants. A shift to lower-emission new installations is here accelerated on the basis of purely microeconomic profitability considerations. However, with a policy of controlled environmental trading, the advantage of a rapid shift to lower emission plants through price incentives may be threatened by unskilled handling on the part of the environmental authorities. If firms expect that the emission rights credited in an environmental bank are more likely to fall victim to devaluations or even confiscation by the governmental environmental authority than rights embodied in old plants, then this asymmetrical risk structure will diminish the attractiveness of an early changeover involving the environmental bank. A permit policy is sometimes even suspected of possibly working "too fast": if firms are forced to rigidly restrict permission to emit to the nominal value of the permits received before they can adjust technically to the new requirements, then this will in the short term lead to high abatement costs and thus high permit prices. The speed with which permits operate may be steadily lowered by modifying the concept, should this happen to seem desirable. If friction in the manner described becomes a serious fear, it might be averted by, say, setting the total emission quota not immediately, but only in stages at lower levels than the emission quantities existing at the time permits are introduced.

3. End-Means Interdependence

In the previous discussion, we always assume *exogenously determined* regional emission standards as the target in environmental policy. This was certainly useful in a first approximation. On further consideration, however, one must ask whether the setting of the emission target can be discussed independently of the properties of the means provided for reaching it.

It might be argued that precisely because of the unfavorable cost effectiveness of a command and control policy, it is hardly possible to impose ambitious targets against the industry affected by the environmental policy (including the employees). After all, emission targets are arrived at not mainly on the basis of purely ecological considerations, but on the basis of attempts to reach a balance between ecological concerns and the burdens on the economy. Of course, this balance has to do not with purely scientific considerations (possible here in any case only to a limited extent), but with a political process in which organized interests exert their influence. If this connection between ecological effectiveness and cost effectiveness is included in the consideration, the ecological attractiveness of a command and control policy looks much less. In contrast, more cost-effective policy variants also look more ecologically promising because the gains in cost effectiveness can be split between business and the environment.[85] They may thus defuse the oft-cited "conflict between economics and ecology."

Analysis of the connections between emission standard and the type of environmental policy instrument chosen to achieve it cannot be confined to the programmatic level. At the level of implementation, too, there are important differences in

---

85 In the United States, the ecologically unsatisfactory outcomes of traditional command and control policy *and* its growth-inhibiting effects on the economy motivated the EPA to look for instruments closer to the market.

this connection between the individual instruments. Because a command and control policy cannot take account of the manifold individual differences in conditions among polluters, the lower authorities that have to apply the policy on the spot have to be allowed discretion. This opens up the possibility for polluters to enter into negotiations with the implementing authorities on achieving the emission targets, which for the previously stated reasons are not convincing. By pointing to resulting economic problems (with alleged consequences for jobs), exceptional permissions, postponements, etc., are arrived at. The prospect of having to spend years in court fighting arguments for maintaining the status quo can greatly depress the enthusiasm of authorities for recourse to retrospective orders for old plants.[86]

Regarding its technical possibilities and their economic effects, the firm has an information advantage over the authority. Big firms are better able here to take advantage of the room for maneuver in the implementation stage than small and midsize ones. The competition policy consequences are obvious. The ecological effectiveness of a cost-ineffective environmental policy is thus limited by the problems arising not only at the stage of defining targets, but also in the implementation stage.

With an emission taxation or tradable permit policy, in contrast, the adaptive flexibility for polluters is so great that the lower authorities need not be equipped with the same flexibility in relation to the requirements set. In contrast with command and control, a uniform pattern for the instrument, advisable on administrative cost grounds, does not with taxation lead to uniform outcomes that then have to be differentiated at a lower level.

4. Emission Reduction with No Fixed Target Value

Part of considering the ecological effectiveness of environmental policy instruments is also the analysis of the dynamic incentive effects, done previously from an economic viewpoint. For many pollutants, precautionary considerations advocate not being content with a preset emission ceiling but attempting, after it is reached, to bring about an ongoing process of emission reduction. This process is to be pushed forward as fast and as far as technically and economically possible. As the discussion in section C.II shows, the development of technical and economic possibilities of cutting emissions can in no way be seen as independent of the nature of the environmental policy instruments chosen. Instead, different instruments produce different incentives to speed up or slow down progress in environmental technology. Seen this way, the instruments with the highest economic incentive effect in terms of dynamic adaptation are at the same time the ecologically most effective ones.

5. Conservation of "Natural" Falls in Emissions

One particular aspect of the ecological effectiveness of environmental policy instruments emerges if attention is directed to cases where the emission level of individual

---

86 Because of their postponement effect, such court proceedings may be profitable for firms, even if they ultimately lose.

installations, individual firms, or whole regions falls in the course of economic development, without this decline having been brought about by environmental regulations. For instance, a firm may shut down on profitability considerations a permitted plant it had been operating and not replace it – or it may replace it with one with a lower emission intensity. Or a firm may decide for purely economic reasons to shift operations or its location to a more attractive region.

In these cases, command and control and emission taxation start off an automatism that leads to a lowering of emissions below the set standard. Government bodies can conserve this effect by, in the case of command and control, not allowing new entitlements to expand emissions, or by providing for a more rigid level of technology for new installations than old ones. In the case of a taxation policy, they can refrain from lowering the emissions tax rate.

This automatism is absent from the tradable permit solution. For instance, if a firm that would in any case shut down a plant or shift location manages to sell its emission rights to another firm, the old emission level is conserved. The dirtier the old plant, the greater the gain for the firm. Emission potential that was dying out is thus filled with new life through permit trading. The same criticism applies to the policy of controlled environmental trading.[87] If in a region overall economic activity falls, this will with taxation or command and control *ceteris paribus* lead to a falling emission level. With a tradable permit solution, instead, the lower demand for permits will be reflected in a fall in their price. If this development is seen as lasting, an incentive will arise to move to business that is harder on the environment.

With these arguments, it must not be overlooked that with a permit arrangement, the emission standard can be tightened. There is an important difference between the tradable permit solution and a command and control (or taxation) one in the case addressed here of the "natural extinction" of emission sources. It lies in the fact that with a permit policy, the environmental authority has to do something in order to make the extinction ecologically effective, whereas with command and control (or taxation) it merely has to refrain from doing something. In the case of the pure permit solution, the action lies in devaluing or buying up permits, and with a controlled trading policy in tightening the reference level in accordance with the line, mentioned previously, of achievable progress.[88] Nonaction in the case of

---

87 The argument just made plays an important part in connection with emissions trading under the Kyoto Protocol (see part five of this book). In the international political debate, it is pointed out that Russia and other East European states have high emission rights obtained by way of "grandfathering." Because of their "collapsed" economies, these rights would allegedly not, without the possibility of trading, be used for the foreseeable future. If, however, the states concerned sell the rights to ones with flourishing economies, the global emission level will rise. The permits that would have been stored environmentally neutrally in (say) Russian filing cabinets thus, as it were, "go up in smoke" (hot air) elsewhere. Cf., e.g., Böhringer/Moslener/Sturm (2007), Klepper/Peterson (2005).

88 The natural rate of emission reduction because of economically based shutdowns might even be a determinant of the extent of emission reduction in the context of the concept of achievable progress (or the rapidity of devaluation of emission rights). One would, of course, have to base

a command and control or taxation policy would consist of refraining from new licenses or from lowering tax rates.

6. Environmental Policy Covering Several Pollutants

Success in reducing a pollutant targeted by environmental policy offers unalloyed joy only, of course, if the polluters refrain from shifting from regulated pollutants to unregulated ones. Yet, this is a danger that exists whatever instrument is used: for if the use of a particular environmentally harmful production factor is limited (directly or by increasing its price), there is by no means any guarantee that the firms affected will shift to environmentally friendly factors. There may instead be undesirable substitutions of pollutants.[89] No environmental policy instrument can, then, be restricted to regulating a single pollutant. Instead, we need a system of instruments covering a broad range of pollutants. Different types of environmental policy instruments can be very well applied to different pollutants. To avoid evasion of the environmental policy network by the development of new substances, new substances have to be tested for their environmental effects and subsequently included among the targets of environmental policy instruments.[90]

An environmental policy covering several pollutants ought not to confine itself to the interdependencies addressed here between individual pollutants in the production process. Instead, connections arising in the environmental medium concerned also have to be taken into account. Allowing for synergisms is known, however, to cause problems in both science and economics.[91] As well as the pollutants, environmental policy instruments must also cover the environmental media. Otherwise, there is a danger that polluters may evade the regulations by moving to a different medium (e.g., shifting from air to water pollution).

7. Immission-Oriented Environmental Policy

In the discussion so far, the suitability of various environmental policy instruments was always discussed on the example of an emission-oriented environmental policy. The analysis could also be done on the basis of an immission-oriented policy. If the targets the instruments are to reach are formulated in immission terms, then their design becomes more complicated for all instruments.

Because immissions can only be affected indirectly through emissions,[92] information must be available on the diffusion of the pollutants. The diffusion

oneself here on an average shutdown rate. Rates based on individual enterprises would discourage operators from shutting down old plants – an ecologically undesirable incentive effect.

89   For instance, the regulations for car exhaust issued in the early 1970s were aimed particularly at carbon monoxide and hydrocarbons. The car industry adapted to these regulations by developing motors that produced less of those substances but more nitrogen oxides.

90   When new substances are introduced, moreover, the application of liability law is in principle able to make polluters be cautious. See chapter B in part two of this book for an economic analysis of environmental liability law.

91   Cf. chapter A in part four.

92   We here ignore the possibility of affecting them through chimney height.

coefficients (immission quantity at point of reception i per emission unit at point of emission j) will depend on many determinants, some of which fluctuate over time. The information on diffusion processes has to be used to reach differentiated regulation for various sources of one and the same pollutant. For instance, an immission-related pollutant tax has to have different emissions tax rates applying to emissions of the same pollutant. This is so because preset immission targets can be efficiently reached only if locations with lower immission intensity of the emissions are subject to lower tax rates than those with less favorable diffusion conditions. Similarly, a command and control regulation of emissions of the same type would have to differentiate the severity of regulations according to immission intensity in order not to add yet another source of inefficiency to the ones already mentioned. With a tradable permit solution, an immission-oriented policy would require every emitter to buy immission rights in line with the diffusion coefficients applying to him in all the regions to which his pollutants may spread.[93]

A system with immission certificates might even solve the oft-discussed problem in the literature of severe local accumulations of environmental burden ("hot spots").[94] Moreover, pragmatic variants of tradable permits (i.e., ones with lower informational and administrative costs) to alleviate hot spot problems are conceivable. For instance, it might be laid down that although emission permits could be transferred within the endangered regions and out of them, they cannot be transferred in. This asymmetrical transferability might in the long run even mitigate hot spot problems that the current command and control policy has not been able to prevent. Another possibility for preventing local accumulations of emissions as a consequence of permit transactions might be to supplement the emission permits policy by a system of immission thresholds. In this sort of system, complying with the immission thresholds in force would be a subsidiary condition for permit trading.[95]

Although, then, account can be taken of the regional distribution of emissions with a permit policy, one thing still has to be clearly stressed: just because a tradable permit policy is more gentle for a plant with high abatement costs in terms of emissions abatement than a corresponding command and control policy (whereas a plant with a more favorable cost profile is more heavily burdened), the emission distribution arising in a permit policy will not be better all over the area than in a command and control policy. The total emission quantity produced may be smaller

93 For more on this, see, e.g., various work reprinted in Tietenberg (2001, vol. II, part 3, sections 15–19).

94 It is somewhat remarkable that "hot spots" have appeared in the debate in the literature (almost) exclusively as a problem for tradable permit policy. However, emissions taxes are just as subject to this problem. With command and control, too, as we know, there are, at least in practical application, problems with protecting the neighborhood.

95 For every restriction on the transferability of permits ordered in the interest of avoiding hot spots (or for other reasons), a "price" has to be paid in the form of a reduction in the cost-effectiveness advantages of permits over command and control. Here, too, it still remains true that "there ain't no such thing as a free lunch."

with a permit policy (because of the gain in cost effectiveness) than with command and control, but at various individual points there may nonetheless be a higher burden.

8. Tradable Emission Permits: Gratification of Environmental Policy Abstinence?

It is sometimes argued in the literature that the high ecological precision of the tradable permit policy is bought at the cost of troubling inequality of treatment among polluters: if firms are allowed the emissions they have caused to date as tradable permits (or even only a proportion of them), then (*ceteris paribus*) a firm receives the more emission rights the less seriously it has taken environmental protection hitherto. Quite otherwise than should be the case for reward systems, thus, it is the sloppy performers that are rewarded and the assiduous that are "punished." One simple way of opposing these difficulties, however, is for the relevant firms to be certified for only a particular proportion of the *allowed* emission load under the current command and control arrangement. Perhaps, however, what is feared from regulation on the basis of allowed emissions is "mobilization of pollutant reserves." That might occur if particular firms had already abated more emissions than prescribed. If they are given permits for allowed emissions, then already "dead" emissions amounting (as a maximum) to the difference between these firms' allowed and actual emissions might be revived again through the sale of emission rights ("Second Life"!).

Yet, even on the basis of *actual* emissions, a solution to the "reward problem" is possible. Here the following calculation pattern might be employed: calculating the permissible total emission value on the basis of actual emission. (With, as in the first proposal, a deduction made.) Each emitter would then, however, receive not its current actual emission (in part) in permits, but the share that the emission quantity allowed it under the current command and control policy constitutes of the total allowed emission quantity. This proposal would *inter alia* solve the "rewarding of the laggards" problem, although the total tolerable emission quantity would be derived from the actual emissions – so that no mobilization of pollutant reserves could occur.

Exercises

Exercise 3.1
Describe the main difference between the internalization and the standard-oriented approach in environmental policy.

Exercise 3.2
Explain the expressions weak and strong polluter pays principle.

Exercise 3.3
Standard-oriented instruments can be evaluated according to several criteria. Now it's your turn to be creative: how would you define the criteria static cost effectiveness

and dynamic cost effectiveness? Explain the relation between these criteria and the criteria cost effectiveness and dynamic incentive effect as they are used in part three of this book.

Exercise 3.4

In part three of this book, standard-oriented instruments are evaluated according to the criteria cost effectiveness, dynamic incentive effect, and ecological precision. List some other possible evaluation criteria.

Exercise 3.5

Apply the criterion of ecological precision: what is the main difference between command and control as well as transferable discharge permits and emission taxes?

Exercise 3.6

Apply the criterion of cost effectiveness: what is the main difference between emission taxes as well as transferable discharge permits and command and control?

Exercise 3.7

Discuss the following statement: "Assume that the marginal abatement cost functions of all firms are identical and the regulator is aware of just that. Then, each of the standard-oriented instruments emission tax, command and control, and permit trading fulfills the criteria of cost effectiveness and ecological precision."

Exercise 3.8

Discuss the following statement: "The higher the number of market participants in a permit market, the higher are the transaction costs of the market system. Hence, the lower the number of involved polluters, the higher is the degree of cost effectiveness of a permit market."

Exercise 3.9

Consider an economy with two firms ($i \in \{1, 2\}$). Let $E_i \in [0, 50]$ denote the emission level of firm i. Marginal abatement cost of firm 1 are given by $MAC_1(E_1) = 25 - \frac{1}{2}E_1$ and of firm 2 by $MAC_2(E_2) = 10 - \frac{1}{5}E_2$.

a) Determine the aggregate marginal abatement cost function $MAC_\Sigma(E)$, and plot the individual and aggregate marginal cost functions in a diagram.

b) To induce the aspired aggregate emission level $\overline{E} = 30$, the government considers assigning the emission ceiling $\overline{E}_i = \overline{E}/2$ to each firm. Determine the firm-specific and aggregate abatement cost in this command and control scenario.

c) To induce $\overline{E}$, the government considers introducing an emission tax, alternatively. Determine the appropriate tax level and the corresponding firm-specific and aggregate abatement cost.

d) As a third variant, the government considers the introduction of a transferable discharge permit system, where each firm receives the amount of $\overline{E}_i = \overline{E}/2$ permits free of charge. Assume that the equilibrium permit price is given by

$MAC_\Sigma(\overline{E})$. Determine the corresponding firm-specific and aggregate abatement cost.

e) Rank the three instruments described in items (b), (c), and (d) from the social point of view and from the individual point of view of the firms 1 and 2.

Exercise 3.10

Consider the economy of exercise 3.9. Now assume that the government neither knows the firm-specific nor the aggregate marginal abatement cost functions but estimates firm-specific abatement cost to be given by $MAC_i^{est}(E_i) = 20 - \frac{2}{5}E_i$.

a) Determine the estimated aggregate marginal abatement cost function, and plot the estimated marginal cost functions in a diagram.

b) Assume that the aspired aggregate emission level is still given by $\overline{E} = 30$. Discuss the effect of the government's estimation error on the policy instruments command and control, emission tax and permit market, corresponding firm-specific and aggregate abatement cost, and the ranking derived in exercise 3.9.e.

Part Four

Extensions of the Basic Environmental Economics Model

A. Environmental Policy with Pollutant Interactions

I. Pollutant Interactions and Environmental Policy Target Setting

In our economic analysis of the use of environmental policy instruments, we assume in part three that the object of environmental policy was to reduce the quantity of an individual pollutant emitted (or several pollutants that can be considered separately from each other). Under this condition, various instruments of environmental policy were looked at for their ability to reach the environmental policy target cost effectively.

Considering single pollutants in isolation is primarily advisable because it enables a simplified presentation of the complex problems of the use of environmental policy instruments. In the long run, though, analysis in environmental economics cannot ignore the fact that pollutants interact in manifold ways in the media that comprise the environment. Where such interactions are present, environmental policy goals can no longer be defined and pursued independently for individual pollutants because the hazardousness of each individual pollutant depends on the quantity of other pollutants emitted. The consequences arising from this complication for the employment of environmental policy instruments are considered here.[1]

Pollutant interactions may be of very varied natures. The simplest case is where several pollutants jointly consume the environment's assimilative capacity, while the environmental burden effect of each additional unit of each pollutant remains constant. Here the environmental burden B produced by two pollutants x, y comes out as $B = a_1 x + a_2 y$, where a_1, a_2 (> 0) are constant coefficients of damage capacity. For every given burden level $\overline{B}$, then, the pollutants are substitutable for each other

---

1 We confine the analysis of pollutant reductions to the previously described type of interaction, arising *after* the emission *in the environment*. But pollutants may also be linked *before* emission on the *production* side. This is, however, a whole separate topic, which we do not go into. Cf., e.g., Pethig (2006).

at a constant rate. This simplest type of pollutant interdependence is termed "linear interaction." It is often assumed for the case of water pollution.

Of course, more complicated types of pollutant interaction cannot be ruled out. For instance, it is conceivable that at constant burden additional emission units of one pollutant are compensated for by increasingly large reductions in emissions of other pollutants. Here the rate at which a pollutant can be substituted for another while maintaining the burden level increases. We call this case "concave interaction." In the converse case, the substitution rate between the pollutants falls ("convex interaction"). Finally, mixed forms where the marginal substitution rate alternately increases and decreases are conceivable ("nonconcave (nonconvex) interaction"). It is even possible for various pollutants to interact at constant burden − not substitutively, but in complementary fashion. This case of reciprocal neutralization of pollutants is not addressed here.

We assume that there is an environmental authority wanting to reduce the environmental burden in the region it regulates to a particular level $\overline{B}$. Its object is, thus, to guarantee that the (regional) economy complies with an environmental policy constraint. The burden is assumed to be caused by two competing industries (established in the same region). Here one industry produces pollutant x, and the other pollutant y. Let the burden index B express the pollutant interdependencies between the two substances, and let these be known to the environmental authority. Linear, concave, and nonconcave interactions are considered on a case-by-case basis.[2]

In a traditional environmental economics analysis dealing with the pollutants independently of each other, the environmental policy objective could be described unambiguously by stating a pair of emission limits $(\overline{x}, \overline{y})$. The task of the environmental policy instrument would in this analytical framework be to provide for distribution of the total emission quantity of $\overline{x}$ $(\overline{y})$ over the individual $x−(y−)$ emitters. However, if pollutant interactions are taken into account, then the environmental policy problem becomes more complicated by one dimension because the environmental policy objective can no longer be formulated by stating independent pollution limits. Because the environmental policy objective of keeping to $\overline{B}$ can be attained with arbitrarily many combinations of pollutants x and y, it must be decided which of these combinations is to be aimed at. We assume that the environmental authorities' intentions are good not only toward the environment, but also toward the economy. Let it aim for that pollutant combination x^{**}, y^{**} that complies with the burden restriction $\overline{B}$ at minimum cost.[3]

Simultaneously with the "new" problem of finding x^{**} and y^{**}, the environmental authority must also solve the "old" problem of distributing emission quantity

2　For space reasons, the case of convex interactions is not dealt with separately; rather, it is contained as a special case in the mixed form of nonconcave interactions.

3　Under certain conditions, cost minimization may be attained by reducing the emissions of one of the two polluters to zero. An example of this kind of a *corner solution* is in Section IV. See Endres (1985) for elaboration.

x^{**} (y^{**}) over the individual $x-$ ($y-$) emitters. Because this problem is already covered exhaustively in part three, it is not given further consideration here. The environmental policy instruments we consider that the authority can use to aim for the environmental policy objective are emission taxes and command and control.[4]

We first consider a situation in which the environmental policy burden limit can be described as a linear combination of pollutant sets (x, y).

II. Linear Interaction

If the model authority wants to use an *emission tax* to reach its target, then, by analogy with the traditional case without pollutant interaction, it must estimate the marginal abatement cost function of each polluting industry. It will thus obtain an idea of the emitters' adjustments to various tax rates on emissions of x and y, respectively. As we know, each polluter is expected to respond to an emission tax set at level t by reducing his emissions far enough for his marginal abatement cost to rise to t. The environmental authority will, then, seek to set tax rates t_x, t_y corresponding to the marginal abatement costs of the industry emitting x or y, respectively, in the environmental policy position aimed at. If the situation aimed at does not occur after the firms adjust to the taxes, then these have to be corrected in a process of *trial and error* until the target level for the burden is reached. In the course of this process, the authority obtains information it can use to improve its picture of the optimum allocation situation. Figure 20 illustrates the environmental authority's procedure for linear pollutant interactions.

The first quadrant of Figure 20 shows the situation of the x industry: with no environmental policy, this industry will emit x^* units of pollutant. The associated marginal abatement costs are denoted MAC_x. The marginal abatement costs (MACs) are assumed (realistically) to increase in the direction of zero emission and (for simplicity's sake) to be linear.

Of course, it is unlikely that the environmental authority will estimate the abatement costs correctly. The first quadrant of Figure 20 accordingly shows the estimated abatement cost functions AC_x^e and MAC_x^e estimated by the environmental authority, as differing from the true functions AC_x and MAC_x. Although the environmental authority correctly assumes progressively rising abatement costs, it is nonetheless wrong about what course they will follow.

The second quadrant analogously presents what occurs in the y industry. The (x, y) combination aimed at, meeting the restriction on environmental burden at minimum cost, is constructed in the third quadrant. The C curves show the combinations of emissions x, y that can be realized at constant abatement cost (along a curve). The further away from the origin this *iso-abatement cost curve* is, the lower are the costs. The convexity of the curves follows from the assumption of increasing marginal abatement costs and the independence of abatement costs

---

4   For space reasons, we must refrain from discussing transferable emission permits here.

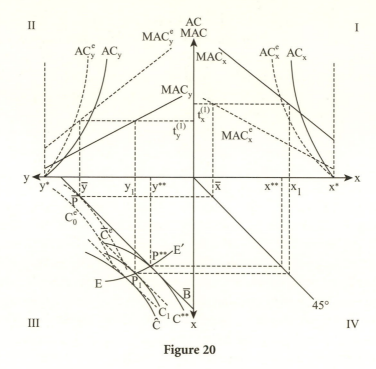

Figure 20

in the x (y) industry from the level of abatement activity in the y (x) industry. The curves marked C are derived from the abatement cost curves AC_x, AC_y and thus reflect the actual circumstances. The curves marked C^e follow from AC_x^e, AC_y^e and thus show the environmental authority's estimate.

The cost-effective allocation sought for is distinguished in the graph by having the linear environmental policy restriction $\overline{B}$ tangent to an iso-cost curve. The solution to the environmental authority's problem is accordingly represented in Figure 20 by point P^{**} (x^{**}, y^{**}). However, the situation the environmental authority aims for on the basis of its abatement cost estimate is $\overline{P}$ ($\overline{x}$, $\overline{y}$). At P^{**} (or $\overline{P}$, respectively), the constant marginal rate of pollutant substitution given by the slope of $\overline{B}$ corresponds with the true (or estimated, respectively) marginal rate of pollutant transformation given by the slope of an iso-cost curve. Under the conditions described here, the environmental authority will set emission taxes of $t_x^{(1)}$, $t_y^{(1)}$, from which it expects emission reductions starting from x^*, y^* that will bring about the situation $\overline{x}$, $\overline{y}$ that it is aiming for. Because it is the estimated marginal abatement costs that are decisive for the adjustment by the polluters that the authority expects, these tax rates are $t_x^{(1)} = MAC_x^e(\overline{x})$ and $t_y^{(1)} = MAC_y^e(\overline{y})$, respectively. They are entered in the first and second quadrants, respectively, of Figure 20.

The polluting firms will respond to the emission taxes by reducing their emissions until their marginal abatement cost corresponds to the relevant tax rate. For the firms' decisions, it is the actual marginal abatement costs (not those estimated by the environmental authority) that count. After adjustment to the set tax rates

$t_x^{(1)}$, $t_y^{(1)}$, accordingly, the emission situation shown in Figure 20 as $P_1(x_1, y_1)$ will arise. The environmental authority's misestimate of the abatement costs thus has the consequence, in the example shown in Figure 20, of missing the environmental policy target. The tax rates must accordingly be corrected.

In this correction, the environmental authority displays its capacity for differentiated self-criticism. It recognizes that in its first attempt it merely chose the absolute level of the tax rates wrongly, but was at any rate able to choose the optimum tax rate relation. That the environmental authorities' considerations are right can be worked out as follows: because the environmental authority knows that the environmental policy restriction $\overline{B}$ has a linear course and (correctly) assumes that the iso-cost curves are convex, it concludes that at the optimum it desires the marginal rate of pollutant transformation (in Fig. 20 the amount of slope of the iso-cost curve) is equal to the marginal rate of pollutant substitution (in Fig. 20, the amount of slope of $\overline{B}$). From reading part three of this book, it knows the nature of the polluter's behavior in adapting to the emission tax (tax rate = marginal abatement cost), and it knows that the marginal rate of pollutant transformation after the response to the taxation has been made corresponds to the reciprocal of the tax rate. Because the marginal rate of pollutant substitution is constant for the case of linear interaction, the environmental authority knows this marginal rate without knowing the optimum allocation. It thus also knows the relative tax rates that will prevail in the optimum. It follows that for the environmental authority, given linear interaction at the adjustment equilibrium that emerges following its first collection of tax, there will be uncertainty only as to the absolute level of the tax rates, but not as to the relation between the tax rates. The authority can accordingly follow a line of conduct that is no more complex than in the case without pollutant interaction. If the environmental policy restriction is breached in the situation brought about by the tax rates initially set, $t_x^{(1)}$, $t_y^{(1)}$ (as at P_1 in Fig. 20), then it must subsequently raise the tax rates (while retaining the relation between them). In Figure 20, this procedure corresponds to a move along the expansion path EE' from P_1 to P^{**}. If the adjustment equilibrium (in contrast with what Fig. 20 shows) is within the restriction, then the authority ought to lower the tax rates accordingly.

This trial-and-error process is equivalent to the classical price standard approach with only one pollutant that has been dealt with in section C.III of part three. Instead of an individual pollutant tax, here the parameter level for a group of taxes is varied.

Of course, the same criticism applies to this trial-and-error process as in the case with no pollutant interaction. In practice, continual correction of tax rates is associated with high transaction costs and is thus hard to implement politically. At any rate, the prior analysis shows that if emission taxes are used, wrong estimates by the environmental authority will automatically be revealed as a consequence of the polluters' adjustments. A further interesting finding is that linear pollutant interaction does not increase the complexity of the problem to be solved by the environmental authority in comparison to the case with no interaction.

The automatic error indication just mentioned does not occur if the environmental authority pursues its goal through *command and control*. Here the authority would have to order the standard $\bar{x}, \bar{y}$ it estimates as efficient (i.e., allocate both polluting industries corresponding emission quotas) and distribute these among the members of the two industries.

Although the burden restriction would be complied with directly (in contrast with the environmental policy with emission taxes), the environmental authority would receive no information as to whether it had achieved its aim at too high a cost. A cost-ineffective (x, y) combination does not automatically call for a correction. Thus, on top of the inefficiency of command and control policy familiar in environmental economics, in distributing a set overall emission limit among individual polluters, where there are pollutant interactions, there is also inefficiency in determining the aggregate pollutant combination aimed at.

III. Concave Interaction

Let us first consider the case of an *emission tax*. In a similar procedure to the one explained in detail for the case of linear interaction, the environmental authority first aims at a situation $(\bar{x}, \bar{y})$ in which, in its estimation, the environmental policy objective will be cost effectively achieved. For this, it imposes emission tax rates $t_x^{(1)}$, $t_y^{(1)}$ on the basis of its knowledge of the burden limit $\bar{B}$ and its assumption about the abatement cost functions AC_x, AC_y. The polluters in both industries adjust to the tax rates on the pattern described previously through emission abatement. If the environmental authority has wrongly estimated the abatement costs, then the equilibrium emission quantities x_1, y_1 will differ from the targets $\bar{x}, \bar{y}$. Figure 21 illustrates this as $\bar{P} \neq P_1$. The actual situation P_1 reached in Figure 21 falls short of the environmental policy objective $\bar{B}$.[5] As in the case of linear interaction, the environmental authority missing its emission standard signals its misestimate of abatement costs. In contrast with the case of linear interaction, the environmental authority cannot, however, correct its error by successively increasing both tax rates by the same percentage. Certainly, the ratio of emission tax rates that leads to the minimum cost situation $P^{**}(x^{**}, y^{**})$ is, as in the case of linear interaction, defined by the marginal rate of pollutant substitution in P^{**}. However, because this marginal rate is, given concave interaction, variable and the authority does not know P^{**}, it cannot derive the optimum ratio of tax rates from this connection.

Although, then, with linear interaction, only the level of emission tax rates is an unknown for the environmental authority, and over- or undershooting $\bar{B}$ with the tax rates first set $t_x^{(1)}$, $t_y^{(1)}$ shows whether the level has to be raised or lowered; with concave interaction, the level and relation of both tax rates are questionable. It is entirely conceivable that if the environmental policy restriction is broken through,

---

5   In addition, abatement costs are caused that lie above those needed in order to comply with the burden restriction ($C_1 > C^{**}$).

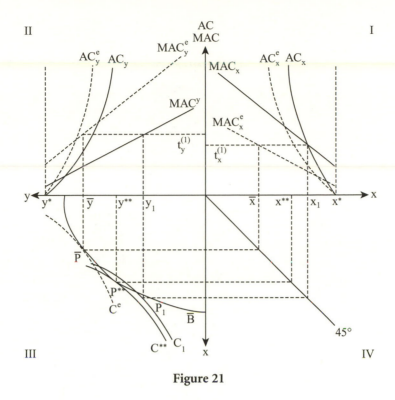

Figure 21

only one of the two tax rates must be raised, but the other lowered in order to reach the optimum position. The "simple" trial-and-error process with linear interaction becomes a "complex" process with concave interaction.

All the same, the position reached with $t_x^{(1)}$, $t_y^{(1)}$ provides certain information that is useful for the environmental authority's further actions: if y_1 is larger (smaller) than $\overline{y}$, then the environmental authority knows that it has under (over-)estimated MAC_y. The same applies to x. Under the conditions of Figure 21, then, it can conclude from the position of the achieved situation P_1 in relation to the expected situation $\overline{P}$ ($y_1 < \overline{y}$, $x_1 > \overline{x}$) that it has overestimated MAC_y and underestimated MAC_x. This information may be useful for a revised estimate of abatement costs, on the basis of which it can then set new tax rates. It does not, however, supply any direct conclusion as to the change in tax rates that will hit the target.

Summarizing, then, it may be said that the compass the environmental authority is using to direct the correction to tax rates is defective in the case of concave interaction. The authority depends on a complicated process of re-estimation of abatement costs and of relative and absolute tax rate adjustments. This reduces the practical applicability of emission taxes in cases of concave interaction.

Using *command and control* gives the same outcome with concave interaction as with linear interaction. The burden limit $\overline{B}$ is complied with, but the authority obtains no information as to whether it has reached a cost-effective combination of the two pollutants.

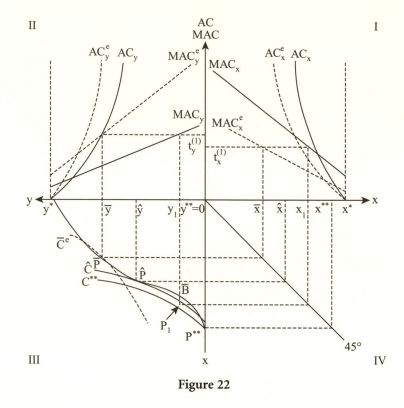

Figure 22

IV. Nonconcave Interaction

Nonconcave interactions may arise in a multiplicity of forms. It is assumed that restriction $\overline{B}$ has a concave and a convex region. We have opted for an "ugly" shape of $\overline{B}$ that causes problems of multiple optima.

By analogy with what we said previously, the authority will first impose *emission taxes* that do not lead to an allocation suited to the target. On the basis of its misestimate of abatement costs, instead of the desired situation $\overline{P}\ (\overline{x}, \overline{y})$, a situation $P_1(x_1, y_1)$ will arise (cf. the third quadrant in Fig. 22). The previously described trial-and-error process (problematic in any case) may lead to a situation $\hat{P}\ (\hat{x}, \hat{y})$ for which restriction $\overline{B}$ is complied with and the marginal rate of pollutant substitution corresponds to the reciprocal of the tax rate ratio. In the situation depicted in Figure 22, $\hat{P}$ is only a local optimum. The global optimum $P^{**}\ (x^{**}, y^{**} = 0)$ lying at the edge may well not be reached by an emission tax.

In the case of a *command and control* policy, as previously described, the situation $\overline{P}\ (\overline{x}, \overline{y})$ regarded as efficient will be ordered. Use of this instrument will not supply any information that enables $\hat{P}$, still less P^{**}, to be found.

V. Conclusion

It can thus be seen that *command and control* is able to achieve the environmental policy target for all forms of interaction. However, it does not generally lead to a cost-effective situation for any interaction form. Instead, it is cost ineffective in two respects: first, as in the case with no pollutant interaction, it generally fails to hit the minimum cost allocation of a given aggregate pollutant quantity over individual emitters. In addition, in the case of pollutant interaction, it is generally not capable of finding the minimum cost quantities of the interacting substances compatible with the burden restriction.

Emission taxes are always efficient in the case of linear pollutant interactions. They reach the environmental policy objective by a trial-and-error process that may well be difficult to handle in practice, but is no more complex than in the traditionally studied case with no pollutant interactions.[6] With concave interaction, the cost effectiveness of the tax is conserved, but the trial-and-error process to lead to the achievement of the environmental policy objective is more complex than in the case with no pollutant interaction. In the case of nonconcave interaction, the cost-effectiveness feature of an emission tax may even get lost. If there are multiple optima, then the local optimum achieved by the emission tax need not be an overall optimum. The more complex the nature of the pollutant interaction becomes, the further the outcomes of emission taxation lag behind the expectations (perhaps) raised by the analysis with no interaction.

B. Environmental Policy with Imperfect Competition

In model building in environmental economics, we usually assume that the observed externality is the only disruption to the economic system. In particular, we assume that those involved act in a competitive manner and (apart from the environmental policy measure considered) no governmental regulations exist. In such an environment, the internalization of externalities is an instrument for reaching a "first-best" solution.[7] Of course, the reality in which practical environmental policy has to prove itself is marked by many departures from this ideal model. We find numerous forms of market power and other market imperfections. The question is now how far the economic analysis and the policy recommendations formulated and derived from the conditions of the ideal model can be conveyed to the friction-filled world of the "second best." In this chapter, we devote ourselves to considering the environmental policy implications of market power for polluters.[8]

We look at adaptation by a monopolistic polluter to an emission tax and its consequences for welfare economics. The monopolistic emitter simultaneously causes two types of market failure. As a monopolist, he supplies the economy with too small a quantity of his product by exploiting the difference between price and marginal revenue. As a polluter, he emits too much because he ignores part of the

---

6   For clarification, the previous statement on the cost effectiveness of a tax refers to the equilibrium position reached after the conclusion of the trial-and-error process.

7   The concepts of "first best" and "second best" are explained in microeconomics textbooks. Cf., e.g., Begg/Fischer/Dornbusch (2008), Friedman (2002).

8   Cf., e.g., Perman et al. (2003, ch. 5.11).

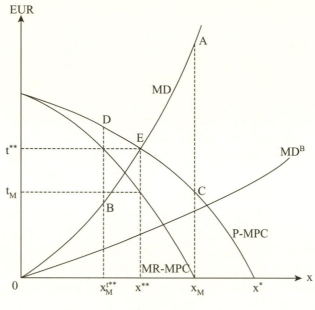

Figure 23

social costs of his activity. What consequences for environmental policy result from this situation? We initially consider this question under the restrictive condition that the only way for the monopolist to cut emissions would be to lower production. We then go on to accept that alongside output reduction, there may be a technical measure available for emission abatement.

We start by showing that for a monopolistic polluter, the Pigovian iron rule "levy a tax at a rate equal to the external marginal costs arising at the social optimum!" cannot be applied. The optimum tax is instead a rule below the Pigovian tax for perfect competition where there is a monopolistic polluter.[9] That the monopolistic polluter is fiscally better off with an environmental policy aiming at internalization than is competitive industry is clear from Figure 23.

Figure 23 contains the traditional portrayal of a monopolistic producer. However, to simplify the graph, the demand curve and the marginal proceeds curve have each been fused with the marginal private cost curve. The profit-maximizing supply quantity in a competitive economy is at x^*, and the equilibrium quantity in the monopoly case is x_M. At x^* (x_M), P – MPC = 0 (MR – MPC = 0) applies. The marginal damage is depicted by curve MD. (MD^B will play a part only later.)

Let us first consider the allocational effects of a Pigovian tax levied at the rate of the marginal damage at the social optimum, t^{**}. The monopolist will respond to this tax by cutting output until his marginal abatement cost corresponds to the tax rate. Because according to the assumptions output reduction is the only way

---

9   Cf. the groundbreaking work of Barnett (1970). Here there is also a reference to the special case where the tax may be higher for the monopolist than with perfect competition (cf. footnote 6, p. 1039).

of reducing the externality, the marginal abatement cost for the monopolist is the marginal foregone profit from production (i.e., is $MR - MPC$). (Marginal profit is the difference between marginal revenue and marginal private cost.) At the Pigovian tax equilibrium, accordingly, the monopolist will produce quantity x_M^{t**}, for which $MR - MPC = t^{**}$ holds.

What now are the welfare effects of this monopolistic adjustment? The benefit from the damage abatement obtained by cutting production is shown in Figure 23 as the area under the MD curve between x_M^{t**} and x_M ($AB x_M^{t**} x_M$). However, society suffers lost benefits from the production cut amounting to $x_M - x_M^{t**}$. These consist of the (unrealized) value to consumers of the products no longer offered. However, they have to deduct from this the value of the productive resources that society can use otherwise when part of the production of x is cut. Last, society's net losses for marginal nonproduction of good x consist of the difference between the price (as a measure of marginal willingness to pay) and the marginal private production cost (as a measure of evaluated consumption of resources) (i.e., they are $P - MPC$). The "price" society has to pay for the emission reduction is thus represented in Figure 23 as the area under the ($P - MPC$) curve between x_M^{t**} and x_M ($CD x_M^{t**} x_M$).

The net welfare effect of the taxation appears in Figure 23 as the difference between the areas ACE and DBE. Even if this difference is positive ($ACE > DBE$), it is still not a maximum. The quantity produced by the monopolist at the Pigovian tax equilibrium, x_M^{t**}, is below the maximum welfare quantity x^{**}. A tax that makes the monopolist move to the optimum output level maximizes net welfare. It lies, at $t_M = (MR - MPC)(x^{**})$, below the marginal damage (decisive for the Pigovian tax) by precisely the difference between the price and the monopolistic marginal revenue.[10]

In the model illustrated here, we must thus adjust the Pigovian "recipe" to the changed market form (in comparison with the case of perfect competition discussed in chapter C of part two). If this is done in the way described previously, then even in the monopoly case the fundamental outcome remains that taxation is suited for bringing about a socially optimum emission equilibrium. We see, however, that this result no longer holds if we abandon the assumption made in the previous argument that the externality can be reduced only by cutting production levels.

Let us first, though, note one interesting implication of taxing a monopoly polluter. It was first formulated by J.M. Buchanan (1969), the economics Nobel Laureate of 1986, in an article that at the time aroused great interest.

What environmental policy consequences follow if at the uncorrected monopolistic equilibrium (in contrast with what has been assumed so far in discussing Fig. 23) the difference between price and marginal private cost is greater than the marginal damage? For this case, Buchanan shows that any taxation of the polluting monopolist would cause a loss of welfare. Buchanan's argumentation can

---

10    $t^{**} = MD$, $t_M = MR - MPC = MD - [(P - MPC) - (MR - MPC)] = MD - (P - MR)$. The functions are to be evaluated at point x^{**}.

be followed by analogy with the foregoing without further explanation if it is not the marginal damage curve, MD, above, but the one running lower than it, MD^B (B for Buchanan), that reflects the actual circumstances. Closer consideration shows that instead of taxing the monopolist, subsidizing him would seem advisable from the welfare theoretical viewpoint.[11]

However, this problem of environmental policy with a monopolistic polluter appears in rather a different light if in our portrayal we (realistically) assume that as well as output reduction there are other ways of cutting emissions.[12] For the following argument, we accordingly assume the existence of an abatement technology that can reduce emissions by the amount ER_a.[13] To represent the monopolistic polluter's emission decision, we add the gross emission function $E^G = ax$ to Figure 23. As before, gross emissions will remain proportional to output.

$E = E^G - ER_a = ax - ER_a$ are the net emissions resulting from the gross emissions after deducting the emission units "caught" by the abatement technology. The second quadrant in Figure 24 contains Figure 23. Using the gross emission function entered in the fourth quadrant, the curves relevant for monopolist evaluation and for social evaluation appear in the second quadrant, with emission (instead of output) as the independent variable.

Let us consider the reference system of perfect competition to illustrate "society's standpoint": at the uncorrected equilibrium, quantity x^* will be produced and thus emission E^* caused. If starting at E^* emissions are cut by reducing output, then society will have to bear opportunity costs amounting to $P - MPC$. If the additional abatement technology is employed, then the costs will fall along the MAC_a curve. The minimum cost combination of the two ways of cutting emissions is reached, for any set reduction quantity, when the methods are employed in such a way that their marginal abatement costs become equal (i.e., $P - MPC = MAC_a$ holds).[14] Society's minimum marginal abatement cost curve (MAC_s^{Min}) for the optimum combination of the two abatement methods follows from the horizontal aggregation (starting at point E^*) of the two marginal abatement cost curves for the two methods. The optimum emission level is given by the point of intersection of society's minimum marginal abatement cost curve and the marginal damage curve. It is at E^{**}. To reduce emissions from the starting level E^* to E^{**}, society cuts

11 Of course, from the competition policy viewpoint, it seems ridiculous to want to cure the market failure caused by the monopolist by subsidizing him.

12 Correspondingly, we again depart from our more usual practice in this book of using the same symbol for emissions and output. (Cf., footnote 28 to part one and footnote 49 to part three.) In the following presentation, x denotes output and E emissions.

13 For simplicity's sake, we assume that the emission abatement technology can be employed additively to output cutting as a way of lowering emissions.

14 The justification is similar to the one for the optimum allocation of a given aggregate emission reduction over various polluting firms as explained (e.g., in sections C.I.2 and C.I.3 of part three). Here we find yet another variant of the "marginal equalization condition" cited previously.

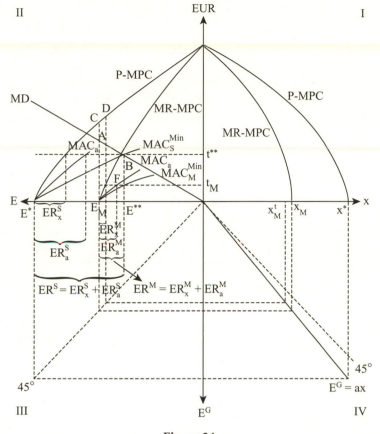

Figure 24

ER_x^s (ER_a^s) emission units by the method of output reduction (or the additional abatement technique, respectively). $E^* - E^{**} = ER_a^s + ER_x^s$ holds.[15]

We now consider the monopolistic polluter. At the uncorrected equilibrium, he does not use the emission abatement technology and produces quantity X_M. He thus causes emissions of E_M. In the graph, we show the "Buchanan" case, allocationally unfavorable for the taxation of the monopolistic polluter, in which at the uncorrected equilibrium the marginal damage lies below the "monopolistic margin" (the difference between price and marginal private cost).[16] The marginal costs arising for the monopolist from the use of each of the two abatement methods are $MR - MPC$ and MAC_a, respectively. The corresponding curve for the monopolist's minimum abatement costs results from the horizontal aggregation of the two curves and is at MAC_M^{Min}.

---

15 Those who so desire can enter the MAC_a curve shifted horizontally rightward by ER_x^s (using a felt pen?). Then the emission quantities cut by the two methods will be beside each other in the graph (instead of "overlapping") and thus represent the sum indicated previously in a more easily visible way. So as to not clutter up Figure 24 with curves, we have not done so.

16 The letter B used in Figure 23 on the MD curve to mark the Buchanan case has been left out in Figure 24.

If society wants to make the monopolist in this position emit the optimum pollutant quantity using an emission tax, then it has to set the tax rate at t_M. t_M corresponds to the minimum monopolistic marginal abatement cost at position E^{**} (and is thus below the marginal damage caused at this position). The reduced emission quantity ER^M by the monopolist in transition from the uncorrected equilibrium emission quantity E_M to the quantity E^{**} emitted after adjustment to the tax is made up as follows: ER_a^M units are cut using the technology, and ER_x^M using the means of output reduction. $ER_x M$ is defined by the equality of tax rate and marginal abatement cost, and ER_a^M by the equality of tax rate and marginal profit (i.e., $MAC_a = MR - MPC = t_M$ holds). The final product quantity X_M^t produced at the equilibrium after adjustment to the tax can be read off in the first quadrant of Figure 24.

The result presented here of taxing a monopolistic polluter with an additional abatement technique differs in two ways from the special case first discussed of emission proportional to output.

First, it should be noted that the emission taxation does not necessarily lead to losses of social welfare, although we had assumed the "Buchanan case" where in the uncorrected starting position the "marginal damage from imperfect competition" is above the marginal damage of the emissions ($P - MPC > MD$). The social welfare effect of the monopoly's adjustment to tax t_M results from the difference between the external damage avoided by the emission reduction (in Fig. 24, $E_M ABE^{**}$) and the social costs of the emission abatement. The latter consist of the net losses of benefit incurred by society from the cut in production (in Fig. 24, $E_M CD$ ($E_M - ER_x^M$)) plus the costs of the equilibrium utilization of the abatement technology (in Fig. 24, $E_M F$ ($E_M - ER_a^M$)).

Whether this difference is positive cannot be answered at the level of abstraction employed here. It will, however, suffice to say that taxation that improves welfare is at any rate *possible* in the "Buchanan case" if the monopoly polluter has another way of cutting emission alongside output reduction. The chances for taxation that improves welfare are *ceteris paribus*, the greater the lower the costs of cutting emissions using the additional technology. As shown in section C.II of part three, the taxation produces incentives to develop and introduce lower-cost technologies. Emission taxation thus even promotes the emergence of conditions under which it can act to promote welfare, even in a particularly unfavorable case of monopoly emission of pollutants.

Second, however, it should be noted that even the best taxation of a monopoly polluter cannot lead to a "truly optimum" outcome (in the sense of a first-best allocation). Instead, it will always be a "lesser optimum" (i.e., a second-best solution). This finding may arouse contradiction: have we not just shown, the gentle reader might object, that the monopolist can be made to emit a quantity of pollutant identical with the one attained at competitive equilibrium with ideal Pigovian taxation? That may be so, is the answer, but the allocation reached is nonetheless suboptimal because the monopolist does not bring about the total emission reduction produced at the socially most cost-favorable distribution between the two reduction methods. Because cost minimization is a necessary condition for maximizing the social surplus, the allocation arrived at by the monopolist cannot be a welfare maximum.[17]

The social suboptimality of the equilibrium mix of abatement methods for the monopolist, with its severe consequences, will now be made even clearer. It is attributable to the monopoly's departure from society's evaluation of the abatement costs. According to the assumptions, in the previous model, two abatement methods are available, a technical one and output reductions. For the abatement technique, we can assume without further ado that there is a perfect market here. The marginal costs paid then by the monopolist as a demander in this market, MAC_a, will correspond with the marginal social costs of the technology.[18] But things are, *by definition*, different with the method of output reduction: precisely because the polluter under study is a monopolist, his valuation of an output reduction will always be different from society's. One unproduced unit for him means a loss of the marginal profit, whereas society has to put up with higher losses, namely, the difference between marginal willingness to pay and marginal private cost. Because output reduction is cheaper for the monopolist than for society, the combination of output reduction and use of technology that is minimum cost for him will always differ from society's minimum cost combination. More exactly, in the monopolistic minimum cost portfolio of abatement methods, there will always from society's viewpoint be too high a proportion of output reduction (too low a proportion of technology use). In the position shown in Figure 24, society would not, starting from the uncorrected monopoly emission equilibrium E_M, use any output reduction to lower emissions to the value E^{**}. The marginal social costs of monopolistic undersupply of the product $(P - MPC)$ are already higher at the uncorrected monopoly equilibrium than the marginal costs of the abatement technology arising if the total quantity to be cut $(E_M - E^{**})$ is eliminated using exclusively the add-on technology. The monopolist will, however, given his cost calculation (a distorted one from society's viewpoint), employ the output reduction method at equilibrium by cutting output from x_M to x_M^t (cf. the first quadrant in Fig. 24).

C. Internalization Negotiations with Asymmetrical Information

In part one of this book, we point out that *externalities*, central in the context of environmental economics, are only one entry in the list of reasons for "market

---

17   This statement stands up even if society takes account of the distortions in the monopolistic portfolio of abatement methods by aiming at a different emission quantity from E^{**}. The problem addressed here might be solved at the most in terms of economic theory, although hardly in those of economic or environmental policy, by the use of combined instruments (output *subsidy* + emission taxation).

18   Here it is also assumed that no externalities result from use of the technology itself.

failure." In introductory environmental economics presentations, it is assumed that the economy observed suffers *exclusively* from the problem of externalities, whereas in all other potential problem areas everything is all right. In a quite similar way (at any rate, so the author presumes), introductory medical works assume that the unfortunate patient is afflicted by *either* lice *or* fleas. Discussion of a simultaneous attack by both types of bug is reserved for the advanced reader. The reason for this limitation in the presentation is, of course, pedagogical. Although interactions of pathologies and therapies are important for practice, they complicate the presentation in a way that does not suit an introduction. Readers of this book who have worked through the three fundamental parts (and thus steeled themselves) are now equipped for the complications dealt with in part four. The accumulation of reasons for market failure is one important type of *extension of the economic basic model* covered in this part.

In chapter B, we combine the problem of externalities with that of market power and consider what consequences follow from this combination for the internalization strategy of a Pigovian tax. Now, we are going to combine externalities with another item on the list of reasons for market failure – asymmetrical information. So as not to exaggerate in the accumulation of allocational problems, we remove chapter B's assumption of the monopolistic polluter again and return to the model of perfect competition. The analysis is done on the example of Coase's internalization negotiations, as explained in chapter A of part two of the book, on the assumption of perfect information.

In the previous discussion, we paid little attention to the question of what informational bases the parties conduct their negotiations on. It was silently assumed in the mainstream of the argument that the negotiating parties know the marginal abatement cost and marginal damage functions decisive for their behavior. It is only in section A.II.4 of part two that reference is made to the possibility of uncertainty regarding the paths of the relevant curves in order to give the model some "plausibility padding" with variable ad hoc transaction costs.[19] In the literature on the *economics of information*, the consequences of imperfect information for the suitability of negotiations as a strategy for internalizing externalities have, however, been systematically studied.[20] Particular attention is paid to the following construction of *asymmetrical* information. Every party involved with an externality knows the function that represents his own situation, but not the corresponding function of the "other side." The polluter thus knows the marginal abatement costs, and the damaged party, the marginal damage. Regarding the function for the respective counterparty, the decision maker knows all *possible* paths of the curve, but not which of these alternatives is the real one for the other party.

---

19   The point here was the allocational consequences of the uncertainty of a negotiating party regarding the path of the curve representing his *own* situation – thus, the uncertainty of the polluter (damaged party) regarding the marginal abatement cost (marginal damage) function.

20   Cf., e.g., Brito et al. (2006).

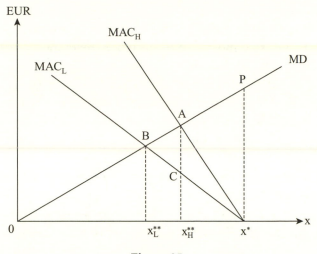

Figure 25

We want to present the effects of this asymmetrical information distribution on the negotiating model in the simplest possible way – and therefore occasionally in somewhat abbreviated fashion. For simplification, we assume that there are only two types of polluters: type H with high marginal abatement costs (MAC_H) and type L with low marginal abatement costs (MAC_L). According to what we have just said, the damaged party does not know in the negotiations whether he has to do with an *H* or an *N*.[21]

Let us first use Figure 25 to illustrate the socially optimum allocation.[22]

From a reading of the foregoing sections, it is clear without further explanation (at any rate, so the author claims) that the socially optimum emission level x^{**} depends on whether the polluter involved is type H or type L. Moreover, it is obviously the case that $x_H^{**} > x_L^{**}$. The question is now whether the socially optimum allocation that applies in each case is reachable through Coase-type negotiations. For space reasons, we consider exclusively the laissez-faire rule and further assume a very simple pattern (although extremely common in the literature) for the distribution of the negotiating gain between the parties. The damaged party offers the polluter a compensation payment for one marginal reduction in the emission that is "a bit" above his marginal abatement cost.[23] Of course, he makes this offer only for emission units for which the marginal damage avoided by the emission reduction

21 But he knows the probability of meeting with an H or L type. For simplification, we assume that the chance of hitting on an H or an L is 0.5 in each case. For further simplification, we assume that there is only one type of damaged party. This saves us considering uncertainties as to the path of the marginal damage curve so that we can confine ourselves to the uncertainties arising from lack of knowledge of the marginal abatement cost curve.

22 To simplify the graph, we assume that both types of polluter emit the same quantity (x^*) of emissions at the uncorrected equilibrium.

23 In the following presentation, for simplicity's sake, the marginal case of a compensation payment exactly equal to the abatement cost will also be allowed and given special consideration. Actually,

is at least as high as the compensation payment. The damaged party will not accept any modification regarding his offer (i.e., the polluter just has to take it or leave it).[24] The polluter gives an indication of his type. The damaged party cannot, on the assumptions, check this and takes it at face value. According to what we have said, a polluter that "identifies himself" as type H will receive payment of MAC_H for a marginal reduction in emissions, and a polluter claiming to be type L will instead receive MAC_L.

Using Figure 25, let us now consider the consequences of this arrangement for the outcomes of a Coase-type negotiating process.

According to the discussion of negotiations in section A.II of part two, it will be clear without further explanation that at the negotiated equilibrium between the damaged party and an honest type H polluter, emission quantity x_H^{**} will be produced. The polluter will receive compensation payments amounting to the area under the MAC_H curve between x^* and x_H^{**} (i.e., $x^*Ax_H^{**}$).[25] The gain from the negotiations (x^*PA) remains with the damaged party.

An honest type L polluter will, according to the same logic, receive a payment of $x^*Bx_L^{**}$. Here, too, the gain from negotiations (this time, x^* PB) remains with the damaged party. If things remained as stated here, then the modifications made to the assumptions previously would change nothing in the validity of the Coase theorem from the basic form of the negotiating model.

However, for a polluter of a particular type, the temptation can exist to sail under a false flag in the negotiations (i.e., pretend to belong to the other type).[26] If an L polluter claims to be an H polluter, he will receive the same compensation payment as an honest H polluter (i.e., as much as it costs the latter to cut his emissions to the optimum level for H polluters; $x^*Ax_H^{**}$ in Fig. 25). By definition, the actual costs to the dishonest L polluter for reducing emissions to x_H^{**} are lower. They amount to only $x^*Cx_H^{**}$. His "profit from deceit" is thus x^*AC. Because deceit is rewarded in this arrangement, the L supplier – as the *Homo economicus* unrestrained by morals that he is (assumed to be!) – will decide to deceive.[27]

It can be shown that within the framework of the previous presentation, no similar incentive to deceive exists for the H polluter. He is, therefore, in our model, condemned to virtue. Of course, the social optimality of the outcome of negotiation (and thus the validity of the Coase theorem) is a thing of the past if the polluter succumbs to the temptations of the incentive structure described, as he is here

---

of course, at least a small additional amount (a sort of "incentive ε") is necessary in order to make the deal attractive to the polluter.

24 The asymmetrical role allocation between polluter and damaged party assumed here recalls (at least to the author) Stackelberg's theory of oligopoly.

25 The "incentive ε" has been left out to simplify the accounting.

26 As you may already know, dear reader, before reading this text, this world is a bad place. And here it is even being modeled!

27 Because the damaged party has, according to the assumptions, no way of directly checking what the polluter says, there is no need here to discuss the influence of the likelihood of discovery and punishment on the allocation.

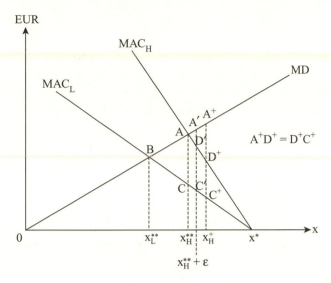

Figure 26

predestined to do. As the outcome of negotiations, the emission quantity x_H^{**} is prescribed, although with the given abatement cost curve for the L polluter social optimality would have required a reduction to emission level x_L^{**}.[28]

In evaluating the previous outcome, however, it must be borne in mind that the underlying argument is based on the assumption that the damaged party simply accepts what the polluter says about his "identity" and adapts himself to that without further ado. Possibly, however, the damaged party will recognize (having been trained in information economics, or simply being astute) the fatal attractiveness of the incentives it sets for the polluter, and therefore not go in for the simple arrangement described in the first place.

A pattern for allocating the gain of negotiations extended in comparison with the type of negotiation described previously can offer the damaged party an "antidote" to the deceitful practices of the polluter. In addition to the offer to compensate for costs (with the incentive ε on top), the damaged party can offer a polluter who claims (admits) to be an L an "honesty premium," the nature of which is now explained. The premium is set at a level that is just sufficient to cause a type L polluter to "come out" as such. For this, it has to be "a bit"[29] above the gain from deceit that the polluter concerned would make by claiming to belong to type H. Figure 26 shows this amount (as in Fig. 25) as the area x^*AC. If the premium is marginally above this amount, then it corresponds to the minimum expenditure

---

28 It is only when the polluter actually belongs to type H that the social optimality of the outcome of negotiation claimed by Coase remains.

29 Here again an incentive ε is necessary to induce the polluter to be honest. For simplicity's sake, we assume in Figure 26 that the polluter is already honest if the subsidy is exactly equal to the gain from deceit. (Jokingly, one might call this a case of "lexicographical preference for honesty.")

at which the damaged party can make honesty into the superior alternative for the polluter.

The secret of the allocational success of a correctly specified honesty premium (i.e., one minimally above the equilibrium gain from deceit) is therefore for it to change the framework conditions for the polluter's decision in such a way that a cost–benefit analysis of deceit will reveal it to be a losing business (in comparison with honesty). The remarkable thing in this model construction is that the damaged party succeeds in setting the incentives in such a way in the negotiating process that the polluter *voluntarily* reveals his type, although the damaged party cannot observe him and thus there would be considerable concealment incentives with a less refined arrangement. Through the instrument of the honesty premium, the damaged party can carry out a successful *screening process* in which a *self-selection mechanism* on the polluter's side replaces selection by the damaged party (which is by definition impossible).[30]

Of course, the damaged party has an interest in limiting the honesty premium he pays to what is just necessary by setting it just slightly higher than the L polluter's gain from deceit. But that does not exhaust his possibilities of freeing himself from premium payments. He will instead direct his attention to the point that the amount of the minimum premium necessary for the behavior-influencing effect he wants depends on the level of the gain from deceit. He can, however, influence this through the level of emission reduction up to which he will promise an H polluter to compensate him for his abatement expenditure. We assumed previously that this happens up to emission level x_H^{**}, the socially optimum one if the H type is the real one.[31] In negotiations with no honesty premium, this is also rational because up to this point the benefit of an emission reduction to the damaged party is above the amount necessary to compensate the H polluter for his abatement costs. But the honesty premium changes the conditions for the damaged party's maximization calculations in a fundamental way. When he includes this premium, the damaged party will be able to check the position of the emission level up to which he will compensate an H polluter for the costs of emission reduction (compensation limit) as follows: a slight move in the compensation limit from x_H^{**} to $x_H^{**} + \varepsilon$ will bring two opposing effects.

First, the damaged party will suffer a loss amounting to $MD - MAC_H$. He has to do without the benefit of a marginal lowering of the emission level (MD), which would have cost him a compensation amount of MAC_H.[32] However, with a marginal shift in the compensation limit from x_H^{**} to $x_H^{**} + \varepsilon$, this loss will be extremely small because x_H^{**} is defined by the fact that marginal damage and

---

30 It can be shown that the honesty premium as described previously establishes no incentive for an H polluter to pretend to be an L.

31 The target emission up to which the polluter is compensated for emission reductions is called the "compensation limit."

32 To simplify, we ignore the fact that the cost to the damaged party of the emission reduction carried out by H is a little above MAC_H (because of the incentive ε).

marginal abatement cost (of the H polluter) are equal to each other. In Figure 26, this small loss that the damaged party has to accept as the consequence of a slight increase in the compensation limit in negotiations with an H polluter is marked by the area $AA'D'$. At the limit, the loss corresponds to the distance $A'D'$. If an H polluter is compensated only for emission reductions from his uncorrected starting emission level x^* to the marginally increased target value $x_H^{**} + \varepsilon$, then the gain from deceit for an L polluter pretending to be an H polluter will automatically shrink. In Figure 26, it will be $x^*D'C'$ at the shifted compensation limit $x_H^{**} + \varepsilon$, instead of x^* AC for the unchanged limit x_H^{**}. Correspondingly, the minimum honesty premium for which the damaged party can induce the L polluter to reveal his type falls by $AD'C'C$. At the limit, the savings for the damaged party correspond in Figure 26 to distance $D'C'$. Because the difference between the marginal abatement costs of the two types of polluter is strictly positive at starting position x_H^{**}, the minimal saving the damaged party can make by marginally shifting the compensation limit for the H polluter is definitely greater than the cost of that shift explained previously. In Figure 26, $D'C' > A'D'$ holds.

An (arbitrarily small) increase in the compensation limit for H polluters is thus always rewarding for the damaged party. Previously, we assumed for simplicity's sake that it is just as likely for the damaged party to meet up with an H polluter as with an L one. On this assumption, the damaged party will weight the loss from shifting the limit that arises if his counterpart is an H polluter just as strongly as the saving he makes if he comes up against an L type. Under these circumstances, at equilibrium, he will set the compensation limit for H polluters at the level for which the difference between the savings with the honesty premium and the cost arising in the form of foregone net benefit from emission reductions is a maximum.

If the curves are well behaved, then this level will be reached when the marginal savings from raising the compensation limit are identical with its marginal cost.[33] This optimum level of the compensation limit from the damaged party's viewpoint we call x_H^+. For x_H^+, $MD - MAC_H = MAC_H - MAC_L$ holds. In Figure 26, correspondingly, $A^+D^+ = D^+C^+$ holds.[34] Of course, this adjustment by the damaged party to the informational structure of the negotiating problem, optimum for his individual economy, will destroy the optimality of the negotiated equilibrium and thus the validity of the Coase theorem. The optimum allocation is reached only if the polluter belongs to the L group. Compensation including the honesty bonus

33 If the marginal damage and marginal abatement cost rise and fall, respectively, monotonically with growing emissions, then the marginal costs will rise steadily starting from 0 if the compensation limit is raised starting from X_H^{**}. In contrast, the marginal savings from this raising of the compensation limit fall, starting from a positive level, if the marginal abatement costs of both polluter groups fall monotonically with rising emissions and come closer to each other.

34 If the damaged party considers it likelier that the polluter is type H, then the equilibrium compensation limit for H polluters will be between X_H^{**} and X_H^+. If instead it is likelier for the damaged party's counterpart to be an L polluter, then the equilibrium limit will lie between X_H^+ and X_X^*.

will induce him to reduce emissions to level x_L^{**}, socially optimum for his type. Things are different if the polluter is an H type. Because he received payments from the damaged party only for emission reductions up to the compensation limit x_H^+, he will not cut his emissions to the level x_H^{**} ($< x_H^+$), which is socially optimum for his type.

It is noteworthy that the room for manipulation an L-type polluter has in negotiations leads to a social suboptimality with the H type (and thus also to a smaller compensation amount paid to this type than at the social optimum). An H type who has no way of convincingly proving himself to be such must at equilibrium "pay the bill" for the room for manipulation his *alter ego* the L type has. The damaged party cannot limit the gain the L type derives from his room for manipulation at the damaged party's expense by direct action on the L type. If he tries this, say, by setting the honesty premium below the gain from deceit, the L type will dodge this attempt by "camouflage." It is only by manipulating the compensation limit for the H type that the damaged party can limit the extent to which the L polluter can capitalize on the advantage he has in information about his type. That the H polluter is thus paying a price for a problem the damaged party has with the L polluter changes nothing in the individual rationality of the equilibrium described here.

The information disclosure mechanism presented here is very trickily designed and therefore particularly intellectually attractive. Nonetheless, one commentary that somewhat qualifies this has to be made. In the previous model construction, the damaged party is on the one hand attributed little information; that is, he does not know what type of polluter he is dealing with. On the other hand, however, he knows a surprising amount. He knows the MAC functions of all existing types of polluters and can on this basis calculate their individual economic optima.[35] Moreover, he knows the proportion of representatives of each type of polluter in the total polluter population. Of course, these elements in the damaged party's information portfolio are not incompatible. All the same, their combination does not seem particularly plausible.

D. The "Double Dividend" of Green Tax

Destruction of the environment and unemployment are among the greatest challenges for modern society. An economic policy instrument that promises to make an important simultaneous contribution to solving both problems can be certain to get a great deal of scientific and political attention. For quite a while in both the scientific and the political debate, the economic policy "wonder weapon" seemed to have been found in the form of an "ecological tax reform."

---

35   We can see from this last point that he must have done at least an undergraduate economics course, and we congratulate him on that.

The idea is to internalize externalities or reach predetermined environmental standards by introducing a system of green taxes.[36]

The resulting welfare gains reaped in the field of ecology constitute the "first dividend" of this economic policy instrument. One central design feature of ecological tax reform is its yield-neutral pattern. The tax proceeds are to be returned to the economy (revenue recycling) by reducing the costs of the production factor labor. This may be done by, for instance, lowering employer contributions to social insurance. The expected employment-enhancing effect of this constitutes the "second dividend."

If a sack of money is lying about ownerless on the street, then a great number of interested parties will quickly appear. It is much the same if a new policy instrument is claimed to be able to generate government revenue, as happens with the introduction of a green tax. From the viewpoint of the new political economy (public choice theory), many of these proposals are worth a brief discussion. From the viewpoint of welfare economics that we prevalently adopt in this book, alongside the use to raise employment just mentioned, one further idea deserves consideration: in the literature of public finance, it has been exhaustively shown that taxation by government puts a particular burden on the economy.[37] This does not mean the grievances that arise for the taxpayer because he has to provide the tax revenue financially through forced payments to the state. That is, so to speak, the normal burden of taxation. The "excess burden" is the allocation-distorting effect of taxes.

In section A.III of part one of this book, we show that an uncorrected market mechanism can in particular ideal conditions bring about socially optimal equilibria. As an example, we take the market for a good x. At this stage of the analysis, we assume that no externalities, market power or other disruptions of the system are present. One essential requirement for optimality of the market observed is that at equilibrium consumers' marginal willingness to pay for x and suppliers' marginal production costs are equal ("equimarginal condition"). This comes about because in the market observed the market price is simultaneously the price that consumers pay for one unit of the good and also the price that producers receive for one unit of x. We now assume that good x is taxed. Let an amount of t Euros be payable per unit. The supply curve would shift upward by the amount t, the equilibrium price would rise, and the equilibrium quantity fall correspondingly along the course of the demand curve. For our context, the decisive thing here is that the price that

---

36 In the political debates, the terms "green tax" and "ecological tax reform" are vaguely defined. It is not always clear whether what is supposed to be involved is an implementation of the internalization idea (as dealt with in part two of this book) or a variant of standard-oriented environmental policy (as dealt with in part three of this book). The criticism has often been made that the associated program does not meet the demands of environmental economics whether in the sense of the internalization idea or in that of the standard-oriented variant. Instead, it is seen as really being an instrument for the state to take in money, shaped in a process of policy formation strongly controlled by interest groups. If nothing else is said, we assume that the green tax we are talking about is a Pigovian tax in the sense of part two of this book.

37 Cf. Ballard/Fullerton (1992).

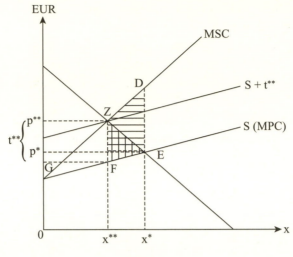

Figure 27

suppliers receive is no longer identical with the one demanders pay for the good. Instead, demanders pay a "gross price" out of which the supplier's marginal costs and the taxes are financed. The suppliers pass the tax proportion on to the state and keep the "net price." Because the price the consumers pay is higher than the price that the suppliers keep for themselves, marginal willingness to pay at equilibrium is above the demander's marginal private costs. At equilibrium, demanders' marginal willingness to pay is identical with the gross price paid by the consumers, whereas the supplier's marginal costs correspond to the lower net price. It is therefore unavoidable for governmental taxation to harm the "equimarginal condition" that is the basis for the efficiency of the market equilibrium. It is the deterioration in allocation caused thereby that is meant by the previously mentioned "excess burden" of taxation.

Here we set out graphically the connection just outlined. However, we turn the argument from the example of the market in consumer good x, directly linked with the discussion in part one of this book, to the labor market. The advantage is that with this example the two particularly interesting variants of the double-dividend thesis mentioned previously can be explained in a single presentation. Let us assume that green tax revenues are used to cut the special taxation on the labor factor; we may then expect both a rise in employment and a lowering of the excess burden of taxation.

We would do best to start by recalling the argument on the Pigou tax from chapter C in part two of this book. In contrast with the previously summarized discussion on the social optimality of an ideally competitive market from part one, it is assumed in part two that production of x was associated with a negative externality. This is internalized by a Pigovian tax. Figure 27 shows the Pigou tax rate as t^{**}; the market equilibrium quantity after adjustment to the tax is x^{**}. The

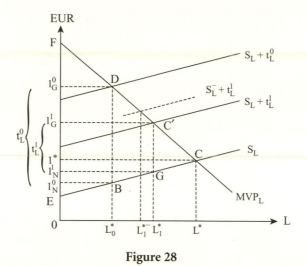

Figure 28

Pigovian tax revenues amount correspondingly to $T = t^{**}x^{**}$. The graph shows the tax revenue as rectangle $p^{**}ZFG$.

We now see what effects arise for employment and for labor market efficiency if the Pigou tax revenues described are used to cut taxation on labor. To do so, we must briefly look at the market for labor in the situation when the Pigou tax proceeds are not yet used to unburden it.

In Figure 28, L denotes the quantity of labor (working hours) offered or demanded in the market. S_L denotes the labor supply curve (corresponding to the curve of marginal opportunity costs of labor). The curve MVP_L is the marginal value product curve for labor, which is identical with the demand curve on the labor market.[38] Without taxation, the equilibrium on the labor market is at the point of intersection of the labor supply curve with the labor demand curve at the equilibrium labor quantity L^*. The corresponding equilibrium price for one unit of labor is the wage rate l^*. As long as labor is not taxed, the wage paid by the firm is identical with the wage received by the worker.

In complete analogy with the previously summarized discussion of social optimality of a market equilibrium in the case of final products, the equilibrium entered here is socially optimal. The marginal opportunity costs of labor supply correspond exactly to the firms' marginal willingness to pay for labor. The marginal willingness to pay for an input is identical to its marginal value product. The "equimarginal condition" for the labor market is met at equilibrium.

Let us now suppose that the state levies tax at a constant rate of t_L^0 on each hour of work done. Correspondingly, the labor supply curve will shift from S_L to $S_L + t_L^0$. This lowers equilibrium employment from L^* to L_0^*, and the wage rate rises from

---

38 For space reasons, the basics of input market economics must be taken as read. A section on it can be found in any intermediate textbook of microeconomics.

l^* to l^0_G (where G stands for "gross").[39] Of course, this sort of wage increase is not exactly what the worker was dreaming of: from the gross wages, the tax per labor unit, namely, t^0_L, is paid, leaving the worker with net wages of l^0_N (where N stands for "net").

After the consequences for employment, let us now look at the welfare economic consequences of this taxation. In the starting position with employment equilibrium L^* and equilibrium wages l^*, the sum of the labor supplier's producer income and the firm's consumer income (as demander of the labor factor) for the whole of the equilibrium labor supply L^* is the difference between the value product of labor and the opportunity cost of the labor supply. Graphically, this amount is shown as the triangle ECF. This is this input market's net welfare contribution to the economy. With the lowering of equilibrium employment from L^* to L^*_0 caused by the taxation, the economy thus loses the net welfare contribution that would be provided by the amount of labor $L_0 - L^*_0$ that is no longer being done. The graph shows the loss as triangle BCD. This is the form the *excess burden of taxation* addressed previously in general terms takes in our example. The tax revenue drawn by the state from the labor considered amounts to "tax rate times equilibrium amount of labor" (i.e., $t^0_L L^*_0$). The graph depicts this as area $1^0_G D B 1^0_N$.

So far, we presented the effects of taxing the use of labor under two criteria – employment and the additional burden. In both viewpoints, the outcome is disappointing: the taxation has negative effects on the "good" indicator (employment) and positive ones on the "poor" indicator (the additional burden).

Clearly, the state needs revenue. Even ignoring the question of its appropriate level for the moment: can the rules of governmental revenue collection not be shaped so as to mitigate the associated undesirable effects (decline in unemployment or creation of additional burdens)?

This is, one might think, precisely the right point in the text to explain the idea of a double dividend from a green tax. As so often happens, though, the right thing is to delay. In the interest of making the presentation more transparent, it is advisable to put the concept of double dividend in somewhat tighter terms as follows.

The academic discussion of the double dividend of a green tax (more precisely, a Pigou tax) is confusing for many reasons.[40] Among these reasons is the fact that the concept of the double dividend has (at least!) *four* meanings in the

39   For reasons of simplification, we use a "neoclassical" stylization of the labor market. The advantage of a trim presentation is bought at the cost of a certain loss of economic policy relevance. Although, depending on the form of the framework conditions, there are differing employment equilibria, there is no involuntary unemployment, which could be portrayed in a presentation using constant labor supply and wage rigidities. However, for the double dividend of the green tax at the center of attention here, no significant differences arise between these alternative models of the labor market. The consequences of negotiating power on the labor market for optimal green taxation are illumined by Wagner (2005).

40   The author hopes that this impression does not become too strong from a reading of the present text.

literature. We previously referred to the interpretation of the second dividend in the form of an increase in employment and/or an improvement in the efficiency of the taxation system. On both interpretations, the literature differentiates between a "strong" and a "weak" version of the hypothesis (strong vs. weak double dividend).[41]

Let us look at the employment dividend: the "strong" version of this interpretation asserts that the employment level rises in absolute terms if the proceeds of a green tax are applied to easing the tax burden on the labor factor. The "weak" version of the employment-oriented interpretation of the double-dividend hypothesis has nothing to say about the absolute change in employment. Instead, the employment effects of the green tax with the use of tax revenue referred to previously are compared with the employment effects of a green tax where the tax revenue is given back wholesale to citizens.[42] The weak double-dividend hypothesis asserts that the employment effects are higher if the tax revenue is used to unburden the input of labor.

The strong and weak dividend hypotheses can be seen similarly in the version that deals with improving the efficiency of the tax system. Here the "strong" version of the hypothesis means that introducing a green tax that is used to lower taxes that distort allocation leads to an increase in welfare, even if in calculating the welfare effects the positive environmental effects are completely ignored. In the "weak" form, this interpretation of the double-dividend hypothesis says that the welfare effects of a green tax with the tax proceeds used as described previously are superior to those of a green tax where the tax proceeds are given back wholesale to citizens. The weak version does not claim that the welfare effects of the green tax are positive if no consideration is given to the environmental effect. It would also be compatible with the weak version if the welfare effect, without taking the environmental effect into account, was less bad with the first mentioned use of green tax proceeds than with the second one.

To deal as usefully as possible with the four different versions of the double-dividend hypothesis, we must start by asking in which context of discussion they are of importance.

The strong double-dividend hypothesis (irrespective of whether the employment-oriented or tax efficiency—oriented interpretation is employed) clearly concerns the question of whether a green tax ought to be introduced at all. Participants in this debate have to cope with the following problem: the decision to introduce an instrument to internalize externalities is greatly hampered by the fact that environmental disruption is difficult to measure in cash terms. If monetization were readily possible, then the question of the social desirability of

41 Mathematical digression: $2 \times 2 = 4$.

42 In defining this term "wholesale," the devil is in the details. What we mean is a way of repaying the tax proceeds that does not lead to any allocational effects. In an absolutely pure form, this sort of transfer (a "lump sum transfer") is probably not possible. The idea perhaps comes closest to that of distributing a "per capita" amount equal for everyone.

internalization could easily be answered by a comparison between the costs and benefits of protecting the environment.[43] In view of the difficulties of justifying the use of environmental policy instruments on a cost—benefit analysis basis, it is a gift of the gods for the ecologically minded participant in the societal discourse if he can say, "Even totally ignoring the environmental effect of the green tax, it is advantageous for society to introduce it. Its positive employment effects alone (the improved efficiency of the tax system) justify using it."

The discussion context in which the weak form of the hypothesis is relevant is cut from quite a different cloth. Here it is obviously no longer a question of whether the environmental tax will be brought in. Instead, the point is how the tax revenue raised from a given environmental tax is to be used. Is it better to apply it to lowering existing taxes, or should it be refunded to citizens wholesale?

It emerges from this consideration that the double-dividend hypothesis in its weak form is not really a specifically environmental economics theme at all. The question of the optimum use of any given tax revenue is important from a social policy viewpoint, but answering it clearly falls within the province of *public economics* rather than environmental economics in the usual division of labor among economic (sub)sciences.[44] Accordingly, we no longer go any further into the double-dividend hypothesis in its weak form. Considerations of public finance are brought in here only where they are inseparably connected with the environmental economics considerations at issue here, but not where they are a "theme in themselves."

Having narrowed our discussion of the double-dividend hypothesis down to the "strong" form, let us now go on with the considerations arising from the two previous graphs.

Taxing labor at a tax rate of t_L^0 has two unpleasant consequences:

- Equilibrium employment falls from L^* to L_0^*.
- An additional burden is generated, illustrated in Figure 28 by area *BCD*.

Now we come to the magic trick for designing a revenue-neutral green tax. The government uses the proceeds of the Pigou tax described previously (and shown in Fig. 27) not for additional expenditure, but to give it back, down to the last farthing, to the economy. More exactly, this is done by appropriately lowering the taxation of labor. By "appropriately," we mean that the tax rate on labor is cut by exactly the amount that makes the tax revenue from the labor market fall by the amount of the

43   In part two of this book, we assume this ideal condition to be met. Because of the manifest problems of this approach, we then assume in part three that monetizing the externalities is impossible.

44   We do not want to arouse the impression that the various subdivisions of economic theory have nothing to do with each other. Nonetheless, it makes sense for the various areas to have differing focuses. The assumption that everything is connected with everything else can hardly be denied, but does not help us much – whether in the world of science or in real life.

proceeds of the green tax. Let us assume that this happens precisely when the tax rate on the labor market is lowered from t_L^0 to t_L^1 and that this is correctly depicted in Figure 28.[45] Correspondingly, the supply curve for the labor factor in Figure 28 falls from $S_L + t_L^0$ to $S_L + t_L^1$. The new equilibrium amount of the labor factor is L_1^*, and the new gross and net wage rates l_G^1 (l_N^1), respectively. For our context, the decisive thing is that the cut in the tax burden on the labor factor made possible at a constant national budget by pulling in the green tax revenue has led to an improvement in the *employment situation* (from L_0^* to L_1^*). This gives us a conclusive description of the second dividend from the green tax in its employment-oriented version.

Matters must be looked at somewhat differently to illustrate the case of double dividend where the focus is on lowering the *excess burden* of taxation on labor. Let us first consider the illustration of the Pigou tax in Figure 27. The "environmental benefit" of the taxation is that with the fall in equilibrium output from x^* to x^{**}, the externalities (assumed to be proportional to the output) also fall. The external costs thus saved are symbolized in the graph by the horizontally hatched area *DZFE*. The environmental benefit is "paid for" by lowering the sum of producer and consumer surplus. This loss that suppliers and demanders on the market suffer is represented in Figure 28 by the vertically hatched area *FEZ*. The correct Pigovian tax rate is defined by the fact that the tax maximizes the difference between the increase in benefit in the "environmental sector" and the losses in benefit in the "goods sector." The positive net benefit from the Pigovian taxation is quantified in the graph as the exclusively horizontally hatched area *ZED*.[46]

---

45 The last phrase is a safeguard clause for the student auxiliaries to the Chair of Economic Theory at the University of Hagen.

46 To simplify, we assume that the level of the Pigovian tax rate established previously remains constant, even if the nature of this tax changes. This "change in nature" occurs when the Pigou tax is no longer used exclusively to pursue the objective of internalization, but a "second dividend" is also aimed at. Closer observation would show that the optimum tax rate changes if the welfare effects on the labor market are included. The optimum tax rate is then no longer distinguished by maximizing the difference between the benefit arising in the environmental sector and the costs incurred in the goods sector. Instead, the sum of the benefit arising in the environmental sector and on the factor market minus the costs to be borne on the goods market is what has to be maximized. In the present context, the tax has to take account not only of a disruption to the market mechanism (namely, the externality), but also of a second disruption (namely, the distortions caused to the labor factor by the tax). In the literature, the optimum tax rate sought under these more complicated circumstances is (somewhat obscurely) termed the "second-best" tax rate. The problem described here has an importance that reaches far beyond the context of interest and is dealt with in the literature under "second-best theory." Some general literature on second-best theory is Begg/Fisher/Dornbusch (2008) and Friedman (2002). And specifically on the second-best green tax rate, see Goulder (1997) and Schöb (2005). We consider another problem of "second-best" environmental policy in the previous chapter. (See the observations there on the optimum ("second-best"!) Pigovian tax rate with a monopoly polluter.)

If the tax revenue is used in the way described to lower the tax burden on labor, as depicted in Figure 28, then the tax rate levied on labor will (as explained previously) fall from t_L^0 to t_L^1. That means the additional costs of taxation in Figure 28 are now only $CC'G$. They have therefore fallen, in comparison with the situation with no green tax, by the amount $BGC'D$. From this "gross welfare increase" attained on the labor market, the welfare losses incurred on the goods market have to be deducted. In its tax efficiency−oriented interpretation, the strong double-dividend hypothesis claims a positive net effect: the welfare losses on the goods market brought about by the environmental taxation work out lower than the welfare benefits obtained on the labor market by "distributing" the green tax revenue. On the strong double-dividend hypothesis, then, the area FEZ in Figure 27 is smaller than area $BGC'D$ in Figure 28.

On green tax reform, many environmentally convinced participants have probably acted on the motto: "The tale of the double dividend is so nice it just has to be true." Looking at the graphic presentations explained previously, too, the double dividend in its employment-oriented interpretation certainly seems to have high plausibility. After all, labor is financially unburdened by the fiscal policy maneuver, so it is hardly surprising if more of it is employed at equilibrium. Instead, in the tax efficiency−oriented variant, a glance is enough to raise doubts. It is anything but easy to see that a particular quantitative relationship will always hold between the welfare-reducing effects on the goods market and the welfare-increasing effects on the labor market.

In the early 1990s, accordingly, considerable doubts were heard in the academic debate as to whether the double dividend actually exists. In particular, the articles by Bovenberg and de Mooij (1994), Bovenberg and van der Ploeg (1994), and Goulder (1995) shook confidence in the double dividend severely and lastingly.[47] The core of the criticism is that the type of economic intuition trained in partial equilibrium models, as presented by way of example in Figures 27 and 28, has led to premature conclusions. With such an important shift for the whole economy as bringing in green taxes, the interdependencies among various markets and sectors in an economy (and even beyond the single national economy!) would have to be systematically studied. Here particular attention would have to be paid to feedback effects. By definition, partial equilibrium analysis is not capable of this. Instead, the effect of a green tax must be chased up using the program of *general equilibrium theory*.[48] So, total analysis instead of partial analysis, then! Illuminating the effects

47   The most important criticisms were tellingly dealt with by Pethig (2003a, 2003b). The reference to Goulder (2002) is meant for readers with more time to devote to this. It brings together the most important (to date) contributions to the discussion, reprinted from the most varied academic journals. Size: 649 pages! A very brief exposition is in Endres (1997a).

48   General equilibrium theory is the keystone of neoclassical microeconomics. Specifically, on the utilization of general equilibrium theory in environmental and resource economics, see Conrad (2002) and Krysiak/Krysiak (2003), and for our specific context, Conrad/Löschel (2005) and (in a dynamic variant) Glomm et al. (2008).

of a green tax with the torch of general equilibrium theory, we see whole sets of effects arguing against the existence of a double dividend that partial equilibrium analysis systematically overlooks. The connections are multifarious and complex. We cannot give them even approximately completely here. But an abbreviated presentation always contains the danger of falsification. If we nonetheless list some viewpoints from a total analysis, this has been done in order to give some insight into the nature of that analysis and its findings.

One important reason for the doubts as to the validity of the double-divided hypothesis resulting from general equilibrium considerations is that green taxes raise the equilibrium prices of goods and thus lower real wages. This changes the equilibrium allocation of the individual decision maker's time budget between work and leisure time against work time, thus reducing the supply of labor. In addition, the fall in the output of environmentally intensive goods might lead to a fall in employment. All in all, it would be uncertain which of the opposing tendencies mentioned would ultimately prevail.

Let us look somewhat more closely at the argument about the change in leisure versus work calculation induced by the green tax, with the help of Figure 28. The increase in the price level of goods lowers the worker's real wages. In Figure 28, the labor supply curve shows the worker's inclination to spend time working as a function of the level of the nominal wage. The fall in the real wage rate indicated shifts the labor supply curve upward (to S_L^-). Including the tax on the labor factor, then, the labor supply curve becomes $S_L^- + t_L^1$ (and not, as argued previously, ignoring the real wages effect, $S_L + t_L^1$). Accordingly, the equilibrium amount of employment at tax rate t_L^1 is not as argued above L_1^*, but L_1^{*-}. This is already bad enough for defenders of the double-dividend hypothesis, but it gets worse.

The fall in equilibrium employment to L_1^{*-} has narrowed the tax base for the tax on the employment of labor. Correspondingly, the tax rate on the labor factor should not be cut from t_L^0 to t_L^1 as assumed in Figure 28, but only to a rate lying between these two. The following consideration facilitates an understanding of this point: if things are as assumed in discussing Figure 28 *without taking the real wage effect into account*, then the tax revenue "earned" on the labor market will amount to "tax rate times equilibrium amount of labor" (i.e., $t_L^1 L_1^*$). *Because of the real wage effect*, however, the same tax revenue has to be raised at the lower equilibrium labor level L_1^{*-}. This can be done at tax rate $\bar{t}$ (not entered in Fig. 28), for which $t_L^1 L_1^* / \overline{L}_1 = \bar{t}_L$ applies. Here $\overline{L}_1$ is defined by the point of intersection of MVP_L with $S_L^- + \bar{t}$ and must be determined simultaneously with $\bar{t}$. Because L_1^{*-} is smaller than L_1^* and $\overline{L}$ smaller than L_1^{*-}, $\bar{t}_L$ must be greater than t_L^1. This adjustment to the tax rate on labor (from t_L^1 to $\bar{t}_L$) necessary in the interest of ensuring the national budget is known in the literature as the *tax interaction effect*. It strengthens the "fiscal wedge" between the marginal opportunity costs of labor and the marginal value product of labor in comparison with the situation shown in Figure 28 and thus increases the additional burden of taxation.

The effects mentioned mean that the labor supply curve used for the "intuitive" presentation of the double-dividend hypothesis, $S_L + t_L^1$ in Figure 28, is "too low", in two ways. A first upward shift is needed because of the fall in real wages associated with the increase in price of goods. A second shift is needed to depict the tax interaction effect. The two effects are added to each other in their employment-lowering effect (which runs counter to the double-dividend argument).

Similar negative arguments as with the employment-oriented interpretation of the double-dividend hypothesis can also be made about the interpretation oriented to the efficiency of the tax system. There have long been discussions in public finance about the criteria for designing a tax system in order to make the additional burden of taxation explained previously as low as possible.[49] Two rules of thumb derived from *optimum taxation theory* are useful for assessing the green tax in our context. The first says that the tax base ought to be as broad as possible. This limits taxpayers' possibilities of substituting other activities for the taxed ones. The second rule demands that the taxation should be aimed at activities that respond inelastically to price increases associated with the taxation.[50] According to both criteria, there is little room for environmental taxes in a tax system aimed at minimizing the additional burden. Because the environmental tax is deliberately aimed at activities that harm the environment, it has a narrow tax base. Moreover, strong substitution effects and strong (negative) level effects are the very objective of green taxation.

Of course, the previous points (and many other arguments put forward in the literature) do not yet prove that a double dividend from green taxation (in one version or the other) definitely does not exist. What has instead been shown is that it does not *necessarily* exist. Its existence depends on a multiplicity of features of the economy considered (or of the model used to analyze this economy). For instance, the previously mentioned Bovenberg and van der Ploeg (1994) article "builds in" a whole series of assumptions that minimize from the outset the chances of a double dividend. In particular, it is there assumed that the tax system is optimum in the sense described previously even before introducing the green tax. It is further assumed that the labor employed in an economy is proportional to the output quantity. Finally, it is assumed that the externality is proportional to output. This makes the losses of benefit on the goods market "heaped on us" by the green tax particularly dramatic. On a more realistic consideration, we should have to include the point that the rational polluter will react to the green tax by a minimum cost combination of output reduction and all the other possibilities of emission abatement.[51] Nor should it be ignored that bringing in the green tax

---

49   Fundamentally, see Diamond/Mirrlees (1971). Sir James A. Mirrlees was awarded the Nobel Prize in Economics in 1996.

50   Clearly, there are connections between the two criteria.

51   See the presentation in section C.I.1 in part three of this book.

will also stimulate technical progress in emission abatement.[52] This, too, will tend (lastingly) to cut the welfare losses from green taxation. The green tax's chances of "scoring" a second dividend are still further reduced if it is assumed that the externality impinges solely on the consumption benefit of households. But in many cases the fact is that environmental damage worsens firms' production conditions. The ecological improvement associated with the green tax would lower marginal production costs in the relevant sectors and thus bring positive effects on welfare and employment.[53]

These qualifications are by no means intended to "pooh-pooh" Bovenberg's and van der Ploeg's model. They are merely intended to make it clear that the question of the existence of the double dividend cannot be answered unambiguously in general. There can only be discussion about specifying the conditions under which the double dividend exists.[54] Considerable progress has been made on this in recent years in the literature.[55] The analysis shows that the welfare and employment effects of a green tax in the double-dividend sense react extremely sensitively to changes in the assumptions used in the model. Particular importance attaches here to the structure of the existing tax system (before introduction of the environmental taxation), the characteristics of the labor market, price-setting behavior on the goods markets considered, and the nature of international interactions. Altogether, though, a look through the numerous studies (particularly the empirical ones) should warn advocates of green tax reforms to be wary of using the double-dividend hypothesis as a slogan. From a welfare economic viewpoint, in the debate over an introduction of green taxes, the hypothesis ultimately looks like an "overkill" argument. The arguments for using environmental policy instruments may be very strong, but they are not so strong that employing them can be justified even if their ecological benefits are completely ignored. Instead, we just have to accept that environmental protection is often not some sort of "win—win" measure that can

---

52   See under the heading "Dynamic incentive effect" in section C.II of part three of this book.

53   One might object to this argument that the double-dividend hypothesis asserts positive net effects from green taxation, even leaving the environmental effects completely out of account. But because the ecology-based improvements in production conditions mentioned here would include environmental effects, we may then want to accept this. However, the concept of excluding the environmental effects of an environmental tax in assessing that tax becomes more odd (than it is anyway) if, in addition to the environmental benefit to households, cost reductions in firms are brought into the definition of the positive environmental effects. Things would then be like this: green taxation might give rise to two effects on supply and demand on the labor market. The first would be an effect tending to lower employment by lowering real wages. The second would tend to promote employment through the increase in the marginal value product of labor brought by the improvement to production conditions. In analyzing the employment effects of the green tax, the first effect would be evaluated, whereas the second "does not count." This way of going about things can hardly be convincing.

54   As Pethig's (2003b) rather conceited observation has it: "Unfortunately interdependence effects in general equilibrium analyses can support just about every pathological result. . . . "

55   For an overview, see Schöb (2005).

be brought in such a way as to "do everyone good and no one ill." Environmental policy is justified when its benefits exceed its costs (estimated to the best of our knowledge and belief). This is the viewpoint that is to the fore in the internalization of externalities dealt with in part two of this book. Moreover, environmental policy should be designed in such a way as to minimize its costs. This is the aspect that is to the fore when considering standard-oriented instruments in part three of this book.

This previously mentioned and extremely important aspect has not yet played any part in the discussion of the double dividend. Focusing on the relevant debates, the question of the double dividend would have to be formulated: "How does the relative advantageousness profile of various standard-oriented instruments change when we take into account the possibility of using the government's revenue from introducing the instrument to promote employment and/or improve the efficiency of the tax system?" Where this sort of consideration will take us can best be grasped by comparing the two variants of tradable emission permits presented in part three (section B.III.1) of this book.

Let us suppose that the alternative is, *ceteris paribus*, to auction emission permits or distribute them free. The negative effects of environmental policy disclosed by the general equilibrium analysis would not (by and large) differ. In both variants, goods prices would rise so that employment would fall. However, with the auction variant, the government would obtain income it could use to reduce the burden on labor. That would at least give it the possibility of compensating (at any rate partly) for the negative employment effect coming from the goods market. The variant of gratis permits does not offer this possibility. Thus, the auction variant has a welfare potential that its rival does not. On this pattern, the environmental policy instruments analyzed in this book (and more) could be compared with each other. This could make a major contribution to the environmental economics analysis of the instruments. All round, the outcome would be an advantage for the instruments that generate government revenue (auctioned permits, green taxes) vis-à-vis the other instruments.[56] The first study focusing on this question is, as far as the author is aware, Conrad/Schröder (1993). The authors look at the employment effects of using environmental policy instruments with a predetermined target. In regard to the "environmental flank" of their model, accordingly, they follow the principle of standard-oriented environmental policy. Specifically, the target would be to cut CO_2 emissions over a particular period by 20%. By using a computable general equilibrium model, they reach the finding that employment ends up higher if the environmental policy is pursued through emission taxes rather than command and

---

56   Because of the double-dividend potential, many authors see "a strong case on efficiency grounds for using carbon taxes or auctioned permits over grandfathered permits" (Parry, 2003, p. 385). An expanded approach is pursued by Wagner (2005). He seeks to optimize a portfolio of environmental policy and labor market policy instruments.

control. Burtraw et al. (2006, p. 267) cite a whole range of empirical studies that support the thesis formulated previously that environmental policy instruments that generate public revenue are superior in welfare terms.

In assessing the environmental policy relevance of such findings, one ought, however, to bear in mind that the argument here has been carried on purely within the framework of welfare economics. The first point is that the revenue-generating instruments create a *potential* for welfare improvements that the instruments with no government revenue lack. If as is usual in welfare economics one sees the state as guardian of the common weal, the question as to whether the state will actually exploit the welfare potential generated becomes superfluous. For this, it would "only" have to take account of the rules of optimum taxation theory, or in designing its revenue recycling, aim at the maximum employment effect. Economists trained in public choice theory, who have always shaken their heads anyway at the naiveté of the welfare economists,[57] now have there hair finally standing on end (as a consequence of particularly vigorous head shaking). They are certain that the *Leviathan* state will ultimately use green tax revenue to expand its share of the national economy. Correspondingly, the state will not, say their expectations, select the green tax rate optimally in the sense of maximizing the net effect of the various dividends, but in such a way as to uphold the interests of the social groups that have the most push. Against this background, the question raised by Zimmermann/Gaynor (1999), "The Double Dividend: Miracle or Fata Morgana?", may confidently be seen as a rhetorical one.

E. The Induction of Advances in Environmental Technology through Environmental Policy

I. Preliminary Remarks

An analysis of the environmental economics literature shows that research interest has in recent years to some extent shifted from the static analysis of internalization strategies and standard-oriented environmental policy instruments to their capacity to induce progress in environmental technologies. The theoretical attractiveness and environmental policy relevance of this aspect is obvious. A long-term—oriented environmental policy cannot be confined to incentivizing decision makers to make "proper" use of a given environmental technology. It must additionally set the framework conditions in such a way that they will develop the "proper" technology. Of course, the issue is not between this approach and the other. Instead, both

---

57 Who would reply to the reproach of naiveté by saying that it involves a regrettable misunderstanding. The state as guardian of the common weal in welfare economics is to be regarded as a normative concept. We do not continue this (friendly?) dispute any further here, although it would certainly be tempting.

problems indicated must be solved simultaneously: in the ideal case, the "proper technology" is at all times employed to the "proper extent."[58]

In the arguments in this book, we base ourselves predominantly on a static economic model. In particular, possibilities of reducing emissions are mostly taken as given. In a simple variant of the model, we assume that emissions are strictly proportional to the output of the firm concerned. That would make output reduction the only available "method" of emission reduction. In somewhat more general modeling, we assume that alongside output reduction there is some other possibility (say, the use of filtering technology) for avoiding emissions. Under these conditions, two objectives of analysis are pursued. The point was, first, to find what emission quantity ought *ideally* to be abated by these given methods (or how this quantity was to be distributed over the various emitters). To define what "ideal" is in this context, we need an operable *standard*. Designing it depends on whether we are thinking in terms of internalization approaches (presented in part two) or in terms of standard-oriented environmental policy (discussed in part three). With the internalization approaches, the standard sought is the emission quantity for which the sum of aggregate emission abatement cost and external damage is a minimum. In a framework of standard-oriented environmental policy, the standard is defined by that allocation of a given emission quantity over individual emitters that minimizes aggregate emission abatement cost.

The second object of investigation was to work out what *means* might be suited to meeting the context-specific goal. In the internalization context, we asked how far the sum of abatement cost and damage could be minimized by Coase-type negotiations, a Pigou tax, or various liability rules. In the context of standard-oriented instruments, we asked whether command and control, emission taxes, or tradable permits best met the objective of cost-effectively allocating a given aggregate emission reduction.

Moving away from this mainstream of our discussion, in section C.II of part three we look at the effects of environmental policy instruments on progress in environmental technologies. This takes us away from the path of the static approach. Here we are guided by the objective of keeping the presentation as simple as possible in the fundamental parts of this book. A price had to be paid. For our context,

---

58   The aspect of the "long run" plays an important part in the debate on sustainable development (see part six of this book) and specifically of climate policy (see part five). Correspondingly, recent research in these two sectors has increasingly turned to the question of the determinants and effects of technical progress. Cf., e.g., the contributions in the special issue titled "Technological Change and the Environment" of the journal *Ecological Economics*, Vol. 54 (2005), No. 2–3, edited by C. Kemfert and H.R.J. Vollebergh, as well as those in the special issue titled "Modeling Technical Change in Climate Policy Analyses" of the journal *Energy Economics*, Vol. 28 (2006), edited by J. Horton, and those in the special issue titled "Technological Change and the Environment" of *Energy Economics*, Vol. 30 (2008), No. 6, edited by K. Fisher-Wanden. Also relevant is the work of Bretschger (2005).

the price was that in evaluating progress in environmental technology we used an extremely rough-cut criterion: we considered as best the environmental policy instrument that, in respect of its performance in inducing progress in environmental technology, displayed the highest dynamic incentive effect. In the model framework of part three, this criterion is not contradictory in itself because innovation costs are not considered. On the more general (and, of course, more realistic) assumption that the stimulation of environmental technological progress also consumes scarce resources, a valuation that amounts to "the more technical progress, the better" is however no longer tenable. It is also possible to invest too much in technical progress.

We accordingly want to take up the theme of induction of progress in environmental technologies again and analyze it rather more precisely.[59] As in the static theory, we distinguish between internalization approaches and standard-oriented environmental policy.

II. Internalization of Externalities and Induced Advances in Environmental Technology

To assess the performance of internalization efforts in the dynamic context at issue here, we need a standard that describes the "ideal state." The procedure is thus fully analogous to the procedure described in the static analysis. To prepare for these expanded considerations, we start by putting what we previously explained in more formal terms.

In the static analysis, the object of internalization efforts is to reach a state where the sum of emission abatement costs and damage is a minimum. The point is thus to find the quantity of emission abatement that will minimize the total cost function $C^T = AC + D$. Here $AC = AC(a)$ (i.e., the amount of abatement cost depends on the quantity of emission abated), $D = D(E)$ (i.e., the amount of external damage depends on the quantity of emitted pollutant), and $E = E^* - a$ (i.e., the emission quantity results from the uncorrected emission equilibrium quantity E^* less the quantity of abated emissions a) all hold. For the optimum emission abatement quantity a^{**}, accordingly, $C^T = AC(a) + D(E^* - a) = $ min will hold. If the abatement cost and damage functions are well behaved in the sense of differential calculus, then the optimum emission abatement quantity is defined by

$$\partial AC/\partial a + \frac{\partial D}{\partial E}\frac{\partial(E^* - a)}{\partial a} = 0$$

or equivalently by $\partial AC/\partial a = \partial D/\partial E$.

The optimality condition amounts to the same as the condition $MAC = MD$ ("marginal abatement cost = marginal damage") already frequently employed in

---

59 Cf. also Fischer/Newell (2008), Goeschel/Perino (2007), Requate (2005a, 2005b), with numerous further references.

this book. The rule of static internalization theory briefly recapitulated here should now be adjusted to the extended objective of our investigations (induction of environmental technological progress). Following the efficiency precept, we seek to find the simplest modeling that meets this objective. We move the total cost function of the static model into a consideration using two periods, 0 and 1, so that we write

$$C^T = AC^{(0)}(a^{(0)}) + AC^{(1)}(a^{(1)}, I^{(0)}) + I^{(0)} + D(E^{(0)}) + D(E^{(1)}).$$

Here $AC^{(0)}$, $AC^{(1)}$ represent the abatement costs in periods 0 and 1, which depend on the respective abatement levels $a^{(0)}$, $a^{(1)}$. D is the damage to be expected in each period, which depends on the period-specific emission level $E^{(0)}$, $E^{(1)}$. (To simplify, we take the damage function as invariant in time.)

So far, then, "not much has happened yet" in comparison with the static model. The situation modeled in the static case "timelessly" is depicted analogously in two periods, 0 and 1. The "trick" is now to combine the two periods, and this is done through the term $I^{(0)}$. $I^{(0)}$ means the amount of money that the firm invests in environmental technological progress. We see the effect of this investment in close analogy to what we said in section C.II of part three of this book: the more resources are invested in environmental technical progress, the more successfully will marginal abatement cost be lowered in comparison with the *status quo ante*. Formulating it more exactly, let us assume that the abatement cost function in period 1 amounts to a particular fraction ($1/f$) of the abatement cost in period 0. How big this fraction is depends on the investment amount. Fed into the graphs from part three, this means that the marginal abatement cost curve turns anticlockwise round the uncorrected emission level E^* ($= E^{(0)*} = E^{(1)*}$) the more in the transition from period 0 to period 1, the higher $I^{(0)}$ is chosen. Writing this formally, we have[60]

$$AC^{(1)}(a^{(1)}, I^{(0)}) = \frac{AC^{(0)}(a^{(1)})}{f(I^{(0)})}.$$

This simple (and therefore also as comprehensible as possible) approach has now specified the standard against which the internalization approaches are to be measured. Optimal are the period-specific emission abatement quantities $a^{(0)**}$, $a^{(1)**}$ and investment amount $I^{(0)**}$ that minimize the previous total

---

60   Here f takes the value 1 when nothing is invested. For positive investment amounts, f is above 1. All functions are well behaved in the differential calculus sense. A more general version of the "production function" for technical progress is used in Endres/Bertram/Rundshagen (2007, 2008) and Endres/Rundshagen (2008). Over and above that, of course, one could conceive of a less deterministic model of technical progress. We refrain from such complications here. An exhaustive discussion of the connections between technical progress and the properties of the marginal abatement cost curve can be found in Baker/Clark/Shittu (2008). Cf. also Bauman/Lee/Seeley (2008), Bréchet/Jouvet (2008), Endres/Friehe (2010).

cost function. The first-order optimality conditions are

$$\partial C^T / \partial a^{(0)} = 0 \leftrightarrow \frac{\partial AC^{(0)}}{\partial a^{(0)}} = \frac{\partial D}{\partial E^{(0)}}$$

$$\partial C^T / \partial a^{(1)} = 0 \leftrightarrow \frac{\partial AC^{(1)}}{\partial a^{(1)}} = \frac{\partial D}{\partial E^{(1)}}$$

$$\partial C^T / \partial I^{(0)} = 0 \leftrightarrow 1 = \frac{AC^{(0)} \partial f / \partial I^{(0)}}{f^2}.$$

The first two lines are perfectly equivalent to the optimality condition in the static model, $MAC = MD$: the *period-specific* abatement costs must be chosen in such a way that the marginal abatement cost in each case corresponds to the marginal damage, $MAC^{(0)} = MD^{(0)}$ and $MAC^{(1)} = MD^{(1)}$. The third line requires the investment level to be chosen in such a way that the marginal costs of investment correspond with the marginal abatement cost reduction attained in the next period. The marginal costs of investment appear with the value 1 because in the target function no physical units of investment are employed, but the money to be spent on the investment (i.e., the investment cost) already is.

The analogous question to the discussion in part two of the book would now be how far Coase-type negotiations, various liability rules, and/or a Pigovian tax are capable of reaching the optimum allocation described here. Putting it differently, in an adequate design of internalization strategies, how can framework conditions for the emitter's decision be set in such a way that *in his own interest* he will decide in both periods to implement the socially optimum abatement activities $a^{(0)**}$, $a^{(1)**}$, and in the starting period make the socially optimum investment $I^{(0)**}$? To answer this question, we must compare the social optimum, defined previously as the minimum of the social cost function, with the equilibrium for a firm. For space reasons, we do the analysis not for all internalization strategies, but only for the Pigou tax.[61]

From the static analysis, we know that at the social optimum the Pigovian tax rate corresponds with the marginal damage. The period-specific tax rates thus amount to

$$t^{(0)} = \frac{\partial D}{\partial E^{(0)}} (E^* - a^{(0)**})$$

and

$$t^{(1)} = \frac{\partial D}{\partial E^{(1)}} (E^* - a^{(1)**}).^{62}$$

---

61   For the dynamics of internalization with various liability law strategies, see Endres/Bertram (2006) and Endres/Bertram/Rundshagen (2007, 2008). On the effects of Coase-type negotiations on environmental technological progress, see Endres/Rundshagen (2008).

62   The part in brackets denotes the point at which the value of the marginal damage function is measured – the socially optimum emission level.

Let us now put ourselves in the position of an emitter aiming at cost minimization and subject to Pigovian taxation. His total costs, C, comprise period-specific abatement costs, investment expenditure, and period-specific taxes. Through the investment expenditure, as described previously, he can influence future abatement costs. Formally, the following problem of cost minimization presents itself to him, with one side condition:

$$C = AC^{(0)}(a^{(0)}) + AC^{(1)}(a^{(1)}, I^{(0)}) + I^{(0)} + t^{(0)}(E^* - a^{(0)}) + t^{(1)}(E^* - a^{(1)}) = min!$$

with

$$AC^{(1)}(a^{(1)}, I^{(0)}) = AC^{(0)}(a^{(1)})/f(I^{(0)}).$$

The first-order equilibrium conditions are

$$\partial C/\partial a^{(0)} = 0 \leftrightarrow \partial AC^{(0)}/\partial a^{(0)} = t^{(0)}$$
$$\partial C/\partial a^{(1)} = 0 \leftrightarrow \partial AC^{(1)}/\partial a^{(1)} = t^{(1)}$$
$$\partial C/\partial I^{(0)} = 0 \leftrightarrow 1 = AC^{(0)}(\partial f/\partial I^{(0)})/f^2$$

The rational emitter will thus extend his abatement activities in both periods up to the point where the period-specific abatement cost is equivalent to the period-specific Pigovian tax rate. He will invest in the new technology to the point where the marginal investment cost equals the marginal abatement cost saving in the next period. The values of the decision variables that meet these conditions (at "equilibrium values") we denote by $a^{(0)*}$, $a^{(1)*}$, $I^{(0)*}$.

Looking at the definition of the period-specific Pigovian tax rate formally expressed (period-specific marginal damage at the social optimum), we can immediately see that the equilibrium conditions for a firm aiming at cost minimization under Pigovian taxation are identical with the conditions for social optimality. With correctly chosen tax rates, the emitter will opt for precisely those abatement or investment amounts that are also socially optimum. So, then,

$$a^{(0)*} = a^{(0)**}$$
$$a^{(1)*} = a^{(1)**}$$
$$I^{(0)*} = I^{(0)**}.$$

We thus obtain a perfect analogy with the static analysis of the Pigovian tax: if the tax rates are properly chosen in the dynamic context with induced environmental technical progress, then it turns out that the Pigovian tax is an *ideal* internalization instrument. In particular, there is no need to take any special government measures alongside emission taxation aimed at inducing optimum technical progress. If the "price" for the emission is set properly, then the emitter will optimize the abatement technology "by himself," with no additional (positive or negative) incentives.

Of course, the word "ideal" used previously has to be seen as highly ambivalent. On the one hand, it means that the instrument is perfectly suited to reaching the objective. On the other hand, it already suggests that there might be problems employing the instrument in the "real" world, which (alas and alack!) is always in a natural relationship of tension with the "ideal" world. This ambivalence is something we are familiar with from the presentation of the static theory of Pigovian taxation in part two of this book. Here, too, Pigovian taxation is an ideal instrument in an ideal world. This is true, in particular, in connection with the assumption that the tax-setting authority knows the marginal damage arising at the social optimum.

In the dynamic context of relevance here, the restrictive information requirements for successful Pigovian taxation are further tightened: the tax-setting authority must know the marginal damage arising at the social optimum in both periods. Here it has to be borne in mind that the social optimum in the future period is also characterized by employment of the *optimum* abatement technique. The tax-setting authority must accordingly know the function shown previously as the constraint in the cost minimization problem, describing the productivity of investment in technical progress. This is essential because the tax-setting body must base the setting of the tax rate on the socially optimal technology. It is not enough to wait and see what technology emitters actually use and then respond by setting the tax. With this procedure, the tax rate would ultimately also depend on firms' decisions as to abatement technology. That would give firms strategic room for maneuver, exploitation of which would give rise to a divergence between equilibrium and optimum.[63]

Furthermore, the modeling assumes that the tax-setting body has no possibilities of manipulation vis-à-vis the firms. In particular, it must be possible for the state credibly to set in the present (when the investments in technical progress are being made) the tax rate to apply in the next period. If this is not the case, then the firms have reason to mistrust the government's present announcements about future tax rates.[64] It cannot then be expected that they will in the way we described previously adjust to this tax rate with the socially optimum investment.

A closer analysis shows furthermore that the internalization properties of the Pigovian tax and other internalization strategies in a dynamic context are subject to a number of problems that typically arise in the intertemporal context of induced technical progress. Among these are, for instance, discrepancies between private and social discount rates and spillovers in research and development.[65]

---

63 Cf. Biglaiser/Horowitz/Quiggin (1995). A similar problem arises with the attempt at internalization through fault liability (the negligence rule), cf. Endres/Bertram (2006).

64 Just let anyone still say economic theory is unrealistic!

65 On the first point, in intertemporal analysis, future effects are often discounted to the time of decision (an aspect we ignore for the sake of simplicity). It is possible for private decision makers and society as a whole to use differing discount rates. On the second point, it was previously implicitly assumed that the individual investor can enjoy the fruits of his investment in technical progress for himself alone ("as a purely private good"). Often, however, with research and development there are positive externalities (spill overs), where decision makers share in knowledge they have themselves contributed nothing to. For more details on this and other problems with the induction of environmental technical progress, cf., e.g., Endres/Bertram/Rundshagen

In this book, we cannot go into the details. It should, however, be stressed that the difficulties addressed here ought not to mislead one into the conclusion that the findings gained from dynamic modeling of internalization instruments are worthless. Instead, here, too, what was said in section B.V of part one, under the heading, "Nonetheless: internalization of externalities as an indispensable component of an environmental policy vision," applies.

III. Standard-Oriented Instruments and Induced Advances in Environmental Technology

In the dynamic analysis of standards-oriented instruments, we can borrow much from the procedure presented previously for internalization strategies. Because of the similarity, the following description has been kept brief.[66]

To assess the performance of standard-oriented instruments in the broader context under discussion here, we need a norm that describes the "ideal state." The procedure is thus again analogous with the considerations in the static analysis dealt with exhaustively in part three of the book and briefly summarized here. To prepare for the expanded considerations, we start by writing what we explained previously in more formal terms. In the static analysis, the object of the standard-oriented instruments is to find a distribution of a firm's individual emission abatement activities that adds up precisely to a set aggregate emission abatement target while minimizing aggregate abatement costs.

Formulating it rather more formally, let us consider n emitters numbered by the indices 1 through n. The standard by which the "performance" of the standard-oriented instruments is measured is that distribution of a firm's individual emission abatement quantities $a_1^{**}, \ldots, a_n^{**}$ that will minimize the aggregate total cost function

$$C^T = \sum_{i=1}^{n} AC_i(a_i)$$

under the constraint

$$\sum_{i=1}^{n} a_i = \overline{a}.$$

Here $\overline{a}$ is the target set by environmental policy for aggregate emission abatement. As we know, among the firms' individual allocations that meet the environmental policy target formulated previously as a secondary condition, the minimum

(2007, 2008), and the survey in Requate (2005b) and the other articles in the special issue titled "Technological Change and the Environment" of *Ecological Economics*, Vol. 54 (2005), No. 2–3.

66 An exhaustive, fully worked out modeling theory version of the argument presented here in abbreviated form and with frequent appeals to the reader's intuition can be found in Endres/Rundshagen (2010).

cost one is the one for which $MAC_i = MAC_j$ holds. At the cost minimum, then, the marginal abatement costs of two arbitrarily chosen firms (here denoted by the indices i and j) are equal to each other, a form of the "equimarginal condition" that played a prominent part in part three when considering cost effectiveness.[67]

Now that we briefly recapitulated the standard for evaluating standard-oriented environmental policy instruments and put it in fairly formal terms, we can now adapt it to the broader objective in our current context of discourse, namely, modeling the induction of environmental technological progress. In accordance with the procedure for internalization strategies, we seek to go about it as simply as possible. To do so, we specify the formulation in the static analysis, by definition "timeless," for two successive periods, 0 and 1, and represent the relation between the two periods, as in the internalization context, using a function depicting how investments in environmental technical progress in period 0 can influence abatement costs in period 1. The object of the standard-oriented environmental policy is, then, to minimize a two-period aggregate cost function consisting of the aggregate abatement costs plus the sum of the investments spent by firms on technical progress. As secondary conditions, we must bear in mind that the aggregate emission abatement targets set by environmental policy in both periods are to be kept to. In addition, the solution sought must keep within the framework of the technically possible reductions in emission abatement cost by investment in technical progress. In formal terms, then, we seek the values $a_i^{(0)**}$, $a_i^{(1)**}$, $I_i^{(0)**}$ that are solutions to the following limited minimization problem:

$$C^T = \sum_{i=1}^{n} AC_i^{(0)} + \sum_{i=1}^{n} I_i^{(0)} + \sum_{i=1}^{n} AC_i^{(1)} = min!,$$

under the constraints

$$\sum_{i=1}^{n} a_i^{(t)} = \overline{a}^{(t)}, \text{ for } t = 0 \text{ and } t = 1, \text{ and also}$$

$$AC_i^{(1)} = \frac{AC_i^{(0)}(a_i^{(1)})}{f_i(I_i^{(0)})},$$

for all values of i between 1 and n inclusive.

The symbols are (as in section II) to be read as in the static formulation. The bracketed superscript numbers to the decision variables of firm i (a_i or I_i), 0 or 1, denote the corresponding period.

Minimizing the Lagrange function associated with this program leads to the optimality conditions

$$\partial AC_i^{(0)}/\partial a_i^{(0)} = \partial AC_j^{(0)}/\partial a_j^{(0)}$$
$$\partial AC_i^{(1)}/\partial a_i^{(1)} = \partial AC_j^{(1)}/\partial a_j^{(1)}$$
$$1 = AC_i^{(0)} \left(\partial f_i/\partial I_i^{(0)} \right) / f_i^2.$$

---

67   We again assume that the underlying functions are well behaved in the differential calculus sense.

The first two lines are nothing but the period-specific equivalent of the cost-effectiveness condition familiar from the static analysis of environmental policy instruments, $MAC_i = MAC_j$. The marginal abatement costs of two arbitrarily chosen firms, i and j, are equal to each other at the cost minimum for period 0. The same applies to period 1.

The third line is identical with the corresponding condition in the analysis of internalization strategies. For each firm, at the cost minimum, the marginal investment costs incurred in period 0 correspond to the abatement cost savings induced thereby in period 1. As with the internalization strategies, the marginal investment costs are standardized to the value 1.

To evaluate the performance of standard-oriented instruments (emission taxes, tradable permits, or command and control), we have to ask whether the period-specific equilibrium values chosen by emitters when these instruments are employed, $a_i^{(0)*}$, $a_i^{(1)*}$, $I_i^{(0)*}$, correspond to the previously cited optimum values $a_i^{(0)**}$, $a_i^{(1)**}$, $I_i^{(0)**}$.

As the more detailed analysis in Endres/Rundshagen (2010) shows, the "performance" of the standard-oriented instruments depends decisively on what information is available to the actors regarding the functions contained in the previously displayed cost minimization program.

- Let us first assume a "perfect information" scenario in which every decision maker, on this assumption, knows the functions contained previously. In this special case, all environmental policy instruments considered are cost effective: if government knows the relevant functions, then it also knows which values meet the previously listed first-order conditions for cost minimization (i.e., knows the cost-effective $a_i^{(0)**}$, $a_i^{(1)**}$, $I_i^{(0)**}$). In a command and control policy, government need merely prescribe the optimum emission abatement level for each firm. It could, of course, with the extremely generous provision of information assumed here, also prescribe the optimum investment amount, but this is by no means necessary. After all, each individual firm is interested in cost minimization and will in its own interest spend the innovation amount for which the sum of its abatement costs and investment expenditure is a minimum. Because we assume no externalities with the innovation, there is a harmony of interests from the outset between government and firm if the emission abatement quantity is set by the state at the minimum cost level.

  In the informational special case considered here, the matter is equally simple for emission taxes. Because the government knows the relevant functions, it also knows how high firms' marginal abatement costs are at the given period-specific cost minimum. It must set the period-specific emission tax rate at this level, and firms will already adjust their emission abatement quantities to this in such a way as to bring about the identity of the equilibrium values $a_i^{(0)*}$, $a_i^{(1)*}$ and the cost minimum values $a_i^{(0)**}$, $a_i^{(1)**}$. The optimum investment here again, as with imposed requirements, comes about "automatically."

With emission permits, things are a bit different because the state neither has to determine individual abatement quantities (as with command and control) nor set period-specific "prices" (as with taxes). The prices for emitting are formed on the market for emission permits. In the outcome, however, with perfect information, there are no differences from the results presented previously for emission taxes and command and control. With permits, it is not the government but the individual emitter that profits from the generous endowment of information in our first scenario. If the relevant functions are generally known (are *common knowledge*), then each emitter knows the demand curve on the permits market in both period 0 and period 1. If the government has fixed on period-specific aggregate emission abatement targets, as we assume, then every emitter also knows the permit prices in both periods. The period-specific permit price then plays the same part for the individual emitter's decision to abate and the amount to invest in technical progress as was explained previously for the emission tax rates.

- Let us now briefly consider a second informational scenario in which the all too generous information endowment of the actors involved is now thinned down a bit. In particular, let us assume that the decision makers no longer know the individual firm's marginal abatement cost functions, but only the total abatement cost function aggregated over all emitters.[68] ("Of course," we always retain the assumption that each firm knows its own marginal abatement cost curve.)

This worsening of the information conditions in the move from the first scenario to the second has a disastrous effect on the efficiency of a command and control policy. Because the state must optimally specify firms' individual abatement quantities in such a policy, the information endowment in scenario 2 is no longer sufficient for a cost-effective command and control policy. The government's problem with cost effectiveness in this scenario for modeling command and control policy with induced environmental technological progress is totally analogous to the cost-effectiveness problems described in part three for the governmental context. Because the requisite information is missing, government must have recourse to a "pragmatic" distribution of emission abatement burdens over firms (e.g., to a "one size fits all" command and control policy in the sense of part three). That means it will miss the cost-effectiveness target.

In contrast, government is not affected by the deterioration in information endowment in the move from the first scenario to the second if it is pursuing an emission tax environmental policy. For emission taxes, knowing firms' individual abatement cost functions is not necessary. The tax rate set by government should be equal for all firms. Only then, of course, will there be the equilibrium

---

68   Only if the firms are identical are the individual marginal abatement cost curves known once the aggregate marginal abatement cost curve is. We ignore this special case.

situation necessary for a cost minimum, at which firms' individual marginal abatement costs have become equal to each other through adjustment of the emission abatement quantity.[69] As long as government knows the aggregate marginal abatement cost curve in both periods, its problems in the dynamic context at issue here are no greater than in the static context illustrated in Figure 18. Government sets the tax rate, as shown in segment (c) of Figure 18, at the level of aggregate marginal abatement costs at the point of aggregate target emission. The firms then adapt appropriately with their individual emission abatement decisions, thus "automatically" bringing about the minimum cost state. In the dynamic context, this is true for both periods. If the "right price" for emitting has been arrived at in this way, then things proceed as in the first information scenario, where firms in their own interest choose the optimum (minimum cost) investment level.

With tradable emission permits, things are much the same as with emission taxes. If the emitters know the aggregate marginal abatement costs in both periods, as assumed in the second information scenario, then they also know the demand curves on the permit market in both periods. If the environmental policy target and thus the supply of permits is known, then firms also know the period-specific equilibrium price on the permits market. This then plays the same role as explained previously for the emission tax rate when it comes to bringing the equilibrium values of firm- and period-specific emission abatement quantities and firm-specific investment amounts into equality with the values of these variables efficient for the whole economy.

• Let us now briefly consider yet a third information scenario, in which the supply of that elixir of life, "information," to the actors in the model is throttled even further back than in the second information scenario. As in the second scenario, the aggregate marginal abatement cost function in period 0 is still supposed to be known to every actor. For the marginal cost in period 1, however, we assume that each emitter knows only his own abatement cost function. The abatement costs in period 1 are, then, *private information*. This diminution of the information supply takes account of the fact that the second information scenario implicitly assumed that the productivity of each firm's investments in technical progress is accessible to every other actor (than the firm considered). This is certainly a restrictive assumption, positively "crying out" to be eliminated.

Under these circumstances, the efficiency of command and control policy is no worse off than in the second information scenario. This is rather meagre consolation because after all in the second scenario the command and control policy was identified as cost ineffective and thus, already in that scenario, landed at the bottom of the evaluation hierarchy. You cannot do worse than

---

69 There is an important distinction to draw here: the marginal abatement cost *curves* of the firms are assumed to differ. At the equilibrium (and at cost minimum), however, it is the case that the marginal abatement costs of all firms take on the same *value*.

that. But although the cost effectiveness of an emission tax stood up to the deterioration in the information conditions in the move from the first scenario to the second, that's all over now. If government does not know the aggregate marginal abatement cost function in period 1, then it cannot be in a position to set the emission tax rate that induces cost effectiveness. However, a wrongly set tax rate means that, as in the static model, the aggregate emission abatement target aimed at will be missed at equilibrium. In addition, a wrongly set tax rate sends out a wrong signal to firms in relation to their decision on investment level in period 0. Last, at equilibrium in the third information scenario, with emission taxation the wrong emission quantity is abated with the wrong technology.

Things are similar with emission permits. If firms do not know the aggregate marginal abatement cost function in period 1, then they will, in contrast with the second scenario, not correctly predict the permit price in the first period. A wrongly anticipated permit price for period 1 will, just like the emission tax set wrongly for period 1, lead to a misallocation in the sphere of investment in technical progress. In contrast with taxation, however, the information deficit with permits cannot have the effect that in period 1 the government's aggregate emission abatement target will be missed. As explained in the static model in part three, this is by definition out of the question with a permits policy.[70]

The only possibility for attaining an efficient allocation even under the conditions of the third information scenario is to think up a permit system in which binding agreements on the transfer of permits in period 1 can already be arrived at in period 0. This is a policy with *permit futures markets*. Because in the third information scenario it is, however, still assumed that each individual emitter knows his own period-specific marginal abatement cost function as well as his own "production function for technical progress," the correct permit price will be arrived at on a futures market for permits (assumed to be perfect). Accordingly, the individual firm's abatement quantities in period 1 and the firm-specific investments in environmental technical progress are in this specific variant of the permit model just as optimal (in the sense of efficient for the whole economy) as in the second information scenario.

In conclusion, we may state that no simple answer is possible to the question of the "dynamic cost effectiveness" of standard-oriented instruments. We can at least say that in the model framework sketched out here, taxes and tradable permits cut a "better figure" than command and control because they are less susceptible to departures from the extreme assumption of perfect information. Of the three information scenarios briefly presented, scenario 2 is the one with the closest analogies to the circumstances assumed in the static textbook literature (here part three of this book). In this framework, it turns out that extending the object of investigation to the dynamic context, including induced technical progress, brings

---

70 As in part three, we assume that the actors stick by the rules of the game for permit policy (just as by those for the other instruments).

no change in the ranking of the standard-oriented instruments: emission taxes and emission permits are efficient, whereas command and control is not.

IV. The Economics of an Ecological Technology Policy

The two foregoing sections briefly set out how environmental policy can induce environmental technological progress. This is true of both the group of internalization strategies and the group of standard-oriented environmental policy instruments. The extent of the induction effect can be influenced by the design of the environmental policy. A more exact analysis can let us see what environmental policy instrumentation can come closest to the dynamically formulated norms of allocational efficiency or cost effectiveness in the given discourse context.

However, it became clear at the conclusion of each of the two sections (and can be pursued in further detail in the literature cited there) that environmental policy alone cannot fully guarantee dynamic efficiency (or cost effectiveness, respectively). Perhaps, then, we should look at how the use of environmental policy instruments can be supplemented by a targeted ecologically oriented technology policy. However, the point is especially the use of government resources to promote invention, innovation, and diffusion of ecologically superior efficient technologies. However, the following must be borne in mind.

We saw in the previous discussion how closely incentives to avoid emissions are bound up with incentives to introduce environmental technological progress. Emission abatement and technical change are two separate issues, which should correspondingly be regulated by the use of separately designed policies. However, environmental policy and ecological technology policy must be closely coordinated with each other, given the interdependencies of their effects. To develop an efficient portfolio of environmental policy and ecological technology policy in the scientific sphere, closer cooperation between *environmental economics* and *industrial economics* (the theory of industrial organization) is required.

But even considered in itself, ecological technology policy has to be "optimized." After all, environmental technological progress can be promoted by various sorts of governmental support. The individual technology policy instruments (and their combinations) must be evaluated according to strict assessment criteria, as is traditionally done in environmental economics in relation to environmental policy instruments.[71] Thus, for instance, the attempt must be made to find a design of promotion that can enable the state to support solutions to problems, instead of plumping from the outset for promoting particular procedures to solve the problem at issue. If this is not successfully achieved, then the principle of cost effectiveness in technology promotion may be missed. With its promotion of *particular* procedures for solving problems, government might even possibly nip the development of alternative and ultimately superior processes in the bud.

71   A good example of the type of analysis is offered by Helm/Schöttner (2008).

Alongside the question of which activities should be promoted by which means, it must also be decided who is to receive the support. If the state "bets on the wrong horse," then severe losses in the efficiency of the promotion measure may result. However, government does not know the "right horse." Here the literature of game theory has developed selection procedures the potential of which for an efficient ecological technology policy ought to be looked at.[72]

We would further recall that objections to subsidies have been raised from the viewpoint of the *new political economy* (public choice). As well as sheer incompetence and lack of care in allocation, these concern *rent seeking, cronyism,* and the *ossification of technical and economic structures.*[73]

Exercises

Exercise 4.1
Give some examples for environmental problems that are caused by pollutant interactions.

Exercise 4.2
Let the environmental burden B produced by two pollutants, x and y, be given by $B = a_1 x + a_2 y$, where $a_1 > 0$ and $a_2 > 0$ are constant coefficients of damage capacity. Further assume that the abatement cost functions of the x and y industry are strictly decreasing and convex.

Determine the optimal tax ratio $(t_x / t_y)^{**}$ inducing polluters to keep a given burden restriction $B \leq \bar{B}$.

Exercise 4.3
Let x and y denote the emission levels of two pollutants. Give an example of an environmental burden function $B(x, y)$ that has concave iso-burden curves.

Exercise 4.4
Consider an environmental burden function $B(x, y)$ with concave iso-burden curves. Further assume that the iso-abatement cost curves are convex. What can be concluded from this information with respect to the number and position(s) of the optimal emission tuple(s) (x^{**}, y^{**})? Illustrate your considerations graphically.

Exercise 4.5
Let the environmental burden B, produced by two pollutants, x and y, be given by $B(x, y)$. Furthermore, let the iso-burden curve defined by $B(x, y) = \bar{B}$ be convex and coincident with an iso-abatement cost curve over its entire length. What can

72 Cf. Che/Gale (2003), each with many further references.

73 Thus, the European Court of Auditors writes in its report published on December 19, 2007, in Luxembourg that there was no recognizable logic pursued in utilization of the funds from the European Union's multibillion-Euro research framework program.

be concluded in this case with respect to the number and position(s) of the optimal emission tuple(s) (x^{**}, y^{**}) ?

Exercise 4.6

A monopolist produces a good x and pollution as a by-product. An abatement technology is not available. Hence, the monopolist can only affect the emission level and thus environmental damages via his production level of good x. The production of x units of the good generates x emission units. Environmental damages are assumed to be given by $D(x) = x^2/2$. The marginal private cost function and the inverse demand function are assumed to be given by $MPC(x) = 1$ and $P(x) = 11 - x$.

Determine the equilibrium supply x_M of the monopolist, the socially optimal supply x^{**} and the optimal tax level t_M. Explain your results and illustrate them graphically.

Exercise 4.7

A monopolist produces a good x and pollution as a by-product. The production of x units of the good generates x gross emission units (i.e., $E_G = x$). Assume the existence of an abatement technology that can reduce emissions by an arbitrary amount $0 \leq ER_a (\leq E_G)$. Hence, net emissions are given by $E = E_G - ER_a$.

Environmental damages are assumed to be given by $D(E) = 5E^2$. The marginal private cost function and the inverse demand function are assumed to be given by $MPC(x) = 10$ and $P(x) = 110 - 5x$. Marginal abatement cost by application of the abatement technology are given by $MAC(ER_a) = 5\,ER_a$.

a) Determine the socially optimal gross and net emission levels E_G^{**} and E^{**}.
b) Determine the unregulated equilibrium (gross) emission level E_M.
c) To induce the socially optimal emission level E^{**}, the government considers charging an emission tax. Determine the appropriate tax level t_M and the corresponding gross emission and abatement level of the monopolist.

Exercise 4.8

Assume that there are two types of polluter, type H with marginal abatement cost $MAC^H(x) = 100 - x$ and type L with marginal abatement cost $MAC^L(x) = (100 - x)/2$. The probability that the polluter is of type H is given by $p = 1/2$. Marginal damages are given by $MD(x) = 2x$. In the following, we consider the laissez-faire rule and assume that the damaged party does not know whether he has to do with an H or L type.

a) Determine the socially optimal emission levels x_H^{**} and x_L^{**} in case the polluter is of type H and type L, respectively.
b) Assume that the damaged party offers the polluter a compensation payment in the amount of his (pretended) abatement cost, provided that the polluter reduces his emissions to the level x_H^{**} or x_N^{**}, respectively. Show that the L type has an incentive to pretend to be of type H.

Exercise 4.9

Assume that a polluter with marginal abatement cost $MAC(x)$ does not know whether the damaged party is of type H with the marginal damages $MD^H(x)$ or of type L with marginal damages $MD^L(x)$, where $MD^H(x) > MD^L(x)$ holds for each emission level x. The polluter only knows the two possible marginal damage functions and the probability $p = 1/2$ of each type. In the following, we consider the polluter rule and assume that the polluter has to compensate the damaged party for his (pretended) damages. Use a graphical illustration to characterize

a) the socially optimal emission levels x_H^{**} and x_L^{**}, respectively.
b) possible incentives to pretend to be of the other type .
c) the (from the point of view of the polluter) optimal combination of compensation limits x_H^+ and x_L^+ and honesty premium P^L.

Exercise 4.10

Discuss the following statement:

The expression "double dividend" of a green tax means that a green tax has two positive welfare effects. The first effect is the increase of the employment level, and the second effect is the improvement in the efficiency of the taxation system. Both effects arise if the tax revenues are applied to easing the tax burden on the labor factor.

Exercise 4.11

Assume that according to the strong interpretation of the employment-oriented variant a green tax leads to the second dividend. Can it then be concluded that the second dividend also arises according to the weak interpretation?

Exercise 4.12

In the following, we consider a two-period model of induced advances in environmental technology with a single firm. The unregulated equilibrium emission level of the firm is given by $E^* = 10$ in each period. The firm may reduce its emissions by an abatement activity a. Abatement costs in period 0 are given by $AC_0(a_0) = \frac{1}{8}a_0^2$. If the firm invests in period 0 the amount I_0 in technical progress, the abatement cost in period 1 are reduced to $AC_1(a_1, I_0) = \frac{1}{8}\frac{a_1^2}{1+\sqrt{I_0}}$. The expected value of environmental damages caused by the firms' emissions in period t, $t \in \{0, 1\}$ is given by $D(a_t) = 10 - a_t$. Simplifying, we assume that costs of period 1 are not discounted.

a) Derive the socially optimal values a_0^{**}, a_1^{**}, and I_0^{**}. Determine the algebraic sign of $a_1^{**} - a_0^{**}$ and explain your result.
b) The government considers the implementation of the strict liability rule to induce the socially optimal investment and abatement levels. Analyze the corresponding optimization problem of the firm, and derive the equilibrium abatement levels a_0^*, a_1^*, and I_0^* under strict liability.

Exercise 4.13

Consider the economy of exercise 4.12, but now assume that future payoffs are discounted.

a) Assume that the society and the firm discount future payoffs with a positive discount rate r. Discuss the consequences for the results from exercise 4.12.a and b.

b) Now assume that the society discounts future payoffs with discount rate r^{**} and the firm discounts future payoffs with rate $r^* > r^{**}$. Discuss the consequences of this discount rate distortion for the results from exercise 4.12.a and b.

(In a first step, you may use your intuition to discuss the consequences. In a second step, try to give a formal analysis.)

Part Five

International Environmental Problems

A. Introduction

In the discussion so far, we have mostly assumed that the *spatial distribution* of emissions is of no particular importance for environmental policy. But where its implications were occasionally considered (e.g., in section C.III.7 of part three), we silently assumed that spatial problems could be dealt with in the context of national environmental policy. However, as we know, pollution flows do not stop at national frontiers. The range of international environmental problems runs from the nameless "neighborhood conflict" in areas near frontiers to "downstream—upstream"problems linking several states (e.g., pollution of the Rhine) and phenomena of large-scale pollutant transport (e.g., "acid rain") to world-embracing ("global") problems such as the "ozone hole" and the "greenhouse effect." In particular, the last-named problems have in recent years received considerable attention from science, politics, and society. We accordingly (and for space reasons) want to confine ourselves to the "extreme case of internationality" in the environmental area, namely, *global* environmental problems. Global pollutants differ from all other pollutants because they are immaterial to their environmental impact where they are produced. Thus, according to current scientific knowledge, the warming of the Earth's atmosphere depends on the total output of *greenhouse gases*[1] and not on their regional emergence profile. Much the same is true of the effects of chlorofluorocarbon (CFC) output on the ozone hole.

The global environmental load thus depends on the total output of the relevant pollutants (i.e., the sum of pollutant outputs of the individual countries). Global environmental quality is produced by all countries jointly, and no country can escape it. On the one hand, the individual emitter of a global pollutant causes an internal effect by deteriorating its own environmental quality and, thus, has to suffer damage. On the other hand, it produces an externality by lowering the

---

1 These are notably carbon dioxide (CO_2), nitrous oxide (N_2O), chlorofluorocarbons (CFCs), methane (CH_4), and ozone (O_3).

environmental quality of all other countries. It is thus both "cause of and victim of" global environmental changes. Because the jointly created environmental quality is consumed by all countries in the same way, it is to be regarded as a *public good*.[2] Now, the consideration of public goods problems is far from new in economics, and in environmental economics, allocation problems arising from the public nature of the environment as a good have long been dealt with. The internalization strategies and pragmatic environmental policy instruments developed here (presented in parts two and three of this book) are largely transferable to global environmental problems. However, they are distinguished by specific features requiring special treatment and leading to modifications of the traditional approach. In particular, in the traditional approach, we (mostly implicitly) assume that there exists a central state body that defines and implements environmental policy. The state is trusted with being willing and able to do this job, even if it thereby worsens the position of individual decision makers (notably, the polluters).

This assumption is nothing special if the analysis is done in the tradition of welfare economics theory, in which the state plays the part of guardian of the common good, irrespective of the policy sphere in question. The matter looks different from the viewpoint of the *public choice theory* (cf., e.g., Mueller 2003, Schneider/Volkert 1999): if the state is seen not as something raised above society, but rather as an actor caught in a jungle of conflicting interests and pursuing its own interests, then the assumptions of welfare economic theory seem somewhat remote from reality, even in the national framework.[3] In connection with international environmental problems, the welfare economics construct of a superordinate actor that would have to maximize aggregate world welfare cannot be maintained (for the positive analysis). We must instead take account of the fact that measures to protect the international environment have to be agreed among sovereign states. Even if we trust every individual state with wanting to maximize its national welfare, a considerable *coordination problem* presents itself if the environmental impact crosses national frontiers. Many environmental problems are typified by the structure of the "prisoner's dilemma" (for more detail, see section B.I.3). This is because although a common effort by all states to protect the international (in the extreme case, global) environmental resources would be in the common interest of all, there are nonetheless incentives for the individual state to act as a *free rider*. The individual state is perhaps tempted not to even join a relevant agreement, or else comply with it only imperfectly or not at all after accession. These severe problems with achieving cooperative environmental policy measures that in themselves enhance worldwide welfare are investigated in international environmental economics using

---

2   This does not mean that the consequences of jointly produced environmental pollution are identical in all countries. But this is not to be seen as differing at all from the "normal" theory of public goods. Ultimately, the utility of a public good is by no means necessarily equal for all individuals consuming it.

3   However, they do (just because of the ideal-type stylization of the state) offer the normative basis for a critical policy analysis.

game theoretic models.[4] We go further into this in later sections of this part. There we also consider how incentive systems to improve states' propensity to cooperate can be constructed.

Game theory is a scientific method for studying the behavior of actors in inter-dependent decision situations: the effect of a decision by A on his utility depends not only on his decision, but also on B's decision. The same is true *mutatis mutandis* for B. How will the actor decide if he is aware of this interdependence and further assumes that his counterpart also knows of it and himself takes it into account in deciding? How can the interaction of the actors be so regulated by setting the framework conditions as to make the individual decisions lead to socially optimal results?

Game theory, the essence of which has been only crudely outlined in the previous observations,[5] has played scarcely any part in the mainstream of environmental economics (the presenting of which is the main focus of this book). This is because environmental impact and environmental policy have been interpreted not on the basis of a theory of interaction and cooperation, but of a regulatory theory (and what is more, a very simple one). According to this, the state has the job of ordering events in the economy and society in accordance with the principle of maximizing the common good. In so doing, it finds that the market mechanism allocates environmental goods wrongly ("market failure because of externalities"). The state now defines environmental policy instruments with which it repairs the flaw in the market mechanism and thus removes contradictions between market events and the setting of common good objectives. In implementing this program, the state lacks neither interest, information, nor power.

In this construction, there is little demand for what game theory can provide. Although the point is not the interaction of symmetrical actors, the state as "master of the procedure" should wisely employ its position for the benefit of the community. (What is "wise" and how this wisdom can be turned to the service of designing environmental policy instruments is discussed in the first four parts of this book, in the spirit of traditional environmental economics.)

It is not just in the relation between the state as regulator and the polluters as regulatory objects that the viewpoint of traditional environmental economics offers little room for "strategic interactions" by those involved (which are what is at the center of game theoretic interest). It is equally true of the relations between the firms involved themselves. In simple environmental economics models, polluters are presented either as firms under perfect competition or as monopolists. Consideration of interdependencies between individual actors is alien to both market forms: with

---

4 From the literature on this scientifically and politically highly topical theme, which has grown by leaps and bounds in recent years, let us mention only: Barrett (2005), Böhringer/Finus/Vogt (2002), Buchholz/Peters (2003), Endres (2004), Finus (2001), Finus/Rundshagen (2006a), C. Helm (2000, 2001), D. Helm (2005), Schmidt (2000, 2001).

5 For an amusing introduction to game theoretic thinking, see Dixit/Nalebuff (1991). For a somewhat more ambitious (although also attractive) one, see Binmore (2007).

perfect competition, an individual firm is a "drop in the ocean." Its activities are imperceptible to the totality of its competitors. Accordingly, the competitors will also not react to what the firm in question does. Correspondingly, that firm need not calculate any response by the others into the planning of its activities. Things are still simpler with a polluter that is a monopolist on its commodity market: it need not consider reactions by its competitors because there are none.[6]

The favorite area for applying game theory in the sphere of microeconomics is *industrial economics.* Here the point is the behavior of firms in oligopoly. This market form is indeed defined by the interdependence of decisions among firms. In addition, interdependencies between state and firms are studied as regulatory problems with asymmetrical information.[7] These problems did not, however, play any part in the previous description. Interdependencies between individual decision makers and the taking account of them in strategic decisions by the individual actors were considered at most marginally. This is, for instance, true of the reference to the possibilities of a strategic innovation policy in part three of this book and for the treatment of Coase-type internalization negotiations with asymmetrical information in part four.

In dealing with national environmental problems, neglecting strategic interdependencies can still be accepted as a simplification admissible in the context of an introductory presentation. According to the generally prevalent view in environmental economics, this is not true of the analysis of international environmental problems. As already explained previously, in the international sphere, no body exists that could even remotely play the role of the state as described in the traditional regulatory approach. Supranational environmental impacts arising initially higgledy-piggledy from the interplay of national activities must be limited by voluntary agreements among sovereign states. Here there is an almost total lack of international jurisdiction that could guarantee the implementation of such agreements and compliance with them. However, the welfare of the various states depends on each other's in precisely the way sketched previously in describing the object of game theory.[8] Recently, there have been intensified efforts to apply the findings of

---

6   Here we have in mind the simple textbook model of monopoly. There are also monopoly models where the firm must in its activities pay attention not to activate any *potential* competition.

7   In contrast with the simple regulatory model, these analyses take into account the point that compliance with governmental (here environmental policy) provisions by the firms regulated will be imperfect. This is attributed in the discussion of the fact that the environmentally relevant conduct of firms, and thus its conformity with statutory provisions and other regulations, cannot be perfectly observed. Around the disclosure of environmentally relevant information and its utilization for environmental policy regulation, there may arise an interplay (that may take the form of a "cat-and-mouse game") between the regulating authority and the polluting firm, which is studied using the means of game theory. Cf., e.g., Macho-Stadler/Pérez-Castrillo (2006), with numerous further references.

8   The part of game theory concerned with the behavior of actors unable to conclude binding agreements with each other is called "noncooperative game theory."

game theory to real negotiating processes in international environmental protection and also to bring insights from the observation of real negotiating processes into the construction of game theoretic models. (For more on this, see chapter B.)

In the practice of international environmental policy, a series of agreements has already been concluded through which governments attempt to address the issues considered here. However, the whole area of international environmental problems is far from being fully covered by agreements. Moreover, the agreements concluded give grounds for criticism, both because of their often unspecific and nonbinding content and because of the smallness of the obligations undertaken.[9] Finally, defects in implementing the agreements can be noted. From the multiplicity of agreements since concluded, let us take two as examples.

One of the best-known international environmental agreements is the 1987 *Montreal Protocol* to protect the Earth's ozone layer. It came into force in 1989, and it laid down a time table for restricting 8 of the substances damaging the ozone layer. Two extensions to the protocol (London, 1990, and Copenhagen, 1992) extended the list of substances regulated to 20. In addition, the reduction objectives were tightened and the deadlines for reaching them brought back. CFCs have not been allowed in production since 1996. Treaty breaches are threatened with tangible trade sanctions. By December 2008, the agreement was ratified by 193 states. Developing countries were induced to join by setting up a fund administered by three agencies of the United Nations (UN) and the World Bank. Between 1991 and 2005, it distributed transfers amounting to $2.1 billion.[10]

Another well-known international agreement, although generally regarded as less successful, is the 1997 *Kyoto Protocol* to limit the greenhouse effect (which came into force on February 16, 2005).[11] At the third conference of contracting states of the UN Climate Protection Convention, 38 industrial and transformation countries listed in Annex 1 to the agreement committed themselves to reducing emissions of six greenhouse gases between 2008 and 2012. The reduction quotas are individually differentiated, but for the most important industrial countries are about 7% below the 1990 emission levels. By May 2009, the protocol was ratified by 184 states. In section B.II, we consider this agreement in more detail and make an attempt at an

---

9   Thus, Finus/Tjøtta (2003) show that in the 1994 Oslo agreement, widely regarded as exemplary, only pollution reductions that would have been in the interest of the contracting parties even without international coordination were agreed. A similarly negative finding is made by Murdoch/Sandler (1997a) for the 1995 Helsinki Protocol and Böhringer/Vogt (2004) and Murdoch/Sandler (1997b) for the Montreal Protocol. However, there are also positive evaluations in the debate on the effectiveness of international environmental agreements (e.g., by Bratberg/Tjøtta/Øines (2005) on the Sofia Protocol and Swanson/Mason (2003) on the Montreal Protocol). On methods of measuring the success of international environmental agreements, see C. Helm/Sprinz (2000).

10   Refer to www.multilateralfund.org/institutional_arrangements.htm.

11   The economics literature on climate change and climate policy is now immense. Cf., e.g., Cogoy/Steininger (2007), Faure/Gupta/Nentjes (2003), Hackl/Pruckner (2001), D. Helm (2005).

economic evaluation of it. To conclude part five of this book, we consider European Union (EU) emissions trading (associated with the Kyoto Protocol) in chapter C.

On the basis of a simple presentation, section B.I studies in terms of economic theory what results are to be expected from international agreements to cut pollutant emissions with global effects. The expected outcomes of negotiations are then compared with the socially optimum allocations. To simplify, the behavior of each individual state is modeled here as if it were a decision maker aiming at maximizing its own net utility. This presentation should bring out the problems in designing a successful international environmental policy; however, we do not enter the jungle of conflicts of interest within an individual state.[12]

B. International Environmental Agreements

It is extremely difficult to conceive of an efficient and ecologically effective international environmental agreement that is *incentive compatible*. An incentive- compatible international environmental agreement is distinguished by two fundamental properties:

- It is attractive for states involved in the international environmental problem at issue to join the treaty.
- It is attractive to signatory states (i.e., the states that have subscribed to the agreement) to keep it.

We seek to explain the nature of these problems in economic terms. In section I.2, the first point is discussed using the term "individual rationality of the agreement" and the second using the term "stability of the agreement." Needless to say, in harmony with the basic constructive approach in this book, we do not stop at discussing the problems. We also give a survey of strategies discussed in the literature that might be able to enhance the incentive compatibility of international environmental agreements. Following the economic theoretical discussion in section B.I, section B.II is devoted to presenting and evaluating a practical international environmental agreement. For this, the analytical machinery developed in section B.I is employed. As an example, we have selected the Kyoto Protocol. This is the international environmental agreement most closely discussed in the academic literature, as well as being best known to the public. A Google search on May 12, 2008 showed 2.8 million hits. No other international environmental agreement can keep up. Indeed, the flood of literature on this topic can hardly be

---

12   Other important aspects of international environmental issues that have had to be left out of the following presentation for space reasons are the connections between environmental and commercial policy and the influence of environmental policy on firms' choices of location. On this, cf. e.g., Engel/Grote, (2004), Kemfert/Lise/Tol (2004), Kirchgässner (2001), Marsiliani/ Rauscher/Withagen (2002, 2003), Rauscher/Gürtzgen (2000), as well as various articles in Schulze/Ursprung (2001).

stemmed. Of course – and the gentle reader of these lines expected nothing else – the author has mastered the challenge with his customary aplomb. The following photo documents the process.

Lateral view 7: "Big Wave Surfing" — first the deluge – *of books. Source:* David Dalla Venezia, no title, oil on canvas, 1998. Reprinted with the artist's kind permission. The author wants to thank the artist warmly for his stimulating thoughts about the relation between art and science.

To conclude part five, which is devoted to international environmental issues, we discuss the peculiarities of the international use of environmental policy instruments in chapter C. As our object of consideration and demonstration, we choose EU emissions trading.

I. The Game Theoretic Interpretation

1. Global Optimum and Nash Equilibrium

Global environmental problems are analyzed using the "standard procedure of welfare economics."[13] In the context of this discussion, we characterize the worldwide *optimum* abatement quantity of a global environmental pollutant and then compare

---

13 This procedure consists of defining and contrasting social optimum and market equilibrium. In the (likely and interesting) case that these two diverge, the development of possible corrections is also part of the program. The standard procedure of welfare economics is already presented in sections A.II–V of part one of this book and is used exhaustively in part two. The comparison between social optimum and market equilibrium led there to a diagnosis of market failure because of externalities. As therapies, various internalization strategies were discussed.

it with the quantity that sovereign states avoid at *equilibrium* without the application of international environmental policy. We then investigate the possibilities of using international cooperation mechanisms to bring the aggregated equilibrium abatement quantity closer to the global optimum one.

We start by using the machinery of economic theory to produce a concept of the global optimum abatement quantity of a global pollutant (e.g., a greenhouse gas). As described previously, we assume that the extent of the global environmental problem observed depends on the quantity of the global pollutant emitted by all states in the world. To make the concept of "extent of the global environmental problem" somewhat more concrete, we assume that damage to be expected from climate change is known and expressible in money terms.[14] If an individual state reduces its emissions of the global pollutant, then "good and ill" are connected in the following fashion. The state is making a contribution to reducing the global environmental problem. The global environmental damage falls *ceteris paribus* to a certain extent. The state that acted itself benefits because it is, according to the assumptions, affected by the global environmental problem. In addition, all other states also profit from the activity of the first state. The positive effects of the measure carried out by the state we selected as an example thus consist in the welfare increase summed over all states, attributable to the improved environmental situation. In contrast, of course, avoiding emissions does not come for free. The state taking the action has to accept abatement costs. This reduces (simply by definition) its welfare. From the viewpoint of the world community as a whole, then, the net welfare effect of the emission lowering carried out by the state taking the action (let us call it "*i*") consists of the difference between the welfare gains summed over all states (including *i*) and the welfare losses borne by state *i*. The net welfare calculation for the environmental policy of an individual state *i* sketched out here applies in principle identically for every other state ("*j*").

We can get from the net welfare calculation for the individual state to the net welfare calculation for the world community if we find for all states the net welfare effect of the emission abatement of an arbitrarily chosen individual state described previously and aggregate these. The positive effects ("benefit") of the emission reduction carried out worldwide lie in the global improvement in environmental quality. This is measured by the fall in environmental damage aggregated over all states. The negative effects ("costs") of the emission reduction carried out worldwide amount to the sum of the emission abatement costs borne by the individual states. The *global optimum emission abatement quantity* is defined as that which

---

14   We initially confine ourselves to a static model framework. This has *inter alia* the consequence that we systematically exclude certain specific features of global warming. This applies particularly to the fact that according to current scientific findings, the Earth's global warming depends on the aggregate *stock* of greenhouse gases in the atmosphere. The period-specific input of these gases ("flow") at the center of the previous observation thus plays only an indirect role. The specific features of the climate problem ignored for the moment are taken up in sections B.II.3 and C.II.5.

maximizes the difference between worldwide benefit and worldwide costs of emission abatement. At this quantity, then, the worldwide net welfare gain from the aggregate emission reduction is a maximum.

But finding the global optimum emission abatement quantity aggregated over all states does not yet adequately describe the global optimum *total* situation. We must instead also look at how the (optimally chosen) aggregate worldwide emission abatement is *distributed* over the individual states. The relevant question is: in the global optimum, who contributes how much to the total emission abatement quantity?

"Why should that be important?" it might be objected. After all, the global environmental problems discussed here are actually defined precisely by the fact that it is immaterial where the pollutants in question are emitted. It must conversely accordingly be equally irrelevant where the emissions are reduced. So far so good – one might answer: the previous statement on the irrelevance of the place of emission relates exclusively to the damage side of global emissions or, in mirror image terms, to the benefit side of emission abatement. However, in defining the global optimum alongside the benefit of emission abatement, its costs are also relevant. The amount of the total emission abatement costs to be incurred certainly does depend on how high the contribution of the individual country to the total quantity to be avoided is. To maximize the worldwide net benefit of emission abatement, not only must the globally optimum quantity of pollutants be avoided, but also the total reduction quantity must be distributed over the individual states in such a way as to minimize worldwide emission abatement costs.[15] Put rather more pragmatically, this means that countries with favorable marginal abatement cost (*MAC*) processes have to avoid more emissions (*ceteris paribus*) in the worldwide optimum than countries with unfavorable abatement terms. To flesh out the concept of the globally optimum emission reduction and associated minimum cost distribution over individual states of the quantity to be reached worldwide, we can refer back to the maxims presented in the first parts of this book regarding national environmental problems. In part one, we already find a definition of the socially optimum quantity of a pollutant (cf., e.g., the discussion of Figure 2). The society associated with the term "social" consists, in the universe of discourse of part one, of the totality of producers, consumers, and environment users in an (unspecified) state. It turns out that the optimum emission level (and, thus, for a given emission in the uncorrected starting position, also the optimum level of emission *abatement*) is characterized by a balance of aggregate marginal abatement costs and aggregate marginal damage (MD). The corresponding condition (in the short form, $MAC = MD$) has already provided useful guidance in this book (or at least the author hopes so). We obtained this condition in part one of the book as the result of net welfare maximization by emission reduction. Welfare increases from emission reduction arise in the form of

15 In fundamental microeconomics (here the theory of the firm), the maxim runs "No profit maximization without cost minimization!" This can be transferred perfectly analogously to the previously described net welfare maximization.

reductions in environmental damage. Welfare losses result from the foregoing of consumer and producer surplus.

In discussing international environmental policy, we now present "the same play with different actors." The actors are now no longer individual consumers, firms, and environment users, but individual states. If in discussing the optimum emission quantity in part one we aggregated the marginal damage, or marginal abatement costs, over all individuals or emission sources involved in a country, then in order to constitute the globally optimum emission rate we must take a further step in aggregation: marginal damage and marginal abatement cost functions must be determined and summed up for all countries. In complete analogy with what was said in part one, the optimum reduction quantity of the global pollutant is then characterized by a balance of total marginal damage caused and aggregate marginal abatement costs. Once again, then, the familiar condition $MD = MAC$ applies.[16]

Just as we abbreviate the description of the global optimum level of emission abatement by recourse to what was said previously, we can do the same for the idea of the optimum distribution of the globally optimum emission quantity over individual states. In part three, we already intensively discussed the problem of the minimum cost distribution of a given emission quantity over individual polluters. This was, to be sure, done in a national context. The state sets an "arbitrarily chosen" emission abatement quantity as an objective and considers how this is to be distributed over the individual emitters of the relevant pollutant to make the aggregate abatement costs a minimum. In the discourse in part three, the polluters were those firms emitting the relevant pollutant in the relevant country. The ideas explained in part three can now be transferred to the international context. The aggregate emission quantity considered is not the national target set by a state, but the previously described global optimum abatement quantity of the global pollutant considered. (Because the discussion in part three applies to any arbitrarily chosen aggregate quantity of emission abatement, it also applies to the globally optimum quantity.) In the model, the emitters of the relevant pollutant are no longer the individual firms, but the states in which these firms are located as "substitutes." Although in part three each individual firm is assigned a marginal abatement cost curve, in the international context of part five, this is done for each individual state. It follows from this total analogy in the model construction that the cost minimality condition for the model world in part three can be transferred without further ado to the one in part five. In the cost minimum of part three, the marginal abatement costs of all firms emitting the relevant pollutant are equal to one another at the cost minimum. In the model for the global environmental problem, the minimum cost distribution of the globally optimum quantity of emission abatement over

16 The high degree of abstraction usual in economic theory is the cause of much puzzlement and the occasion for much criticism. However, the analogy presented previously does bring out one advantage that makes up for a lot: the abstract analytical machinery is so flexible that it can easily be transferred from a discourse about individuals as decision makers to one with states as decision makers.

individual states is attained when the marginal abatement costs of all states have been equalized. Accordingly, the condition for cost minimality we know from part three, $MAC_1 = MAC_2$ (cf., e.g., Fig. 18) applies. In part three, actors 1 and 2 are firms; in part five, they are states.[17]

We previously attempted to clarify the idea of the globally optimum level of emission abatement and its optimum (here minimum cost) distribution over individual countries by analogy with the basic environmental economics model confined to one state. In our search for analogies, we may find useful things even in the area of traditional microeconomics (without externalities). We briefly explain this to show our gentle readers the "comprehensiveness of microeconomic theory" (and show environmental economics as applied microeconomics).

At the beginning of part one of this book, the discussion of the economic theory fundamentals of environmental economics in sections A.I and A.II was concerned with explaining the optimum provision of a private good x in a model without externalities. We said about the production of x that, on the one hand, it created utility for the consumer, but, on the other hand, it incurred costs to the producer. The socially optimal supply of x is defined by the equality of marginal willingness to pay and marginal production costs. Alongside the description of the optimum supply quantity of x, the optimum (here minimum cost) distribution of this quantity over various firms producing x was also tested. The analysis brought equalization of firm-specific marginal production costs in as a further optimality condition.

How similar the pictures are: both in the economic discussion of global environmental problems and in the economic discussion of provision of a private commodity, the *first* point is the optimum level of an aggregate quantity. In the context of global environmental problems, this is the globally optimum emission abatement quantity; in the context of private supply of commodities, it is the socially optimum production quantity. In both cases, the property of the optimum sought consists of its equalizing marginal benefits and marginal costs. In the environmental context, the marginal benefit consists of the environmental quality improvement aggregated over all states attributable to a marginal reduction in emissions. The marginal costs appear as the corresponding marginal abatement costs. In the context of the private commodity, the marginal benefit consists in the marginal willingness to pay of consumers, and the marginal costs consist of the marginal production costs.

Second, in both the environmental context and that of private provision of goods, the point is the minimum cost distribution of the aggregate quantity over the various actors contributing something to its production. In the environmental context, these producers (of emission abatement efforts) are the individual states; in the context of the private good, the actors are the individual suppliers of x. In both contexts, the condition for cost minimization is that the marginal costs of the individual actors should be equalized. In the environmental context, this means

---

17 For a critique of this analysis (upheld by the economic mainstream), see Sheeran (2006).

that the marginal abatement costs of two arbitrarily chosen states are equal to each other at the optimum. In the context of the private good, it means that the marginal production costs of two arbitrarily chosen firms are equal to each other at the optimum.

The previous determination of the globally optimum abatement quantity and its distribution over individual states constitutes the welfare economics norm by which the equilibrium conduct of states is evaluated. Of course, the equilibrium depends on which objective the individual state is pursuing and under which framework conditions it can pursue its objective. We assume that the individual state is pursuing the goal of maximizing its own welfare (corresponding to the aggregate welfare of its citizens). Regarding the framework conditions, we initially assume that each state decides in sovereign fashion over its own emission quantity and that no environmental policy embracing many states exists. In these conditions, the individual state looks at its measures to reduce the global pollutant with "one smiling and one weeping eye." The emission reduction increases national welfare by contributing a little to alleviating the global environmental problem, from which the state considered is, according to the assumption, suffering. In contrast, it reduces national welfare by causing abatement costs. The state aiming for national welfare maximization will reduce emissions of the global pollutant to an extent that maximizes the difference between national benefit and national cost. If the relevant damage and abatement cost functions behave properly in terms of differential calculus,[18] then it follows, for the equilibrium quantity of emission abatement, that the marginal damage of country i considered is equal to the marginal abatement cost borne by this country, $MD_i = MAC_i$. This consideration also applies to every state j. A situation in which all states reduce their emissions enough to meet this condition is termed a *Nash equilibrium* in the literature.[19]

Of course, the readers of these paragraphs trained in the theory of externalities will immediately pick out the difference between the "profitability calculation" carried out by the individual state when reducing the global pollutant and the profitability calculation from the viewpoint of the world community explained previously. The costs and benefits estimated by the individual state are exclusively those arising for itself. In the worldwide calculation, these are also present. Over and above that, however, the worldwide calculation also contains the benefit that

18 We always assume this because we want to avoid unnecessary trouble. The inclusion of "unconventional" functions may, in particular, produce corner solutions that do not meet the first-order conditions known from differential calculus for an extreme value. This procedure would complicate the analysis without bringing any corresponding added value to the discussion context. The restriction made here thus pursues the goal of net benefit–maximizing modeling. Surprise, surprise – even the design of economic models is an economic problem!

19 John Nash, b. 1928, won the Nobel Prize for Economics in 1994 (together with J. Harsanyi and R. Selten). for his groundbreaking contributions to game theory. The concept of the Nash equilibrium is transferable to all interdependent decision situations; negotiations among states over global environmental policy is only one example. The roots of the concept lie in the oligopoly theory model developed by A.A. Cournot (1801–1877).

all other states derive from the emission abatement by the state considered. That constitutes a positive externality of the activity of the state considered on all other states. In perfect analogy with the "market failure" caused by externalities discussed in part one, we have to do with an allocation failure conditioned by the absence of an international coordinating mechanism. Because the individual state does not take into account the positive externalities caused by its activities, the equilibrium level of its emission abatement does not correspond to the globally optimum level. Intuitively, we may suppose that the equilibrium emission reduction of the individual state ignoring positive externalities will lie below the globally optimum emission reduction.[20] Because this applies to all states, the aggregate equilibrium emission reduction will also be smaller than the global optimum. In addition, we can assume simply *prima facie* that the (suboptimal) global emission reduction attained altogether at equilibrium is "produced" with too high aggregate abatement costs into the bargain. At this point in the discussion, there is no coordinating mechanism that could ensure that the marginal abatement costs of the individual states would be equalized in the equilibrium brought about by "autistic" optimization.

Figure 29 illustrates the global optimum and the Nash equilibrium for the case of two countries. Figure 29a and 29b, respectively, show each given country's marginal abatement costs as a function of the pollutant quantity reduced by this country.[21] Figure 29d and 29e show *inter alia* the relevant marginal damage curves for country 1 and country 2 as a function of the total emission level x. Figure 29c shows the aggregated country-specific function curves. For the sake of simplicity, we assume in Figure 29 that the two countries are identical (i.e., have identical marginal abatement and marginal damage cost curves).

The globally optimum situation is illustrated in Figure 29c by the point where the aggregate marginal abatement cost and marginal damage curves intersect ($MAC = MD$): the globally optimum emission quantity is x^{**}, so that, starting from an uncorrected emission quantity x^*, the optimum quantity of emission abatement is then $x^* - x^{**}$. The globally optimum emission quantity is distributed in minimum cost fashion over the two countries if the countries' individual marginal abatement costs shown in Figure 29a and 29b are equalized ($MAC_1 = MAC_2$). This occurs if country 1 reduces its emissions from x_1^* to x_1^{**} and country 2 from x_2^* to x_2^{**}.

Let us now, for a comparison with the globally optimum abatement level and its minimum cost distribution, look at the equilibrium situation given "autistic optimization" (i.e., the Nash equilibrium). Each country reduces its emission as

20 In fact, this need not be so in every case (cf. Finus (2001, p. 138f)). For simplicity reasons, however, we do not go further into this counterintuitive and (for that very reason) intellectually attractive possibility.

21 One might equally well say that the marginal abatement cost is shown as a function of the pollutant quantity *emitted*. However, the formulation depends on whether the curve is read (starting at zero) "from left to right" or (starting from the uncorrected equilibrium emission level x_1^*) "from right to left."

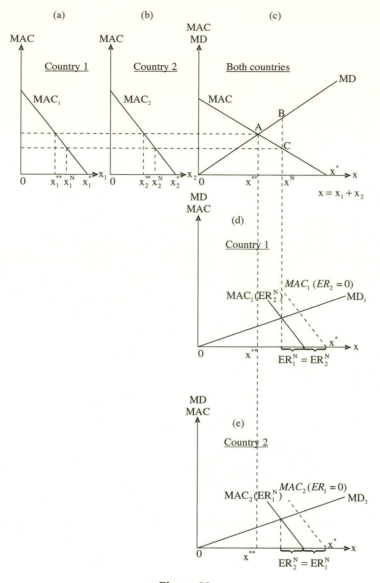

Figure 29

explained previously far enough until its own marginal abatement costs equal its own marginal damage. Accordingly, $MAC_1 = MD_1$ and $MAC_2 = MD_2$ hold.

In Figure 29d and 29e, the corresponding equilibrium quantities are each represented by the intersection of the marginal abatement cost curve of each country and its own marginal damage curve. We must, however, take account of the fact that for each individual country, the marginal damage depends as much on its own emission as that of the other country. A country's pollutant reduction thus reduces the emission quantity to which the other country is exposed correspondingly. Graphically, this fact is shown by shifting the marginal abatement cost curve of each country to the left by the abatement amount of the other country.

Excursus on graphic presentation technique:

Note the difference in graphic presentation between "shifting a curve" and "moving along a curve": in relation to the marginal abatement cost of country 1, a reduction in country 2's emissions results in Figure 29 as a parallel leftward shift in the MAC_1 curve. For this, consider Figure 29d. MAC_1 ($ER_2 = 0$) is country 1's marginal abatement cost curve applying on the condition that country 2 does not reduce its emissions at all and, thus, emits its uncorrected starting emission x_2^*. If country 2 reduces its emissions from x_2^* to x_2^N, (thus raising the emission reduction from $ER_2 = 0$ to ER_2^N), then country 1's marginal abatement cost curve is correspondingly shifted leftward from $MAC_1(ER_2 = 0)$ to $MAC_1(ER_2^N)$. In contrast, the effect of country 1's emission abatement on its own marginal abatement costs is shown in Figure 29d as movement along the respective MAC_1 curve.[22]

"Shifting *the* curve/moving *along* the curve – why the hell is it all so complicated?"

The reason is that Figure 29d and 29e each show two curves *for country i concerned* (where $i \in \{1, 2\}$), namely MD_i and MAC_i. The abscissae of the two diagrams each show x (i.e., the emission quantity *aggregated over both countries*). No problem arises for curve MD_i because by the assumptions each country's marginal damage depends, for global environmental problems, on the aggregate emission quantity. However, it is different for curve MAC_i.

The marginal abatement costs of the individual country i depend not on aggregate emission, but on the emission by country i. The independent variable of country i's marginal abatement cost function (namely, x_i) thus does not correspond with the variable to be read off from the abscissa in the diagram (namely, x). Of course, there is a close connection between the two variables: the aggregate emission is after all the sum of the country-specific emissions (i.e., $x = x_1 + x_2$). Let us consider the consequences of the discrepancy noted for the presentation. As an example, we select country 1 and imagine a situation where this country carries out no emission reductions ($ER_1 = 0$). Country 1 thus emits its uncorrected equilibrium emission quantity x_1^*. Let us consider Figure 29a, which shows country 1's marginal abatement costs in isolation. Figure 29a is familiar because it corresponds with the presentation in part three of the book, where the complications arising from considering international environmental problems do not yet play a part. This marginal abatement cost curve has its abscissal intercept at x_1^*. The marginal abatement costs are estimated for reductions in emissions starting from x_1^*, and it is assumed, for the starting point where nothing has yet been reduced, that the marginal abatement cost is zero ($MAC_1(ER_1 = 0) = 0$). The question is now where the abscissal intercept of country 1's marginal abatement cost curve is to appear *in Figure 29d*. We cannot simply take the same point as the "starting point" of the curve on the abscissa as in Figure 29a. This is because, in contrast with Figure 29a, Figure 29d shows on the abscissa not the emissions by country 1 (x_1), but the aggregate

---

22 Of course, the considerations for country 1 given here apply correspondingly to country 2.

emissions (x). The abscissal intercept in Figure 29d we are looking for denotes the total emission quantity on condition that country 1 emits the uncorrected starting quantity x_1^* and is thus at $x = x_1^* + x_2^*$. The position of the abscissal intercept of the MAC_1 curve in Figure 29d thus also depends, in contrast with Figure 29a, on how much country 2 is emitting. It is only for the special case that country 2 completely avoids its emissions, so that $x_2 = 0$ holds, that the abscissal intercept of the MAC_1 curve in Figure 29d is at the same point as in segment (a), namely, at x_1^*. If instead country 2 produces positive emission quantities, then the abscissal intercept of the MAC_1 curve will be rightward of x_1^*, and the bigger x_2 is, the farther right it will be. In the extreme case where country 2 makes no reductions and thus emits its uncorrected equilibrium quantity x_2^*, the abscissal intercept of MAC_1 will be at $x^* = x_1^* + x_2^*$.

The previous argument, here presented exhaustively for the abscissal intercept of the MAC_1 curve, applies correspondingly to *each point* on the MAC_1 curve. Altogether, it thus emerges that the *position* of the MAC_1 curve in Figure 29d depends on country 2's emission quantities. Because the uncorrected equilibrium level of country 2's emissions is given as the value x_2^*, this statement is equivalent to the position of the MAC_1 curve depends on country 2's emission *abatement quantity* (ER_2). After all, $ER_2 = x_2^* - x_2$ holds. Correspondingly, in Figure 29d, the label of each MAC_1 curve contains an addition showing what emission reduction quantity of country 2 the curve shown applies to. Curve $MAC_1(ER_2 = 0)$ is thus the marginal abatement cost curve for country 1 applying on condition that country 2 avoids no emissions $(ER_2 = 0)$. The notation $MAC_1(x_2^*)$ would be equivalent: country 1's marginal abatement cost curve shown applies on condition that country 2 emits its uncorrected equilibrium emission x_2^*. (For $ER_2 = 0$, it immediately follows from $ER_2 = x_2^* - x_2$ that $x_2 = x_2^*$.)

End of excursus

The total emission quantity generated at the Nash equilibrium is shown in Figure 29c as x^N. The country-specific pollutant quantities emitted at the Nash equilibrium are shown in Figure 29a and 29b as x_1^N and x_2^N, respectively. The equilibrium emission reduction quantities of both countries are correspondingly ER_1^N and ER_2^N, respectively. Because the two countries are identical, and thus make the same reduction in emission quantity at equilibrium, $ER_2^N = ER_2^N$. (Correspondingly, $x_1^N = x_2^N$ holds.)

The graphic presentation supports the previous intuitively based assumption: although uncoordinated action by both countries leads to certain efforts at abatement, we nonetheless remain below the globally optimum value.[23] Correspondingly, the Nash equilibrium emission level (x^N) is above the globally optimum level (x^{**}).

---

23 Moving away from the limitation to only two countries made for simplicity's sake in the previous example, we find that the larger the number of countries involved, the smaller, *ceteris paribus*, will be the emission reduction made by each country at Nash equilibrium.

2. The Problem of Incentive Compatibility: The Individual Rationality and Stability of International Environmental Agreements

Given this finding, the question that arises is: what consequences follow if the countries recognize the suboptimality of their uncoordinated action? The possibilities of reaching agreement on some further-reaching emission abatement are obvious in the model. The incentive for the states involved to think about them consists in the gap between the global optimum and the Nash equilibrium. Because at the global optimum, aggregate welfare is higher than at the Nash equilibrium, the attempt would suggest starting from the Nash equilibrium to seek to change the actual situation in the direction of the global optimum. The reward for such efforts would be the exploitation of the welfare potential associated with this shift.[24] In environmental policy reality, the calls for cooperation in the interest of common fundamentals of life have also long been unmistakable. Therefore, we turn to the possibilities and consequences of cooperative behavior to protect global environmental resources.[25]

Initially, we retain the assumption that the countries are identical. This makes the analysis simpler. That is beneficial. In addition, it is a likely presumption that the highest possible harmony of interests guaranteed by the identity of the countries is favorable to the attainment of a globally optimum environmental position. We accordingly investigate the chances of cooperative solutions in international environmental policy starting with a model framework that creates favorable conditions for it. In a second step, we do away with the identity of the states involved.

How then would the chances be for both countries simply to agree that each should make its contribution to the globally optimum solution? More specifically, the agreement would be that each country would reduce its emission quantity from the initial level by an amount of ER_i^{**} to x_i^{**}. (Here i again stands for the "postcode" of the countries shown in the diagram, 1 and 2.) Each country would then make precisely the contribution that is necessary to reach the globally optimum situation. In the special case of identical countries, it is the case that the emission abatement quantities ER_i^{**} be added to reach the optimum, and that both countries' residual emissions x_i^{**} remaining at the global optimum, are equal to each other.

The globally optimum emission reduction by country i, ER_i^{**}, can be defined in two ways: the simpler would be (also for graphic presentation) to take as the basis for reducing emissions the emission level x_i^*, at which no emission reductions have yet been made. The overall emission reduction of country i would then be defined as $ER_i^{**} = x_i^* - x_i^{**}$. Alternatively, i's Nash equilibrium emission level could be taken as a reference point. Then the globally optimum emission reduction by country i would be defined as $ER_i^{**} = x_i^N - x_i^{**}$. This definition complicates the

---

24 Note the analogy to the Coase theorem dealt with in part two of this book. There, too, it is unexploited welfare potential that drives the motor of internalization negotiations.

25 Cf., e.g., Barrett (1994a, 1994b, 2002), Buchholz/Peters (2003), Cogoy/Steininger (2007), Endres (2004), Endres/Finus (2002), Finus/Altamirano-Cabrera/van Ierland (2005), Heister (1998), C. Helm (2000), Hoel/Schneider (1997), Rubio/Ulph (2006), Stähler (1996), Weikard/Finus/Altamirano-Cabrera (2006).

graphic presentation a little, but has the advantage of greater plausibility. If we detach ourselves a little from the (static) model, then the following notion will help understanding. "First," each state reduces its emissions to meet its interests without communication with the other state. That means the lowering of emissions from the uncorrected initial level x_i^* to a Nash equilibrium emission level x_i^N. "Then" a globally optimum agreement is reached. If it is implemented, then "as a second stage" the reduction in emissions from the Nash equilibrium x_i^N to the treaty-agreed emission quantity x_i^{**} follows. The terms marking the successive steps "first," "then," and "as a second stage" have been put in quotation marks because the temporal sequence is, strictly speaking, not covered by the model at all. The concept of the sequence is merely a heuristic (albeit a useful one pedagogically). It allows the simple model presented to be interpreted in such a way as to be helpful for understanding the processes taking place in practice over time. After considering the advantages and drawbacks of the two possibilities sketched previously for defining the globally optimum level of emissions reduction (ER_i^{**}), we decide in favor of the latter alternative. The Nash equilibrium will therefore act as the baseline from which the emission reduction will be measured, so that $ER_i^{**} = x_i^N - x_i^{**}$ holds.

We referred previously to one specific feature of international environmental issues: there is no superordinate body that can take those involved and "force them to be happy." No one can order the countries to actually conclude the globally optimum treaty considered here and (to make their happiness really perfect) also keep it. Instead, the "reality test" for the construction imagined here is that it has to be in every participant's *own interest* to conclude the agreement and keep it. Correspondingly, following the literature, we demand in the preamble to chapter B that the agreement would have to be incentive compatible (or self-enforcing). As already briefly set out, the criteria for seeing whether an agreement is incentive compatible are individual rationality (profitability) and stability. The profitability criterion is met if every potential signatory state is better off in a situation created by universal compliance with the treaty than in the initial state with no agreement. The agreement is, moreover, stable if, starting from a situation of compliance with it on all sides, there is no incentive for any state to depart in its actual conduct from the conduct agreed on in the treaty.

Let us test the *individual rationality* of the agreement of two states imagined previously, whereby each has to act in relation to emission abatement in the way necessary to achieve the global optimum. For this, we have to compare the welfare of each state in the initial situation with no treaty (Nash equilibrium) and in the state of treaty compliance (global optimum). If the state's welfare is higher in the second situation, then the agreement is profitable. That the *aggregate* welfare is higher in the state of treaty compliance than at the Nash equilibrium follows, as noted previously, from the mere definition of the equilibrium and the social optimum. It follows from the assumption of the identity of the two countries that the welfare of each individual state is also higher at the global optimum than at the Nash equilibrium. The increase in aggregate welfare is achieved half each in the case of identical countries, if both move from their (identical) Nash equilibrium emission level to their (also identical) globally optimum emission level. There is no "leak" in the model through which aggregate welfare gains could trickle in the course of implementation into individual welfare gains, nor does the model allow identical countries to distribute the welfare gains asymmetrically.

Figure 30 starts by depicting the globally optimum agreement graphically. The upper part of the diagram repeats Figure 29c. The lower part is a modified presentation of Figure 29d. What is shown here is the situation of country 1 at the global optimum as it would be reached by the agreement imagined here. (We could portray the situation of country 2 analogously. Because the two countries are identical, we have not bothered to do so.) As in Figure 29d, $MAC_1(ER_2 = 0)$ denotes the marginal abatement cost curve of country 1 in the condition where country 2 does not reduce its emissions. Correspondingly, $MAC_1(ER_2^N)$ denotes the marginal abatement cost curve of country 1 on the condition that country 2 lowers its emissions to the Nash equilibrium level x_i^N. In the context of the globally optimum agreement, however, country 2 would reduce its emissions by the globally optimum amount ER_2^{**} from x_2^N to x_2^{**}. Because Figure 30 is intended to depict the situation created by the globally optimum agreement, we must take account of the beneficial action of country 2 by shifting the marginal abatement cost curve of country 1 leftward in parallel, from $MAC_1(ER_2^N)$, by the amount ER_2^{**}. On the assumption that country 2 acts in compliance with the treaty, the relevant marginal abatement cost curve of country 1 is correctly portrayed by the straight line $MAC_1(ER_2^N + ER_2^{**})$. Country 1 must now, in accordance with the treaty, reduce its emissions by ER_1^{**}. Altogether, then, there is an emission abatement of $ER_1^{**} + ER_2^*$. That means the globally optimum emission level x^{**} has been reached. The globally optimum agreement creates the situation for country 1 in which marginal damage has fallen from $MD_1(x^N)$ to $MD_1(x^{**})$, and the marginal abatement costs have risen from $MAC_1(x_1^N)$ to $MAC_1(x_1^{**})$. The associated overall utility for country 1 (i.e., the fall in environmental damage caused in country 1) is illustrated in Figure 30b as the area $x^{**}x^N AB$. The total abatement costs the state has to bear as a consequence of the agreement are shown in Figure 30b as the area $x^{**}DEF$. It follows from the previous considerations that the first area is bigger than the second (i.e., a change from the initial situation to the globally optimum situation increases the welfare of state 1). The globally optimum international environmental agreement is thus *individually rational* for country 1. Because of the identity of the two countries assumed here, the same applies to country 2. This finding gives us hope and also provides us with just the right impetus to answer the question of the *stability* of the globally optimum international environmental agreement. That question is: on the condition that the other state complies with the agreement, is it an equilibrium for the state considered to comply with the agreement in its turn?

Unfortunately, the chances for "equilibrium treaty keeping" in the model considered here are poor, even with the condition that the countries are identical. A

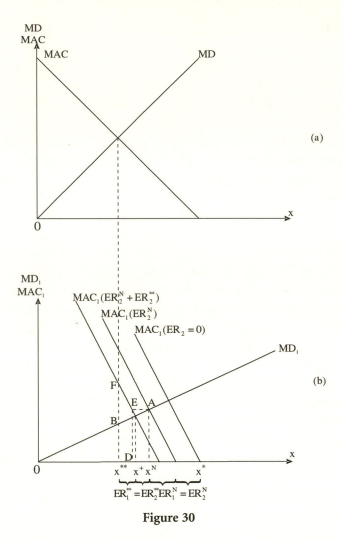

Figure 30

glance at the situation of the first country in the treaty-compliant situation shown in Figure 30 shows immediately why this is so. Point F is higher than point B. In the treaty-compliant situation, the marginal abatement costs of the country considered are thus above its marginal damage ($MAC_1(x_1^{**}) > MD_1(x^{**})$). This infringes the condition for a Nash equilibrium ($MAC_1 = MD_1$) in the treaty-compliant situation. The Nash equilibrium is the "theoretical point of rest" in the model at which an actor has no reason to make changes as long as the other party does not either. Conversely, it can be seen that in the treaty-compliant situation, it is attractive for the country considered to change its emission quantity. On the condition that the other country keeps the agreement, the first country could make itself better off by increasing its emissions to an extent such that its marginal abatement costs correspond to its own marginal damage. That would mean it would be adopting a free rider position. In Figure 30, country 1 would increase its emissions by $x^+ - x^{**}$. The condition $MAC_1(ER_2^N + ER_2^{**}) = MD_1$ would then be met.

The same incentive problem arises for the other country. Although the position x^{**} is optimum for the community of the two countries, each country could accordingly be tempted to make itself better off at the expense of the other. If both countries succumb to the temptation indicated to breach the treaty, then there will be an ever-increasing erosion of the agreement. Ultimately, each would be emitting its Nash equilibrium emission quantity. The overall environmental quality attained would not differ from the one without the treaty. So, it was just a lot of trouble for nothing. Considered all around, the test of the incentive compatibility of the globally optimum international environmental agreement with identical countries leads to a negative result. Although the agreement's incentive structure stands up to the test of the first criterion ("individual rationality"), it nonetheless fails at the second stage of testing ("stability"). Because for incentive compatibility both criteria must be met simultaneously, the positive outcome from the first test criterion hardly brightens up the overall result. If the countries anticipate the missing stability of the globally optimum treaty construction, then they will not even conclude the relevant agreement. This is true even if, considered in isolation, it meets the criterion of individual rationality. In sections 4 and 5, we seek to conceive of various possibilities for improving the incentive compatibility of international environmental agreements. However, to conclude this section, we briefly show what consequences arise for the previous modeling if the assumption of identical countries is dropped. We also (in section 3) present a description explaining the incentive problems of international environmental agreements at issue that is very popular in the literature – the prisoner's dilemma in the normal form.

Let us consider the implications of differences between the two states for the previous model. Of course, the differences can be modeled in multiple ways within the model framework: the countries may differ in regard to their marginal damage and/or their marginal abatement costs.

We here confine ourselves for the sake of simplicity to a representative of the first-mentioned case. We assume that the countries continue to have identical marginal abatement costs, but that one country (2) is much more damaged by the global environmental changes than country 1. (It may thus, for instance, be expected that *ceteris paribus* countries will be more harmed by the Earth's global warming the closer they are to the equator and the bigger and flatter their coastal areas.[26])

In investigating the effects of the differences in environmental damage caused in individual countries, we make things easier for ourselves by a simplifying assumption on the form of this difference. We select a special case where the aggregate marginal damage over the two countries considered remains unchanged by comparison with the previously presented model with identical countries. It is only in

26 The island and delta states, as the group *Members of the Alliance of Small Island States*, presented a joint catalog of demands at the negotiations for the Kyoto Protocol that had the highest demands of the whole conference. The group sought a 20% reduction in greenhouse gas emissions by the year 2005. It took 1990 as the base year.

the model's "fine structure" that something changes: the contribution by country 1 to the total marginal damage arising falls in comparison with the model with identical countries, and the contribution by country 2 rises *correspondingly*. What we mean by the word "correspondingly" is that the marginal damage to country 1 in the model with differing countries lies, for every emission quantity, below the marginal damage in the model with identical counties by precisely the same amount as the marginal damage to country 2 lies *above* it.

We can also make the position clear by looking at Figure 30b. After all, it depicts the case of identical countries. However, we could easily move from the portrayal of identical countries to the case of differing countries described here. For this, the ordinate values of the individual marginal damage curve for country 1 would have to be multiplied by a constant factor (e.g., one third). By showing this marginal damage curve "devalued" in comparison with the model for identical countries, we would then have depicted the situation for the less-affected country in the model with differing countries. In a second step, we could correspondingly "upgrade" the individual marginal damage curve show in Figure 30b by multiplying the ordinate values by the complement of the correction factor employed previously (in the context of this example, then, the factor 5/3). That would depict the situation of a more strongly affected country (country 2), which for the purposes of the simplified construction employed here exactly fits that of the less strongly affected country depicted previously. The *individual* marginal damage functions of the two countries are differentiated from each other in comparison with the model with identical countries, without the *aggregate* marginal damage function having changed from the first model to the second.

The special form of differentiation chosen here enables the effects of departure from the model with identical countries initially presented on the individual rationality of the globally optimum environmental agreement to be explained as simply as possible. Let us, for example, look at the less affected country (country 1) and denote the model with identical countries for short as "scenario 1" and the one for countries differing in the way described as "scenario 2." With the move from scenario 1 to scenario 2, the marginal abatement costs of the first country remain unchanged, but its marginal damage falls. Accordingly, this country's Nash equilibrium level of emission abatement will fall with the move from the first to the second scenario. The corresponding equilibrium condition ($MAC_1 = MD_1$) is *ceteris aribus* met by a lower emission abatement the flatter is the MD_1 curve.[27] In contrast, with the Nash equilibrium emission level, the global optimum (and, thus, the globally optimum agreement) remains completely unaffected by the move from the first scenario to the second. This is because, in the condition that fully describes

---

27 The special form of differentiation of the two countries taken here has the property that all statements made for country 1 apply equally to country 2 with the opposite sign. Correspondingly, the Nash equilibrium emission abatement rises for country 2 with the move from the first scenario to the second.

the optimum ($MD = MAC_1 = MAC_2$), the *distribution* of aggregate marginal damage over the two countries does not appear. However, it is only this distribution that distinguishes the second scenario from the first. What constitutes the global optimum is purely the country-specific marginal abatement costs and the *aggregate* marginal damage.

Summarizing the individual elements of the previous argument for the situation of country 1, we find that the emission level that country 1 ought to still achieve through conclusion of the globally optimum agreement does not differ between the two scenarios. The Nash equilibrium emission level is, in contrast, higher in the second scenario than in the first. The emission quantity that country 1 would have to cut on the move from a Nash equilibrium to treaty-compliant behavior is accordingly higher in the second scenario than in the first. Because the marginal abatement cost function does not change with the move from one scenario to another, the costs arising for country 1 from the globally optimum agreement are higher in the second scenario than in the first. In contrast, however, the benefit for country 1 from the agreement in the second scenario is smaller than in the first because the environmental damage to country 1 falls with the move from the first scenario to the second. Considered all around, then, the attractiveness of the globally optimum agreement for country 1 is smaller in the second scenario than in the first.[28] It is easy to conceive that the attractiveness becomes negative if the effects addressed previously are strong enough. To make this clear, imagine the extreme case of a difference between the countries such that country 1 does not suffer (hardly) at all from the environmental problem, so that its marginal damage curve is (almost) identical with the abscissa. Then the country concerned gains (only a little more than) nothing from a move to the global optimum starting from the Nash equilibrium. All the same, if it were to comply with a globally optimum agreement, then it should emit only the same emission quantity as country 2 ($x_1^{**} = x_2^{**}$). This is because we have assumed that the marginal abatement costs of both countries are equal to each other. It follows that the two countries must make the same emission-reducing contributions (starting from zero) in order to achieve the global optimum. It is not surprising that country 1 (aiming at maximizing the welfare of its own citizens) would be anything but enthusiastic about the prospect of concluding the globally optimum agreement.

Of course, in reality, circumstances will mostly not be as they are in the special case presented here (or in any other special case!). Nonetheless, presenting the special case is relevant in practice. It enables us to state that a globally optimum environmental agreement for the case of differing countries is not *in general* individually rational for each country. In fact, many circumstances departing from the situation presented previously can be imagined, in which at least one state would be a net loser as a result of a move from the Nash equilibrium to global optimum.

---

28 For the reasons given previously, it follows that for country 2 there is a "mirror image" rise in attractiveness with the move from the first scenario to the second.

Moreover, the optimum agreement is unstable. For this, what was already set out for the case of identical countries applies.

3. An Alternative Description: Global Environmental Problems as a Static Prisoner's Dilemma in Normal Form

In the foregoing sections, the concepts of the optimum and equilibrium emission level for a global pollutant are developed. In addition, the problems of incentive compatibility of international environmental agreements have been explained from the viewpoint of economic theory. Here the method of presentation was chosen so as to be directly comparable with the "standard presentation" in environmental economics in the first three parts of this book, as well as with the presentation of a few special problems in part four. As is usual in mainstream environmental economics, optima and equilibria have been defined using continuous functions, in particular, marginal abatement costs and marginal damage functions. The emission quantities (or emission abatement quantities) appear as independent variables in these functions. They can take on any arbitrary (nonnegative) value.

In contrast, international environmental problems are often presented in the literature in a highly simplified form. States' possibilities of action are no longer presented in the literature as a continuum of possibilities of emission abatement ranging from not avoiding any emissions to avoiding all. Instead, the decision problem is narrowed down into a dichotomy, a yes-or-no alternative. In the context of this discussion, "yes" stands for accession by a particular country to an international environmental treaty and compliance with it. This alternative is often called "cooperation" in the literature. The "no" alternative in this context stands for a state's possibility of refusing international environmental cooperation and going for its "autistic optimum" (Nash equilibrium). For this, the term customary in the literature is "defection." This presentation grossly simplifies the structure of the problem, but does have pedagogical advantages. It enables incentive problems of international environmental policy to be depicted by recourse to a particularly simple way of presenting a game. Interdependencies between the various states are shown as a "game in normal form."[29] In this simple form, we now present a particularly drastic version of the position that it is impossible to achieve the optimum level of global environmental quality without a supranational authority. This is the so-called prisoner's dilemma.[30]

To simplify, we assume a world of two states. Each state is faced with the alternative of either compelling its CO_2-emitting industry, the transport sector, and/or

---

29 To avoid misunderstandings, it should be noted that game theory is by no means restricted to this simple mode of portrayal.

30 The dilemma is traditionally explained using an example from American criminal law, which is also where its name originates. It is, in general, suited to illustrating problems of decentralized supply of purely public goods. Global environmental quality is only one example among many of this sort of public good.

Table 1. *The prisoner's dilemma – an example*

2 \ 1	Cooperation	Defection
Cooperation	10 — 10	15 — 0
Defection	0 — 15	5 — 5

private households to do some costly restructuring in the interest of climate protection, or else completely refraining from this measure. Following the terminology used in literature on the prisoner's dilemma in general, we call the first alternative "cooperation" and the second "defection" (abstaining). We assume that each state's aim is to maximize its own population's social welfare. Let this welfare be quantifiable through a social welfare function in which both the benefit of climate stabilization and the costs arising from climate protection measures for one's own economy are considered. As described previously, a state's *own* costs for climate protection have a negative sign in its social welfare function. The costs arising for the other state, however, play no part in the welfare of the first state. The case is different with the benefit of climate protection. The benefit of climate protection goes into the social welfare function irrespective of whether it arises from activities of this state or the other. Ultimately, in this example, climate protection is a purely public good. Now the social welfare function attributes a welfare value to each combination of decisions by the two states. Because we are here considering two states that each have two alternative actions, four welfare values occur. In Table 1, we show these values, for simplicity's sake, as numbers. The size of these numbers is arbitrary; what matters is the relation between them.

To simplify, the social welfare functions of both countries are assumed to be identical. The top right figure in each of the four boxes indicates the social welfare of country 1 for the given combination of decisions by the states ("cooperation or defection"), and the bottom left figure, the social welfare of country 2. The upper left box in the figure is accordingly to be read as follows: if both states decide to implement the climate protection measure at issue (i.e., both "cooperate"), then they produce a social welfare value of 10 units each. The other boxes are to be interpreted correspondingly. A glance at the numerical values in Table 1 shows that it would be better for the community of both states as a whole if they were to cooperate because the sum of the social welfare values (20) is a maximum for this situation. Bilateral cooperation is, then, the *globally optimum* situation in the sense explained previously. We assume that this position has been reached, and test whether it is a stable equilibrium.

Let us put ourselves in the position of state 1. However nice the starting position, it would be even nicer for this state if, with the given conduct of 2, it shifted from cooperation to defection. Although it would then lose the benefit arising from its own contribution to climate protection, it would also save its climate protection costs. Because this would make its welfare rise from 10 to 15, we can see that the second effect overcompensates for the first. It is accordingly attractive to 1 in the given incentive structure to adopt a *free rider position*. Of course, the interest position of both states is completely symmetrical. State 2 would similarly improve its position if with the given cooperative behavior of 1, it were to move from cooperation to defection. However, if both states succumb to the incentive to free riding described here, then they "land" in a situation of bilateral defection in which they only reach welfare of 5. Ultimately, the effort of each individual to secure advantages at the expense of the other has meant a deterioration of the welfare of both. Nor is it possible to free oneself from the dungeon of bilateral defection by unilateral action. For instance, if in a starting position of bilateral defection state 1 were to shift to unilateral cooperation, its welfare would fall still further (namely, from 5 to 0).

It is in the divergence between the global optimum and equilibrium and the impossibility of overcoming this without an effective coordinating institution that the *dilemma* in the incentive structure addressed here consists. Of course, the representatives of both states depicted could endeavor to make joint efforts to overcome the allocational dilemma by agreeing to act cooperatively. However, such an agreement is always threatened with instability. For each of the two treaty partners, there is an incentive not to comply with the agreements reached (in practice, to also comply imperfectly). In game theoretic literature, a whole series of possible solutions to the prisoner's dilemma has been discussed. We go into these solutions later in this part.

The prisoner's dilemma should be presented in rather more general terms (i.e., detached from the specific features of the numerical example offered previously). For this, let us denote the individual state's welfare as W_1 or W_2, and the aggregate welfare as $W = W_1 + W_2$. Then we write the welfare of a state as a function of the alternative action chosen by itself and the other state in each case (i.e., cooperation or defection). Then the quintessence of the incentive structure in the prisoner's dilemma that works on the individual decision maker (and here we are taking the example of country 1) can be portrayed by the inequalities $W_1(DC) > W_1(CC) > W_1(DD) > W_1(CD)$. In this particularly simple notation, the first position of the combination of activities in the brackets denotes the activity of the state whose preference order is denoted here. Because we have written the inequalities for the first state, *DC* means a combination in which the first state defects and the second cooperates. For this combination, the first state achieves a higher welfare level than in the combination *CC* (i.e., in the event of bilateral cooperation). The argument and the notation apply *mutatis mutandis* to the other state.

The dilemma lies in the fact that each of the two states would like to defect irrespective of what the other does. In game theoretic terminology, defection is the *dominant strategy*. If each follows this incentive, then the resulting equilibrium is position *DD*, suboptimal for both, in which global environmental quality is below optimum. If the two cannot conclude a binding treaty, then there is no escape for them from this trap, although both can see the situation of bilateral cooperation that would be better for both of them. This dilemma position, briefly presented here, has long typified the perception of the problem of the private production of public goods in general and the problem of global environmental policy specifically. Economics has not, however, for the following reasons, stopped at this description of the problem:

- In reality, in certain areas, thoroughly cooperative behavior is observed in the production of public goods. In the area of global environmental problems, too, there are many efforts at cooperation, and perhaps even some successes. If economic theory wants to achieve "interpretive leadership" among the social sciences (or keep it, if it already has it), then it has to explain human behavior as completely as possible, using economic means. If economics is not in a position to explain cooperative behavior (especially perhaps if it is a new development arising in society and politics), then it will lose ground in the face of competition from other social sciences.[31]
- Where there is no cooperation in the production of public goods (here, no successes in global environmental policy), economics wants to help. It would like to contribute to designing an institutional framework where the chances for cooperation can be improved. The sciences compete for a leading role not only in the interpretation of observations, but also in policy advice.

Contrary to what a classic somewhat out of fashion in recent years thought, then, the point is not either to interpret the world or to change it. Economists at any rate want both.[32]

We now look briefly at the game theoretic discussion beyond the simple prisoner's dilemma. First, we seek to explain why individuals sometimes act cooperatively, although the conceptualization in the prisoner's dilemma would predict an equilibrium with defection on all sides. Second, we look for possibilities of overcoming the unsatisfactory outcome of equilibrium defection by supplementing or restructuring the "ground rules" applying to the parties involved.

4. Generalization of the Game Structure

Every model is unrealistic. The point of one is to define the optimum degree of abstraction from real facts, and this is possible only in a way specific to a context. It depends on the model's explanatory objective and the state of development of the science at the time the model is constructed. Considered this way, the static

---

31 Readers acquainted with interdisciplinary dialog will of course understand that the author (an economist!) is not taking up arms against the other social sciences here. It is after all modern to discover positive relations between competition and cooperation ("co-opetition").

32 It is in any case (in the world's interest) advisable for those wanting to change it to first attempt to understand it.

prisoner's dilemma is today still suited as a pedagogical means for explaining dilemma structures. It can, however, at the present state of the game theoretic art, be adjusted better to real events at little cost (low model development costs) and thus supply better results (high model development benefit). In particular, for the construction, as simple as possible, sketched in section 3, two features strike one:

- Its static nature
- The given payoff structure (known to the players)

In the game theoretic literature, both special assumptions have been generalized. It has emerged that equilibria respond sensitively to the model extensions made in this way. By including dynamic games and risk-loaded payoffs, the game structure is generalized in the sense that the model world in which the actors are deciding takes on a greater resemblance to the real world.[33] The procedure here is analogous to parameter variation in the context of comparative static analysis. The point is to analyze the effects of differences in the pattern of fixed elements in the model structure on the outcome of the model.

a) **Dynamic Games.** The extension of observation from one round (the static model) to several rounds (the dynamic one) is associated in the literature with the hope of improving the chances of attaining cooperative equilibria. This expectation can be explained without going into detail: extending observation to more than one round allows the decision makers to pursue a *conditionally cooperative strategy*. In contrast with the one-round model, the decision to cooperate can be made dependent on how the other behaves. For instance, a decision maker may undertake to cooperate as long as the other also acts cooperatively. If the "opponent" defects, then the decision maker considered can also abandon cooperation. This opens the possibility for each decision maker to reward cooperative behavior of the other party by its own cooperation, and punish defecting behavior by its own defection. This sort of interaction by definition does not exist in the static context. We briefly clarify the point that actors can use the room for maneuver in the multiround model under certain conditions in order to support cooperative behavior. When we have completed the move from the static prisoner's dilemma to dynamic modeling, the question then arises as to whether the actors are to decide in relation to a finite or infinite planning horizon. It turns out that for a finite planning horizon, the chances of cooperation in the prisoner's dilemma are no better than in the static

---

33 Here, for the sake of example, we pick out two particularly important extensions to the model from the wealth of possible ones. We present the extensions within the framework of the prisoner's dilemma in the normal form. The same extensions could also be implemented in the model of global environmental problems with a continuum of emission abatement possibilities, as explained in sections 1 and 2. Limiting the prisoner's dilemma in the normal form to two alternatives for decision (cooperation or defection), however, enables a simpler presentation.

game. This is at any rate true where the end of the planning period is known with certainty.[34]

Given the need for brevity, we then shift the view immediately to the next model variant: the prisoner's dilemma with an infinite planning horizon. Here it turns out that cooperation can be an equilibrium strategy for the participants if future welfare effects of the decision to cooperate are not discounted "too strongly." Then it is conceivable for countries to comply with an agreement to always act cooperatively, even if the treaty is not binding. This is true when (but not only when) a state breaching the treaty expects the duped treaty partner to apply the "trigger strategy", i.e., to abandon cooperative relations for all time. With this condition, the following "cost—benefit analysis of breach of treaty" applies: on the benefit side stands the surplus of national welfare that the *DC* combination brings the treaty-breaching state by comparison with the *CC* combination during the period of breach of treaty. On the cost side of breach of treaty, in contrast, in each of the following periods there is the net increase in welfare that the state would have had from implementing the agreement. These are then the welfare consequences of the difference between combination *CC* and combination *DD*.

We normally start from the position that net welfare flows lying in the future are discounted for the state at issue (as for every other decision maker) to the time of decision. It is intuitively obvious that the cost—benefit analysis sketched out here will come out in favor of complying with a cooperation treaty if the discount rate used in the discounting is low enough. Of course, the conditions for this highly optimistic outcome are restrictive: the trigger strategy used as a punishment mechanism here presumes that the punishing state is engaging in irrational behavior if it damages itself by employing it. After all, in the long run it will have to pay for using the strategy by the certain loss of all welfare gains conceivable for it from subsequent implementation of the agreement. That is what the credibility of a threat to use the trigger strategy suffers from.[35] However, this

---

34 The forecast derived from the theory that the incentive structure will not be improved by a move from the static prisoner's dilemma to a dynamic prisoner's dilemma with a finite and known planning horizon is not confirmed in experimental economics. However, in experiments, the propensity to cooperate as a rule falls off sharply toward the end of the game. Cf., e.g., Weimann (1994).

35 This has the (apparently paradoxical) consequence that it may be strategically advantageous for a player, say, A, to have a certain reputation for irrationality. Let us assume that A convinces the opponent, B, that he (A) is *irrational* enough to use the trigger strategy in the event of treaty breach by B, even though he (A) would damage himself thereby. This makes breach of treaty unattractive to B. Let B, in contrast, assume that he has to deal with a partner (contracting party) (C) known not to have its rationality impinged on by feelings. If C threatens the trigger strategy in the event of treaty breach by B, then B will not take it seriously. B does not believe that the rational C will do something to put itself in a worse position. Because C's threat lacks credibility, it contributes nothing to stabilizing the agreement. (The circumstances briefly addressed here are discussed in the literature under the heading "strategic importance of feelings"; cf., e.g., Frank (2004, 2008) and Bolle/Braham (2006).)

strategy is not a constitutive element of a model with an infinite planning horizon. Instead, the literature considers a number of other punishment mechanisms, which we briefly return to later in this part.

b) Risky Payoffs. We have so far assumed that the welfare effects of the activity combinations of the states involved are fixed and known to those involved. Now we depart from that and assume that only the probability distributions are known to the states. We thus move from the simple static prisoner's dilemma to a game with the *expectation value structure* of the simple static prisoner's dilemma. For the resulting equilibria, the risk preference of the states involved is decisive. For risk-neutral decision makers, nothing changes. If we instead consider the example of risk aversion, the following results.[36]

In analyzing the welfare effects of combinations of strategies, not only the mean values, but also the spreads have to be considered. This viewpoint is most simply grasped by assuming that the states endeavor to maximize a *risk utility function* that takes account of mean values and spread. Although the effects of the states' strategy choices on the mean values are given by the focus on the prisoner's dilemma, nothing can be said about the dependency of the spread on the country's strategies without additional assumptions. Here scientific information (presumably differing according to which real world problem is being studied) would have to be incorporated into the economic analysis. Although this need not necessarily be the case, let us assume for the sake of example that the spread declines with the intensity of cooperative efforts. Applied to the object of our discussion, this means that the spread of risks associated with global warming will be smaller the more successful the efforts at lowering CO_2 emissions are. In this case, accordingly, the spread for the combination *DD* would be greater than for the combination *CC*. The larger spread is assessed negatively by risk-averse states. Thus defection loses attractiveness by comparison with cooperative behavior in the model with risk-averse actors vis-à-vis a model with welfare effects that are certain. In the prisoner's dilemma the mean values constitute a fatal structure regarding the incentives to cooperate. In the model allowing for risk aversion, the "fear of risk" constitutes a certain counterweight to these fatal incentives. A more exact model theory analysis shows that a game with the expectation value structure of a prisoner's dilemma is transformed into a game with a higher likelihood of cooperation if the risk aversion of the states involved exceeds a critical threshold. Depending on the intensity of the risk aversion, the transformation process may lead to a game of chicken (with a certain unilateral incentive to cooperate) or even to a no conflict game (with bilateral incentives to cooperate).[37]

---

36   Cf. Endres/Ohl (2001, 2002, 2003).

37   In general (i.e., without reference to risk preference), on these types of games, cf., e.g., Finus (2001).

c) Consequences. We can thus see that the dismal forecast of the prisoner's dilemma originally used in the literature regarding the possibilities of cooperation is at least partly brought about by the fact that the world in which the model actors are acting has an extremely restricted form. If in building the model we take account of the fact that in the real world actions take place over time, and moreover that nothing is certain, then the possibilities of explaining cooperation increase.

5. Instruments to Enhance the Propensity to Cooperate

a) Internal Incentives to Participation and Stabilization. Alongside the drastic, but in some circumstances noncredible, trigger strategy, there are other measures for enhancing the *individual rationality* of agreements on cooperative behavior and their stability.[38] These strategies – termed *internal* participation and stabilization mechanisms – have in common that they link the cooperative behavior of each state to the cooperative behavior of every other state. If one state breaks the treaty, the other states are no longer bound by their promises. The variants of the principle of internal stabilization differ only in how the states concerned use this room for maneuver. As well as breaking off cooperative relations with the treaty-breaking state for all time, as the trigger strategy provides, the following variants are discussed in the literature:

- *Reoptimization Strategy.* The optimum emission reduction quantity to be agreed on for each state depends on how many states join the relevant agreement. If a treaty with a particular number of signatory states comes about, then each state's individual reduction quantity agreed in that it is optimum only for that coalition. If one member state breaks the treaty and leaves it, then the agreed emission quantities for the remaining states are no longer optimum. In the reoptimization strategy, the remaining states are now entitled to adjust their emission quantities to the new circumstances (i.e., to reoptimize). If the aggregate equilibrium emission of the coalition members rises in this process, then the fact that the treaty-breaking coalition member will suffer from this increase in emissions can be seen as "punishment" for it. This punishment is credible because it is a mere consequence of the optimization by the states remaining in the coalition. More precise game theoretic modeling shows, however, that the effects of this stabilization strategy are limited. In the very cases in which coordinated action by states would be particularly desirable, only coalitions with disappointingly small memberships are stable for this stabilization strategy.[39] Even if the reoptimization strategy does not seem particularly effective as a stand-alone instrument to enhance the propensity to cooperate, the idea of reoptimization is nonetheless significant for the whole theory (and practice?!)

---

38 Cf., e.g., Schmidt (2000, 2001), Endres (2004).

39 Cf. already Barrett (1994a, 1994b), Carraro/Sinsicalco (1993), and Hoel (1992), as well as the more recent contributions by Eyckmans/Finus (2006a, 2006b), Rubio/Ulph (2006), and Weikard/Finus/Altamirano-Cabrera (2006).

of international environmental problems. Reoptimization is a consequence of the universal interdependence among the states affected by the global environmental problem. This connection will often be important in the following sections, up to and including the economic analysis of the Kyoto Protocol.

- *Extended Tit-for-Tat Strategy.*[40] Here defection by one coalition member is initially, as with the previous strategy, "punished" by reoptimization. However, the defecting state is taken back into the coalition if it has done sufficient "penance." This may be by paying a fine or taking on extra obligations to cut emissions.[41] It turns out, though, that this stabilization mechanism can accomplish only very little. Often, only coalitions with small numbers of participants are stable, or the emission reductions the coalition members agree to are small.[42]

- *Ratification Clause.* In this mechanism, there is a provision that an international environmental treaty will enter into force only once a particular number of states have ratified it.[43] This clause results in a twofold incentive to participate: an "honest state" does not have to fear committing itself to costly reduction measures, the positive effects of which will "go up in smoke" because other states do not join in. A state playing with the idea of free rider advantages has to reckon that its free rider behavior will endanger the whole treaty structure if it does not join. It will therefore also damage itself. Yet, it should be noted that the participation incentives briefly presented here are not necessarily associated with stabilization incentives. It is not granted in any case that each country which signs an agreement will also fully comply with the terms of this agreement.[44] The connection between joining a treaty and keeping it is, however, strengthened by ratification. Ratification converts the obligations of an international treaty into national law, which binds the state more strongly than its agreement with other states.

All in all, it emerges that although internal mechanisms may provide some incentive to cooperative behavior, the ones presented here are generally insufficient to solve the problem of the prisoner's dilemma.

40   That is, "what you do to me I'll do to you."

41   Strictly speaking, the element of the fine in the extended "tit for tat" strategy goes beyond the range of internal stabilization. For this is defined by the fact that states' cooperative behavior is linked to the condition of cooperative behavior by the other states. The fine, however, adds an extra element borrowed from the area of external stabilization. This is dealt with in the following section.

42   Cf. Barrett (2002) and Finus/Rundshagen (1998a, 1998b).

43   The best-known example from practice is the Kyoto agreement. For more, see section II in this part.

44   The skepticism as to states' treaty compliance expressed in these lines has empirical support. Falkner et al. (2005) study compliance with obligations taken on by EU member states. The findings are (depending on the reader's state of mind) sobering to devastating. The analysis by Falkner and coauthors is confined to the area of European social policy. It would be rash to expect the findings to be any better in other policy areas (in our context, international environmental agreements).

b) External Incentives to Participation and Stabilization. From the previously mentioned shortcomings of internal incentives, there follows a need to develop additional instruments. In detail, these possibilities exist:

- *Transfer Payments.* If the interests of various decision makers in relation to a particular object cannot be adequately harmonized, then the first thing an economist thinks of is bringing in compensation payments. The social optimum is defined by maximizing the summed welfare of the participants. To bring about a consensus move from a suboptimal to an optimum state, it is "merely" necessary to develop a system of side payments to turn the potential Pareto improvement into an actual Pareto improvement. This is ultimately, after all, the basic idea of the Coase theorem dealt with in detail in part two of this book. Applied to our topic, this means that states that would profit from implementation of a globally optimum environmental treaty ought (at least) to compensate the losers from such a treaty. It follows from the definition of a globally optimum agreement that the welfare gains arising from implementing the agreement are at least sufficient for the necessary compensation.

  However, in attempting to implement this idea, good in itself, problems arise that we are familiar with from the preceding discussion of the Coase theorem: for the countries providing the transfers, the induced abatement efforts by the recipient countries induced by the transfers are a public good. It is anything but obvious that it will be possible to find a way of determining the proportions in which the individual donor countries should contribute to financing this public good. Instead, the usual free rider problems are to be expected inside the group of donor countries. Alongside these fundamental considerations, there is the problem with transfer payments that recipient states do not reliably comply with the reduction obligation associated with the transfer payment. The transfer payment, supposedly aimed at stabilizing treaties, is perhaps itself in need of stabilization.[45]

  The model state in the game theoretic analysis measures its benefits and costs from emission reductions with no problem at all. Mostly, it also knows the other states' benefits and costs. It is therefore, in principle, unproblematic to determine which state must make a (marginal) compensation payment to which other states in order to aim at the optimum. All that can be disputed in the model is how the proceeds arising from the move to the optimum situation are to be distributed.

  In reality, however, the country-specific benefits and costs are unknown, even if they were accepted as the criterion for redistribution measures. Because the benefits and costs determine the transfer payments, incentives arise to strategic conduct in states' information policies, which would then become effective for the allocation. Both transfer donors and recipients are exposed to the incentive to estimate their benefits from environmental protection measures low and

---

45 Cf. Finus (2002).

their abatement costs high in order to receive high transfer payments, or else make smaller payments. Furthermore, transfer donors have an incentive to keep the transfers low or avoid them in order not to set up any precedents and perhaps appear in future negotiations as a weak negotiating partner.[46] The incentive to manipulation would not be confined to the falsification of cost–benefit data from available technologies, but would perhaps develop effects on the choice of technology itself. It would be entirely conceivable for a state to omit particular environmental protection measures or take particular technology policy decisions in order to turn itself into a recipient state for transfer payments.[47]

Things become still more difficult where states do not even think of making economic cost–benefit magnitudes the criterion for their action at all (explicitly). We cannot ignore the fact that especially the economic evaluation of environmental damage (or the benefit from avoiding it) meets with extreme resistance as soon as we leave the protected area (!!) of debate among economists. Even economists admit that considerable methodological and empirical problems exist.[48]

The difficulties in agreeing on monetary transfer payments have led to attempts to think up alternative forms of transfer. The simplest form would be real transfers. For instance, an industrialized state would like to induce a developing country to reduce emissions. Then, the industrialized country could make the technology necessary to achieve the intended abatement available to the developing country and pay for it. This would act against the danger of misuse that is strongly present with monetary transfers. Of course, this does not solve all problems of transfers. For instance, the installation of environmental technologies does not yet guarantee that they will also be properly used. This is particularly true of add-on ("end-of-pipe") technologies. Moreover, there will certainly have to be additional incentives in order to interest the recipient state in the agreement effectively.

• *Issue Linkage.* From a game theoretic viewpoint, it is particularly interesting if an agreement on emission efforts can be made incentive compatible by linking it with another agreement.[49] This occurs in ideal fashion where both agreements are related to each other *mirror*wise. That is, a country losing national welfare in the environmental sphere from a move to the socially optimum agreement gains precisely in this sphere from the object of the second agreement if there is an advance from the suboptimum position without an agreement to the socially optimum one. It is, of course, easy in the model to dream up agreements that fit each other in this sense like bits of a jigsaw. In reality, however, it is extremely

---

46 Cf. Mäler (1990) on this last argument.
47 Cf. Buchholz/Konrad (1995).
48 Cf., e.g., Smith (2004), Turner et al. (2003).
49 Cf., e.g., Kemfert (2003), Mohr/Thomas (1998). The idea of issue linkage is also important outside the theory and practice of international environmental agreements. Cf., e.g., the political and economic analysis of linked issue petitions as an instrument of direct democracy in Goeschl (2005).

difficult, especially where multilateral problems are involved. Moreover, it must be asked whether the pooling of different policy areas has only advantages. It is likely that the joining up of problem areas that constitutes issue linkage will also bring difficulties. An exact analysis of these is not made otiose by the mere fact of calling them "transaction costs."

- *Penalties.* One special way of linking various factual areas is penalties. The form most commonly dealt with in theory and applied in practice is trade sanctions. Here states not joining an environmental agreement or breaking it are threatened with the breakage of trade relations or the elimination of benefits from international trade. If applying trade sanctions is advantageous to the punishing states themselves, then the penalty is at any rate credible. It is, however, in this very case difficult to distinguish actual sanctions for lack of cooperation from purely protectionist measures. If, instead, the trade sanction is disadvantageous for the punishing states, then it is appropriate to doubt whether the relevant threat will actually be acted on in the event of failure to cooperate in the environmental sphere.[50]

6. Coalition Formation in International Environmental Negotiations

Previously, we illustrated a few possibilities and problems of international environmental negotiations using a very simple model. Simplification of the presentation was served particularly by restricting those involved to only two states.

The procedure so far can be summarized as follows. First, we describe the position in which the summed welfare of the two countries is maximized ("global optimum"). Second, we describe the position arising where each state maximizes its own welfare without considering the effects of its action on the other ("Nash equilibrium"). The divergence between global optimum and Nash equilibrium led to a third step in the analysis: answering the question as to whether the two states would be likely to succeed through cooperative behavior in leaving the Nash equilibrium and moving to the global optimum. The chances of success were assessed according to two criteria:

- *Is the individual state's welfare at the global optimum higher than at the Nash equilibrium?* It is then *individually rational* for the individual state to conclude a globally optimum treaty with the other one. This would provide that each state has to bring about the emission reduction required to produce the globally optimum situation.
- *Is it attractive for the individual state to comply with the globally optimum agreement on the condition that the other complies?* Then the treaty is *stable*.

Limiting the model to two states enabled us to analyze essential features of the economics of international environmental problems in a comparatively simple way. However, the presentation in this book should not be confined to the case of two states. After all, the model with only two participants is remote from reality,

---

50 Cf., e.g., Kirchgässner/Mohr (1996).

particularly when treating worldwide problems. This is not a book about international environmental problems; it merely treats them as part of a general course in environmental economics. Nonetheless, the fundamentals of the modeling of international environmental problems with many states is set out here.[51] For more details, we would, however, refer to the specialized literature.[52]

Of course, the problems (in the model and in reality) are considerably complicated if a multiplicity of states is involved in the negotiations. The landscape of interests not only has to be portrayed with much more variance, but is also harder to grasp than in the two-state model. In particular, problems of coalition forming by subgroups of states arise here, and we briefly turn to them later in this part. Let us consider a large number of states jointly causing a global environmental problem and suffering from it (in the general case, to differing extents). What predictions for these countries' coalition behavior follow from the economic model theory depends on a range of assumptions. With the type of model so far most popular in the literature, two groups of countries are distinguished: signatory states and nonsignatory states. The signatory states cooperate with each other in ideal fashion: they choose their action variables (in our context, mostly the emission level) in such a way as to maximize their common welfare. In relation to the nonsignatory states, however, they act uncooperatively. For the nonsignatory states, we assume that they each strive in isolation to maximize their own welfare. They act uncooperatively to all other states, irrespective of whether they belong to the group of signatory or nonsignatory states. The process of coalition formation, on the one hand, and agreements within the coalition as well as decisions by nonmembers, on the other hand, are as a rule presented as two stages of a game. In the first stage, a simultaneous decision is taken on membership. In this phase, each state takes the dichotomous decision: "do I join the coalition or not?" In the second stage, the members of both groups of countries (signatories and nonsignatories) choose their emission levels simultaneously. Here the concept of the Nash equilibrium developed in the previous sections comes to bear.[53]

The two-stage nature of the approaches addressed here means that they are among the dynamic models. In the light of what we said in sections 4 and 5, the relevant models are thus from the outset better suited for explaining cooperative

51 My understanding of the problems covered in the following discussion has been clarified by numerous talks with Michael Finus, University of Exeter (something that was urgently necessary in the interest of the readers of this passage). For his many suggestions, I am particularly grateful.

52 The account here is based, in particular, on Finus (2001, 2003a, 2003b). Cf. also, e.g., Barrett (2005), Finus/Rundshagen (2006b, 2009), Wagner (2001).

53 Approaches with sequential decisions are, however, also common. Cf., e.g., Barrett (1994a, 1994b). The models often assume that signatory states have an information lead over the nonsignatory states. They take advantage of this by calculating the nonsignatory states' responses they predict into their decision on emission levels. That means that we are here dealing with a Stackelberg interaction model with "emission leadership" by the signatory states, familiar *mutatis mutandis* from oligopoly theory. For recent developments in sequential modeling, see Finus/Rundshagen (2006a), Rubio/Ulph (2006).

behavior than their static predecessors. The mere existence of a second stage opens up the possibility of reacting correspondingly if particular states have not acted cooperatively in the first stage. This makes defection less attractive than in a model where "for lack of a future," there is no possibility of punishing uncooperative behavior in the present. In the models dealt with here, a coalition to reduce global pollutant emissions can come about only if the following conditions are met:

- The coalition must be *individually rational* for each country (i.e., the net welfare attainable as a coalition partner must be higher for each country than the net welfare at the Nash equilibrium).
- The coalition must be stable in the sense that no country belonging to it has an incentive to leave it (internal stability) and, moreover, that there is no incentive for any country to come into the coalition from outside it (external stability).

Let us now briefly pause and check: what has really changed significantly from the move from the model limited to two states to one of many states? The first thing that strikes us is that the move from two to several states means it no longer makes sense to confine observation to comparing two alternative situations (global optimum and Nash equilibrium). The distinction previously introduced between states joining a coalition (signatory states) and states staying outside as loners (nonsignatory states, singletons) necessarily brings into view arrangements that in "degree of cooperation" lie between the Nash equilibrium (no cooperation) and the global optimum (complete cooperation). This makes the analysis not only more realistic, but also (as so often with greater realism) more complicated: "complete cooperation" and "no cooperation" are clear concepts. In contrast, the concept of "partial cooperation" is vague. Partial cooperation can take on many forms: who cooperates with whom, in what respect, and how intensively?

The restriction to two situations (global optimum or Nash equilibrium) in the previous sections has a further simplifying implication. If we find that those involved are not able to bring about the global optimum, then we need not bother ourselves about what they might do otherwise: all that is left is arriving at the Nash equilibrium. *Tertium non datur* — at least not in this model. With the extension of consideration to several participants, things are quite different: what does a state not complying with the coalition agreement do? Perhaps it stays in the coalition and just fudges compliance with its obligations. Perhaps it leaves the coalition and decides for the *Lonesome Rider* option. Perhaps it even leaves the coalition to join another one (if provided in the model). It turns out that the questions raised by all this are so complex that they cannot be explained within the framework of a single model. "The supermodel does not yet exist" (as Michael Finus assures us).

The literature therefore splits the overall problem into subareas covered by different types of models. In particular, a distinction is drawn between *compliance models* and *membership models*. The former do not study coalition *formation*, but presuppose it as given. The question treated with this type of model runs: given a particular coalition, how is it to be secured that the agreements reached among its members on emission reductions are actually kept? The membership models take a "mirror image" approach: given that the parties keep the agreements reached, what coalitions are stable?[54]

The question of stability raised here leads to a further distinction between the two-state model used in the foregoing sections and the model with several states. Clearly, in the model with only two states, it is superfluous to distinguish between external and internal stability, as was done previously in the introductory explanation of the coalition issue. If there are only two states, cooperation always refers to all those involved. The accession of an additional participant (external stability) need not be dealt with because there is no third participant. It is only with the move to the model with many states that it becomes possible for only a subset of the countries "appearing" in the model to join a coalition. This is what makes the division of the stability into an external and internal segment meaningful (and also necessary).

We have now sketched out the model framework developed in the literature for analyzing coalitions and distinguished it from the simple world with only two states. We now look more closely at coalition-forming processes and their outcomes in relation to emission of a global pollutant. To simplify, we do this on the basis of a numerical example. For further simplification, we assume a world with five identical states. The observed welfare function for an individual state is $W_i = (200 - 0.5x^2) - 5(10 - x_i)^2$, with $i \in \{1, \ldots, 5\}$. Here x denotes the aggregate emission level, and x_i that of state i.

Table 2 shows the welfare levels these countries obtain if coalitions of varying sizes are brought about. The two polar cases of coalition size are where all five states are loners (no coalition) and a coalition of all participants (complete coalition). Table 2, to make it easier to read, arranges the countries with the ones with the higher index numbers always acting as coalition members. The remaining countries are then the nonsignatories. A coalition of two is, then, made up of countries 5 and 4, a coalition of three of countries, 5, 4, and 3, etc.[55] The numerical values entered in Table 2 are determined on the assumption that all countries decide on their emission levels simultaneously. L_i denotes the ith country, N the number of coalition participants, and the column headed $\sum$ shows welfare summed over all the countries.

To understand this better, let us look at our hypothetical initial situation, where each state maximizes its welfare without considering the others (i.e., no coalition

---

54 A detailed presentation of the differences between the two types of model would go beyond the bounds of a general textbook in environmental economics. Cf. here Finus (2003a). For the simplified presentation proper in this section, the *membership models* are followed.

55 Because the countries are assumed to be identical, this order has to be arbitrary (ad hoc). If we wanted to answer the question as to which countries will join a coalition endogenously to the model, we would have to include differing propensities to cooperate in the model (say, through risk preference). Readers who have already paid their game theory dues will know these things from the game of chicken; cf., e.g., Finus (2001).

Table 2. *Individual and Aggregate Welfare for Alternative Sizes of Coalition*

N/L_i	L_1	L_2	L_3	L_4	L_5	$\sum$
1^a	−411	−411	−411	−411	−411	−2055
2	−275	−275	−275	−405	−405	−1638
3	−111	−111	−338	−338	−338	−1239
4	11	−245	−245	−245	−245	−971
5	−181	−181	−181	−181	−181	−909

Note: ^{a} No coalition: each country acts as a singleton.

comes about). We can see that in this initial position, it is advantageous in every respect if two of the five states join as a coalition[56]: the aggregate welfare rises from −2055.5 to −1638.4, the individual welfare of each coalition member rises from −411.1 to −405.5, and the welfare of the nonsignatories rises from −411.1 to −275.8 for each of them.[57] We see here that the nonsignatories even profit more from coalition formation than the signatories. This is not surprising because given the global nature of the pollutant concerned, they are after all benefited because the two coalition members, in their endeavor to maximize their common welfare, cut emissions. The nonsignatories value this all the more because they do not have to share the costs of this beneficial activity. This coalition of two is also the solution (equilibrium) to our little coalition game in the numerical example given. The coalition of two countries already meets the previously mentioned conditions of individual rationality and stability. It is *individually rational* because each member of the coalition secures higher welfare than in the initial position with no coalition. The coalition is *internally stable* because neither of its members has an incentive to leave it. It would then reach the lower welfare of the initial position. Moreover, the coalition of two is also *externally stable* because there is no incentive for a third country to join the coalition and thus convert it into a coalition of three. For although this step would increase the welfare of the "old" coalition members (from −405.5 to −338.5) and improve the welfare of the nonsignatories (from −275.8 to −111.8), it would itself pay a price for that in the form of a deterioration in welfare (from −275.8 to −338.5). The country (as a "homo oeconomicus") would not decide on such self-injury in the interests of the other countries. This outcome (a coalition of two), although an improvement over the original condition with no coalition, is, however, on the whole, perhaps rather disappointing. After all, aggregate welfare (and even the welfare of each individual country) is considerably higher if all five countries join a coalition. The common welfare is a maximum for this full coalition because by definition it constitutes the socially optimum position.

56　According to the assumptions, these are states 4 and 5.

57　In assessing Table 2, only the relations between the welfares attainable with different sizes of coalition are of importance. Readers troubled by the negative welfare values appearing in Table 2 are welcome to augment the underlying function W_i by the absolute term "+500."

Yet, in the model framework discussed here, we cannot expect the full coalition as an equilibrium. Although it does meet the condition of individual rationality ($-181.9 > -411.1$), it does not meet that of internal stability. Instead, country 1 has an incentive to leave a full coalition. For with this step, it would raise its individual welfare (from -181.9 to 11.38) at the expense of the other countries. Once the full coalition has shrunk to a coalition of four, there is no stopping: the second country has an incentive to leave the coalition of four and pursue its happiness as a nonsignatory in the penumbra of the remaining coalition of three. As it does ($-111.8 > -245.8$). Similarly, country 3 will denounce the coalition of three and leave countries 4 and 5 in the coalition of the two already discussed.

This numerical example portrays a number of theoretical analyses from the literature that suggest that the formation of stable coalitions is extremely difficult if they are to include more than a small number of participants. Somewhat more optimistic outcomes may emerge if one looks "over the edge" of the very simple model on which the previous discussion is based.

- For instance, in our previous argument concerning internal coalition stability, we have implicitly assumed that the country contemplating leaving the coalition bases its decision on the effects of this single step only. It is acting very shortsightedly. If the countries' mental purview is somewhat broader, their propensity to cooperate is greater, and a situation with a larger coalition and better welfare effects will be in equilibrium. In light of Table 2, this connection becomes clear when considering a coalition of four. Country 2 improves itself "in the short term" if it leaves the coalition of four (from -245.8 to -111.8). If, however, it foresees that the third country will "consequently" leave the remaining coalition of three, then it will compare its welfare in the coalition of four (-245.8), not with the welfare it can secure as a nonsignatory in the penumbra of a coalition of three (-111.8), but with the welfare it gets as a nonsignatory in the penumbra of a coalition of two (-275.8). It thus takes account of the fact that following the third country's response, it will end up worse off as a nonsignatory in the penumbra in the coalition of two than as a signatory in a coalition of four. This foresight will prevent it leaving the coalition of four. If we apply the underlying concept, "far-sighted coalition stability," going back to Michael Chwe (1994), then bigger coalitions and thus a higher welfare level than from the viewpoint of the "standard model" presented previously appear within the range of possibility.
- A further departure from the basic model comes from discarding the assumption of "atomistic" behavior by the nonsignatory states. Here the strict separation of the world into two groups, coalition members and an (atomistic) group of nonsignatories, is transcended. This gives us a picture of several partial coalitions existing alongside each other. Recent results of game theory research show that such situations may very well be equilibria and, in some

circumstances, lead to welfare improvements over the initial model.[58] These results might prove particularly important in designing international environmental agreements. To date, it has been taken as undisputed that agreements must be so designed that as large a number of states as possible will join them. It might, however, turn out that the environmental and welfare effects would be better if groups of states came together in subagreements, which would take better account of the heterogeneity of individual state interests.[59]

Let us end by further pointing out that not every type of expansion of the model leads to greater optimism regarding the environmental and welfare properties of the model's results. Thus, the basic model implicitly assumed that countries' adjustments to a decision by a particular country (e.g., to join a coalition or leave it) come about with no time delay. This means that the model is by its very design not capable of grasping one free rider incentive that may be important in reality. For instance, a country might capitalize on the fact that between its infringement of the treaty, discovery of the infringement and punishment by the signatory states, time will pass. In the literature, a number of coalition models that depart from the basic model focused on here have been developed. Here the incentives to treaty breach arising from time delay are presented using the theory of repeated games.[60]

If we take a little distance from the details discussed in the past sections, we see the following picture: for international environmental problems, states' uncoordinated endeavors at maximum welfare lead to severe environmental damage and losses of welfare. The previous presentation shows that international environmental protection agreements can improve the position vis-à-vis the Nash equilibrium. However, the outcomes in general fall short of a globally optimum resource allocation. Moreover, there are doubts whether international environmental protection agreements will always be kept. These problems look all the tougher the more states' interests differ, and the higher the number of participants. It should particularly be noted that the previous problems arise even though (because?) we assume that every country acts in negotiations in such a way as to best serve the interests of promoting national welfare. It should be emphasized that from the outset the

---

58 For more details, see Eyckmans/Finus (2006a, 2006b), Finus (2001, esp. ch. 15), and Finus/Rundshagen (2003). In another model framework (namely, a compliance model, rather than the membership models used in the other sources cited), Asheim et al. (2006) reach similar findings.

59 The previous reference to the heterogeneity of states is made with an eye to the actual circumstances in the world. After all, the preceding model has assumed that the states are identical. It can be shown that even under this condition, multiple coalitions may exist. This is because the incentive to leave a coalition rises *ceteris paribus* with its size. For the "defectors," it is in certain circumstances more attractive to form a (or several) coalition(s) of their own rather than stick it out as loners. The alternative is no longer "all or nothing"; instead, one can decide what coalition to join (for more details, see Finus (2003b), Finus/Rundshagen (2003)).

60 Cf., e.g., Barrett (2002), Finus/Rundshagen (1998a, 1998b), Stähler (1996).

concept of welfare included the interest in an intact environment. The problems disclosed by our considerations are, then, not necessarily attributable to a lack of environmental awareness by decision makers. After this discussion, it will perhaps no longer be quite so easy to attribute the slow progress and mostly modest results of international environmental negotiations to the incapacity of politicians or the pernicious influence of industry.[61]

7. Prospects for the Game Theoretic Analysis of Global Environmental Problems

Wherever it is important to model environmental policy as an interaction between various actors and groups of actors, game theory is an indispensable analytical aid. The use of game theoretic methods has brought considerable advances in knowledge in recent years. All the same, it is necessary to develop the game theory approach further and extend it:

- Game theory demands of actors a high capacity for strategic thought and, in its mainstream, a high degree of rationality. It should not be ignored that game theory forecasts about human behavior are only partly confirmed in experiments.[62] The game theory approach has to be extended intensively by bounded rationality models. It must be confessed, though, that this is rather easier to say than to do. Although rationality is a sufficiently clearly defined concept, when it comes to irrationality, things are fairly wide open. The point cannot be to explain a single social phenomenon unexplained by classical game theory using a particular narrowly defined conception of irrationality. What is missing is a general concept of irrationality that explains a set of real world phenomena that is of higher cardinality than the traditional theory.[63]

- Most game theory models start by assuming that states' behavior can be explained as maximization of a welfare function. Apart from the rationality problem already addressed, the criticism should be made that clashes among interest groups in policy formation within an individual state are left completely out of account. It is not to be ruled out that this view can lead to a distortion of perceptions of decision processes at the supranational level. In the literature, there are already a few promising approaches toward a new political economy of international environmental negotiations.[64]

- In (noncooperative) game theoretic models, states interact in a context that does not admit of binding agreements. For actual politics, however, a web of bonds of differing intensity and reliability plays a great part. The relations among states

---

61   This is not intended to excuse all political rapacity and/or dilatoriness in international environmental negotiations. Nor should the previous statement be confused with a claim that there are no incapable politicians or powerful industrial interests.

62   This does not yet say whether this is the fault of game theory or (and?!) of the experimental design.

63   Advances in understanding the concept of bounded rationality and its modeling are documented by, e.g., Rubinstein (2002) and Gigerenzer/Selten (2001).

64   See various articles in Buchholz/Haupt/Peters (2005) and Schulze/Ursprung (2001, esp. ch. 4.11).

show a range from nonbinding declarations of intent up to partial or even complete surrender of national sovereignty. Often, the relation between states on particular topics goes through various stages of bindingness over the course of time. In the course of this evolution, information is gained, trust established (or deceived), and preferences changed. The analysis of such processes and their control constitutes not only one of the most ambitious, but also one of the most attractive future tasks for game theory. Economic research will, alongside perfecting game theory models, have to concern itself more intensively with bringing institutional and international law aspects into consideration, with the aim of pragmatically improving the design of international agreements. Here an integration of economic, legal, and political science approaches seems particularly fruitful.

8. Epilogue: The Prisoner's Dilemma – A Phantom Pain of Game Theorists?

Previously, global environmental problems have been stylized using simple game theory resources. It was assumed, in the mainstream of the argument, that the incentive structure to which the actors in global environmental policy are exposed corresponds to that of the prisoner's dilemma.

However, an assumption is by no means a finding of fact. It has, then, also been doubted in the literature that states in international environmental negotiations (more generally, actors act in solving cooperation problems) act the way prisoners do in the now proverbial dilemma. In this view, game theorists are racking their brains to solve a problem that does not actually exist (or is at any rate not very important in practice), when they try to think up ways out of the maze of the prisoner's dilemma.

Is the prisoner's dilemma a phantom? As already mentioned, experiments have shown that decision makers in dilemma situations often act more cooperatively than the simple model presented previously would suggest.[65] The causes of this "divergent behavior" are mostly seen in the fact that human nature is less egocentrically (not to say "chaotically individualistically") disposed than in the stylized version of the model. Instead, individuals are seen as having internalized social norms that facilitate human coexistence and thus the overcoming of social dilemmas. In detail, the following factors are regarded as important[66] :

---

65 The difficult questions of how far experimental economics can yield insights on how individuals will behave outside the experiment ("running free") cannot be discussed within the limits of this book. An exhaustive discussion on the possibilities and limits of experimental economics, with applications to the environmental area, can be found in Sturm/Weimann (2006).

66 In the economic theory of international environmental agreements there are opposing views regarding the possibility of cooperation, some optimistic and some pessimistic. A very enlightening comparison of these differing approaches is in Buchholz/Peters (2005). Bolle/Kritikos (2006), Bolle/Tan (2006), and Buchholz/Cornes/Peters (2006) discuss optimism and pessimism regarding cooperation in a general context (i.e., not in relation to international environmental agreements).

- *Goodwill (Kindness)*. Individuals consider their fellow humans with respect and friendliness. This concept is close to "loving one's neighbor," but not confined to a Christian framework. Here the famous imperative "let Man be noble, helpful and good!" is unobtrusively converted into the (assertion of a) fact: "Man is noble, helpful and good." The importance of "goodwill" in human coexistence in practice can probably best be seen in relation to the treatment of people from whom no return can be expected for good deeds, notably, the elderly and the severely disabled.
- *Reciprocity*. This concept is that individuals follow a *mutuality principle*. On a basis of reciprocal trust, cooperation is responded to with cooperation.[67] The reciprocity principle has been attributed fundamental importance in economics literature in recent years. This ranges far beyond the context of international environmental agreements.[68]
- *Aspiration to Justice (Fairness)*. Decision makers do not consider their own utility alone, but place value on participating in a just arrangement.[69]

It is easy to see that these three qualities will favor cooperative conduct in the prisoner's dilemma if they constitute character traits of the actors involved. Let us take as an example the last-mentioned aspiration for justice and interpret the concept in the sense of equality. If to simplify the argument we look at the presentation given in Table 1 of the static prisoner's dilemma in the normal form, then if an actor is aiming (at least also) at justice in the sense briefly defined here, he is not interested solely in the payoff value as entered in Table 1. Instead, he values his own payoff less the higher above the average payoff it is. The combination *DC* favored in the textbook case of the prisoner's dilemma, in which the defecting decision maker obtains a payoff of 15 and his cooperating opponent (sorry, partner) only zero, takes on a bitter taste if the actor considered is justice oriented in the previous sense. He has a *bad conscience* because he is better off in a highly asymmetrical situation.

If we assume that the actor is in a position to measure his pleasure at the payoff and dislike of the inequality along one and the same dimension, then we can include the inequality aversion just described in Table 1 by changing the payoffs. We can then see that it will depend on the strength of the inequality aversion whether the aspiration for justice can show a way out of the prisoner's dilemma. Let us, for instance, assume that payoffs received by individual 1 have only half the nominal value for this actor once they exceed the average payoff. Then, in the previously considered *DC* situation, a corrected payoff would amount to 11.25. This figure

---

67   "How you shout at the hill is how the echo comes back" (proverb). "And in the end, the love you take /Is equal to the love you make" (The Beatles). For more details, see Falk/Fischbacher (2006), with many other references.

68   We already refer to the possibilities of conditional cooperation (and its portrayal in dynamic game theory models) in section 4a.

69   Cf. for our discourse Buchholz/Peters (2005), Lange (2006), Lange/Vogt (2003), Lange/Vogt/ Ziegler (2006), Peters/Schuler (2005).

is made up of two components. The first component is the average payoff, which counts at its full amount of 7.5. The second component is the part of the payoff lying above the average payoff. This also amounts to 7.5 (15 − 7.5), but from the viewpoint of a bad conscience is weighted by a factor of 0.5, so that it falls to 3.75. In the numerical example chosen, it follows accordingly that the values in Table 1 look a little friendlier, but nothing fundamental is changed about the basic problem of the prisoner's dilemma. In the nonsocial (from the viewpoint of individual 1) combination DC, individual 1, at 11.25, still receives a payoff higher than the one he would receive at the *just equilibrium, CC*. Of course, this thought experiment allows us to let the inequality aversion we attribute to the actor rise sufficiently far as to make the *DC* combination less attractive than *CC*. If we measure the height of the inequality aversion by the coefficient α with which the decision maker discounts the part of his payoff lying above the average payoff, it follows that for any degree of aversion α lying above two thirds, cooperation of both sides is more attractive to decision maker 1 than the free rider position.[70] If this is true of both decision makers (previously, we assumed identical individuals), then the prisoner's dilemma is overcome by the aspiration to justice.[71] Of course, the same applies to the model actor aspiring to justice as for the individualist traditionally appearing in the drama of the prisoner's dilemma. The fact that we have correspondingly specified the utility function in the model does not yet allow us to say anything about reality. If we look at reality, we will undoubtedly see a heterogeneous picture with numerous examples for and against the importance of inequality aversion for human action. One extremely important example of the latter is undoubtedly the drastic welfare differences between industrial and developing countries. That these differences have for decades been unanimously and vigorously complained of might point to the fact that greater importance attaches to inequality aversion in speaking than in acting. All the same, heuristic observations (which would then suggest polemical remarks) cannot replace a systematic treatment of the importance of inequality aversion. What would be important would be how far inequality aversion is context-specifically determined. From that one might derive, in relation to international environmental negotiations (and other cooperation problems), bases for how negotiations would have to be designed (regarding negotiating process, object of negotiation, participants in negotiation) in order in actuality to mobilize the cooperative potential inherent in human nature.

---

70 We are looking for the value of α in $7.5 + (1 − \alpha)(15 − 7.5) \leq 10$, with $0 \leq \alpha \leq 1$. Solution: $\alpha \geq 2/3$. It should be noted that the dichotomic choice between cooperation and defection creates favorable conditions for equity preferences to overcome free rider incentives.

71 The finding that the inequality aversion must exceed a given threshold value in order to overcome the prisoner's dilemma constitutes an analogy with the finding from the prisoner's dilemma model with risk discussed in section 4b. There it emerged that participants' risk aversion must be above a certain threshold value in order to resolve the prisoner's dilemma. The same applies, moreover, to the capacity of environmental awareness to overcome the prisoner's dilemma: cf. Endres (1997b), Endres/Finus (1998).

II. The Kyoto Protocol from an Economic Viewpoint

1. Presentation

The start of international efforts to protect the climate was marked by the "Earth Summit" in Rio de Janeiro in 1992.[72] This conference led to the United Nations Framework Convention on Climate Change (UNFCCC), which has so far (as of May 2009) been ratified by 184 states and came into force in 1994. In it, the community of states for the first time termed climate protection a serious problem and declared its willingness to reduce greenhouse gas emissions. States' self-commitment was the trigger for further climate protection negotiations, which have taken place in 14 conferences of the parties (COPs) to date (May 2009), including the 1997 Kyoto Conference. At this climate change conference (COP 3), the states were for the first time able to agree on a *binding* quantitative objective for the reduction of six greenhouse gases.[73] The decisions taken there are laid down in the so-called *Kyoto Protocol.* The protocol is by now also known to the public (at least by name) and enjoys cult status in the climate change scene. The Kyoto Protocol commits industrial states to lower their emission of total greenhouse gases between 2008 and 2012 (the first commitment period) by at least 5% below the 1990 level.[74] To reach the aggregate target level for the first commitment period, industrialized countries have accepted limitation or reduction targets. The relevant agreements are contained in Annex B to the Kyoto Protocol.[75]

- Bulgaria, Estonia, all EU states, Latvia, Lithuania, Monaco, Romania, Switzerland, Slovakia, Slovenia, Czech Republic: −8%
- United States: 7%
- Japan, Canada, Poland, Hungary: −6%
- Croatia: −5%
- New Zealand, Russia, Ukraine: ±/−0%
- Norway: ±1%
- Australia: ±8%
- Iceland: ±10%

---

72 The following presentation of the content of the Kyoto Protocol and its embedding in international climate diplomacy closely follows section 3.1 of Endres/Ohl (2005b). The author would like to thank *FernUniversität in Hagen* for permission to use this material.

73 These are carbon dioxide (CO_2), methane (CH_4), nitrous oxide (N_2O), hydrofluorocarbons (HFCs), perfluorated hydrocarbons (PFCs), and sulphur hexafluoride (SF_6).

74 Negotiations are currently going on regarding further commitment periods.

75 Annex B to the Kyoto Protocol lists the countries that have undertaken specific targets during the period from 2008 to 2012. It names the countries mentioned in Annex 1 to the Framework Convention, except Belarus and Turkey. To them, it adds the following countries not in Annex 1: Croatia, Slovenia, Monaco, and Liechtenstein. The term "Annex B countries" is therefore often used as a synonym for "industrial countries," whereas "non–Annex B countries" as a rule means developing and threshold countries.

From these country-specific emission targets, we can calculate a total reduction of greenhouse gases in the countries mentioned by -5.2%.

For the entry into force of the Kyoto Protocol, two hurdles had to be crossed. *First*, the protocol had be ratified by at least 55 countries. *Second*, the ratifying states together had to be responsible for at least 55% of the CO_2 emissions (referring to the base year 1990) of the countries mentioned in Annex 1 to the 1992 Framework Convention. The required minimum number of ratifying countries was quickly reached, but the second hurdle was crossed only after much procrastination. After Russia ratified the protocol, it finally came into force on February 16, 2005. The Kyoto Protocol also opened the way to the employment of the three *flexible mechanisms*, by which the emission targets in the Kyoto Protocol (KP) could be reached at the lowest cost:[76]

- Clean Development Mechanism (Art. 12 KP)
- Joint Implementation (Art. 6 KP)
- Emissions Trading (Art. 17 KP)

The *Clean Development Mechanism* (CDM) allows industrial countries to carry out climate protection projects (e.g., setting up solar power or wind energy plants) in developing countries. All CDM projects must be registered with the CDM Executive Board.[77] If a project is then carried out, it has to be funded by the industrial country involved in it. In return, it can write off the emissions the project has saved in the developing country. This write-off may take the form of either an emission credit or a discount on the national emission target for the first commitment period. This means that the industrial country concerned can in fact emit more than it was originally allowed. The national emission target can thus be met either by emission reductions at home (internal reduction) or as it were by an emission reduction credit abroad (external reduction).

Joint Implementation (JI) allows the industrial counties listed in Annex B to the Kyoto Protocol to carry out climate-saving projects jointly. As with CDM, with JI, too, a particular climate protection project is funded by an industrial country. However, implementation is not in a developing country, but in another industrial country. For the emission reduction from the project, the industrial country financing it, as with CDM, either receives an emission credit or can during the first commitment period additionally emit the emission saved in the partner country. In contrast, though, with CDM, in the country where the project is implemented, a corresponding amount of emission rights are deducted. The deduction of emission rights in the implementing country with JI is because a binding emission target was laid down for both the implementing and the financing industrial country.[78]

---

76 Cf., e.g., Faure/Gupta/Nentjes (2003), Schwarze (2001a), Schwarze/Barrera (2005).

77 More details at www.netinform.de.

78 With CDM projects, in contrast, the project partner is a developing country. No emission targets have yet been agreed on for developing countries; thus, no emission rights can be deducted from them either.

Emissions Trading (ET) allows the industrial countries listed in Annex B to the Kyoto Protocol to trade with other Annex B countries the emission quantity of greenhouse gases (or parts of it) allotted to it in the first commitment period but not used at home. In contrast with the two previously mentioned mechanisms, JI and CDM, trading in emission rights is not mandatorily bound up with a specific climate protection project. Referring to the statements in section B.III.2 of part three of this book, the project-related Kyoto mechanisms (CDM and JI) can accordingly be termed *cautious variants* of the concept of tradable emission certificates. In contrast, ET can be termed a *bold variant.*

The following description of the details of the Kyoto Protocol and the international political negotiating process that ultimately led to it focus on the system of interstate emissions trading because it is particularly interesting from the economic viewpoint. Emissions trading under the Kyoto Protocol is also instructive for the EU's emissions trading system discussed in the next section.

According to the Kyoto Protocol, emissions trading is to extend to all six greenhouse gases. To reach the climatologically correct "exchange rate" among the various gases when trading different pollutants, the "CO_2 equivalent" is defined as a single "currency." This is to be taken to mean the "greenhouse potential" of CO_2 (operationalized through the time the CO_2 stays in the atmosphere). The greenhouse potential of all other gases is converted into CO_2 equivalents. For instance, reduction by 1 ton of methane brings 21 CO_2 equivalents. The conversion to CO_2 equivalents gives states an agreed method, enabling them to equate reductions in different gases with each other. The calculation method is an essential precondition for being able to reach states' reduction obligations set down in the Kyoto Protocol by a differing combination of gas compositions.

Trade in emission rights under the Kyoto Protocol is possible exclusively among those contracting states for which an emission limitation target has been set (Annex B states). For Europe, a reduction in emissions by 8% was agreed. Within the EU member states, the national reduction obligations may have different levels (refer to chapter C for more detail). For instance, Germany has declared its intention to achieve a national contribution of −21%. This practice is based on the so-called *bubble concept* regulated in Art. 4 of the Kyoto Protocol. The bubble concept is also called "trading without rules" and enables a group of Annex B countries to meet their obligations under the Kyoto Protocol jointly. The combination of these states ("bubble") through a declaration on the rules of their free integration is completed by presentation of the ratification document to the Climate Secretariat. The EU member states are accordingly also termed "bubble states."

The combination of states into a bubble is intended mainly to meet goals of distributive policy. Thus, although the Kyoto Protocol sets the EU reduction target at −8% altogether, how this target is to be reached by the member states can be decided by these bubble states autonomously. A further advantage of the bubble concept is that the distribution of the reduction burden within the bubble need not already be defined definitively at the time of the protocol negotiations, but may also be negotiated later internally. From this construction, it follows that the EU reduction targets set in the Kyoto Protocol can be met even if individual member states have not complied with their internal obligation undertaken within the bubble. To meet the Kyoto agreement, it is sufficient for the planned greenhouse gas reduction of 8% to be attained by the member states as a whole. Country-specific advantages in cutting particular gases can accordingly be exploited.

In the course of the diplomatic negotiations and confrontations over the Kyoto Protocol, there were attempts by the United States, together with Australia, Canada, Japan, New Zealand, Russia, and the Ukraine, likewise to form a bubble (the bubble of "umbrella states"). No agreement was ever reached among these states. However, a common interest continues to exist, particularly regarding the development of rules for trading in emission rights at state level.

At the sixth conference of treaty states in The Hague in the year 2000, the countries of the EU, together with the developing countries, developed massive opposition to the umbrella states in relation to the shape of the international trading rules. Although the group of bubble states advocated a restrictive application of the flexible mechanisms allowed in the Kyoto Protocol, the umbrella states pushed for a broad interpretation. In this clash, the bubble states called for a limitation of the volume of market-tradable emission rights by an upper limit (cap). The umbrella states instead favored unlimited trading.

The advocates of a restriction in trading argue that incentives to innovation in the area of reduction technologies and renewable energies are indispensable for a long-term strategy to protect the climate, and that these incentives can only arise if the bulk of reductions has to be made in one's own country. To provide the required incentives, emissions trading would have to be restricted. The opponents of trading restrictions argue against this, stating that trade limitations would considerably increase the costs of implementing national reduction targets and might thus undermine acceptance of them (and thus also the system's overall efficiency). Alongside the controversy over details of "cap and trade," the states often also argued over "hot air." This is not as surprising as it might at first sound; the term means an allocation of emission rights going beyond the actually needed emission volume.

Hot air is an issue, particularly in Russia and the Ukraine. For these countries, the reduction target was set at 0%. These states have accordingly to keep emissions at the level of the base year 1990. However, the economic collapse in the Eastern European countries has made emissions fall below the level of the base year. It is not expected that these states will have fully used up their emission rights by the end of the Kyoto Protocol's term. This makes it possible, without any further climate change measures at home, to buy rights from states (buy hot air) that in the Kyoto Protocol received such low emission obligations that they remain below the target level.

This is the background that explains the fear (particularly among Europeans) that with unrestrained trade in emission rights, the Kyoto Protocol might lose credibility. For in the case of unrestrained emissions trading, hot air could be offered on the market *de facto*, putting the industrial countries in a position to buy themselves exemptions from the reduction obligations. An argument brought against unrestricted emission trading was accordingly that it would undermine the assumption of responsibility by industrial countries for anthropogenic global warming in accordance with the "polluter pays" principle, reducing the ecological effect to zero. Advocates of unrestrained trading in emission rights counter this by saying that the economic collapse in Eastern Europe was a temporary phenomenon that ought not be made the basis for designing a long-term—oriented trading system. In addition, trade in hot air would have the advantage of keeping prices of traded rights low, which might ease entry into a climate protection system by the developing countries. Moreover, it was seen as possible within the framework of the Kyoto Protocol to transfer unclaimed rights to a future commitment period. A trade restriction would accordingly not solve the hot air problem, but merely postpone it. Nor should it be overlooked that selling the rights would give the Eastern European states financial resources that could be used to promote investments in low pollutant technologies. The Europeans claimed, though, that solving the climate problem required such far-reaching technological change that there should be incentives to it in all Organisation for Economic Co-operation and Development (OECD) states. However, the greater the trading volume, the smaller would be the incentives at home to research favorable abatement measures.

One further point of dispute that could not be settled at Kyoto was the extent of the crediting of *sinks*.[79] Counting sink activities as a form of emission reduction also opens up the possibility of generating emission rights. This reduces the incentives to initiate other (innovative) abatement measures at the national level. The Europeans advocated accordingly that sink activities not be countable as credits toward the Kyoto targets. In contrast, the umbrella states emphasized that the ecological effect of sink activity was equal to emission reduction and ought to be credited accordingly.

The opposing positions of the umbrella and bubble states at the sixth contracting states' conference in The Hague show that efficiency considerations clashed with arguments of ecological precision and dynamic incentive effects. Although the Europeans wanted to intensify incentives to technical advances in the area of low emission technologies through restricted emission trading, the umbrella states put the cost argument to the fore in their considerations.

The intentions as described previously were discharged with a big bang before the contracting states' conference to be held in July 2001 in Bonn: the U.S. government headed by George W. Bush announced it was leaving the Kyoto Protocol. This

---

79 A sink means an ecosystem that draws carbon out of the atmosphere. Examples are forests. Countries' reforestation projects are accordingly able – at least until the woods are cut again – to bind liberated carbon emissions. The debate is still running and has received new impetus from the need to plan beyond the first commitment phase of the Kyoto Protocol. Cf. Schwarze (2001b), Sedjo/Amano (2006), and the special focus on "post-Kyoto" in (Spring 2005) No. 157 of the journal *Resources*, published by *Resources for the Future* in Washington, DC.

led to vehement protests from the other states. The United States was accused of dodging its responsibility as the largest emitter to date of greenhouse gases. What happened would seem a general human phenomenon: if a member of a group leaves it, then solidarization occurs among the remaining ones. In our specific case, the (genuine or pretended) indignation at U.S. conduct led to a "we'll show 'em" mood among the remaining states. This greatly facilitated agreement as to how to implement the protocol, even without the United States. In this process, Russia, in particular, still hesitating over ratification, managed to improve its position – *honi soit qui mal y pense.*

Considered from an economic viewpoint, the fact is that the value of Russian ratification assurances rose sharply with U.S. withdrawal. This is because of the previously mentioned ratification conditions for the entry into force of the protocol. Particularly, the EU states had nailed the Kyoto Protocol to their standards. They wanted success in their negotiations at all costs. With the United States on board, Russian assent was not absolutely necessary to cross the ratification hurdle. With the United States, the 55% condition would have been met even if Russia and Japan had rejected the Kyoto process. After U.S. departure, the Kyoto process was at the mercy of those countries that had not yet decided. It is therefore hardly surprising that Russia, in particular, being able to throw considerable weight in terms of emissions into the balance, made its ratification assurance dependent on conditions being met.[80] *Inter alia*, during the ratification debate, pressure on the rebel states to drop their restrictive position on the design of the emission trading system was intensified. The Europeans' concessions on the design of the trading system are embodied in the *Bonn Resolution* of July 2001 (and the supplementary accords reached in Marrakesh, Morocco, in November 2001 (the Marrakesh Accords)).

For trading in emission rights, the picture arising from a consideration of the outcome of Bonn and Marrakesh is as follows:

- Emission rights created by the three flexible mechanisms and emission credits from "sink activities" can be used both to meet national reduction obligations and for trading with other contracting states. Here an emission credit procured by trading with other countries is *de facto* equated with a correspondingly large emission reduction at home.

- Transferring emission credits from "sink activities" to later commitment periods ("banking") is not possible. For credits from JI and CDM, transfer is instead in principle permitted (although particular restrictions have to be complied with).

- The different types of emission rights (allotted rights and project-related rights from CDM or JI measures) can be traded with each other. To prevent uncovered

---

80 As well as the concessions to be explained here on the Kyoto agreement itself, it should be pointed out that during the decisive phase of the ratification process, Russia conducted successful negotiations for inclusion in the World Trade Organization. See Baker (2004).

sale of emission rights, however, every country is obliged to retain a certain quantity of rights as a reserve.[81]

From an ecological viewpoint, it is particularly noteworthy that the unlimited transferability of emission rights means that a major part of the Kyoto commitment can be met by trading in "hot air." Quantitative indications on this are found in the following section under the term "ecological effectiveness." In Marrakesh, the preconditions under which a state can use the flexible mechanisms provided for in the Kyoto Protocol were also settled. It must

- Have ratified the Kyoto Protocol
- Subject itself to the sanction system decided on in Marrakesh
- Inventory its national emissions
- Make a timely and correct report on annual greenhouse gas emissions
- Present an inventory of sinks
- As from the second commitment period, make timely and accurate reports on carbon binding in the sinks

2. Environmental Economics Assessment

With the Kyoto agreement, for the first time a group of industrial states committed itself to limiting their greenhouse gas emissions and setting quantitative targets for it. The agreement has accordingly been celebrated as a milestone in world climate policy. In detail, the Kyoto agreement displays a number of features that are excellent from an economic viewpoint. In particular, the protocol contains, in the flexible mechanisms explained previously, elements of a policy of tradable emission permits. Despite much criticism of the details of design, we can welcome this, after decades of misery with command and control policies in environmental protection, as a step in the direction of environmental policy efficiency. That is something that has always been close to the heart in environmental economics. Moreover, the approach embracing various pollutants in the protocol follows environmental economics principles. This approach averts the danger of undesirable pollutant substitution (as addressed in section C.III.6 of part three of this book) and is, in particular, a requirement for efficiency. Countries can cut their emissions in their portfolio of greenhouse gases where their marginal abatement costs, referred to CO_2 equivalent, are lowest. This leads to utilization of cost minimization potential as described in chapter A of part four for the case of linear pollutant interactions. Again, the monitoring guidelines (laid down in Articles 5, 7, and 8) belong among the achievements of the Kyoto Protocol. The details on emission reporting were laid down unambiguously by the "conference of the parties." This narrows room for interpretation and enables treaty breaches to be disclosed quickly (particularly because of the annual reporting obligation). A weakness in the monitoring system

---

81 This brings the same effect *de facto* from an economic viewpoint as the introduction of a trade restriction.

Table 3. *Baseline emissions and emission reduction targets for annex B regions*

Region[a]	Baseline Emissions (MtC)[b]		Kyoto Targets (% Vis-à-Vis 1990)[c]		*Effective* Targets (% Vis-à-Vis 2010)		*Effective* Targets (MtC)	
	1990	2010	Old	New	Old	New	Old	New
AUN	88	130	+6.8	+10.2	−27.7	−25.4	−36	−33
CAN	127	165	−6,0	+7.9	−27.7	−17.0	−46	−28
EUR	929	1,041	−7.8	−5.2	−17.7	−15.4	−184	−160
JPN	269	331	−6.0	−0.8	−23.6	−19.4	−78	−64
CEA	301	227	−7.1	−3.9	+23.2	+27.5	+53	+62
FSU	1,036	713	0.0	+6,4	+45.3	+54.6	+323	+389
Total U.S. out[d]	2,750	2,607	−5,0	−0.5	+0.7	+3.8	+32	+166
USA	1,347	1,809	−7.0	−3.2	−30.8	−27.9	−556	−505
Total U.S. in[e]	4,097	4,416	−5.0	−0.5	−11.9	−7.7	−525	−339

Notes: [a] For reasons of data availability, we apply the greenhouse gas reduction targets only to CO_2, which is by far the most important greenhouse gas among industrialized countries. AUN, Australia and New Zealand; CAN, Canada; EUR, OECD Europe (including EFTA); JPN, Japan; CEA, Central and Eastern Europe; FSU, former Soviet Union (including the Ukraine); USA, United States of America. [b] Based on U.S. Energy Information Administration, U.S. Department of Energy (2001): reference case. [c] Estimates by the European Commission (Nemry, 2001). [d] Annex B without U.S. compliance (assuming full trade in "hot air"). [e] Annex B with U.S. compliance (assuming full trade in "hot air").
Source: Böhringer/Finus, 2005, p. 268.

is, however, the fact that monitoring is done by each country for itself. A stronger confidence-building measure would undoubtedly have been to set up an independent institution. The previously mentioned positive aspects of the Kyoto Protocol deserve to be emphasized and valued. It should not be overlooked that the protocol shows a number of fundamental weaknesses from an economic viewpoint. On the whole, the agreement cannot be seen as a successful institution of international climate protection. For this on the whole rather skeptical position, the following points are decisive[82]:

- *Ecological effectiveness.* Table 3 shows the Kyoto targets, referred to CO_2.

    Table 3 is to be read as follows. The first column lists the industrial states (or groups of states) most important in terms of the greenhouse effect, line by line.[83] The third-last line (total U.S. out) sums the figures for all states mentioned up until this line. The U.S. is so far not included. The U.S. figures come in the second-last line. The last line (total U.S. in) is the sum of the third-last and second-last lines, and thus sums the figures for the United States and for the "rest of the world" without the United States.

    The column "baseline emissions" lists CO_2 emissions (in million tons) by the states concerned: *first* as actually emitted in 1990, and *second* as they would

82 Cf., e.g., Böhringer/Finus (2005).
83 AUN, Australia and New Zealand; CAN, Canada; EUR, European Union; JPN, Japan; CEA, Central and Eastern Europe; FSU, former Soviet Union, including the Ukraine.

likely be emitted in 2010 (on an estimate constituting the state of the art) if the Kyoto agreement did not exist. The "1990" column thus shows historical figures, whereas the figures under "2010" portray a "business as usual" scenario. The historical sequence is important because the Kyoto agreement itself takes 1990 emissions as a reference line from which the emissions reductions aimed at in the Kyoto agreement are measured. However, the last-mentioned column of figures is important in assessing the reduction effort to actually be made by states: the effort a state has to make in, say, 2010 to meet its Kyoto obligation is not in fact measured from the difference between the emissions by the state for 2010 compatible with its Kyoto obligations minus its 1990 emissions. Instead, the actual reduction burden is the difference between the Kyoto-compatible 2010 emissions and the quantity of emissions it *would* produce in 2010 were it *not* bound by the Kyoto agreement.

The third column, "Kyoto targets" (percent vis-à-vis 1990) now measures the difference between a country's emissions compatible with its Kyoto obligation and the historical emissions in 1990. Here the figures in the first subcolumn ("old") refer to a comparison of the historical emissions with the targets originally provided for in the Kyoto agreement. The second subcolumn ("new") shows the result of comparing the historical emission data and the targets laid down as a compromise in the previously mentioned subsequent negotiations at Bonn and Marrakesh. This shows the "softening effect" of the negotiating process (differing in magnitude for the individual countries) caused particularly by the United States dropping out.[84]

The fourth column ("effective targets" (% vis-à-vis 2010)) shows the corresponding comparison between the Kyoto targets and the emission quantities to be expected from "business as usual" developments. The subcolumn "old" again refers to the original targets in the Kyoto agreement, whereas "new" again refers to what was left of these targets after the Bonn and Marrakesh erosion process. The individual entries in Table 3 speak for themselves, but we want to single out two figures: the fifth figure in the last line of the table (-11.9) shows that with the Kyoto Protocol as originally designed, a considerable reduction in CO_2 emission by the totality of contracting states (including the United States) would have been reached. What is actually left of that can be seen from the sixth figure in the seventh line ($+3.8$). This shows the extent of the climate policy disruption brought by U.S. withdrawal and the ensuing softening of targets among the remaining contracting states. Instead of achieving a considerable emission reduction of well more than 10% from the "business as usual" scenario, there is even a rise in CO_2 emissions from Kyoto states by a total of almost 4%. The asymmetrical distribution over the remaining contracting states is striking.[85] The increase in emissions from the former Soviet Union

84 Cf. also Böhringer/Vogt (2004), Klepper/Peterson (2005).

85 The asymmetrical distribution is attenuated by the fact that the (at first sight apparently particularly burdened) EU can probably meet its reduction obligations rather cheaply in Russia, the

and other states of Eastern Europe (compatible with the Kyoto agreement as it currently stands) overcompensates for the considerable (contemplated) efforts by the other contracting states.

A mere glance at Table 3 thus leads to the finding that the Kyoto agreement has not brought any reversal of the trend to global warming of the Earth's atmosphere. This impression becomes still stronger if we shift our gaze beyond the edge of Table 3. For what then heaves into sight is that many CO_2 emitters very important in the future (besides the United States) are not covered by the Kyoto agreement. There was much fuss in public about the U.S. withdrawal. However, it must also be borne in mind that such CO_2 emitters as China and India were absent from the outset from the reduction obligations of the Kyoto agreement. Of course, these states and the other developing and threshold countries brought good, in their view, arguments to bear for their abstention.[86] One may regard this reluctance by the countries concerned as justified or (as in the prevailing U.S. opinion) not; it changes nothing as to the catastrophic effects for climate policy.

• *Incentive Compatibility.* We referred previously to the comprehensible public furore raised by U.S. withdrawal from the Kyoto process. Sober consideration, however, suggests the conclusion that the Kyoto Protocol is not attractive from the viewpoint of the United States. Quite apart from the fairness considerations, it is also not advisable from a viewpoint of national welfare maximization for countries like China and India to join the agreement. That means that the Kyoto agreement fails from the outset to meet the conditions specified previously for a successful global environmental policy instrument. This estimate is supported by several model calculations presented in the economics literature. We give an extract from one such work, namely, Finus/van Ierland/Dellink (2006).[87]

Table 4 is to be read as follows. The first column lists 12 countries or groups of countries.[88] The next three columns have self-explanatory headings.

Ukraine, and other Eastern European states through the flexible Kyoto mechanisms. Ultimately, there will not be an emission reduction in EU states, but an income transfer from the EU to the Eastern European area.

86   Briefly, the greenhouse effect depends basically on the *stock* of CO_2 and other gases in the atmosphere accumulated over long periods. The industrial countries contributed almost all of this, and the developing and threshold countries almost none. Against this background, it seems hardly fair for the latter countries now to have to help pull the chestnuts out of the fire, restricting their development possibilities by cutting back on their emission flows. (Note the distinction between the sizes of stocks and flows in this argument.)

87   The presentation here is an expanded version of Table 4 in Finus/van Ierland/Dellink (2006, p. 280). I want to thank Professor Michael Finus for the enlargement. The empirical figures contained in the study cited are based on various works (cited within) by Ellerman, Fankhauser, Nordhaus, and Tol. More details on calibrating the functions used for the costs and benefits of emission abatement can be found at www.enr.wur.nl/uk/staco.

88   The 12 regions are USA (USA), Japan (JPN), European Union (EEC), other OECD countries (OOE), Central and Eastern European countries (EET), former Soviet Union (FSU), energy-exporting countries (EEX), China (CHN), India (IND), dynamic Asian economies (DAE), Brazil

Table 4. *Industrialized countries coalition structure*

Regions	total emission reduction	Total abatement costs	Total benefits from abatement	Payoff	Payoff no cooperation	Marginal abatement costs	Marginal benefits	Incentive to change membership strategy
(1)	(2)	(3)	(4)	(5)	(6)	(7)	(8)	(9)
	Gton over 100 years	bln US$ over 100 years	bln US$ over 100 years	bln US$ over 100 years	bln US$ over 100 years	US$/ton	US$/ton	bln US$ over 100 years
(1) USA	32	332	906	574	415	28.0	8.5	65.3
(2) JPN	3	38	691	653	354	28.0	6.5	−46.9
(3) EEC	14	147	945	798	464	28.0	8.8	−52.8
(4) OOE	9	83	138	55	71	28.0	1.3	70.5
(5) EET	9	85	52	−33	27	28.0	0.5	80.3
(6) FSU	17	157	270	113	135	28.0	2.5	114.6
(7) EEX	1	0	120	120	62	1.1	1.1	−113.5
(8) CHN	15	16	248	232	112	1.1	2.3	−794.9
(9) IND	3	3	200	197	101	2.3	1.9	−172.7
(10) DAE	1	0	100	99	51	1.9	0.9	−93.9
(11) BRA	0	0	61	61	32	0.9	0.6	−6.5
(12) ROW	4	4	272	268	137	0.6	2.5	−137.8
World	107	865	4,005	3,140	1,960	2.5		

Source: Finus/van Ierland/Dellink, 2006, p. 280.

Columns 5 to 9 are explained further in the course of the ensuing arguments. The calculations underlying Table 4 divide the 12 regions into signatory and nonsignatory states. The first six regions (in italics) constitute a coalition to combat the greenhouse effect. These are the signatory states. The other six regions (nonsignatory states) each act "autistically."

This starting position can be taken as a stylized presentation of an international environmental agreement similar in its main points to the Kyoto agreement at the stage before U.S. withdrawal. The calculations assume that coalition members will act on the pattern explained in section B.I.6: each member chooses its emission level so as to maximize the aggregate welfare of the coalition group. Thus, each makes the contribution to aggregate emission reduction by the group needed to achieve the "constrained global optimum" for the coalition group. Correspondingly, the emission abatement quantities indicated in Table 4 for coalition members meet the condition for a global optimum (confined to this group). As we know from section B.I.1, these conditions are, *first*, that the marginal abatement costs of individual states be equal to each other. A glance at column 7 confirms this for coalition members (the first six regions covered by Table 4). Individual marginal abatement costs here amount to 28.0 each.

The *second* optimality condition addressed previously requires the marginal abatement cost of each individual state to correspond with the marginal damage aggregated over all states (here, all states in the coalition) ($MAC_i = MD$, where $MD = MD_1 + \cdots + MD_6$). Whether these conditions are met can be checked by adding the individual marginal damage for the six coalition members given in column 8.[89] The result is $8.5 + 6.5 + 8.8 + 1.3 + 0.5 + 2.5 - \varepsilon = 28$.[90] The second optimality condition is thus also met if coalition members act as portrayed in Table 4. The loners are also, in the model on which the values in Table 4 are based, stylized in exactly the way explained in the foregoing sections: each chooses its emission abatement quantity so as to maximize its own welfare with the given conduct of the other states. The loners thus act as in a Nash equilibrium.[91] In section I.1, a state *i* autistically maximizing its

---

(BRA), and "rest of the world" (ROW). The EU here means the 15 states that were members in 1995.

89 Table 4 lists the marginal benefits of the emission reduction. The marginal benefit consists in the avoidance of the environmental damage that would occur if the marginal emission unit considered were emitted. The marginal benefits of emission abatement considered in Table 4 are thus exactly the same as the marginal damage from emission mentioned in the previous text.

90 The term ε merely corrects errors that arise because the figures entered in Table 4 are rounded up or down to one digit after the decimal.

91 Although the nonsignatory states all act *as* in the Nash equilibrium, the position presented in Table 4 is not to be seen overall as a Nash equilibrium. This is because the six coalition members act differently. As indicated previously, they aim at maximizing the net joint welfare of the coalition group. A position that would be a Nash equilibrium overall would require *all* participants to act according to the criterion: I maximize my net welfare without regard to the consequences of my conduct for others, given the condition of a given conduct by those others.

net welfare, as assumed in this context for the singletons ("loners"), acts in such a way that its marginal damage at equilibrium corresponds to its marginal abatement cost ($MD_i = MAC_i$). Comparing the marginal abatement costs for the six nonsignatory states entered in column 7 with the marginal damage for these states entered in column 8, we can see that the condition repeated previously is met in each case.

Let us pause for a moment and establish what we have so far read from Table 4: it is assumed that a group of states has joined in an anti-greenhouse coalition similar to the Kyoto agreement (including the United States). Others have refused. The behavior of the coalition members and the outsiders has been determined by applying the theory explained in the previous sections.

The question now is whether the position assumed is attractive to the states: can they actually agree on it? If so, will they actually keep to what they have agreed? From the viewpoint of economic theory, this means asking the "question of all questions" in the economics of international environmental agreements: is the proposed arrangement (inspired by the Kyoto agreement) *incentive compatible*? The question of incentive compatibility can best be answered by splitting it into subquestions about individual rationality and stability, just as we practice in section B.1.6. As likewise prepared previously, we go on to split the stability criterion further into the subcriteria of internal and external stability.

As to individual rationality, according to what was said previously, an international agreement is individually rational for an (arbitrarily selected) state if its net welfare in the agreed situation is higher than at the Nash equilibrium. To test this, look at columns 5 and 6 in Table 4. Column 5 shows the net welfare (payoff) for the individual regions under the condition that the coalition of six members explained previously exists. In contrast, column 6 shows the net welfare of the individual states on the condition that all states act as loners (Nash equilibrium). The comparison shows that the three coalition members listed last (OOE, EET, FSU) are worse off in the coalition than in a world of loners. For them, the agreement assumed in the initial position is not individually rational. Thus, we already have a negative answer to the question of the attractiveness of the arrangement inspired by the Kyoto agreement.

For the sake of completeness, however (and of the (hopefully) associated gain in knowledge for the reader), we also check stability.

Let us consider internal stability. Here the point is whether it pays a particular (arbitrarily selected) coalition member to leave the coalition and act as a loner (free rider). In these considerations, we assume that all countries retain their status as signatory or nonsignatory states, except the one (i) for which internal stability is being tested. In the literature, the phrase used is that all states involved except i retain their "membership strategy" in the thought experiment.

However, if all states (except i) maintain their membership strategy if i leaves the coalition, this does not mean that they will also retain their emission level. On the contrary, it was explained in the previous sections how states optimize their emission levels *under the condition of a coalition of six states*. The relevant emission quantities now lose optimality if the framework conditions are altered by the departure of *i* from the coalition. Following the change in conditions from a six-state to a five-state coalition, all states have to *reoptimize* their emission levels.[92] When the first six lines in column 9 show how the net welfare of a coalition member changes if it leaves the coalition, the effect of the reoptimization by all other states on the net welfare of the "deserter" state has already been included in the calculation.

We can see that column 9 shows positive figures for four of the six coalition members. This means that it pays these states to leave the coalition. Here, then, the condition of internal stability is infringed, and for the three previously mentioned coalition members (OOE, EET, FSU), it is not now surprising that they have an incentive to leave the coalition. For here, after all, the test of individual rationality of the coalition gave a negative result. However, for the United States, too, for which the coalition passed the test of individual rationality, no internal stability follows. This is anything but a contradiction. Although on this model calculation the United States is better off in the coalition than in a world without any cooperation, it is even better off if the others cooperate while it adopts a free rider position. It is only for the EU and Japan that column 9 shows negative figures for the area of the coalition members. A change in membership strategy (i.e., leaving the coalition) is unattractive for these two regions. That makes the coalition internally stable from their viewpoint.

Analogously (so we are quite brief), the coalition's external stability can be tested. Here the question is: is it attractive to an (arbitrarily selected) nonsignatory state to give up its loner stance and join the coalition? A glance at the values entered for nonsignatory states in column 9 shows negative figures everywhere. A change in membership strategy is unattractive. China and India, in particular, would do themselves considerable hurt by joining the coalition. Therefore, the coalition is externally stable (which sounds better than it is – the reality is that none of the outsiders want to join).

Of course, some may have found it rather venturesome to criticize the Kyoto Protocol with the highly stylized argumentation presented here. It is clear that a model calculation does not depict reality precisely – it cannot do so and does not seek to. However, analyses on the pattern presented here do grasp essential structural features of reality (in our context, of the Kyoto agreement), at least according to the view overwhelmingly supported in the literature. The analysis offers at least *one* plausible explanation for the problems of failure to participate arising with the Kyoto process. If the model calculation portrays

---

92 The idea of reoptimization of the emission quantities of all states j ($j \neq i$) as a response to a change in behavior by state i is explained in section I.5a.

individual states' interest positions in the context of the Kyoto agreement even only a little (accuracy is not claimed by the authors), then it is no wonder that the results of the Kyoto process are as sobering as presented previously. Both the U.S. decision not to ratify the agreement and the decision by the Eastern European states to make their accession dependent on considerable concessions become understandable if we accept that a state pursues policy oriented to the national interest. It is equally comprehensible on looking through the figures given in Table 4 that developing and threshold countries fight tooth and nail against being drawn into the obligations of the Kyoto framework.

• *Sanctions.* The literature has often criticized the fact that international (environmental) agreements often lack any possibility of sanctions against treaty breaches. It should thus be positively stressed that the Kyoto Protocol does provide for sanctions. To discuss, decide, and implement sanctions, a special "compliance committee" is competent, not (directly) dependent on the individual contracting states. The Kyoto Protocol allows two forms of punishment.

First, a state emitting more than is compatible with its Kyoto commitment must later reduce its excess emissions further. It has an additional punishment, consisting of an increase in its future reduction obligation by 30% of the amount of the illicitly emitted pollutant. Because the reduction obligation under the Kyoto Protocol does not have to be met by a particular deadline but over the average of a period of 5 years (currently, during the first commitment stage, running from 2008 to 2012), an infringement may possibly be established only after this phase is over. The obligation provided for to make up for the reduction omitted with an extra 30% on top can therefore refer only to the next commitment phase (from 2013 to 2017, at present only announced).

The *second* sanction is that a country breaching the treaty may have its right to take part in emission trading taken away.

Let us now briefly consider the first sanction mechanism mentioned. From an economic viewpoint, it should be noted that the threat of appropriate punishment meets the criterion of credibility to the extent that treaty-compliant states do not worsen their welfare position by insisting on the sanction. On the contrary, if the state accepts its punishment and carries out the corresponding measures, the other states benefit from improvements in environmental quality. On the negative side, though, it should be noted that the punishment contains no particular incentive for the treaty-breaching state to actually accept the punishment (i.e., actually implement the raised emission abatement). It might, after all, simply let its list of sins grow from one period to another by always pushing its reduction obligations pronounced in the sanction process further into the future by one period. The Kyoto Protocol is defenseless against this. In the sanction process, there is no special response to lasting treaty breach and accumulation of reduction obligations imposed on the state. In addition, the "deterrent effect" of the sanction is reduced by the previously mentioned time lag between treaty breach and punishment. Governments that heavily discount the future (say, because of election periods spreading over only a few years) are not very impressed by punishments lying in the future.

The two critical points mentioned here take on greater weight from the fact that each state can, by complying with a notice period of 3 years (pursuant to Art. 27 of the Kyoto Protocol), terminate its membership in the treaty arrangements. It can thereby escape threatened punishment. Obviously, awareness of this "back door" for states in breach of the treaty hardly enhances the incentive for treaty-compliant states to consistently use the sanction possibilities created with the Kyoto agreement. Finus/Herzog (2006) thus recommend extending the notice periods in the protocol and letting punishments start during the same commitment period as the transgression occurred. Meanwhile, speedy and extensive reductions by the state in breach could be honored by abatements of punishment.

Let us now consider the second sanction mechanism mentioned previously. How do things stand with the credibility of punishment through excluding the country in breach of treaty from emissions trading? In the perfect competition model, there is no effect on the equilibrium permit price if an individual country joins the permits market or withdraws from it. In this scenario, the threat of excluding a country in breach of treaty from permits trading is credible because the welfare position of the treaty-compliant states involved in the trade would not change by its exclusion. Of course, this scenario can be put into practice only if the country sanctioned is "very small" in relation to the totality of countries involved in the permit system. For bigger countries, exclusion of the state in breach of treaty affects the equilibrium price on the permits market. If it is a net supplier of permits, then the equilibrium rate rises; if it is a net demander, then it falls. In the first case, those treaty-compliant states who appear on the market as net demanders are negatively affected; in the second case, the net suppliers are negatively affected. If a "big" country, as at issue here, is sanctioned for a breach of treaty, then some of the sanctioning countries would be harming themselves. So considered, the sanction of "exclusion from permits trading" can be seen as having its credibility restricted. However, the reduction in deterrent effect to be seen here is (at least partly) avoided in the Kyoto system. The application of the sanction instrument is not decided by a vote among the treaty-compliant countries (perhaps with a unanimity requirement). Instead, the decision is delegated to the previously mentioned *Compliance Committee*.

Reviewing the numerous arguments over assessing the Kyoto Protocol in the literature, we can see "good marks" for the Kyoto Protocol, particularly for its instruments borrowed from the idea of tradable emission permits, its monitoring, and its sanction system. Irrespective of all criticism in detail, the Kyoto Protocol is in this connection better designed than most other international environmental agreements. Altogether, though, there is an anything but euphoric bottom line: a limited number of states have committed themselves to reducing greenhouse gases for a limited period to a limited extent. Positive effects on worldwide climate cannot be expected from this. Hopes for better times can feed only on the fact that the Kyoto Protocol can be seen as one step in a process of institutional evolution. It was the Kyoto Protocol that for the first time succeeded in bringing a few states to agreement on a binding quantitative target for reduction of greenhouse gases. The hope is rooted in a belief in states' capacity to learn: may they recognize the shortcomings of the current regulations and take the ensuing first step of a number of others (and, moreover, in the right direction). This kind of "positive thinking" is not, however, made easy by a look at states' behavior. For according to the current data position, it is not to be expected that all Kyoto signatory states will even meet the (hardly ambitious, as we said previously) abatement targets. If this turns out to be true, then the idea that Kyoto signatories would by their "good example" lead other states to imitate them would certainly collapse. If the signatory states destroy the credibility of the Kyoto agreement by poor treaty compliance, then the attempt to bring, in particular, the United States and CO_2-intensive threshold countries to join is doomed to failure. The developing countries will conclude that for all the preaching, it is probably not really possible to pursue effective climate protection together with a growing economy.

3. Prospects

Currently, the debate on the future of the Kyoto Protocol is being carried on intensively in society, politics, and science. This is understandable because although the first commitment period was begin in 2008, its end in 2012 is already coming into view. The portfolio of proposals ranges from improvements in individual areas of shortcomings to replacement by an agreement of an entirely different nature. Its replacement by a number of agreements between individual states is also being intensively discussed. Thus, Böhringer/Finus (2005) suggest various changes that might enhance signatory states' treaty compliance. Barrett (2005) would like to see, instead of quantitative reduction targets, an agreement promoting climate-friendly technologies. Other authors want to see the emission permits theme that marks the Kyoto Protocol replaced by a system of taxes on emissions of greenhouse gases. This was called for by economics Nobel Prize winner Joseph Stiglitz at the *World Congress of Environmental and Resource Economics* held in Kyoto in summer 2006. Now the role of Nobel Prize winners in economics is much the same as that of saints in the Catholic Church: as merely one of the faithful, one should be rather cautious with one's criticisms. Nonetheless, from the wealth of proposals for changes we want to single out the idea of replacing the permit system by one of levies. (An exhaustive discussion of the reform (or revolution) debate would go beyond the bounds of this general textbook.) The plea to replace the permit-oriented Kyoto Protocol by an agreement on a global greenhouse gas tax can be pared down to the following three arguments:

- Permits can (as set out in part three of this book) fix the quantity of greenhouse gases emitted by each state in a period (according to the rules) exactly. This instrument thus has the advantage of high ecological precision. The price is, though, that the marginal abatement cost functions for future periods are unknown: if the emission targets are set years in advance and kept to by a "loss regardless" permit system (i.e., here abatement costs), then it may turn into an expensive matter if the marginal abatement costs in the future lie considerably above forecasts. With emission taxes, in contrast, an upper limit is set by the tax rate to the marginal abatement costs that count at equilibrium. No one need budget for higher marginal abatement costs; one can after all pay the taxes instead of cutting emissions. Looked at from a distance, though, this consideration is not yet an unambiguous argument in favor of the superiority of emissions taxes over emission permits. With uncertain future courses of marginal costs, politics has the choice between a situation where an upper limit for the cost burden on firms can be kept to with certainty (but no upper limit exists for specific emissions over the period) or a situation where the specific emission level for the period is certain (whereas abatement costs may, in the worst case, run completely off the charts). The first position is established with taxation, and the second with a permit system. This is a bit like the choice between cholera and the plague.[93] At best, it should be pointed out that with the phenomenon of global warming, the specific ecological precision over a period (i.e., the strength of a permit policy) does not seem particularly important because the extent of the greenhouse effect depends not on pollutant inputs specific to the period, but on the total *stock* of these gases accumulated in the atmosphere. But if it happens that with a system of greenhouse gas taxes the announced specific targets for a period are broken period by period over a long time because firms prefer paying taxes to cutting emissions, then this will have an effect on greenhouse gas stocks that will damage the climate. If this connection is not recognized, one has to entirely give up pursuing climate policy through the regulation of specific pollutant inputs for a period.

- A related argument used in the literature in favor of a levy solution for climate protection takes up a finding of the theory of environmental policy instruments under uncertainty. The losses in welfare brought by misestimating aggregate marginal abatement cost functions are larger with a quantity-controlling policy (tradable permits) than with a price-controlling one (taxes) if the slope of the marginal damage curve is less than that of (more exactly, than the absolute value of the slope of) the marginal abatement cost curve. The following illustration illustrates this argument.

    Here the marginal damage function has deliberately been kept "flat" and the marginal abatement cost function instead deliberately "steep." For it is just for this situation that the argument presented here applies. The marginal abatement cost curve appears in two variants. MAC^{est} denotes the curve the policy making body takes as a basis for its decisions in accordance with an estimate to the

---

93 As a way out, a combination between permits and levies has been suggested in the literature. Cf., e.g., B. Böhringer/Finus (2005).

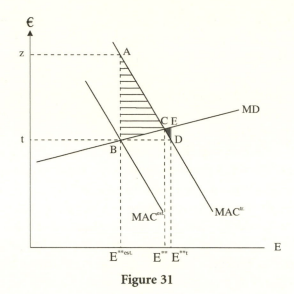

Figure 31

best of its knowledge and belief. The "est" here stands for "estimated." MAC^{tr} is, in contrast, the actual ("true") curve. On the basis of the marginal damage function, assumed to be known, and the estimated marginal abatement cost function, the policy making institution believes that the emission level $E^{**\,est}$ is optimum. $E^{**\,est}$ is defined as the intersection of the marginal damage curve and the estimated marginal abatement cost curve. If environmental policy is pursued by the instrument of taxes, this means that per emission unit the tax rate t, defined by the intersection of the two curves, is required. If the policy is implemented through tradable permits, then correspondingly $E^{**\,est}$ emission rights will be issued. Let us now consider the environmental policy equilibrium for the two variants.

If emission tax rate t applies, then the model actors will adjust their emission behavior in the way explained in part three of the book. For the firms, of course, it is not the abatement cost function estimated by policy but the actual function that counts. The emission equilibrium for emission taxation accordingly lies at the quantity E^{**t} for which the actual marginal abatement cost MAC^{tr} has risen to the emission tax rate. For the case of permit policy, the equilibrium course is defined by the level of the actual marginal abatement costs at point $E^{**\,est}$. This is shown in Figure 31 as z. In the terminology of Figure 31, then, the economy is at equilibrium for an emissions taxation policy at point D and for a permits policy at point A. The optimum allocation is instead marked by point C (the intersection of the marginal damage and real marginal abatement cost curves). It can clearly be seen from Figure 31 that the losses in welfare induced by the misestimate of the marginal abatement cost curve (the difference between maximum and equilibrium welfare) depend on which environmental policy instrument is chosen. The welfare loss for a tradable permit policy is illustrated by triangle ABC, and for a taxation policy, by triangle CDE. The way things are in Figure 31, the welfare loss for a permit policy is considerably higher than for a tax policy. In the debate on continuation or replacement of the Kyoto Protocol, this presentation is now regarded as politically relevant. Just because the greenhouse effect depends on the stock of greenhouse gases and not the specific input of them in a period, it seems plausible that the marginal damage curve runs "very flat" (i.e., just the way it is shown in Figure 31). Despite the plausibility of the foregoing presentation, there is certainly still some need for clarification before guidelines for action can be derived from this simple model. In particular, it does not necessarily follow from the flat course of the *MD* curve that it will be *flatter* than the marginal abatement cost curve. But this is a requirement for the previous argument. It is at any rate rather risky to make a statement that may have weighty consequences about the course of the slope of the relevant functions in a context that consists precisely of the fact that the future course of at least one of the two curves (namely, the marginal abatement cost curve) is unknown.

- The third element put forward in the literature in favor of emission taxation in climate protection consists of the presumed better political implementability. The criterion of justice, seen as particularly helpful to acceptance by the community of states, is claimed to be better met here.[94] In contrast with the tradable permit system, developing and threshold countries can no longer justifiably argue that they are to be forced to pay for sins by industrial countries in the past. With a global emission tax, fairness would rule because every country would in the same way have to call on its own polluters for the amount of the external marginal costs caused at the global optimum.

  Of course, the author of these lines can only speculate as to how easily the developing countries may be persuadable of the global fairness inherent in this proposal. Possibly they might point out the following: with increasing external marginal damage and a problem such as global warming defined by the *stock* of pollutants, although the marginal damage curve specific to a period may run flat as previously assumed, its *location* is as important as its *slope*. The latter depends on the quantity of pollutants accumulated in the past. A procedure whereby each country levied taxes at the amount of the worldwide aggregate marginal damage would attain the equal treatment intended only superficially. Because the industrial countries are responsible with their past emissions for the (highly exposed!) position of the marginal damage curve, the developing countries are, with this system of emission taxation, paying for the sins of the past committed by the industrial countries. Considered this way, no improved chances for global acceptance of the instrument of greenhouse gas taxation by comparison with tradable greenhouse gas permits emerge. Furthermore, the argument that tax receipts would stay in the country concerned and could be used in it to do good is scarcely suitable for differentiating between the two

---

94 Here we give the opinion by Joseph E. Stiglitz mentioned previously. Generally, on the criterion of fairness in international environmental policy, see Buchholz/Peters (2005), C. Helm/Bruckner/Tóth (1999), C. Helm/Simonis (2001), Lange/Vogt/ Ziegler (2006).

instruments. The same effect could be reached using emission permits that are auctioned. Böhringer/Finus (2005) point out a further problem with global emission taxation. The individual countries may be tempted to mitigate the burden of emission taxation through compensatory measures hard to see from outside. Moreover, an extremely nontransparent race to get credit for energy and environment taxes in existence before the introduction of the global taxation system might occur.

In discussing political feasibility, it may also do no harm to recall that in the course of the 1990s, there were energetic, prolonged attempts (by the Commission of the European Communities, among others) to bring in an all EU system of emission taxes. As we know, the project failed. Of course, history need not necessarily repeat itself in this respect. However, a certain skepticism remains. The reason for the failure of the efforts mentioned was resistance by interest groups. This resistance has not got any less since then. Has the strength to overcome it grown?

C. Instruments of International Environmental Policy – The Example of the European Union's Emissions Trading

I. Presentation

The Kyoto Protocol supplies the framework for European emissions trading.[95] It defines reducing greenhouse gases in the EU by a total of 8% from the emission level in the base year 1990 over the period from 2008 to 2012 as an ecological target. How this target is to be reached can be decided autonomously by member states. When they converted the Kyoto mechanisms into a trading system of their own, EU member states were in agreement that without coordinated action at the European level, progress in reaching the Kyoto targets could hardly be expected. Some countries, for instance, Britain and Denmark, had already developed various trading systems so that there was a danger of fragmenting the markets in the course of a gradual creation of national trading systems. This danger was to be averted through common trading rules that guaranteed smooth functioning of the internal market and prevented distortions of competition.

The "Directive of the European Parliament and of the Council establishing a Scheme for Greenhouse Gas Emission Allowance Trading within the Community" of November 27, 2002, adopted in July 2003 with minor amendments, set the pointers for meeting the Kyoto obligations within the framework of an EU-wide coordinated strategy. Trading began on January 1, 2005. The directive on emissions trading was intended to implement the principles of European climate policy

---

95 The following text gives the presentation in section III.2 of Endres/Ohl (2005b) in abbreviated form. The author wants to thank FernUniversität Hagen for permission to use this material.

both ecologically and effectively, and as economically as possible. This means that European climate strategy (like the previously mentioned compromise from the Bonn and Marrakesh conferences on interstate emissions trading) sets the goals of cost effectiveness and ecological precision to the fore in designing its scheme.

The introduction of the European trading system is intended to make the sum of absolute greenhouse gas emission quantities by EU member states fall to the highest level allowed under the Kyoto Protocol. Here, the EU reduction target is, in accordance with the bubble concept, reached by distributing the burdens among member states (EU burden sharing). In accordance with an EU internal agreement of June 1998, the reduction obligations of EU member states in relation to the 1990 emissions were distributed as follows:

- Luxembourg: −28%
- Germany, Denmark: −21%
- Austria: −13%
- Great Britain: −12.5%
- Belgium: −7.5%
- Italy: −6.5%
- Netherlands: −6%
- Finland, France: ±0%
- Sweden: +4%
- Ireland: +13%
- Spain: +15%
- Greece: +25%
- Portugal: +27%

The differentiated emission rates within the EU are intended to enable low-income countries to increase their emissions in future. The European emissions trading system thus aims at flexibilizing the emission targets set for member states in the Kyoto Protocol.

European emissions trading differs from the interstate emissions trading under the Kyoto Protocol (ET) discussed previously. The following three points should be stressed:

- EU emissions trading started with a system of CO_2 emission permits only. In contrast, emissions trading according to the Kyoto Protocol may be used for all six greenhouse gases mentioned previously. Within the EU system, the inclusion of greenhouse gases except for CO_2 has been allowed since 2008. However, it is up to each individual member state to decide whether it makes use of this option. Currently, greenhouse gases other than CO_2 do not play any role in the practice of EU emissions trading.
- Trading in emission permits already happened at EU level in the period from 2005 to 2007 (first phase). In contrast, the emissions trading regulated by the Kyoto Protocol became relevant only in the commitment period from 2008 to

2012. This period is covered in the European trading system by a second trading phase. This means that before the start of Kyoto trading EU states should have been able to "practice a bit."

- The emissions trading under the Kyoto Protocol is (at least so far) possible only among contracting states for meeting the emission targets set in the Kyoto Protocol. Participation in emissions trading is, in principle, a free choice. The establishment of the EU trading system is, in contrast, binding on member states and occurs at the level of firms.[96]

Firms' initial endowment of emission rights comes overwhelmingly from a free allotment under the *grandfathering principle*, as explained in part three.[97] Here member states issue factory-related *permits* for emitting greenhouse gases in the sectors affected by the directive (listed in more detail later in this part). They receive instructions for monitoring, reporting, and testing greenhouse gas emissions. They are, furthermore, tied to a particular installation or location; hence, they are not transferable. However, the permits are to be coupled with ownership of a corresponding quantity of *entitlements* for greenhouse gas emissions, which are tradable among firms.

In issuing permits, it is essentially left up to member states themselves to decide on the total quantity of entitlements and on the national allocation plan. The fact that the allocation quantity can be decided autonomously by the states may at first sight seem surprising. After all, the national reduction obligation has already been set in the EU burden-sharing agreement. However, this agreement does not automatically imply that the state also has to distribute the whole emission reduction volume as tradable permits. The trading strategy is only *one* measure in the portfolio of climate instruments brought to bear in individual EU member states. For instance, the German federal government's climate program includes implementation of ecological tax reform (ÖSR), the Renewable Energy Act (EEG), the Heat Protection Order, the Combined Heat and Power Act (KWKG), and self-commitments by German industry.

II. Environmental Economics Assessment[98]

The EU emissions trading system can be interpreted as a pragmatic variant of the theoretical concept of tradable emission permits, as presented in part three of this

---

96 However, not all emitters of greenhouse gases can take part in trading. For more details, see section II.

97 More precisely, in the first trading phase, at least 95% of rights had been given out free, and in the second phase, this rate is down to about 90%. Currently, there is heated discussion going on within the EU on whether the allocation system is to be switched to one in which all permits are auctioned off instead of being given away for free. The author expects the discussion to result in a compromise: "in principle," the system will be an auction, but there will be many exceptions for certain industries.

98 For more details, see Endres/Ohl (2005a). Cf. Hansjürgens (2005), Woerdman (2004).

book. The question is, of course, how far the specific design of the permit concept in the European directive is capable of meeting the high expectations placed on the effectiveness of emission permits aroused by the discussion of an ideal permit system (offered previously in this book and in many other environmental economics textbooks). The brief evaluation below uses the assessment criteria explained in part three as guidelines.

1. Ecological Precision

The object of international climate policy is inarguably to limit the temperature rise on Earth. In relation to this objective, EU emissions trading is certainly not precise, nor can it be, more than any other environmental policy instrument. For the development of world climate is not determined exclusively anthropogenically, and we are moreover uncertain as to the quantitative connection between economic activity and climate change.

According to the present state of scientific knowledge, however, we can take it that the world's climate is at least negatively *affected* by the emission of greenhouse gases. To that extent, the target of reducing worldwide emissions of greenhouse gases is a suitable substitute for the target actually pursued although not properly operable, namely, climate stabilization. But EU emissions trading cannot be precise even in relation to this "substitute goal." The fact is that the target quantity has to include greenhouse gas emissions produced worldwide, and the EU is not the world. Moreover, the objective of stabilizing greenhouse gas emissions is not completely compatible with the means of EU emissions trading to the extent that in the EU (at least so far), not all greenhouse gases (only CO_2) are traded.

Even were we to set the target level "one floor down" and define the aim as reducing the EU's CO_2 figure, the instrument of EU emissions trading cannot be asserted to possess ecological precision. After all, the fact is that not all sectors in which CO_2 is emitted are covered by trading, only the energy economy and most of the industrial sector. Transport, households, crafts, trade, and services are left outside. Even disregarding possible infringements of the rules, then, the result is that European emissions trading can be ecologically precise in its outcome only in a very reduced sense. It is at best in a position to precisely control the aggregate CO_2 contribution of those European firms entitled to trade and actually doing so. This may sound highly sobering, but it is not quite as negative as it may sound. The "performance" of an instrument assessed by a particular criterion must always be considered in relation to the corresponding performance of other instruments. For instance, a CO_2 tax on the firms covered by EU emissions trading as an alternative instrument would not even be ecologically precise in the reduced sense emissions trading was previously said to be.

Regarding ecological precision, we must point out one particularly critical aspect. It results from the fact that the Kyoto Protocol (which constitutes the basis for EU emissions trading) has not been signed by all states and, in particular, provides no reduction obligations for developing countries. That means that only part of the world's countries are making reduction efforts in accordance with the Kyoto Protocol.

One might imagine the operation of this arrangement as follows: the total input of climate-damaging gases to the atmosphere is made up of the inputs of the individual countries or groups of countries in the world. It is thus a sum of emissions, the individual elements that are more or less controlled by international agreements. If it is not possible to cut back the inputs, then we can be happy with reducing some of them and at least making a contribution toward reducing the total sum. This image implies that reducing some of the inputs does not lead to others being increased. However, this is not unrestrictedly the case. Instead, there is a negative feedback, mediated through the market mechanism, between the greenhouse gas emissions of the states committed to climate protection and other states. The climate protection efforts of participating states in particular bring a change in economic structures that induces reduced use of fossil energy sources. Here a number of measures and programs are aimed at cutting overall energy consumption and replacing fossil fuels with other (preferably renewable) energy sources. These activities have the result of damping down demand on world markets for fossil fuels and thus *ceteris paribus* exercising downward pressure on prices. However, falling world market prices will stimulate demand for fossil fuels from the uncommitted states. The increased use of these will *ceteris paribus* lead to a rise in the relevant emissions. It is important to note that the point here is not that demand for fossil fuels may, for all sorts of reasons that have nothing to do with the Kyoto Protocol or the EU trading system, rise elsewhere. It is instead that the splitting of the world into states active in climate policy and the "rest of the world" is *causal* for the fact that, in other states, emissions rise. This interdependence, which the economics literature calls the *leakage effect*, sharpens the strong criticism of the partial nature of regulations such as the Kyoto Protocol or EU emissions trading. In pointing out this deficit in ecological precision, we nonetheless want to stress that this is not a point specific to tradable permits. Every partial regulation has to combat leakage effects, quite irrespective of what environmental policy instruments it employs.[99]

99 The phenomenon of leakage arises not just through the mechanisms explained previously. A game theoretic analysis instead shows that a state aiming at welfare maximization increases its equilibrium emission if the other states reduce theirs. The "emission reaction functions" thus have a negative slope. For this, it is sufficient for the marginal damage to rise with increasing emission quantity and abatement costs to rise with increasing quantity of reduced emissions. These are conventional assumptions and are not without a certain plausibility. Of course, leakage also arises when firms under pressure from environmental policy regulation move their activities to non-(or less-) regulated other countries. For more details on the leakage problem, see, e.g., Finus (2001) and Rauscher/Lünenbürger (2004).

2. Cost-Effectiveness

In part three of the book, we explain cost-effective emission abatement as follows: the object of environmental policy is to lower the aggregate emission of a particular pollutant. This pollutant is emitted by two firms. In this example, there are two ways the policy objective can be achieved and pursued to totally different extents. It is possible to achieve the aggregate emission abatement by making heavy impositions on firm A and light ones on firm B, or conversely. More exactly, the emission abatement target can be met by arbitrarily many combinations of burden spreading between the two firms. We explain that the minimum cost distribution is characterized by the fact that the marginal abatement costs will become equal. In chapter A of part five, we apply this idea to the goal of reducing emissions of a global pollutant (e.g., greenhouse gases) to a particular amount.

Of course, there are a multiplicity of ways this goal could be attained. There are an immensely large number of decision makers able to make significant contributions toward reducing worldwide greenhouse gas emissions. These decision makers emit various *pollutants* from various *installations* belonging to various *sectors* in various *locations*. The efficient mixture of these contributions is the one that achieves the goal of stabilizing worldwide greenhouse gases at minimum cost. The cost minimum is reached when all specific marginal abatement costs of contributions become equal. The analysis in part three shows that permit trading does constitute an instrument for reaching the equalization of marginal abatement costs required for cost effectiveness. In our example with two pollutant firms, the equalization would be achieved from the fact that the two firms could exchange emission rights with each other. Applying this to the example of the reduction of worldwide greenhouse gas emissions means that the permit system must be ideally so designed that emitters of greenhouse gases can supply and demand emission rights on the market, irrespective of which gas they emit, what sector they belong to, and where in the world they do it. An ideal type of emission permit system is, then, *comprehensive* in the sense that there are no restrictions on the transferability of rights to cause emissions of equivalent effect. Only then is it possible for there to be a sorting out at market equilibrium of the quantitative climate-affecting contributions of the individual emitters of greenhouse gases through the equalization of marginal abatement costs over all installations and activities, pollutants, sectors, and regions. As soon as regulations restraining trade are laid down, the outcome is no longer an unrestrained cost minimum, but only a cost minimum with qualifications. This *restricted cost minimum* departs further from the unrestricted cost minimum the higher the number of binding restrictions. It is plain that the system of EU emissions trading does not in this sense meet the requirement of being comprehensive:

- The EU system initially narrows the set of pollutants declared greenhouse relevant by the Kyoto Protocol down to CO_2. But it is obvious that it may be more favorable in cost terms to avoid a particular CO_2 equivalent by reducing another gas than CO_2 itself. On the criterion of efficiency in the sense of minimizing abatement costs, then, there should be calls for the number of pollutants covered by trading to be extended as soon as possible, with the aim of ultimately doing without any restrictions at all.[100] The plausibility considerations presented here are supported by empirical studies. The marginal abatement costs arising at equilibrium would likely be around one third lower in a trading system covering all pollutants than the corresponding marginal abatement costs for a system limited to CO_2.[101]

- The EU system regulates trading and emission rights on the territory of the member states. How far it is possible to include member states' emission rights generated by them in connection with project-related mechanisms (JI and especially CDM) outside the EU if the trading has not yet been fully clarified in all states.[102] In Germany, the currently available revised *second national allocation plan* provides that the proportion of such rights generated by using project-related mechanisms in the total trading volume be limited.[103] In other EU states, similar considerations may have been made. It can immediately be deduced from what has just been said that such limitations hamper the minimization of abatement costs. It may be possible that greenhouse gas emissions can be reduced more cheaply by using a project-related mechanism than by transferring emission rights within the EU. If the use of project-related mechanisms is restricted in the context of emissions trading, this brings an additional proviso into the cost minimization problem and prevents the equalization of marginal abatement costs. In particular, a situation would presumably arise in which marginal abatement costs in developing countries are lower than in EU member states. In addition, there might be an internal differentiation of marginal abatement costs in various EU countries if the latter adopt different regulations on the possibility of including project-related emission rights in

100 On the economics of environmental policy covering all pollutants, see Michaelis (1997), Moslener (2004), and the explanations in chapter A of part four.

101 More precise indications with corresponding bibliographical references can be found in Endres/Ohl (2005a, p. 23).

102 Unrestricted inclusion has been settled with a "definite maybe": on the one hand, the EU directive says credits from the Kyoto mechanisms can be included in trading "without restriction," and on the other hand, the Marrakesh agreements require that the mechanisms "shall be supplemental to domestic action." In addition, the EU Commission has announced that it will start a review process as long as more than 6% of the emission rights allotted by a member state arise from the use of flexible Kyoto mechanisms. It has furthermore approved national plans for implementing the EU trading system in which member states announce they do not want to make any use of the Kyoto mechanisms. (More details and references to sources can be found in Endres/Ohl (2005a, pp. 24–25). Cf. Anger (2008) and Böhringer/Moslener/Sturm (2007) on the economic evaluation of various possibilities of combining EU emission trading with other trading systems ("Linking Schemes").

103 See pp. 40 and 41 of the Second German National Allocation Plan (2008–2012) published by the Federal Ministry for Environment, Nature Protection and Reactor Safety, at www .emissionshandel-fichtner.de/pdf/Revidierter_NAP_II_Stand_13.02.2007.pdf.

EU emissions trading. According to an empirical study by Hillebrand et al. (2002), the marginal abatement costs at equilibrium in a system incorporating the Kyoto mechanisms without restriction would be only about one fifth of the marginal abatement costs in a system without the Kyoto mechanisms.

• What has been said applies *mutatis mutandis* to restrictions of emissions trading to firms belonging to particular sectors or to particular types of installation. The EU system limits trading possibilities to "activities and installations" listed in Annex 1 in the relevant directive. In the upshot, this means that some 98% of CO_2 emissions from the energy industry and about 60% of those from industrial activities are covered by trading. However, households and transport are not covered. Equalization of the marginal costs of emission abatement thus comes about only within a subset of firms.[104] However, no complete equalization is reached among firms belonging to different sectors. This leads to a further movement away from the goal of cost minimization.[105] Nor does this problem disappear if those states not included in emissions trading are regulated by some other instrument of climate policy, say, a green tax. At equilibrium, a situation then arises where marginal abatement costs correspond to the tax rate. Efficiency across all sectors arises here, however, only in the (unlikely) special case where the tax rate is identical with the permit price. Accordingly, the current considerations in Germany on how far a program of national equalization projects can manage to create the possibility of making the boundaries between sectors of industry more permeable to emission rights are to be welcomed. For a comprehensive gain in efficiency, however, it would be needful for this possibility, first, to be very broadly designed, and second, to apply in all member states.

Previously, we discussed the principle of the completeness of emission trading in terms of restrictions detrimental to the efficiency objective in relation to pollutants, locations, and sectors. Alongside the principle of completeness, the principle of *smooth* (or at least low-friction) operation must also be considered. Friction may arise in many ways, particularly where regulations of the emissions trading system come into conflict with other regulations. Here attention should be paid particularly

---

104 It is extremely unlikely that a distribution of the reduction obligation over sectors not linked with each other by emissions trading can "hit" the minimum cost allocation. If the initial allocation is not minimum cost, then it cannot be improved by trading between these sectors. Even if it were initially minimum cost, that should not set us at ease. In the dynamics of economic events, the minimum cost allocation between sectors shifts over time. In Germany, there has indeed been a particularly unfortunate distribution, from the economic viewpoint, of reduction obligations over the "trade" and "nontrade" sectors; cf. Endres/Ohl (2005a, p. 26).

105 Cf. Böhringer/Hoffmann/Manrique-de-Lara-Peñate (2006), Böhringer/Löschel/Rutherford (2007) on the quantitative significance of the separation into a "trade" and "nontrade" sector. Frenz (2003) criticizes the exclusion of the chemical industry and the nonferrous metal and aluminium industries from a legal viewpoint, on the basis that it constitutes an infringement of the principle of equality before the law.

to whether public policy provisions restrict the transferability of emission rights and thus might endanger the attainment of the efficiency goal. This second group of restrictions acting on cost minimization is harder to see because it cannot be deduced simply from reading the EU directive on emissions trading. It might instead be findable in other directives. In this connection, one tends to recall public policy environmental protection provisions that, like the German Water Pollution Levy Act (*Abwasserabgabengesetz*) or U.S.-controlled emissions trading, heavily restricted the efficiency characteristics of market-oriented environmental policy instruments.[106] In connection with EU emissions trading, it is not so much technical standards, which as far as we know do not exist for CO_2 emissions (for lack of an affordable separation technique), that we need think about here. However, that might change as soon as other greenhouse gases were included in the trading, as called for previously. It would then be necessary to take stock with the object of finding out how far technical standards in individual member states for these gases might hamper emissions trading. We are not here *a priori* calling for all of these to disappear. That would be going too far because it might be that they were adopted for other reasons than those of climate policy, which continue to exist even after the introduction of EU emissions trading. However, the taking of stock should have the goal of establishing *compatibility* between EU emissions trading and the environmental policy regulating other climate gases than CO_2. In light of what we say in part three of this book, we would from an environmental economics viewpoint, repeat our plea to replace command and control–oriented instruments by market-oriented ones wherever possible.

It is mainly (although not solely) technical standards that might come into conflict with the EU emissions trading system. Regulations obliging firms to get a particular proportion of their energy from renewable sources might also amount to a restriction of the transferability of emission rights and thus hamper the goal of attaining efficiency.[107] In the legal literature, the viewpoint of consistency of the various elements of environmental and energy policy regulatory systems is stressed. Here, however, it is not the efficiency aspects presented previously that are to the fore, but arguments as to burdens and considerations of legal systematics.

3. Dynamic Incentive Effect

For the dynamic incentive effect, some of the points mentioned for efficiency apply *mutatis mutandis*. If the area of application of emissions trading is confined to particular pollutants, installations, sectors, and regions, then we cannot (and here cost effectiveness resembles dynamic incentive effect) expect it to work beyond the limits defined by these restrictions. This is particularly regrettable bearing in mind

---

106   See the account of this in part three of this book.

107   Cf. Böhringer/Koschel/Moslener (2009) on the economic evaluation of the coexistence (or indeed clash) of various instruments in climate protection. Pittel/Rübbelke (2008) and Rübbelke (2003) extend the analysis to environmental policy measures with multiple effects (e.g., climate protection, reduction of local environmental pollution).

the fact that the real strength of the market mechanism is not by many economists even seen as its ability to bring about static cost effectiveness, which was at the center of our attention previously. The market mechanism is instead seen more as a *discovery procedure*.[108] If a tendency to scarcity becomes visible and tangible for economic subjects in a functioning market system through a rising price, then this initiates an incentive to develop and apply new processes that use the resources becoming scarce in smaller quantities. This incentive is distinguished particularly by its *breadth*. It is not necessarily worthwhile to replace the scarce resource *in one particular way*, as happens with many governmental promotions programs. Instead, the rising price makes it attractive to replace the scarce resource *in any profitable way*. In our context, the resource becoming scarce is the atmosphere's capacity for assimilating greenhouse gases. The rising price that signals this scarcity and is made tangible to decision makers is the price of tradable emission rights. Thus, we are taking away from the market its outstanding advantage, in comparison with other allocation mechanisms, of stimulating innovation efforts *broadly* if we design the market for emission permits *narrowly* by all sorts of regional, sectoral, installation-based, or pollutant-specific limitations.

4. Conflicts of Objectives

We have dealt with the three criteria of cost effectiveness, dynamic incentive effect, and ecological precision in such a way, for simplification reasons, as if they had nothing to do with each other. From the example of efficiency and dynamic incentive effect, however, it can be seen from our discussion that conflicts among objectives may arise here. Thus, in the course of the Kyoto process, the EU asked to make only part of the reduction obligations of a particular country coverable by transferring emission rights across its frontiers. Another part of the emission reduction obligation would have to be met in the country itself. For the reasons stated previously, this is a demand that runs counter to the cost-effectiveness objective. However, it may be positive for the dynamic incentive effect. The proposed regulation would have had the consequence of setting a bar against efforts by industrial countries to meet their emission obligations in developing countries. Demand for emission rights that otherwise would have flowed to the developing countries is thus kept back in the industrial countries. This leads *ceteris paribus* to a higher equilibrium permit price in these countries. The higher the permit price, however, the greater the dynamic incentive effect of this instrument. If one believes the industrial countries have a higher potential for introducing environmental technical progress than the average country in the world, then the trade restriction brings a greater growth of dynamic incentive effect in the industrial countries than it takes away in the other countries. In the upshot, then, this sort of trade restriction leads, on the assumption stated,

108　This view goes back to F.A. von Hayek (1899–1992). Hayek, who won the Economics Nobel Prize in 1974 (together with G. Myrdal), is one of the most important representatives of the Austrian School of Economists.

to an increase in the dynamic incentive effect.[109] Ultimately, the EU states did not manage to push their demand through in the Kyoto process. Economically, this could be interpreted as attributing higher priority to the criterion of the system's cost effectiveness than to its dynamic incentive effect.[110]

To conclude this point, let us note that the conflict of objectives mentioned arises only if cost-effective and cost-ineffective environmental policies are compared with each other by the criterion of dynamic incentive effect for *one and the same environmental policy goal*. Of course, this precondition (a given emission reduction target level) is met in our context of discourse, the Kyoto Protocol and EU emissions trading. However, it is not systematically binding at all. Cost effectiveness and dynamic incentive effect could be reconciled with each other by tightening up the environmental policy target correspondingly in moving from a cost-ineffective (i.e., limited in regional terms or in regard to the greenhouse gases covered) emissions trading system to a cost-effective one (i.e., "derestricted" in every respect). One and the same, cost pressure on polluters, with all its beneficial effects on inducing environmental technological progress, can be exercised with both the cost-effective and the cost-ineffective policy variant. Of course, the cost-effective policy variant (the defining feature of cost effectiveness) can at any given cost reach a higher target (here emission reduction) than the cost-ineffective policy.

It is, then, important not to confuse a *context-specific* conflict of objectives between cost effectiveness and dynamic incentive effect with a *general* (applying in all contexts) conflict of objectives allegedly lying in the essence of the concepts of cost effectiveness and dynamic incentive effect.

5. Emissions Trading and Specific Features of Climate Protection

The climate protection problem relevant for our discussion differs from other international environmental problems in a few specific features. These have not been thoroughly discussed in the mainstream of the previous analysis. It was only occasionally (in particular, in the discussion of the proposed replacement of the permit-oriented Kyoto Protocol by a system of greenhouse gas taxes) that peculiarities of the climate situation played a part. We now want to go further into this aspect. Previously, we mostly acted as if what climate policy was about was limiting the emission of greenhouse gases over a particular period. This is all the more justified the better the effect of a particular pollutant can be grasped by its emission over a specific period (i.e., in the form of a *flow magnitude*). In such a viewpoint, cumulative effects by definition play no part. But in climate protection (according to the current state of scientific knowledge), the fact is that the extent of damage from pollutant inputs depends less on the input over a particular period

---

109 However, it also leads to an increase in the leakage effect and thereby reduces the system's ecological precision.

110 The preceding argumentation is rather crude because of its brevity. A more differentiated analysis of the impact of restraints on trading emissions permits on cost effectiveness and technical progress can be found in Matschoss/Welsch (2006).

than on the *stock* of such gases formed over a period as a sum of the inputs specific to periods. This is of particular importance for the criteria of ecological precision and efficiency.

If the period-specific emission flow is not the real target quantity, but the cumulative stock over time, then a shortcoming in *ecological precision* is not all that dramatic. Poor control in one period can then, in principle, be corrected by steering in the opposite direction in another. Accordingly, the familiar criticisms of emission taxation in the literature because of its lacking ecological precision need not be weighted so heavily in the area of climate protection policy as would be the case for a pollutant for which the period-specific emissions really did have to be precisely controlled.

Regarding the *cost-effectiveness criterion*, the significance of a target defined in terms of an accumulated stock level is that on top of the possibilities already mentioned of securing efficiency gains by equalizing marginal costs, a completely new dimension comes along. This is the equalization of marginal abatement costs between different periods.[111] For instance, if it is foreseeable that marginal abatement costs in period 2 will be lower than in period 1, it makes sense to reach an emission stock level aimed at for period 3 by making heavier reduction efforts in period 2 than in period 1. Against this background, it would seem desirable from the viewpoint of the cost-effectiveness criterion to allow a transfer of emission rights between various periods (*Emission Banking and Borrowing*).[112]

6. Conclusion

Previously, we interpreted the EU directive on trading in greenhouse gas emissions as one variant in practice of the idea of tradable environmental permits. As such, the EU system is, in principle, and pragmatically well suited to furthering environmental protection at lower cost than would be the case with many other environmental policy systems. Moreover, it might be possible to moderately induce progress in environmental technology with this system. This is to be welcomed not only from the economic point of view, but also ecologically. The more inexpensively climate protection is pursued, the more ambitious are the climate policy objectives that are from an economic viewpoint to be aimed at and (still more important) that are politically feasible. Finally, it should further be pointed out that climate policy is an "ideal area of application" for tradable permits insofar as here the dispersion

---

111 Cf., e.g., Feng/Zhao (2006). The importance of "when flexibility" is rated low in Godal/Klaassen (2006) and Stephan/Müller-Fürstenberger (2004).

112 From the viewpoint of political economy, however, caution would seem appropriate in relation to "borrowing." "Frivolous" recourse by today's emitters to tomorrow's emission rights might mean that emission rights become very scarce in future. One might then take the position that the market in intertemporal claims will equalize, as often happens in pragmatic fashion on other futures markets. However, it is conceivable that the interest groups involved in the political process will burst the tight corset of the framework of availability of emission permits in a future period, if permits become scarce.

characteristics of a pollutant, right up to hotspot problems, play no part at all. It is precisely these aspects that complicated the debate on the applicability of the tradable permits mechanism so much in the past. Greenhouse gases are global pollutants. For their effect on the climate is, according to the present state of scientific knowledge, irrelevant where they are emitted.

In contrast, the EU system is quite far off an ideal type of system of "climate protection certificates." Between the two systems, there are many imperfections and limitations that mark the EU system.

Of course, it is a wise principle not to reject a practical political instrument just because it does not fit some ideal system. Ideal systems, as we know, cannot be converted into practice simply, and in any case, that is not what they are there for. Instead, the ideal system has the function of giving guidance in the political process in relation to the direction that the development of systems of instruments should take. Without this guidance, it is more difficult to see where politics turns into a game of special interests.[113]

Let us hope that politics takes the right path and advances along it rapidly.

D. Epilogue: The Vision of a U.S. Emissions Trading System

Not having ratified the Kyoto Protocol earned a lot of negative comments for the United States from both national and international critics. In recent years, however, U.S. climate policy has gained considerable momentum. In the American public, there is increasing awareness of the problems of global warming and its anthropogenic origin. Moreover (and in response to the "winds of change" in society), politicians are, well, increasingly willing to act.

In the U.S. environmental economics community, it is completely undisputed that the country needs a convincing federal climate policy. Moreover, there is a wide consensus that market-based policies should be used. There is also a lively debate on whether a tradable permit system or an emissions tax constitutes the superior instrument of climate policy. There have been numerous proposals for the design of either of the two systems. However, it is beyond the scope of this book to explore more than one of these proposals. The proposal of our choice is the recent vision of a nationwide federal permit trading system as the instrument of the U.S.'s climate policy. The idea was suggested by Robert N. Stavins, one of the most prominent American environmental economists, in his 2008 paper.[114]

The reason for devoting our precious space in this book to the aforementioned idea is twofold. First, the proposed U.S. system would be a welcome complement to

---

113 Cf. Svendsen (2005) on EU emissions trading from the viewpoint of the New Political Economy.

114 Among the rivaling concepts is the proposal of a federal greenhouse gas tax presented by Metcalf (2009). Other recent contributions to the discussion on U.S. climate policy instruments can be found in Cramton/Stoft (2010), Keohane (2009), and Murray/Newell/Pizer (2009).

the EU emissions trading system discussed in the previous chapter. Linking two cap and trade systems, each of which has a wide coverage, would open up tremendous gains from cost-effective greenhouse gas reduction. This is due to the fact that the pool of greenhouse gas emitters with different marginal abatement cost functions would be very large in a combined U.S. and EU system. As we saw in the third part of this book, differences in marginal abatement cost functions are the key to the superior cost effectiveness of market-based environmental policy instruments compared to command and control.[115] This argument already points to the second ("didactic") reason for considering the proposed U.S. tradable permit system. The criteria for its design, as discussed here, present a nice application of the theory of environmental policy as explained previously. This is particularly true regarding not only what has been said on standard-oriented environmental policy in part three, but also with respect to the analysis of Coasean bargains in part two and on the "double dividend hypothesis" in part four.

Let us sketch what a U.S. emissions trading system should look like in order to be an ecologically effective and cost-effective tool of national climate policy. This exposition closely follows that given in Stavins (2008) and has the following key elements:

- *Greenhouse Gas Trading (GHG) Trading, Not Just CO_2 Trading.* The focus of the public discussion on the greenhouse effect is on CO_2 emissions generated by burning fossil fuels as the source of global warming. However, there are other GHGs contributing to the problem, as explained previously in this book. Accordingly, the proposed system would be a multi-GHG trading system, covering as many non-CO_2 GHGs as possible at a reasonable administrative cost.

- *Tightening the Belt.* The number of emission permits annually provided by the system should be gradually reduced, following a trajectory that is made public far in advance. This trajectory is designed to serve as a reliable indicator for the parties involved. It makes the available quantity of emission rights predictable and contributes to the predictability of future permit prices. The economic advantages of this procedure are obvious: reduced frictions in the economy and more time to use technological progress compared to a quick

---

115 Vol. 9 (2009), No. 4, of the journal *Climate Policy* contains several articles on linking various cap and trade systems. Linkage of the EU-ETS to proposed U.S. cap and trade systems is discussed in Sterk/Mehling/Tuerk (2009). These envisioned U.S. systems are the Waxman-Markey and the Lieberman-Warner U.S. Congressional Proposals. There is a brief assessment of several market-based climate change bills as introduced in the 111th U.S. Congress on the webpage of *Resources for the Future*, a Washington, DC–based brain trust in environmental economics. See www .rff.org/news/features/documents/110th_legislation_table_graph.pdf (draft as of May 26, 2009; accessed June 17, 2010). A European environmental economics perspective on U.S. climate policy can be found in Moslener/Sturm (2008).

tightening of the economy's emissions frame.[116] It is argued by Stavins that the ecological implications of realizing the potential of economic advantages can be well tolerated. The reason given for this assessment is that climate change is a problem of pollution stocks, rather than pollution flows. Any goal of attaining a certain stock of pollutants (*accumulated* flow of pollutants) in the future can be reached via different trajectories of pollution reduction connecting the present and the future point in time at which the target must be reached. The abatement costs associated with these alternative trajectories will be diverse. The trajectories with the lowest costs are characterized by an initially modest pace of emission reduction followed by a subsequent gradual acceleration.

- *Upstream Approach.* The flow of a river may be understood as an allegory for the economic process. The source represents the extraction of natural resources used as productive inputs. The mouth of the river is analogous to the consumption of final products (and, well, waste disposal). Choosing an *upstream approach* for the nationwide greenhouse gas emissions trading system means that permits have to be surrendered by economic agents that are "located" close to the origin of the flow. In particular, greenhouse gas content is to be measured and accounted for at the point of fuel extraction, refining, distribution, or importation.

  The reason for opting in favor of this approach is that it keeps the number of parties involved in the trading system to a minimum. Obviously, holding agents operating at the "mouth of the river" responsible for surrendering permits for the greenhouse gas content of the commodities they consume would unnecessarily inflate the transaction costs of the cap and trade system.

- *Making Abatement Cost More Predictable.* In part three of this book, alternative environmental policy instruments are evaluated according to, among other criteria, that of ecological accuracy. Tradable discharge permits fared particularly well in this context because the quantity of pollutants (lawfully) emitted is under the direct control of the environmental agency issuing the permits. However, we also hinted at the flipside of this coin: future demand for tradable discharge permits is uncertain because it depends on the future overall pulse of the economy and on the development of abatement technology.[117]

  The proposed U.S. federal greenhouse gas emissions trading program contains several elements that aim to reduce this problem of cost uncertainty. One is the provision that emission permits are to be intertemporally transferable:

---

116 However, the speed and the direction of technical progress will depend on the temporal path environmental policy will take. We refer to what has been said on induced technical change in section C.II of part three and chapter E of part four of this book.

117 Issues of cost uncertainty in tradable permit systems and (emission) quantity uncertainty in emission tax systems are discussed in Murray/Newell/Pizer (2009).

"Banking" allows unused present allowances to be saved and used at a later date. "Borrowing" allows future emission allowances to be drawn on at the present time. This kind of "when flexibility" attenuates undesirable year-to-year cost fluctuations. However, these rules do not help in cases of dramatic permit price fluctuations, which may occur in the short run. To cope with these problems, the proposed system includes a particular "cost containment mechanism" as a second tool to reduce cost uncertainty:

Using this mechanism, polluters may buy additional permits at a fixed price. This price must be set sufficiently high to confine the use of the mechanism to extreme cases of permit shortage. Moreover, the revenues generated by the cost containment mechanism are to be strictly earmarked for the use of greenhouse gas reduction purposes only. These reductions may, for example, be brought about by buying back permits from the polluters in the future.

• *Hybrid System of Auctions and Grandfathering.* In part three of this book, two possibilities are presented in regard to initial allocation: auctioning permits and giving them away for free. We also discuss grandfathering, a specific form of free allowance allocation. This procedure is designed to make sure that established polluters receive a sufficient number of permits to allow them to sustain their businesses.

In a world without frictions, the initial allocation of permits is irrelevant for the market equilibrium distribution of emission rights among the participating firms. Here, the game is played according to "Coasean rules." In the real world (and in more sophisticated economic models), the game is played with many imperfections. This may have the consequence that the equilibrium allocation of emission rights depends on the mode chosen for initial allocation. The first issue worth noting in this context is that initial allocation using grandfathering is quite different from the situation in the market equilibrium. A lot of trading has to be done before the market equilibrium is reached. In a world of positive transaction costs, this might lead to the result that the market equilibrium implies an allocation of permits that is quite different from cost-effective allocation. Let us refer back to what we say in section A.II.4. of part two of this book, where we discuss what remains of the Coase theorem if we switch to a model with positive transaction costs. Compared to such a model, initial allocation achieved using an auction is closer to the situation in the market equilibrium. In addition, less trading is needed to adjust the initial permit allocation, reducing transaction costs in comparison to the grandfathering alternative. All in all, it is more likely that the market equilibrium is closer to cost-effective allocation under a system of auctions than it is under a system of grandfathering (see Stavins (1995)).

Another concern regarding the grandfathering alternative is that new firms are treated unfairly in comparison with established polluters. They must pay for permits in the market that others have been allocated free of charge. To counter this problem, the environmental agency must hold a "permit reserve" to satisfy the demand of future newcomers. However, the optimal size of this reserve is difficult to determine because future demand generated by newcomers is highly uncertain.

A third argument in the literature in favor of the auction method is that auctions generate public revenue that may be used to attenuate imperfections in the economy. The *double dividend* discussion in part four of this book may provide a helpful point of reference here.[118]

A final argument worth mentioning is that experience with the EU emissions trading system suggests that grandfathering favors *rent seeking* by interest groups. Grandfathering seems to have stirred up the creativity of interest groups, arguing that they deserve all kinds of special treatment when it comes to getting hold of free emission allowances.

The arguments summarized previously speak in favor of auctions instead of grandfathering. However, grandfathering seems to improve the probability that a transferable discharge permit system is accepted in society. There is stiff opposition against the introduction of an auctioning system, just as there is against the introduction of a greenhouse gas tax. In the EU, an initiative to introduce a comprehensive greenhouse gas tax failed, and it might be argued that the EU emissions trading system would never have been introduced if it had been designed as a system of auctions in the first place.

In light of these arguments and experiences, it is intended that the proposed U.S. Federal Emissions trading System will start with a 50–50 auction-free allocation mixture. Then, the share of auctions is suggested to be increased to 100% over 25 years.

Stavins (2008) estimates the costs of the proposed system for the U.S. economy using the *National Energy Modeling System* (NEMS) of the U.S. Department of Energy and the *Emissions Prediction and Policy Analysis* (EPPA) model of the Massachusetts Institute of Technology.[119] If the program is used to reduce emissions from their 2008 level to 50% below the level from 1990 by 2050, the costs are estimated to be about 1% of the U.S. gross domestic product per year. It is emphasized in the proposal discussed here that these costs are considerably lower compared to a program that would serve the same ecological goal using a command and control policy. Of course, this result is perfectly in line with what we would expect according to what has been said about the cost effectiveness of alternative environmental policy instruments in section C.I of part three of this book.

---

118 Of course, we are aware that this argument in favor of auctions should be taken with a grain of salt considering what has been said in this section.

119 EPPA has also been used to assess a set of cap and trade programs considered by U.S. Congress in Spring 2007, as well as a set of bills proposing taxes to limit U.S. greenhouse gas emissions. See Metcalf et al. (2008) and Paltsev et al. (2008, 2009).

Exercises

Exercise 5.1

Which relations hold in the optimal allocation of a global pollutant

a) between aggregate marginal damages and aggregate marginal abatement costs?
b) between country-specific marginal abatement costs and aggregate marginal abatement costs?
c) between country-specific marginal damages and aggregate marginal damages?

Exercise 5.2

Assume that, *ceteris paribus*, exogenous technical progress causes a decrease of country i's marginal abatement costs (for any given abatement level), whereas marginal abatement costs of country j, $j \neq i$, remain unaffected. What affect would you expect to see on the Nash equilibrium emission level of country j?

Exercise 5.3

a) Assume that the world is composed of two countries, $i \in \{1, 2\}$, which produce a global pollutant. Marginal abatement costs of countries 1 and 2 are given by $MAC_1 = 100 - x_1$ and $MAC_2 = 100 - 10x_2$, respectively. Marginal damage cost are given by $MD_1 = 10(x_1 + x_2)$ and $MD_2 = x_1 + x_2$, respectively, where x_i denotes the emission level of country i. Show that the socially optimal emission level of country 1 *exceeds* the Nash equilibrium level, and explain this result.

b) Assume that the two countries initially choose their Nash equilibrium emission levels. Starting from this point, they bargain over an international contract that allows each country to choose the socially optimal emission levels. Is this contract individually rational? Determine for each country the corresponding welfare change.

Exercise 5.4

List some possible causes for a shift of a country's marginal abatement cost and marginal damage curve, respectively.

Exercise 5.5

Which of the following statements is/are correct?

a) A contract on the emission reduction of a global pollutant is individually rational, if each country's welfare is higher than in the situation where each country chooses its uncorrected emission level x_i^* (with $MAC_i(x_i^*) = 0$).

b) If a contract on the emission reduction of a global pollutant is individually rational, then each country's welfare is higher than in the situation where each country chooses its uncorrected emission level x_i^* (with $MAC_i(x_i^*) = 0$).

Exercise 5.6

Give some examples for environmental problems that suffer from the incentive structure of the prisoner's dilemma.

Exercise 5.7

Do you think that the assumption of risk-averse countries is adequate in the context of environmental problems?

Exercise 5.8

Assume an international contract that does not enter into force until each country of the world has signed it. Give some reasons why this kind of ratification strategy is not able to provide a general solution to the global prisoner's dilemma.

Exercise 5.9

Assume that there are n countries, $i \in \{1, \ldots, n\}$, and let W_i^N and W_i^{**} denote the welfare of country i in the noncooperative and socially optimal allocation (without transfers).

Give an example for a transfer scheme that assures the individual rationality of the socially optimal allocation.

Exercise 5.10

Give an example of an international environmental agreement that includes trade sanctions.

Exercise 5.11

Consider a world that is composed of $n \geq 3$ identical countries, and assume that some of them form a coalition. Further assume that each member of the coalition chooses the level of its activity variable in order to maximize the joint welfare of the coalition members. Nonsignatories are assumed to behave as singletons. This means that each nonsignatory maximizes its own welfare, given the strategies of the other countries.

Which of the following statements is correct?

a) If a coalition of size $j > 1$ is externally stable, then a coalition of size $j - 1$ is internally stable.
b) If a coalition of size $j > 1$ is internally stable, then a coalition of size $j - 1$ is externally stable.
c) If a coalition of size $j < n$ is externally stable, then a coalition of size $j + 1$ is internally stable.
d) If a coalition of size $j > 1$ is not internally stable, then a coalition of size $j - 1$ is externally stable.

Exercise 5.12

Which objective could a government pursue instead of national welfare maximization?

Exercise 5.13

What is the main feature that hampers the solution of international environmental problems compared with national environmental problems?

Exercise 5.14

In the Kyoto Protocol, emission targets are formulated in terms of CO_2 equivalents. Explain what this means, and what it implies with respect to the cost effectiveness of emission reductions.

Exercise 5.15

Does the Kyoto Protocol allow the trade of emission reduction duties between industrialized and developing countries?

Exercise 5.16

Assume for the example presented in Figure 31 that the policy maker chooses command and control (i.e., emission reduction quotas) instead of tradable permits or emission tax. Which welfare loss compared to the social optimum would you expect?

Exercise 5.17

List some additional criteria that could be used besides ecological precision, cost effectiveness, and the dynamic incentive effect to evaluate the EU emission trading system from the economist's point of view.

Exercise 5.18

Which consequences on the cost effectiveness, ecological precision, and dynamic push of EU emissions trading should be expected from the fact that CDM projects (up to a certain amount) are countable within the EU emissions trading system?

Exercise 5.19

Discuss the following assertion: The EU emissions trading system is a pilot project of the flexible mechanism "emissions trading" of the Kyoto Protocol, allowing for *learning by doing* of institutions.

Part Six

Natural Resources and Sustainable Development

In this part, the economics of natural resources and sustainable development are presented in an overview. Specific aspects can be addressed only briefly in the space available here. Following the literature, we divide natural resources into exhaustible and renewable ones. The former are defined by the fact that the total stock of them in the Earth is a constant within the time frame of relevance to human planning. A unit of an exhaustible resource used in the present thus reduces the stock available in the future by precisely one unit. Here the present and the future are in total rivalry over the utilization of the resources.

The standard examples of exhaustible resources come from the area of mining, with fossil fuels and mineral raw materials being frequently mentioned. For exhaustible resources such as metals, the rivalry between present and future utilization can be mitigated by recycling.

Renewable (also called regenerable) resources can be increased in the time frame of relevance to human planning. The growth rate of the stock depends on many determinants, particularly the size of the stock itself. The connection between present utilization and future possibility of utilization is thus more complex for renewable resources than for exhaustible ones. Important examples of resources in this category are forestry and fish stocks.

A. Resource Exhaustion – The End of Humankind?

I. Introduction

One of the central questions that excited the public and the scientific world in the 1970s and beyond was: will humanity decline and fall because of a shortage of resources? The debate has slackened somewhat in the meantime, but continually flares up again.

The notion underlying this concern can be outlined as follows: humanity has a given stock of natural resources available. We draw on it continuously – and indeed at an increasing rate. One (not terribly remote!) day, everything will be used up. Because the economy depends on the supply of resources, much like humans depend on a supply of oxygen, it will eventually collapse.

The general concern at issue here was nourished by the experience of the world economy's dependency on petroleum in the crisis years 1973–1974 and 1979–1980, as well as by extremely pessimistic forecasts (derived from scientific simulation calculations). A particularly spectacular example at the time was the report by Meadows et al. (1972) to the Club of Rome. This continued the tradition started by Malthus in 1798 of "doomsday economics." It calculated, in various scenarios, that the world economy would come up against restrictions defined by the size of resource stocks and/or the environment's limited capacity for assimilation before the end of the second millennium and would therefore collapse. The report was translated into 29 languages and sold more than 9 million copies worldwide.[1]

Of course, it is a bit cheap to simply point out that the threatened collapse has not come about. As we know, we always see better with hindsight. Moreover, the decline and fall may still come. This statement is unscientific, to the extent that it is not falsifiable, yet it may nonetheless be true![2]

However, it should be emphasized that the scientific method employed by the Club of Rome (and later by other groups of authors) was criticized by economists immediately after publication. In particular, it was pointed out that the simulation calculations had taken no account of market reactions to the predicted scarcity processes. But it is the belief of most economists that the market is an extremely capable instrument for coping with scarcity problems. Specifically, the market mechanism is trusted to be able to signal increasing scarcity of resources and other goods through rising prices. It is expected that rational economic subjects will react to the rising prices with efforts to expand the supply of the resource becoming scarcer and cut back the demand. This is true both with current technology and with incentives to develop technologies whereby the expansion of supply or limitation of demand may be made possible. In a study that appeared in 1977, economics Nobel Prize winner Wassily Leontief looked at how the Club of Rome's models change if the scarcity-reducing effect of the market mechanism is incorporated in the analysis. With otherwise identical assumptions, Leontief showed that much more optimistic findings appear. Of course, not even economic Nobel Prize winners (far less "normal" economists!) can see into the future. An evaluation of the developments

---

1 As an author of textbooks, one might comment, with a sigh: "How enviable!"

2 Let me offer readers who may be unhappy at this a bit of "decline and fall" aesthetics by way of consolation: "New York was not that unpleasant, she replied; since the time of the Great Drying Up there was lots of wind, the sky was constantly changing, she lived high up and spent a lot of time observing the movements of the clouds. Some chemical factories, probably situated in New Jersey, judging from the distance, continued to function, and at sunset the pollution gave the sky strange pink and green hues; and the ocean was still present, far to the east, unless it was an optical illusion, but in good weather you could sometimes make out a vague shimmering." (Found in Michel Houellebecq, *La Possibilité d'une île*, 2005; trans. by Gavin Bowd as *The Possibility of an Island* (New York: Vintage Books), 2007.)

in the area of natural resources that have occurred since the 1970s shows, however, that every forecast about the availability of such resources went wrong if it failed to include the role of the market mechanism in solving scarcity problems.

For similar reasons as with the model calculations just mentioned, the reserve stock indicator frequently used as an early warning system that particular resources are becoming scarce can lead to error. The indicator is constructed by quantifying the reserves of a particular raw material known and economically and technically exploitable at the time of the survey, and dividing that by the (actual or predicted) annual consumption quantity. This gives the number of years for which the resource will according to the criterion of the indicator still be available. It has emerged, however, that this construction has no predictive force. Quite the contrary, empirical studies have shown that the reserve stock of important raw materials has in the course of time increased, despite sizeable annual consumption rates.[3] One cause is presumably that exploration activities intensify once a scarcity of existing reserves looms over the horizon. Moreover, in the course of technical progress, increasingly more deposits "move up" from the set of known (but technically and/or economically inaccessible) resources to the category of directly utilizable resources.

Because of the lack of forecasting capacity of purely "technocratic" (i.e., constructed without including market mechanisms) availability indicators, a totally differently formed indicator has been sought in the *resource price*. Because in economics price is regarded as the scarcity indicator *par excellence*, the idea suggested itself of looking at the development of real resource prices of important raw materials over the course of time and drawing conclusions from them in relation to scarcity tendencies that might emerge. Here, too, however, the indicator has not shown serious scarcity signals so far. For the most important exhaustible resources in the years considered, the prices have by no means dramatically risen; indeed, they have often fallen.[4]

It would be careless to conclude from the fact that the price, as a scarcity indicator, is not moving into an alarming area that there is no scarcity problem for natural resources. In particular, the price can indicate future scarcity only if that is expected by the economic actors. After all, prices are formed from supply and demand decisions in the markets. Their expectations may, however, be illusory. Moreover, it may be that the planning horizon of individual actors on the resource markets is narrower than society might like in regard to the forecasting value of an indicator for resource scarcity.

II. Social Optimum and Competitive Equilibrium in the Exploitation of Exhaustible Resources – The Hotelling Rule

As explained previously, the question of resource exhaustion has become reduced in public debate to a "to be or not to be." In the theoretical economics debate, in

---

3   Details on this can be found in Simpson/Toman/Ayres (2005) and Tahvonen/Kuuluvainen (2000).
4   Cf. the literature cited in footnote 3.

contrast (and the reader of this book would not have expected anything else!), the topic has been dealt with in rather more differentiated fashion. Here the point was to find the laws of motion of market exploitation of natural resources and compare them with the laws of motion of a utilization of them that would be desirable for the whole of society. Put more technically, and concentrating on the area of exhaustible resources, the path of utilization of resources in a competitive economy is described over time and compared with the path of utilization over time that would be a welfare optimum. The relevant work is rooted in the pioneering article by Harold Hotelling[5] (1931), who put the problem as follows. Let a strictly limited stock of an exhaustible resource be available. Now, how should this stock be distributed over the periods of utilization of the resource in order to maximize the cash value for society of net welfare from the resource? Net welfare is here understood as the difference between gross welfare and utilization costs.

Of course, the real problems of optimal exploitation of exhaustible resources are rather more complicated than in Hotelling's stylization. In the literature, numerous variants of Hotelling's model have been developed so as to take account of the various complications of the real world. All the same, the model does reflect fundamental features of the allocation problem for exhaustible resources. The model accordingly still forms the basis today for all scientific effort in resource economics, and the *Hotelling Rule* explained in more detail here can with full right be called the "first principle of resource economics."

From the results of Hotelling's considerations, we single out two main features:

- It becomes clear from Hotelling's analysis that the limitation of the resource stock (alongside the exploitation costs) establishes an additional type of cost. Because at a particular point in time a resource unit withdrawn from the fixed stock reduces possibilities of using the resource in future by precisely this unit, there arise *temporal opportunity costs* (or *utilization costs*). The nature of these costs becomes plainly clear if we compare the cost of using a fossil fuel with that of using solar energy. For both forms of energy, costs arise for making the energy "offered" by nature usable for people. In a very broad sense of the term, we might for simplicity call these "exploitation costs." For solar energy, in contrast with fossil fuels, our use of today's solar radiation does not in the slightest affect the quantity of such energy available in future. The temporal opportunity costs (utilization costs) mentioned previously, "discovered" by Hotelling, thus do not exist with solar energy, whereas for the exploitation of fossil energy sources they are the very essence of the problem.

    If we apply welfare economics considerations to these specific circumstances, then the outcome is that for a maximum welfare allocation of the exhaustible resource it is necessary to exploit it in such a way that at any arbitrarily

---

5   Harold Hotelling (1895–1973), founder of the modern theory of exhaustible resources, and also the author of pioneering works on the theory of oligopoly and of business location.

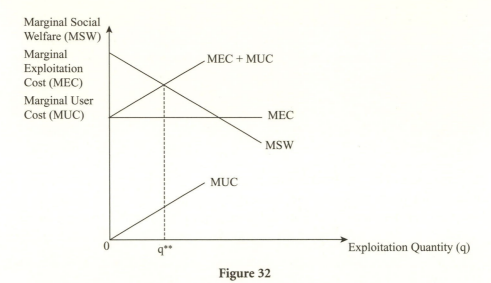

Figure 32

selected point in time the marginal gross welfare corresponds to the sum of the marginal exploitation costs and the marginal utilization costs.[6]

This property of the optimum resource allocation is illustrated in Figure 32. In it, *MEC* indicates the marginal exploitation cost, *MUC* the marginal user cost, and q^{**} the socially optimum exploitation amount over the period considered.[7]

- The next element in Hotelling's theory provides illumination about the development of marginal utilization costs over time. Hotelling showed that the marginal utilization costs on an optimum welfare time path of resource exploitation rise at a rate corresponding to the social discount rate obtained in the society considered. This connection has since been known in the literature as the *Hotelling Rule*. Formally, the Hotelling Rule is nothing other than the conditions for intertemporal allocational efficiency in resource utilization. If the income from the resource rises at the rate indicated, then this is also true of the difference between gross welfare and exploitation cost (i.e., society's net welfare).[8]

However, if net welfare rises over time at the social discount rate, then the last unit exploited in every period will contribute the same amount to the total cash value of the net welfare arising from utilization of the resource. It is therefore impossible to increase the total cash value by shifting utilization of a particular unit from one period to another. The objective of finding a path of

---

6 Assuming that the underlying functions are "well behaved" in the sense of differential calculus. Obviously, this is a special case of the general microeconomic optimality condition "marginal utility = marginal cost." This condition frequently appears in this book in the most varied "disguises."

7 The exploitation quantity related to a point in time is often referred to in the resource economics literature as the "exploitation rate."

8 For a well-behaved marginal welfare function, rising welfare over time goes hand in hand with a decreasing exploitation quantity.

resource exploitation over time that maximizes the cash value of net welfare from exploitation of the resource through the whole period of utilization has thus been resolutely grasped.

Of course, in a market economy (and elsewhere), there is no omniscient, benevolent dictator who not only knows the socially optimum path of resource expectation described previously, but also can and wants to implement it. In a market economy, the time path of resource exploitation is instead a consequence of the decisions of the resource owners and their (market-guided) interaction with the demanders of it. The driving force in the decisions of the resource owners is the endeavor for profit maximization and not the objective that was the basis for the previous considerations of allocational theory, namely, maximizing social welfare. However, the findings about the maximum welfare exploitation of a resource define the standard by which the equilibrium exploitation arising in a market system is evaluated.[9]

To understand a market pattern of exploitation of an exhaustible resource, let us put ourselves in the interest position of an individual supplier of the resource and pay particular attention to the incentives he is exposed to in the environment of a competitive economy. Because we are aiming at as simple as possible a presentation of the intertemporal allocation problem, we assume the existence of a perfect system of futures markets. In this system, all economic actors can conclude contracts for the present moment in time and the whole of the future on the basis of the equilibrium prices obtained in each case. The individual supplier must decide how to allocate the exploitation of his resource over time. In as close analogy as possible with the traditional static model of the firm that has already so often been helpful to us in this book, we assume that the supplier aims to find the profile of exploitation over time for which the value of the profit flow coming from selling the resource over time is a maximum. He must accordingly take account of the fact that present exploitation and sale of a unit of the resource, while bringing current profits, reduces future profit possibilities (i.e., causes utilization costs).

Because the firm can invest the profits from current exploitation of the resource on the capital market (assumed to be perfect) at the market interest rate, it will, in considering between present and future exploitation of the resource, discount profits to be expected in the future at this interest rate. Future profits will accordingly be weighted lower than current ones. This speaks in favor of rapid exploitation of the resource. However, the profit from a unit of the resource will be higher in the future than in the present because the resource will *ceteris paribus* rise in value in the course of time as it becomes scarcer. This is in favor of slow exploitation of the resource.

The question of the optimum exploitation path over time for the firm thus amounts to the same as the question of the balance between the two opposing

---

9 The procedure thus follows the standard welfare economics analysis already frequently employed in this book.

trends for profit, namely, discounting and rise in value. The time path of resource exploitation sought by the firm that will maximize the cash value of profit from the resource is defined by the fact that the discounted marginal profit from exploiting the resource (price for the period concerned less marginal exploitation cost) is equal for all periods.[10] With this temporal distribution, the marginal profit from exploitation of one marginal unit of the resource in the present will precisely cover the foregoing of (discounted) future profit caused by that exploitation. Marginal profit and marginal utilization cost thus always coincide at equilibrium.

The condition of a discounted marginal profit equal for all periods is met precisely when the marginal profit over time rises at the rate of the interest rate employed as a discounting factor. Here the opposing effects of discounting of future profits and increasing resource value over time balance out. At equilibrium, the supplier is always indifferent to the alternative of leaving a (marginal) unit of the resource in the ground – and thus being able to enjoy the increase in value – or exploiting it, and thus being able to draw interest on the profit on the capital market. The quantity produced will here be guided by demand.

The fact that on the equilibrium time path of resource exploitation the marginal profit grows at a rate equal to the interest rate had already been deduced by Hotelling (1931).[11] This is a second version of the "Hotelling Rule" already addressed. In the previous context, the Hotelling Rule meant the conditions for the *socially optimum* intertemporal exploitation profile for an exhaustible resource. In the form just mentioned, in contrast, it denotes the *maximum profit* intertemporal exploitation profile of the same resource, in a market system assumed to be perfect. We might also say that the Hotelling Rule can be formulated in either a *normative* or a *positive* version. Against the background of these considerations, it is clear what *conditions* must be met for a market equilibrium development of resource exploitation over time to be identical with the socially optimum development (i.e., for the two variants of the Hotelling Rule to describe one and the same exploitation profile):

- The aggregate marginal willingness to pay of the resource consumers is accepted as a quantity approximating to the gross social marginal welfare from the resource.[12] In addition, in consuming the resource, no externalities arise. Because the aggregate marginal willingness to pay, as we know, corresponds with the

---

10 If the discounted marginal profit for period t is higher (lower) than the discounted marginal profit for period $t + 1$, then the present value of the sum of all profits for periods can be increased by increasing (lowering) the planned exploitation of the resource in t at the expense of period $t + 1$ (in favour of period $t + 1$).

11 In the simple model employed by Hotelling, without marginal exploitation costs, the equilibrium *price* rises at the interest rate. In the model with positive, constant marginal exploitation costs, the price rises at a lower rate than the interest. Because of the negligible importance of the constant marginal exploitation cost for marginal profit, the rate of change in price comes ever closer to the interest rate in course of time.

12 This condition corresponds fully with the procedure employed in section B. II of part one of this book: social welfare is operationalized through aggregate willingness to pay.

demand function, the curve for marginal gross social welfare contained in the Figure 32 is identical with the demand curve, if both conditions are met. That means the resource is valued by the market in one and the same way as by society.

- The production factors employed in exploiting the resource are supplied and demanded under competitive economic conditions. Moreover, no externalities arise in exploiting the resource. If both are true, then the curve of marginal exploitation costs employed for social welfare maximization corresponds with the marginal exploitation cost relevant to decisions on allocation through the market. As argued previously for the benefit side of using the preceding resource, it will be true, as for the cost side, that society's and the market's valuation are made with one and the same "vision."

- The social discount rate corresponds to the market interest rate. That would mean the rate at which the income from the resource rises over time (which indirectly guides the rate of exploitation) is identical in the maximum welfare time path and the competitive equilibrium time path. The equality of social discount rate and market interest rate mentioned here guarantees that market and society are employing one and the same "intertemporal exchange rate" when calculating future effects in terms of effects in the present. For this, it is *inter alia* necessary that the owners of the resource believe that their property rights are guaranteed in the long run. If they doubt that because they feel threatened by government measures or military conflicts, then they will discount the future effects at a rate that is too high from a welfare economics viewpoint.[13]

Of course, the previous conditions for the identity of the maximum welfare path of resource exploitation and the market equilibrium one are extremely restrictive. This is no surprising finding. After all, the static theory of externalities (and other areas of economics) presented in this book show that market equilibria are socially optimum only under very tight conditions. The advantage of this analysis is that knowing it opens the way to rational discussion of the possibilities of improving the welfare properties of market outcomes.

We show the "dynamic law" of the Hotelling Rule graphically. In doing so, we choose the positive version of the Hotelling Rule (i.e., Figure 33 shows the intertemporal path of price development in a competitive economy and the associated path of exploitation). Let us consider the second quadrant of the following illustration.

The price of the resource at the beginning of exploitation in period 0 is at an (endogenously determined) level $p(0)$. The marginal exploitation costs, assumed to be constant (and unchanging over time), are entered as MEC. $p(0) - MEC$ shows the marginal profit (marginal utilization cost) in the initial period. In line with the Hotelling Rule, the marginal profit rises over time at the private discount rate

---

13 Cf. Welsch (2008) on the connection between resource endowment and armed conflict.

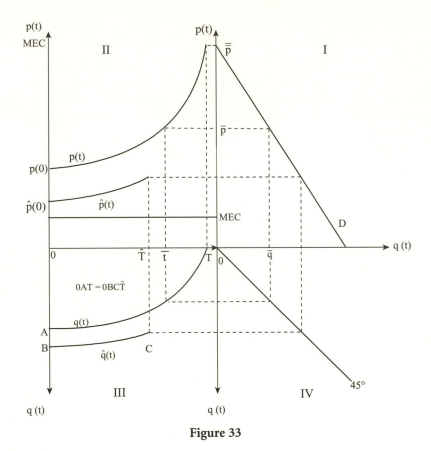

Figure 33

(the interest). This results in time path $p(t)$ for the price. Let us now look at the first quadrant. D denotes the demand curve (assumed to be unchanging over time) for the exhaustible resource considered. Along this curve, we read off the quantities demanded in each case at the prices obtained in the various periods. In period $\bar{t}$, for instance, price $\bar{p}$ applies, at which quantity $\bar{q}$ is produced and sold.

Using the 45-degree line in the fourth quadrant, we obtain in the third quadrant the time path of resource exploitation $q(t)$, which corresponds according to the Hotelling Rule with the price path $p(t)$. It shows for each point in time what quantity of the exhaustible resource is being exploited. The integral below the curve of exploitation quantities at specific points in time, measured from the beginning of utilization ($t = 0$) up to the point of exhaustion ($t = T$), shows the total stock of the resource. (If you drink a glass sip by sip, then the content of the glass corresponds with the sum of the amounts of the individual sips. The condition is that you must not spill any.) A look at the second quadrant shows that at the time of exhaustion T the price path defined by the Hotelling Rule has risen to the prohibitive price $\bar{\bar{p}}$ and ends there (caution: blind alley!). That describes the equilibrium prevailing at any point in time.

Because one can also imagine the individual points in time being extended into small periods of time, in this context the literature often also talks about a *period equilibrium* (flow equilibrium). Moreover, it becomes clear that as well as the period equilibrium in intertemporal resource exploitation a *stock equilibrium* has to be upheld too. The equilibrium time path is also characterized by the fact that the resource is fully exploited (no more and no less) at that point in time T at which the price reaches its prohibitive level $\overline{\overline{p}}$.

The alternative time path $\hat{p}(t)$ entered as an alternative to the Hotelling path $p(t)$ in the second quadrant of Figure 33 makes it clear that the price is not set arbitrarily in the initial period: if we start from an initial price $\hat{p}(0) < p(0)$, then the time path $\hat{p}(t)$, fixed by the marginal profit rising at the interest rate, leads to the position that in each period more is demanded (exploited) than with the higher time path $p(t)$. This is shown by the exploitation path $\hat{q}(t)$ in the third quadrant. Because along this path more is exploited at any point in time than on the Hotelling path $q(t)$, the resource is exhausted earlier if development $\hat{q}(t)$ is followed than if $q(t)$ is. We call the time of exhaustion $\hat{T}$, in case the relevant time path follows $\hat{q}(t)$. $\hat{T} < T$ holds. Because it is one and the same stock of resources that is being exploited along path $q(t)$ between $t = 0$ and T and on path $\hat{q}$ (t) between $t = 0$ and $\hat{T}$, the integral of the function $q(t)$ between the limits 0 and T must be identical to the integral of function $\hat{q}(t)$ between the limits 0 and $\hat{T}$. In Figure 33, areas $0AT$ and $0BC\hat{T}$ are equal in size. The price $\hat{p}(\hat{T})$ necessarily lies below the prohibitive price $p(T)$ so that a positive quantity $(\hat{q}(\hat{T}))$ is still being demanded when the resource has already been exhausted. Because the time path of prices starting from $\hat{p}(0)$ thus leads to a situation in which the demand is not met by any supply, it cannot be an equilibrium one. Also not equilibrium would be a price development (not shown in Fig. 33) in which resources would ultimately be left *in situ*, which would not (because of too high prices) be demanded any more. Under competitive conditions, all suppliers will endeavor, observing the interest rule discussed previously, to prevent being "left sitting" on their goods by exploiting the resource faster in the previous periods.[14]

In the literature, the empirical validity of the Hotelling Rule has frequently been investigated.[15] The findings are very predominantly negative. This need not surprise us too much in view of the restrictive construction of Hotelling's model. In particular, Hotelling assumed – as we explained previously – a given fixed stock of the resource. In reality, however, successes in *exploration* regularly led to a steady improvement from one period to another in the state of knowledge of available reserves. For a new state of knowledge, a larger reserve stock is then relevant. With greater reserves, however, the scarcity problem is abated, lowering the temporal marginal opportunity costs of resource exploitation, and thus also the Hotelling path. Similar effects that damp down or even overcompensate for the rise in utilization costs derive from *technical progress* in methods of exploitation. These lower the

14   The connections just discussed were the reason why previously, denoting the price at the initial period "$p(0)$", we made the rather sibylline comment that this price was "endogenously determined". (So that's that cleared up, too, then.)

15   Cf., e.g., Livernois (2009), Slade/Thille (2009).

marginal exploitation costs and/or raise reserve stocks, and raw materials in hitherto inaccessible positions or too-low concentrations become economically exploitable. It would be possible for every given set of such informational, technical, and economic conditions of exploitation of exhaustible resources to imagine a Hotelling path. The actual development, however, does not follow *one* such path, but would – with continual change in the informational, technical, and economic conditions – be conceivable as a movement *between various* Hotelling paths. Jokingly, we might say that the Hotelling Rule is a *self-destroying prophecy*: as soon as the price rise for the relevant resource arising along the Hotelling path emerges (or is even only anticipated by agents), these agents respond to this scarcity signal by many and varied activities of resource exploration and substitution, as well as encouragement of technical progress. This slows down the scarcity process so that a price rise of the amount corresponding to the Hotelling Rule does not come about. The previously addressed factors of "exploration" and "technical progress in exploitation procedures" have been exhaustively modeled in the literature. This is also true of many other determinants of the exploitation of exhaustible resources that are very important in practice but ignored in the simple Hotelling model. Among examples we might mention are differing quality of resource deposits, the dependency of exploitation costs on the stocks, the existence of "backstop technology,"[16] and uncertainty about future developments.

The continuing importance of the simple Hotelling model lies in the fact (apart from its pedagogical qualities) that it laid the foundation for these extensions of models important in practice.

III. Climate Policy in Light of the Economics of Exhaustible Resources

In part five of this book, global warming was described as a public bad. It is from this description that the theoretical economic literature taken as a basis there starts, and correspondingly, the problems of climate protection are portrayed as problems of the decentralized allocation of a purely public good and analyzed using game theory. But this description leaves one important aspect "off the table."

Climate problems arise from the emission of greenhouse gases, one of the most important of which is CO_2. That CO_2 emissions arise from burning fossil fuels is generally known, but plays absolutely no part in the previously mentioned game theoretic modeling. The allocation of the public good (bad) is treated in isolation; the fact that the emissions arise as a by-product of the consumption of private goods

16 By this, we mean procedures whereby nonexhaustible resources can be made utilizable in such a way as to overcome the finiteness of the exhaustible resources. Here we might think of two cases. Either the exhaustible resource is substituted directly by a nonexhaustible resource (e.g., oil by solar energy). Or raw materials used by society are rendered out of date by the use of nonexhaustible energy sources in a closed (and thus never-ending) recycling cycle.

(oil, coal) is irrelevant to the negotiation theory models. If, however, we bring the genesis of greenhouse gas emissions under the spotlight, then the climate problem can be interpreted as a market failure in the exploitation of exhaustible resources, at any rate to the extent that greenhouse gas emissions arise from burning fossil fuels. We can learn something about the structure of this problem through the economic theory of exhaustible resources briefly dealt with in the previous two sections.

Thus, we have seen previously that the market equilibrium time path of resource exploitation is, under particular (restrictive) conditions, identical with the welfare optimum time path.

Most divergences between the simple model addressed in the previous section and reality (or between the simple model and more complicated models that take account of those divergences) have the effect that the equilibrium exploitation of the resource runs faster than the socially optimum one. On the one hand, this may be because the socially optimum exploitation happens slower in the realistic model than in the basic ideal model. On the other hand, it may be the case that the equilibrium exploitation rate in the realistic model is higher than in the simple basic model. An example of the first of these phenomena is that the socially optimum exploitation slows down if negative externalities are incorporated in the model. The characteristic example of the second effect mentioned is poor property rights. They increase the equilibrium exploitation rate in comparison with the ideal model with fully protected rights.

There are, however, also complications of the basic model from which contrary tendencies may arise, to the extent that they may lower the rate of equilibrium resource exploitation (without affecting the rate of socially optimum exploitation). Thus, *market power* on resource markets may produce an effect in relation to exploitation rate that tends to compensate for the enhancement effect of negative externalities and poor property rights. Ultimately, in certain circumstances, the monopolist is known to be "the conservationist's friend" (*the Hotelling-Solow paradox*).[17]

As briefly indicated here, a glance at the literature on the economics of exhaustible resources will show that the market equilibrium exploitation path and the socially optimum exploitation path depart from each other once we allow model conditions that are more realistic than those of the simple basic model. Many flaws in the market mechanism have the effect that the market equilibrium implies too fast resource consumption by comparison with the socially optimum exploitation path. Because there are also contrary tendencies, it cannot be said with certainty which effect will have the upper hand. Moreover, the summary treatment (customary in the literature) of several of these departures is to be taken with a pinch of salt because it ignores possible interactions among the various reasons for

---

17 On the conditions mentioned previously, cf., e.g., Katayama/Abe (1998), with numerous further references.

market failure. In the literature, however, the prevailing opinion is that the uncorrected market mechanism takes too little account of the social concern for resource conservation.

If we accept this majority opinion, we must also believe that the CO_2 emission associated with the burning of fossil fuels would come about earlier at equilibrium than at the social optimum. This is particularly unfortunate for our discourse because the climate effect of CO_2 depends on the pollutant stock accumulated over time from contributions in the various periods. (We pointed this out specially in our previous treatment of European Union (EU) emissions trading; cf. section C.II.5 of part five of this book.)

It gets worse, though.[18] Let us assume – suppressing the objections presented in chapter B of part five of this book – that the community of states has recognized the fatal connections evident from the resource economics analysis and decided to slow down the consumption of fossil fuels. For this, it would undertake programs that "accelerate" in course of time, for instance, a dynamically patterned "green tax." The rising tax rate would be supposed to increasingly suppress the *demand* for fossil fuels. This should stop the market system's trend suggested previously to exploit resources too fast and emit pollutants too quickly. However, in such programs, you cannot write the bill without the host – and that means the resource *suppliers*! If they anticipate that the noose placed around their necks by "green politics" will be pulled ever tighter in course of time, they will on certain conditions[19] escape this imposition in a way that will make "green politics" reach the opposite of what it intends. Because the profits to be obtained in the future by exploiting fossil fuels are reduced due to the "green tax," it will pay resource suppliers to *anticipate* that exploitation. The suppliers' market reaction will, in sum, mean that the intertemporal price path for the exhaustible resource initially runs flatter than without political measures. The quantities exploited early will thus rise, as will the CO_2 emissions caused by their burning – a *paradox* of green climate policy.[20]

The argument given previously using the example of a dynamic green tax brings out one *general principle* of intertemporal profit maximization: if storm clouds on the temporal horizon threaten the profitability of the exhaustible resource, then the producers will take refuge under the protective roof of "immediate" resource exploitation. This effect is often illustrated in the resource economics textbooks by the example of development of a *backstop technology* (anticipated by resource

18   Cf. Sinn (2007), (2008).
19   Cf. Sinn (2008).
20   To avoid misunderstandings, the paradox does not arise with climate policy interventions that make constant claims over time (e.g., resource taxation at a constant tax rate). The "trick" is when tightening exceeds a certain proportion and is correctly anticipated by the resource owners. The environmental policy regulation assumed in the previous argument, intensifying monotonically over time, would presumably not necessarily meet the criterion of welfare optimality. Cf., e.g., Hoel and Kverndokk (1996) on the intertemporal course of optimum emission tax rates in an integrated climate and resource economics model.

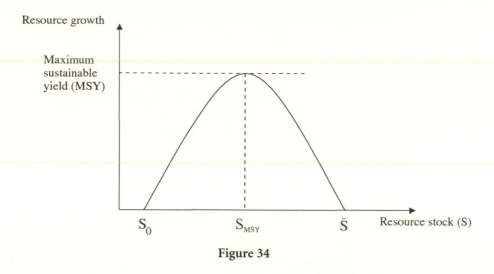

Figure 34

owners). It also applies, however, to any other development that makes resource stocks less valuable in the future. Developments that lower the profitability of future resource exploitation are thus very similar to expropriations threatened in the future and have the same consequence for resource suppliers: those who perceive the developments at issue will prefer to exploit the resource in the present. This line of thought, presented previously using the example of a green tax, can thus be extended to other variants of green policy such as promoting the use of renewable energy sources, better isolation of buildings, energy-saving light bulbs, and hugging instead of heating.

B. Renewable Resources

I. Bioeconomic Foundations

As explained previously, renewable resources differ from exhaustible ones in that the former can be increased in a time frame of relevance to human planning. The growth of the resource stock depends on many determinants, for instance, environmental conditions. In the biological literature, the size of the stock itself is treated as a central determinant of growth. For the relationship between these two quantities, it is (ideally) typical that for a positive regeneration rate a particular nonzero minimum population must be present. Starting from this minimum size of the stock (S_0), growth initially increases as the stock does, then falls, and finally at the saturation level of the stock ($\bar{S}$) reaches the value zero again. Figure 34 illustrates these connections.

We can see that in contrast with the circumstances obtained for exhaustible resources, with renewable ones it is perfectly possible to harvest a particular quantity in each period without reducing the stock. For this, one must "merely" observe the restriction that the quantity harvested may not be above the natural net growth of the stock. On the basis of the connection presented previously between growth in the stock and size of stock, the sustainably harvestable yield depends on stock size. In Figure 34, maximum growth is attained at a stock of S_{MSY}. This quantity is the *maximum sustainably harvestable yield* (maximum sustainable yield).

In harvesting a renewable resource, two different kinds of cost arise, namely, harvesting cost and utilization cost. Let us take as an example fisheries. Every fish caught causes costs to arise proportionately for building a fleet with the appropriate equipment, crew, etc. These catching costs can be called, using the more general term that also embraces fisheries, "harvesting costs." In addition, costs are incurred because the fish caught today can no longer be caught tomorrow and will no longer be able to contribute to regeneration of the relevant stock. These temporal opportunity costs are called "utilization costs." In particular, we point out that the term "utilization cost" employed in the area of renewable resources coincides with the term "utilization cost" in the theory of exhaustible resources to the extent that it denotes future scarcity effects of today's exploitation decisions. These consequences arise, however, in a different guise for renewable resources than for exhaustible ones. For the latter, the point is exclusively that a unit consumed today will, in view of the fixed total stock, diminish future consumption possibilities by precisely that unit. This aspect also applies in the case of renewable resources.[21] With renewable resources, however, it is *additionally* the case that today's consumption of one unit reduces consumption in the future by the biomass that today's catch would have contributed to the regeneration of the resource.

II. The Open Access Problem

For many renewable resources, the fact is that they are harvested in a context without precisely specified property rights.[22] In the extreme case, there is no institutional framework at all, and the resource belongs to whoever first takes control of it. Thus, fishes in the high seas belong to no one (everyone?) and whoever catches a fish can make economic use of it.[23] The circumstances so described are termed an "open access regime" in the literature.

It is immediately clear that open access regimes lead to severe misallocations. For a view trained in general microeconomics, it is clear that the relevant resource

---

21 Because the renewable resources, in contrast with exhaustible resources, have a limited life expectancy even without human exploitation, this intertemporal effect has a smaller temporal reach with the former than with the latter.

22 To a smaller extent, this is also true of exhaustible resources.

23 International fisheries agreements running counter to that are full of gaps. Moreover, they are a reaction to the problem described previously and are thus not taken into account in explaining it. Alongside the usual textbook example of fisheries, the problem of misallocation because of the absence of allocation of property rights is particularly virulent in connection with the preservation of biodiversity. Cf., e.g., Goeschl/Igliori (2006), Goeschl/Swanson (2000).

ought to be so exploited that the market price to be obtained for it covers both the marginal harvesting costs and the marginal utilization costs. The individual fisher in an open access regime has, however, no incentive to take the utilization costs into account in his decision on the amount of his activity. He will instead extend his activity until it meets the price of the marginal harvesting costs.[24] It is not attractive to the individual decision maker to refrain from fishing with the object of leaving part of the stock behind for future possibilities of utilization and for the sake of its future contribution to the growth of the stock. For in an open access regime, the actor will be unable to secure the return on his reticence for himself. Rather, he has to expect that other fishermen will today or tomorrow benefit from his self-restraint. All he would have done then would be to produce a positive externality in favor of his colleagues at the expense of private opportunity costs. Putting it differently, fishermen in an open access regime are in a *prisoner's dilemma*.[25] It would be best in the general interest for all to exercise some restraint in catching in order to guarantee the stock of the resource from which they all live. Irrespective of whether the others restrain themselves or not, it is best for the individual decision maker, in terms of his private optimization, not to impose any restraint on himself. Because this incentive applies to all, the stocks will be overfished (sometimes to the point of extermination). At equilibrium, things go badly for everyone: the fishermen, the consumers of fish – not to mention the fish themselves.[26] After the misallocation sketched out here had been worked out in the economic literature, the question naturally arose of possible ways to correct it. These can be divided into two subissues:

- First, we have to ask what the *objective* of the corrective activity is to be. Here the obvious thing would seem to be to stabilize the stock at a level at which the maximum sustainable harvest is obtained. This objective of resource policy plays the predominant part in the scientific (especially biological) literature and the attempts at governmental regulation influenced by it. However, economists have pointed out that the point is perhaps less to maximize the physical flow of biomass harvested over time. Instead, it is the net contribution accruing to welfare from the harvest over time that should be maximized. This rather different objective leads notably to two trends departing from the maximum sustainable yield. On the one hand, economic analyses discount effects lying in the future to the time of decision. This sets up a tendency toward an optimum fish stock that is smaller than the stock associated with the maximum sustainable yield. On this view, it is worthwhile to consume stock in the present to some

---

24 Here conditions of a competitive economy are assumed.
25 The incentive structure resembles the one discussed in part five of this book in connection with global environmental problems.
26 More exhaustive presentations of the open access problem addressed only briefly here, including many empirical references, can be found in Tahvonen/Kuuluvainen (2000) and Wilen (2000).

extent and thus live at the expense of the future because the present benefits associated therewith weigh heavier in a cash value calculation than the lost possibilities of utilization in the future. The falling marginal utilities regularly assumed in the models prevent this preference for the present from becoming immeasurably strong in its effects.

On the other hand, however, for the economic optimization of harvest figures, the harvesting costs are also taken into account. In particular, it makes sense to assume that the harvesting costs depend not only on the quantity harvested, but also on the size of the stock from which the catch is made. In light of this consideration, it is plausible that the costs of any considered unit of catch are smaller the bigger the fish stock is. For the economic optimum, these circumstances lead to a tendency to leave the stock at a higher level than would be necessary for the maximum sustainable yield. Refraining from reducing the stock to the biologically most productive level is rewarded by savings on the costs of catching.

We can thus see that the economic consideration differs from the "biological" one (particularly) on two major points. These two differences compensate each other qualitatively, however, in terms of their effect on the differences between the economically optimum stock of the natural resource and the stock with the highest biological productivity. Of course, how far the two opposing tendencies actually compensate each other *quantitatively* to such an extent that the economic optimum is close to the biologically most productive stock cannot be said at the level of abstractness of discussion chosen here.

• The second question relates to the choice of instruments with which the equilibrium misallocation in the open access regime is to be corrected. In the literature on fisheries and much government regulation based on that literature, administrative rules play a prominent part. This means that such things as limitation of the times when harvesting the relevant natural resource is allowed (fishing seasons). Moreover, there are many restrictions regulating catching capacity and/or catching techniques, or the amount caught. From an economic viewpoint, such "command and control" strategies are inefficient, and their effect doubtful.[27]

In the economic literature, levies on the catch or transferable catch rights are favored. The economic debate on the instruments for protecting renewable resources and exploiting them efficiently is extremely analogous with the debate on instruments for protecting the environment. For the reasons explained in part three of this book, economists, chiefly on efficiency grounds, favor compensation payments, levies, and transferable rights over administrative measures.[28]

---

27 For more details, see Tahvonen/Kuuluvainen (2000) and Wilen (2000).

28 Outside the fisheries context, cf. the case studies done by Engel/López/Palmer (2006) and Engel/Palmer (2008) for the field of forestry in Indonesia.

C. Sustainable Development

Where I actually went was the locksmith's store, which is Frazer and Sons, on Seventy-Ninth.

. . .

I said, "I have a question that I was just wondering."
He said, "Shoot."
"Shoot?"
"Shoot. Go ahead. Ask."
"Are you Frazer, or are you Son?"
"I'm Grandson, actually. My grandfather started the shop."
"Cool."
"But I suppose I'm also Son, since my dad ran things when he was alive. I guess I'm Frazer, too, since my son works here during the summers."

　　– Jonathan Safran Foer, *Extremely Loud and Incredibly Close*, London, 2005

I. Introduction

The Chief Superintendent of Mines of Freiberg, Germany, Carl von Carlowitz, proclaimed about the year 1700, we are told, that it was anything but sensible to cut down more wood in the forest than grows back. The fascination of this insight remained confined to remote forestry circles for nearly three centuries. Since the Brundtland Commission interpreted the principle universally in its famous final report[29] and labeled it "sustainable development," everything is different: the term has had a unique career in ordinary language usage. Today you can find hardly a company or a social institution that does not claim to support the goal of sustainable development. In 2002, a "World Summit on Sustainable Development" was held in Johannesburg, involving the highest representatives of many states and organizations. However, we have to admit that comprehensive agreement on the goal of sustainability exists only as long as the term is defined in the most general way. The wide-ranging but most unspecific concept among the public has both advantages and drawbacks. A general concept sends out a signal to which the most varied groups and interests can initially at least respond positively. The general concept has – something we are familiar with from the formulas deliberately couched in general terms in party political programs of principle – a "grab all" character. Various tendencies that move at least to some extent in the same direction can be channeled and together develop a political undertow effect. This initially integrative effect then loses meaning if the troops marching behind the same banner are so heterogeneous that the coalition breaks up as soon as the vaguely formulated goal is made specific and has to be implemented.

---

29 World Commission on Environment and Development, *Our Common Future*, Oxford, 1987.

Apart from these considerations (which could be taken further in political and economic terms), a vague concept of sustainability is unsuited to scientific treatment. If science is to give advice on the measurement of sustainability, the design of a sustainability policy, and the critical assessment of that policy, then the concept of sustainability has to be defined as sharply and operationally as possible. What is common to the numerous different definitions of sustainability is the basic idea that "something" ought to be preserved (i.e., increase or remain constant over time, but at any rate not decline). The time frame envisaged here stretches far beyond that of everyday economic and political decisions. A typical feature of the idea of sustainability is always the intergenerational view.

What this "something" actually is that sustainable development cannot let decline has been the object of the most varied views in the literature. One important trend interprets the "preservation" aspect addressed here of the sustainability idea in such a way that social welfare must for sustainable development be at least constant over time. Putting it a bit closer to the ground, the demand becomes that future generations should not have things worse than us.[30] Another (equally important!) part of the literature understands the demand that "something" must be preserved as meaning that the capital stock available to humanity must at least remain conserved. Behind this is the intention to leave future generations *possibilities* of development that are no worse than our own. Within the group of capital stock – oriented sustainability concepts, three main currents can be discerned. They differ in the underlying concept of capital.

We briefly present the welfare-oriented and then the capital-oriented concepts of sustainability. We go on to discuss basic features of sustainability policy and incentive problems of sustainable development.

II. Sustainability as Nondeclining Welfare

In allocation theory (welfare economics), the aim of every policy is seen as maximizing social welfare. The concept of internalization of externalities discussed in part two of this book is one application of this idea. Applying the idea to the question of sustainability means that for sustainable development, welfare must remain at least constant over time.[31] One well-known and justified criticism of this

---

30 The preservation aspect is rooted in a Rawlsian norm of intergenerational justice. Cf. the monumental Rawls (1971), and, e.g., Asheim/Buchholz (2003), Baumgärtner/Faber/Schiller (2006), Bretschger/Pittel (2005), Buchholz/Dasgupta/Mitra (2005), Helm/Simonis (2001).

31 Consequentially, the concept of sustainable development plays an important part in modern growth theory. Even the neoclassical growth theory strongly developed as long ago as the 1960s paid intensive attention to the question of the durability of growth processes. Of course, this meant "merely" maintaining the *standard of living* in a very narrow sense of the word for today's tastes. In particular, the ecological reference central today is absent. And the word *sustainability* itself had not yet become a magic one.

interpretation is that welfare is conceptually and empirically hard to measure. Economics endeavors in the following ways, among others, to cope with these difficulties.

Following Sir John Hicks' (1946, p. 172) definition, an individual's *period income* is the maximum consumption he can have without detriment to his assets. Here durability is a component of the concept of income. It is accordingly not surprising that Hicks' concept has been transferred from the individual to the social context and used as a welfare indicator when discussing sustainability.[32]

To make the idea concrete, we have to derive the calculation of the sustainable national income from the net national product (NNP). For this, the NNP has to be diminished not only by writing off the reproducible capital, but also by write-offs from the natural capital.[33] To be sure, it is one thing to analyze a concept of income purified on the Hicks pattern in theoretical model terms, and quite a different one to fill that concept with life empirically. As Partha Dasgupta (2001, p. 154) whimsically observes, the relevant literature has less to do with the "green net national product" than the "green Hamiltonian." What he means is that such writers are getting high on the aesthetics of mathematical description rather than worrying about the pressing problems of humankind.[34] Economics Nobel Laureate of 1987 Robert Solow (1993) instead sees this approach as "an almost practical step toward sustainability." However, the practical endeavors meet with criticism because the selection of corrections made to the net national product and their weighting is not done on an adequately sound theoretical basis. A particularly controversial point about making the concept practical is the necessary monetization of ecological effects.

One concept for defining social welfare that has received much attention in economics only recently is the *happiness approach*.[35] This approach uses representative surveys to find the population's self-perceived contentedness with their lives. Here the influence of individual determinants (e.g., income, employment status) and social ones (e.g., social product per capita, inflation rate) on happiness is estimated econometrically. This approach has not so far – as far as the author is aware – played any significant part in the sustainability debate. It will be for future research to ask how far it can be made more useful for operationalizing the sustainability concept in the sense of nondeclining welfare. It is presumably possible to

32　This theme in the literature goes back to Weitzman (1976). From the wealth of contributions, we would single out Asheim (1997) and Hartwick (1990).

33　There are many other objections to the suitability of the social product as a welfare indicator than those relevant to our discussion about neglect of consumption of natural capital. However, we cannot go into these here for space reasons.

34　Hamiltonians are a special class of differential equation with applications, especially in broad areas of physics (but also in advanced resource economics models).

35　Cf., e.g., Frey/Stutzer (2002a, b), with many other references. Welsch/Kühling (2009) use the happiness approach to make an economic evaluation of environmental goods.

estimate the effect of natural resources on happiness just as has already been done for other determinants. This also opens up the possibility of quantifying trade-offs between the levels of individual determinants (e.g., income and environmental quality improvements) at constant happiness. The first steps in this direction have been taken by Rehdanz/Maddison (2005), (2008), Schneider/Wagner (2006), and Welsch (2002, 2007). Here, in particular, the connection between specific forms of environmental pollution and contentedness with one's life is estimated econometrically. For the sustainability context, the "resource basis" of these approaches would have to be expanded. It would be still more important to incorporate the intertemporal aspect that is basic to sustainability.

Both national income in a sense purified in accordance with Hicks' idea and contentedness with life in the sense of the happiness approach are one-dimensional indicators of welfare. To that extent, they are better suited to assessing the sustainability of a development than the numerous multidimensional indicators offered in the literature.[36] For the basic differences between the two approaches, they are also linked to the extent that empirical happiness studies have shown income to be a major determinant of contentedness with one's life, alongside other important factors.[37]

One important difference between the two approaches just mentioned, however, is that happiness measures a subjective factor, whereas subjective and objective factors enter together into the calculation of income.[38]

Irrespective of whether income or happiness is employed as the measure of welfare, the following should be borne in mind: to operationalize the concept, it is necessary not only to measure welfare in the present, but also to estimate the consequences of today's activities for the welfare of people living in future. The needed predictive capacity for this has to be greater the farther forward into the future we look. In the literature on the concept of sustainable income, considerable efforts have been made to solve this problem. Rules have been sought that if complied with in the present would be sufficient to ensure nondeclining welfare in future. These would be a number of variants of "Hartwick's Rule" (Hartwick 1977) that the income from natural resources must be reinvested in anthropogenic capital.

---

36 Cf., e.g., Atkinson et al. (2002). Here there is no longer any intertemporal comparability as long as even only two components of the multipart indicator system move in different directions in course of time. Ebert/Welsch (2004) developed, on the basis of the *social choice* approach, a criterion for choosing environmental indicators. Cf. also Walz (2000).

37 For a more differentiated look at the importance of income to happiness, see Welsch (2003, 2007).

38 The statement that subjective elements enter into the calculation of income may surprise some. What we mean is that income comes about as a product of equilibrium factor prices and quantities. These are formed on factor markets. Because factor demand is a derived demand, end-product markets also play a part. For what happens on markets, *inter alia* the preferences of suppliers and demanders are important. Preferences are subjective.

However, a general criterion for sustainability in the sense of nondeclining welfare cannot yet be derived from these rules.[39]

III. Sustainability as Constant Capital

1. Weak Sustainability

This notion of sustainability is based on the idea that guaranteeing the welfare of future generations depends on humanity's whole capital stock. By this stock, we mean an aggregate value made up in particular of the capital made by people and natural capital. First, the aggregation of such different components of capital presumes that they are more or less mutually replaceable in their function of guaranteeing welfare. Second, it must be possible to determine the "exchange rate" at which units of one particular type of capital can be converted into units of another type in a sustainability equivalent way.[40]

As we already know from the discussion of a "net welfare product" for the measurement of flows of relevance to welfare, with this approach a sort of net asset calculation (sizes of stocks of relevant to welfare) would lead to a single figure. The indicator would then to the fullest extent meet the demand for interpretability. It would without further ado make it possible to diagnose the sustainability (or not, as the case may be) of a development and compare various developments for their degree of sustainability. However, it is obvious that severe problems of principle and empirical evaluation are associated with this procedure. It is extremely difficult to find the "clearing prices" between various capital goods necessary for this approach in connection with sustainability. Because the prices of goods depend on the course of an economy's developmental path, employing the prices actually observable might lead into error if the path being followed by the economy at the time of observation is not sustainable. To be correct, the "exchange rates" between various capital goods would have to be evaluated along a sustainable development pathway. However, the properties of this path are unknown. Evaluating the total capital stock is supposed to be the thing that makes the concept of sustainability operational in the first place. Strictly speaking, then, the construction of an indicator for aggregate capital stock in connection with sustainable development requires the presence of the very information that the indicator is supposed to reveal. It would need abilities worthy of no less than a Baron von Münchhausen[41] to get out of this vicious circle.

---

39 Cf. the critical assessments in Asheim/Buchholz/Withagen (2003), Pezzey/Toman (2002) with many further references. An interesting empirical study of the consequences of following or ignoring Hartwick's Rule for practical politics can be found in Hamilton/Ruta/Tajibaeva (2006).

40 Atkinson/Hamilton (2007) and Markandya/Pedroso-Galinato (2007) summarize recent theoretical developments with this approach and empirical estimates. For a pessimistic view of the substitution, see Ayres (2007).

41 Baron von Münchhausen ("The Baron of Lies") is a somewhat doubtful hero of German folklore. In the story alluded to previously, he claimed, "I fell with my horse in a puddle of mud which

2. Strong Sustainability

According to the concept of strong sustainability, it is impossible to consider humanity's total capital stock as an aggregate. Humanity's total capital is instead to be seen as a vector containing components strictly separate from each other. A particularly noteworthy thing about this approach is the insuperable separation between capital made by people and natural capital. The sustainability requirement in the form of nondeclining capital stock here means that each component contained in the vector must at least remain constant. This approach is supposed to work against the danger that parts of humanity's assets that cannot be compared to each other because they have different dimensions are set off against each other. Otherwise, it might come about that natural capital gets "crushed under the wheels" because of substitution by manmade capital in the course of economic development. However, it must be admitted that the concept of strong sustainability cannot get by without a high degree of aggregation. Otherwise, the list of the specific types of capital to be conserved with a view to sustainability would lead to a jungle of perhaps thousands (millions?) of indicators pointing in various directions. The concept of sustainability would then disappear in the white noise of the enormous system of indicators, which would hardly permit a comparison of different situations in terms of the degree of sustainability that they have each reached.

3. Critical Sustainability

As a compromise between these two polar approaches, the concept of "critical natural capital" has been suggested in the literature.[42] This requires that particular parts of the natural capital stock remain physically conserved. This feature (borrowed from the concept of strong sustainability) is intended to guarantee that the physical minimal conditions necessary for survival are not harmed. For all components of humanity's assets present over and above this minimal endowment, the rules of the weak sustainability concept apply.

This approach does not avoid the problems explained previously of the two polar approaches, although it does presumably make them more bearable in combination. Thus, in the context of critical sustainability, it is probably easier for humanity to put up with mistakes being made in calculating the assets for the purposes of the weak sustainability concept. After all, respect for the safe minimum standards at least guarantees that the mistakes will not take on fatal proportions. However, the problems of the incomprehensibility of a multidimensional system of physical indicators are mitigated by the fact that this system is not, in contrast with strong sustainability, applied in critical sustainability to the whole of the assets, but only to the parts of them regarded as vital to survival. The restriction of freedom is correspondingly smaller, although it can never entirely be avoided (and is also

turned out to be surprisingly deep. I was on the verge of drowning and my horse was bound to fare no better. However, with my strong arms I succeeded in pulling myself out by taking a firm grip on my pigtail. (In the process, I saved my horse, too, clutching it firmly between my knees.)"

42   Exhaustively on this, see Neumayer (2004, 2010).

deliberately accepted here) if physical restrictions are to be interpreted as policy imperatives. Of course, it will be controversial what the minimal requirements on humanity's capital stock to guarantee humanity's survival actually are. Science may provide assistance here, but cannot take the decision away from society.

In its emphasis on standards fixed in advance, the concept of critical sustainability shows remarkable analogy with the concept of standard-oriented environmental policy explained previously in part three of this book. As explained there, the environmental policy objective is exogenous in this tradition of thought (in contrast with that of internalization presented in part two) (i.e., here set "extraeconomically"). The role of economics is confined to developing strategies for reaching this goal at minimum cost. Correspondingly, the "ecological crash barriers" in the system of critical sustainability can be regarded as determined extraeconomically. The role of economics is confined to the search for strategies, the pursuit of which can guarantee compliance with these restrictions at minimum loss of welfare.

In the mainstream of environmental economics literature, the question addressed previously of the minimum cost strategy for reaching a given environmental policy goal is investigated in the framework of a static conceptual structure. This means that the technical conditions underlying the economic activity observed (e.g., emission abatement technology) are assumed as given. Because of the long-term nature of the sustainability concept, however, the question has to be broadened if the basic idea of standard-oriented environmental policy is to be transferred to the sustainability context. For in the long term, the point is not just to employ given technologies of resource protection optimally. Instead, it must further be asked how a sustainability policy has to be patterned in order to incentivize the development of resource-bearing technologies in satisfactory fashion. Correspondingly, the more recent literature has shifted its focus from looking at static efficiency properties to their capacities for inducing resource-saving technical progress.[43]

IV. Sustainability Policy

In this section, we want to consider the possibilities for government policy to promote sustainable development.[44] Here we are particularly interested in how far this sort of sustainability policy differs from an environmental and resource policy

---

43   In chapter E of part four, we present such approaches, even if without direct reference to the problem of sustainable development. On the importance of technological progress for sustainable development, cf., e.g., Bretschger (2005), Kemfert/Vollebergh (2005), Lehmann-Waffenschmidt (2006).

44   Other decision makers than the state are not barred from putting themselves at the service of sustainable development. In the literature, the ecologically (and socially) responsible conduct of firms plays an important part in this context (*corporate responsibility*). For more, cf., e.g., Ziegler/Schröder/Rennings (2007) and the contributions to the "Symposium on Corporate Social Responsibility and the Environment" in the *Review of Environmental Economics and Policy*, Vol. 2 (2008), pp. 219–275. As in other parts of this book (and as justified in chapter A of part three), we confine the concept of policy (here sustainability policy) to governmental efforts.

oriented by the criterion of welfare maximization, such as has hitherto characterized the presentation in this book. This aspect is significant for an assessment of the sustainability idea as a separate paradigm of relevance to practice.

For a discussion of the policy relevance of the sustainability idea, a comparison between sustainable development paths and socially optimum paths is not enough. Instead, we must include in our considerations the fact that the situation we find in reality (in the terminology of model theory, the equilibrium) does not coincide with the social optimum (see section A.4 of the first part of this book). We want to first go through all conceivable patterns of the resource consequences of sustainable, maximum welfare, and market equilibrium allocation.[45] Let the idea of sustainable development be represented here by the minimum stock of a renewable resource, R^{sus}. Let the market equilibrium stock be R^* and the welfare optimum R^{**}. We start with the case where, at equilibrium, no complete internalization of externalities has been brought about and open access problems exist. This means the equilibrium resource stock will be below the socially optimum one: ($R^* < R^{**}$). We have chosen this situation in order to work out the possibly differing "requirement strength" of the welfare maximization concept and the sustainability concept on economic policy interventions in the market. The stock that is barely still compatible with sustainable development may lie either below the equilibrium stock, or between the equilibrium stock and the optimum welfare stock, or above the optimum welfare stock. We distinguish the three possible cases in terms of their consequences for sustainability policy:

Case I: $R^{sus} \leq R^{*}$[46]

In this situation, the objective of sustainability implies no binding restriction on the economic process. The minimum resource stock to be conserved for sustainability will not be undershot, even at the uncorrected (or only inadequately corrected) market equilibrium. In this case, then, no special "sustainability policy" is necessary. That the demand for welfare maximization requires a correction to the market equilibrium allocation by internalizing externalities is irrelevant from the viewpoint of sustainability.

Case II: $R^* < R^{sus} \leq R^{**}$[47]

In this case, the sustainability requirement that the resource stock R^{sus} must unconditionally be respected over time is infringed at market equilibrium development of the economy. However, the departure between the market equilibrium development and the optimum welfare development in relation to resource stock

---

45   For the sake of simplicity, we assume that the three allocations mentioned here are known. On the relationship between welfare maximization and sustainability, cf. also Heal (2003).

46   We formulated the three cases constructed statically. In a dynamic context, case I is present where the minimum stock of the resource is never above the equilibrium stock.

47   The dynamic formulation of case II is: the minimum stock is above the equilibrium stock in at least one period, but never exceeds the socially optimum stock.

R is at least as large. The requirement that a welfare-maximizing policy places on the economic process is thus more intensive than that from sustainable development. In this case, the concern for sustainability is "suspended" in the restrictive policy (aiming at maximizing welfare). If welfare maximization is regarded as the traditional policy objective and the upholding of sustainability as the new one, then the genesis of the new objective has no policy consequences. This changes with the move to the third case.

Case III: $R^{**} < R^{sus}$[48]

Here the principle of sustainability requires a bigger stock of the natural resource than the objective of social welfare maximization. Sustainability puts the strongest requirements on the economic process; that is, a sustainability policy is being called for that is tighter than the maximum welfare policy and, in particular, includes internalization of all externalities. It is only in this case that the requirement of sustainability becomes significant as a factor shaping social development.

It must be clearly stressed that the sustainability principle implies restrictions on the economic process that cannot be derived from the preferences of the present generation. These preferences, including the time preference, are already contained in the social welfare function. It is obvious that an extremely restrictive policy in this sense would meet with severe resistance to its implementation. In democratic societies, it is difficult to pursue policy against the citizens' preferences, and dictatorships are no guarantee of sustainability either. Unfortunately, it thus turns out that the chances of implementing a separate sustainability policy are at their worst precisely where it would be most urgently required in the interest of conserving humanity's life support system.

However, preferences (and the technologies that enable the sustainability principle to be achieved) are not constant. Preferences may change in social discourse and in the course of the competition of ideas, and technologies may be adapted through the induction of technical progress (even though (similarly) not to an infinite extent). It cannot then be ruled out that through social discourse, the ethical quality of the present generation may be improved (in the form of a higher sense of responsibility for future generations) and the costs of a sustainability policy lowered through the induction of resource-saving technological progress. If that succeeded, then the welfare function and the intergenerational welfare transformation curve would change in such ways as to blunt the conflict between the objective of social welfare maximization and of sustainability.[49] Technically speaking, consciousness-raising and resource-sparing technical progress would shift a situation in the area of what we call case III into the area of case II, due to increasing R^{**}.

48   Formulated dynamically, this runs: there exists at least one period for which the minimum stock exceeds the socially optimum stock.

49   The intergenerational transformation curve shows the maximum welfare in the future compatible with any given welfare level in the present.

In discussing the power of technological progress that may potentially shift the intergenerational welfare transformation curve, economics can fall back on some degree of tradition. For the transformation of preferences, however, the analytical (and policy-advising) arsenal of economic theory is more poorly equipped. Economics has extremely predominantly explained changes in individuals' decisions by changes in the restrictions decision makers act under, at constant preferences. Changes in the preferences themselves were, however, treated marginally at best.[50] We are not seeking to talk up at a new version of the attempt to create new socialist man (in this case, "new ecological man"). Nor do we want to fall in behind the call of American preachers to "do the right thing!" Instead, we want to encourage economists to devote more study to the effects of given changes in preferences (step one), and beyond that, also develop economic approaches to explain changes in preferences (step two). Here collaboration between economists and psychologists would be particularly desirable. The enormous social policy explosiveness of the conflict in case III previously between maximizing social welfare and sustainability should be reason enough for the discipline to move in this direction.

Having asked how intensively a sustainability policy or a welfare-oriented environmental and resource policy would change uncorrected market equilibrium allocations, let us now look at the means that can, according to the criteria of the two rival ideals, be employed to achieve the objective. Here the two concepts show only slightly differing implications. The endeavor for efficiency that dominates welfare-oriented environmental and resource economics is not in contradiction with the guiding principle of sustainable development. On the contrary, inefficient instrumentalization of environmental and resource policy would waste resources that would be lost for future generations, too. At least in the long term, moreover, it is presumably the case that more ambitious objectives of protecting the environment and resources become implementable in social policy terms if these goals can be achieved with smaller sacrifices. Thus, many authors see the intensified and more consistent use of the instruments proposed by traditional environmental and resource economics as a particularly good way of following the new ideal (sustainable development).[51] This also explains why authors strongly committed to the principle of sustainability prefer incentive-oriented instruments (e.g., ecological tax reform) in much the same way as this overwhelmingly happens in welfare-oriented environmental and resource economics.[52]

Anyway, a special affinity can be noted between particular sustainability conceptions and particular features of the range of instruments offered by welfare-oriented environmental and resource economics. Thus, strategies for internalizing externalities are, as explained previously in part two, especially compatible with the weak sustainability concept. Both require an economic valuation of losses in the area

50   See 1992 Economics Nobel Laureate Gary Becker (1993) for a discussion of this approach.

51   We discuss these issues in parts two and three of this book.

52   Of course, all the currents in the literature ought not to be simply lumped together here. It is hard to make general statements, and there are departures from the trend just noted.

of natural resources. The internalization of externalities as sole policy strategy is compatible with the critical sustainability concept only if the physical restrictions defined by the ecological corridor are complied with. If not, the internalization must be supplemented by corresponding quantitative restrictions.[53] The internalization concept is least compatible with the idea of strong sustainability. The monetization of natural capital implicit in internalization is foreign in nature to the idea of strong sustainability.

The "standard-oriented" instruments discussed in part three of this book do correspond to the concept of strong sustainability. Within the category of efficient standard-oriented approaches, one could presumably derive from the critical sustainability concept's strict orientation to protecting stocks a preference for quantity-controlling over price-controlling approaches. As explained previously, transferable discharge permits, for instance, have higher *ecological precision* than emission taxes. This finding ought to be generalizable to deciding between price-controlling and quantity-controlling approaches to managing substance flow. In general, it should follow from the central position of the long-term aspect from the viewpoint of sustainable development that the capacity of environmental policy instruments to induce resource-saving technological progress should play a key role in the apparatus for evaluating environmental policy instruments. For economists, it is only "natural" to use economic approaches for reaching a given goal – including sustainability. Thus, the list of guiding principles of action in Tietenberg/Lewis (2009, pp. 594–599), intended to promote the transition to a sustainable economy, shows only a few (and, if at all, in the fourth point) differences from a traditional welfare economics list[54]:

- *Full Cost Principle* (internalization principle). All users of environmental resources should bear the full costs caused by them.
- *Cost-Effectiveness Principle* (cost minimization principle). Any environmental policy should be carried out cost effectively so as to achieve maximum environmental quality for the given expenditure.
- *Property Rights Principle* (ownership principle). Property rights in natural resources should be allotted in such a way as to encourage responsible action.
- *Sustainability Principle* (intergenerationality). The present utilization of resources should come about in such a way as to be compatible with the needs

53 The need for supplementation would disappear if the (negative) value of breaking a restriction were set at "infinite." In the example of a Pigou tax, this would mean that the tax rate would tend toward infinity if the economic development were threatening to come into conflict with the restriction. A Pigou tax on this pattern would admittedly go beyond the framework of the traditional internalization idea (oriented toward social optimization) if a socially optimum welfare development were (precariously) to infringe the restrictions of critical sustainability.

54 The decision whether there is really a closeness here between the practical implications of sustainability and welfare maximization or merely the inability of an economist trained in welfare theory to see anything else in a new paradigm than his traditional model, may be left to our esteemed readers to make.

of future generations. Maximization of the present value of utility flows should be a guide for action only to the extent that it serves to choose among various allocations that meet the sustainability criterion.

* *Information Principle* (principle of "enlightened consumer sovereignty"). All members of society should be as well informed as possible about the ecological consequences of present decisions so that they can collaborate in the transition to sustainable development.

In conclusion, we want to point to one further piece of relatedness of the two rival paradigms in terms of the environmental and resource policies that they imply. Just like welfare-oriented policy, sustainability policy will become increasingly aware of the limitations of national possibilities of action. Quite irrespective of whether global environmental and resource problems are interpreted as a misallocation because of externalities and open access arrangements or as a threat to the sustainability of development, they cannot be solved by any nation going it alone. As explained in detail in part five of this book for the special case of climate protection, it is also true for all other questions of worldwide sustainable development that it is difficult to find a way toward international cooperative behavior by states. This is true even on the favorable assumption that all governments are interested in correcting the misallocation or in the sustainability of development. Worldwide optimum management of global natural resources or worldwide sustainable development are public goods for which, if they are offered in decentralized fashion, supply problems caused by free rider incentives arise. There is no supranational institution endowed with the necessary powers (and the requisite competence) to make supply central. The difficult problems to be solved here of expedient design of international treaties arise for a policy aiming at sustainability in similar fashion as for a policy aiming at improving allocations in a welfare economics direction. Even from a merely instrumental viewpoint, accordingly, Nutzinger (1998) has to be agreed with when he writes that the former boundary drawn between (orthodox) environmental economics and (heterodox) ecological economics has lost must of its importance. This is an important piece of progress for giving guidance to practical economic policy in the direction of sustainability.[55]

To conclude this brief discussion of sustainability policy, we must still mention the management rules presented in the literature for sustainable economic activity. They have to do with the attempt to shift the debate on sustainability policy from its often abstract level to one of practical instructions for action. Typically, a rule is defined for each exhaustible resource and renewable resource, and

---

55   By "environmental economics," we mean the orientation mainly toward the goal of maximizing social welfare, and by "ecological economics" the economic theory committed to the ideal of sustainable development and concerned with problems of the relation between humans and nature. Cf. Ayres (2008) and Venkatachalam (2007) on the possibilities of a convergence between the two "schools."

the environment's pollutant-absorbing capacity. We present the rules (*R*) for these "sectors," talking about the aspects specific to each sector, and then go on to deal with problems that cover several areas.

- *R1: Exhaustible Resources.* Exhaustible resources can be exploited only as long as the associated absence of them for future generations is compensated for. This can be done by building up anthropogenic capital, human capital, or renewable resources. The substitution rule appearing here reflects a weak sustainability conception.[56] The stock of exhaustible resources is seen as part of a capital stock that also includes other parts. For this, marginal substitution rates between the various components of the capital stock have to be established. What would have to be found in order to comply with the rule mentioned here would be the extent of consumption of exhaustible resources in a particular period and its value. This would then have to be compared with the value of net investments in anthropogenic capital, human capital, and/or renewable resources. If the value of the consumption of exhaustible resources is above the value of the investments, resource consumption would have to be throttled back and/or the investment level raised.

- *R2: Renewable Resources.* The relevant management rule prescribes that the harvest/catch quantity cannot exceed the stock growth produced by natural regeneration. This rule leaves some room for interpretation regarding whether it is to apply to each individual renewable resource, subsets within the category of renewable resources, or the whole stock of these resources. Depending on how the rule is interpreted, it is an expression of a more or less strong sustainability conception *within* the category of renewable resources. What would have to be found for this indicator would be the regeneration and harvest quantities for the individual resources or for the aggregates pointed to by the various interpretations of the rules. (In forming an aggregate, the question would again arise of the value-equivalent weighting of the individual components of the aggregate. If quantities harvested exceed the regrowth of the stock, then a reduction in the harvest and/or promotion of regeneration capacity (e.g., by improving environmental quality) would be required.

  Even if the management rule presented here is – when considered within the category of renewable resources compatible with a broad spectrum of assessments that are optimistic or pessimistic toward substitution – all the same in assessing the substitution possibilities *between* various categories of the Earth's capital stock, it is tied to a pessimistic position in the strong sustainability sense. Obviously, a harvest that goes beyond the regrowth of the resource cannot be compensated for by capital accumulation (in the area of anthropogenic capital or human capital).

---

56 This is also true of representatives of *ecological economics*, who otherwise sharply reject this concept.

- *R3: The Environment's Absorption Capacity.* On this management rule, emissions must always be below the environment's capacity to assimilate them. Here one implicit special case is the instruction to cause no emissions that cannot be assimilated by the environment. This rule does not allow any (*direct*) substitutions whether within the environmental area or between the environmental area and other areas. Overuse of the assimilation capacity for a particular pollutant cannot be balanced either by not using all the capacity for another pollutant or by building up stocks in the area of renewable resources (or of anthropogenic capital). To implement the instruction considered here, the pollutant-specific assimilation capacity and the emission quantities of the individual substances would have to be found. If the emissions are above the capacity, they would as a rule have to be lowered. Sometimes there may also be a possibility of raising the assimilation capacity. In particular, the capacity for one particular pollutant may depend on the contribution from a different pollutant. Then an *indirect* possibility of substitution could exist in the environmental sphere.

The rules briefly presented here are aimed at providing rough guidance in answering the question of how an economy is to behave in order to comply with the sustainability principle. This is certainly useful. However, we must point out the following problems and open questions:

- Some features of the rules admit differing interpretations regarding the substitution possibilities existing in the context of sustainable development. Differing interpretations lead to differing instructions for action. To that extent, the rules are rather sibylline. Where there is no room for interpretation, the implied fixity need not always be plausible.
- The rules give no indication as to what consumption level they are to be met at. This is particularly critical for the rules affecting renewable resources and the environment's assimilative capacity. Cynically (if only for pedagogical reasons), one might say that the rule for sustainable exploitation of renewable resources is complied with even for extinct species: nothing regrows, and nothing more is harvested.
- The rules ignore sustainability-relevant interdependencies between the three areas of rules and within them. Let us consider an example of an *intra*sectoral interdependency: the harvesting volume for one particular renewable resource may obey rule R2, but the stock that is conserved thereby may be so small that another species that uses the former as prey (or anyway, basis for living) dies out. For this, it is not even necessary for humanity to catch the predator species in the period concerned. The extinction of the predatory species is not even necessarily the last link in the chain of cause and effect threatening the sustainability of development, the starting point for which was a human activity that did not infringe sustainability for the species concerned.

    Let us consider an example of an *inter*sectoral interdependency: a particular emission may be assimilable by the environment in the long term. However, this need not contradict the possibility of its destroying the viability of a renewable resource and thus ending its existence.

The examples show that even strict compliance with the rules formulated previously is not necessarily enough to ensure sustainability of development. If the management rules approach is nonetheless to be followed, then they have to be supplemented and refined in order to take account of the intrasectoral and intersectoral interdependencies of relevance to sustainability. Where the rules amount to limiting human consumption to a natural capacity (assimilative capacity, regeneration capacity), it must be verified whether this capacity itself depends on human action. Where that is the case, the management rules approach requires supplementation by restrictions compliance that will ensure a minimum level of this capacity.

- It seems noteworthy that none of the very different sets of management rules given in the literature contain statements about value-conserving principles for anthropogenic capital or human knowledge.
- Finally, the measurement and valuation problems mentioned previously for other indicators should also be recalled.

V. Incentive Problems of Sustainability

Let us simply assume that the problems of the conception of sustainability and sustainability policy mentioned previously have been solved. That would mean humanity could say precisely what sustainable development consists of and what policy measures could bring it about. However, there will still be the question of whether it would necessarily aim at sustainable development. With an eye to relations between various generations, from an economic viewpoint two important obstacles arise:

- It seems to be part of human nature that future satisfaction of needs is rated lower than present satisfaction. Thus, the saver expects to receive the amount saved on the due date together with interest. The reason for this "discounting" of future events from the viewpoint of the present lies in humans lacking "telescopic" abilities – so, at any rate, thought the famous economist Arthur C. Pigou (1932), praised in part two of this book. As long ago as 1881, Eugen von Böhm-Bawerk found that it was regrettable, albeit understandable, for a decision maker to discount future effects. He could not be sure that he would be able to enjoy the consumption tomorrow as much as today. After all, he could be dead.[57] Whatever the causes of the habit of undervaluing future effects of present decisions, it is poison to sustainable development.[58]

---

57 The debate over discounting has not fallen silent yet. Cf., e.g., Bayer (2003), Frederick/Loewenstein/O'Donoghue (2002), Hampicke/Ott (2003), Weitzman (2001).

58 For a more differentiated look, see Sáez/Requena (2007), Stephan/Müller-Fürstenberger (1998), and Winkler (2006).

Decisions that increase enjoyment of the present but that will bring grave negative consequences in the future are more favorably assessed at the time of decision the higher the rate at which future effects are discounted. It might be observed that the reasons that make discounting by the individual decision maker understandable, indeed, even rational, do not apply to society as a whole. Thus, although the individual's life is limited, society itself can, however, with appropriate lifestyles, continue to exist into the distant future – albeit with ever-changing personnel. Although this objection is normatively convincing, the question nonetheless arises as to who is to take the decisions in society's long-term interest if society, naturally, consists only of individual decision makers of the current generation.

• Does economics not – it is sometimes objected – paint too dark a picture of reality in basing itself on decision makers that have only their own welfare in mind? Closer consideration shows, however, that a little more faith in the goodness of man does not decisively brighten the forecast for a sustainable mode of economics. If, for instance, a decision maker concerned for his own children and grandchildren decides to use less energy, then he spares humanity's energy resources (of course, only marginally, but let us ignore this for the moment). He cannot, however, by any means be certain that this saving bought by him at a certain cost will benefit his "target group," that is, his children and grandchildren. Instead, he has to expect that the resources he has spared will be consumed by his own contemporaries. The fraction of the decision maker's savings that can actually benefit his descendants is negligibly small. Accordingly, the incentive to act in energy-saving fashion for this reason is small, even for the *selectively altruistic* decision maker assumed here. The incentive problem is precisely the same as the one (already discussed in section B.II) of individual restraint in exploiting freely accessible natural resources ("self-service resources"). Thus, the appeal to the individual fisherman to remember while working that he wants to fish tomorrow also goes unheard – but above all, unheeded. The decision maker knows that his restraint will tend to benefit the present consumption of others more than it will provide for his own future. Thus, we reach the familiar result of the individually rational but collectively totally irrational overexploitation of freely accessible fish resources.

Unfortunately, the incentives to behavior by the whole society altruistic toward the future are no more favorable than for the single individual. Let us assume that the present generation is considering whether it wants to accept considerable hardship for the sake of development that will last sustainably for generations. The unfortunate thing is that it can never be certain whether its savings formed by self-restraint in consumption of natural resources will in fact be used to maintain sustainable development. For even in the next generation, the fatal temptation exists to exploit the present generation's restraint and snaffle the resources for itself. Because the generations are not freely moveable over time, there is nothing with which generation 1 could protect its altruistic sacrifice for the future against desecration by generation 2.[59] This constitutional unprotectedness of generation-spanning investment in the future is a major hindrance to making the investment in the first place. The investment structure is just as depressing as the one facing an investor pondering an involvement in a country with uncertain political circumstances. Because he cannot be sure how long it will, given the unstable conditions, be possible for him to draw the proceeds of his investment, he either will not invest at all or will invest in projects that pay off in the very short term.

Is it, in view of the Herculean extent of the effort required for sustainable development, sensible for the present generation to trouble itself with concerns about the future? Perhaps we should simply enjoy things as long as they last and leave the rest to fate. Economic theory lets us derive the following arguments against this path of resignation:

- In the sustainability debate, market processes appear overwhelmingly as *causes* of unsustainable developments. As explained previously, this view is only partly justified: where markets are functional, they certainly produce a tendency to *spare* resources. If a resource traded in a functioning market becomes scarce, then that will be reflected in a rising price. This will induce processes of limitation of demand, expansion of supply, and a multiplicity of forms of technical progress that will reduce the scarcity of the more expensive resource and thus, in general, help the goal of sustainability.

- Of course, not all markets are functional in the sense just mentioned. Instead, due to free rider problems in the provision of public goods, failed internalization of negative externalities and the openness of resources in "self-service" regimes to exploitation, numerous and severe misallocations come about, often termed "market failure" in the literature. The present generation has every occasion to improve the suboptimum use of scarce resources *in its own interest*. Resource-sparing corrections to the present's "thoroughly selfish" way of doing business have as a by-product positive effects for the future. It does not have to be well meant to do good.

- Experimental economics has shown that individuals certainly do depart in their conduct from the predictions of the sort of economic theory underlying the previous statements. (We already considered this point in the context of international environmental problems; see section B.I.8 of part five of this book.) Many believe that economics should concern itself more with the behavior of a *Homo sustinens*[60] and, finally, demobilize good (?) old *Homo oeconomicus*.

---

59   Because of the fundamental asymmetry between different generations, the *mutuality principle* ("reciprocity") discussed in part five of this book as a "glimmer of hope" is not applicable in the sustainability context. What can future generations do for us, after all – except perhaps pray?

60   Among the alternatives to *Homo oeconomicus*, there is now a pleasing (and increasing) multiplicity of varieties. Cf., e.g., Bolton/Ockenfels (2000), Fehr/Schmidt (1999). The spectrum now goes as far as *Homo sportivus oeconomicus* (Maennig 2003). Perhaps the circle might be closed with

Of course, attention always has to be paid not to let enthusiasm over the construction of alternative behavioral types come down to mere wishful thinking. The fact that we can dream up for ourselves a decision maker for whom the striving for sustainability is a component of his preferences does not yet make sustainable development a reality.

How, then, do future generations' chances look from an economic viewpoint?[61] If the community of the unborn is wrinkling its brow over what the present generation is cooking, then it is probably not placing its hopes too much in its capacity for altruism toward the future. The future people might do better to base their optimism on the consideration that the present generation might in its own interest like to get a grip on its own problems. If the present generation can manage to internalize negative externalities and protect natural resources from the overexploitation "rational" in self-service regimes, then it will thereby produce positive externalities for the future. Whether this will be sufficient to guarantee the survival of future generations is more a question for prophets than for economists.

Exercises

Exercise 6.1
Give some examples for exhaustible and renewable energy resources.

Exercise 6.2
Discuss the following statement: Renewable resources are resources that cannot be depleted.

Exercise 6.3
List some conditions that are required for the social optimality of the intertemporal market equilibrium in the exploitation of exhaustible resources.

Exercise 6.4
Consider an economy that is endowed with $Q = 1345$ units of an exhaustible resource. The resource may be used for energy production in three periods $t \in \{0, 1, 2\}$. In each period, marginal willingness to pay for q_t resource units is given by $MWP(q_t) = 1010 - q_t$. Marginal exploitation costs are constant and given by $MEC(q_t) = 10$. The social rate of discount equals $r = 0.1 = 10\%$. Derive the socially optimal time path of resource exploitation.

Exercise 6.5
Use your intuition to describe the following comparative static effect. How does an increase of the social discount rate affect the socially optimal time path of resource exploitation?

> *Homo anti-oeconomicus* (not called that in the following work): "His day was filled with aimless hurry" (Joseph Roth, *Das Spinnennetz*, 1923). Nice one, that – no?!?

61 More cautiously formulated: "from the viewpoint of the economic mainstream?"

Exercise 6.6

The resource growth of a renewable resource is assumed to be given by $G(S_t) = \frac{2}{5}(S_t - 100)\left(1 - \frac{S_t}{1000}\right)$, with S_t denoting the resource stock in period t. Determine the maximum sustainable yield (MSY) and the minimum stock (S_{min}) that are necessary for a positive rate of regeneration.

Exercise 6.7

Discuss the following statement: The socially optimal yield of an exhaustible resource is identical to the maximum sustainable yield.

Exercise 6.8

What is meant by an *open access regime* in the context of exhaustible resources?

Exercise 6.9

What is a main difference between the concept of welfare maximization and the sustainability approach?

Exercise 6.10

Assume that the concept of strong sustainability would be applied to exhaustible resources. How would the strong sustainable extraction path of an exhaustible resource look like?

Epilogue

Three Types of Externality and the Increasing Difficulty of Internalizing Them

This book's readers have accompanied the author on a long journey through the (sometimes impracticable) terrain of environmental economics. Many thanks for your company: without you (or, more exactly, without the vision of an addressee), I could not have managed it. In conclusion (as a reward?!), we offer you a bird's-eye view of our journey.

The simplest models in economic theory contain only households and firms as actors. The *households* aim to maximize utility. In doing so, they decide on their demand for consumer goods and the supply of production factors (especially labor) they offer. The objective of *firms* is seen as profit maximization. They can approach this objective in their role as suppliers of end products and demanders of factors of production. The activities of the individual households and firms are coordinated through markets. On certain conditions, the market mechanism is an extremely efficient instrument for coping with scarcity problems. One (of the many possible) complication(s) is that although many of the economically relevant relations among the actors are market relations, not all of them are. Often, the activity of one decision maker will affect the situation (the welfare) of another decision maker, without the market being the mediating mechanism. Such processes outside the market are called "externalities." The literature of economics has shown that externalities can encroach severely on the capacity of the market mechanism to increase a society's welfare. Putting it in technical jargon, externalities lead to *misallocation* (i.e., they disrupt the social optimality of market equilibria). In this situation, the *state* now comes along as the third type of actor on the stage. It is typical for the traditional scenario in welfare economics that the state is not seen as part of the mêlée of rival interest groups, nor politicians as pursuers of interests of their own. Instead, in the drama set by welfare economics, the state appears as guardian of the common weal. It attempts to maximize social welfare by internalizing the externalities arising from uncorrected economic actions. The state, as it were, takes the social "total perspective" and makes corrections where individual efforts at optimization come into contradiction with social optimization.

Of course, this sort of scenario can be satisfactory at best where the activities and effects observed are confined to the framework of a single state. However, this is not the case with global environmental problems because what marks them out is their massive border-crossing effects; the all-embracing "total viewpoint" cannot be adopted by a single state. Instead, the nation-state is only one of many actors – just as, in the previously described basic model, the individual firm and the individual household were.

Considering the individual state as one actor among many and doing the same with firms as actors has one fundamental difference, however. As described previously, for the individual firms (and, similarly, the individual households), we have an analytical construct in the market mechanism we can use to show coordination processes and problems within a uniform theoretical framework. Although real economic markets may not be identical with the concept of the market in economic theory, the prevailing view in the literature is nonetheless that the theoretical construct can grasp basic structural features of real markets and that analyzing it is therefore useful for making statements about reality.

In contrast with this, there is no general economic theory for coordination among various states. In reality, it seems to be more of an immense web of customs, agreements, and treaties of the most varying degree of bindingness and specificity, rather than a uniform coordination mechanism. Undoubtedly, it is also the case that the economic activity of one state and the economic and environmental policies that govern such activities have direct effects on the welfare situation of other states. Although things are not the same here as in the case of a firm harming a household without the intermediary of the market mechanism by producing emissions, here we can talk about "externalities." We conceive of the country a harmful border-crossing environmental effect comes from, with its government and its millions of firms and households, as a single decision maker that harms another country, without a coordination mechanism (of whatever kind) having acted as a mediator. If in economics we usually consider direct effects between individual decision makers as externalities of the first kind, then direct border-crossing effects between states are externalities of the second kind. If a state's activities affect not just one other state but all other states, then the merely border-crossing externality becomes a global externality.

Global environmental problems have been understood and discussed in the economic literature by analogy with externalities between individual decision makers within a state. In practice, a number of states linked with each other through externalities and each aiming to maximize national welfare is modeled. As with the familiar model of externalities, the totality of national welfare maximization efforts does not lead to maximizing the welfare of the totality of all states. However, the analogy ends there. A "superstate" that could play the same role for the community of states as the national state does for the community of its households and firms does not exist. However, if there is no "state of states," then the individual states must themselves take on the task of coordination. Through international environmental treaties, they may seek to correct the misallocation arising from their isolated optimization. Just as the concept of the "globality" of environmental damage has been used here, it can be seen as the "extreme case of internationality": the point is not that an externality crosses the frontiers between two neighboring states, but that the environmental actions of each individual state may have worldwide consequences.

On top of this spatial globalization, however, we also have to consider a temporal globalization. The consequences of present environmental actions do not often arise immediately, but rather in the future. The farther forward that consideration of damage has to be directed, the more uncertain are statements about its size. Having spoken of two kinds of externalities (those between individual economic subjects and those between states), we now have to deal with a third kind: externalities the present generation produces for future generations. For this third kind of externality, the internalization problem takes on a much more fundamental form than for the first two kinds. Some imagination is already required to see the nation-state as guardian of the national common weal. It takes even more to imagine the individual states as being capable of coordination with an eye to upholding the common weal of the whole community of states. And perhaps it boggles all imagination to conceive of the present generation taking the welfare of future generations into account in its decisions in such a way as to bring about generation-spanning maximization of the common weal.

Achieving the common weal in its first two variants (the national one and that of the community of states) is favored at least by the fact that all those whose individual welfare is a component of the overall welfare at issue in each case are actually present. In the process of maximizing total welfare, the point here is "only" for them to articulate themselves appropriately and be taken into account "correspondingly" in the aggregation process necessary on the path from maximizing individual welfare to maximizing total welfare. But with total welfare of the third kind (intergenerational total welfare), those, apart from the present generation, whose welfare has to be taken into account in aggregating individual interests are not present at the negotiating table at all – future generations. To reach a solution here, present generations would have to uphold the interests of future generations even where these are directed against their own short-term interests. That this sort of self-restraint is called for is a specific feature of externalities of the third kind. Neither had we, at the first stage of internalization, asked individual firms to cut their emissions by way of self-restraint, out of consideration for neighbors suffering damage, nor at the second stage was self-restraint by an individual state in relation to border-crossing environmental pollution a part of the internalization idea. It is instead the case that the nation-state as the bearer of internalization policy at the first stage, and the designing of international treaties at the second stage, are necessary only because the individual actor is not trusted to exercise self-restraint. For the problems of intergenerational globalization, from an economic viewpoint, all we are left with is the "principle of hope" already mentioned at the end of part six of this book:

- Internalization efforts of the first and second kinds will let future generations profit from them, too, indirectly. Although this is not the same thing as total intergenerational internalization, perhaps the worst consequences of the lack of a third level of internalization will nonetheless be avoided.
- The ideas underlying economic model building, of the utility-maximizing individual, the state that maximizes national welfare and the present generation maximizing present benefit, are too pessimistic.

One might add, may humanity grow to meet the size of its tasks.

I know there's always a certain kind of reader who will be compelled to ask, But what really happened? The answer is simple: the lovers survive and flourish.

— Ian McEwan, *Atonement*, London, 2001

Solutions to Exercises

Solution to exercise 1.1
i) Positive analysis: "What is?"
A positive analysis explains the equilibrium behavior of the individual decision makers in a given policy environment (without judging this behavior).
ii) Normative analysis: "What should be?"
A normative analysis characterizes the social optimum and analyzes which policy instruments are able to induce socially optimal activity levels of the individual decision makers.

Solution to exercise 1.2
Much as a map that has a scale of 1:1 is not suitable for putting in the trouser pocket, a model that approximates reality as close as possible is intractable due to its too high complexity. The analyst's task is to construct a model that is as simple as possible, but that reflects all important aspects of the problem by appropriate assumptions. What is considered to be "important" depends on the questions the model is designed to answer.

Solution to exercise 1.3
Only assumption (a) is necessary. The simplest model to formalize the free rider incentive in public good provision is the so-called prisoners' dilemma. Its basic design is a model with two identical players, which decide once and simultaneously whether they cooperate. They may have the possibility to contact each other, but may not be able to make binding agreements.

Solution to exercise 1.4

a) The (inverse) individual supply function of a firm corresponds to its marginal cost function. Horizontal aggregation of the individual supply functions gives the market supply function. Solving $MC_A = x + 10$ with respect to x gives $x = MC_A - 10$. Hence, the supply function of a type A firm is given by $x_A =$
$$\begin{cases} P - 10 & \text{if } P \geq 10, \\ 0 & \text{if } P < 10. \end{cases}$$

The supply function of a type B firm is given by $x_B = \dfrac{P}{2}$.

Thus, market supply equals $S = 50x_A + 50x_B = \begin{cases} 75P - 500 & \text{if } P \geq 10, \\ 25P & \text{if } P < 10. \end{cases}$

The (inverse) individual demand function of a consumer corresponds to his marginal willingness to pay function. Horizontal aggregation of the individual demand functions gives the market demand function. Solving $MWP_C = 20 - \dfrac{5}{3}x$ with respect to x gives $x = 12 - \dfrac{3}{5}MWP_C$. Hence, the demand function of a type

C consumer is given by $x_C = \begin{cases} 12 - \dfrac{3}{5}P & \text{if } P \leq 20, \\ 0 & \text{if } P > 20. \end{cases}$

Correspondingly, the demand function of a type D consumer is given by

$$x_D = \begin{cases} 8 - \dfrac{2}{5}P & \text{if } P \leq 20, \\ 0 & \text{if } P > 20. \end{cases}$$

Hence, market demand equals $D = 50x_C + 50x_D =$
$$\begin{cases} 1,000 - 50P & \text{if } P \leq 20 \\ 0 & \text{if } P > 20. \end{cases}$$

b) Note that the intersection of S and D lies in the range $P \in [10, 20]$. Solving $75P - 500 = 1,000 - 50P$ gives $P^* = 12$. Inserting $P^* = 12$ in the supply (or demand) function gives $x^* = 400$.

c) We use the following notation: $S_A = 50x_A$, $S_B = 50x_B$, $D_C = 50x_C$, $D_D = 50x_D$.

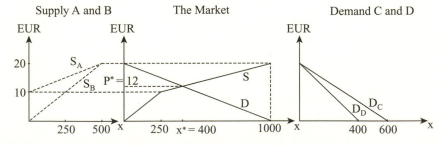

d) In the market equilibrium, the consumer surplus is given by $CS = \int_{x=0}^{x^*} MWP \, dx - x^* P^*$ with MWP denoting the aggregate marginal willingness to pay function ($\rightarrow$ inverse demand function) given by

$$MWP = 20 - \frac{1}{50}x. \quad \text{Hence, \; we \; get} \quad CS = \int_0^{400} 20 - \frac{1}{50}x \, dx - 400 \cdot 12$$

$$= 20 \cdot 400 - \frac{1}{100}400^2 - 4{,}800 = 1{,}600.$$

The producer surplus is given by $PS = x^* P^* - \int_0^{x^*} MC \, dx$ with MC denoting the aggregate marginal cost function ($\rightarrow$ inverse supply function) given by $MC = $

$$\begin{cases} \dfrac{x}{75} + \dfrac{20}{3} & \text{if } x \geq 250, \\ \dfrac{x}{25} & \text{if } x < 250. \end{cases}$$

Thus, $PS = 400 \cdot 12 - \left(\int_0^{250} \dfrac{x}{25} \, dx + \int_{250}^{400} \dfrac{x}{75} + \dfrac{20}{3} \, dx \right) = 1{,}900.$

Social net welfare is given by $W = CS + PS = 1{,}600 + 1{,}900 = 3{,}500.$

Solution to exercise 1.5

a) $AC(a) = 10a^2 \Rightarrow \quad MAC = 20a = 20(10 - x) = 200 - 20x.$

$$D(x) = 10x^2 \Rightarrow \quad MD = 20x.$$

b) The socially optimal emission level x^{**} is determined by $MAC = MD$.

$$MAC = MD \Leftrightarrow \quad 200 - 20x = 20x. \text{ Hence, } x^{**} = 5.$$

Solution to exercise 1.6

a) A positive/negative externality of an economic transaction is a positive/negative impact on a third party that is not directly involved in the transaction.
b) Examples for positive externalities:
   - Knowledge spillovers
   - Apiculture of a beekeeper

   Examples for negative externalities:
   - Greenhouse gas emissions
   - Waste and smell generated by industrial farm animal production

Solution to exercise 1.7

a) Marginal damages are given by $MD = 2$. The socially optimal production level is determined by $MWP = MC + MD$. The intersection of MWP and

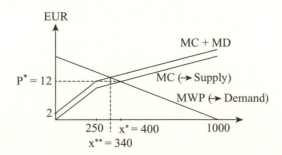

$MC + MD$ lies in the range $x \geq 250$. Hence, from $20 - \dfrac{1}{50}x = \dfrac{x}{75} + \dfrac{20}{3} + 2$, we get $x^{**} = 340$.

b) The social welfare level in the market equilibrium is given by

$$W^* = CS(x^*) + PS(x^*) - D(x^*) = 3{,}500 - 800 = 2{,}700, \text{ with } CS \text{ denoting}$$
the consumer surplus and PS denoting the producer surplus.

The socially optimal welfare level is given by

$$W^{**} = \int_0^{x^{**}} MWP - MC - MD \; dx = \int_0^{250} MWP - MC - MD \; dx$$

$$+ \int_{250}^{340} MWP - MC - MD \; dx = \int_0^{250} \left(20 - \frac{1}{50}x\right) - \left(\frac{x}{25}\right) - 2 \; dx$$

$$+ \int_{250}^{340} \left(20 - \frac{1}{50}x\right) - \left(\frac{x}{75} + \frac{20}{3}\right) - 2 \; dx$$

$$= \int_0^{250} 18 - \frac{3}{50}x \; dx + \int_{250}^{340} \frac{34}{3} - \frac{1}{30}x \; dx = 2{,}625 + 135 = 2{,}760.$$

Solution to exercise 1.8

The production tax does not only influence the production level of good x, but also the production level of substitutive and complementary goods. The demand for substitutive goods increases, whereas the demand for complementary goods decreases. This results in indirect effects on the environmental quality if the production of substitutive and/or complementary goods also damages the environment.

Moreover, it might be cheaper to reduce pollution by other means than the reduction of the production level. Examples include switching to cleaner production processes or installing filters and other additive devices.

Solution to exercise 1.9

A Pareto optimum is a state in which it is impossible to improve the situation of a member of the economy without negatively affecting another member.

The social optimum is the allocation that maximizes social welfare of an economy.

Hence, the social optimum is a Pareto optimum.

This statement can easily be proven by contradiction: if it would be possible to increase the welfare of a member of the economy without decreasing the welfare of another member in the social optimum, then social welfare would not be maximal in the optimum.

Solution to exercise 1.10

The statement is wrong. The willingness to pay of an individual i for a certain level of environmental quality q is a function of individual income I_i and generally differs between individuals (i.e., $WTP_i(q, I_i)$). Only in (unrealistic) special cases is aggregate willingness to pay independent from the individual income distribution. For example, a sufficient condition would be that the WTP function is linear in I_i and identical for all individuals. In this case, we would have $\sum_i WTP(q, I_i) = \sum_i f(q) \cdot I_i = f(q) \sum_i I_i$.

Solution to exercise 2.1

a) No transaction costs are incurred.
b) There are no income effects.

Solution to exercise 2.2
In the Coasean bargaining model, the individuals are not price takers as in the competitive market model. Instead, the price is negotiated. The bargaining result may be influenced by strategic behavior, and the bargaining power depends on the property rights.

Solution to exercise 2.3
If the state does not assign the property rights, the situation equals the bargaining situation under the laissez-faire rule. For the conclusion of a contract, it is only necessary that the government provides instruments that can assure the fulfillment of a contract.

Solution to exercise 2.4
a) The socially optimal emission level maximizes the sum $\Pi_U + \Pi_D$. From the corresponding first-order condition $ba - (b + c)E = 0$ follows $E^{**} = \dfrac{ab}{b+c} = 5$.

b.i) Laissez-faire rule: In the noncooperative situation, the factory maximizes its profit function Π_U. From the first-order condition $ba - bE = 0$ follows $E^* = a = 10$.

The maximum payment the fisher could pay is given by

$$P_{\max}^{LR} = \Pi_D(E^{**}) - \Pi_D(E^*) = \left(d - \frac{c}{2}(E^{**})^2\right) - \left(d - \frac{c}{2}(E^*)^2\right)$$

$$= \frac{c}{2}(a)^2 - \frac{c}{2}\left(\frac{ab}{b+c}\right)^2 = 100 - 25 = 75.$$

The minimum demand of the factory is given by

$$P_{\min}^{LR} = \Pi_U(E^*) - \Pi_U(E^{**}) = \left(b\left(aE^* - \frac{1}{2}(E^*)^2\right)\right) - \left(b\left(aE^{**} - \frac{1}{2}(E^{**})^2\right)\right)$$

$$= \left(b\left(a \cdot a - \frac{1}{2}(a)^2\right)\right) - \left(b\left(a\frac{ab}{b+c} - \frac{1}{2}\left(\frac{ab}{b+c}\right)^2\right)\right)$$

$$= \frac{1}{2}a^2 b - b\left(a\frac{ab}{b+c} - \frac{1}{2}\left(\frac{ab}{b+c}\right)^2\right)$$

$$= 100 - (100 - 25) = 25.$$

b.ii) Polluter rule: In the noncooperative situation, the factory is not allowed to dump its emissions into the river. Hence, $E^0 = 0$.

The maximum payment of the factory is given by

$$P_{\max}^{PR} = \Pi_U(E^{**}) - \Pi_U(0) = \left(b\left(aE^{**} - \frac{1}{2}(E^{**})^2 \right) \right) - 0$$

$$= b\left(a\frac{ab}{b+c} - \frac{1}{2}\left(\frac{ab}{b+c} \right)^2 \right) = 75.$$

The minimum demand of the fisher is given by

$$P_{\min}^{PR} = \Pi_D(0) - \Pi_D(E^{**}) = \left(d - \frac{c}{2}(0)^2 \right) - \left(d - \frac{c}{2}(E^{**})^2 \right)$$

$$= d - \left(d - \frac{c}{2}\left(\frac{ab}{b+c} \right)^2 \right) = \frac{c}{2}\left(\frac{ab}{b+c} \right)^2 = 25.$$

c.i) Under strict liability, the factory has to compensate the fisher for its profit reduction.

Hence, the objective function of the factory is given by

$$P^{SL} = \Pi_U(E) - (\Pi_D(0) - \Pi_D(E)) = \Pi_U(E) + \Pi_D(E) - \Pi_D(0).$$

The first-order condition is given by $\Pi'_U(E) + \Pi'_D(E) = 0$ and thus is identical to the first-order condition of the socially optimal emission level. Hence, the factory chooses the socially optimal emission level $E^{**} = \dfrac{ab}{b+c} = 5$.

c.ii) Under the negligence rule with emission standard E^{**}, the objective function of the factory is given by

$$P^{NR} = \begin{cases} \Pi_U(E) & \text{if} \quad E \le E^{**} \\ \Pi_U(E) - (\Pi_D(0) - \Pi_D(E)) & \text{if} \quad E > E^{**} \end{cases}.$$

The objective function is strictly increasing in the range $E \le E^{**}$, has a discontinuity (downward) at $E = E^{**}$, and is strictly decreasing in the range $E > E^{**}$. Hence, also under the negligence rule, the factory chooses the socially optimal emission level $E^{**} = \dfrac{ab}{b+c} = 5$.

For the parameter values $a = 10$, $b = c = 2$, and $d = 200$, the objective functions are given by

$$P^{SL} = 2\left(10E - \frac{1}{2}E^2 \right) - (200 - (200 - E^2)) = 20E - 2E^2$$

under strict liability and

$$P^{NR} = \begin{cases} 20E - E^2 & \text{if} \quad E \le 5 \\ 20E - 2E^2 & \text{if} \quad E > 5 \end{cases}$$

under the negligence rule.

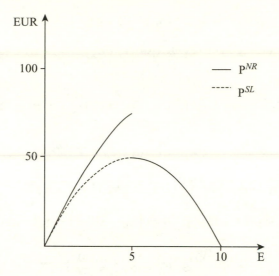

Solution to exercise 2.5

The involved parties have higher degrees of freedom in the Coasean bargaining model, where the government specifies only the property rights.

Moreover, both liability law and the property rights approach allow arrangements that are not producible in the other one.

Using liability law under the negligence rule, the socially optimal activity level may be induced without any transfers between the involved parties, which is not possible in the property rights approach.

Using the property rights approach under the laissez-faire rule, the polluter can claim compensation, which is not possible under liability law.

Solution to exercise 2.6

a) The socially optimal emission levels may be derived by minimizing the aggregate cost function

$$AC_1(10 - x_1) + AC_2(10 - x_2) + D(x_1, x_2)$$
$$= 50(10 - x_1)^2 + 100(10 - x_2)^2 + 50(x_1 + x_2)^2.$$

Differentiation with respect to x_1 and x_2 leads to the first-order conditions

$$-100(10 - x_1) + 100(x_1 + x_2) = 0 \text{ and}$$

$$-200(10 - x_2) + 100(x_1 + x_2) = 0.$$

Solving the system of equations gives $x_1^{**} = 2$, $x_2^{**} = 6$ and, hence, $x^{**} = 8$.

b) The relevant cost functions for $i \in \{1, 2\}$ are given by

$$C_1^T = AC_1(10 - x_1) + \frac{1}{2}D(x_1, x_2) = 50(10 - x_1)^2 + \frac{1}{2} \cdot 50(x_1 + x_2)^2,$$

$$C_2^T = AC_2(10 - x_2) + \frac{1}{2}D(x_1, x_2) = 100(10 - x_2)^2 + \frac{1}{2} \cdot 50(x_1 + x_2)^2.$$

The first-order conditions are given by

$$\partial C_1^T/\partial x_1 = -100(10 - x_1) + 50(x_1 + x_2) = 0 \text{ and}$$

$$\partial C_2^T/\partial x_2 = -200(10 - x_2) + 50(x_1 + x_2) = 0, \text{ from which follows}$$

$$x_1^* = \frac{30}{7} > x_1^{**} \text{ and } x_2^* = \frac{50}{7} > x_2^{**}.$$

Hence, both firms choose emission levels that are higher than the socially optimal ones.

c) The socially optimal emission levels are determined by $MAC_1 = MD$ and $MAC_2 = MD$.

Hence, the firms choose the socially optimal emission levels if both firms have to pay for the total damages. Under this liability rule, the relevant cost functions are given by

$$C_1^T = AC_1(10 - x_1) + D(x_1, x_2) = 50(10 - x_1)^2 + 50(x_1 + x_2)^2,$$
$$C_2^T = AC_2(10 - x_2) + D(x_1, x_2) = 100(10 - x_2)^2 + 50(x_1 + x_2)^2.$$

The first-order conditions are

$$\partial C_1^T/\partial x_1 = -100(10 - x_1) + 100(x_1 + x_2) = 0 \text{ and}$$

$$\partial C_2^T/\partial x_2 = -200(10 - x_2) + 100(x_1 + x_2) = 0, \text{ from which follows}$$

$$x_1^* = 2 = x_1^{**} \text{ and } x_2^* = 6 = x_2^{**}.$$

Note, however, that under this variant of strict liability, the damaged parties are overcompensated.

Solution to exercise 2.7

a) To be able to determine the socially optimal care standard, the government needs a lot of information.
  • The government has to know the dimension and probability of possible damages.
  • The government has to know the monetary equivalent of the potential damages.

- The costs for the care activity must be known.

  Another reason for a suboptimal standard could be that the objective function of the government differs from the social welfare function and, for example, instead seeks reelection.

b) Let x^S denote the care standard chosen by the government and x^{**} the socially optimal care level.

   In the case of $x^S \leq x^{**}$, the firm complies with the standard. Thus, in case of $x^S < x^{**}$, the equilibrium care level differs from the socially optimal one.

   In the case of $x^S > x^{**}$, the firm complies with the standard if $C(x^S) \leq C(x^{**}) + D(x^{**})$. If $C(x^S) > C(x^{**}) + D(x^{**})$, then the firm does not comply with the standard and chooses x^{**}.

c) Possible reasons are as follows:
   - Causality between the firm activity and damage can be difficult to prove.
   - Temporal or spatial distances between damage cause and effect.

d) The firm only complies with the standard if $C(x^{**}) \leq \min\left[C(x) + a \cdot D(x)\right]$, with damage discount factor $a < 1$. Otherwise, the firm chooses the care level $\tilde{x}(< x^{**})$, which minimizes $C(x) + a \cdot D(x)$.

e) The socially optimal care level x^{**} can be determined by minimizing the aggregate cost function $C(x) + D(x) = 2x + 8/x$. From the first-order condition $2 - 8/x^2 = 0$ follows $x^{**} = 2$.

   If A complies with the standard, its corresponding cost is given by $C(x^S) = 7$. If A does not comply with the standard and instead chooses $x^{**} = 2$, the corresponding costs are given by $C(x^{**}) + D(x^{**}) = 4 + 4 = 8$. Hence, A chooses $x = x^S$.

f) If A complies with the standard, the corresponding costs are again given by $C(x^S) = 7$. If A does not comply with the standard, it chooses the care level $\tilde{x} = 3/2$, which minimizes $C(x) + \dfrac{9}{16} D(x)$. Because the corresponding costs are given by $C(\tilde{x}) + \dfrac{9}{16} D(\tilde{x}) = 3 + 3 = 6 < 7$, A does not comply with the standard and chooses $\tilde{x} = 3/2$.

g) In the social optimum, aggregate costs are given by $C(x^{**}) + D(x^{**}) = 4 + 4 = 8$. Social costs in part e are given by $C(x^S) + D(x^S) = 7 + \dfrac{16}{7} = 9\dfrac{2}{7}$, and in part f by $C(\tilde{x}) + D(\tilde{x}) = 3 + \dfrac{16}{3} = 8\dfrac{1}{3}$. Hence, in parts e and f, social costs are higher than in the social optimum. The chosen care level differs from the socially optimal one in both cases. However, total costs are lower in part f with two distortions than in part e with one distortion.

Solution to exercise 2.8

The introduction of the Pigou tax results in an additional term of the private cost function of the polluter. For any emitted unit of the pollutant, he has to pay the tax level. If the tax level exceeds the marginal emission abatement cost of the polluter, then the polluter can decrease his total cost by (additional) emission reductions. In the private optimum, marginal abatement costs equal the emission tax level. If the government succeeds in choosing the socially optimal tax level that is determined by $t^{**} = MD(x^{**}) = MAC(x^{**})$, then the private optimum coincides with the social one.

Solution to exercise 2.9

Generally, the implementation of a Pigou tax is impossible due to the extremely high information requirements. To determine the Pigou tax, the government has to know not only the aggregate abatement cost function (which is composed of the abatement cost functions of all polluters), but also the aggregate damage functions.

Solution to exercise 2.10

a) $AC(a) = 50a^2 \Rightarrow \quad MAC = 100a = 100(6 - x) = 600 - 100x.$

$$D(x) = 25x^2 \Rightarrow \quad MD = 50x.$$

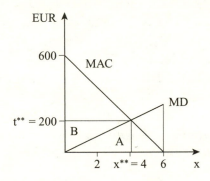

b) The socially optimal emission level x^{**} is determined by $MAC = MD$.

$$MAC = MD \Leftrightarrow \quad 600 - 100x = 50x. \text{ Hence, } x^{**} = 4.$$

The corresponding value of expected damages is given by $D(x^{**}) = 25 \cdot 4^2 = 400$.

c) The Pigou tax level t^{**} equals marginal damages and marginal abatement cost in the socially optimal allocation $t^{**} = MD(x^{**}) = MAC(x^{**})$. Hence, $t^{**} = MD(4) = MAC(4) = 200$. The tax load of the firm is given by $x^{**}t^{**} = 4 \cdot 200 = 800$.

d) Under strict liability, the firm minimizes the cost function

$$C^{T,SL}(x) = AC(6 - x) + D(x) = 50 \cdot (6 - x)^2 + 25x^2.$$

From the first-order condition

$$C^{T,SL'}(x) = -100 \cdot (6 - x) + 50x = 0 \text{ follows } x = x^{**} = 4.$$

Under the negligence rule, the firm minimizes the cost function

$$C^{T,N}(x) = \begin{cases} 50 \cdot (6 - x)^2 + 25x^2 & \text{if} \quad x > x^{**} = 4 \\ 50 \cdot (6 - x)^2 & \text{if} \quad x \le 4. \end{cases}$$

This function is strictly decreasing in the range $x \in [0, 4]$, has a discontinuity (upward) at $x = 4$ (because for $x > 4$, the damage term has to be added), and is strictly increasing in the range $x > 4$. Thus, also under the negligence rule, the firm chooses the emission level $x = x^{**} = 4$, which minimizes $C^{T,N}$.

e.i) Information requirements of the government: To be able to determine the Pigou tax or the socially optimal emission standard under the negligence rule, the government has to know the marginal abatement cost function of the firm and the marginal damage function. Under strict liability, there are no information requirements.

e.ii) Planning security of the firm: Under the Pigou tax and the negligence rule, total costs of the firm only depend on the *ex ante* known socially optimal level of expected damages, not on the *ex post* realized damages. Under strict liability, the firm *ex ante* only knows its expected value of total cost. However, this insecurity might be avoided by insurances.

(*Note*: It is assumed that the government knows the socially optimal tax level or emission standard. If this is not the case, there might be additional planning insecurities (e.g., in case of an emission tax, the government might approach the Pigou tax using a trial-and-error process).)

e.ii) Distributional effects: Whereas the polluter bears the social damage cost under strict liability, the damaged parties have to bear the damage costs under the negligence rule. The tax load of the firm (areas $A + B$ in the figure) under the Pigou tax exceeds total damages (area A). Thus, even if the government compensates the damaged parties, it remains a surplus.

Solution to exercise 3.1

The internalization approach differs from the standard-oriented approach in that, in the former, the target level of environmental quality is determined by economic optimization, and, in the latter, it is given exogenously. The standard-oriented approach is less ambitious in economic terms because social optimization is substituted by constrained cost minimization.

Solution to exercise 3.2

According to the *weak polluter pays principle*, a polluter who complies with the regulations only bears abatement cost.

According to the *strong polluter pays principle*, a polluter also has to bear costs for his residual emissions. (*Note*: These costs do not necessarily equal external costs. Even though this section is dedicated to solutions (instead of exercises), another question exists: what are some reasons for deviations between what the polluter pays for residual emissions and external costs?)

Solution to exercise 3.3

Static cost effectiveness means the capacity of an instrument to reach the emission target at minimum cost, given the current state of technology. The term *cost effectiveness* in part three is used in this spirit.

Dynamic cost effectiveness means the capacity of an instrument to reach a future emission target or a multiperiod overall emission target at minimum total cost (see part four). Thereby, total cost is composed of investments in environmentally advantageous technical progress and present and future emission abatement cost. In particular, dynamic cost effectiveness implies an instrument's ability to induce the socially optimal level of technical progress or, in other words, to induce the socially optimal level of the *dynamic incentive effect*. In addition, given the optimal abatement technologies for each period, dynamic cost effectiveness implies *cost-effective* abatement in each period.

Solution to exercise 3.4
Other evaluation criteria are

a) (market)system compatibility
b) acceptability and political feasibility
c) informational requirements
d) transaction costs

Solution to exercise 3.5
Command and control and transferable discharge permits allow a precise implementation of an exogenous emission standard. (In the case of command and control, the requirements have to be formulated as absolute emission ceilings for each firm to achieve precise implementation.) In the case of emission taxes, the precise implementation of an exogenous emission standard is left to chance if the regulator does not know the aggregate marginal abatement cost function.

Solution to exercise 3.6
Under transferable discharge permits and emission taxes, marginal abatement costs of different polluters are equalized in equilibrium. Hence, emission reductions are cost effective. In case of command and control, cost effectiveness is left to chance if the regulator does not know the individual marginal abatement cost functions.

Solution to exercise 3.7
If the government has the information that the marginal abatement cost functions of all firms are identical but does not know the marginal abatement cost function, then the government is able to assure cost effectiveness and ecological precision under command and control (by choosing uniform quotas) and permit trading. However, the choice of the ecologically precise emission tax requires the information of the aggregate marginal abatement cost for the aspired emission level.

Solution to exercise 3.8
It has to be mentioned that the evaluation criterion *cost effectiveness* is often used in a narrower sense that does not consider transaction cost. However, if we understand the term "cost effectiveness" in a wider sense and take transaction cost into account, the following two arguments counter the statement:

- It is correct that the transaction cost of a market system tends to increase with the number of market participants. However, the transaction cost per market participant tends to decrease.
- If the number of market participants is small, then there might be inefficiencies due to the fact that some participants have enough market power to influence the permit price.

Solution to exercise 3.9

a) From $MAC_1(E_1) = 25 - \frac{1}{2}E_1$ follows $E_1 = 50 - 2MAC_1$ with $MAC_1 \leq 25$,

and from $MAC_2(E_2) = 10 - \frac{1}{5}E_2$ follows $E_2 = 50 - 5MAC_2$ with $MAC_2 \leq 10$.
Hence, the aggregate marginal cost function is given by

$$E = \begin{cases} 100 - 7MAC & \text{if} & MAC \leq 10, \\ 50 - 2MAC & \text{if} & 10 < MAC \leq 25, \\ 0 & \text{if} & MAC > 25, \end{cases}$$

or, equivalently,

$$MAC_\Sigma = \begin{cases} 25 - \frac{1}{2}E & \text{if} & 0 \leq E \leq 30, \\ \frac{100}{7} - \frac{1}{7}E & \text{if} & 30 < E \leq 100. \end{cases}$$

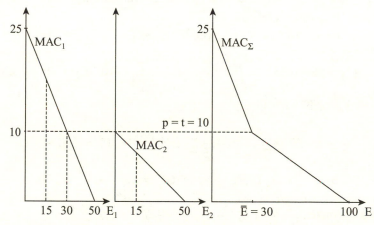

b) $\overline{E} = 30 \Rightarrow \overline{E}_1 = \overline{E}_2 = 15$. Under command and control, the firm-specific cost equals the firm's abatement cost.

(Abatement) costs of firm 1 are given by

$$C_1^{CC} = AC_1 = \int_{15}^{50} MAC_1 \, dE_1 = \int_{15}^{50} 25 - \frac{1}{2}E_1 \, dE_1 = 306.25.$$

(Alternative calculation: $AC_1 = \frac{1}{2} \cdot (50 - 15)\left(25 - \frac{15}{2}\right) = 306.25$.)

(Abatement) costs of firm 2 are given by

$$C_2^{CC} = AC_2 = \int_{15}^{50} MAC_2 \, dE_2 = \int_{15}^{50} 10 - \frac{1}{5}E_2 \, dE_2 = 122.5.$$

(Alternative calculation: $AC_2 = \frac{1}{2} \cdot (50 - 15) \left(10 - \frac{15}{5}\right) = 122.5$.)

Hence, aggregate abatement costs under command and control are given by $C_\Sigma^{CC} = AC_\Sigma = AC_1 + AC_2 = 306.25 + 122.5 = 428.75$.

c) The appropriate tax level is determined by $t = MAC_\Sigma\left(\overline{E}\right) = 10$. The corresponding emission levels of firms 1 and 2 are given by $E_1 = 30$ and $E_2 = 0$.

Firm-specific costs are composed of the abatement cost and the tax load. For firm 1, we get

$$C_1^T = t \cdot E_1 + AC_1 = 10 \cdot 30 + \int_{30}^{50} 25 - \frac{1}{2} E_1 \, dE_1 = 300 + 100 = 400.$$

For firm 2, we get

$$C_2^T = t \cdot 0 + AC_2 = \int_0^{50} 10 - \frac{1}{5} E_2 \, dE_2 = 250.$$

Aggregate abatement costs are given by the sum of firm-specific cost less tax revenues. That is,

$$C_\Sigma^T = C_1^T + C_2^T - t\overline{E} = 350.$$

d) As under the tax regime, equilibrium emissions are given by $E_1 = 30$ and $E_2 = 0$. That is, firm 2 sells its total amount of emission allowances at price $p = MAC^\Sigma(\overline{E}) = 10$ to firm 1.

That is, total costs of firm 1 are given by

$$C_1^P = AC_1 + p \cdot (E_1 - 15) = \int_{30}^{50} 25 - \frac{1}{2} E_1 \, dE_1 + 10 \cdot 15 = 100 + 150 = 250.$$

Total costs of firm 2 are given by

$$C_2^P = AC_2 - p \cdot 15 = \int_0^{50} 10 - \frac{1}{5} E_2 \, dE_2 - 10 \cdot 15 = 250 - 150 = 100.$$

Aggregate abatement costs are given by $C_\Sigma^P = C_1^P + C_2^P = 350$.

e) *Aggregate abatement cost:* $C_\Sigma^T = C_\Sigma^P < C_\Sigma^{CC}$.

Because the tax regime and the permit regime are cost effective, aggregate abatement costs are minimal under these two regimes. The welfare loss under the cost-ineffective command and control regime is given by 78.75.

Firm-specific cost: $C_1^P < C_1^{CC} < C_1^T$ and $C_2^P < C_2^{CC} < C_2^T$.

Both firms prefer command and control over the tax regime because the tax load outweighs the firm-specific welfare losses due to cost-ineffectively chosen emission quotas under command and control.

Furthermore, both firms prefer the permit regime over command and control because the initial permit allocation (without trade) equals the situation under command and control. Starting from this benchmark, both firms benefit from the voluntary permit trading.

Solution to exercise 3.10

a) From $MAC_i^{est}(E_i) = 20 - \dfrac{2}{5}E_i$ follows $E_i = 50 - \dfrac{5}{2}MAC_i^{est}$ with $MAC_i^{est} \leq$ 20. Hence, the estimated aggregate marginal cost function is given by

$$E = 100 - 5\,MAC^{est} \text{ or, equivalently, } MAC_{\Sigma}^{est} = 20 - \frac{1}{5}E.$$

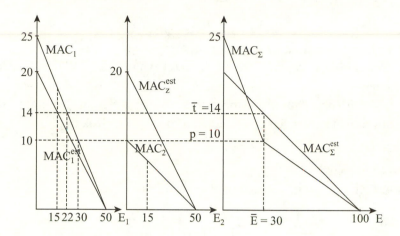

b) The estimation error of the government has no effect under the command and control and the permit regime.

Under the tax regime, the tax level chosen by the government is determined by $\bar{t} = MAC_{\Sigma}^{est}\left(\bar{E}\right) = 14$. The corresponding emission levels of firms 1 and 2 are given by $E_1 = 22$ and $E_2 = 0$.

Total costs of firm 1 are given by

$$C_1^T = \bar{t} \cdot E_1 + AC_1 = 14 \cdot 22 + \int_{22}^{50} 25 - \frac{1}{2}E_1 \, dE_1 = 308 + 196 = 504.$$

For firm 2, we get

$$C_2^T = \bar{t} \cdot 0 + AC_2 = \int_0^{50} 10 - \frac{1}{5}E_2 \, dE_2 = 250.$$

Aggregate abatement costs are given by the sum of firm-specific costs less tax revenues. That is,

$$C_{\Sigma}^T = C_1^T + C_2^T - \bar{t}E = 754 - 308 = 446.$$

Social cost: $C_{\Sigma}^P < C_{\Sigma}^{CC} < C_{\Sigma}^T$.

The overfulfillment of the emission standard under the tax regime involves aggregate abatement costs that are even higher than aggregate abatement costs under command and control. Note, however, that the model of standard-oriented environmental policy does not contain a social cost function that accounts for the positive welfare effect due to reduced damages.

Firm-specific cost: $C_1^P < C_1^{CC} < C_1^T$ and $C_2^P < C_2^{CC} < C_2^T$.

The firm-specific rankings are the same as in exercise 3.9. In particular, the tax regime again generates the highest firm-specific cost. The estimation error makes the tax regime even more unfavorable to the firms due to the higher tax level.

Solution to exercise 4.1
Examples are

- *global warming*, caused by greenhouse gases
- *the respirable dust exposure*, caused by diesel exhaust particulates and airborne particulates
- *the forest dieback*, caused by the interaction of different pollutants such as sulphur dioxide, nitrogen oxides, and ammonium hydroxide

Solution to exercise 4.2
Total differentiation of the restriction $B = \overline{B}$ yields

$$\frac{\partial B}{\partial x}dx + \frac{\partial B}{\partial y}dy = a_1 dx + a_2 dy = 0.$$

Hence, the constant marginal rate of pollutant substitution ($=$ slope of $B = \overline{B}$) is given by

$$MRS = \frac{dy}{dx} = -\frac{a_1}{a_2}.$$

In the optimum, the marginal rate of pollutant substitution equals the marginal rate of pollutant transformation ($=$ slope of an iso-cost curve), which is given by $MRT = \frac{dy}{dx} = -\frac{MAC_x}{MAC_y}$, with MAC denoting marginal abatement cost.

Given the tax levels t_x and t_y, the industries adjust their emissions according to $MAC_x = t_x$ and $MAC_y = t_y$. Hence, the optimal tax ratio is given by $(t_x/t_y)^{**} = a_1/a_2$.

Solution to exercise 4.3
An example of an environmental burden function with concave iso-burden curves is $B(x, y) = x^2 + y^2$. In this case, the iso-burden curves $\overline{B} = x^2 + y^2$ are circular arcs with radius $\sqrt{\overline{B}}$.

Solution to exercise 4.4
In the case of concave iso-burden curves and convex iso-abatement cost curves, there is a unique optimal emission tuple (x^{**}, y^{**}). The optimal emission tuple can either be an inner solution (see Fig. a) or a corner solution (see Fig. b).

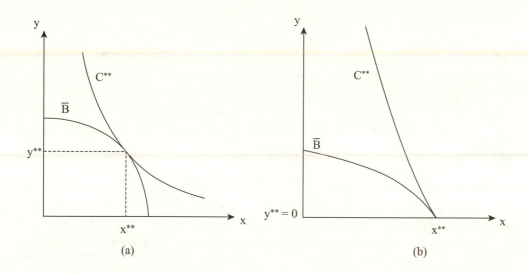

(a)   (b)

Solution to exercise 4.5

Each emission tuple (x^{**}, y^{**}) that fulfills the burden restriction $B(x, y) = \overline{B}$ yields identical cost and, hence, is socially optimal.

Solution to exercise 4.6

The equilibrium supply of the monopolist is determined by $MR = MPC$, with MR denoting marginal revenues and MPC denoting marginal private cost.

The revenue function is given by $R(x) = P(x) \cdot x = (11 - x)x$. Deriving the revenue function yields $MR(x) = 11 - 2x$. From $MR(x_M) = MPC(x_M) \Leftrightarrow 11 - 2x_M = 1$ follows $x_M = 5$.

At the social optimum, the price (as a measure of marginal willingness to pay) equals the sum of private marginal cost and marginal damages, $P(x^{**}) = MPC(x^{**}) + MD(x^{**})$. From which follows $x^{**} = 5$.

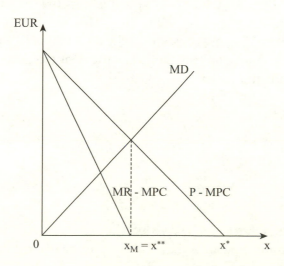

Hence, the equilibrium supply of the monopolist is socially optimal, which can be explained as follows: due to the negative externality, the socially optimal production level x^{**} is lower than the competitive equilibrium production level $x^* = 10$, determined by $P(x^*) = MPC(x^*)$. However, an unregulated monopolist also chooses a production level x_M, which is lower than the competitive equilibrium level. For the given functions, both deviations have the same size (i.e., we have $x^* - x^{**} = x^* - x_M$ from which follows $x^{**} = x_M$). Hence, the optimal tax rate is given by $t_M = 0$.

Solution to exercise 4.7

a) Marginal opportunity cost of an output reduction (or, equivalently, of a gross emission reduction) are given by $(P - MPC)(E_G) = 110 - 5E_G - 10 = 100 - 5E_G$. In the social optimum, these marginal opportunity costs equal the marginal technological abatement costs $MAC(ER_a) = 5\,ER_a$. In addition, both marginal costs coincide with marginal damages $MD(E) = 10E$. Summarizing, the socially optimal emission levels are determined by

$$MD(E_G^{**} - ER_a^{**}) = MAC(ER_a^{**}) = (P - MPC)(E_G^{**})$$

$$\Leftrightarrow 10(E_G^{**} - ER_a^{**}) = 5\,ER_a^{**} = 100 - 5\,E_G^{**}, \text{ from which follows}$$

$$E_G^{**} = 12, \quad ER_a^{**} = 8 \text{ and } E^{**} = 4.$$

b) In the unregulated equilibrium, the monopolist makes no use of the abatement technology. The monopolistic marginal opportunity costs of an output reduction are given by $(MR - MPC)(E)$ with $MR(E) = 110 - 10E$. From this follows $110 - 10E_M - 10 = 0 \Leftrightarrow E_M = 10$.

c) If the government chooses the tax level t_M, the monopolist adjusts his gross emission level E_G and his emission abatement level ER_a according to $t_M = MAC(ER_a) = (MR - MPC)(E_G) \Leftrightarrow t_M = 5\,ER_a = 100 - 10E_G$. Together with $E_G - ER_a = E^{**} = 4$, we get $t_M = 20$, $ER_a = 4$, and $E_G = 8$. Note that, even though the corresponding net emission level equals the socially optimal one, the output level and the emission reduction via abatement technology are lower than in the socially optimal situation.

Solution to exercise 4.8

a) $MAC^H(x_H^{**}) = MD(x_H^{**}) \Leftrightarrow 100 - x_H^{**} = 2x_H^{**} \Leftrightarrow x_H^{**} = 33\frac{1}{3}.$

$$MAC^L(x_L^{**}) = MD(x_L^{**}) \Leftrightarrow \frac{100 - x_L^{**}}{2} = 2x_L^{**} \Leftrightarrow x_L^{**} = 20.$$

b) An honest polluter of type L reduces his emission level from $x^* = 100$ to $x_L^{**} = 20$ and is compensated for the corresponding abatement cost.

If a polluter of type L pretends to be of type H, he reduces his emission level from $x^* = 100$ to $x_H^{**} = 33\frac{1}{3}$. Corresponding abatement costs are

$$AC^L(x_H^{**}) = \int_{x_H^{**}}^{x^*} MAC^L(x)\,dx = \int_{100/3}^{100} \left(50 - \frac{1}{2}x\right) dx = 1{,}111\frac{1}{9}.$$

As compensation payment, however, he receives the pretended abatement cost

$$AC^H(x_H^{**}) = \int_{x_H^{**}}^{x^*} MAC^H(x)\,dx = \int_{100/3}^{100} (100 - x)\,dx = 2{,}222\frac{2}{9}$$

and, hence, makes the profit $AC^H(x_H^{**}) - AC^L(x_H^{**}) = 1{,}111\frac{1}{9}$.

Solution to exercise 4.9

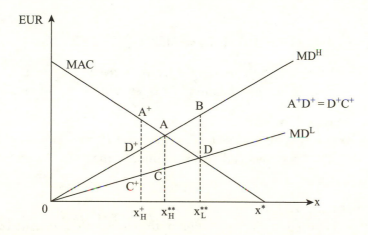

a) The socially optimal emission levels x_H^{**} and x_L^{**} are determined by $MAC(x_H^{**}) = MD^H(x_H^{**})$ and $MAC(x_L^{**}) = MD^L(x_L^{**})$.

b) If a damaged party of type L is honest and allows the polluter to emit x_L^{**}, he is compensated for his damage, represented by the area $0x_L^{**}D$.

   If a damaged party of type L pretends to be an H type, he allows the polluter to emit x_H^{**}. The corresponding damages are $0x_H^{**}C$ and lower than the compensation payment $0x_H^{**}A$. Hence, the profit of a dishonest type L party is represented by the area $0AC$.

   If a damaged party of type H is honest and allows the polluter to emit x_H^{**}, he is compensated for his damage, represented by the area $0x_H^{**}A$.

   If a damaged party of type H pretends to be of type L and allows the polluter to emit x_L^{**}, the corresponding damages are $0x_L^{**}B$ and thus higher than the compensation payment, which equals the pretended damage $0x_L^{**}D$.

   Hence, only a damaged party of type L has an incentive to be dishonest.

c)   A decrease of the compensation limit for a damaged party of (pretended) type H
     from x_H^{**} to x_H^+ has two effects for the polluter. On the one hand, his bargaining
     profit in the case that the damaged party is of type H decreases by

$$\int_{x_H^+}^{x_H^{**}} (MAC(x) - MD^H(x))dx.$$

On the other hand, the cheating profit of a dishonest L type (and accordingly
the honesty premium for an honest L type) decreases by

$$\int_{x_H^+}^{x_H^{**}} (MD^H(x) - MD^L(x))dx.$$

Because the probability of each type is $\frac{1}{2}$, the polluter weights both effects
equally. Hence, the optimal compensation limit x_H^+ of the H type is determined
by

$$MAC(x_H^+) - MD^H(x_H^+) = MD^H(x_H^+) - MD^L(x_H^+).$$

The optimal compensation limit of the L type is given by $x_L^+ = x_L^{**}$.
The corresponding honesty premium P^L is represented by the area $0C^+D^+$.

Solution to exercise 4.10

The statement is wrong because both described effects are elements of the "second dividend." The "first dividend" refers to improvements of the environmental
quality.

Solution to exercise 4.11

Interpretation A: The strong interpretation of the employment-oriented variant of
the second dividend asserts that the employment level rises in absolute terms if tax
revenues are used to ease the tax burden on labor.

Interpretation B: The weak interpretation asserts that the employment effects are
higher if tax revenues are used to ease the tax burden on labor instead of giving
them back as lump sum payments to the citizens.

Theoretically, the case may occur that the employment level also increases if
tax revenues are distributed as lump sum payments to the citizens and that the
employment effect in case of the lump sum distribution is even higher.

However, the theoretical construct described previously does not seem to be
realistic because a lump sum distribution involves only indirect effects on the labor
market (e.g., via demand changes or the influence of the income effect on labor
supply), whereas the tax unburdening of the factor labor has a direct positive effect
on the labor demand.

Hence, the terms "weak" and "strong interpretation" are appropriate.

Solution of exercise 4.12

a) The total cost function of the society is given by

$$C^T(a_0, a_1, I_0) = \frac{1}{8}a_0^2 + (10 - a_0) + I_0 + \frac{1}{8}\frac{a_1^2}{1 + \sqrt{I_0}} + (10 - a_1).$$

Note that the total cost functions can be divided into two parts as follows:

$$C^T(a_0, a_1, I_0) = C_0^T(a_0) + C_1^T(a_1, I_0) \text{ with}$$

$$C_0^T(a_0) = \frac{1}{8}a_0^2 + (10 - a_0) \text{ and } C_1^T(a_1, I_0) = I_0 + \frac{1}{8}\frac{a_1^2}{1 + \sqrt{I_0}} + (10 - a_1).$$

The corresponding first-order conditions are given by

$$\partial C_0^T / \partial a_0 = \frac{1}{4}a_0 - 1 \Rightarrow a_0^{**} = 4$$

$$\partial C_1^T / \partial a_1 = \frac{1}{4}\frac{a_1}{1 + \sqrt{I_0}} - 1 = 0$$

$$\partial C_1^T / \partial I_0 = 1 - \frac{1}{16}\frac{a_1^2}{(1 + \sqrt{I_0})^2 \sqrt{I_0}} = 0.$$

From the last two equations follows $I_0^{**} = 1$ and $a_1^{**} = 8$.

For the sake of completeness, note that $\dfrac{\partial^2 C_0^T}{\partial a_0^2} > 0$ holds and that $H =$

$$\begin{pmatrix} \dfrac{\partial^2 C_1^T}{\partial a_1^2} & \dfrac{\partial^2 C_1^T}{\partial a_1 \partial I_0} \\ \dfrac{\partial^2 C_1^T}{\partial I_0 \partial a_1} & \dfrac{\partial^2 C_1^T}{\partial I_0^2} \end{pmatrix}$$ is positive definite (i.e., also the sufficient conditions for

the inner optimum are fulfilled).

Hence, the socially optimal activity levels are given by $a_0^{**} = 4$, $I_0^{**} = 1$, and $a_1^{**} = 8$.

Furthermore, we have $a_1^{**} - a_0^{**} > 0$ (i.e., the investment in technical progress reduces (marginal) abatement cost in period 1). Hence, the equilibrium abatement level of period 1 is higher than that of period 0.

b) Under strict liability, the private cost function of the firm equals the social cost function. Accordingly, the equilibrium abatement levels a_0^*, a_1^*, and I_0^* coincide with the socially optimal ones (i.e., we have $a_0^* = 4$, $I_0^* = 1$, and $a_1^* = 8$).

Solution of exercise 4.13

a) The socially optimal investment level, I_0^{**}, and the abatement level in period 1, a_1^{**}, are lower than in the situation without discounting because, with discounting, society puts more weight on the (marginal) investment cost of period 0 compared to the (marginal) utility in terms of decreasing (marginal) abatement cost in period 1.

As in the situation without discounting, the private cost function of the firm equals the socially cost function under strict liability. Accordingly, the equilibrium abatement levels a_0^*, a_1^*, and I_0^* coincide with the socially optimal ones.

Formal analysis:
The total cost function of the society is given by

$$C^T(a_0, a_1, I_0) = C_0^T(a_0) + C_1^T(a_1, I_0) \text{ with}$$

$$C_0^T(a_0) = \frac{1}{8}a_0^2 + (10 - a_0) \text{ and } C_1^T(a_1, I_0)$$

$$= I_0 + \frac{1}{1+r}\left(\frac{1}{8}\frac{a_1^2}{1+\sqrt{I_0}} + (10 - a_1)\right).$$

Note that only $C_1^T(a_1, I_0)$ has changed compared to the situation without discounting. Hence, we again get $a_0^{**} = 4$. The corresponding first-order conditions with respect to a_1 and I_0 are given by

$$\partial C_1^T / \partial a_1 = \frac{1}{1+r}\left(\frac{1}{4}\frac{a_1}{1+\sqrt{I_0}} - 1\right) = 0,$$

$$\partial C_1^T / \partial I_0 = 1 - \frac{1}{1+r}\frac{1}{16}\frac{a_1^2}{(1+\sqrt{I_0})^2\sqrt{I_0}} = 0,$$

from which follows $I_0^{**} = \frac{1}{(1+r)^2}$ and $a_1^{**} = \frac{4}{1+r} + 4$.

Again, $H = \begin{pmatrix} \dfrac{\partial^2 C_1^T}{\partial a_1^2} & \dfrac{\partial^2 C_1^T}{\partial a_1 \partial I_0} \\ \dfrac{\partial^2 C_1^T}{\partial I_0 \partial a_1} & \dfrac{\partial^2 C_1^T}{\partial I_0^2} \end{pmatrix}$ is positive definite.

Hence, the socially optimal activity levels are given by $a_0^{**} = 4$, $I_0^{**} = \frac{1}{(1+r)^2} < 1$ and $a_1^{**} = \frac{4}{1+r} + 4 < 8$.

Under strict liability, the equilibrium abatement levels a_0^*, a_1^*, and I_0^* coincide with the socially optimal ones (i.e., $a_0^* = 4$, $I_0^* = \frac{1}{(1+r)^2}$, and $a_1^* = \frac{4}{1+r} + 4$).

b) If the society discounts future payoffs with discount rate r^{**} and the firm discounts future payoffs with rate $r^* > r^{**}$, the firm chooses an investment level in period 0 and an abatement level in period 1, which are too low from the socially optimal point of view. The relevant cost functions of the society and the firm differ only with respect to the discount rate. Because the firm puts relatively more weight on the (marginal) investment cost of period 0 compared to the (marginal) utility in terms of decreasing (marginal) abatement cost in period 1, its investment level is too low compared to the socially optimal one. Correspondingly, the marginal abatement cost function in period 1 is too steep compared to the social one, from which follows $a_1^* < a_1^{**}$.

Formal analysis:

If the society discounts future payoffs with discount rate r^{**} and the firm discounts future payoffs with rate $r^* > r^{**}$, then the socially optimal activity levels are given by $a_0^{**} = 4$, $I_0^{**} = \dfrac{1}{(1 + r^{**})^2}$, and $a_1^{**} = \dfrac{4}{1 + r^{**}} + 4$.

Under strict liability, however, the firm chooses $a_0^* = a_0^{**} = 4$, $I_0^* = \dfrac{1}{(1 + r^*)^2} < I_0^{**}$, and $a_1^* = \dfrac{4}{1 + r^*} + 4 < a_1^{**}$.

Solution to exercise 5.1

a) In the optimal allocation of a global pollutant, aggregate marginal abatement costs are equal to aggregate marginal damages (i.e., $MAC = MD$).

b) In the optimal allocation of a global pollutant, country-specific marginal abatement costs are identical for each country and equal to aggregate marginal abatement costs (i.e., $MAC = MAC_i$).

c) In any allocation of a global pollutant (and thus also in the optimal one), aggregate marginal damages are equal to the sum of country specific marginal damages (i.e., $MD = \sum MD_i$).

Solution to exercise 5.2

Given the benefit and damage functions are well behaved, the technical progress leads to a reduction of the Nash equilibrium emission level of country i. The influence on the emission level of country j depends on the slope of this country's marginal damage function. If this function is strictly increasing in the aggregate emissions, the Nash equilibrium emission level of country j rises due to the emission reduction of country i. This effect is called leakage effect. (See also section C.II.1.)

Solution to exercise 5.3

a) The socially optimal emission levels are determined by

$$MAC_1 = MAC_2 = MD_1 + MD_2 \Leftrightarrow 100 - x_1 = 100 - 10x_2 = 11(x_1 + x_2).$$

The solution of this system of equations is given by $x_1^{**} = \dfrac{1000}{131}$, $x_2^{**} = \dfrac{100}{131}$. The Nash equilibrium emission levels are determined by

$$\begin{array}{cc} MAC_1 = MD_1 \\ MAC_2 = MD_2 \end{array} \Leftrightarrow \begin{array}{c} 100 - x_1 = 10(x_1 + x_2) \\ 100 - 10x_2 = x_1 + x_2 \end{array}.$$

The solution is given by $x_1^N = \dfrac{100}{111}$, $x_2^N = \dfrac{1000}{111}$.

Whereas aggregate emission levels are higher in the Nash equilibrium than in the socially optimal allocation $\left(\dfrac{1100}{111} > \dfrac{1100}{131} \right)$, the emission level of country 1 is higher in the socially optimal allocation $\left(\dfrac{1000}{131} > \dfrac{100}{111} \right)$.

Compared with country 2, country 1 suffers from high environmental damages. Correspondingly in the Nash equilibrium, country 1 chooses a rather low emission level and country 2 a rather high emission level, although marginal abatement costs of country 1 are also higher. This difference in the marginal abatement cost, however, implies that country 2 should bear the main part of the emission reductions from the socially optimal point of view.

b) The change from the Nash equilibrium to the socially optimal emission levels decreases total environmental damages in countries 1 and 2 by

$$\Delta D_1 = \int_{x_1^N + x_2^N}^{x_1^{**} + x_2^{**}} MD_1(x)dx = -138.49, \quad \Delta D_2 = \int_{x_1^N + x_2^N}^{x_1^{**} + x_2^{**}} MD_2(x)dx = -13.85.$$

Total abatement costs of country 1 decrease by

$$\Delta AC_1 = -\int_{x_1^N}^{x_1^{**}} MAC_1(x_1)dx_1 = -644.54.$$

Total abatement costs of country 2 increase by

$$\Delta AC_2 = -\int_{x_2^N}^{x_2^{**}} MAC_2(x_2)dx_2 = 421.67.$$

Thus, the welfare of country 1 increases by $\Delta W_1 = 783.03$, and the welfare of country 2 decreases by $\Delta W_2 = -407.82$.

The contract is not individually rational because the welfare of country 2 decreases.

Solution to exercise 5.4

Possible causes for a shift of the marginal abatement cost curve are as follows:

- Technical progress
- Environmental regulation (e.g., eco-tax)

Possible causes for a shift of the marginal damage curve are as follows:

- Change of the society's environmental awareness
- New natural scientific insights with respect to the emission–damage correlation

Solution to exercise 5.5

Statement (b) is correct, and statement (a) is wrong if the starting point of the negotiations is the Nash equilibrium.

Starting from the uncorrected emission levels, the welfare of country i increases if the other countries choose the Nash equilibrium emission levels instead of their uncorrected emission levels due to the positive externality of emission reductions.

The welfare of country i further increases if country i itself chooses its best reply (i.e., its own Nash equilibrium emission level). Thus, the welfare of country i (and any other country) is higher in the Nash equilibrium than in the situation without any emission reductions.

Hence, the condition that under the contract each country's welfare is higher than in the situation where each country chooses its uncorrected emission level is a necessary but not sufficient condition for the individual rationality of a contract.

Solution to exercise 5.6
Some examples are as follows:

- Global warming
- Overfishing
- Road congestion
- Extinction of species

Solution to exercise 5.7
In the environmental economics literature that deals with local environmental problems, the society as a whole is usually assumed to be risk neutral, even if individuals are risk averse. The reason is that individuals may contract insurances, and thus the risks are diversified. However, the insurability against global risks is (if at all) only given within narrow limits. Therefore, the assumption of risk-averse countries is plausible in the context of global environmental problems such as climate change.

Solution to exercise 5.8
Provided that the contract is individually rational, each country prefers the situation where all countries have ratified the contract and comply with the rules over the situation without cooperation. However, there are (at least) two incentive problems.

First, if the contract has entered into force, the incentive for a country to breach the rules still remains and must be eliminated through additional stabilization mechanisms (sanctions).

Second, the threat to play the noncooperative equilibrium in the event that one country rejects the ratification is not credible because the residual countries have an incentive to renegotiate the contract and weaken the ratification rules.

Solution to exercise 5.9
A possible transfer scheme would be the scheme that assures that each country receives the same proportion of the global welfare improvement.

Thus, the transfer T_i of country i would be defined by

$$W_i^{**} + T_i = W_i^N + \frac{1}{n} \left(\sum_{j=1}^{n} \left(W_j^{**} - W_j^N \right) \right),$$

which is equivalent to

$$T_i = W_i^N - W_i^{**} + \frac{1}{n}\left(\sum_{j=1}^{n}\left(W_j^{**} - W_j^N\right)\right).$$

Solution to exercise 5.10
The Montreal Protocol on Substances that Deplete the Ozone Layer is one of the first international environmental agreements that includes trade sanctions (e.g., the protocol contains provisions banning trade in some ozone-depleting substances with nonsignatories).

Solution to exercise 5.11

a)   The assertion is wrong (e.g., in the example presented in Table 2, a coalition of size 4 is externally stable, but a coalition of size 3 is not internally stable).
b)   The assertion is wrong (e.g., in the example, a coalition of size 2 is internally stable, but a coalition of size 1 is not externally stable).
c)   The assertion is wrong (e.g., in the example, a coalition of size 3 is externally stable, but a coalition of size 4 is not internally stable).
d)   The assertion is correct. If a coalition of size $j > 1$ is not internally stable, then the welfare of a signatory of a size j coalition is lower than the welfare of a nonsignatory of a size $(j-1)$ coalition. Hence, the welfare of a nonsignatory of a size $(j-1)$ coalition is at least as high as the welfare of a signatory of a size j coalition.

Solution to exercise 5.12
The government could pursue the objective to gain maximal voters' support.

Solution to exercise 5.13
In the national context, the government is able to regulate environmental problems. In the international context, there is no corresponding world government with enough enforcement power to enforce globally optimal solutions. Instead, the regulation of international environmental problems demands coordinated actions of sovereign countries, which are hampered by free rider incentives.

Solution to exercise 5.14
Carbon dioxide equivalency is a quantity that describes, for a given amount of greenhouse gas, the amount of CO_2 that would have the same global warming potential. Thus, by means of CO_2 equivalent, the global warming potential of different greenhouse gases is converted into a single unit.

The formulation of global and national emission targets in form of CO_2 equivalents provides the basis for a cost-effective emission reduction because the reduction targets may be divided on the different greenhouse gases in such a way that marginal abatement costs are equalized.

Solution to exercise 5.15

Whereas the flexible mechanisms emission trading and joint implementation are restricted to annex B (i.e., industrialized) countries, the clean development mechanism establishes a kind of trade between industrialized and developing countries.

Solution to exercise 5.16

Because the policy maker believes that the optimal emission level equals E^{**est}, he chooses this level as aggregate emission target. If the policy maker succeeds in dividing the aggregate emission target cost effectively on the different polluters, then the welfare loss is given by the triangle ABC (which is the lower bound for the welfare loss under command and control). However, the cost-effective division is very unlikely because the policy maker does not know the individual marginal abatement cost functions. Thus, under command and control, the welfare loss presumably exceeds the area of the triangle ABC.

Solution to exercise 5.17

Additional evaluation criteria could be as follows:

- Competition effects
- Transaction cost (related to the criterion of cost effectiveness)
- Enforceability (related to the criterion of transaction cost)

Solution to exercise 5.18

The integration of CDM into European Union emissions trading works in favor of (static) cost effectiveness because it helps equalize marginal abatement cost between developing and industrial countries. The quantitative restriction hampers cost effectiveness if it is binding.

Because there are no obligations for developing countries to reduce their emissions, the usage of CDM hampers ecological precision. This holds especially true if the addition of emission reductions from CDM in developing countries cannot always be assured.

The usage of CDM lowers the equilibrium permit price and thereby decreases the industrialized countries' incentive to invest in technological progress. However, note that this does not necessarily imply that investments decrease below the socially optimal level.

Solution to exercise 5.19

Because the emission reduction obligations of the Kyoto Protocol refer to 2008–2012, whereas the European Union (EU) emissions trading system started in 2005, the EU emissions trading system offered the possibility to gain experience with permit trading in advance.

However, a main difference between the Kyoto emissions trading and the EU emissions trading is that the Kyoto emissions trading system is a trading system between countries, whereas in the EU permit market trading occurs among polluters.

Solution to exercise 6.1
Exhaustible energy: coal, oil, natural gas
Renewable energy: solar energy, water power, wind power, biofuel, geothermal energy

Solution to exercise 6.2
Indeed, some renewable resources that cannot be depleted do exist, such as solar energy or wind power. However, other kinds of renewable resources, such as fish stocks, can be depleted. For these kinds of resources, a positive regeneration requires a minimum stock. If the stock falls short of this minimum level due to excessive exhaustion (or other causes) in a certain period, then the stock will completely disappear in the future. Hence, the statement is wrong.

Solution to exercise 6.3

- Perfect competition
- Existence of (a perfect system of) future markets
- No external effects
- Identity of market interest rate and social rate of discount

Solution to exercise 6.4
With *WP* denoting willingness to pay and *EC* denoting exploitation cost, the welfare maximization problem of the social planner is given by

$$\max_{q_0, q_1, q_2} W = WP(q_0) - EC(q_0) + (WP(q_1) - EC(q_1))(1+r)^{-1}$$

$$+ (WP(q_2) - EC(q_2))(1+r)^{-2}$$

$$\text{s.t. } q_0 + q_1 + q_2 \leq Q.$$

The first-order conditions are given by

$$MWP(q_0) - MEC(q_0) + \lambda = 0,$$
$$(MWP(q_1) - MEC(q_1))(1+r)^{-1} + \lambda = 0,$$
$$(MWP(q_2) - MEC(q_2))(1+r)^{-2} + \lambda = 0, \text{ and}$$
$$q_0 + q_1 + q_2 - Q = 0.$$

From the first three conditions follows the rule (Hotelling Rule)

$$MWP(q_0) - MEC(q_0) = \frac{MWP(q_1) - MEC(q_1)}{1+r}$$

$$= \frac{MWP(q_2) - MEC(q_2)}{(1+r)^2}.$$

Inserting the given functions gives

$$1,000 - q_0 = (1,000 - q_1) \cdot 1.1^{-1} = (1,000 - q_2) \cdot 1.1^{-2} \text{ and}$$

$$q_0 + q_1 + q_2 = 1,345$$

As can be easily verified, the solution of this system of equations is given by $q_0 = 500$, $q_1 = 450$ and $q_2 = 395$.

Solution to exercise 6.5

An increase of the social discount rate accelerates the socially optimal extraction of the resource.

Solution to exercise 6.6

We first have to determine the stock S_{MSY} at which maximum growth is attained. From the first-order condition,

$$\frac{\partial G}{\partial S_t} = \frac{2}{5}\left(1 - \frac{S_t}{1000} - \frac{S_t - 100}{1000}\right) = \frac{11}{25} - \frac{S_t}{1250} = 0$$

follows $S_{MSY} = 550$.

Inserting S_{MSY} in the growth function gives $MSY = G(S_{MSY}) = \frac{2}{5}(550 - 100)\left(1 - \frac{550}{1000}\right) = 81$.

Because $G(S_t) = \frac{2}{5}(S_t - 100)\left(1 - \frac{S_t}{1000}\right) > 0 \Leftrightarrow 100 < S_t < 1000$ holds, the minimum stock is given by $S_{\min} = 101$.

Solution to exercise 6.7

The statement is wrong. First, the socially optimal yield may be lower than the maximum sustainable one if marginal extraction costs are positive and marginal utility from consumption of the resource is decreasing. Second, the socially optimal yield may be higher than the maximum sustainable one if the social welfare function only accounts for the welfare of the current generation.

Solution to exercise 6.8

The expression *open access regime* means that the property rights of a resource are not specified.

Solution to exercise 6.9

The concept of social welfare maximization discounts the interests of future generations by a positive discount rate (if they are considered in the welfare function at all). The sustainability approach accommodates the interests of future generations and, in particular, weights them equally.

Solution to exercise 6.10

Strong sustainability asks for a constant (or nondecreasing) capital stock over time and also assumes that natural capital cannot be substituted by manmade capital or other kinds of natural capital. Hence, no positive extraction of an exhaustible resource would be acceptable.

References

Ackerman, F., L. Heinzerling (2004): *Priceless: On Knowing the Price of Everything and the Value of Nothing*, New York.

Ahlheim, M., F. Schneider (2002): Allowing for Household Preferences in Emission Trading, *Environmental and Resource Economics* Vol. 21, 317–342.

Akerlof, G.A. (1970): The Market for "Lemons": Quality Uncertainty and the Market Mechanism, *Quarterly Journal of Economics* Vol. 84, 488–500.

Anger, N. (2008): Emission Trading Beyond Europe: Linking Schemes in a Post-Kyoto World, *Energy Economics* Vol. 30, 2028–2049.

Arguedas, C. (2008): To Comply or Not To Comply? Pollution Standard Setting under Costly Monitoring and Sanctioning, *Environmental & Resource Economics* Vol. 41, 155–168.

Asheim, G. (1997): Adjusting Green NNP to Measure Sustainability, *Scandinavian Journal of Economics* Vol. 94, 355–370.

Asheim, G., W. Buchholz (2003): The Malleability of Undiscounted Utilitarianism as a Criterion of Intergenerational Justice, *Economica* Vol. 70, 405–422.

Asheim, G., W. Buchholz, C. Withagen (2003): The Hartwick Rule – Myths and Facts, *Environmental and Resource Economics* Vol. 25, 129–150.

Asheim, G. et al. (2006): Regional versus Global Cooperation for Climate Control, *Journal of Environmental Economics and Management* Vol. 51, 93–109.

Atkinson, G., K. Hamilton (2007): Progress along the Path: Evolving Issues in the Measurement of Genuine Saving, *Environmental & Resource Economics* Vol. 37, 43–61.

Atkinson, T. et al. (2002): *Social Indicators*, Oxford.

Aumann, R.J., S. Hart (2003): Long Cheap Talk, *Econometrica* Vol. 71, 1619–1660.

Ayres, R.U. (2007): On the Practical Limits to Substitution, *Ecological Economics* Vol. 61, 115–128.

Ayres, R.U. (2008): Sustainability Economics: Where Do We Stand?, *Ecological Economics* Vol. 67, 281–310.

Baker, P. (2004): Russia Backs Kyoto to Get on Path to Join WTO, The Washington Post, May 22, 2004, A15.

Baker, E., L. Clarke, E. Shittu (2008): Technical Change and the Marginal Cost of Abatement, *Energy Economics* Vol. 30, 2799–2816.

Baksi, S., P. Bose (2007): Credence Goods, Efficient Labelling Policies, and Regulatory Enforcement, *Environmental & Resource Economics* Vol. 37, 411–430.

Ballard, C.L., D. Fullerton (1992): Distortionary Taxes and the Provision of Public Goods, *Journal of Economic Perspectives* Vol. 6, 117–131.

Bansal, S. (2008): Choice and Design of Regulatory Instruments in the Presence of Green Consumers, *Resource & Energy Economics* Vol. 30, 345–368.

Barnett, A.H. (1970): The Pigouvian Tax Rule under Monopoly, *American Economic Review* Vol. 70, 1037–1041.

Barrett, S. (1994a): Self-Enforcing International Environmental Agreements, *Oxford Economic Papers* Vol. 46, 878–894.

Barrett, S. (1994b): The Biodiversity Supergame, *Environmental and Resource Economics* Vol. 4, 111–122.

Barrett, S. (2002): Consensus Treaties, *Journal of Institutional and Theoretical Economics* Vol. 158, 529–547.

Barrett, S. (2005): *Environment and Statecraft: The Strategy of Environmental Treaty-Making*, 2nd edition, New York.

Bauman, Y., M. Lee, K. Seeley (2008): Does Technological Innovation Really Reduce Marginal Abatement Costs? Some Theory, Algebraic Evidence, and Policy Implications, *Environmental & Resource Economics* Vol. 40, 507–527.

Baumgärtner, S., M. Faber, J. Proops (2002): How Environmental Concern Influences the Investment Decision, *Ecological Economics* Vol. 40, 1–12.

Baumgärtner, S., M. Faber, J. Schiller (2006): *Joint Production and Responsibility in Ecological Economics*, Cheltenham.

Baumol, W.J., W.E. Oates (1971): The Use of Standards and Prices for Protection of the Environment, *Swedish Journal of Economics* Vol. 73, 42–54.

Baumol, W.J., W.E. Oates (1988): *The Theory of Environmental Policy*, 2nd edition, Cambridge.

Bayer, S. (2003): Generation Adjusted Discounting in Long-Term Decision-Making, *International Journal of Sustainable Development* Vol. 6, 133–149.

Becker, G.S. (1974): A Theory of Social Interactions, *Journal of Political Economy* Vol. 82, 1063–1094.

Becker, G.S. (1993): Noble Lecture: The Economic Way of Looking at Behavior, *Journal of Political Economy* Vol. 101, 395–409.

Becker, G.S. et al. (1991): Economics of Drugs, Rational Addiction and the Effect of Price on Consumption, *American Economic Review* Vol. 81, 237–241.

Begg, D., S. Fischer, R. Dornbusch (2008): *Economics*, 9th edition, Boston.

Berg, V., J. Tschirhart (1988): *Natural Monopoly Regulation*, Cambridge.

Bergstrom, T.C. (2006): Benefit–Cost in a Benevolent Society, *American Economic Review* Vol. 96, 339–351.

Biglaiser, G., J.K. Horowitz, J. Quiggin (1995): Dynamic Pollution Regulation, *Journal of Regulatory Economics* Vol. 8, 33–44.

Binmore, K. (2005): *Natural Justice*, Oxford.

Binmore, K. (2007): *Playing for Real – A Text on Game Theory*, Oxford.

Blume, A., T. Arnold (2004): Learning to Communicate in Cheap-Talk Games, *Games and Economic Behavior* Vol. 46, 240–259.

Böhringer, C., M. Finus (2005): The Kyoto Protocol – Success or Failure? In: D. Helm (Ed.), *Climate-change Policy*, Oxford, 253–281.

Böhringer, C., M. Finus, C. Vogt (Eds.) (2002): *Controlling Global Warming – Perspectives from Economics, Game Theory and Public Choice*, Cheltenham.

Böhringer, C., T. Hoffmann, C. Manrique-de-Lara-Peñate (2006): The Efficiency Costs of Separating Carbon Markets under the EU Emissions Trading Scheme, *Energy Economics* Vol. 28, 44–61.

Böhringer, C., H. Koschel, U. Moslener (2009): Efficiency Losses from Overlapping Economic Instruments in European Carbon Emissions Regulation, *Journal of Regulatory Economics* Vol. 33, 299–317.

Böhringer, C., A. Löschel, T.F. Rutherford (2007): Efficiency Gains from "What" – Flexibility in Climate Policy – An Integrated CGE Assessment, *The Energy Journal* Vol. 28, 405–424.

Böhringer, C., U. Moslener, B. Sturm (2007): Hot Air for Sale: A Quantitative Assessment of Russia's Near-Term Climate Policy Options, *Environmental & Resource Economics* Vol. 38, 545–572.

Böhringer, C., C. Vogt (2004): The Dismantling of a Breakthrough: The Kyoto Protocol as Symbolic Policy, *European Journal of Political Economy* Vol. 20, 597–617.

Bolle, F., M. Braham (2006): A Difficulty with Oaths – On Trust, Trustworthiness, and Signalling, *European Journal of Law and Economics* Vol. 22, 219–232.

Bolle, F., A. Kritikos (2006): Reciprocity, Altruism, Solidarity: A Dynamic Model, *Theory and Decision* Vol. 60, 371–394.

Bolle, F., J. Tan (2006): On the Relative Strengths of Altruism and Fairness, *Theory and Decision* Vol. 60, 35–67.

Bolton, G.E., A. Ockenfels (2000): ERC – A Theory of Equity, Reciprocity and Competition, *American Economic Review* Vol. 90, 166–193.

Bovenberg, A.L., R.A. de Mooij (1994): Environmental Levies and Distortionary Taxation, *American Economic Review* Vol. 84, 1085–1089.

Bovenberg, A.L., F. van der Ploeg (1994): Environmental Policy, Public Finance and the Labour Market in a Second-Best World, *Journal of Public Economics* Vol. 55, 349–390.

Bramhall, D.F., E.S. Mills (1966): A Note on the Asymmetry Between Fees and Payments, *Water Resources Research* Vol. 2, 615–616.

Bratberg, E., S. Tjøtta, T. Øines (2005): Do Voluntary International Environmental Agreements Work? *Journal of Environmental Economics and Management* Vol. 50, 583–597.

Bréchet, T., P.-A. Jouvet (2008): Environmental Innovation and the Cost of Pollution Abatement Revisited, *Ecological Economics* Vol. 65, 262–265.

Brennan, T.J. (2006): "Green" Preferences as Regulatory Policy Instrument, *Ecological Economics* Vol. 56, 144–154.

Bretschger, L. (2005): Economics of Technological Change and the Natural Environment, *Ecological Economics* Vol. 54, 148–163.

Bretschger, L., K. Pittel (2005): Innovative Investments, Natural Resources and Intergenerational Fairness, *Swiss Journal of Economics and Statistics* Vol. 141, 355–376.

Brito, D.L. et al. (2006): Private Information, Coasian Bargaining, and the Second Welfare Theorem, *Journal of Public Economics* Vol. 90, 871–895.

Buchanan, J.M. (1969): External Diseconomies, Corrective Taxes and Market Structure, *American Economic Review* Vol. 59, 174–177.

Buchholz, W., R. Cornes, W. Peters (2006): Lindahl Equilibrium vs. Voluntary Contribution to a Public Good, *Finanzarchiv* Vol. 62, 28–49.

Buchholz, W., S. Dasgupta, T. Mitra (2005): Intertemporal Equity and Hartwick's Rule in an Exhaustible Resource Model, *Scandinavian Journal of Economics* Vol. 107, 547–561.

Buchholz, W., A. Haupt, W. Peters (2005): International Environmental Agreements and Strategic Voting, *Scandinavian Journal of Economics* Vol. 107, 175–195.

Buchholz, W., K.A. Konrad (1994): Global Environmental Problems and the Strategic Choice of Technology, *Journal of Economics* Vol. 60, 299–321.

Buchholz, W., K.A. Konrad (1995): Strategic Transfers and Private Provision of Public Goods, *Journal of Public Economics* Vol. 57, 489–505.

Buchholz, W., W. Peters (2003): International Environmental Agreements Reconsidered: Stability of Coalitions in a On-Shot Game, In: Marsiliani/Rauscher/Withagen (Eds.), *Environmental Economics in an International Perspective*, Dordrecht, 81–92.

Buchholz, W., W. Peters (2005): A Rawlsian Approach to International Cooperation, *Kyklos* Vol. 58, 25–44.

Burrows, P. (2008): Nonconvexities and the Theory of External Costs, In: Bromley (Ed.), *The Handbook of Environmental Economics*, 2nd edition, Oxford and Boston.

Burtraw, D. et al. (2006): Economics of Pollution Trading for SO_2 and NO_X, *Annual Review of Environment and Resources* Vol. 30, 253–289.

Calabresi, G. (1968): Transaction Costs, Resource Allocation and Liability Rules – A Comment, *Journal of Law and Economics* Vol. 87, 67–73.

Calcott, P., S. Hutton (2006): The Choice of a Liability Regime When There Is a Regulatory Gatekeeper, *Journal of Environmental Economics and Management* Vol. 51, 153–164.

Carlson, C.P. et al. (2000): SO_2 Control by Electric Utilities: What Are the Gains from Trade?, *Journal of Political Economy* Vol. 108, 1292–1326.

Carraro, C., D. Siniscalco (1993): Strategies for the International Protection of the Environment, *Journal of Public Economics* Vol. 52, 309–328.

Carson, R. et al. (2004): Valuing Oil Spill Prevention, *A Case Study of California's Central Coast*, Dordrecht.

Challen, R. (2000): *Institutions, Transactions Costs and Environmental Policy*, Cheltenham.

Chang, H.F., H. Sigman (2000): Incentives to Settle under Joint and Several Liability: An Empirical Analysis of Superfund Litigation, *Journal of Legal Studies* Vol. 29, 205–236.

Chang, H.F., H. Sigman (2007): The Effect of Joint and Several Liability under Superfund on Brownfields, *International Review of Law and Economics* Vol. 27, 363–384.

Che, Y.K., I. Gale (2003): Optimal Design of Research Contests, *American Economic Review* Vol. 93, 646–671.

Chwe, M.S.-Y. (1994): Farsighted Coalitional Stability, *Journal of Economic Theory* Vol. 63, 299–325.

Coase, R. (1937): The Nature of the Firm, *Economica* Vol. 4, 386–405.

Coase, R. (1960): The Problem of Social Cost, *Journal of Law and Economics* Vol. 3, 1–44.

Cogoy, M., K.W. Steininger (Eds.) (2007): *The Economics of Global Environmental Change*, Cheltenham.

Cohen, M.A., V. Santhakumar (2007): Information Disclosure as Environmental Regulation: A Theoretical Analysis, *Environmental & Resource Economics* Vol. 37, 599–620.

Conrad, K. (2002): Computable General Equilibrium Models in Environmental and Resource Economics, In: Tietenberg/Folmer (Eds.), *The International Yearbook of Environmental and Resource Economics 2002/2003*, Cheltenham, 66–114.

Conrad, K., A. Löschel (2005): Recycling of Eco-Taxes, Labor Market Effects and the True Cost of Labor – A CGE Analysis, *Journal of Applied Economics* Vol. 8, 259–278.

Conrad, K., M. Schröder (1993): Choosing Environmental Policy Instruments Using General Equilibrium Models, *Journal of Policy Modeling* Vol. 15, 521–543.

Cooter, R. (1991): Lapses, Conflict and Akrasia in Torts and Crimes, *International Review of Law and Economics* Vol. 11, 149–164.

Cowen, T., E. Crampton (2002): *Market Failure or Success*, Cheltenham.

Coyle, D. (2007): *The Soulful Science – What Economist Really Do and Why It Matters*, Princeton and Oxford.

Cramton, P., S. Stoft (2010): Price Is a Better Climate Commitment, *The Economists' Voice*, February, 1–7.

Dales, J.H. (1968a): *Pollution, Property, and Prices*, Toronto.

Dales, J.H. (1968b): Land, Water and Ownership, *Canadian Journal of Economics* Vol. 1, 797–804.

Dasgupta, P. (2001): *Human Well-Being and the Natural Environment*, Oxford.

Dellink, R., M. Finus, N. Olieman (2008): The Stability Likelihood of an International Climate Agreement, *Environmental & Resource Economics* Vol. 39, 357–377.

Diamond, P., J.A. Hausman (1994): Contingent Valuation: Is Some Number Better Than No Number? *Journal of Economic Perspectives* Vol. 8, 45–65.

Diamond, P., J. Mirrlees (1971): Optimal Taxation and Public Production. I. Production Efficiency, *American Economic Review* Vol. 61, 8–27.

Dietz, T., P.C. Stern (Eds.) (2002): *New Tools for Environmental Protection*, Washington, DC.

Dixit, A.K., B.J. Nalebuff (1991): *Thinking Strategically – The Competitive Edge in Business, Politics and Every Day Life*, New York.

Ebert, U. (2008): Approximating WTP and WTA for Environmental Goods from Marginal Willingness to Pay Functions, *Ecological Economics* Vol. 66, 270–274.

Ebert, U., O. von dem Hagen (2002): Exogenous Preferences and Endogenous Tastes, *Jahrbücher für Nationalökonomie und Statistik* Vol. 222, 513–530.

Ebert, U., H. Welsch (2004): Meaningful Environmental Indices, *Journal of Environmental Economics and Management* Vol. 47, 270–283.

Ellerman, D.A. (2003): Ex Post Evaluation of Tradable Permits: The US SO_2 Cap-and-Trade Program. Work. Pap. MIT/CEEOR 03-003, Mass. Inst. Technol., Cent. Energy Environ. Policy Res.

Endres, A. (1985): Environmental Policy with Pollutant Interactions, In: Pethig (Ed.), *Public Goods and Public Allocation Policy*, Frankfurt a.M./Bern/New York, 165–199.

Endres, A. (1989): Liability and Information, *Journal of Institutional and Theoretical Economics* Vol. 145, 249–274.

Endres, A. (1991): The Economics of Accident Law: Discounted Expected Damage, Suboptimal Due Care Standards, and the Role of a "Negligence Tax", *Public Finance* Vol. 46, 198–207.

Endres, A. (1997a): Incentive-Based Instruments in Environmental Policy: Conceptual Aspects and Recent Developments, *Konjunkturpolitik* Vol. 43, 299–343.

Endres, A. (1997b): Increasing Environmental Awareness to Protect the Global Commons – A Curmudgeon's View, *Kyklos* Vol. 50, 3–27.

Endres, A. (2004): Game Theory and Global Environmental Policy, *Poiesis & Praxis* Vol. 3, 123–139.

Endres, A., R. Bertram (2006): The Development of Care Technology under Liability Law, *International Review of Law and Economics* Vol. 26, 503–518.

Endres, A., R. Bertram, B. Rundshagen (2007): Environmental Liability Law and Induced Technical Change – The Role of Discounting, *Environmental & Resource Economics* Vol. 36, 341–366.

Endres, A., R. Bertram, B. Rundshagen (2008): Environmental Liability Law and Induced Technical Change – The Role of Spillovers, *Journal of Institutional and Theoretical Economics* Vol. 164, 254–279.

Endres, A., M. Finus (1998): Playing a Better Global Emission Game: Does It Help To Be Green?, *Swiss Journal of Economics and Statistics* Vol. 134, 21–40.

Endres, A., M. Finus (2002): Quotas May Beat Taxes in a Global Emission Game, *International Tax and Public Finance* Vol. 9, 687–707.

Endres, A., T. Friehe (2010): R&D and Abatement under Environmental Liability Law – Comparing Incentives under Strict Liability and Negligence if Compensation differs from Harm, *Universities of Hagen and Konstanz*, mimeo.

Endres, A., A. Lüdeke (1998): Limited Liability and Imperfect Information – On the Existence of Safety Equilibria und Products Liability Law, *European Journal of Law and Economics* Vol. 5, 153–165.

Endres, A., J. Martiensen (2007): *Mikroökonomik – Eine integrierte Darstellung traditioneller und moderner Konzepte in Theorie und Praxis*, Stuttgart.

Endres, A., C. Ohl (2001): International Environmental Cooperation in the One Shot Prisoners' Dilemma, *Schmollers Jahrbuch* Vol. 121, 1–26.

Endres, A., C. Ohl (2002): Introducing "Cooperative Push" – How Inefficient Environmental Policy (Sometimes!) Protects the Global Commons Better, *Public Choice* Vol. 111, 285–302.

Endres, A., C. Ohl (2003): International Environmental Cooperation with Risk Aversion, *International Journal of Sustainable Development* Vol. 6, 378–392.

Endres, A., C. Ohl (2005a): Kyoto, Europe? – An Economic Evaluation of the European Emission Trading Directive, *European Journal of Law and Economics* Vol. 19, 17–39.

Endres, A., C. Ohl (2005b): Der Europäische Handel mit Treibhausgasemissionen, in: Interdisziplinäres Fernstudium Umweltwissenschaften/Infernum (Hg.), *Klimafolgenforschung* Vol. 2, Hagen und Oberhausen.

Endres, A., I. Querner (1995): On the Existence of Care Equilibria under Tort Law, *Journal of Institutional and Theoretical Economics* Vol. 151, 348–357.

Endres, A., B. Rundshagen (2008): A Note on Coasean Dynamics, *Environmental Economics and Policy Studies* Vol. 9, 57–66.

Endres, A., B. Rundshagen (2010): Standard Oriented Environmental Policy – Cost Effectiveness and Incentives for 'Green Technology', *German Economic Review* Vol. 11, 86–107.

Engel, S. (2004): Achieving Environmental Goals in a World of Trade and Hidden Action – The Role of Trade Policies and Eco-Labeling, *Journal of Environmental Economics and Management* Vol. 48, 1122–1145.

Engel, S. (2006): Overcompliance, Labeling, Lobbying: The Case of Credence Goods, *Environmental Modelling and Assessment* Vol. 11, 115–130.

Engel, S., U. Grote (2004): Trade Liberalization and Environmental Standards in the Agricultural Sector, *Quarterly Journal of International Agriculture* Vol. 43, 89–110.

Engel, S., R. López, C. Palmer (2006): Community-Industry Contracting over natural Resources Use in a Context of Weak Property Rights: The Case of Indonesia, *Environmental and Resource Economics* Vol. 33, 73–98.

Engel, S., C. Palmer (2008): Payments for Environmental Services as an Alternative to Logging under Weak Property Rights: The Case of Indonesia, *Ecological Economics* Vol. 65, 799–809.

Eriksson, C. (2004): Can Green Consumerism Replace Environmental Regulation? – A Differentiated-Products Example, *Resource and Energy Economics* Vol. 26, 281–293.

Eyckmans, J., M. Finus (2006a): New Roads to International Environmental Agreements: The Case of Global Warming, *Environmental Economics and Policy Studies* Vol. 7, 391–414.

Eyckmans, J., M. Finus (2006b): Coalition Formation in a Global Warming Game: How the Design of Protocols Affects the Success of Environmental Treaty-Making, *Natural Resource Modeling* Vol. 19, 323–358.

Falk, A., U. Fischbacher (2006): A Theory of Reciprocity, *Games and Economic Behavior* Vol. 54, 293–315.

Falkner, G. et al. (2005): *Complying with Europe*, Cambridge.

Faure, M., J. Gupta, A. Nentjes (Eds.) (2003): *Climate Change and the Kyoto Protocol*, Cheltenham.

Faure, M.G., T. Hartlief (2003): *Insurance and Expanding Systemic Risks*, Paris.

Feess, E. (1999): Lender Liability for Environmental Harm: An Argument against Negligence Based Rules, *European Journal of Law and Economics* Vol. 8, 231–250.

Feess, E. (2004): *Mikroökonomie*, 3rd edition, Marburg.

Feess, E., U. Hege (1998): Efficient Liability Rules for Multi-Party Accidents with Moral Hazard, *Journal of Institutional and Theoretical Economics* Vol. 154, 422–450.

Feess, E., U. Hege (1999): The Role of Insurance in the Adjudication of Multiparty Accidents, *International Review of Law and Economics* Vol. 19, 69–85.

Feess, E., U. Hege (2000): Environmental Harm and Financial Responsibility, *The Geneva Papers on Risk and Insurance* Vol. 25, 220–234.

Feess, E., U. Hege (2002): Safety Regulation and Monitor Liability, *Review of Economic Design* Vol. 7, 173–185.

Feess, E., C. Schumacher (2006): Why Costless Auditing May Reduce Social Welfare, *Economics Letters* Vol. 90, 407–411.

Fehr, E., K. Schmidt (1999): A Theory of Fairness, Competition and Cooperation, *Quarterly Journal of Economics* Vol. 114, 817–868.

Feldman, A.M., R. Serrano (2005): *Welfare Economics and Social Choice Theory*, Berlin.

Feng, H., J. Zhao (2006): Alternative Intertemporal Permit Trading Regimes with Stochastic Abatement Cost, *Resource and Energy Economics* Vol. 28, 24–40.

Finus, M. (2001): *Cooperative Solutions for International Environmental Problems: A Game Theoretical Inquiry*, Cheltenham.

Finus, M. (2002): Game Theory and International Environmental Cooperation: Any Practical Application? In: Böhringer/Finus/Vogt (Eds.), *Controlling Global Warming*, Cheltenham, 9–104.

Finus, M. (2003a): Stability and Design of International Environmental Agreements: The Case of Global and Transboundary Pollution, In: Folmer/Tietenberg (Eds.), *International Yearbook of Environmental and Resource Economics 2003/4*, Cheltenham, 82–158.

Finus, M. (2003b): New Developments in Coalition Theory: An Application to the Case of Global Pollution. In: Marsiliani/Rauscher/Withagen (Eds.), *Environmental Economics in an International Perspective*, Dordrecht, 19–49.

Finus, M., J.-C. Altamirano-Cabrera, E.C. van Ierland (2005): The Effect of Membership Rules and Voting Schemes on the Success of International Climate Agreements, *Public Choice* Vol. 125, 95–127.

Finus, M., O. Herzog (2006): Sanktionen zur Durchsetzung von Vertragspflichten in Internationalen Umweltabkommen, *Zeitschrift für Umweltpolitik & Umweltrecht* Vol. 29, 25–60.

Finus, M., B. Rundshagen (1998a): Renegotiation – Proof Equilibria in a Global Emission Game, *Environmental and Resource Economics* Vol. 12, 275–306.

Finus, M., B. Rundshagen (1998b): Toward a Positive Theory of Coalition Formation and Endogenous Instrument Choice in Global Pollution Control, *Public Choice* Vol. 96, 145–186.

Finus, M., B. Rundshagen (2003): Endogenous Coalition Formation in Global Pollution Control: A Partition Function Approach, In: Carraro (Ed.), *The Endogenous Formation of Economic Coalitions*, Cheltenham, 199–243.

Finus, M., R. Rundshagen (2006a): Participation in International Environmental Agreements: The Role of Timing and Regulation, *Natural Resource Modeling* Vol. 19, 165–200.

Finus, M., R. Rundshagen (2006b): A Micro-Foundation of Core-Stability in Positive Externality Coalition Games, *Journal of Institutional and Theoretical Economics* Vol. 162, 329–346.

Finus, M., R. Rundshagen (2009): Membership Rules and Stability of Coalition Structures in Positive Externality Games, *Social Choice and Welfare* Vol. 32, 389–404.

Finus, M., S. Tjøtta (2003): The Oslo Protocol on Sulfur Reduction: The Great Leap Forward? *Journal of Public Economics* Vol. 87, 2031–2048.

Finus, M., E. van Ierland, R. Dellink (2006): Stability of Climate Coalitions in a Cartel Formation Game, *Economics of Governance* Vol. 7, 271–291.

Fischer, C., R.G. Newell (2008): Environmental and Technology Policies for Climate Mitigation, *Journal of Environmental Economics and Management* Vol. 55, 142–162.

Frank, R.H. (2004): *What Price the Moral High Ground? Ethical Dilemmas in Competitive Environments*, Princeton.

Frank, R.H. (2008): *Microeconomics and Behavior*, 8th edition, Boston.

Frederick, S., G. Loewenstein, T. O'Donoghue (2002): Time Discounting and Time Preference, *Journal of Economic Literature* Vol. 40, 351–401.

Frenz, W. (2003): Freiwillige Unternehmensleistungen und spätere Inpflichtnahme, *Verwaltungsarchiv* Vol. 94, 345–370.

Frey, B.S. (2001): *Inspiring Economics*, Cheltenham.

Frey, B.S., M. Benz, A. Stutzer (2004): Introducing Procedural Utility: Not Only What, But Also How Matters, *Journal of Institutional and Theoretical Economics* Vol. 60, 377–401.

Frey, B.S., M. Osterloh (Eds.) (2002): *Successful Management by Motivation – Balancing Intrinsic and Extrinsic Incentives*, Berlin.

Frey, B.S., A. Stutzer (2002a): What Can Economists Learn from Happiness Research? *Journal of Economic Literature* Vol. 40, 402–432.

Frey, B.S., A. Stutzer (2002b): Economics of Happiness, *World Economics* Vol. 3, 25–41.

Frey, B.S., A. Stutzer (2005): Beyond Outcomes: Measuring Procedural Utility, *Oxford Economic Papers* Vol. 57, 90–111.

Friedman, L.S. (2002): *The Microeconomics of Public Policy Analysis*, Princeton.

Geoghegan, J., W.B. Gray (2005): Spatial Environmental Policy, In: Folmer/Tietenberg (Eds.), *The International Yearbook of Environmental and Resource Economics 2005/2006*, Cheltenham, 52–96.

Gigerenzer, G, R. Selten (2001): *Bounded Rationality*, Cambridge, Mass.

Glomm, G. et al. (2008): Green Taxes and Double Dividends in a Dynamic Economy, *Journal of Policy Modeling* Vol. 30, 19–32.

Godal, O., G. Klaassen (2006): Carbon Trading across Sources and Periodes Constrained by the Marrakesh Accords, *Journal of Environmental Economics and Management* Vol. 51, 308–322.

Goeschl, T. (2005): Non-Binding Linked-Issues Referenda: Analysis and an Application, *Public Choice* Vol. 124, 249–266.

Goeschl, T., D. Igliori (2006): Property Rights for Biodiversity Conservation and Development, *Development and Change* Vol. 37, 427–451.

Goeschl, T., G. Perino (2007): Innovation without Magic Bullets: Stock Pollution and R&D Sequences, *Journal of Environmental Economics and Management* Vol. 54, 146–161.

Goeschl, T., T. Swanson (2000): Property Rights Issues Involving Plant Genetic Resources, *Ecological Economics* Vol. 32, 75–92.

Goodstein, E.S. (1995): *Economics and the Environment*, Englewood Cliffs, NJ.

Goulder, L.H. (1995): Environmental Taxation and the Double Dividend: A Reader's Guide, *International Tax and Public Finance* Vol. 2, 157–183.

Goulder, L.H. (1997): Environmental Taxation in a Second-Best World, In: Folmer/ Tietenberg (Eds.), *The International Yearbook of Environmental and Resource Economics 1997/1998*, Cheltenham, 28–54.

Goulder, L.H. (Ed.) (2002): *Environmental Policy Making in Economies with Prior Tax Distortions*, Cheltenham.

Goulder, L.H., A. Schmutzler (1997): The Choice between Emission Taxes and Output Taxes under Imperfect Monitoring, *Journal of Environmental Economics and Management* Vol. 32, 51–74.

Hackl, F., G.J. Pruckner (2001): *The Economics of the Kyoto Protocol*, In: Welfens (Ed.), *Internationalization of the Economy and Environmental Policy Options*, Berlin, 205–222.

Halbheer, D., S. Niggli, A. Schmutzler (2006): What Does It Take to Sell Environmental Policy? An Empirical Analysis for Switzerland, *Environmental and Resource Economics* Vol. 33, 441–462.

Hamilton, K., G. Ruta, L. Tajibaeva (2006): Capital Accumulation and Resource Depletion, *Environmental and Resource Economics* Vol. 34, 517–533.

Hampicke, U., K. Ott (Eds.) (2003): Reflections on Discounting, *International Journal of Sustainable Development* Vol. 6, Special Issue.

Hansjürgens, B. (2005): *Emissions Trading for Climate Policy*, Cambridge.

Harrington, W. et al. (Eds.) (2004): *Choosing Environmental Policy*, Washington, DC.

Harris, J.M. (2006): *Environmental and Natural Resource Economics*, 2nd edition, Boston.

Harrison, D. (2002): Tradable Permits for Air Quality and Climate Change, In: Tietenberg/Folmer (Eds.), *The International Yearbook of Environmental and Resource Economics 2002/2003*, Cheltenham, 311–372.

Hartwick, J.M. (1977): Intergenerational Equity and the Investing of Rents from Exhaustible Resources, *American Economic Review* Vol. 67, 972–974.

Hartwick, J.M. (1990): Natural Resources, National Accounting and Economic Depreciation, *Journal of Public Economics* Vol. 43, 291–304.

Hartwick, J., N. Olewiler (1998): *The Economics of Natural Resource Use*, 2nd edition, Reading, Mass.

Heal, G. (2003): Optimality or Sustainability?, In: Arnott et al. (Eds.), *Economics for an Imperfect World*, Cambridge, Mass., 331–348.

Heister, J. (1998): Who Will Win the Ozone Game? On Building and Sustaining Cooperation in the Montreal Protocol on Substances That Deplete the Ozone Layer, In: Michaelis/Stähler (Eds.), *Recent Policy Issues in Environmental and Resource Economics*, Heidelberg and New York, 121–154.

Helm, C. (2000): *Economic Theories of International Environmental Cooperation*, Cheltenham.

Helm, C. (2001): On the Existence of a Cooperative Solution for a Coalitional Game with Externalities, *International Journal of Game Theory* Vol. 30, 141–146.

Helm, C., T. Bruckner, F.L. Tóth (1999): Value Judgments and the Choice of Climate Protection Strategies, *International Journal of Social Economics* Vol. 26, 974–998.

Helm, C., A. Schöttner (2008): Subsidizing Technological Innovations in the Presence of R&D Spillovers, *German Economic Review* Vol. 9, 339–353.

Helm, C., U.E. Simonis (2001): Distributive Justice in International Environmental Policy, *Environmental Values* Vol. 10, 5–18.

Helm, C., D. Sprinz (2000): Measuring the Effectiveness of International Environmental Regimes, *The Journal of Conflict Resolution* Vol. 44, 630–652.

Helm, D. (Ed.) (2005): *Climate-Change Policy*, Oxford.

Hicks, J. (1946): *Value and Capital*, 2nd edition, Oxford.

Hillebrand, B. et al. (2002): *Zertifikatehandel für CO₂-Emissionen auf dem Prüfstand*, Münster.

Hiriart, Y., D. Martimort, J. Pouyet (2004): On the Optimal Use of Ex Ante Regulation and Ex Post Liability, *Economics Letters* Vol. 84, 231–235.

Hirshleifer, J., A. Glazer, D. Hirshleifer (2005): *Price Theory and Applications*, 7th edition, Cambridge.

Hoel, M. (1992): International Environment Conventions: The Case of Uniform Reductions of Emissions, *Environmental and Resource Economics* Vol. 2, 141–159.

Hoel, M., S. Kverndokk (1996): Depletion of Fossil Fuels and the Impacts of Global Warming, *Resource and Energy Economics* Vol. 18, 115–136.

Hoel, M., K. Schneider (1997): Incentives to Participate in an International Environmental Agreement, *Environmental and Resource Economics* Vol. 9, 153–170.

Holmström, B. (1982): Moral Hazard in Teams, *Bell (today: Rand) Journal of Economics* Vol. 13, 324–340.

Hotelling, H. (1931): The Economics of Exhaustible Resources, *Journal of Political Economy* Vol. 31, 137–175.

Hutchinson, E., K. van't Veld (2005): Extended Liability for Environmental Accidents, *Journal of Environmental Economics and Management* Vol. 49, 157–173.

Israel, D. (2007): Environmental Participation in the U.S. Sulfur Allowance Auctions, *Environmental & Resource Economics* Vol. 38, 373–390.

James, H.S. (2005): Why Did You Do That? An Economic Examination of the Effect of Extrinsic Compensation on Intrinsic Motivation and Performance, *Journal of Economic Psychology* Vol. 26, 549–566.

Jenkins, R.R., E. Kopits, D. Simpson (2009): The Evolution of Solid and Hazardous Waste Regulation in the United States, *Review of Environmental Economics and Policy* Vol. 3, 104–120.

Kahnemann, D., J.L. Knetsch, R.H. Thaler (1990): Experimental Tests of the Endowment Effect and the Coase Theorem, *Journal of Political Economy* Vol. 98, 1325–1348.

Katayama, S., F. Abe (1998): Is the Monopolist the Friend of the Conservationist? Two Remarks on the Hotelling-Solow Paradox, *Journal of Economic Behavior & Organization* Vol. 33, 493–505.

Kemfert C. (2003): International Climate Coalitions and Trade, *Energy Policy* Vol. 32, 455–465.

Kemfert, C. (2005): Induced Technological Change in a Multi-Regional, Multi-Sectoral, Integrated Assessment Model (WIAGEM), *Ecological Economics* Vol. 54, 293–305.

Kemfert, C., W. Lise, R. Tol (2004): Games of Climate Change with International Trade, *Environmental & Resource Economics* Vol. 28, 209–232.

Kemfert, C., H.R.J. Vollebergh (2005): The Role of Technical for a Sustainable Development, *Ecological Economics* Vol. 52, 133–147.

Keohane, N.O. (2009): Cap and Trade, Rehabilitated: Using Tradable Permits to Control U.S. Greenhouse Gases, *Review of Environmental Economics and Policy* Vol. 3, 42–62.

Kirchgässner, G. (2001): Trade Neutrality of National Environmental Policy: Some Theoretical Considerations and Simulation Results for Switzerland, In: Welfens (Ed.), *Internationalization of the Economy and Environmental Policy Options*, Berlin, 125–152.

Kirchgässner, G., E. Mohr (1996): Trade Restrictions as Viable Means of Enforcing Compliance with International Environmental Law: An Economic Assessment, In: Wolfrum (Ed.), *Enforcing Environmental Standards*, Berlin, 199–226.

Kirchgässner, G., F. Schneider (2003): On the Political Economy of Environmental Policy, *Public Choice* Vol. 115, 369–396.

Klaassen, G., A. Nentjes (1997): Sulfur Trading under the 1990 CAA in the U.S., *The Journal of Institutional and Theoretical Economics* Vol. 153, 384–410.

Klepper, G., S. Peterson (2005): Trading Hot-Air, *Environmental and Resource Economics* Vol. 32, 205–227.

Kolstad, C.D. (2000): *Environmental Economics*, New York and Oxford.

Körber, A. (2000): *The Political Economy of Environmental Protectionism*, Cheltenham.

Kornhauser, C.A., R.L. Revesz (2009): Joint and Several Liability, In: M. Faure (Ed.), *Encyclopedia of Law and Economics – Tort Law and Economics*, Cheltenham.

Krarup, S., C.S. Russell (Eds.) (2005): *Environment, Information and Consumer Behaviour*, Cheltenham.

Krysiak, F.C. (2008): Ex-Post Efficient Permit Markets: A Detailed Analysis, *Environmental & Resource Economics* Vol. 39, 397–410.

Krysiak, F.C., D. Krysiak (2003): Production, Consumption, and General Equilibrium with Physical Constraints, *Journal of Environmental Economics and Management* Vol. 46, 513–538.

Laffont, J.-J. (2002): Public Economics Yesterday, Today and Tomorrow, *Journal of Public Economics* Vol. 86, 327–334.

Landes, W.M., R.A. Posner (1980): Joint and Multiple Tortefeasors: An Economic Analysis, *Journal of Legal Studies* Vol. 9, 517–555.

Landes, W.M., R.A. Posner (1987): *The Economic Structure of Tort Law*, Cambridge, Mass./London.

Landsburg, S.E. (2002): *Price Theory and Applications*, 5th edition, Cincinnati.

Lange, A. (2006): The Impact of Equity-Preferences on the Stability of International Environmental Agreements, *Environmental and Resource Economics* Vol. 34, 247–268.

Lange, A., C. Vogt (2003): Cooperation in International Environmental Negotiations Due to a Preference for Equity, *Journal of Public Economics* Vol. 87, 2049–2067.

Lange, A., C. Vogt, A. Ziegler (2006): On the Importance of Equity in International Climate Policy: An Empirical Analysis, *Energy Economics* Vol. 29, 545–562.

Lehmann-Waffenschmidt, M. (2006): *Innovations Towards Sustainability*, Dresden.

Leijonhufvud, A. (1981): *Life among the Econ*, In: A. Leijonhufvud (Ed.), *Information and Coordination – Essays in Macroeconomic Theory*, New York/Oxford, 347–359.

Livernois, J. (2009): On the Empirical Significance of the Hotelling Rule, *Review of Environmental Economics and Policy* Vol. 3, 22–41.

Macho-Stadler, I., J.D. Pérez-Castrillo (2001): *An Introduction to the Economics of Information*, 2nd edition, Oxford.

Macho-Stadler, I., J.D. Pérez-Castrillo (2006): Optimal Enforcement Policy and Firms' Emissions and Compliance with Environmental Taxes, *Journal of Environmental Economics and Management* Vol. 51, 110–131.

Maennig, W. (2003): From the Mature Athlete to the *Homo Sportivus Oeconomicus*, In: Krüger (Hg.), *Menschenbilder im Sport*, Schorndorf, 174–193.

Mäler, K.-G. (1990): International Environmental Problems, *Oxford Review of Economic Policy* Vol. 6, 80–108.

Mäler, K.-G., J. Vincent (Eds.) (2005): *Handbook of Environmental Economics, Vol. 2: Valuing Environmental Changes*, Amsterdam.

Markandya, A., S. Pedroso-Galinato (2007): How Substitutable Is Natural Capital?, *Environmental & Resource Economics* Vol. 37, 297–312.

Marsiliani, L., M. Rauscher, C. Withagen (Eds.) (2002): *Environmental Economics and the International Economy*, Dordrecht.

Marsiliani, L., M. Rauscher, C. Withagen (Eds.) (2003): *Environmental Economics in an International Perspective*, Dordrecht.

Matschoss, P., H. Welsch (2006): International Emissions Trading and Induced Carbon-Saving Technological Change: Effects of Restricting the Trade in Carbon Rights, *Environmental & Resource Economics* Vol. 33, 169–198.

Meadows, D.H. et al. (1972): *The Limits to Growth*, London.

Menges, R., C. Schröder, S. Traub (2005): Altruism, Warm Glow, and the Market for Green Electricity, *Environmental and Resource Economics* Vol. 31, 431–458.

Metcalf, G.E. (2009): Designing a Carbon Tax to Reduce U.S. Greenhouse Gas Emissions, *Review of Environmental Economics and Policy* Vol. 3, 63–83.

Metcalf, G.E. et al. (2008): Analysis of US Greenhouse Gas Tax Proposals, NBER Working Paper No. W13980.

Mohr, E., J.P. Thomas (1998): Pooling Sovereign Risks: The Case of Environmental Treaties and International Debt, *Journal of Development Economics* Vol. 55, 173–190.

Moslener, U., B. Sturm (2008): A European Perspective on Recent Trends in U.S. Climate Policy, *European Environment* Vol. 18, 257–275.

Mueller, D.C. (2003): *Public Choice III*, Cambridge.

Murdoch, J.C., T. Sandler (1997a): Voluntary Cutbacks and Pretreaty Behavior – The Helsinki Protocol and Sulfur Emissions, *Public Finance Review* Vol. 25, 139–162.

Murdoch, J.C., T. Sandler (1997b): The Voluntary Provision of a Pure Public Good: The Case of Reduced CFC Emissions and the Montreal Protocol, *Journal of Public Economics* Vol. 63, 331–349.

Murray, B.C., R.G. Newell, W.A. Pizer (2009): Balancing Cost and Emissions Certainty: An Allowance Reserve for Cap-and-Trade, *Review of Environmental Economics and Policy* Vol. 3, 84–103.

Nemry, F., (2001): LULUCF39 v4-Quantitative Implications of the Decision CP.7 on LULUCF, personal communication to the authors Böhringer and Finus.

Neumayer, E. (2004): Indicators of Sustainability, in: Folmer/Tietenberg (Eds.), *The International Yearbook of Environmental and Resource Economics 2004/2005*, Cheltenham, 189–217.

Neumayer, E. (2010): *Weak versus Strong Sustainability*, 3rd edition, Cheltenham.

Nutzinger, H.G. (1998): Indikatoren einer nachhaltigen Entwicklung, *Kyklos* Vol. 51, 429–430.

Nyburg, K., R.B. Howarth, K.A. Brekke (2006): Green Consumers and Public Policy: On Socially Contingent Moral Motivation, *Resource & Energy Economics* Vol. 28, 351–366.

Oates, W.E. (2000): From Research to Policy – The Case of Environmental Economics, *University of Illinois Law Review* Vol. 1, 135–154.

Organisation for Economic Co-operation and Development (OECD) (2004): *Tradeable Permits*, Paris.

Ott, C., H.-B. Schäfer (1997): Negligence as Untaken Precaution – Limited Information and Efficient Standard Formation in the Civil Liability System, *International Review of Law and Economics* Vol. 17, 15–29.

Paltsev, S. et al. (2008): Assessment of US GHG Cap-and-Trade Proposals, *Climate Policy* Vol. 8, 395–420.

Paltsev, S. et al. (2009): The Cost of Climate Policy in the United States, *Energy Economics* Vol. 31, 235–243.

Parry, I.W.H. (2003): Fiscal Interactions and the Case for Carbon Taxes over Grandfathered Carbon Permits, *Oxford Review of Economic Policy* Vol. 19, 385–399.

Perloff, J.M. (2007): *Microeconomics*, 4th edition, Boston.

Perman, R. et al. (2003): *Natural Resource and Environmental Economics*, 3rd edition, Harlow.

Peters, W., C. Schuler (2005): IEA: Stability of the Grand Coalition, European University Viadrina Frankfurt (Oder), Working Paper.

Pethig, R. (2003a): Corrective Environmental Taxation and Distortionary Taxation Revisited, In: Pethig/Rauscher (Eds.), *Challenges to the World Economy – Festschrift for Horst Siebert*, Berlin, 293–307.

Pethig, R. (2003b): Ecological Tax Reform and Efficiency of Taxation: A Public Good Perspective, In: Böhringer/Löschel (Eds.), *Empirical Modeling of the Economy and the Environment*, Heidelberg, 261–289.

Pethig, R. (2006): Non-Linear Production, Abatement, Pollution and Materials Balance Reconsidered, *Journal of Environmental Economics and Management* Vol. 51, 185–204.

Pezzey, J., M.A. Toman (2002): Progress and Problems in the Economics of Sustainability, In: Folmer/Tietenberg (Eds.), *The International Yearbook of Environmental and Resource Economics 2002/2003*, Cheltenham, 233–277.

Pigou, A.C. (1932): *The Economics of Welfare*, 3rd edition, London.

Pindyck, R.S. (2007): Uncertainty in Environmental Economics, *Review of Environmental Economics and Policy* Vol. 1, 45–65.

Pittel, K., D.T.G. Rübbelke (2008): Climate Policy and Ancillary Benefits: A Survey and Integration into the Modelling of International Negotiations on Climate Change, *Ecological Economics* Vol. 68, 210–220.

Polk, A., A. Schmutzler (2005): Lobbying against Environmental Regulation vs. Lobbying for Loopholes, *European Journal of Political Economy* Vol. 21, 915–931.

Rauscher, M., N. Gürtzgen (2000): Environmental Policy, Intra-Industry Trade, and Transfrontier Pollution, *Environmental and Resource Economics* Vol. 17, 59–71.

Rauscher, M., B. Lünenbürger (2004): Leakage, In: Böhringer/Löschel (Eds.), *Climate Change Policy and Global Trade*, Heidelberg/New York, 205–230.

Rawls, J. (1971): *The Theory of Justice*, Cambridge, Mass.

Rehdanz, K., D. Maddison (2005): Climate and Happiness, *Ecological Economics* Vol. 52, 111–125.

Rehdanz, K., D. Maddison (2008): Local Environmental Quality and Life-Satisfaction in Germany, *Ecological Economics* Vol. 64, 787–797.

Reksulak, M. et al. (2004): Economics and English – Language Growth in Economic Perspective, *Southern Economic Journal* Vol. 71, 232–259.

Requate, T. (2005a): Commitment and Timing of Environmental Policy, Adoption of New Technology, and Repercussions on R&D, *Environmental & Resource Economics* Vol. 31, 175–199.

Requate, T. (2005b): Dynamic Incentives by Environmental Policy Instruments – A Survey, *Ecological Economics* Vol. 54, 175–195.

Rhoads, T., J.F. Shogren (1998): Current Issues in Superfund Amendment and Reauthorization, *Duke Environmental Law and Policy Forum* Vol. 8, 245–257.

Rübbelke, D.T.G. (2003): An Analysis of Differing Abatement Incentives, *Resource and Energy Economics* Vol. 25, 269–294.

Rubinstein, A. (2002): *Modeling Bounded Rationality*, 2nd printing, Cambridge, Mass.

Rubio, S., A. Ulph (2006): Self-Enforcing International Environmental Agreements Revisited, *Oxford Economic Papers* Vol. 58, 233–263.

Russell, C.S. (2001): *Applying Economics to the Environment*, Oxford.

Sáez, C.A., J.C. Requena (2007): Reconciling Sustainability and Discounting in Cost–Benefit Analysis: A Methodological Proposal, *Ecological Economics* Vol. 60, 712–725.

Schäfer, H.-B., C. Ott (2004): *The Economic Analysis of Civil Law*, Cheltenham.

Schaltegger, S., R. Burritt (2005): Corporate Sustainability, In: Folmer/Tietenberg (Eds.), *The International Yearbook of Environmental and Resource Economics 2005/2006*, Cheltenham, 185–222.

Schaltegger, S., M. Wagner (2006): *Managing the Business Case for Sustainability*, Sheffield.

Schmidt, C. (2000): *Designing International Environmental Agreements*, Cheltenham.

Schmidt, C. (2001): *Incentives for International Environmental Cooperation*, In: Schulze/Ursprung (Eds.), *International Environmental Economics*, Cheltenham, 209–240.

Schmutzler, A. (1996a): Pollution Control with Imperfectly Observable Emissions, *Environmental and Resource Economics* Vol. 7, 251–262.

Schmutzler, A. (1996b): Pollution Control with Imperfect Information, *Environmental and Resource Economics* Vol. 7, 251–262.

Schneider, F., J. Volkert (1999): No Chance for Incentive-Oriented Environmental Policies in Representative Democracies? A Public Choice Analysis, *Ecological Economics* Vol. 31, 123–138.

Schneider, F., A. Wagner (2006): Satisfaction with Democracy and the Environment in Western Europe – A Panel Analysis, CesIfo Working Paper No 1660.

Schneider, F., H. Weck-Hannemann (2005): Why Isn't Economic Theory Considered in Environmental Policy Practice? In: Böhringer/Lange (Eds.), *Frontiers of Applied Environmental and Resource Economics*, Heidelberg, 257–276.

Schöb, R. (2005): The Double-Dividend Hypothesis of Environmental Taxes: A Survey, In: Folmer/Tietenberg (Eds.), *The International Yearbook of Environmental and Resource Economics 2005/2006*, Cheltenham, 223–279.

Schulze, W., R.C. d'Arge (1974): The Coase Proposition, Information Constraints and Long Run Equilibrium, *American Economic Review* Vol. 64, 763–772.

Schulze, G.G., H.W. Ursprung (Eds.) (2001): *International Environmental Economics*, Oxford.

Schwarze, R. (2001a): *Law and Economics of International Climate Change Policy*, Dordrecht.

Schwarze, R. (2001b): The "Crunch Issue" of Additional Sinks, *Climate Policy* Vol. 1, 397–401.

Schwarze, R. (2005): Umwelthaftungsgesetz und Umwelthaftpflichtversicherung – Eine Bilanz nach zehn Jahren, In: Hansjürgens/Wätzold (Eds.), *Umweltpolitik und umweltökonomische Politikberatung in Deutschland*, Berlin 247–260.

Schwarze, R., J. Barrera (2005): Does the CDM Contribute to Sustainable Development?, *International Journal of Sustainable Development* Vol. 7, 353–368.

Schwarze, R., P. Zapfel (2000): Sulfur Allowance Trading and the Regional Clean Air Incentives Market, *Environmental and Resource Economics* Vol. 17, 279–298.

Sedjo, R.A., M. Amano (2006): The Role of Forest Sinks in a Post-Kyoto World, *Resources*, Issue 162, 19–22.

Segerson, K. (2000): Liability for Environmental Damages. In: Folmer/Gabel (Eds.), *Principles of Environmental and Resource Economics*, Cheltenham, 420–444.

Shavell, S. (1987): *Economic Analysis of Accident Law*, Cambridge, Mass./London.

Sheeran, K.A. (2006): Who Should Abate Carbon Emissions? A Note, *Environmental and Resource Economics* Vol. 35, 89–98.

Sigman, H. (2010): Environmental Liability and Redevelopment of Old Industrial Land, *Journal of Law and Economics* Vol. 53, 289–306.

Simpson, D.R., M.A. Toman, R.U. Ayres (Eds.) (2005): *Scarcity and Growth Revisited*, Washington, DC.

Singh, R. (2003): Efficiency of "Simple" Liability Rules When Courts Make Erroneous Estimation of the Damage, *European Journal of Law and Economics* Vol. 16, 39–58.

Sinn, H.-W. (2007): Pareto Optimality in the Extraction of Fossil Fuels and the Greenhouse Effect: A Note, CESifo Working Paper No. 2083.

Sinn, H.-W. (2008): Public Policies against Global Warming, *International Tax and Public Finance* Vol. 15, 360–394.

Slade, M.E., H. Thille (2009): Whither Hotelling – Tests of the Theory of Exhaustible Resources, *Annual Review of Resource Economics* Vol. 1, 239–260.

Smith, V.K. (2004): Fifty Years of Contingent Valuation, In: *The International Yearbook of Environmental and Resource Economics 2004/2005*, Cheltenham, 1–60.

Sohmen, E. (1976): *Allokationstheorie und Wirtschaftspolitik*, Tübingen.

Solow, R. (1993): An Almost Practical Step toward Sustainability, *Resources Policy* Vol. 19, 162–172.

Stähler, F. (1996): Reflections on Multilateral Environmental Agreements, In: Xepapadeas (Ed.), *Economic Policy for the Environment and Natural Resources*, Cheltenham, 174–196.

Stavins, R. (1995): Transaction Costs and Tradeable Permits, *Journal of Environmental Economics and Management* Vol. 29, 133–148.

Stavins, R. (2008): Addressing Climate Change with a Comprehensive US Cap-and-Trade System, *Oxford Review of Economic Policy* Vol. 24, 298–321.

Stavins, R.N., A. Pratt (2004): *The Political Economy of Environmental Regulation*, Cheltenham.

Steiniger, K.W., B. Friedl, B. Gebetsroither (2007): Sustainability Impacts of Car Road Pricing – A CGE Analysis for Austria, *Ecological Economics* Vol. 63, 59–69.

Stephan, G., G. Müller-Fürstenberger (1998): Discounting and the Economics of Altruism in Greenhouse Gas Abatement, *Kyklos* Vol. 51, 321–338.

Stephan, G., G. Müller-Fürstenberger (2004): Does Distribution Matter? Efficiency, Equity and Flexibility in Greenhouse Gas Abatement, *Environmental & Resource Economics* Vol. 27, 87–107.

Sterk, W., M. Mehling, A. Tuerk (2009): *Prospects of Linking EU and US Emission Trading Schemes*, Climate Strategies Working Paper.

Sturm, B. (2008): Market Power in Emissions Trading Markets Ruled by a Multiple Unit Double Auction: Further Experimental Evidence, *Environmental and Resource Economics* Vol. 40, 467–487.

Sturm, B., J. Weimann (2006): Experiments in Environmental Economics and Some Close Relatives, *Journal of Economic Surveys* Vol. 20, 419–457.

Svendsen, G.T. (2005): *Lobbying and CO_2 Trade in the EU*, In: Hansjürgens (Ed.), *Emissions Trading for Climate Policy*, Cambridge, 151–161.

Swanson, T., A. Kontoleon (2004): What Future for Environmental Liability? In: Vig/Faure (Eds.), *Green Giants? Environmental Policies of the United States and the European Union*, Cambridge, Mass., 183–204.

Swanson, T., R. Mason (2003): The Impact of International Environmental Agreements: The Case of the Montreal Protocol, In: Marsiliani/Rauscher/Withagen (Eds.), *Environmental Economics in an International Perspective*, Dordrecht, 51–80.

Tahvonen, O., J. Kuuluvainen (2000): The Economics of Natural Resource Utilisation. In: Folmer/Gabel (Eds.), *Principles of Environmental and Resource Economics*, Cheltenham, 665–699.

Tietenberg, T.H. (1989): Indivisible Toxic Torts: The Economics of Joint and Several Liability, *Land Economics* Vol. 65, 305–319.

Tietenberg, T.H. (2001): *Emissions Trading Programs*, 2 vols., Burlington.

Tietenberg, T.H. (2008): *Environmental and Natural Resource Economics*, 8th edition, Boston.

Tietenberg, T.H., L. Lewis (2009): *Environmental and Resource Economics*, 9th edition, Boston.

Turner, R.K., J. Paavola, P. Cooper, S. Farber, V. Jessamy, S. Georgiou (2003): Valuing Nature: Lessons Learned and Future Research Directions, *Ecological Economics* Vol. 46, 493–510.

U.S. Energy Information Administration, U.S. Department of Energy, (2001): *International Energy Outlook 2001*, www.eia.doe.gov/oiaf/archive/ieo01/index.html.

van Egteren, H., R.T. Smith, D. McAfee (2004): Harmonization of Environmental Regulations When Firms Are Judgement Proof, *European Journal of Law and Economics* Vol. 17, 139–164.

van Velthoven, B.C.J., P.W. van Wijck (2009): Additive and Non-Additive Risk Factors in Multiple Causation, *Review of Law and Economics* Vol. 5, Article 2.

Varian, H.R. (2006): *Intermediate Microeconomics – A Modern Approach*, 7th edition, New York.

Vatn, A. (2005): *Institutions and the Environment*, Cheltenham.

Venkatachalam, L. (2007): Environmental Economics and Ecological Economics: Where They Can Converge?, *Ecological Economics* Vol. 61, 550–558.

Wagner, T. (2005): Environmental Policy and the Equilibrium Rate of Unemployment, *Journal of Environmental Economics and Management* Vol. 49, 132–156.

Wagner, U.J. (2001): The Design of Stable International Environmental Agreements: Economic Theory and Political Economy, *Journal of Economic Surveys* Vol. 15, 377–411.

Walz, R. (2000): Development of Environmental Indicator Systems: Experiences from Germany, *Environmental Management* Vol. 25, 613–623.

Weikard, H.-P., M. Finus, J.-C. Altamirano-Cabrera (2006): The Impact of Surplus Sharing on the Stability of International Climate Agreements, *Oxford Economic Papers* Vol. 58, 209–232.

Weimann, J. (1994): Individual Behavior in a Free Riding Experiment, *Journal of Public Economics* Vol. 54, 185–200.

Weitzman, M. (2001): Gamma Discounting, *American Economic Review* Vol. 91, 261–271.

Weitzman, M.L. (1976): On the Welfare Significance of National Product in a Dynamic Economy, *Quarterly Journal of the Economics* Vol. 90, 156–162.

Welsch, H. (2002): Preferences over Prosperity and Pollution, *Kyklos* Vol. 55, 473–494.

Welsch, H. (2003): Freedom and Rationality as Predictors of Cross-National Happiness Patterns, *Journal of Happiness Studies* Vol. 4, 295–321.

Welsch, H. (2007): Environmental Welfare Analysis: A Life Satisfaction Approach, *Ecological Economics* Vol. 62, 544–551.

Welsch, H. (2008): Resource Abundance and Internal Armed Conflict: Types of Natural Resources and the Incidence of "New Wars," *Ecological Economics* Vol. 67, 503–513.

Welsch, H., J. Kühling (2009): Using Happiness Data for Environmental Valuation: *Issues and Applications, Journal of Economic Surveys* Vol. 23, 285–406.

Wesseler, J. H.-P. Weikard, R. D. Weaver (2003): *Risk and Uncertainty in Environmental and Natural Resource Economics*, Cheltenham.

Wilen, J.E. (2000): Renewable Resource Economists and Policy – What Differences Have We Made? *Journal of Environmental Economics and Management* Vol. 39, 306–327.

Winkler, R. (2006): Does "Better" Discounting Lead to "Worse" Outcomes in Long-Run Decisions? The Dilemma of Hyperbolic Discounting, *Ecological Economics* Vol. 57, 573–582.

Woerdman, E. (2004): *The Institutional Economics of Market-Based Climate Policy*, Amsterdam.

Xepapadeas, A.P. (1997): *Advanced Principles in Environmental Policy*, Cheltenham.

Young, R., M. Faure, P. Fenn (2004): Causality and Causation in Tort Law, *International Review of Law and Economics* Vol. 24, 507–523.

Young, R., M. Faure, P. Fenn, J. Willis (2005): Multiple Tortfeasores: An Economic Analysis, Paper presented at: 22nd Annual Conference of the European Association for Law & Economics, Ljubljana.

Young, R.A. (2005): *Determining the Economic Value of Water*, Washington, DC.

Zervogianni, E. (2004): Remedies for Damage to Property, *International Review of Law and Economics* Vol. 24, 525–541.

Ziegler, A., M. Schröder, K. Rennings (2007): The Effect of Environmental and Social Performance on the Stock Performance of European Corporations, *Environmental & Resource Economics* Vol. 37, 661–680.

Zimmermann, K.W., J.D. Gaynor (1999): The Double Dividend: Miracle or Fata Morgana?, *Public Choice* Vol. 101, 39–58.

Index